The Complete

Chi's Sweet Home

Part 4

Konami Kanata

contents
homemade 165~218 +

165 a cat guides   5

166 a cat feels certain   13

167 a cat is watched   21

168 a cat is concerning   29

169 a cat communicates   37

170 a cat is misread   45

171 a cat has signals
crossed   53

172 a cat is told   61

173 a cat goes to see   69

174 a cat ponders   77

175 a cat realizes   85

176 a cat queries   93

177 a cat is briefed   101

178 a cat trains   109

179 a cat holds   117

180 a cat masters   125

181 a cat joins up   133

182 a cat begins to
change   141

183 a cat calls   149

184 a cat is distressed   157

185 a cat is feeling gloomy 165

186 a cat receives a shock 173

187 a cat is in denial 181

188 a cat notices 189

189 a cat hangs her head 197

190 a cat is called upon 205

191 a cat becomes sensitive 213

192 a cat communes 221

193 a cat is surprised 229

194 a cat is compelled 237

195 a cat recalls 245

196 a cat is lost in thought 253

197 a cat is looked for 261

198 a cat is rejected 269

199 a cat is irritable 277

200 a cat has a chance meeting 285

201 a cat chases her memories 293

202 a cat's spirits lift 301

203 a cat meets trouble

309

204 a cat runs   317

205 a cat helps   325

206 a cat snuggles   333

207 a cat bonds   341

208 a cat goes back   349

209 a cat accepts   357

210 a cat fits in   365

211 a cat separates   373

212 a cat confirms   385

213 a cat has to pick   393

214 a cat makes up her mind   401

215 a cat runs off   409

216 a cat continues to run   417

217 a cat dwells   425

218 a cat comes home

433

homemade special 456

extras   465

The Kitten and the Mole   473

homemade 165: a cat guides

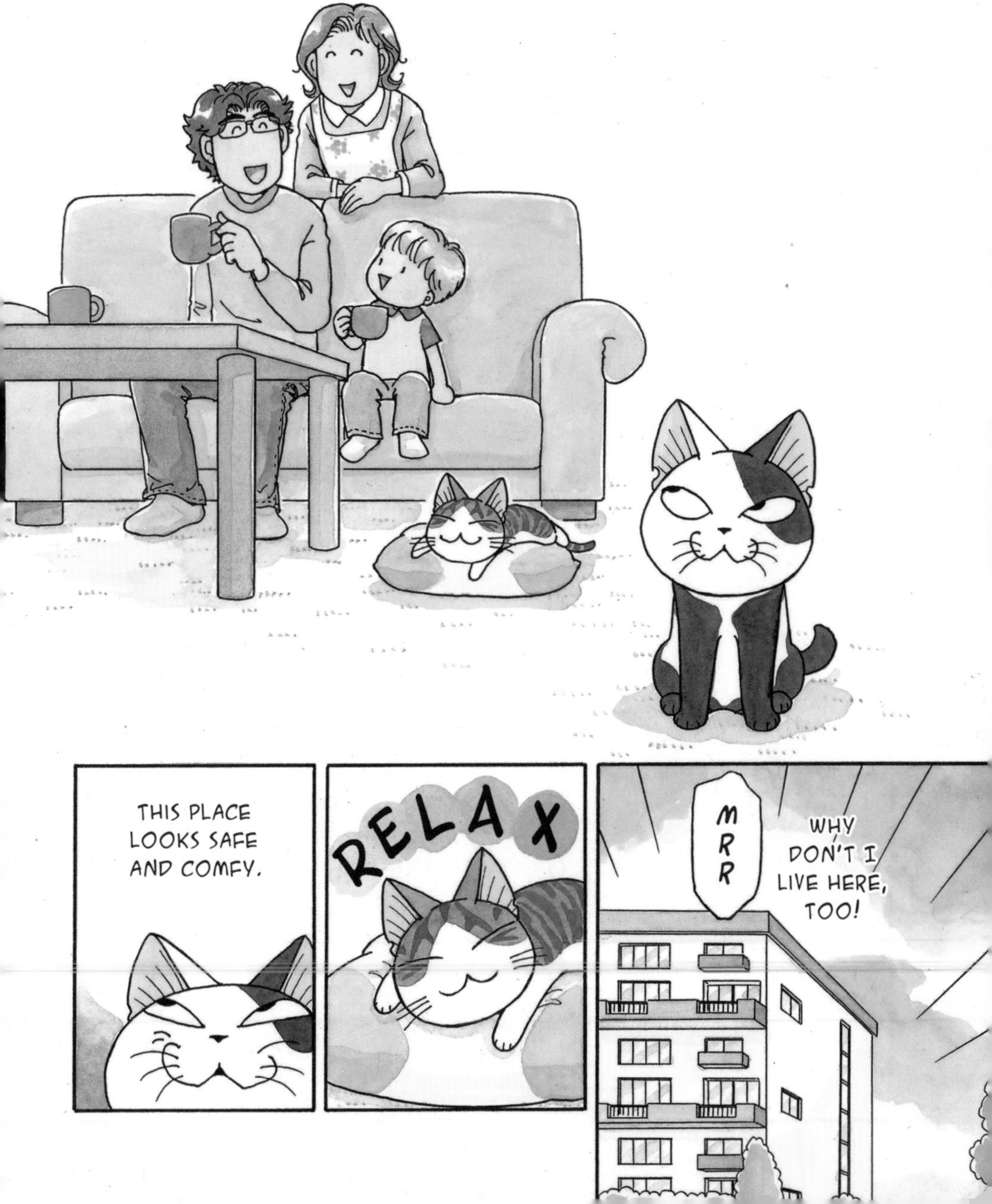
THIS PLACE LOOKS SAFE AND COMFY.
RELAX
MRR
WHY DON'T I LIVE HERE, TOO!

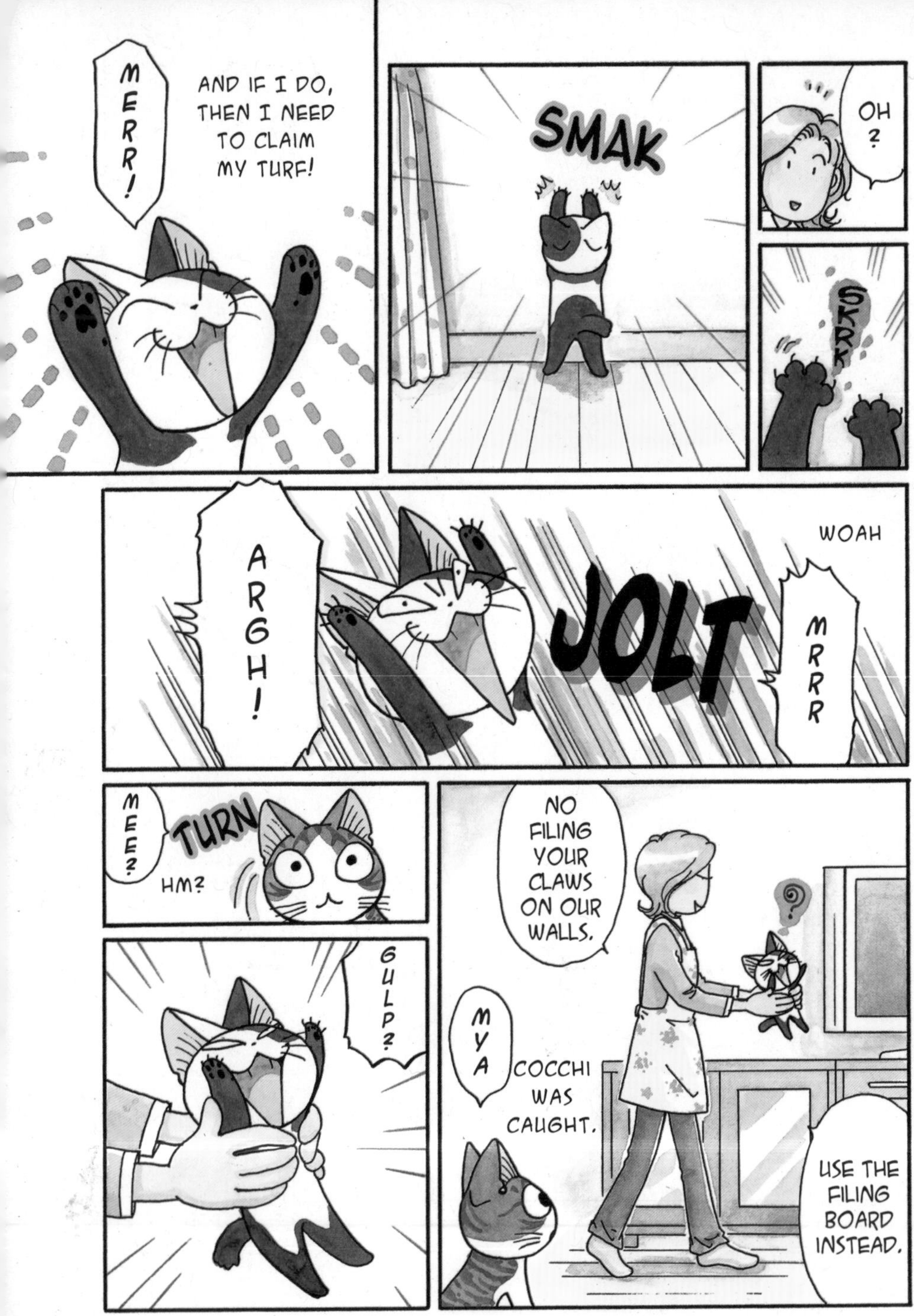
MERR!
AND IF I DO, THEN I NEED TO CLAIM MY TURF!
SMAK
OH?
SKRK
ARGH!
JOLT
WOAH
MRRR
MEE?
TURN
HM?
NO FILING YOUR CLAWS ON OUR WALLS.
GULP?
MYA
COCCHI WAS CAUGHT.
USE THE FILING BOARD INSTEAD.

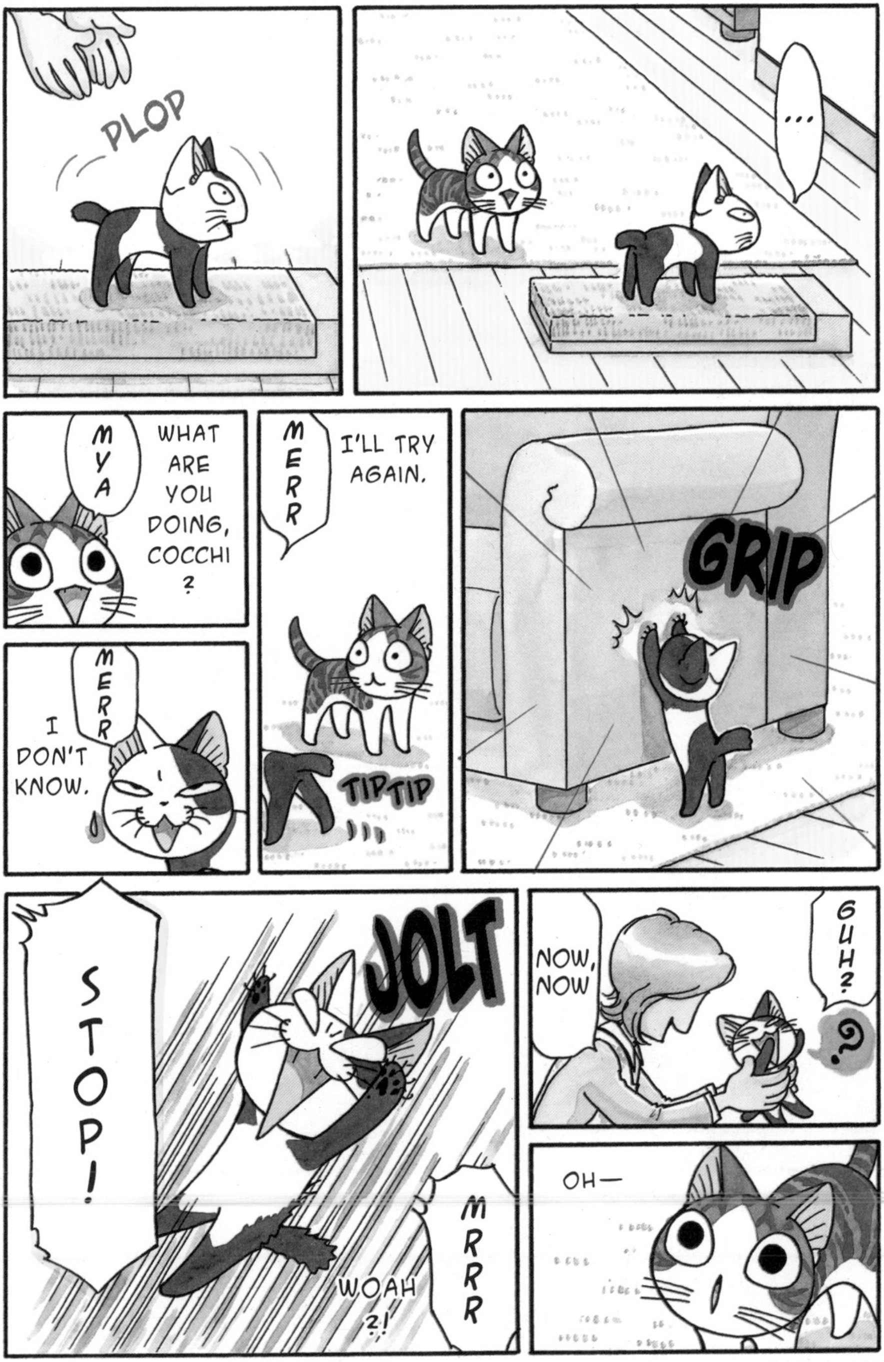
PLOP
...
MYA
WHAT ARE YOU DOING, COCCHI?
MERR
I DON'T KNOW.
MERR
I'LL TRY AGAIN.
TIP TIP
GRIP
STOP!
JOLT
MRRR
WOAH?!
NOW, NOW
GUH?
?
OH—

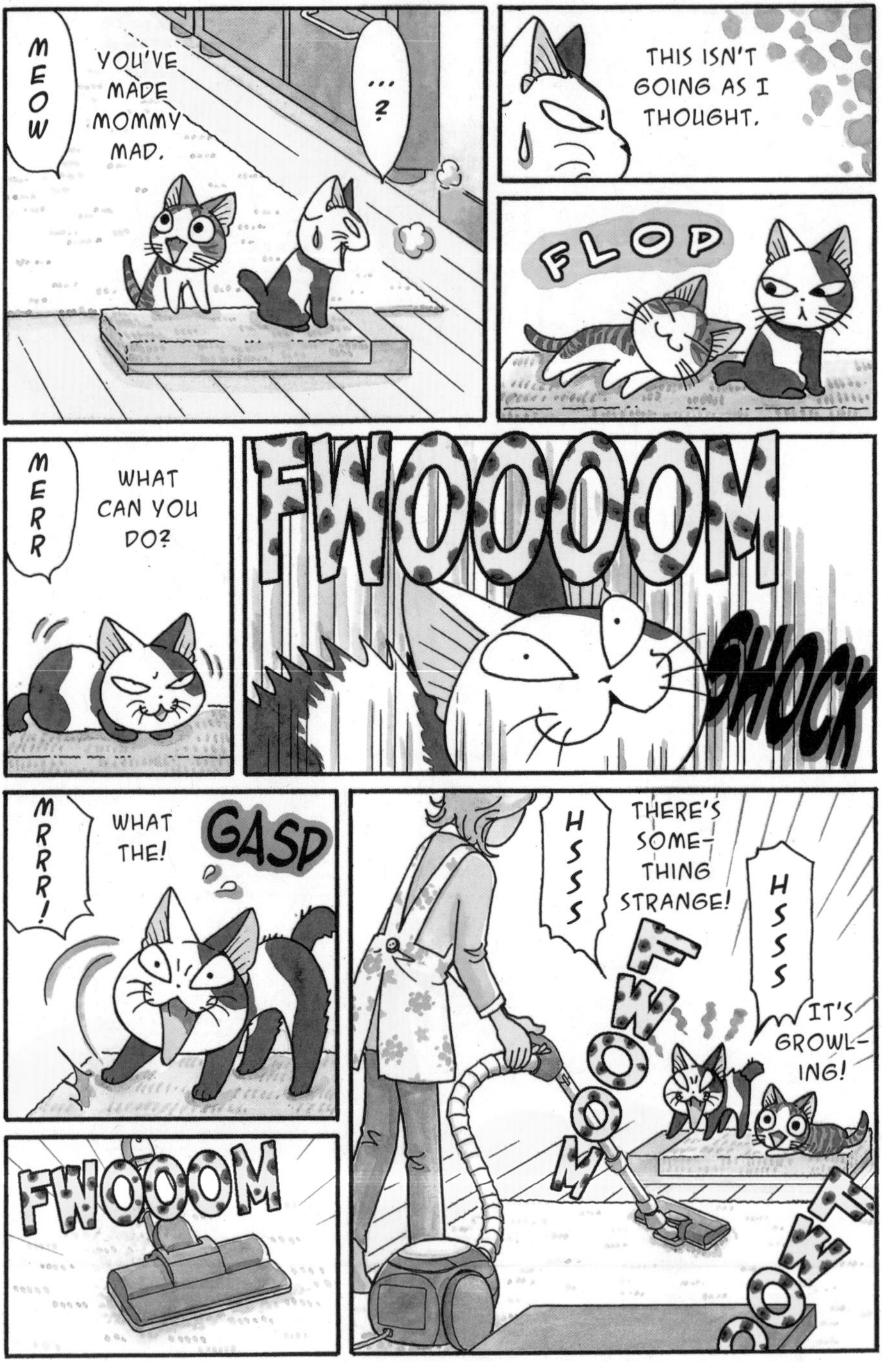
MEOW
YOU'VE MADE MOMMY MAD.
...?
THIS ISN'T GOING AS I THOUGHT.
FLOP
MERR
WHAT CAN YOU DO?
FWOOOOM
SHOCK
MRRR!
WHAT THE!
GASP
FWOOOM
HSSS
THERE'S SOME-THING STRANGE!
HSSS
IT'S GROWL-ING!
FWOOOM
FWOOOOM

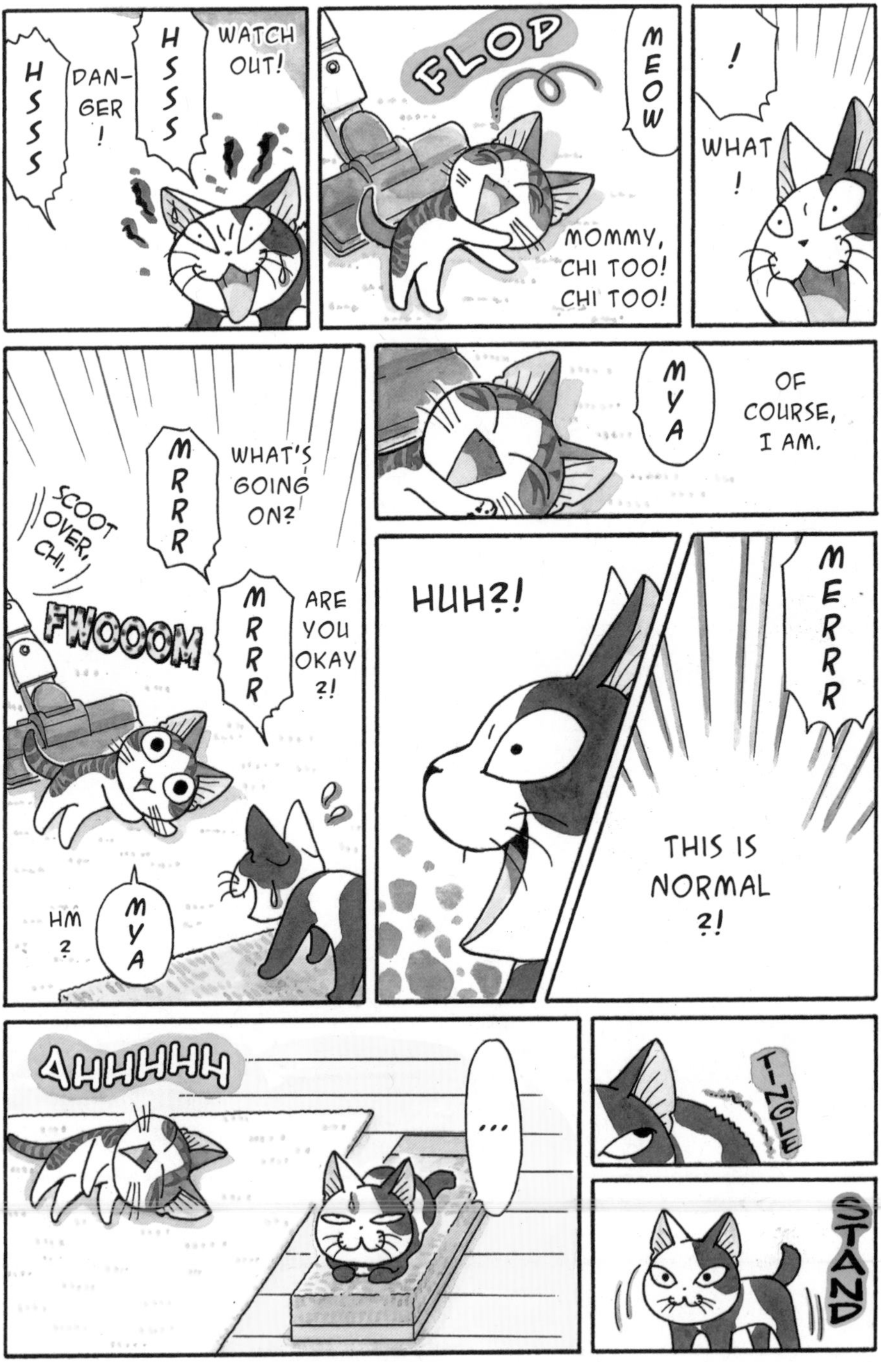
HSSS
DAN-GER!
HSSS
WATCH OUT!
FLOP
MEOW
MOMMY, CHI TOO! CHI TOO!
!
WHAT!
SCOOT OVER, CHI.
MRRR
WHAT'S GOING ON?
FWOOOM
MRRR
ARE YOU OKAY?!
HM?
MYA
MYA
OF COURSE, I AM.
HUH?!
MERRRR
THIS IS NORMAL?!
AHHHHH
...
TINGLE
STAND

AMBLE AMBLE
AMBLE
AMBLE AMBLE

AMBLE AMBLE AMBLE

7

MYA?

WHAT'S UP?

I'M LOOKING FOR A PLACE TO GO WEE.

MERR

MYA

IS THAT ALL?

HUP

MIYA

IN THAT CASE, IT'S THIS WAY.

TIP TIP TIP

GREAT! WHERE?

MERR

TAP TAP TAP

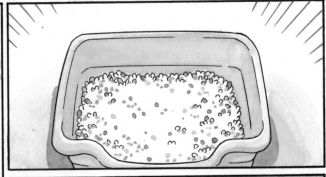

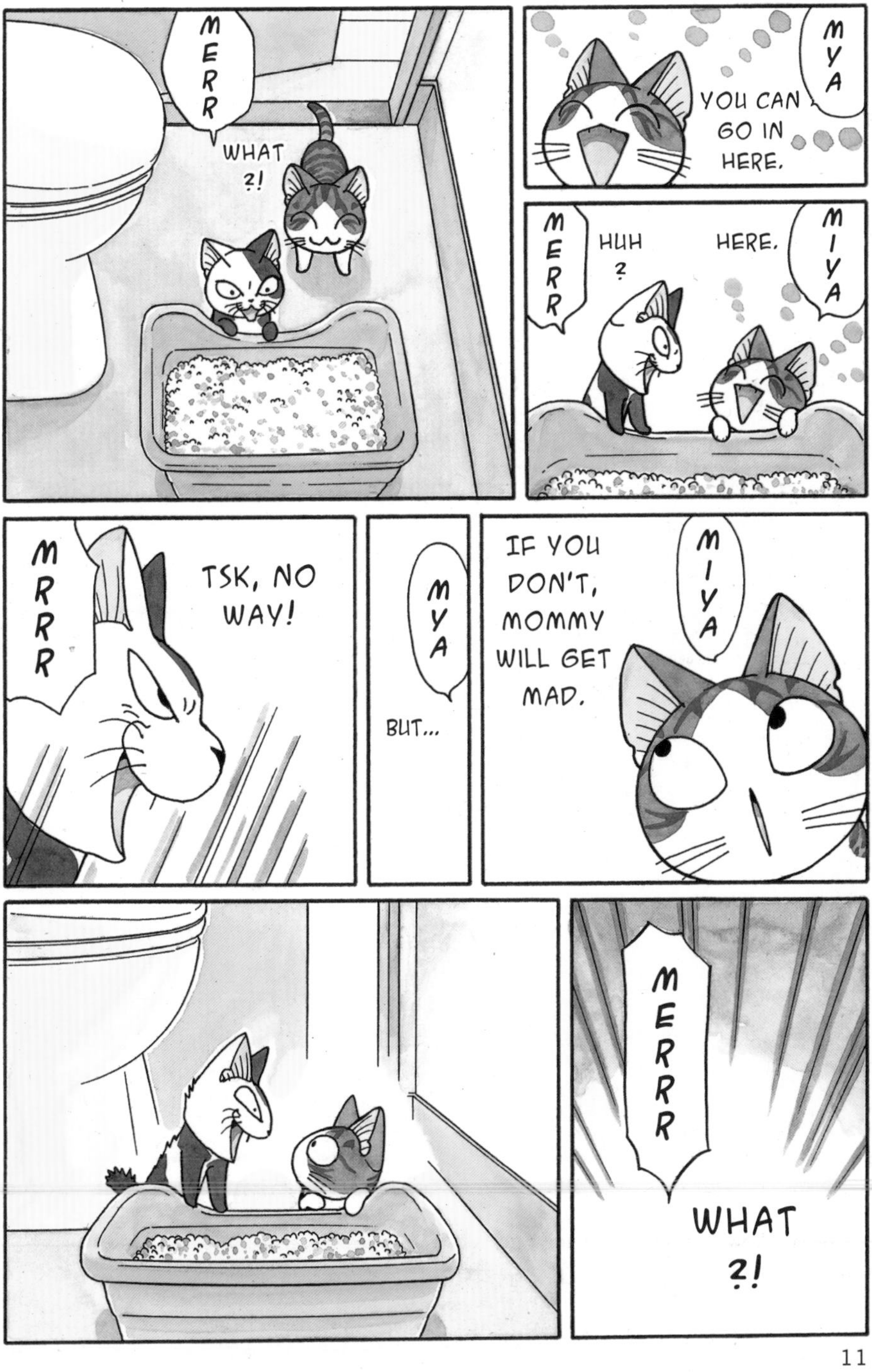
MERR
WHAT ?!
MYA
YOU CAN GO IN HERE.
MERR
HUH ?
HERE.
MIYA
MRRR
TSK, NO WAY!
MYA
BUT...
IF YOU DON'T, MOMMY WILL GET MAD.
MIYA
MERRR
WHAT ?!

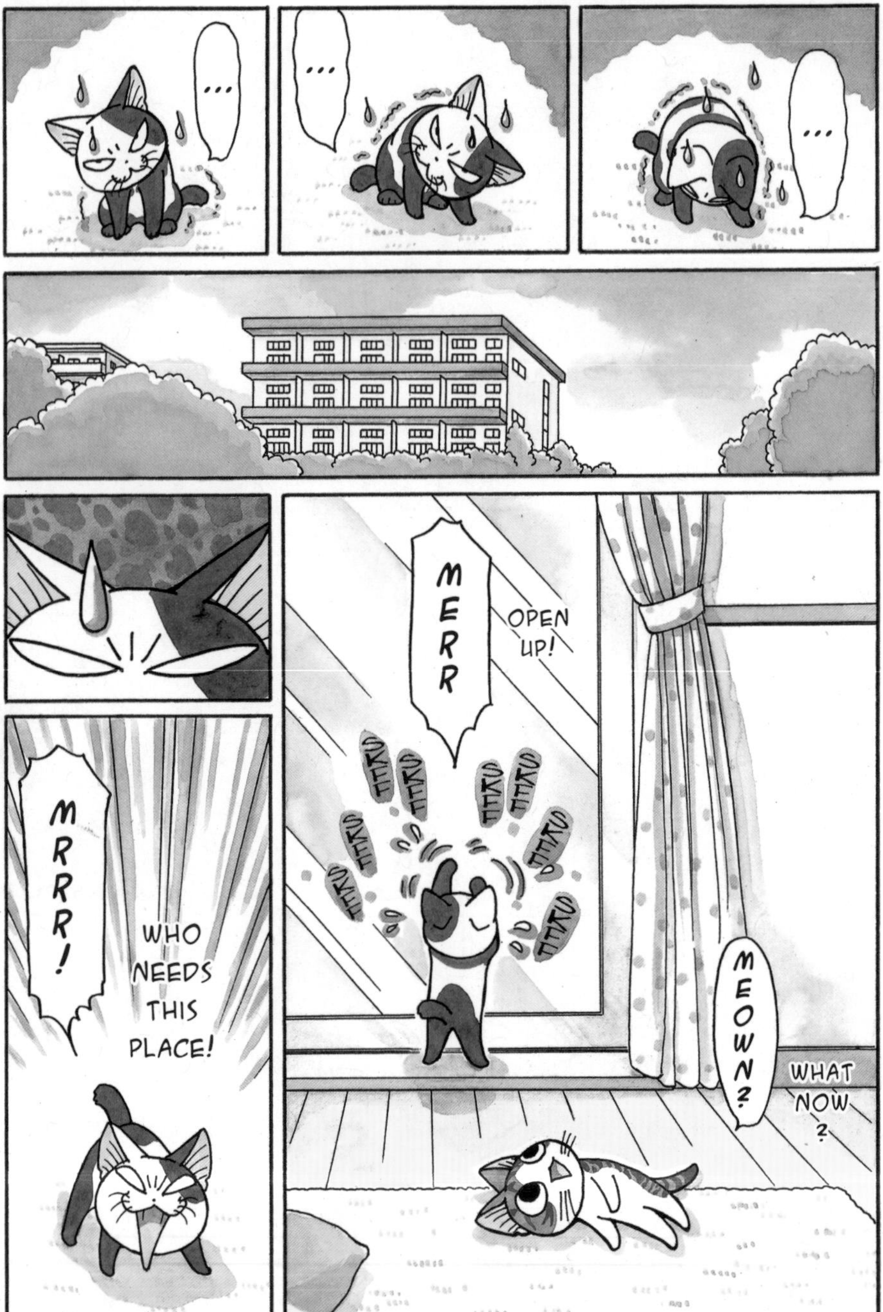
...
...
...
MERR
OPEN UP!
SKEE SKEE SKEE SKEE SKEE SKEE SKEE SKEE
MRRR!
WHO NEEDS THIS PLACE!
MEOWN?
WHAT NOW?

the end

homemade 166: a cat feels certain

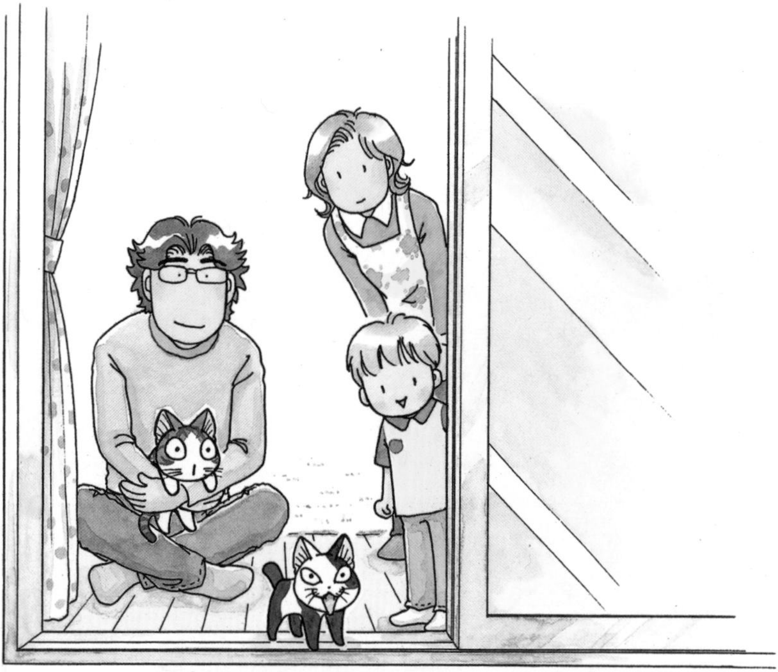

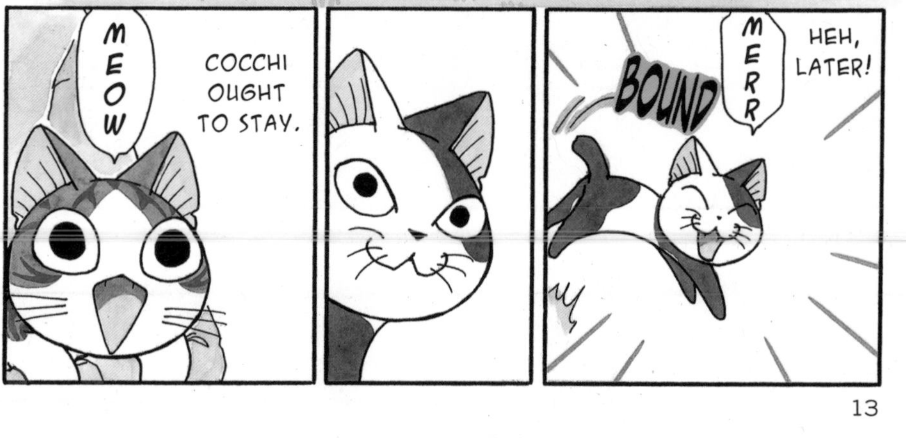
MEOW
COCCHI OUGHT TO STAY.
BOUND
MERR
HEH, LATER!

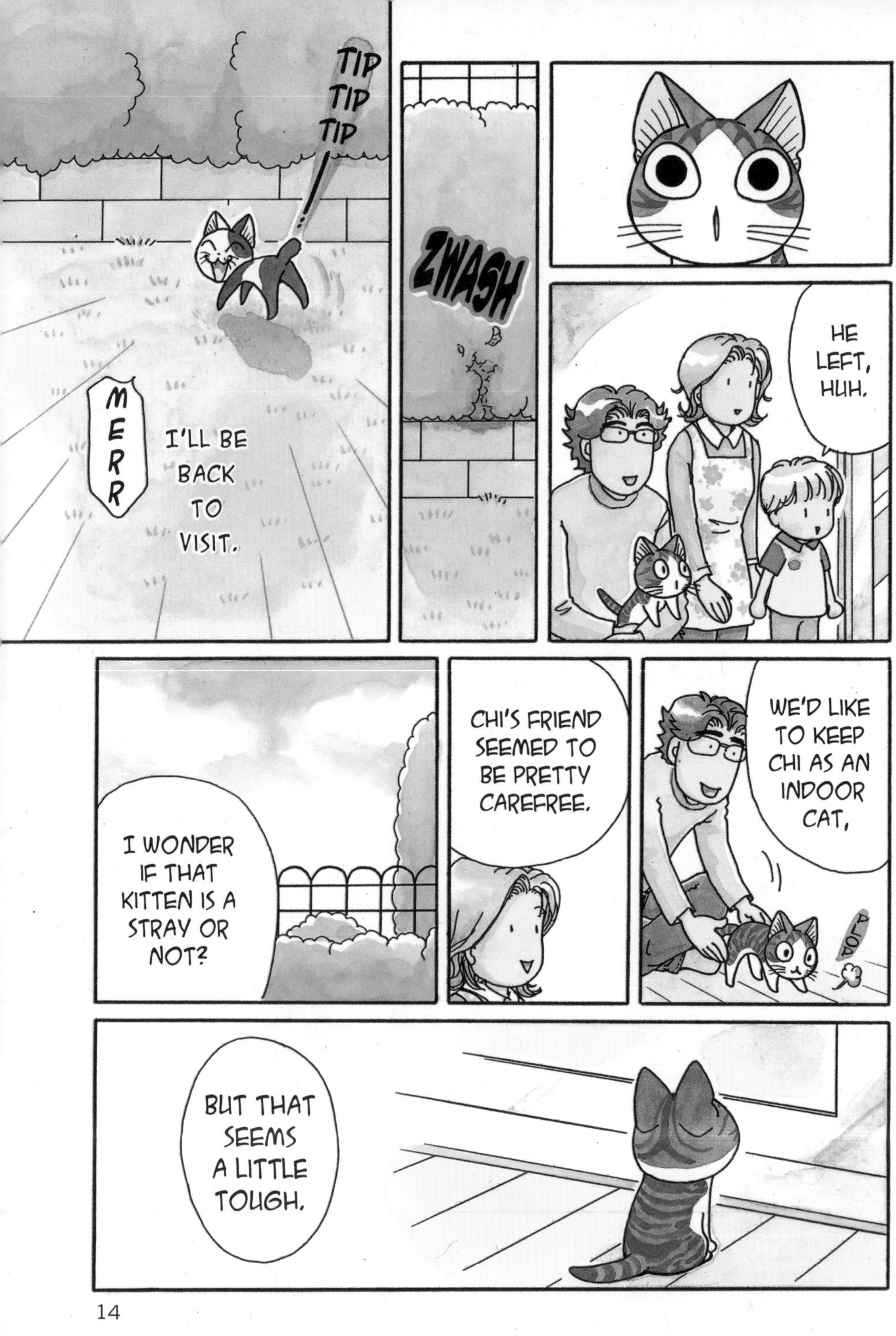
TIP
TIP
TIP
MERR
I'LL BE BACK TO VISIT.
ZWASH
HE LEFT, HUH.
I WONDER IF THAT KITTEN IS A STRAY OR NOT?
CHI'S FRIEND SEEMED TO BE PRETTY CAREFREE.
WE'D LIKE TO KEEP CHI AS AN INDOOR CAT,
PLOP
BUT THAT SEEMS A LITTLE TOUGH.

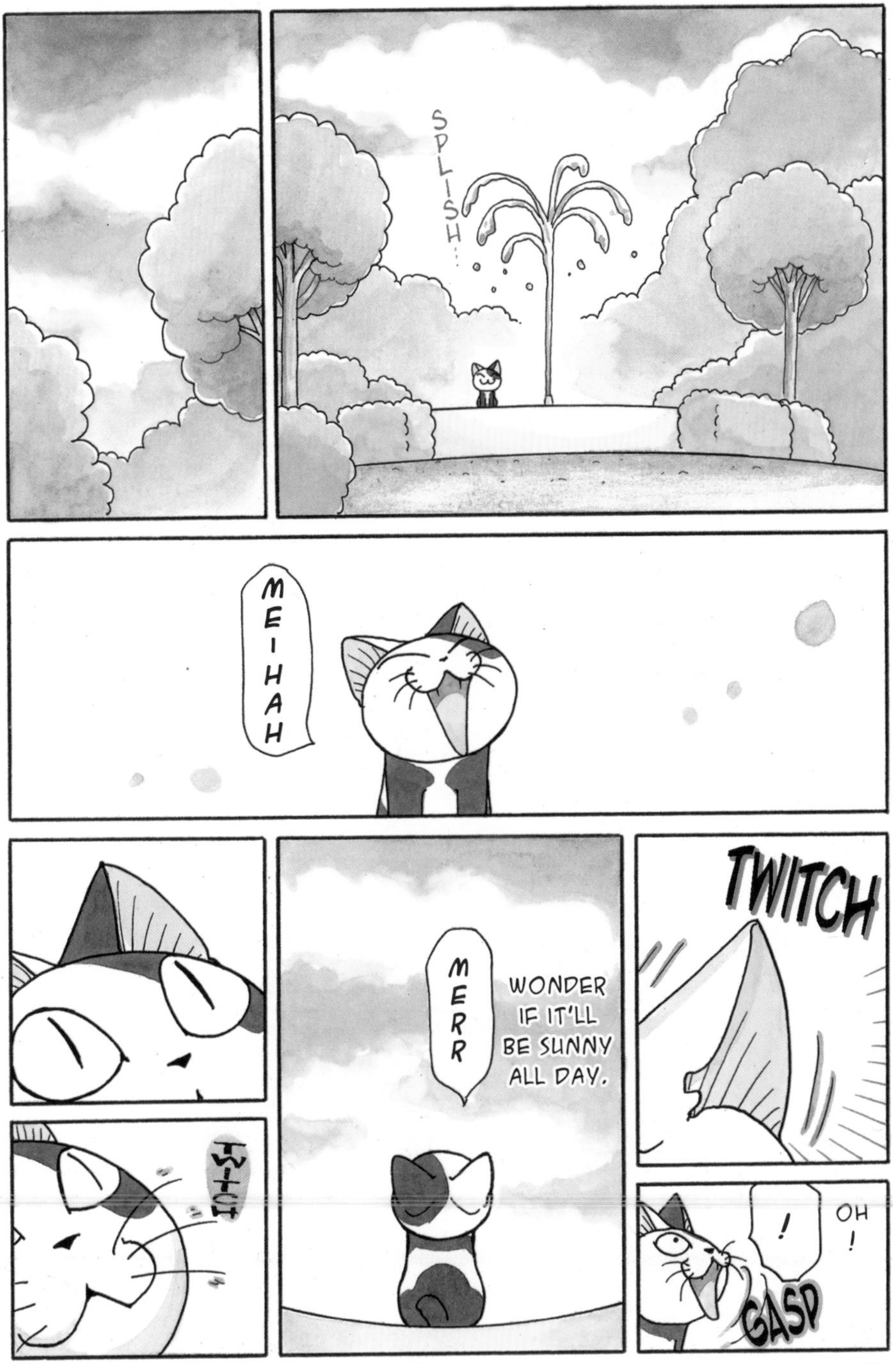
SPLISH...
MEIHAH
TWITCH
MERR
WONDER IF IT'LL BE SUNNY ALL DAY.
TWITCH
!
OH!
GASP

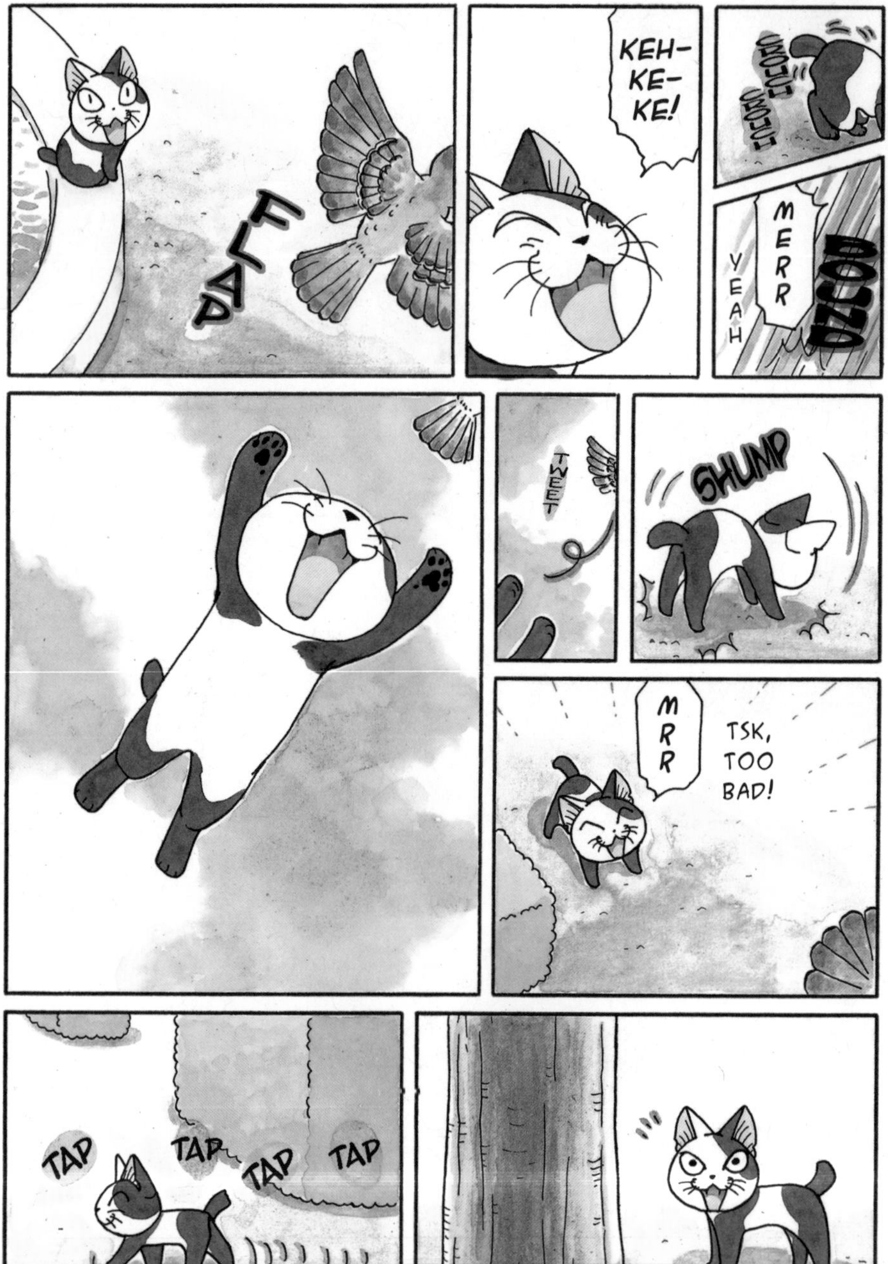
FLAP
KEH-KE-KE!
CROUCH CROUCH
MERR
YEAH
BOING
TWEET
SHUMP
MRR
TSK, TOO BAD!
TAP TAP TAP TAP

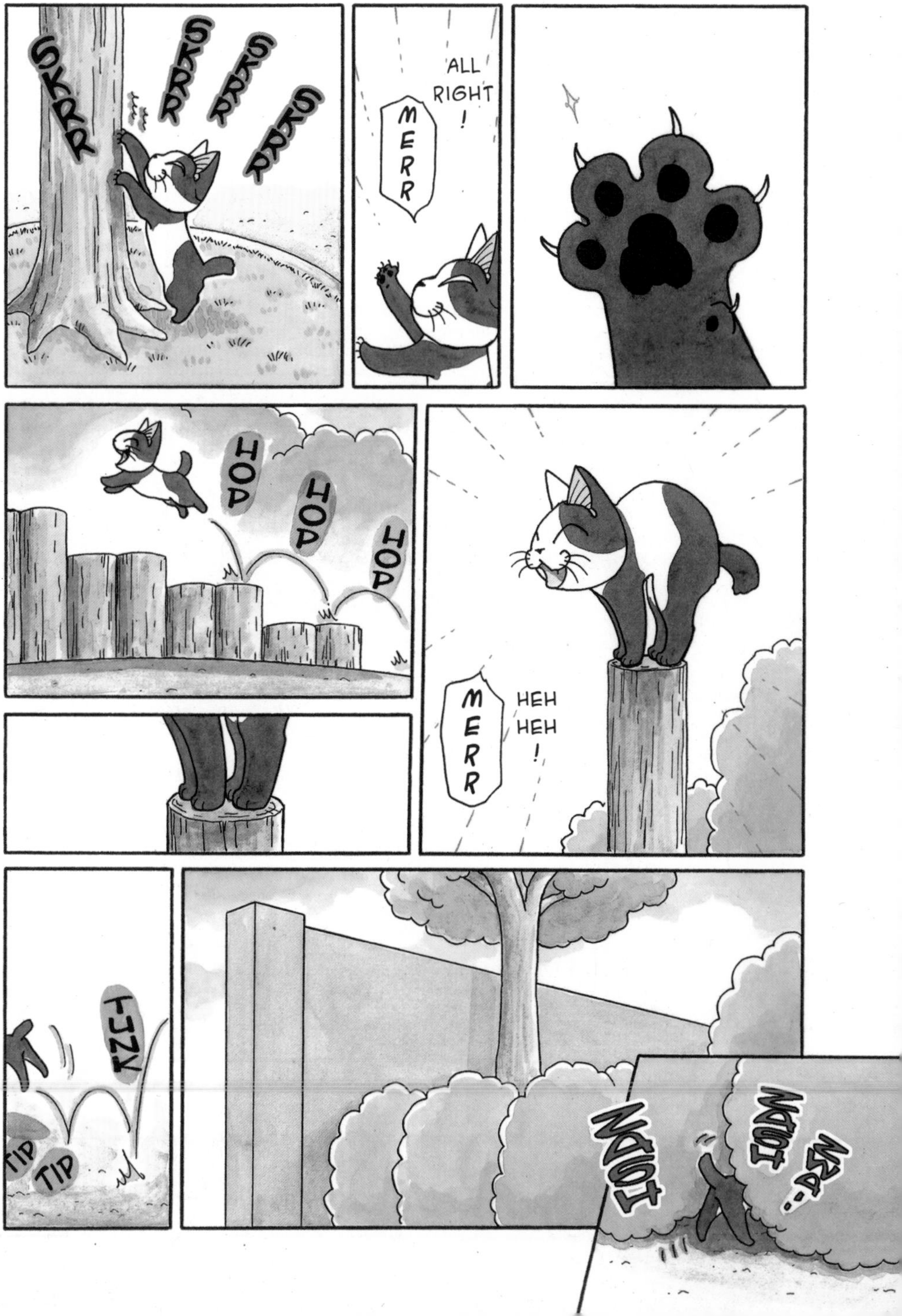
SKRR
SKRR
SKRR
SKRR
MERR
ALL RIGHT!
HOP
HOP
HOP
MERR
HEH HEH!
TUNK
TIP
TIP

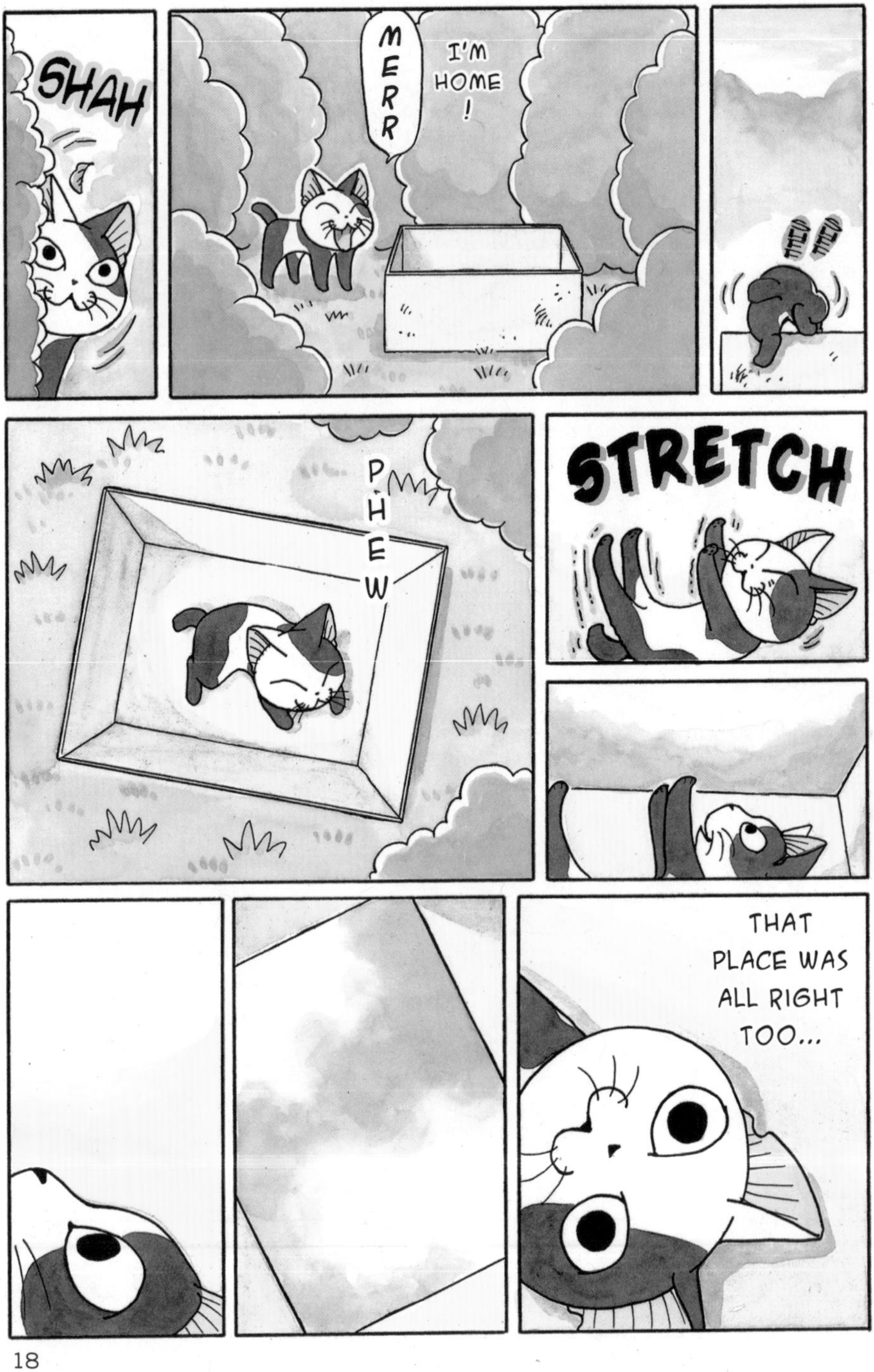
SHAH
MERR
I'M HOME!
PHEW
STRETCH
THAT PLACE WAS ALL RIGHT TOO...

BUT I CAN
REALLY CHILL
IN MY OWN
TERRITORY.

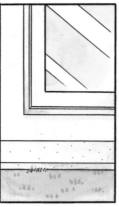

ROLL ROLL ROLL

BOP

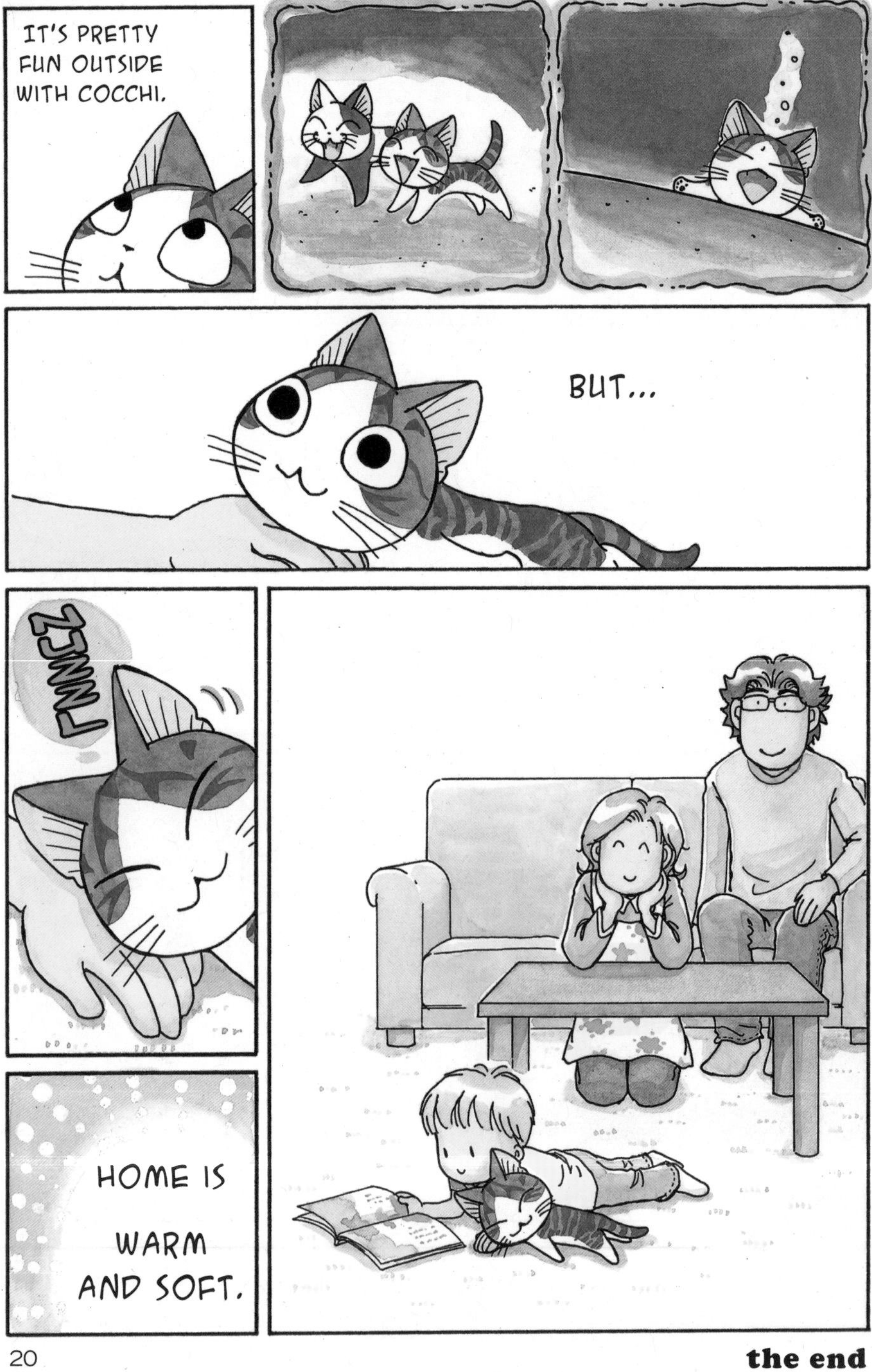
IT'S PRETTY FUN OUTSIDE WITH COCCHI.
BUT...
HOME IS WARM AND SOFT.

the end

homemade 167: a cat is watched

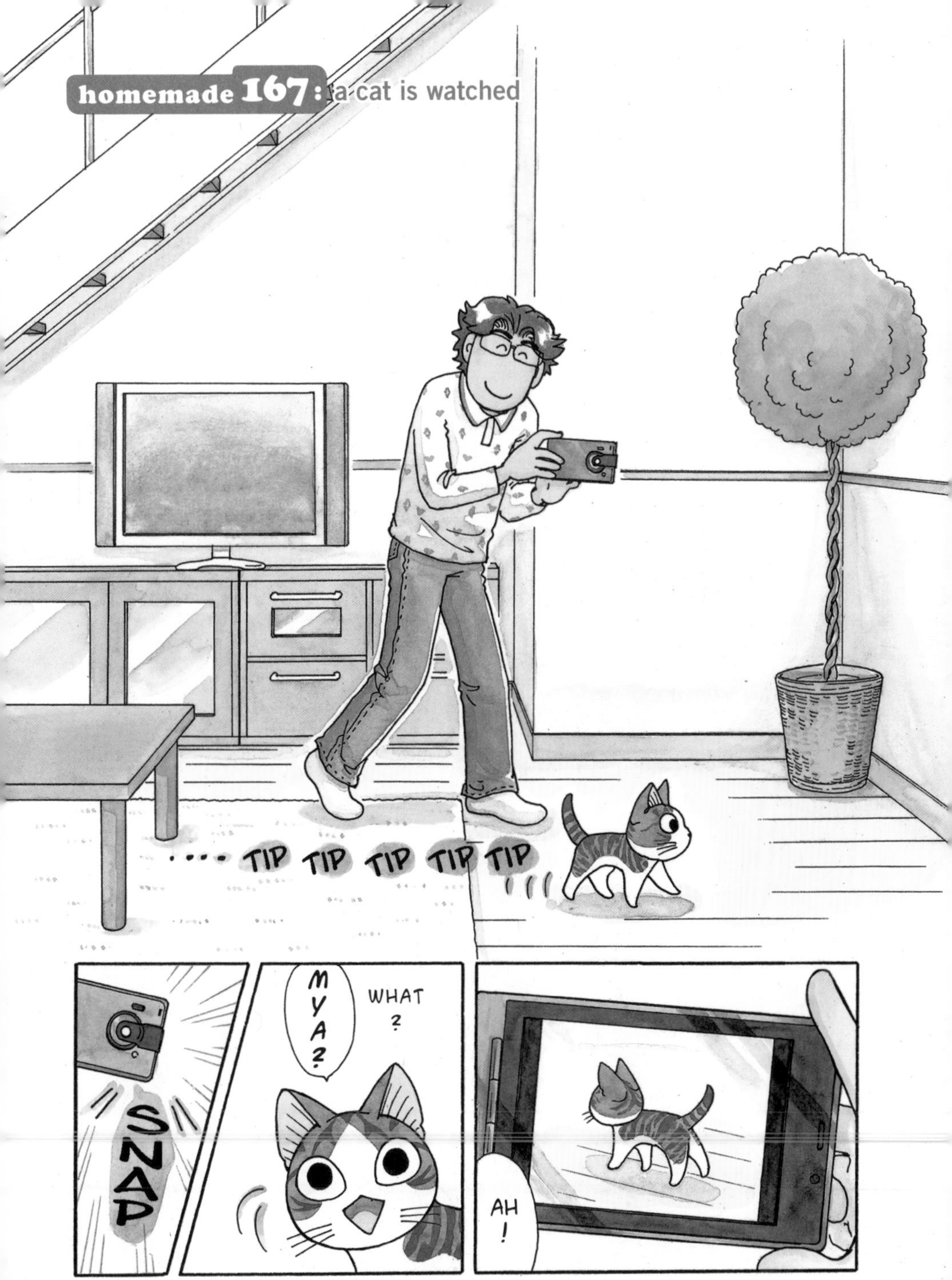
....TIP TIP TIP TIP TIP
SNAP
MYA?
WHAT?
AH!

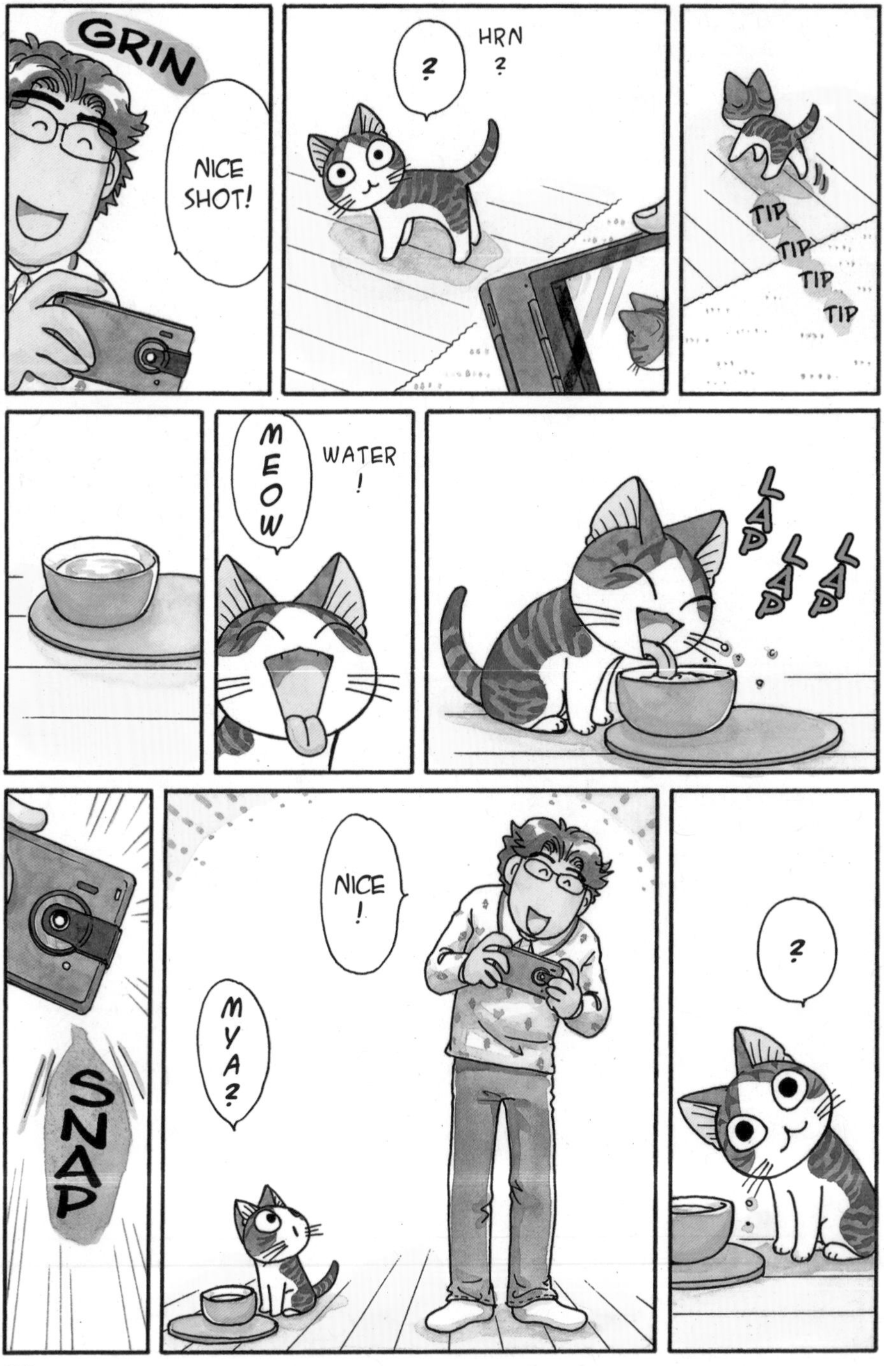
GRIN
NICE SHOT!
?
HRN ?
TIP
TIP
TIP
TIP
MEOW
WATER !
LAP
LAP
LAP
SNAP
NICE !
MYA?
?

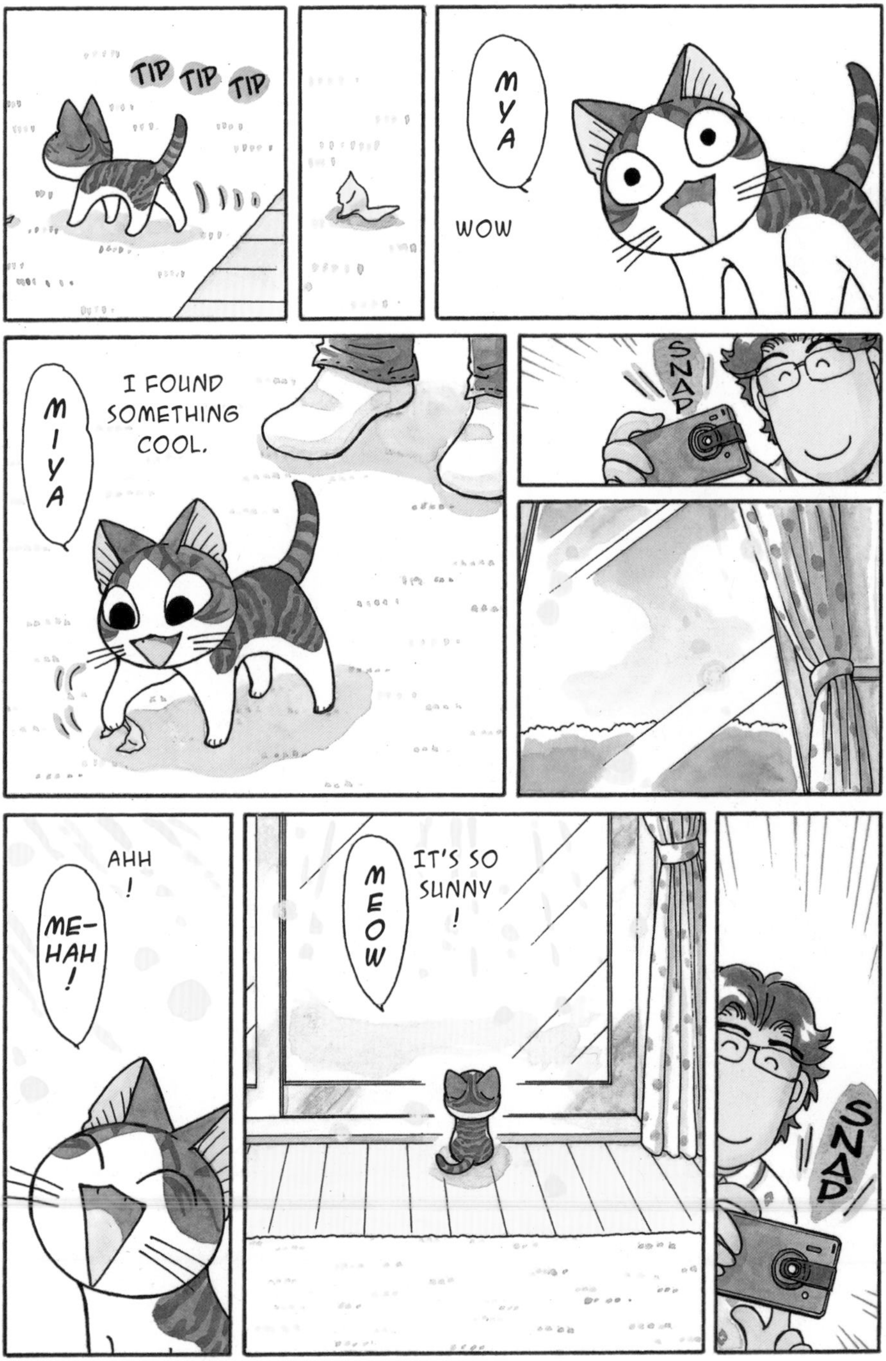
TIP TIP TIP
MYA
WOW
MIYA
I FOUND SOMETHING COOL.
SNAP
AHH!
ME-HAH!
MEOW
IT'S SO SUNNY!
SNAP

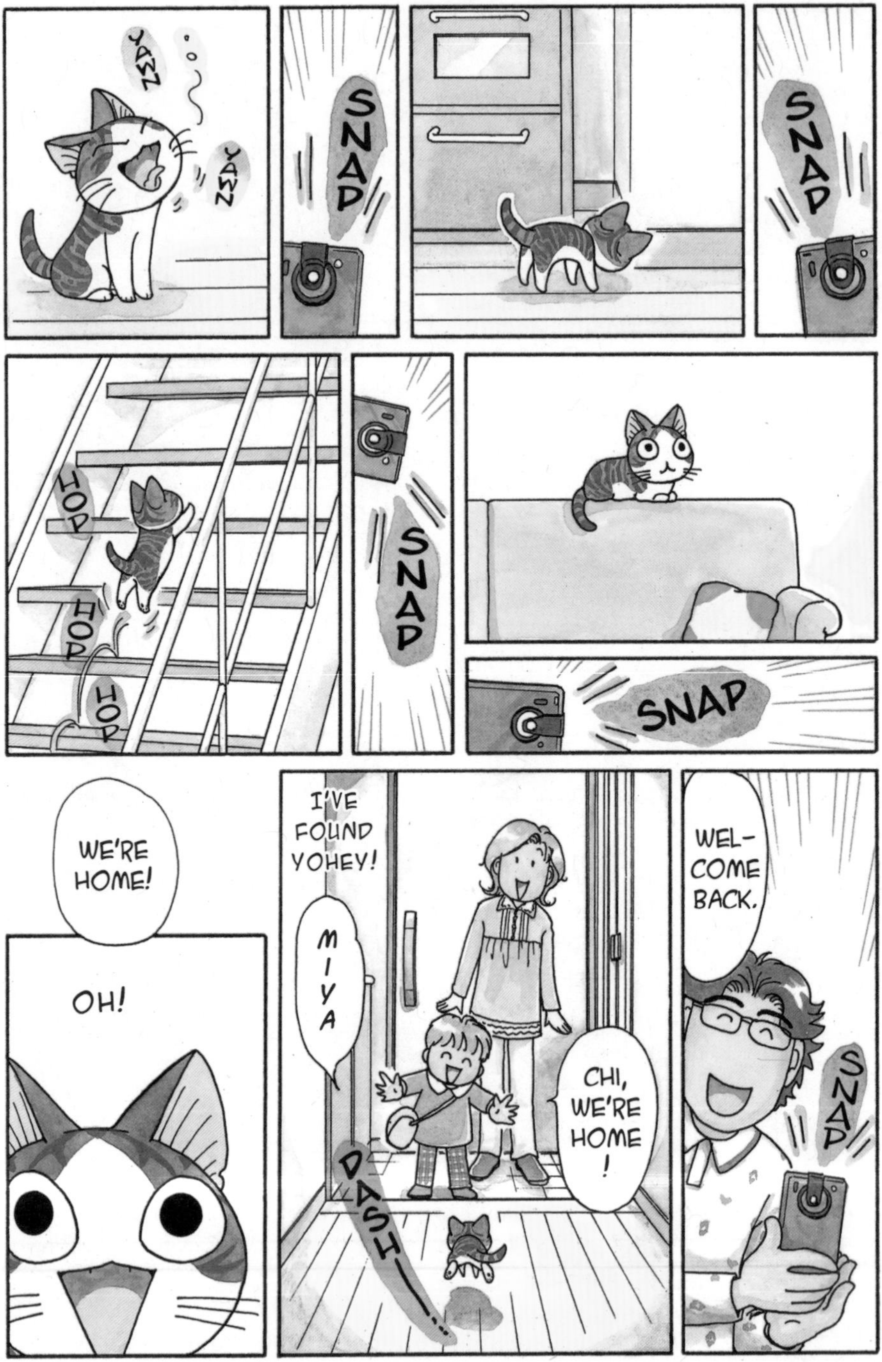
YAWN
YAWN
SNAP
SNAP
HOP
HOP
HOP
SNAP
SNAP
WE'RE HOME!
OH!
I'VE FOUND YOHEY!
MIYA
CHI, WE'RE HOME!
DASH
WEL-COME BACK.
SNAP

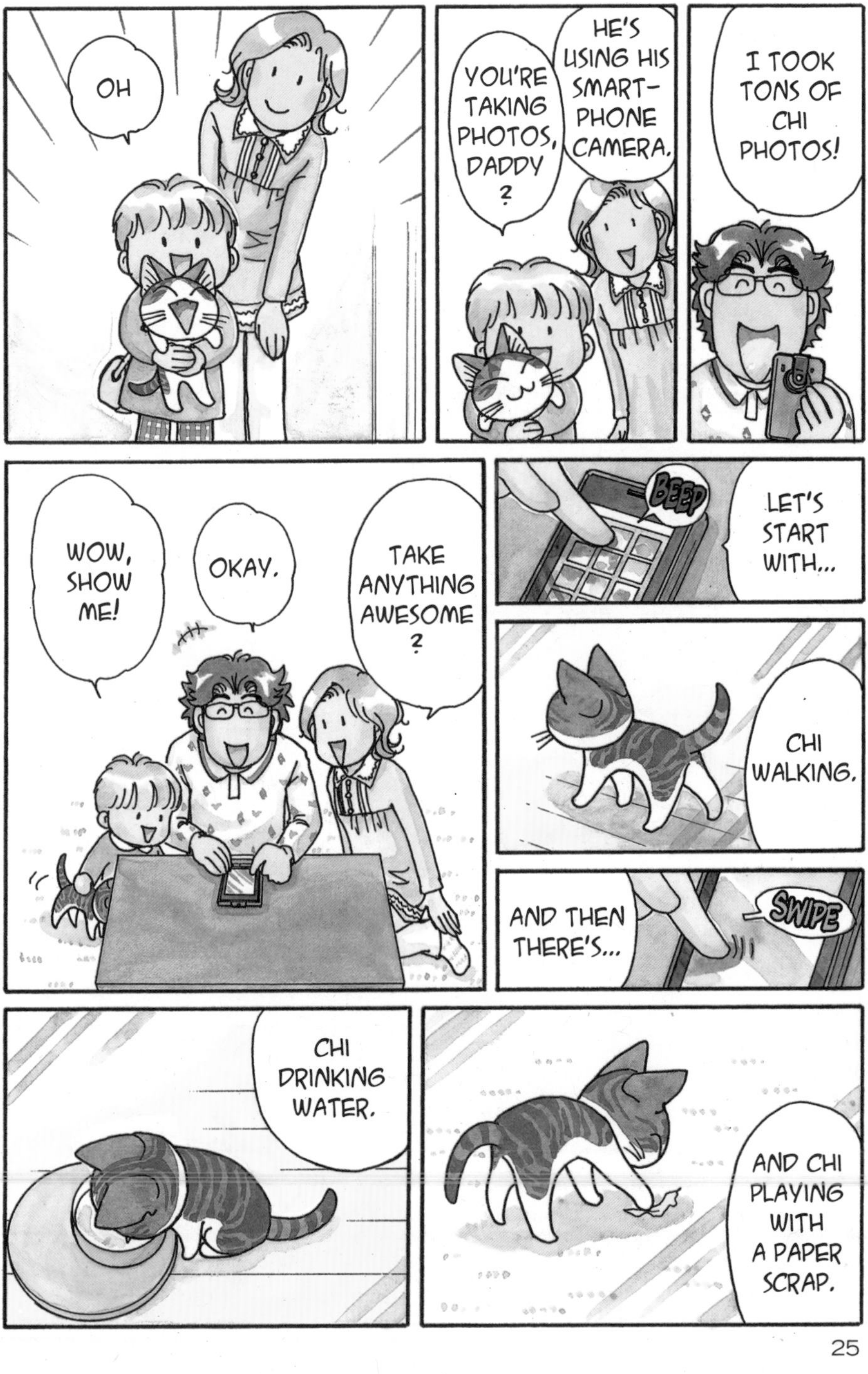
OH
YOU'RE TAKING PHOTOS, DADDY?
HE'S USING HIS SMART-PHONE CAMERA.
I TOOK TONS OF CHI PHOTOS!
WOW, SHOW ME!
OKAY.
TAKE ANYTHING AWESOME?
BEEP
LET'S START WITH...
CHI WALKING.
AND THEN THERE'S...
SWIPE
CHI DRINKING WATER.
AND CHI PLAYING WITH A PAPER SCRAP.

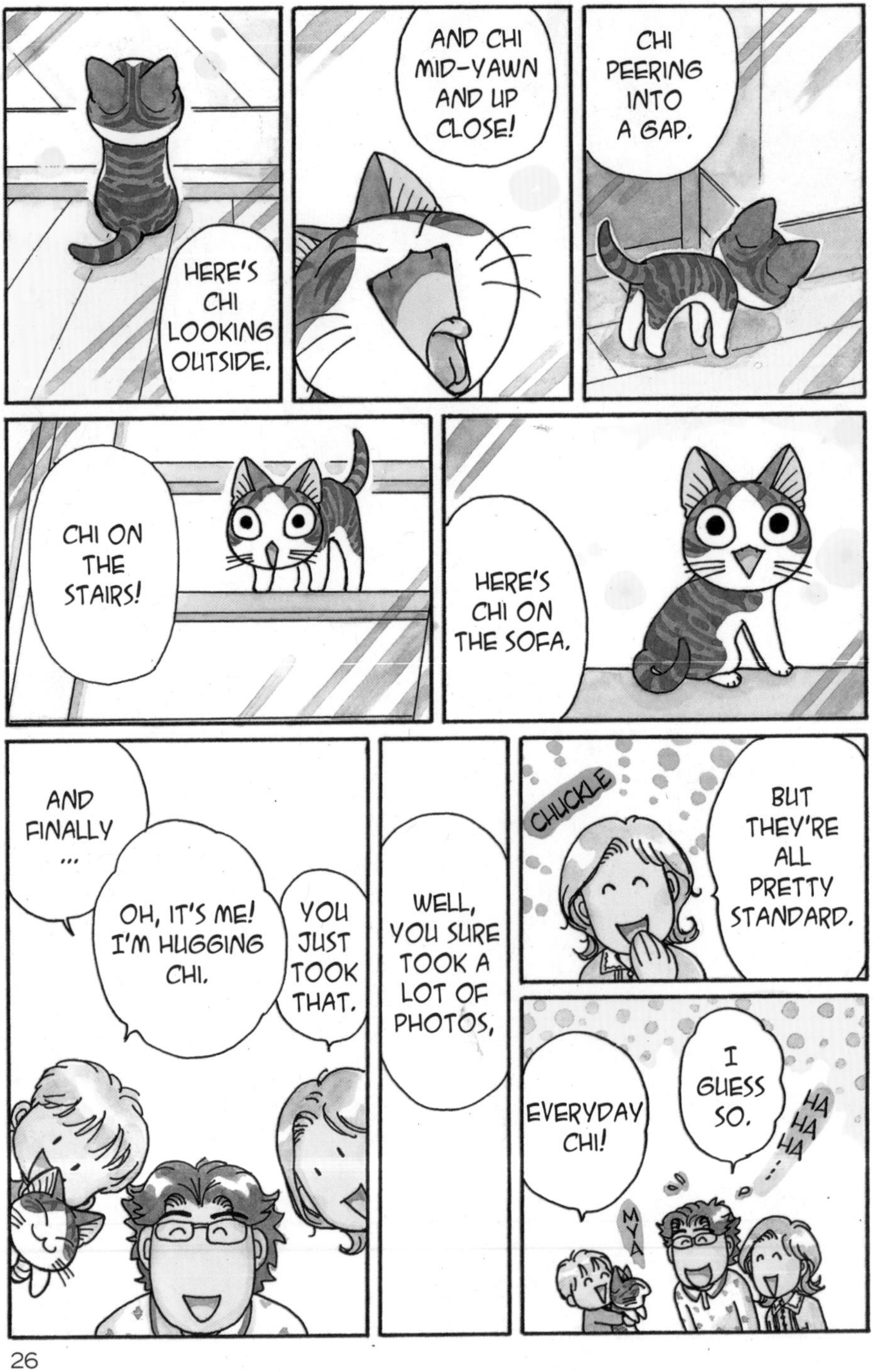
HERE'S CHI LOOKING OUTSIDE.
AND CHI MID-YAWN AND UP CLOSE!
CHI PEERING INTO A GAP.
CHI ON THE STAIRS!
HERE'S CHI ON THE SOFA.
AND FINALLY ...
OH, IT'S ME! I'M HUGGING CHI.
YOU JUST TOOK THAT.
WELL, YOU SURE TOOK A LOT OF PHOTOS,
CHUCKLE
BUT THEY'RE ALL PRETTY STANDARD.
EVERYDAY CHI!
I GUESS SO.
HA HA HA ...
MYA

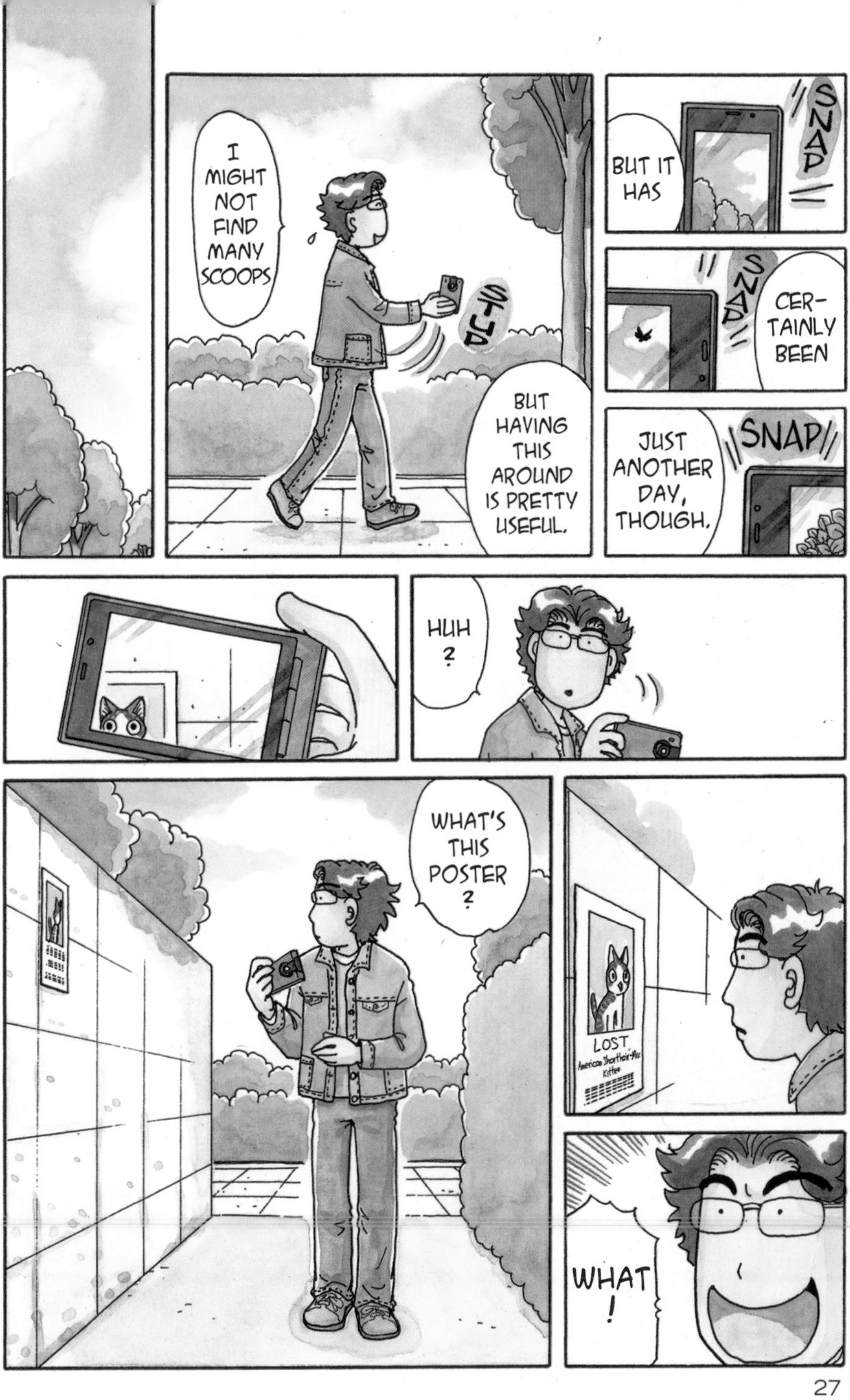
I MIGHT NOT FIND MANY SCOOPS
STUP
BUT HAVING THIS AROUND IS PRETTY USEFUL.
BUT IT HAS
SNAP
SNAP
CER-TAINLY BEEN
SNAP
JUST ANOTHER DAY, THOUGH.
HUH?
WHAT'S THIS POSTER?
LOST
American Shorthair-Mix Kitten
WHAT!

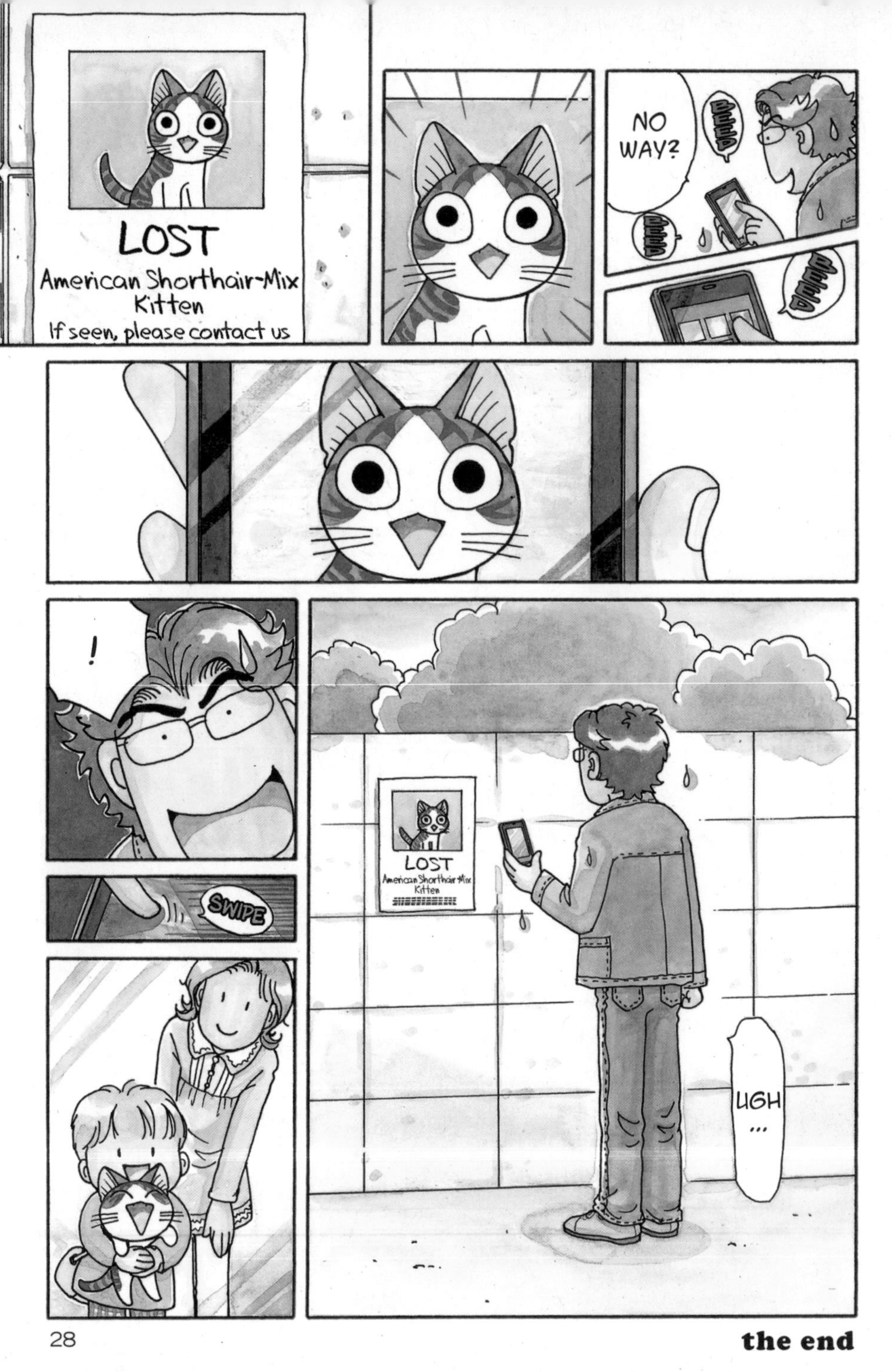
LOST
American Shorthair-Mix Kitten
If seen, please contact us
NO WAY?
BEEP
BEEP
BEEP
!
SWIPE
LOST
American Shorthair-Mix Kitten
UGH ...

the end

homemade 168: a cat is concerning

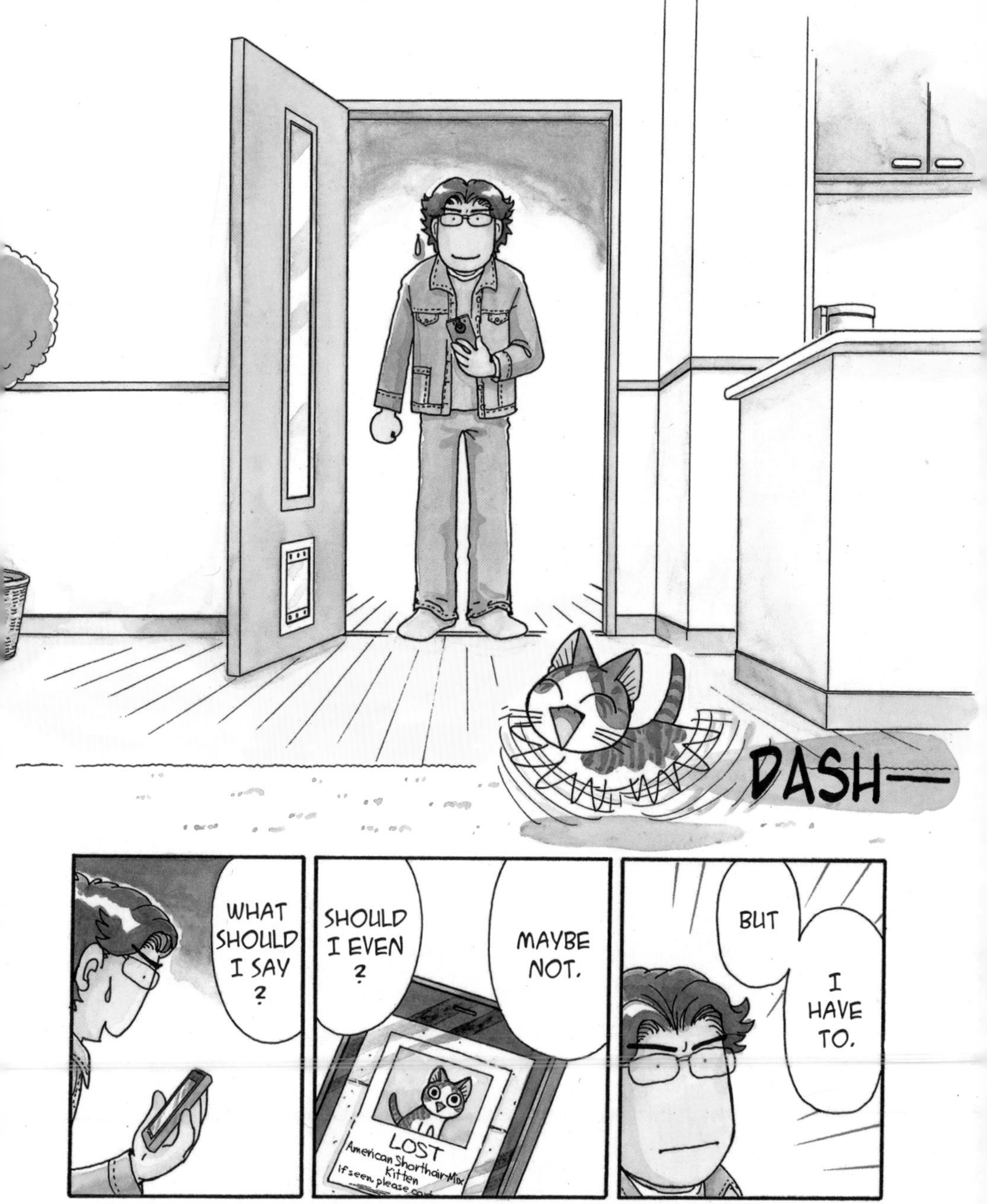

DASH—
WHAT SHOULD I SAY ?
SHOULD I EVEN ?
LOST
American Shorthair Mix Kitten
If seen, please
MAYBE NOT.
BUT
I HAVE TO.

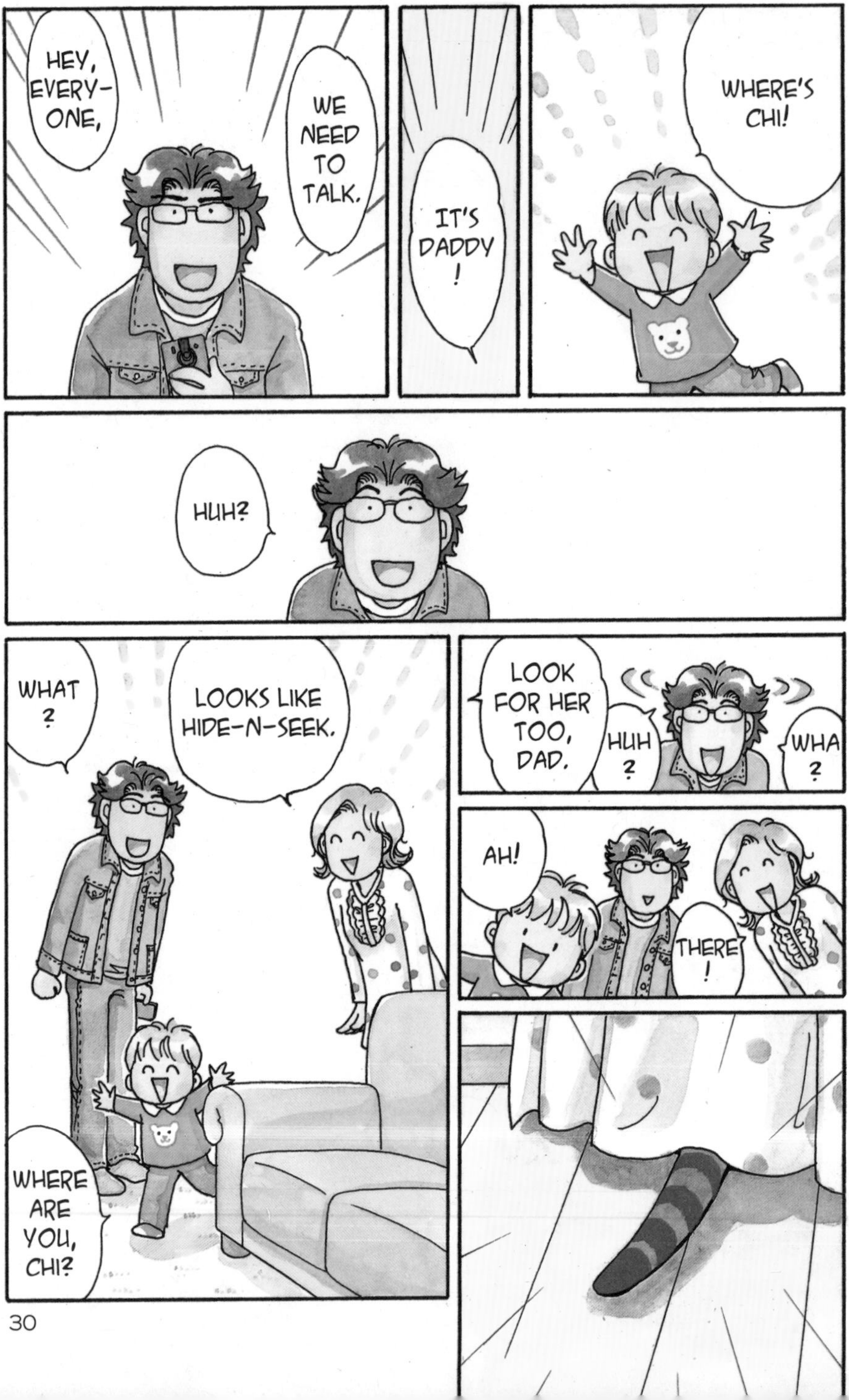
HEY, EVERY-ONE,
WE NEED TO TALK.
IT'S DADDY!
WHERE'S CHI!
HUH?
WHAT?
LOOKS LIKE HIDE-N-SEEK.
WHERE ARE YOU, CHI?
LOOK FOR HER TOO, DAD.
HUH?
WHA?
AH!
THERE!

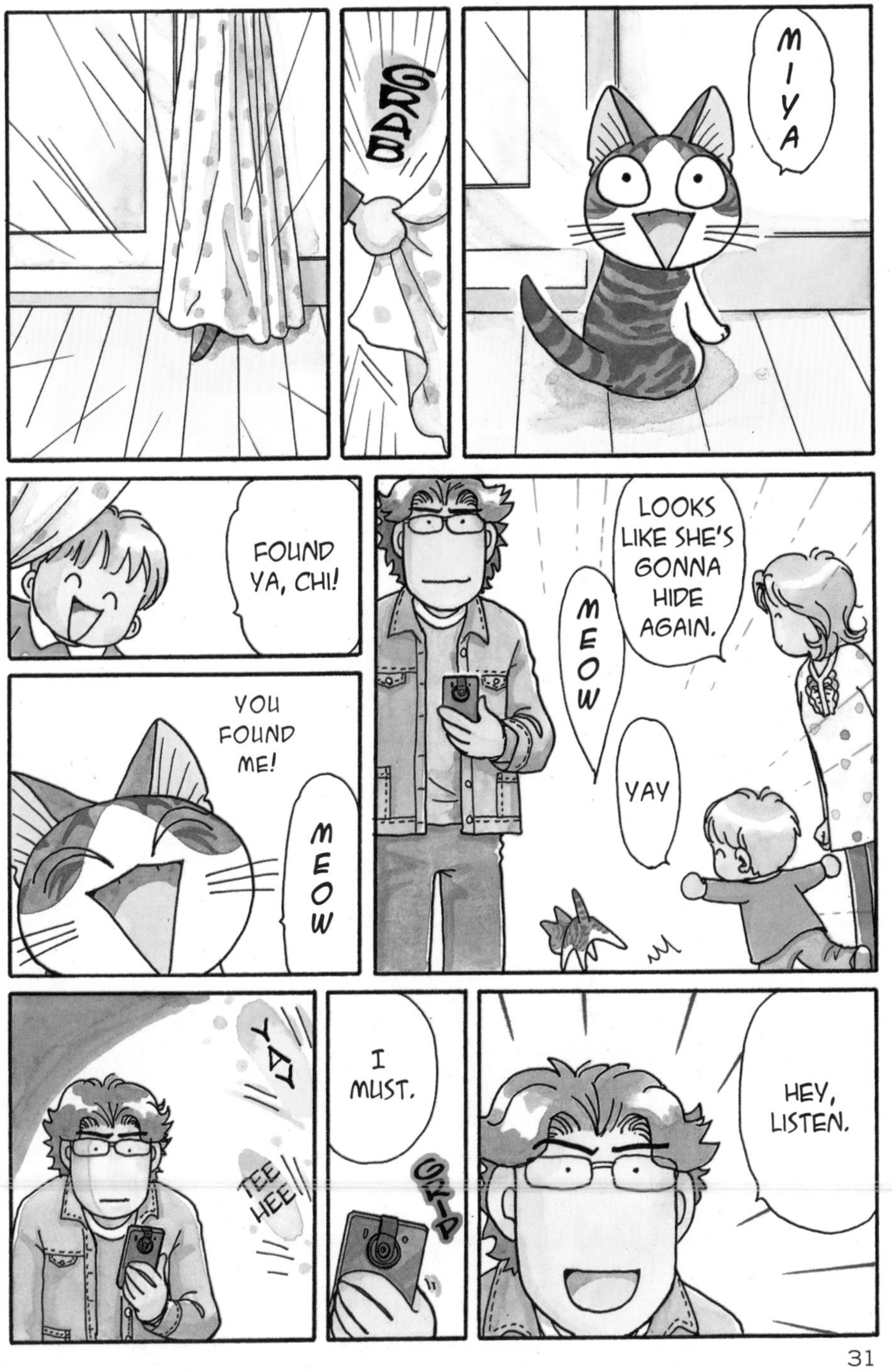

GRAB
MIYA
FOUND YA, CHI!
YOU FOUND ME!
MEOW
LOOKS LIKE SHE'S GONNA HIDE AGAIN.
MEOW
YAY
YAY
TEE HEE
I MUST.
GRIP
HEY, LISTEN.

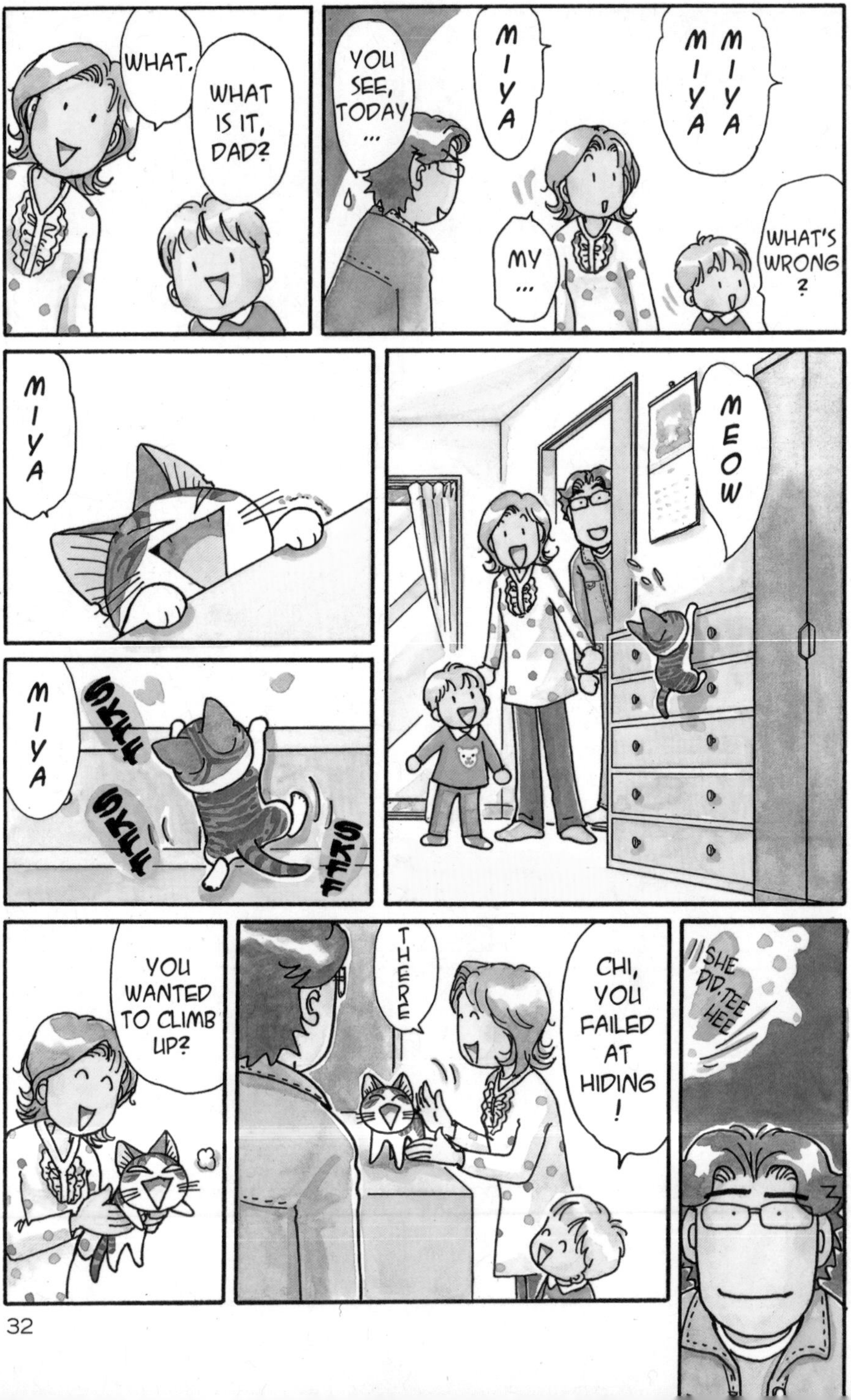
WHAT.
WHAT IS IT, DAD?
YOU SEE, TODAY ...
MIYA
MY ...
MIYA MIYA
WHAT'S WRONG?
MIYA
MIYA
SKFF SKFF
SKFF
MEOW
YOU WANTED TO CLIMB UP?
THERE
CHI, YOU FAILED AT HIDING!
SHE DID. TEE HEE

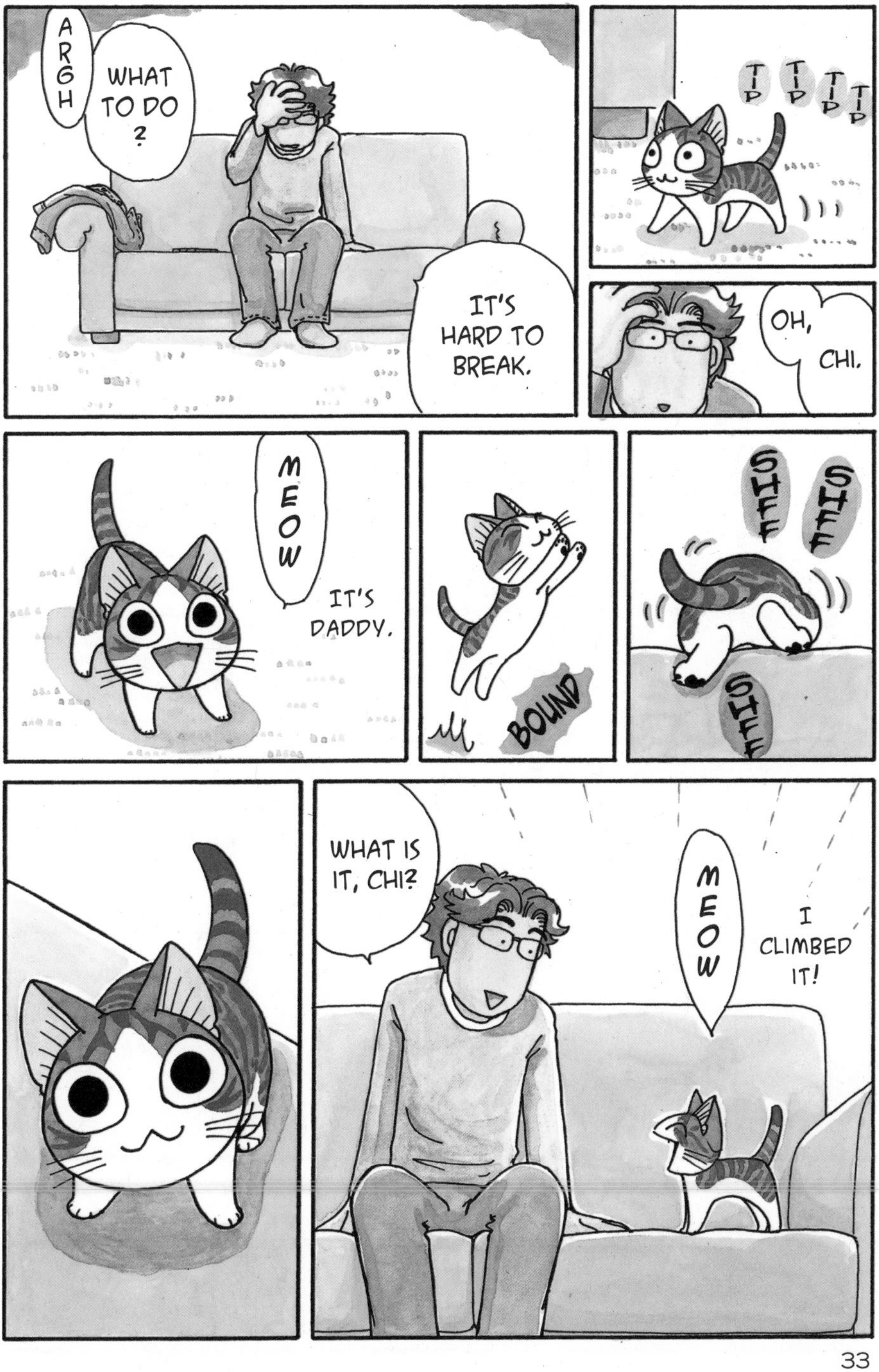
ARGH
WHAT TO DO?
IT'S HARD TO BREAK.
TIP TIP TIP TIP
OH, CHI.
MEOW
IT'S DADDY.
BOUND
SHFF SHFF
SHFF
WHAT IS IT, CHI?
MEOW
I CLIMBED IT!

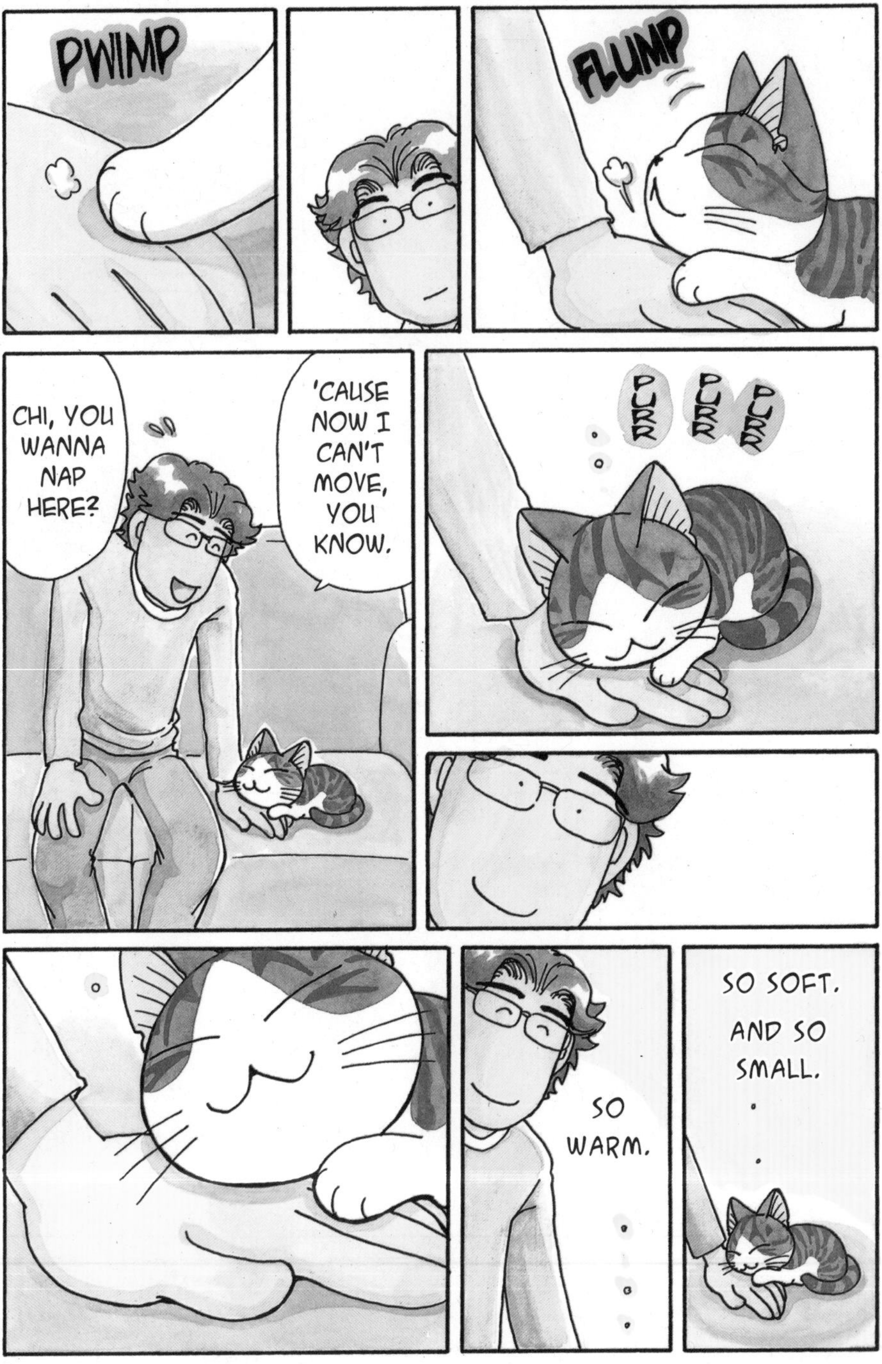
PWIMP
FLUMP
CHI, YOU WANNA NAP HERE?
'CAUSE NOW I CAN'T MOVE, YOU KNOW.
PURR PURR PURR
SO WARM.
SO SOFT.
AND SO SMALL.

FOR THE TIME BEING, MAYBE I'LL KEEP QUIET.

MEOW

YAY

YEAH, EVERYONE IS DOING WELL.

AND CHI?

HA HA

LIKE THIS.

CHI'S FINE, TOO.

I'LL SEND SOME PHOTOS SOON.

GRAB

NOT LIKE THAT, CHI!

MEOW MEOW

ROLL KLUNK

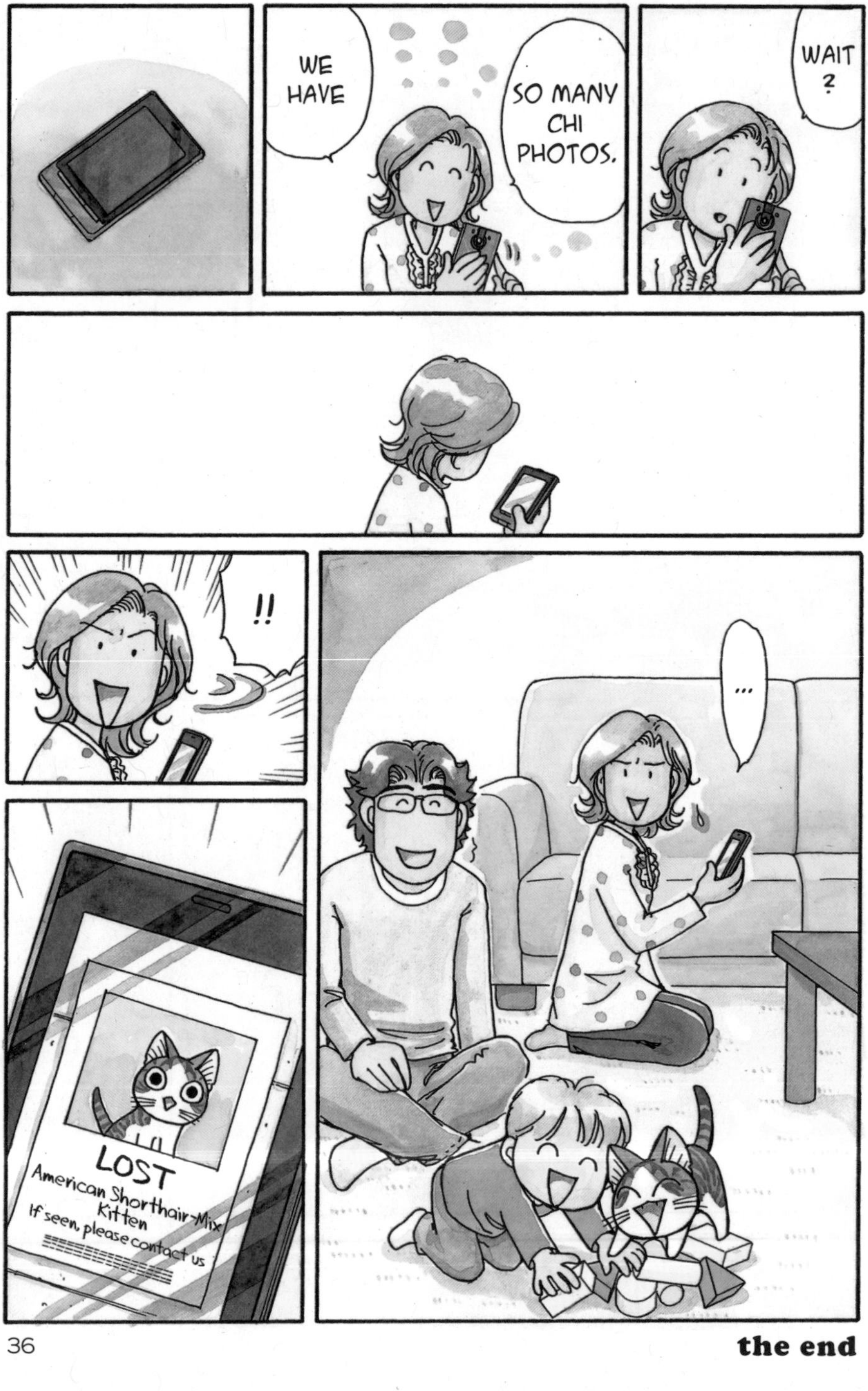

WE HAVE
SO MANY CHI PHOTOS.
WAIT ?
!!
LOST
American Shorthair-Mix Kitten
If seen, please contact us
...

the end

homemade 169: a cat communicates

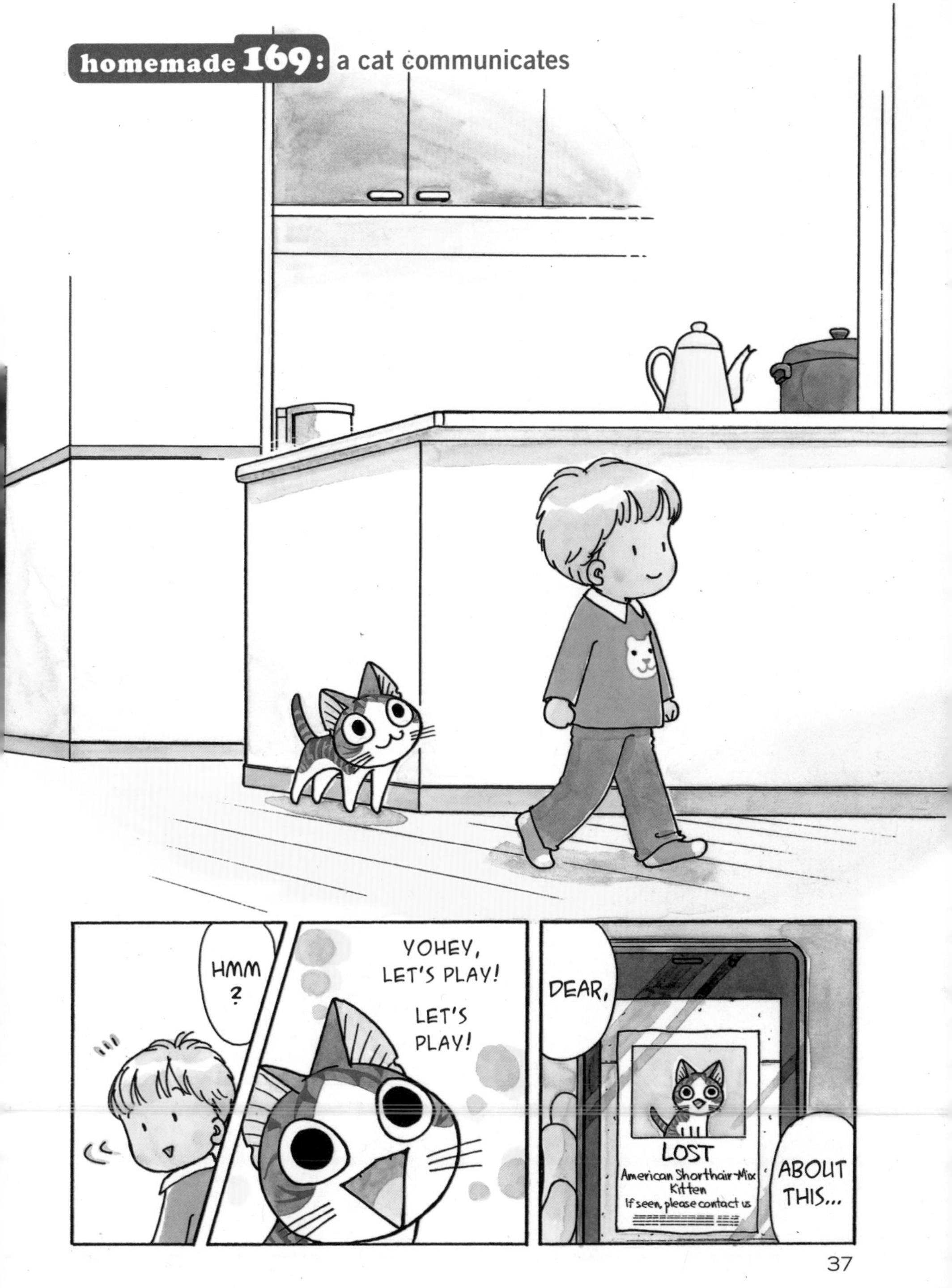

HMM ?
YOHEY, LET'S PLAY!
LET'S PLAY!
DEAR,
LOST
American Shorthair-Mix Kitten
If seen, please contact us
ABOUT THIS...

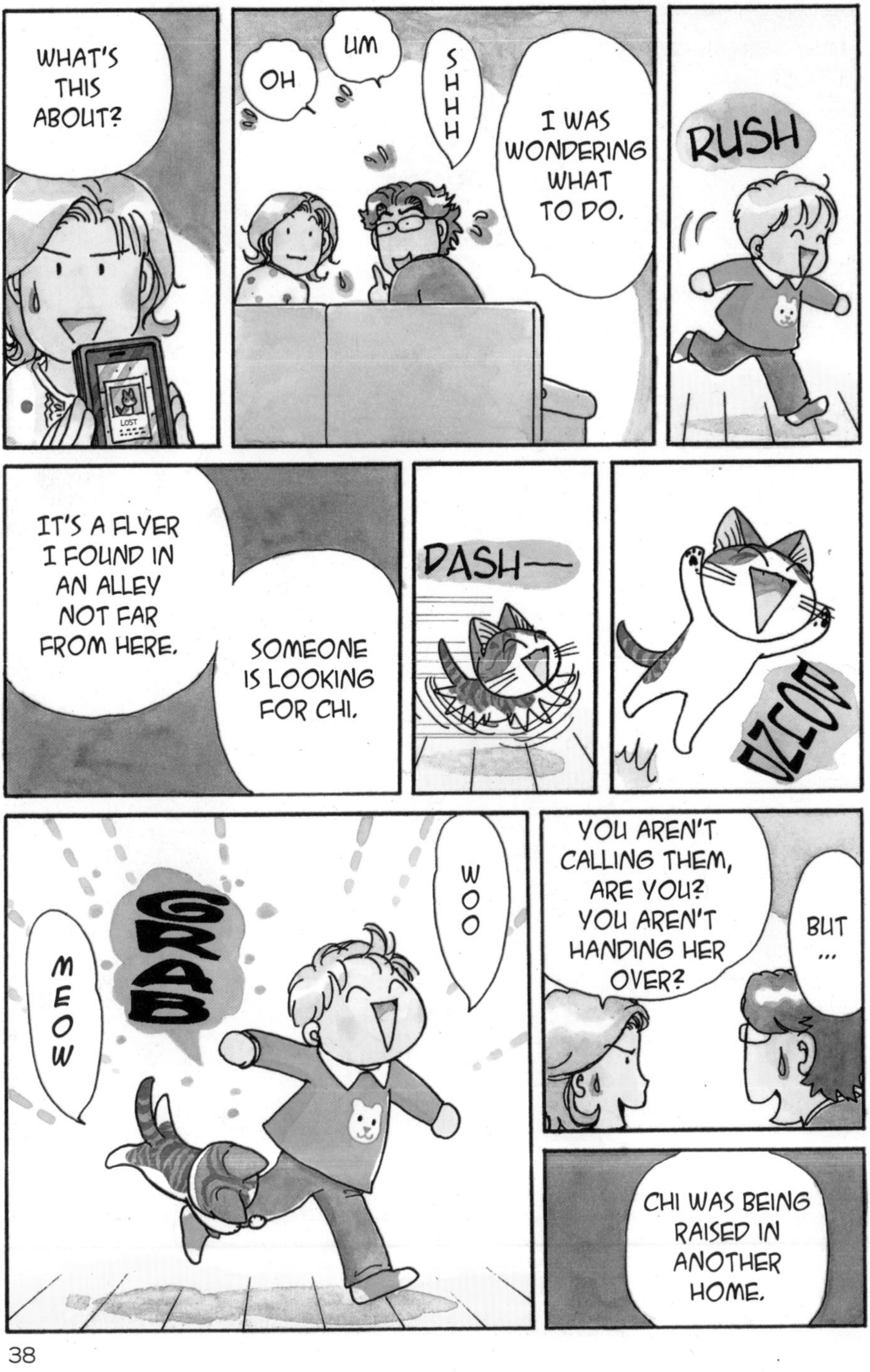
WHAT'S THIS ABOUT?
LOST
OH
UM
SHHH
I WAS WONDERING WHAT TO DO.
RUSH
IT'S A FLYER I FOUND IN AN ALLEY NOT FAR FROM HERE.
SOMEONE IS LOOKING FOR CHI.
DASH—
VZOOM
MEOW
GRAB
WOO
YOU AREN'T CALLING THEM, ARE YOU? YOU AREN'T HANDING HER OVER?
BUT ...
CHI WAS BEING RAISED IN ANOTHER HOME.

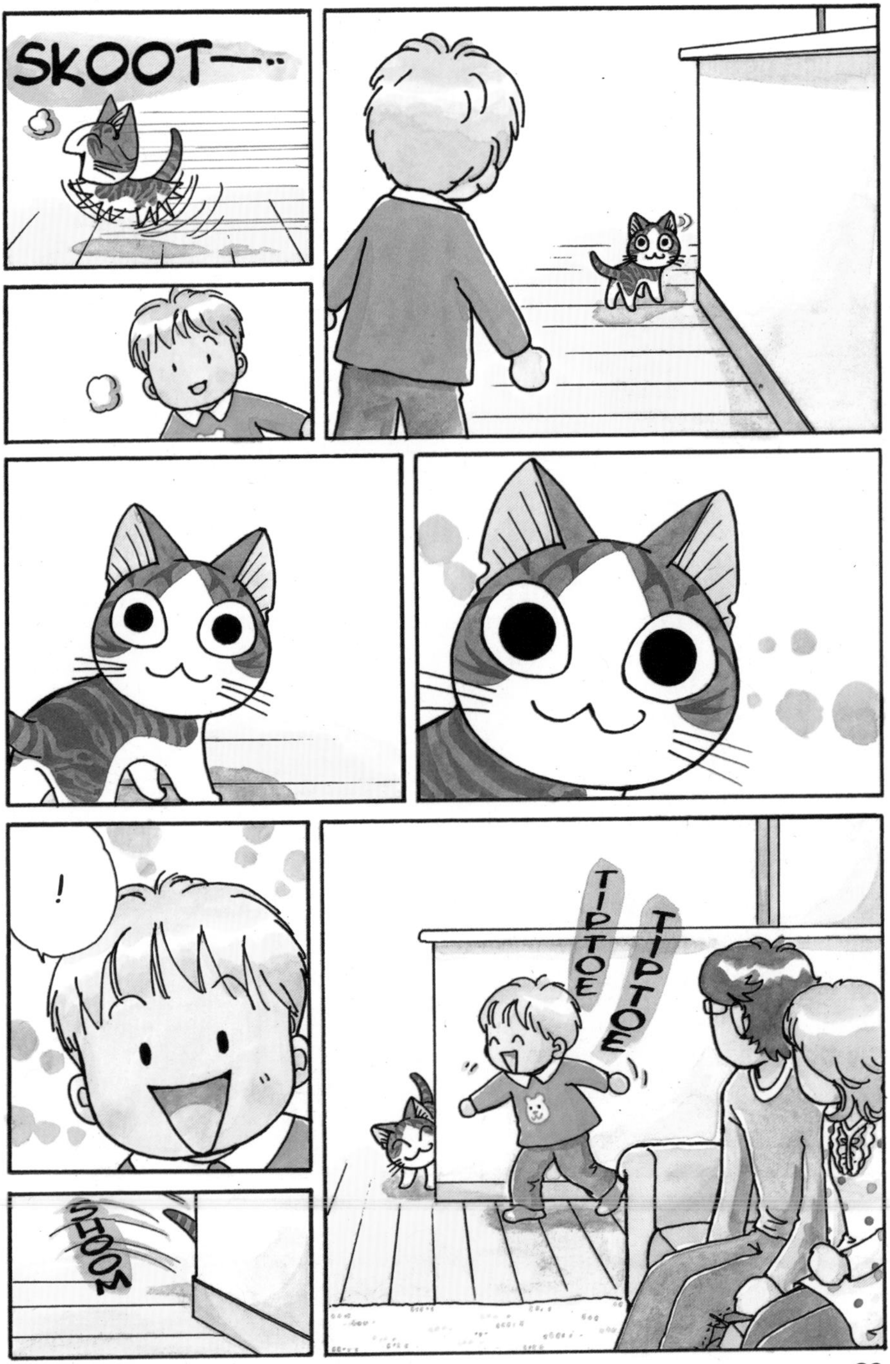
SKOOT—..
!
TIPTOE TIPTOE
SHOOM

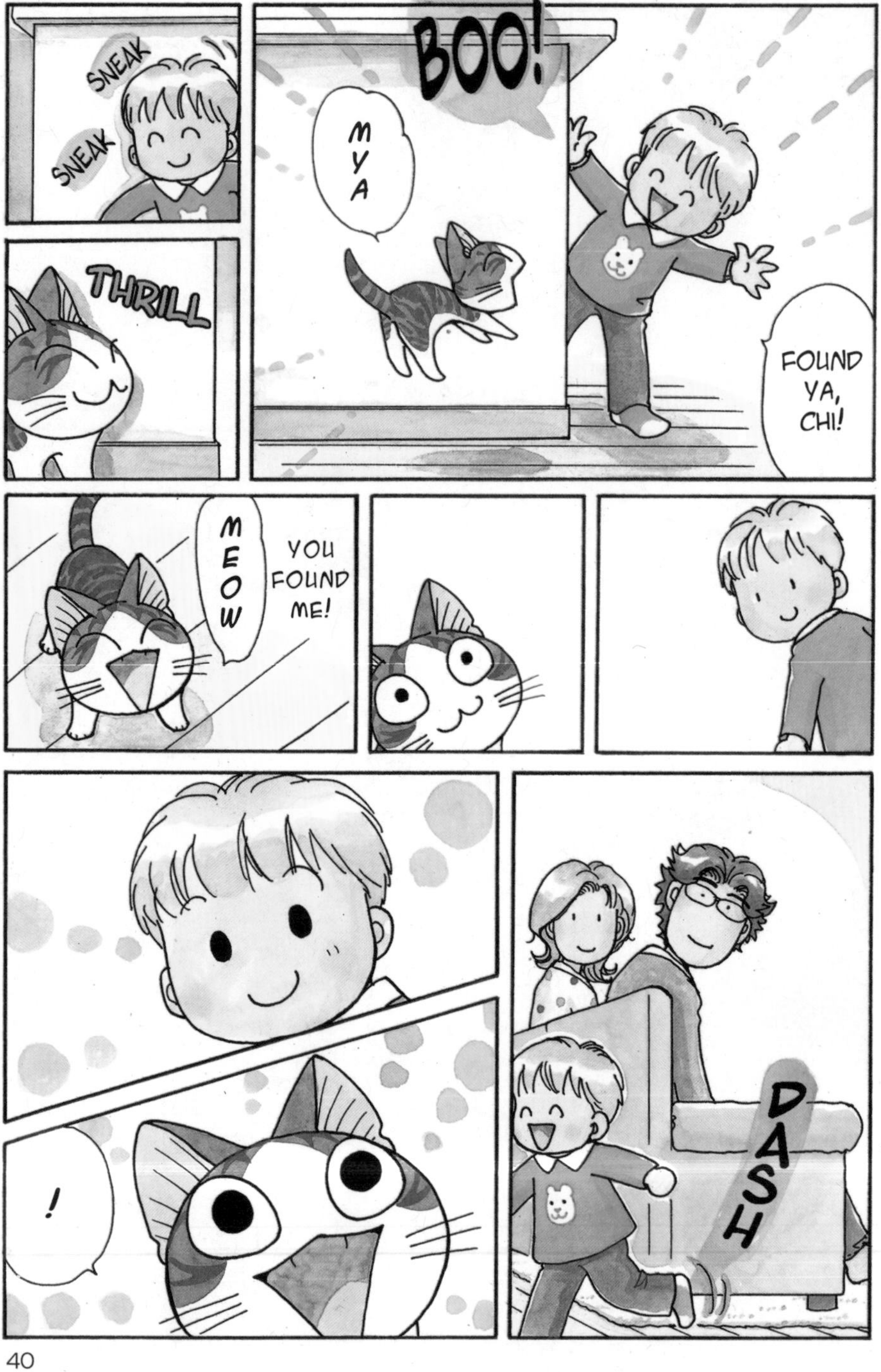
SNEAK
SNEAK
THRILL
BOO!
MYA
FOUND YA, CHI!
MEOW
YOU FOUND ME!
!
DASH

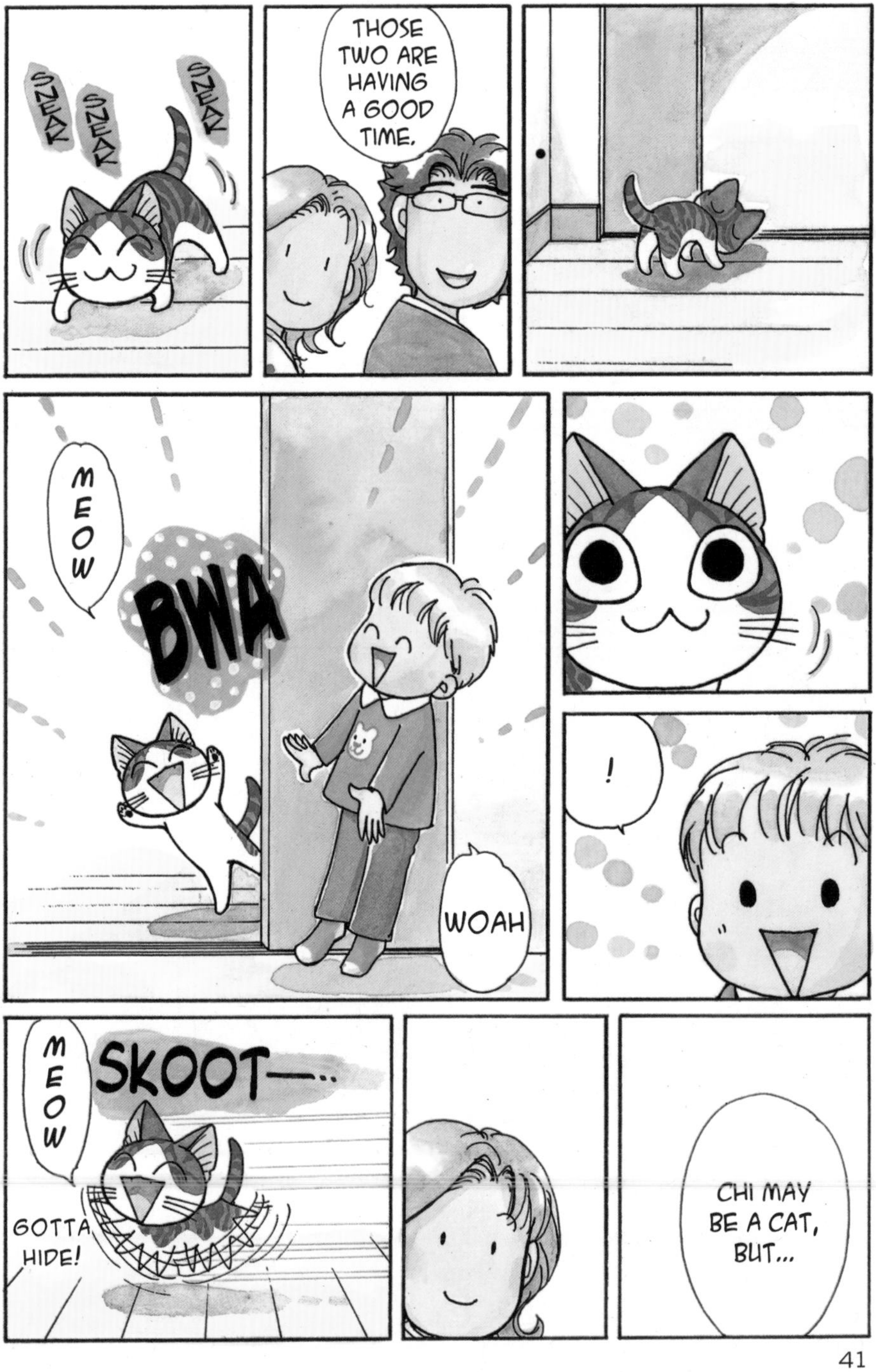
SNEAK
SNEAK
SNEAK
THOSE TWO ARE HAVING A GOOD TIME.
MEOW
BWA
WOAH
!
MEOW
SKOOT—..
GOTTA HIDE!
CHI MAY BE A CAT, BUT...

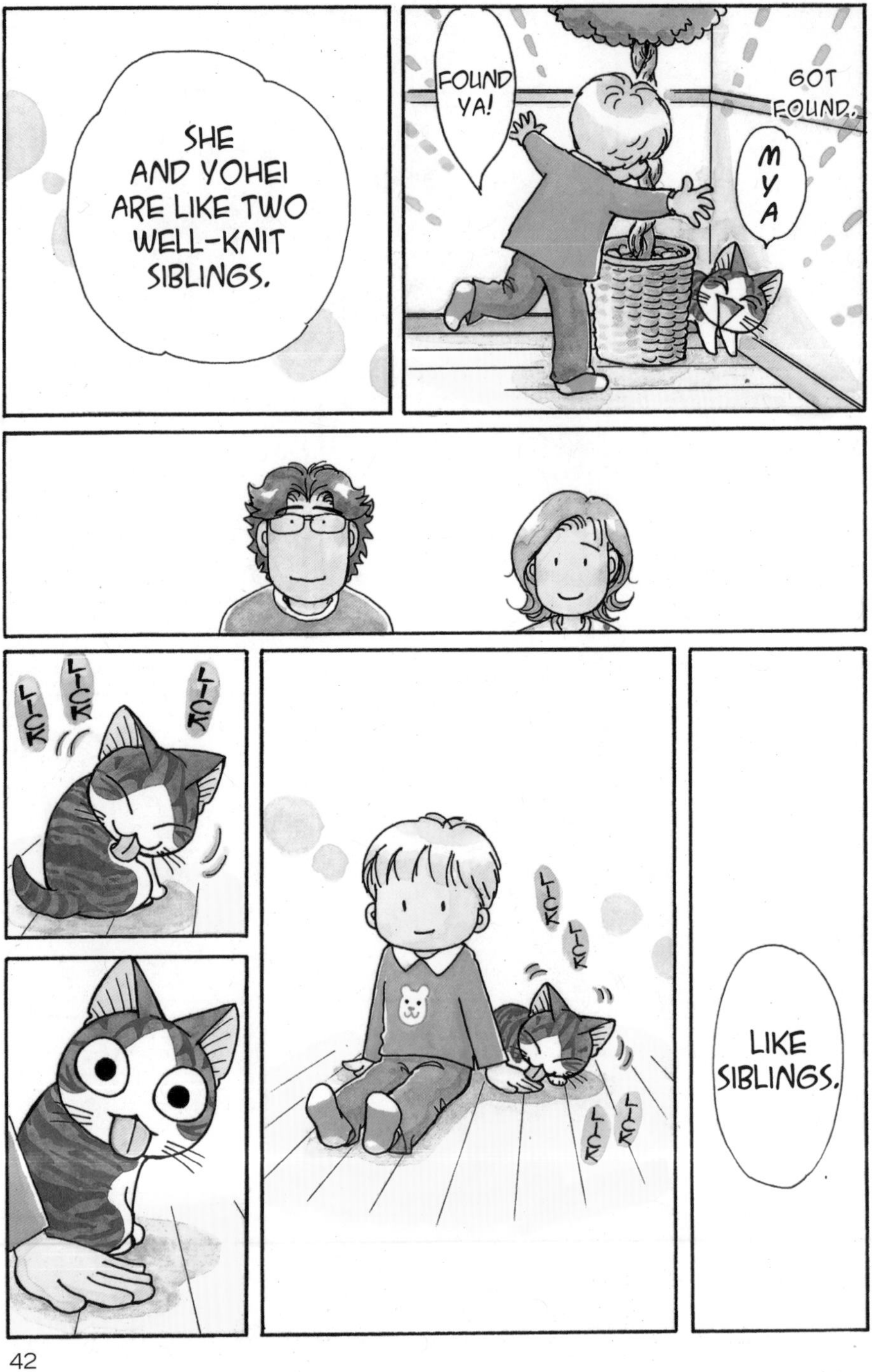
SHE AND YOHEI ARE LIKE TWO WELL-KNIT SIBLINGS.
FOUND YA!
GOT FOUND.
MYA
LICK LICK LICK
LICK LICK
LICK LICK
LIKE SIBLINGS.

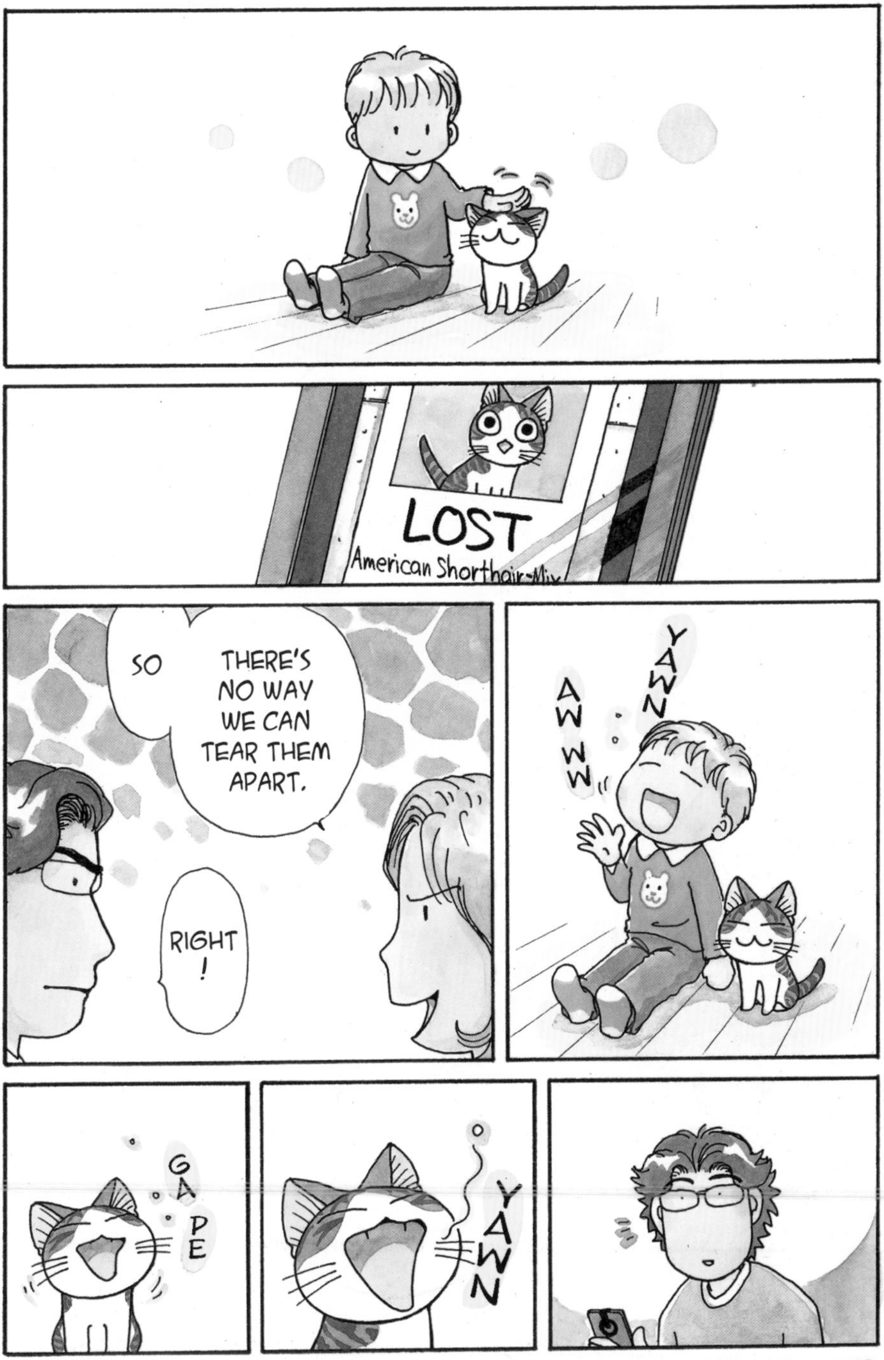
LOST
American Shorthair-Mix
SO THERE'S NO WAY WE CAN TEAR THEM APART.
RIGHT!
YAWN
AWWW
GAPE
YAWN

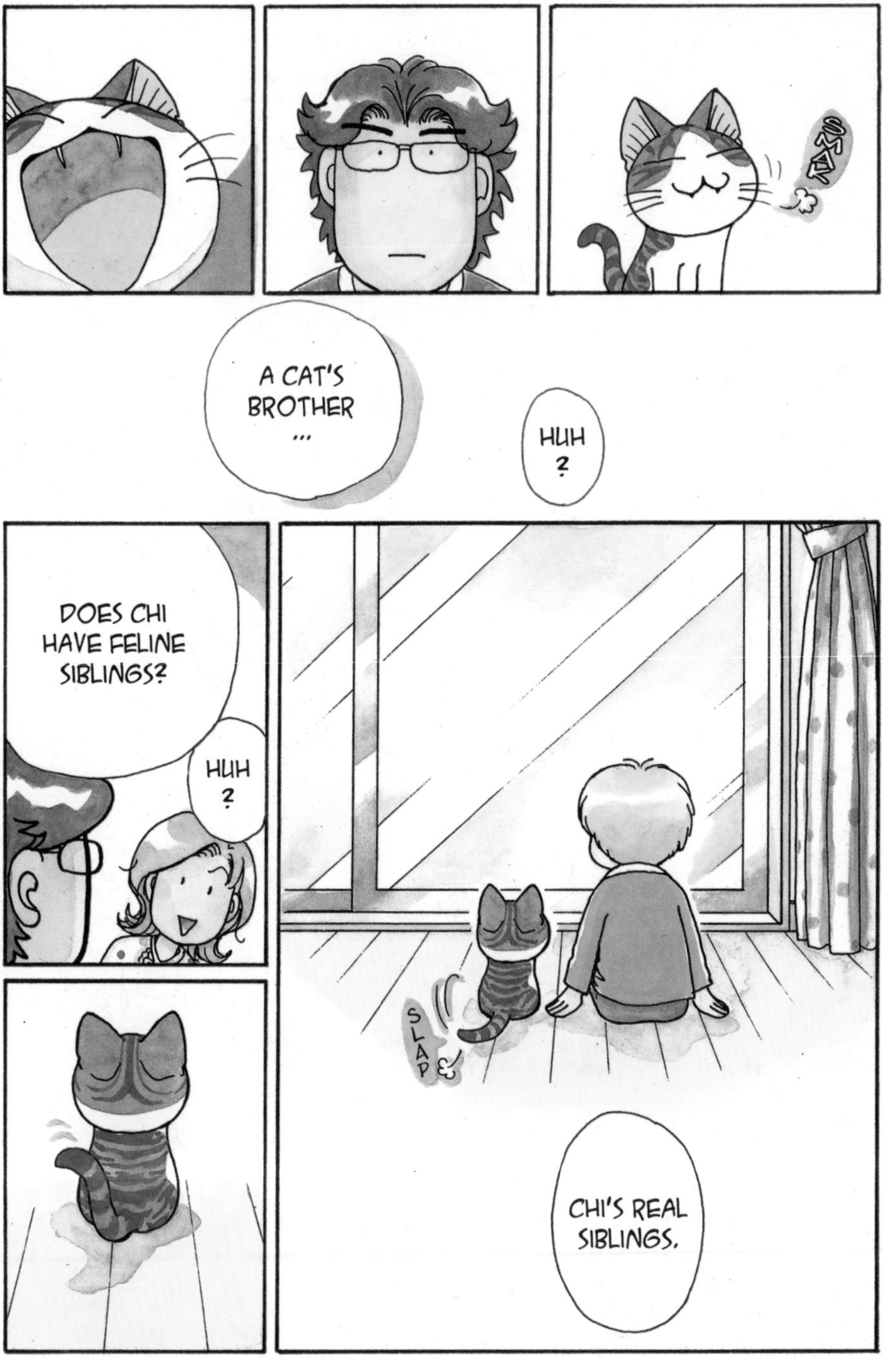
SMAK
A CAT'S BROTHER ...
HUH ?
DOES CHI HAVE FELINE SIBLINGS?
HUH ?
SLAP
CHI'S REAL SIBLINGS.

the end

homemade 170: a cat is misread

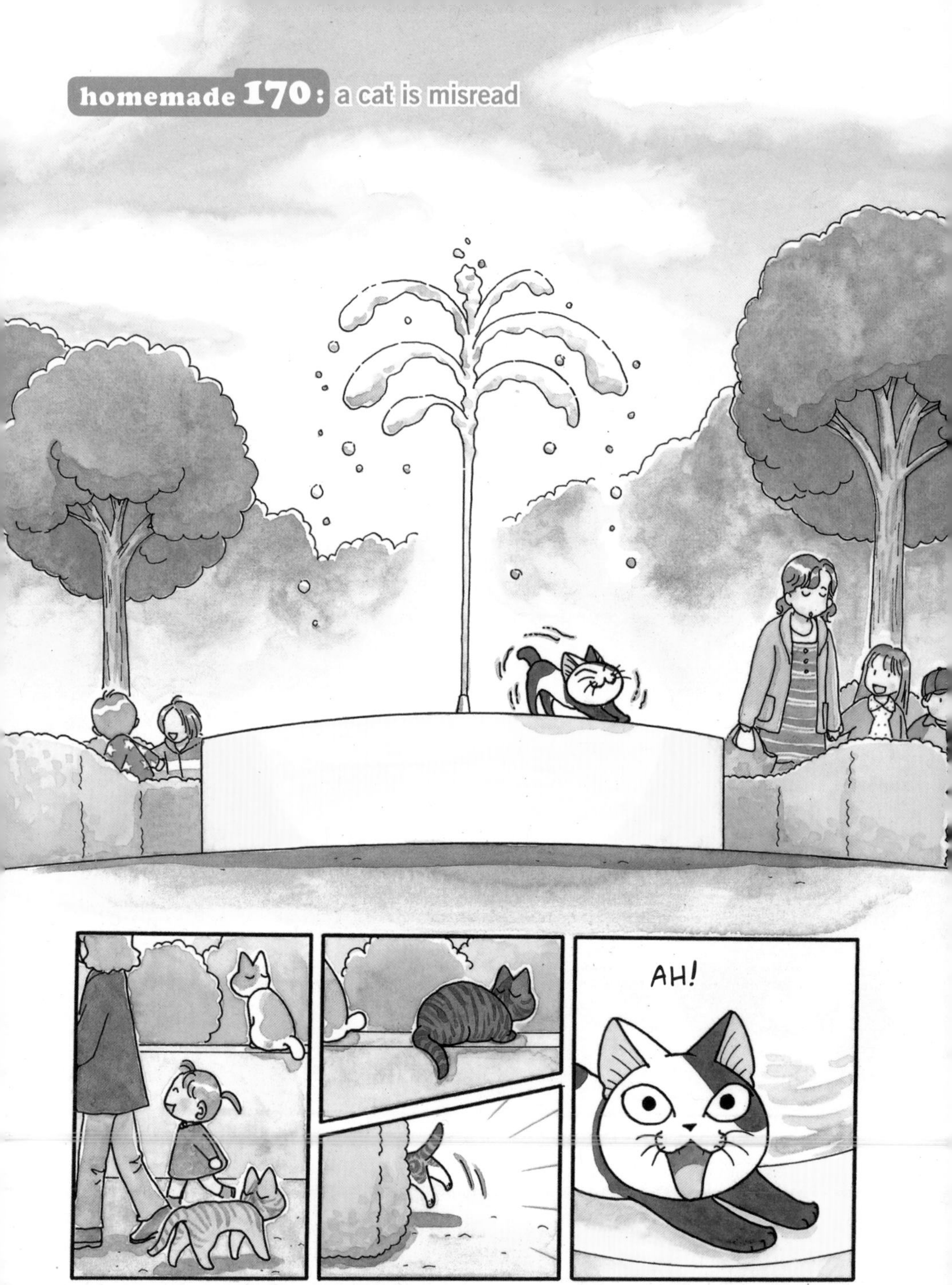

AH!

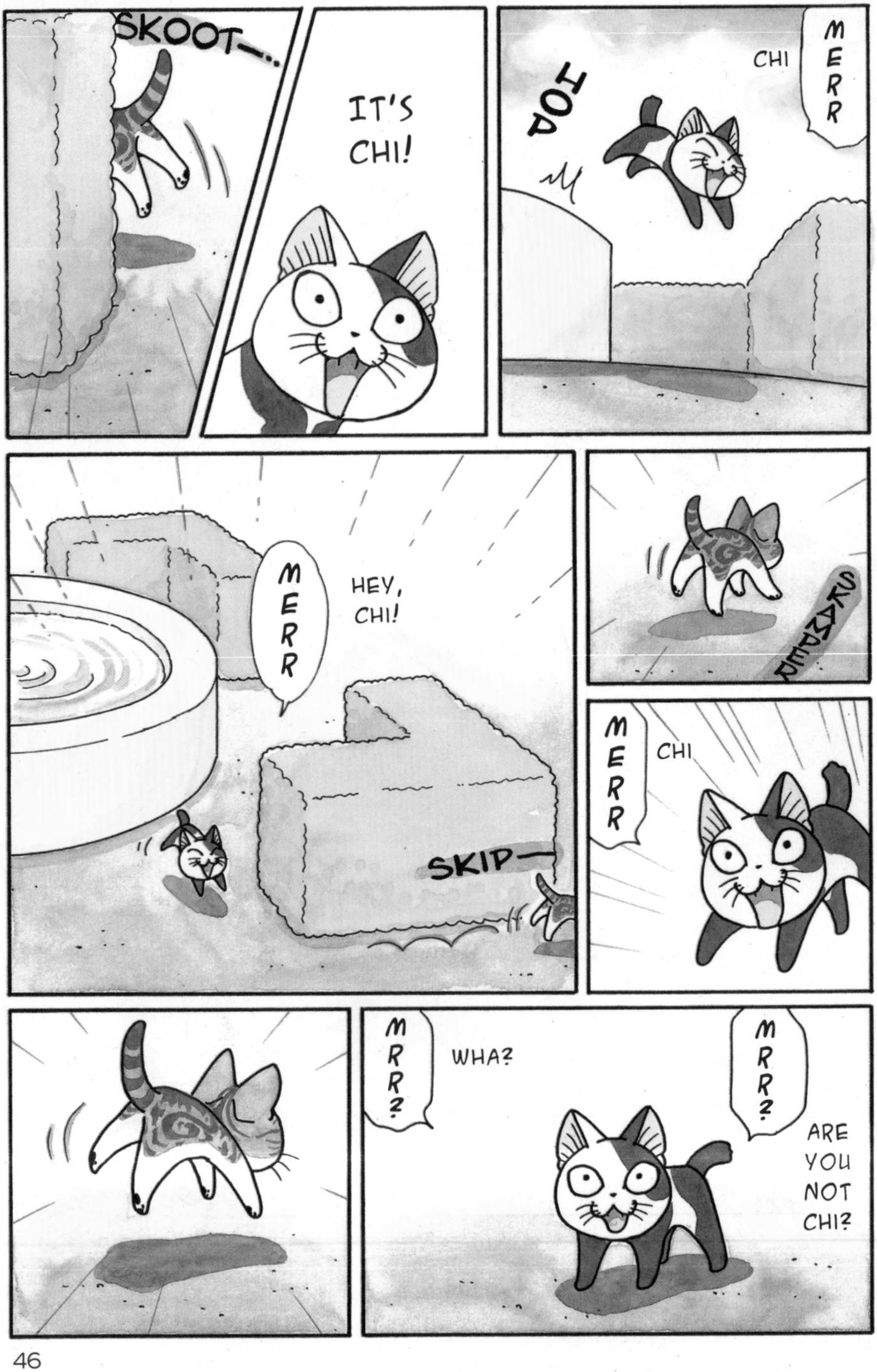
SKOOT—..
IT'S CHI!
HOP
MERR
CHI
MERR
HEY, CHI!
SKIP—
SKAMPER
MERR
CHI
MRR?
WHA?
MRR?
ARE YOU NOT CHI?

MEWN
LEAP
FLAP FLAP
CHIRP
...
MERR
SO BAD ...
MYA?!
WHAT?!
TURN
WOAH...
PEER
MYA
WHAT'S UP?

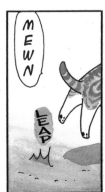

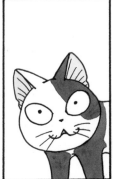

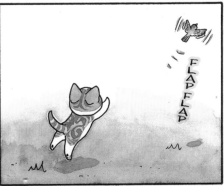

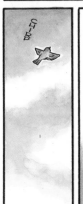

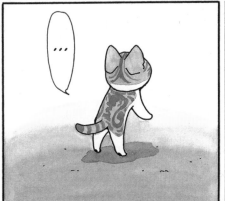

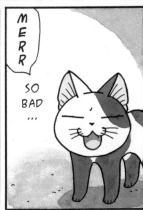

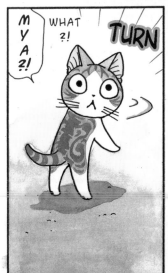

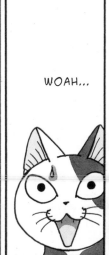

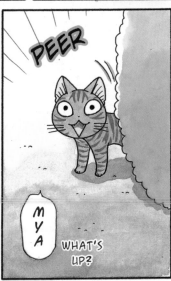

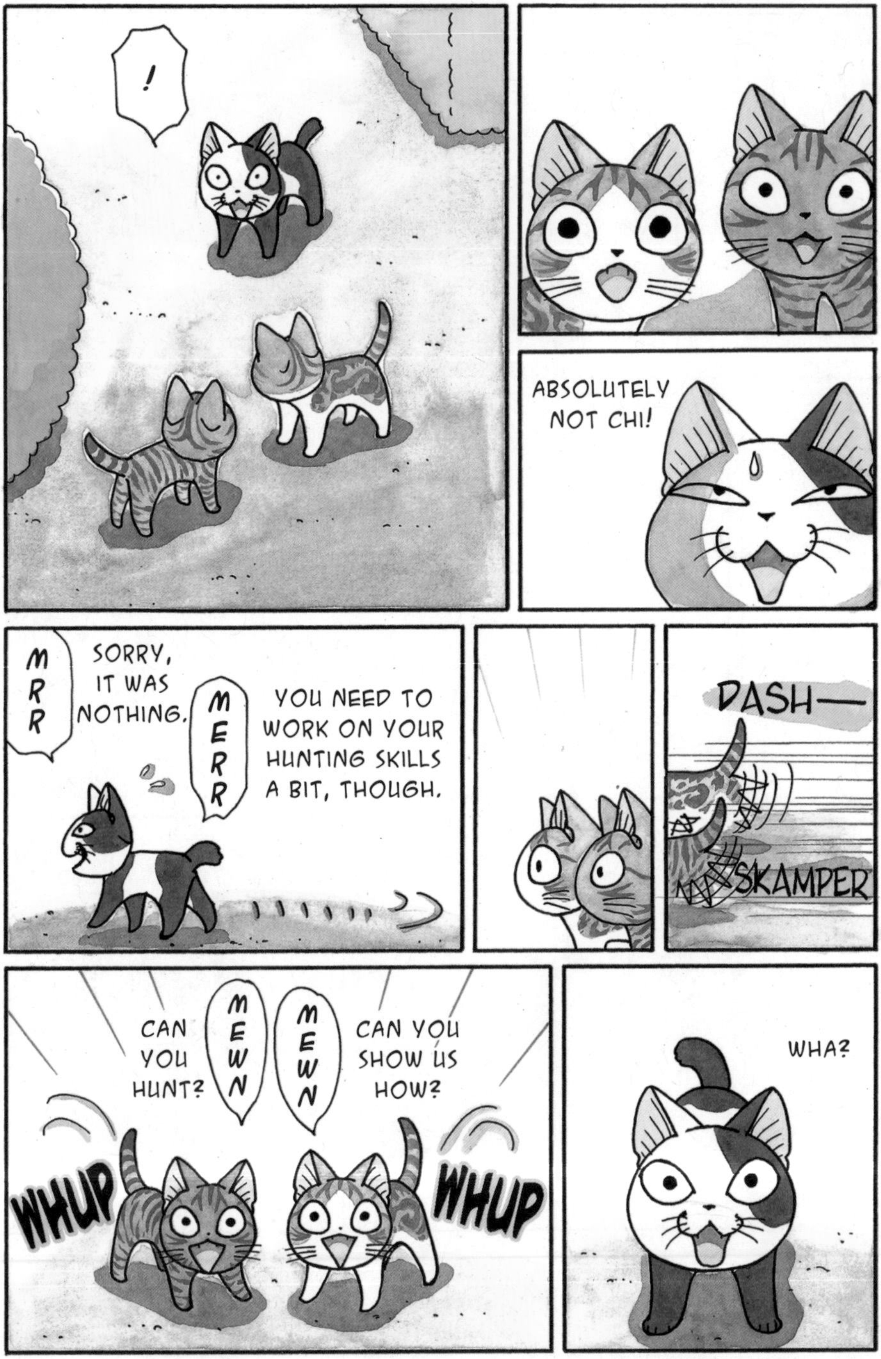
!
ABSOLUTELY NOT CHI!
MRR
SORRY, IT WAS NOTHING.
MERRR
YOU NEED TO WORK ON YOUR HUNTING SKILLS A BIT, THOUGH.
DASH—
SKAMPER
CAN YOU HUNT?
MEWN
MEWN
CAN YOU SHOW US HOW?
WHUP
WHUP
WHA?

DO YOU KNOW HOW ?!

MEWN

MEWN

DO YOU KNOW HOW ?!

DO YOU KNOW HOW ?!

HEH... YOU COULD SAY SO.

MERR

MRR

THAT GUY'S ALWAYS WATCHING WHAT'S UP.

MRR

YOU CAN'T RUSH IT.

MRR

YOUR TARGET MUST NOT NOTICE YOU.

MRR

WAIT FOR SLIP-UPS.

PEER PEER

MRR

LIKE NOT NOW.

49

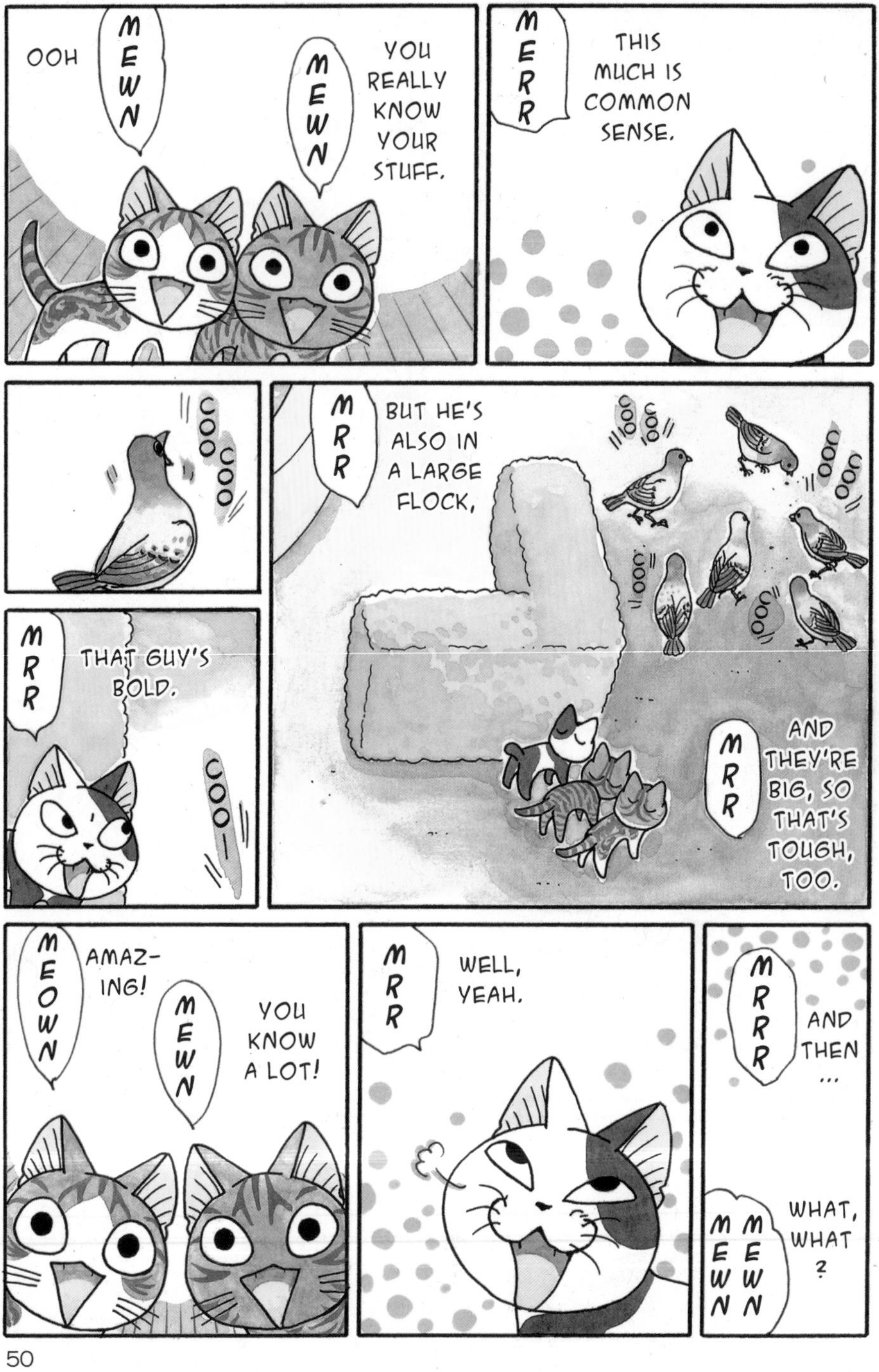
OOH
MEWN
MEWN
YOU REALLY KNOW YOUR STUFF.
MERR
THIS MUCH IS COMMON SENSE.
COOO
COOO
MRR
THAT GUY'S BOLD.
COOO—
MRR
BUT HE'S ALSO IN A LARGE FLOCK,
COOO
COOO
COOO
COOO
MRR
AND THEY'RE BIG, SO THAT'S TOUGH, TOO.
MEOWN
AMAZ-ING!
MEWN
YOU KNOW A LOT!
MRR
WELL, YEAH.
MRRR
AND THEN ...
MEWN
MEWN
WHAT, WHAT?

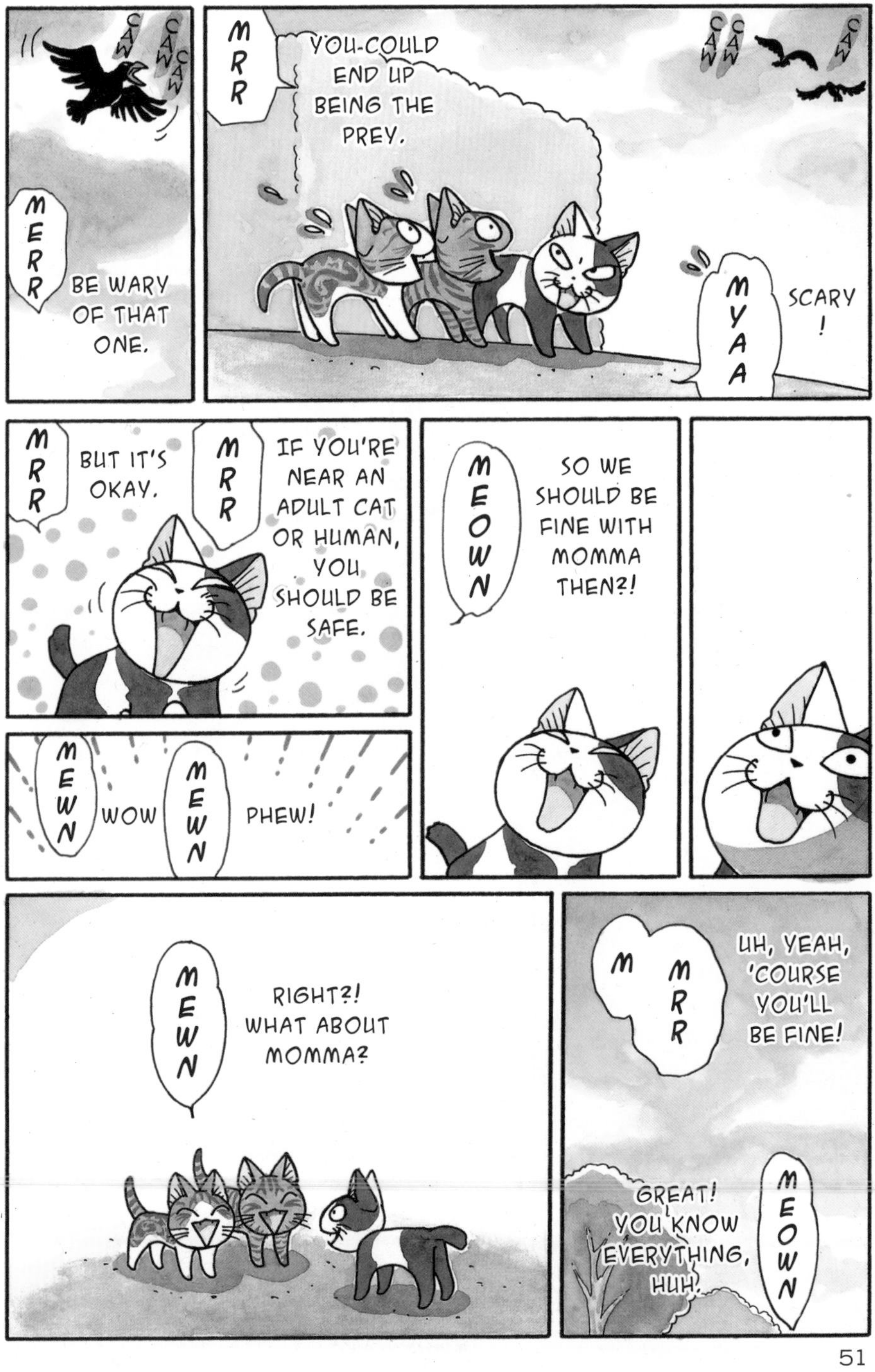
CAW
CAW
CAW
MERR
BE WARY OF THAT ONE.
MRR
YOU-COULD END UP BEING THE PREY.
CAW
CAW
CAW
MYAA
SCARY!
MRR
BUT IT'S OKAY.
MRR
IF YOU'RE NEAR AN ADULT CAT OR HUMAN, YOU SHOULD BE SAFE.
MEWN
WOW
MEWN
PHEW!
MEOWN
SO WE SHOULD BE FINE WITH MOMMA THEN?!
MEWN
RIGHT?! WHAT ABOUT MOMMA?
M
MRR
UH, YEAH, 'COURSE YOU'LL BE FINE!
GREAT! YOU KNOW EVERYTHING, HUH.
MEOWN

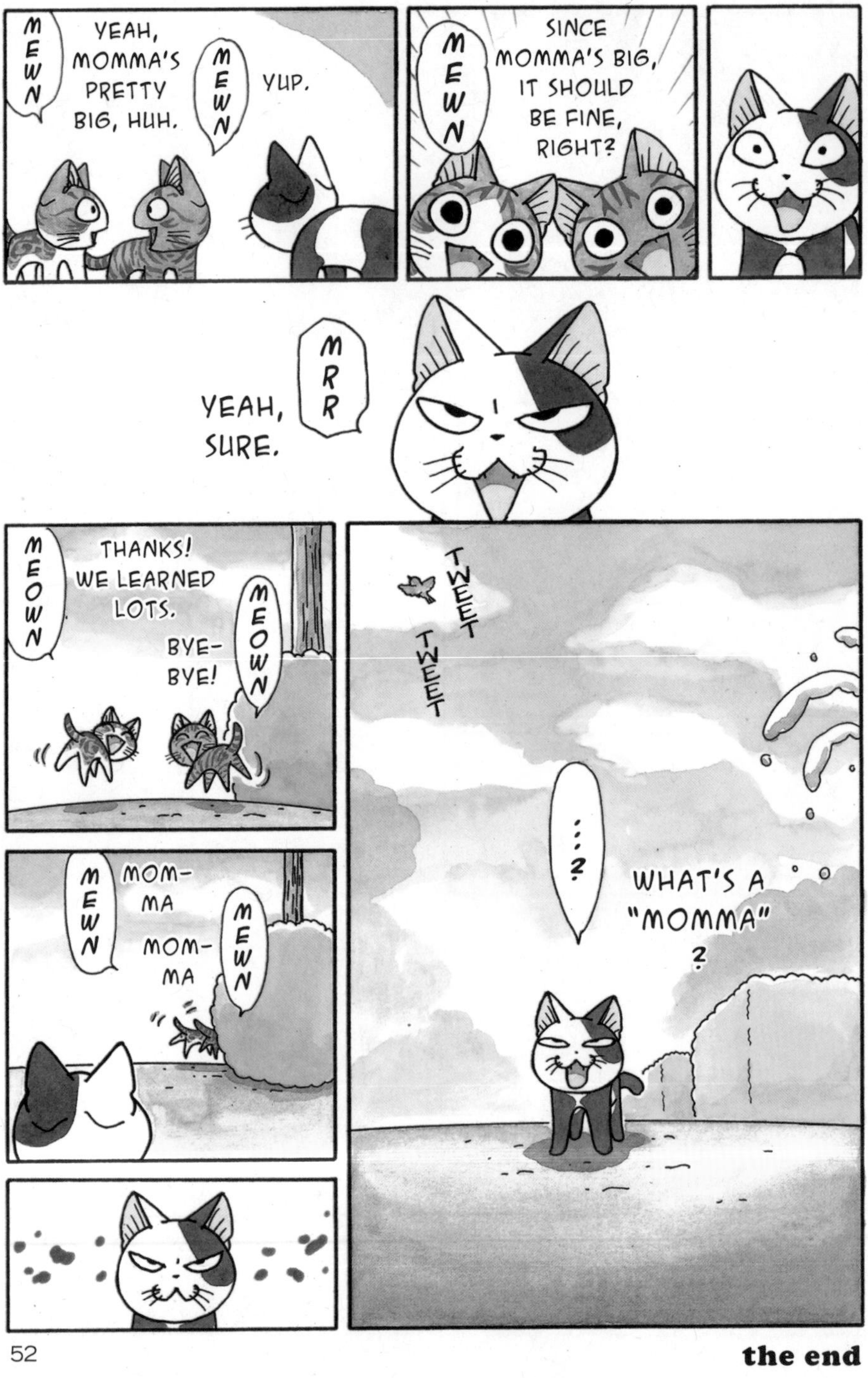
MEWN
YEAH, MOMMA'S PRETTY BIG, HUH.
MEWN
YUP.
MEWN
SINCE MOMMA'S BIG, IT SHOULD BE FINE, RIGHT?
MRR
YEAH, SURE.
MEOWN
THANKS! WE LEARNED LOTS.
MEOWN
BYE-BYE!
TWEET
TWEET
...?
WHAT'S A "MOMMA"?
MEWN
MOM-MA
MEWN
MOM-MA

the end

homemade 171: a cat has signals crossed

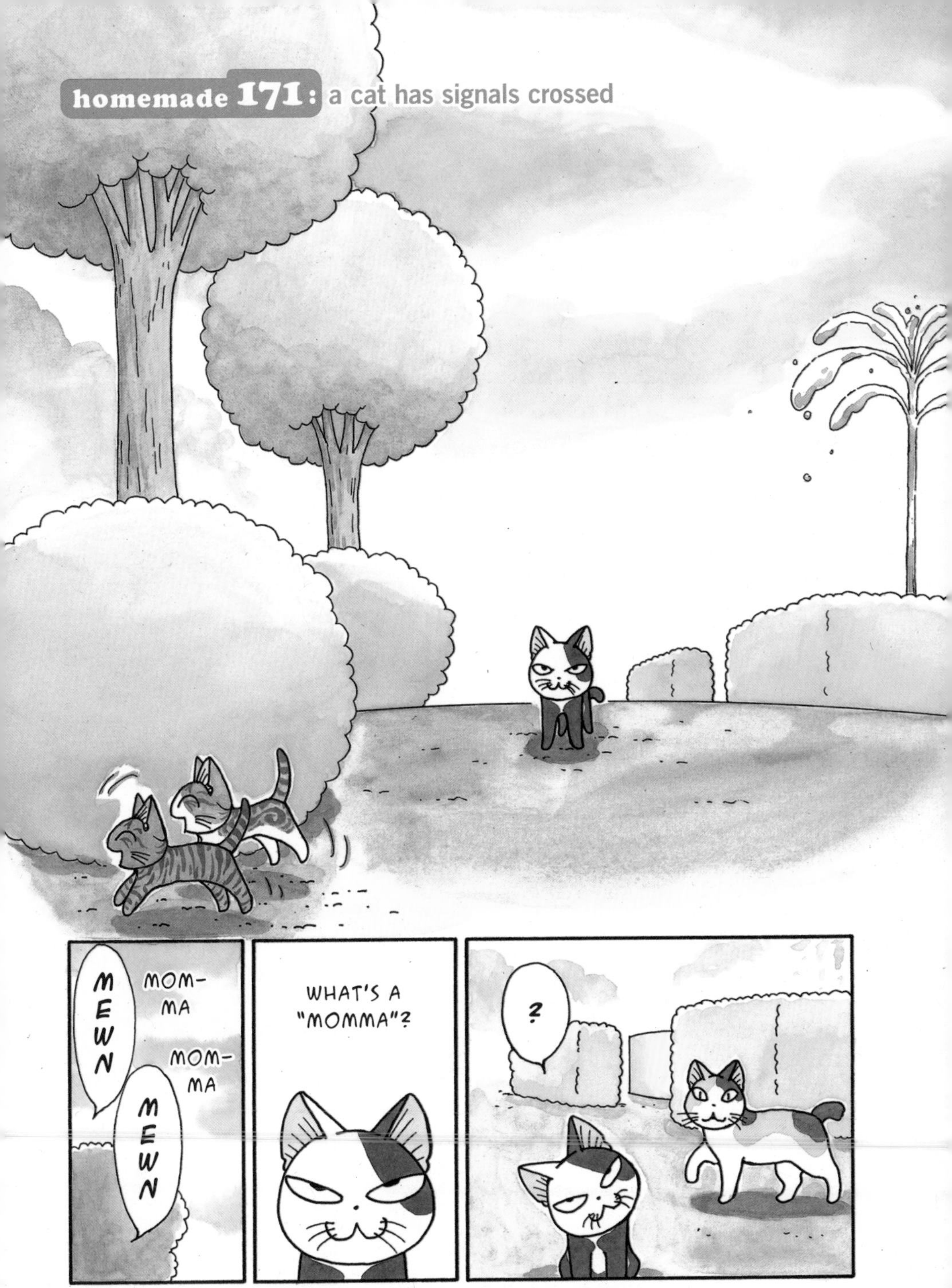
MEWN
MOM-MA
MOM-MA
MEWN
WHAT'S A "MOMMA"?
?

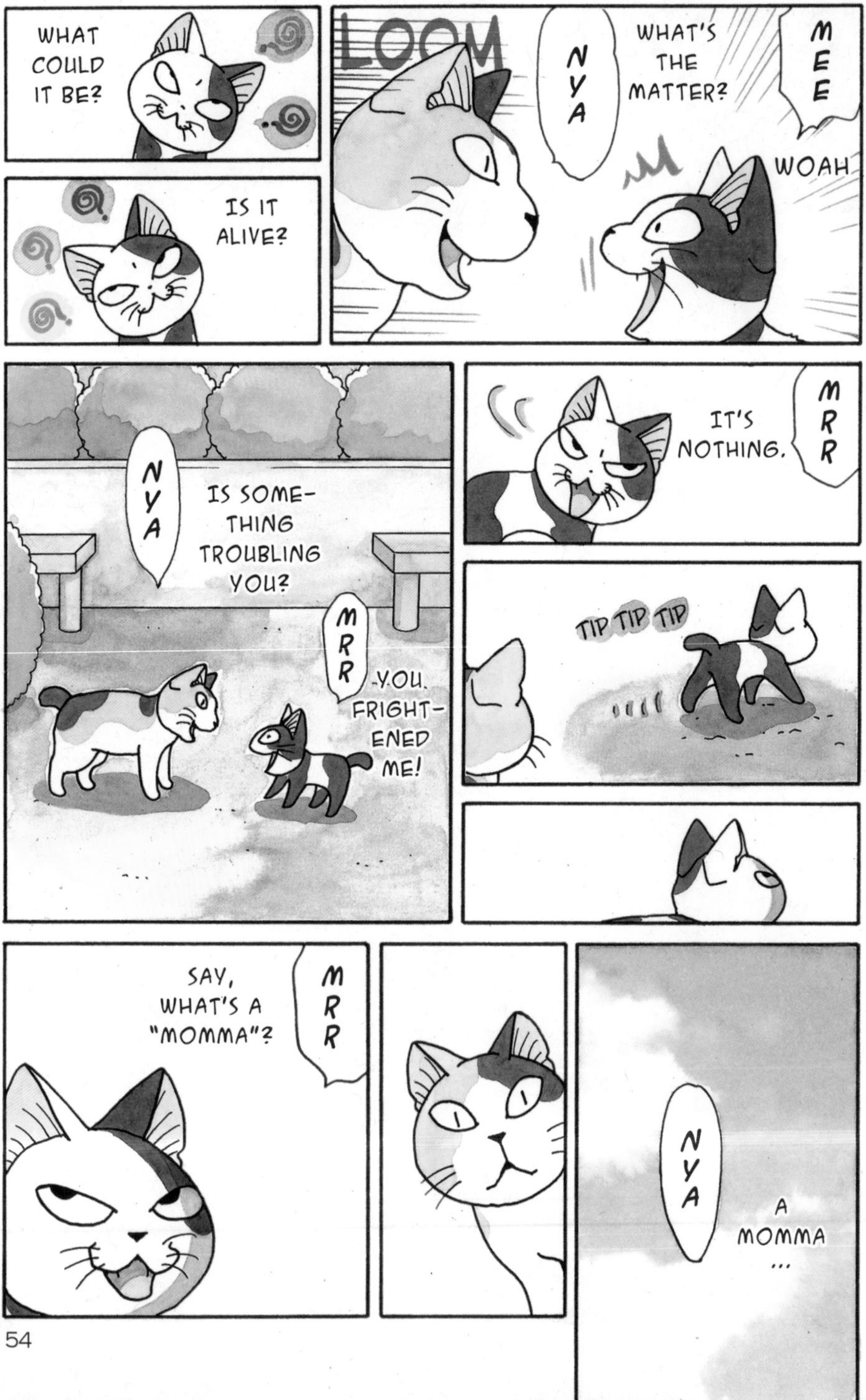
WHAT COULD IT BE?
IS IT ALIVE?
LOOM
NYA
WHAT'S THE MATTER?
MEE
WOAH
NYA
IS SOME-THING TROUBLING YOU?
MRR
YOU FRIGHT-ENED ME!
IT'S NOTHING.
MRR
TIP TIP TIP
SAY, WHAT'S A "MOMMA"?
MRR
NYA
A MOMMA ...

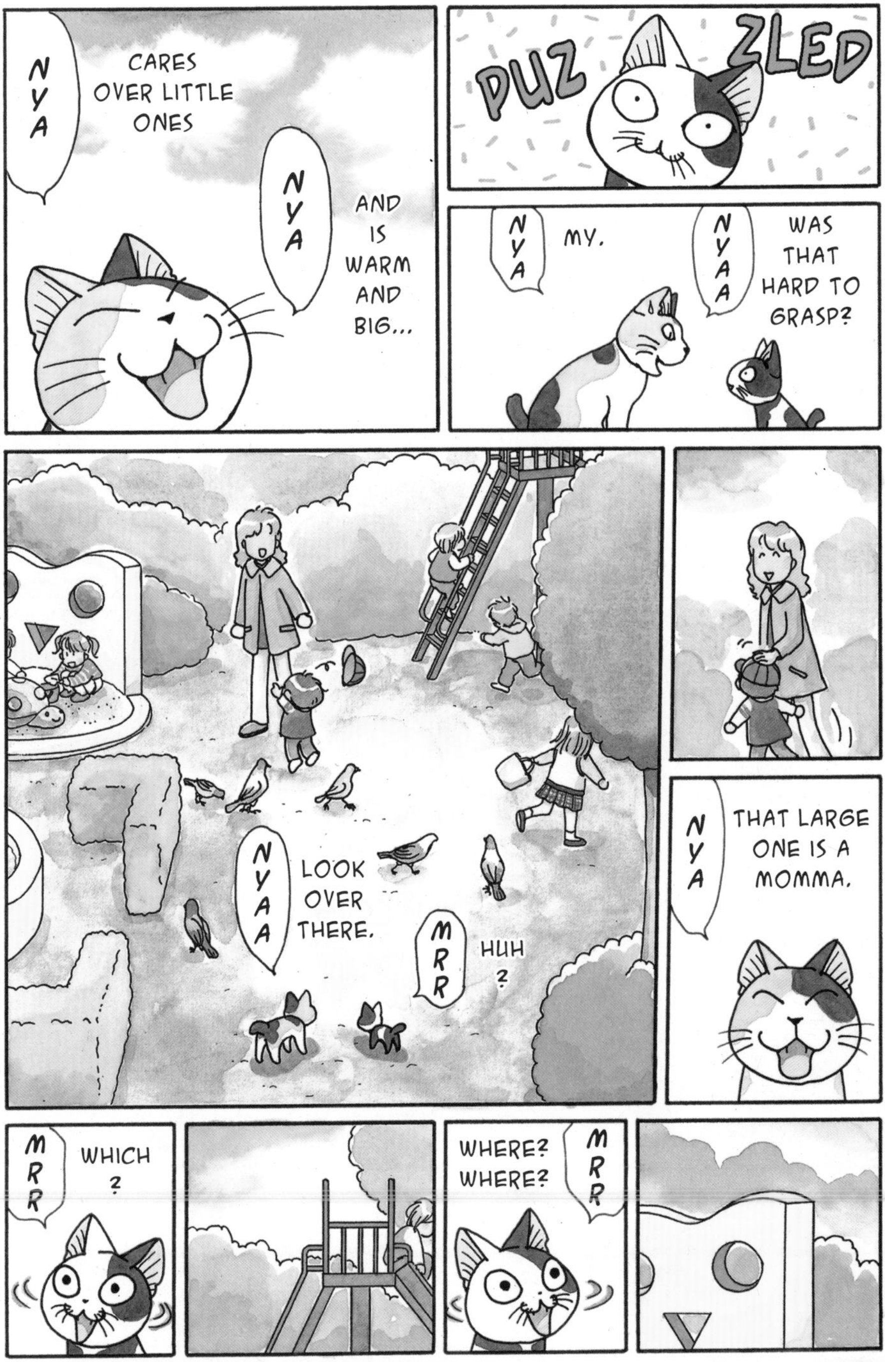
NYA
CARES OVER LITTLE ONES
NYA
AND IS WARM AND BIG...
PUZZLED
NYA
MY.
NYAA
WAS THAT HARD TO GRASP?
NYAA
LOOK OVER THERE.
MRR
HUH?
NYA
THAT LARGE ONE IS A MOMMA.
MRR
WHICH?
WHERE? WHERE?
MRR

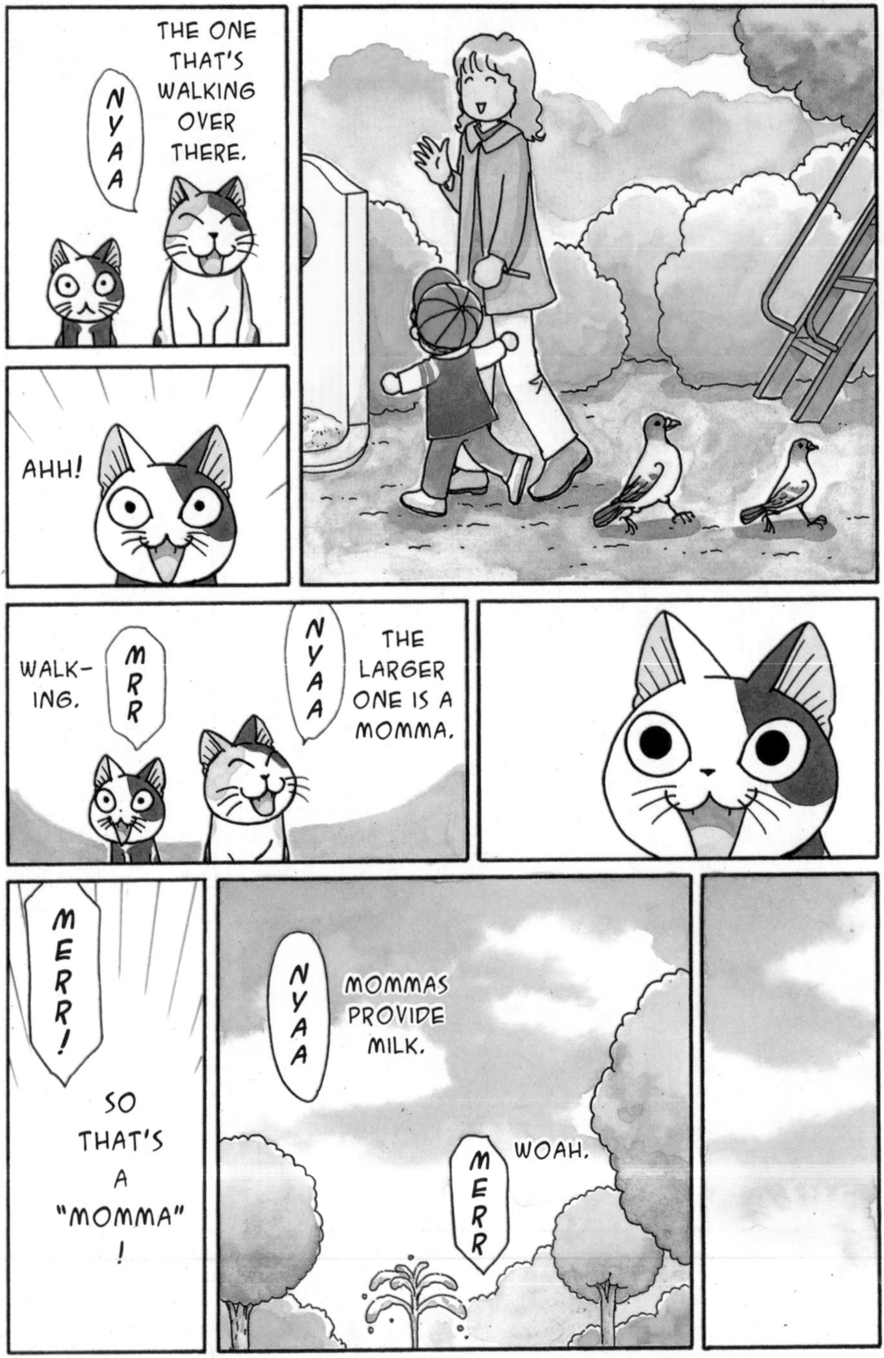
NYAA
THE ONE THAT'S WALKING OVER THERE.
AHH!
WALK-ING.
MRR
NYAA
THE LARGER ONE IS A MOMMA.
MERR!
SO THAT'S A "MOMMA"!
NYAA
MOMMAS PROVIDE MILK.
MERR
WOAH.

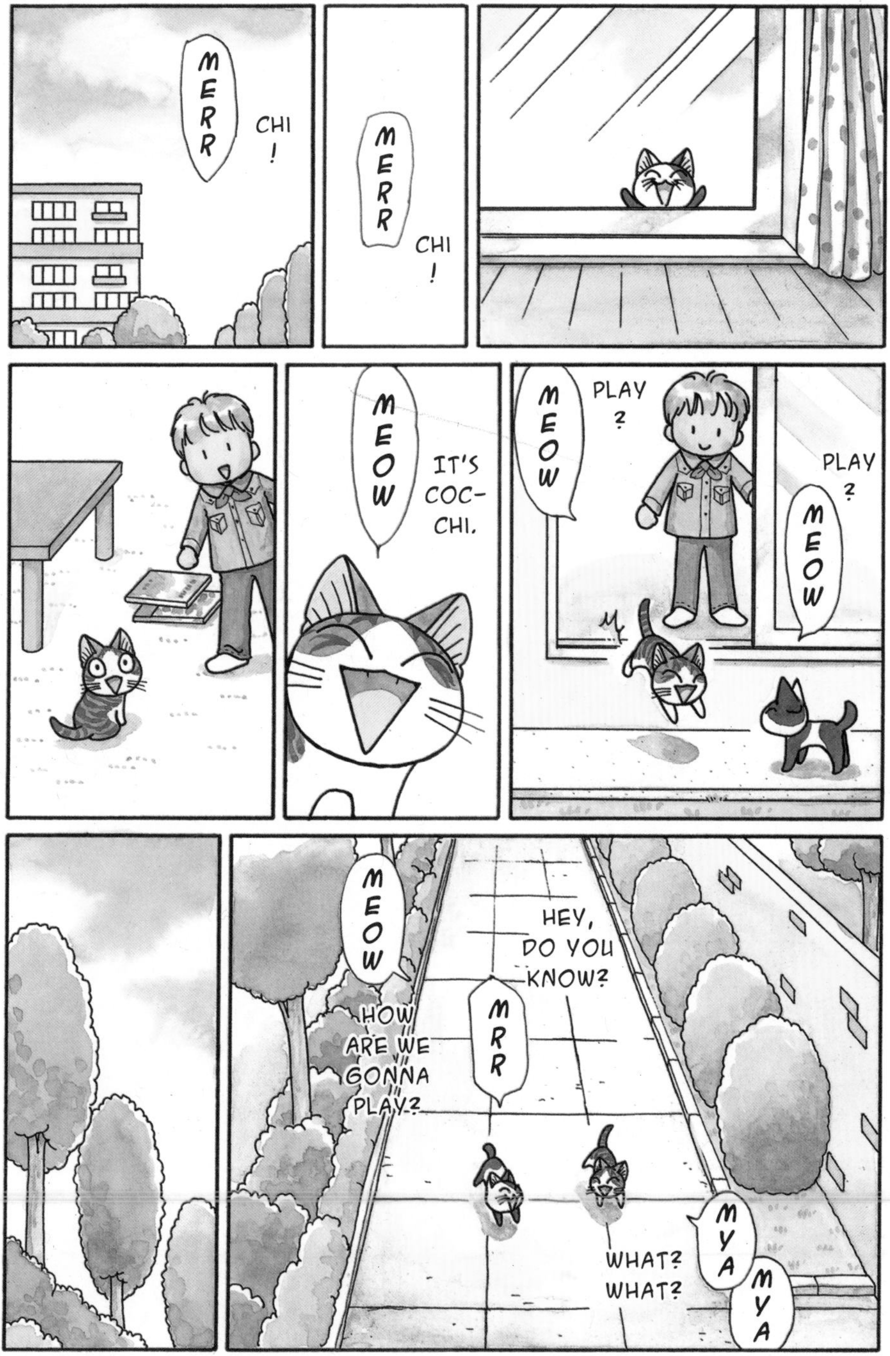
MERR
CHI!
MERR
CHI!
MEOW
MEOW
IT'S COC-CHI.
MEOW
PLAY?
PLAY?
MEOW
MEOW
HEY, DO YOU KNOW?
HOW ARE WE GONNA PLAY?
MRR
WHAT? WHAT?
MYA
MYA
MYA

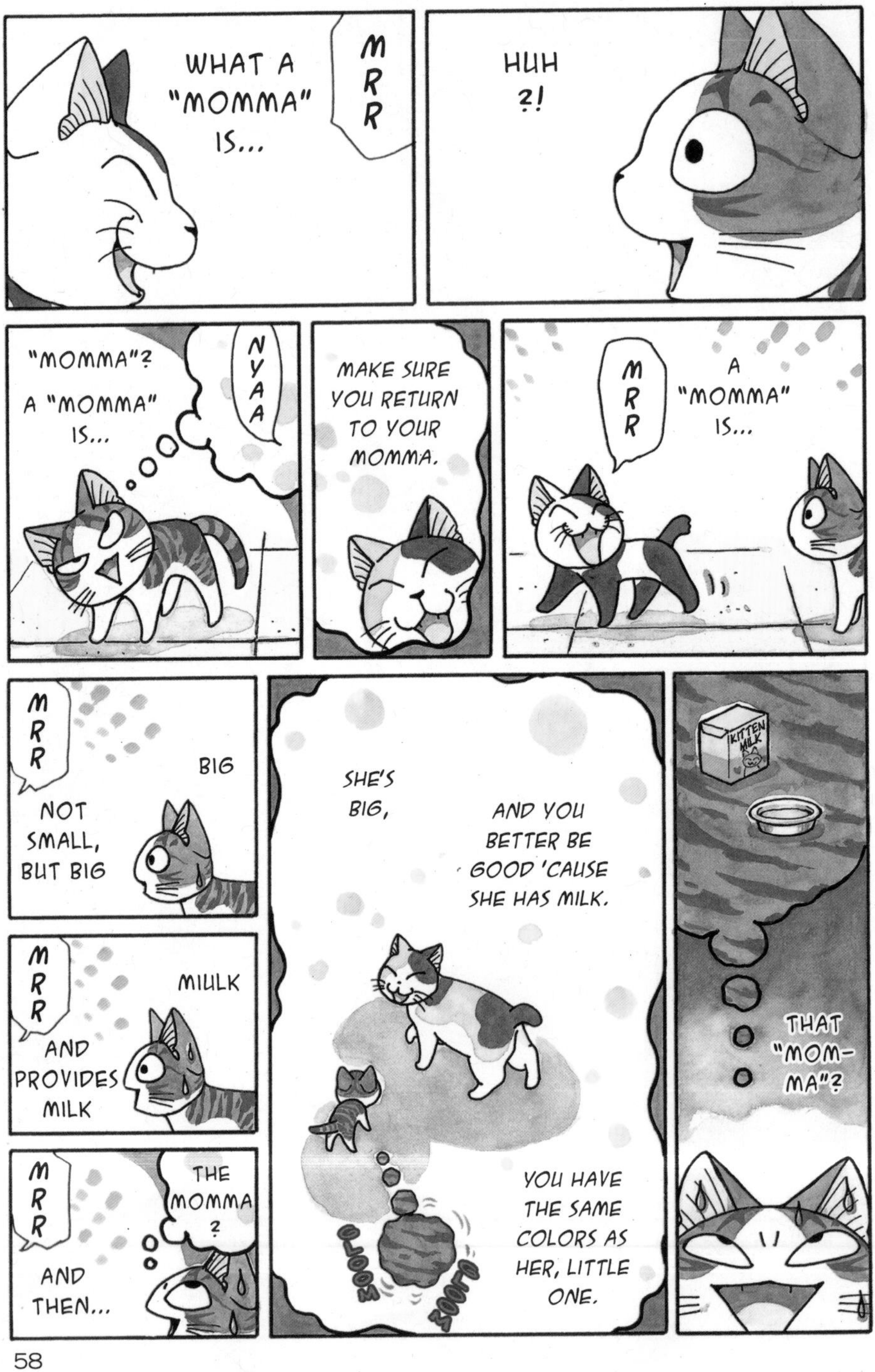
WHAT A "MOMMA" IS...
MRR
HUH ?!
"MOMMA"?
A "MOMMA" IS...
NYAA
MAKE SURE YOU RETURN TO YOUR MOMMA.
MRR
A "MOMMA" IS...
MRR
BIG
NOT SMALL, BUT BIG
MRR
MIULK
AND PROVIDES MILK
MRR
THE MOMMA ?
AND THEN...
SHE'S BIG,
AND YOU BETTER BE GOOD 'CAUSE SHE HAS MILK.
YOU HAVE THE SAME COLORS AS HER, LITTLE ONE.
GLOOM
GLOOM
KITTEN MILK
THAT "MOM-MA"?

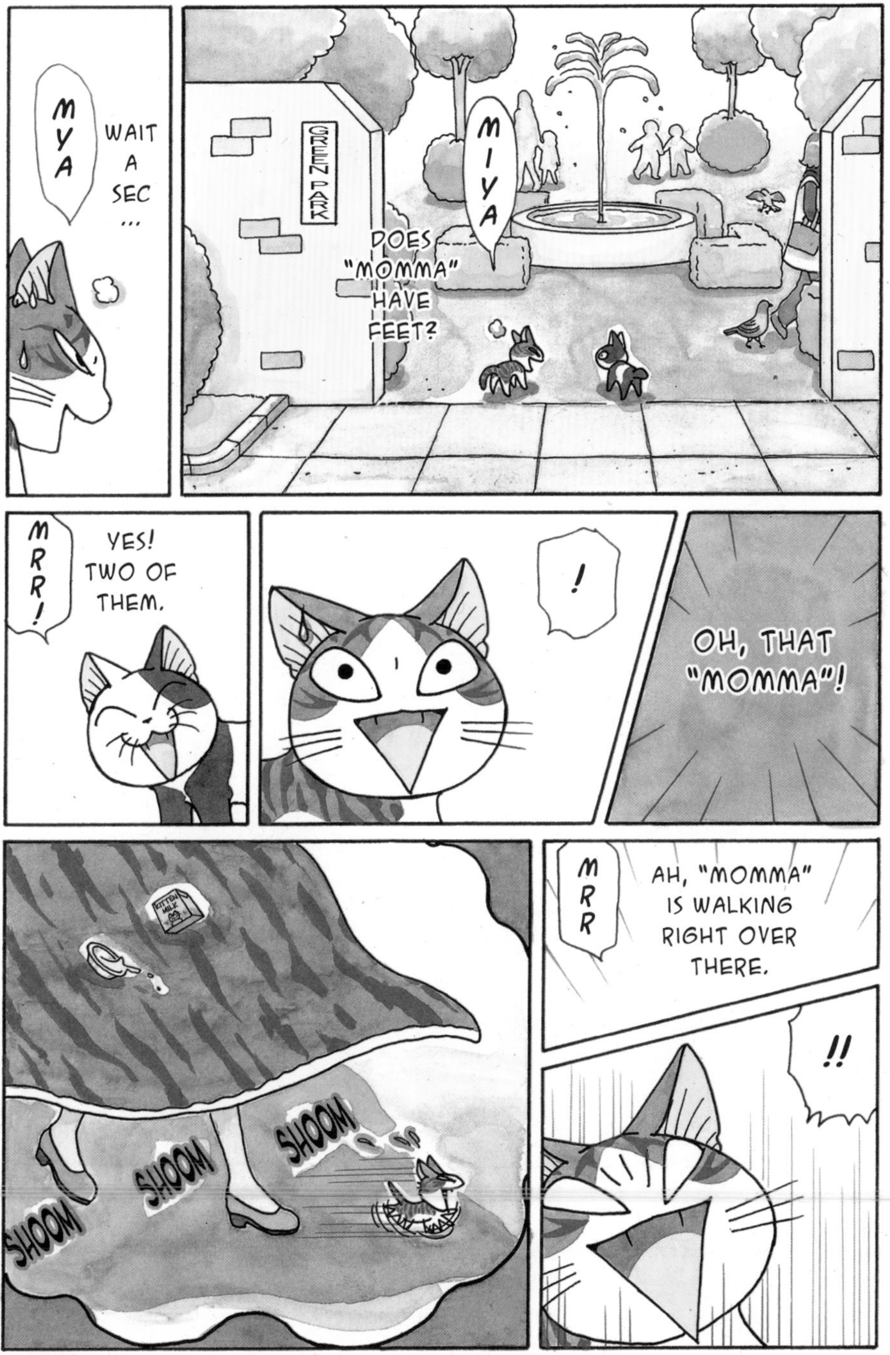
MYA
WAIT A SEC ...
GREEN PARK
MIYA
DOES "MOMMA" HAVE FEET?
MRR!
YES! TWO OF THEM.
!
OH, THAT "MOMMA"!
SHOOM
SHOOM
SHOOM
MRR
AH, "MOMMA" IS WALKING RIGHT OVER THERE.
!!

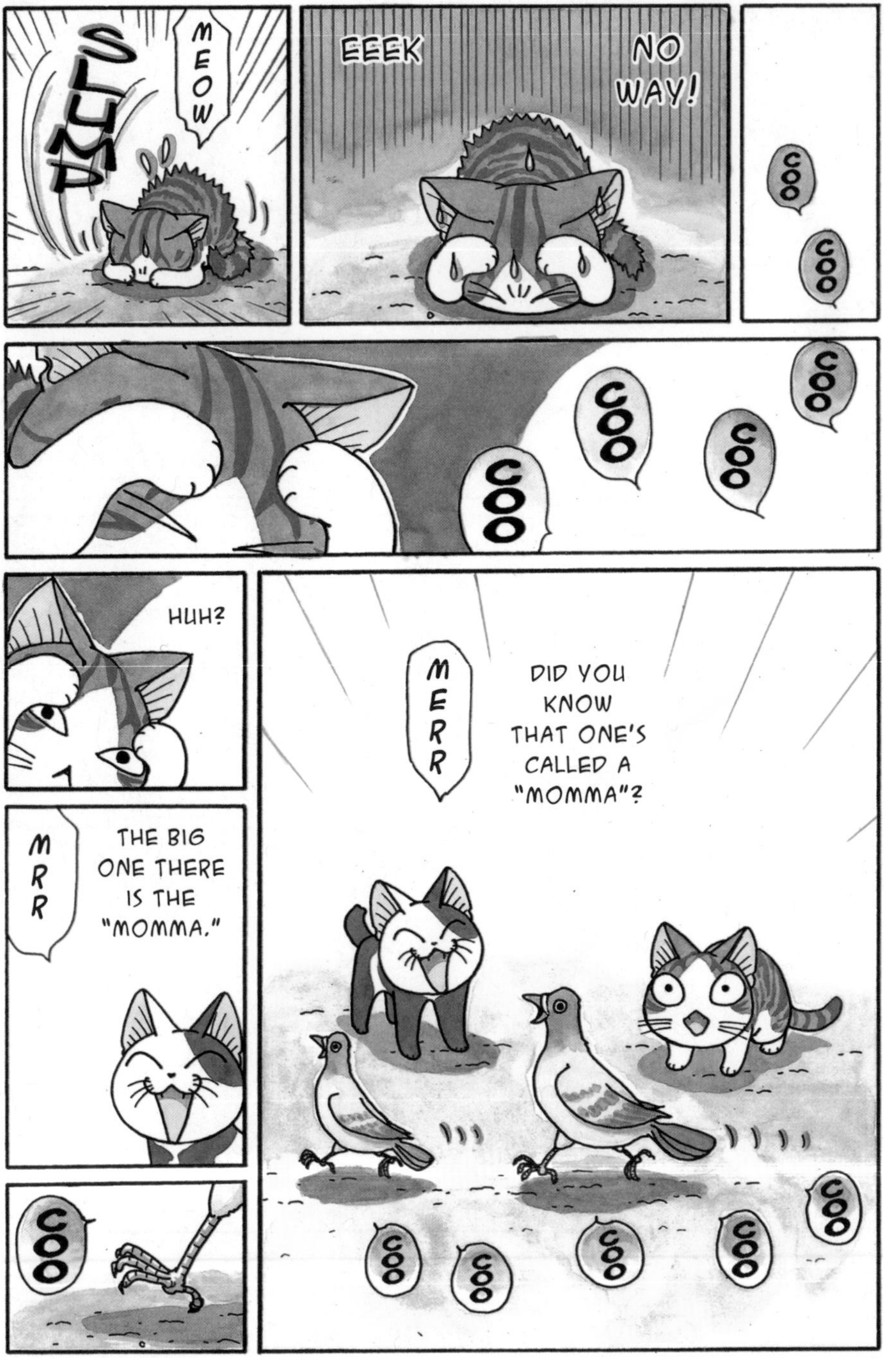
SLUMP
MEOW
EEEK
NO WAY!
COO
COO
COO
COO
COO
COO
HUH?
MRR
THE BIG ONE THERE IS THE "MOMMA."
COO
MERR
DID YOU KNOW THAT ONE'S CALLED A "MOMMA"?
COO
COO
COO
COO
COO
COO

the end

homemade 172: a cat is told

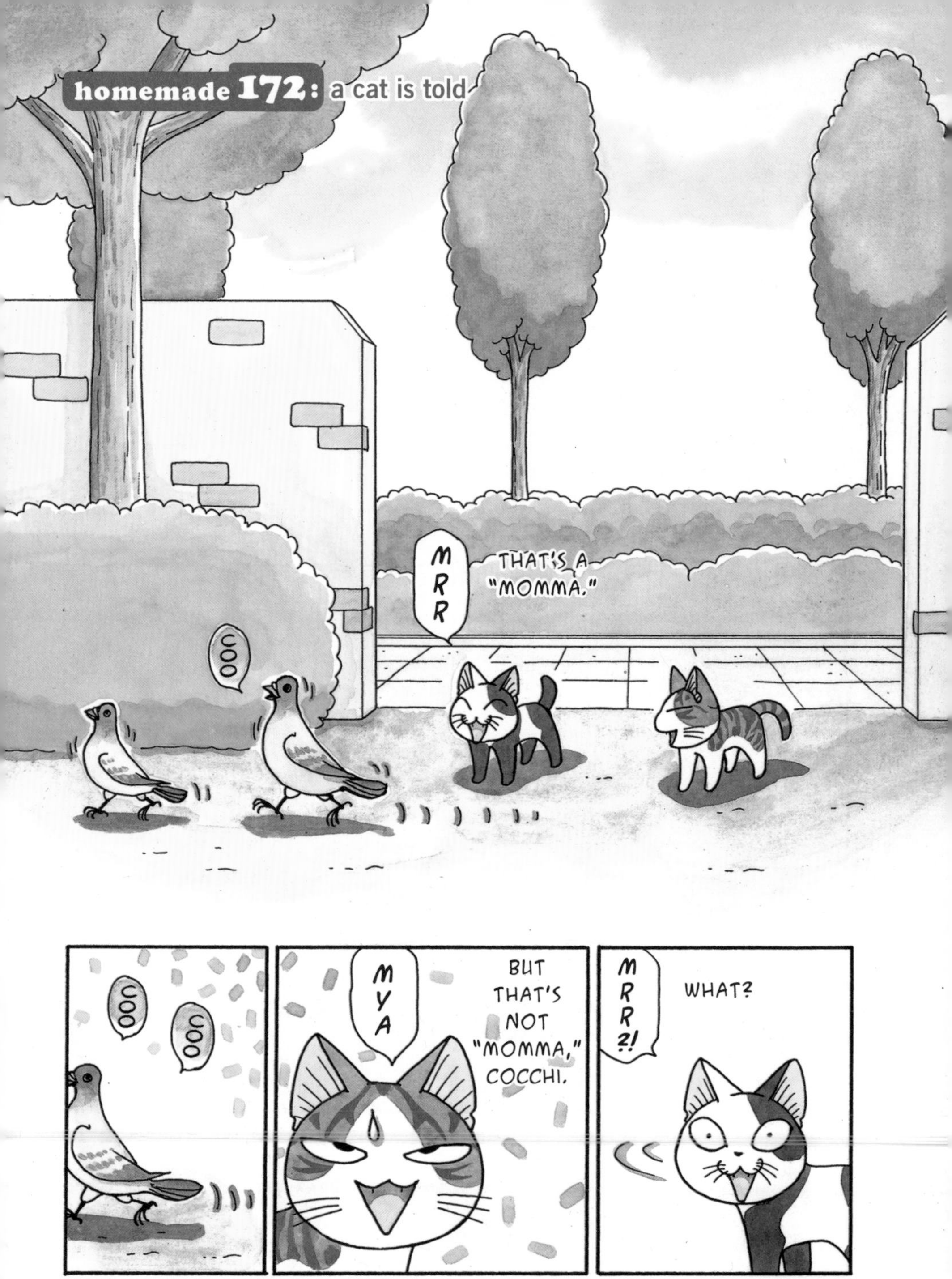

MRR
THAT'S A "MOMMA."
COO
COO
COO
MYA
BUT THAT'S NOT "MOMMA," COCCHI.
MRR?!
WHAT?

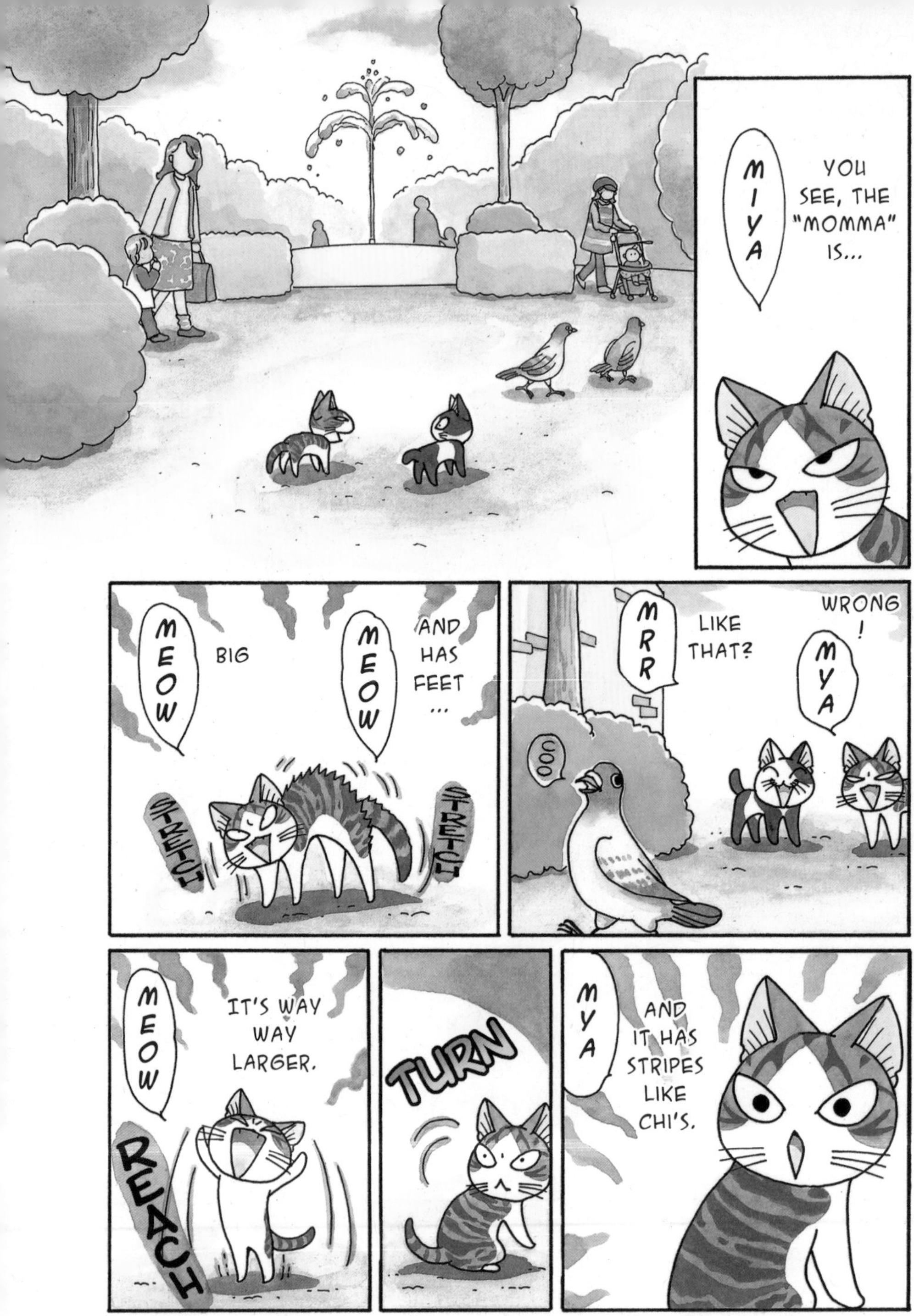
MIYA
YOU SEE, THE "MOMMA" IS...
MEOW
BIG
MEOW
AND HAS FEET ...
STRETCH
STRETCH
MRR
LIKE THAT?
COO
WRONG!
MYA
MEOW
IT'S WAY WAY LARGER.
REACH
TURN
MYA
AND IT HAS STRIPES LIKE CHI'S.

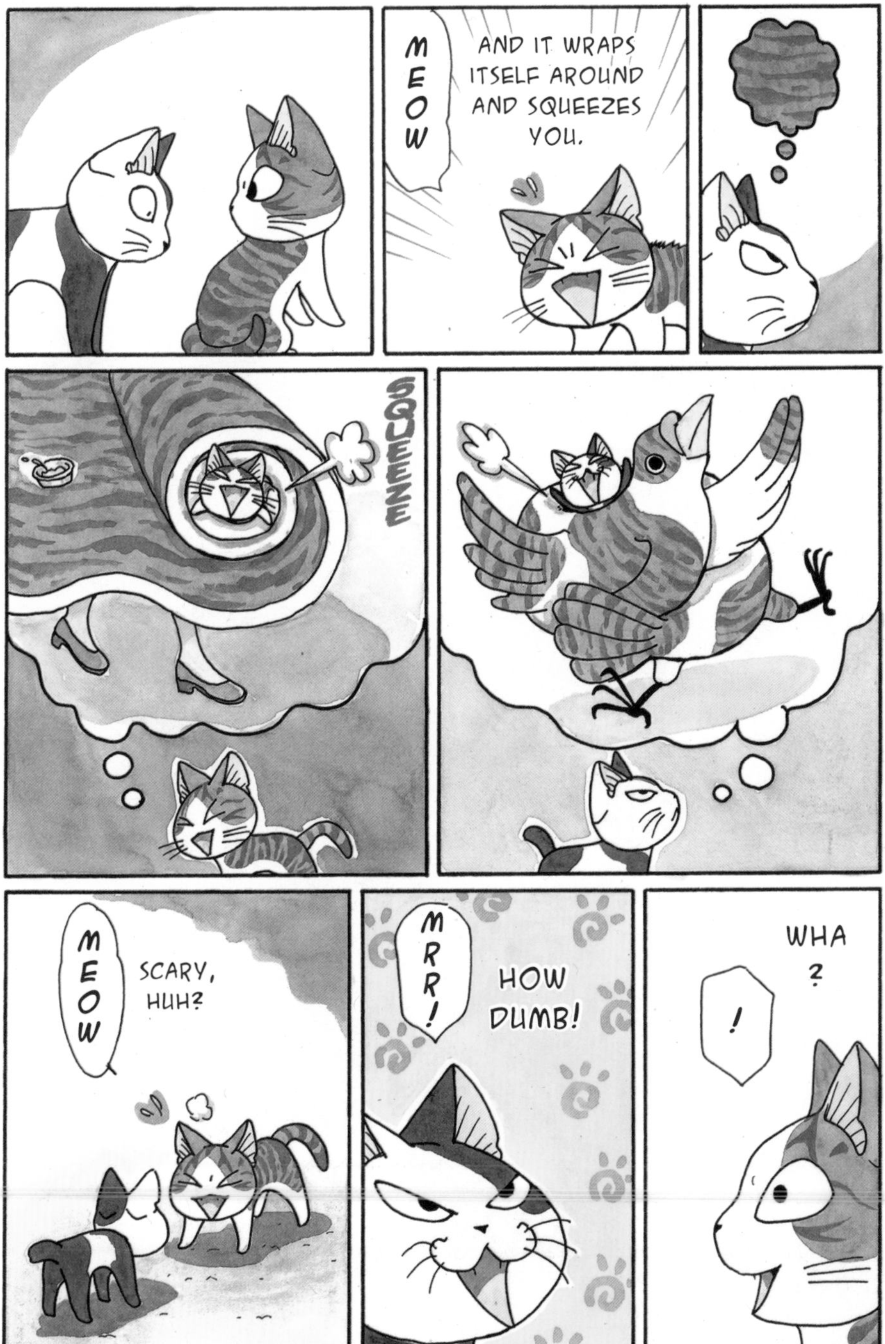
MEOW
AND IT WRAPS ITSELF AROUND AND SQUEEZES YOU.
SQUEEZE
MEOW
SCARY, HUH?
MRR!
HOW DUMB!
!
WHA?

MEOW?

DUMB?

THERE'S NO WAY SUCH A THING EXISTS.

MERR

TIP TIP TIP

DASH—

HALT

MEOW

BUT AUNTIE CALICO TOLD ME.

WELL, I HEARD FROM AUNTIE CALICO TOO.

MERR

SO WHAT ARE YOU SAYING?

MRR

MYA

SHE TOLD CHI!

BUT THAT'S JUST DUMB.

MERR

MEOW

COCCHI'S THE WEIRD ONE.

MERR

WHAT'D YOU SAY?

MEOW

WHAT?

NYA

OH MY, WHAT IS THE MATTER?

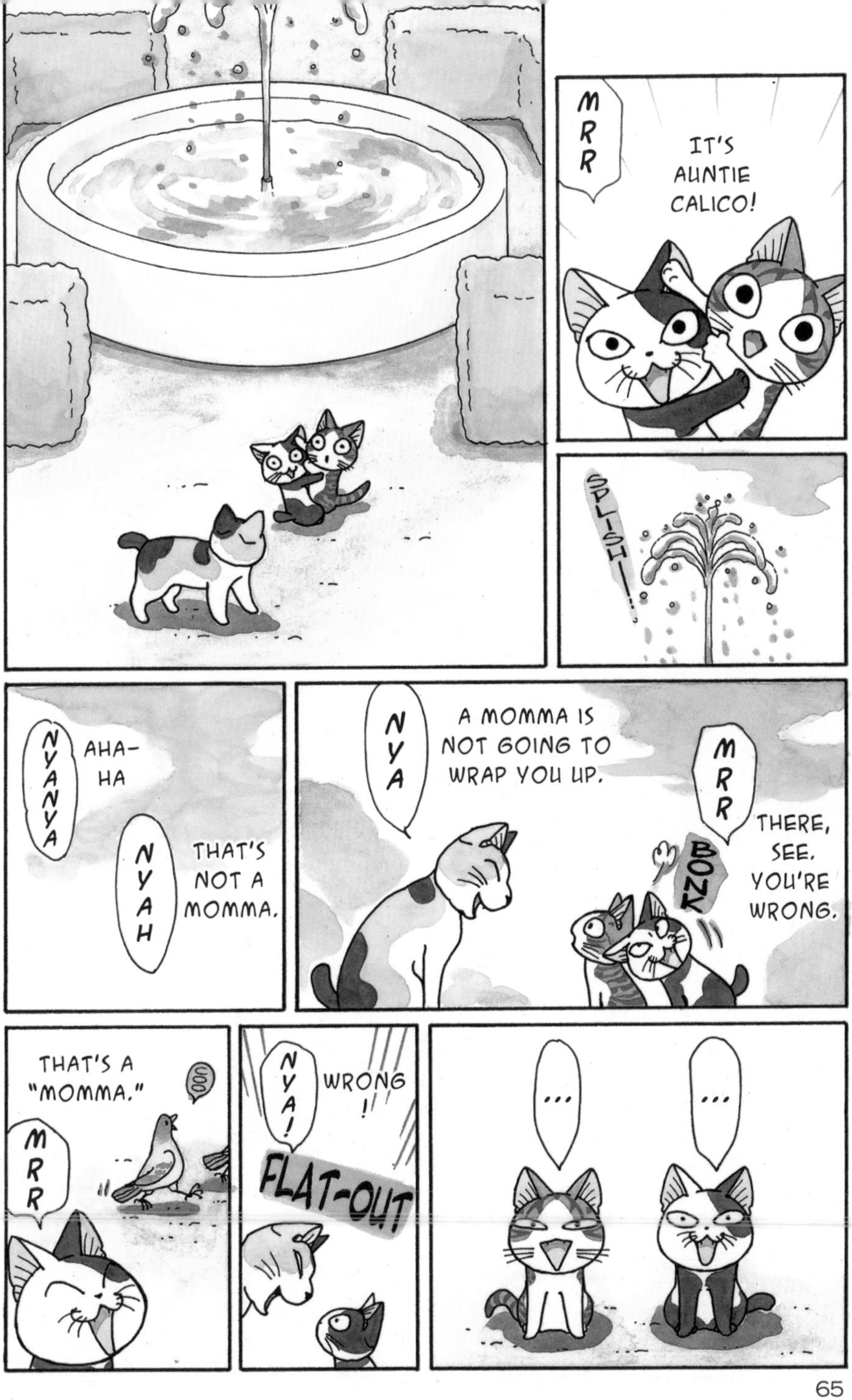
MRR
IT'S AUNTIE CALICO!
SPLISH!!
NYANYA
AHA-HA
NYAH
THAT'S NOT A MOMMA.
NYA
A MOMMA IS NOT GOING TO WRAP YOU UP.
MRR
BONK
THERE, SEE. YOU'RE WRONG.
THAT'S A "MOMMA."
MRR
NYA!
WRONG!
FLAT-OUT
...
...

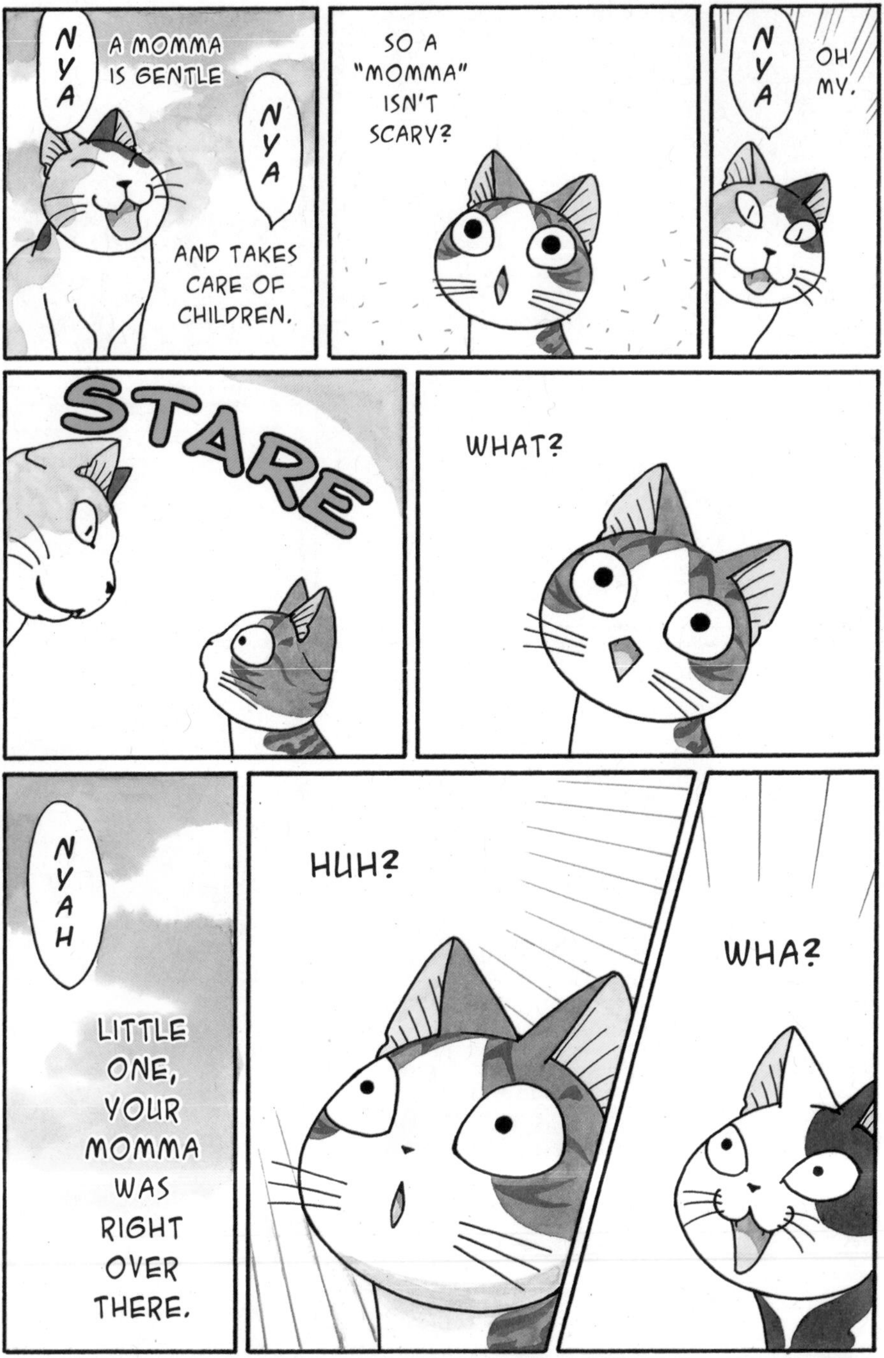
NYA
A MOMMA IS GENTLE
NYA
AND TAKES CARE OF CHILDREN.
SO A "MOMMA" ISN'T SCARY?
NYA
OH MY.
STARE
WHAT?
NYAH
LITTLE ONE, YOUR MOMMA WAS RIGHT OVER THERE.
HUH?
WHA?

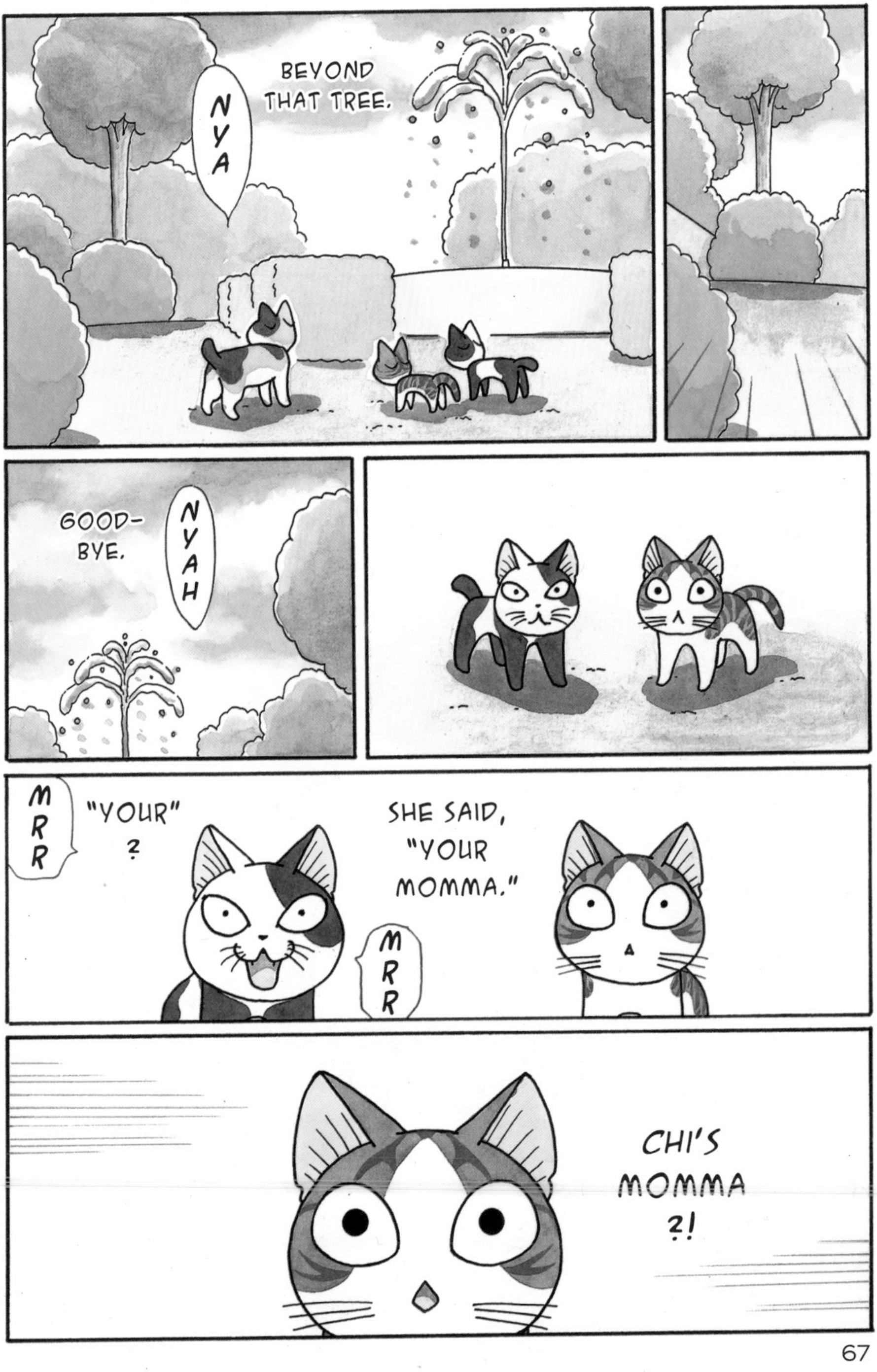
NYA
BEYOND THAT TREE.
GOOD-BYE.
NYAH
MRR
"YOUR"?
SHE SAID, "YOUR MOMMA."
MRR
CHI'S MOMMA?!

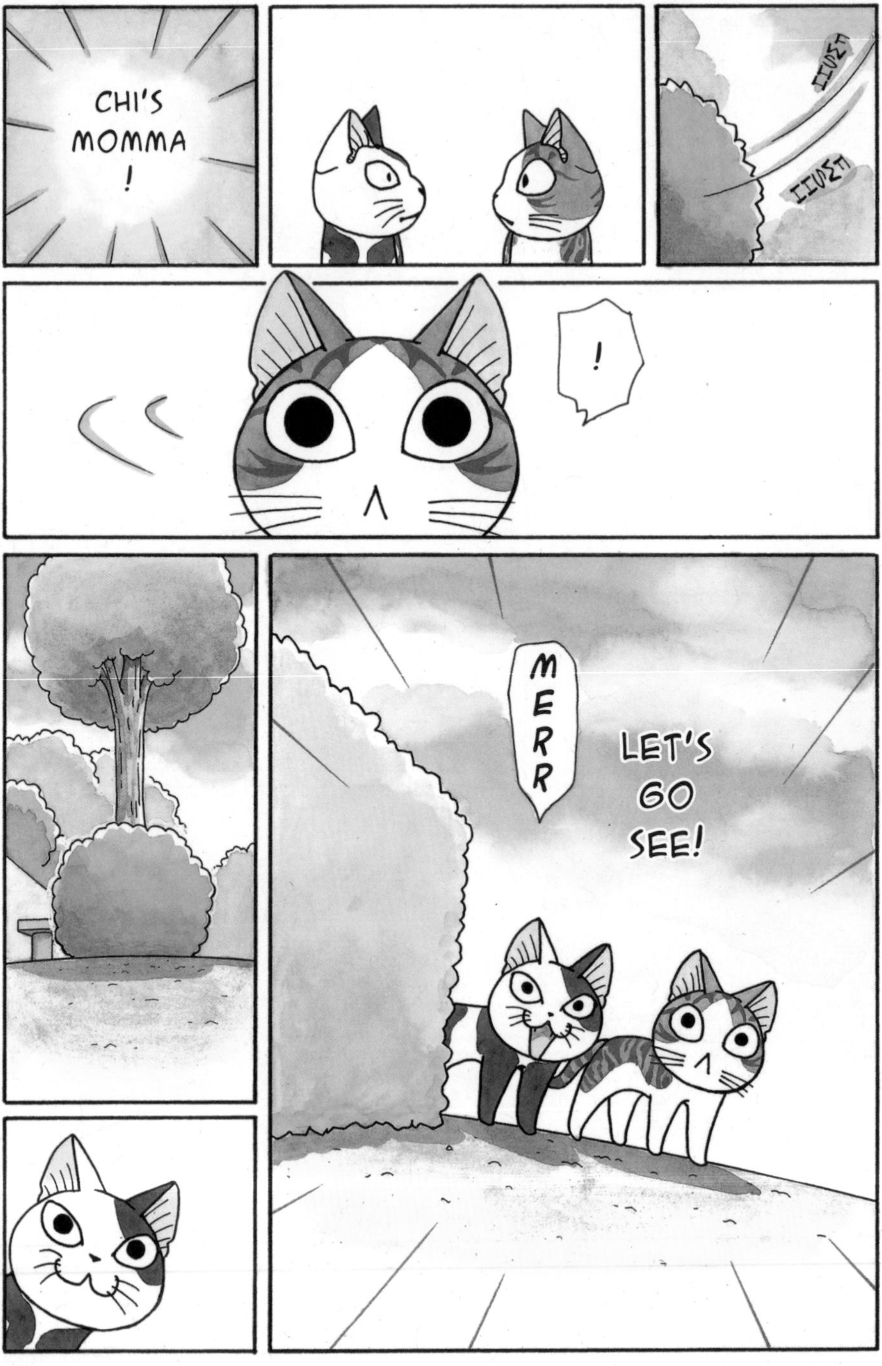
CHI'S MOMMA !
!
MERR
LET'S GO SEE!

the end

homemade 173: a cat goes to see

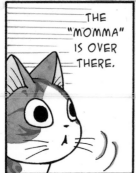

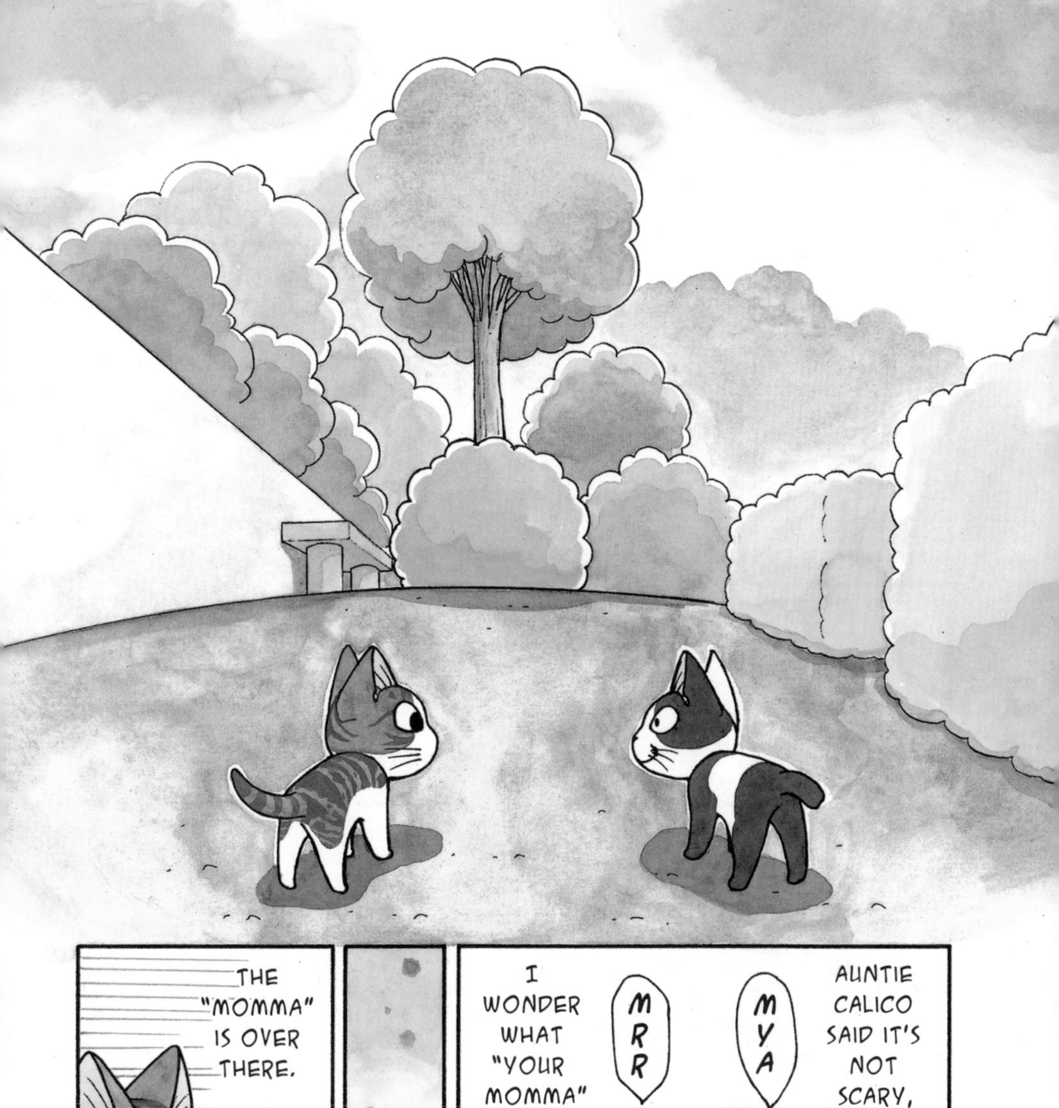
THE "MOMMA" IS OVER THERE.
... "MOM-MA"?
I WONDER WHAT "YOUR MOMMA" IS LIKE?
MRR
MYA
AUNTIE CALICO SAID IT'S NOT SCARY, RIGHT?
SLINK
SLINK

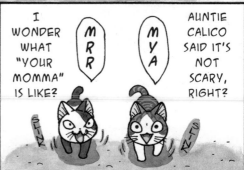

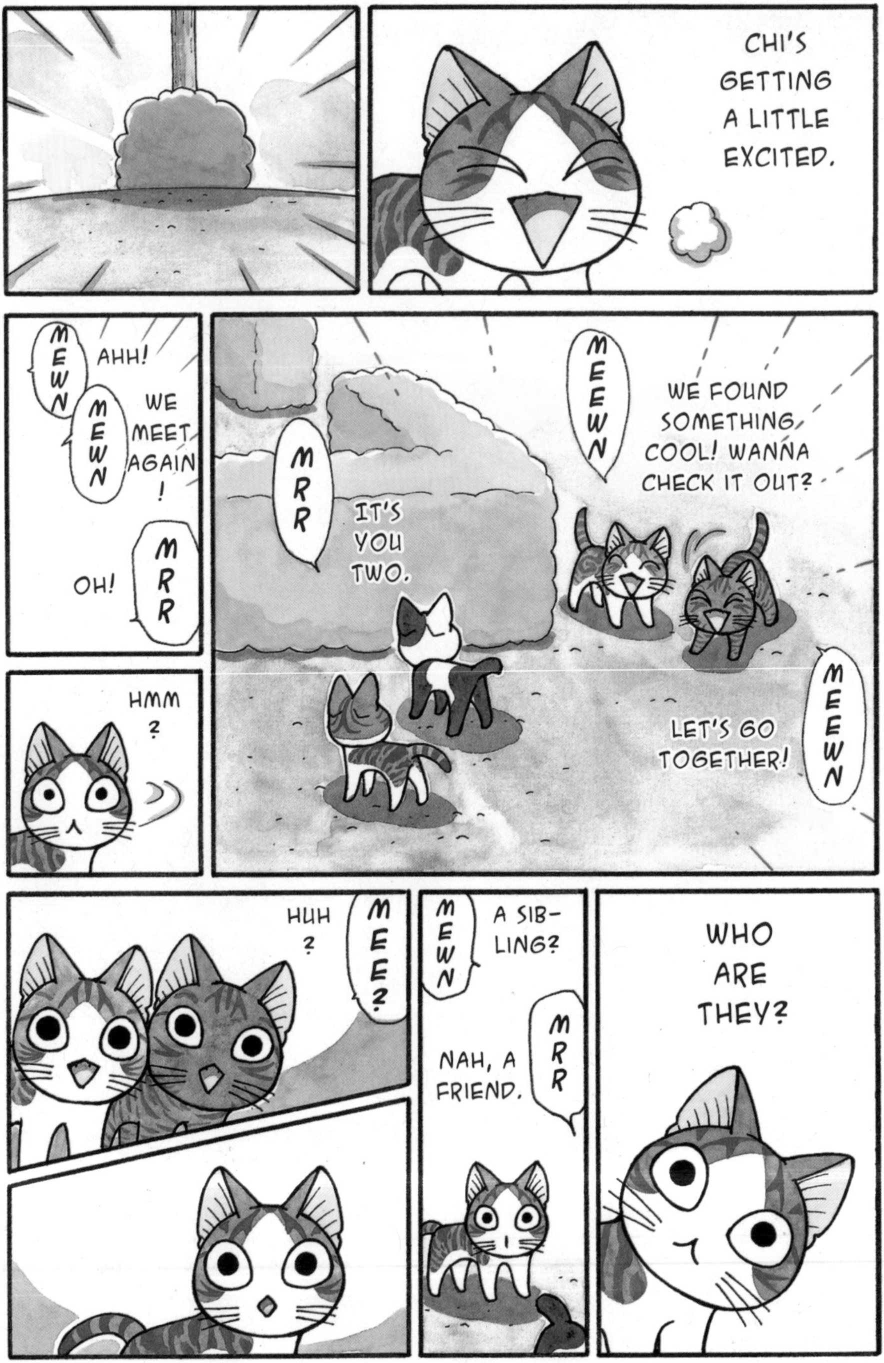
CHI'S GETTING A LITTLE EXCITED.
MEWN
AHH!
MEWN
WE MEET AGAIN!
MRR
OH!
MRR
IT'S YOU TWO.
MEEWN
WE FOUND SOMETHING COOL! WANNA CHECK IT OUT?
MEEWN
LET'S GO TOGETHER!
HMM?
HUH?
MEE?
MEWN
A SIB-LING?
MRR
NAH, A FRIEND.
WHO ARE THEY?

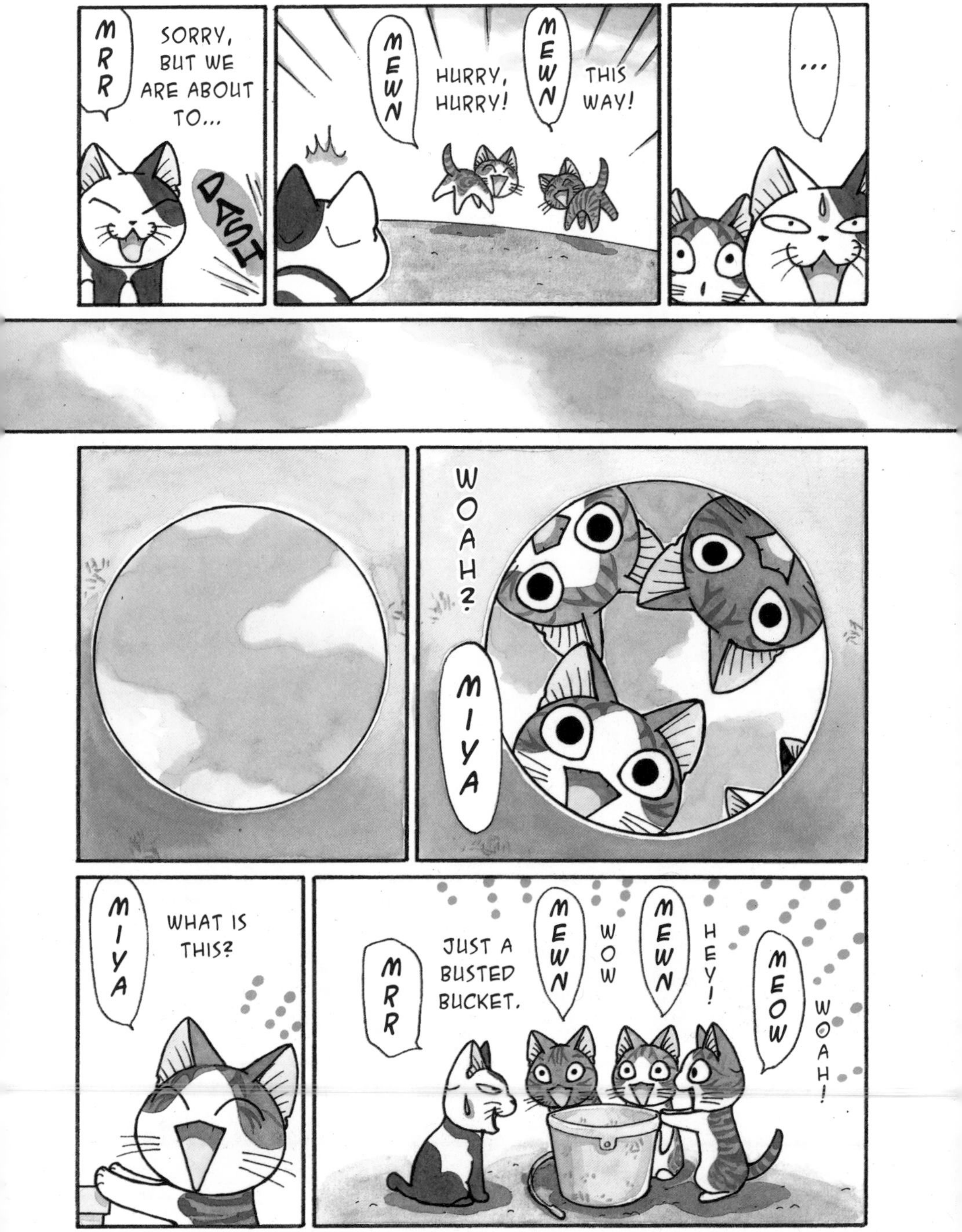
MRR
SORRY, BUT WE ARE ABOUT TO...
DASH
MEWN
HURRY, HURRY!
MEWN
THIS WAY!
...
WOAH?
MIYA
MIYA
WHAT IS THIS?
MRR
JUST A BUSTED BUCKET.
MEWN
WOW
MEWN
HEY!
MEOW
WOAH!

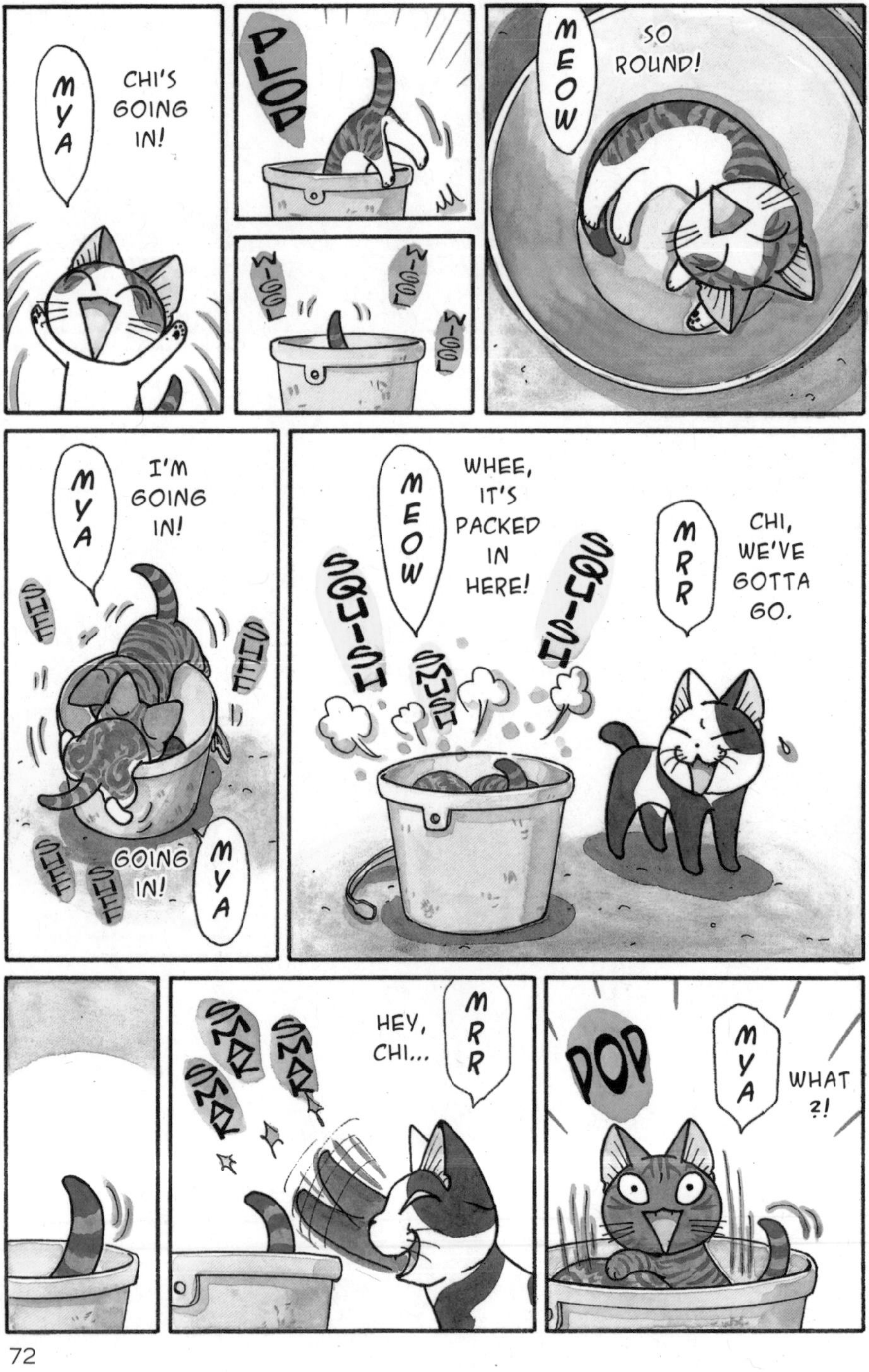
MYA
CHI'S GOING IN!
PLOP
WIGGL
WIGGL
WIGGL
MEOW
SO ROUND!
MYA
I'M GOING IN!
SHFF
SHFF
MYA
GOING IN!
SHFF
SHFF
MEOW
WHEE, IT'S PACKED IN HERE!
SQUISH
SMUSH
SQUISH
MRR
CHI, WE'VE GOTTA GO.
SMAK
SMAK
SMAK
HEY, CHI...
MRR
POP
MYA
WHAT ?!

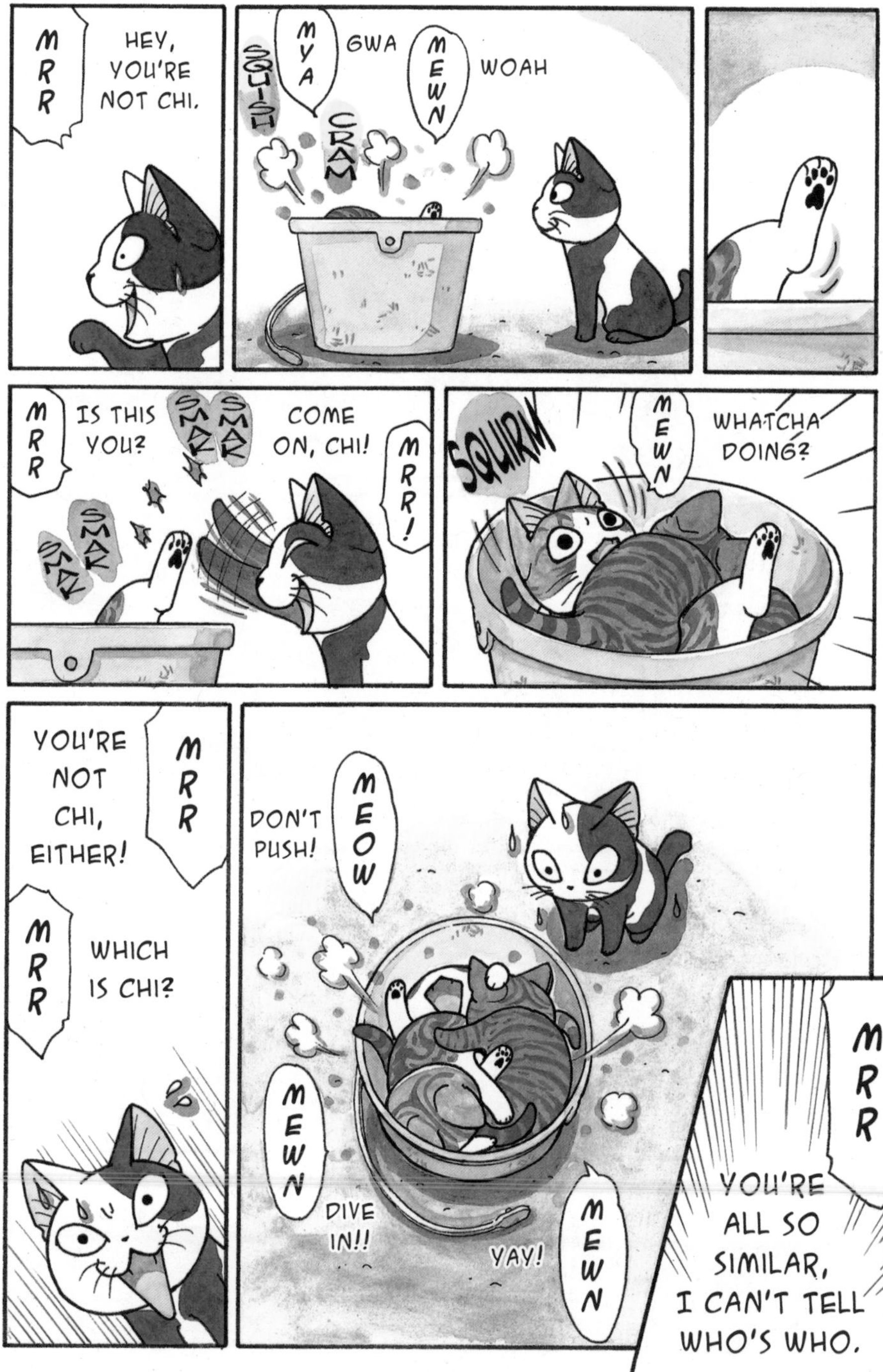
MRR
HEY, YOU'RE NOT CHI.
MYA
GWA
SQUISH
MEWN
WOAH
CRAM
MRR
IS THIS YOU?
SMAK SMAK
COME ON, CHI!
MRR!
SMAK SMAK
SQUIRM
MEWN
WHATCHA DOING?
YOU'RE NOT CHI, EITHER!
MRR
MRR
WHICH IS CHI?
DON'T PUSH!
MEOW
MEWN
DIVE IN!!
YAY!
MEWN
MRR
YOU'RE ALL SO SIMILAR, I CAN'T TELL WHO'S WHO.

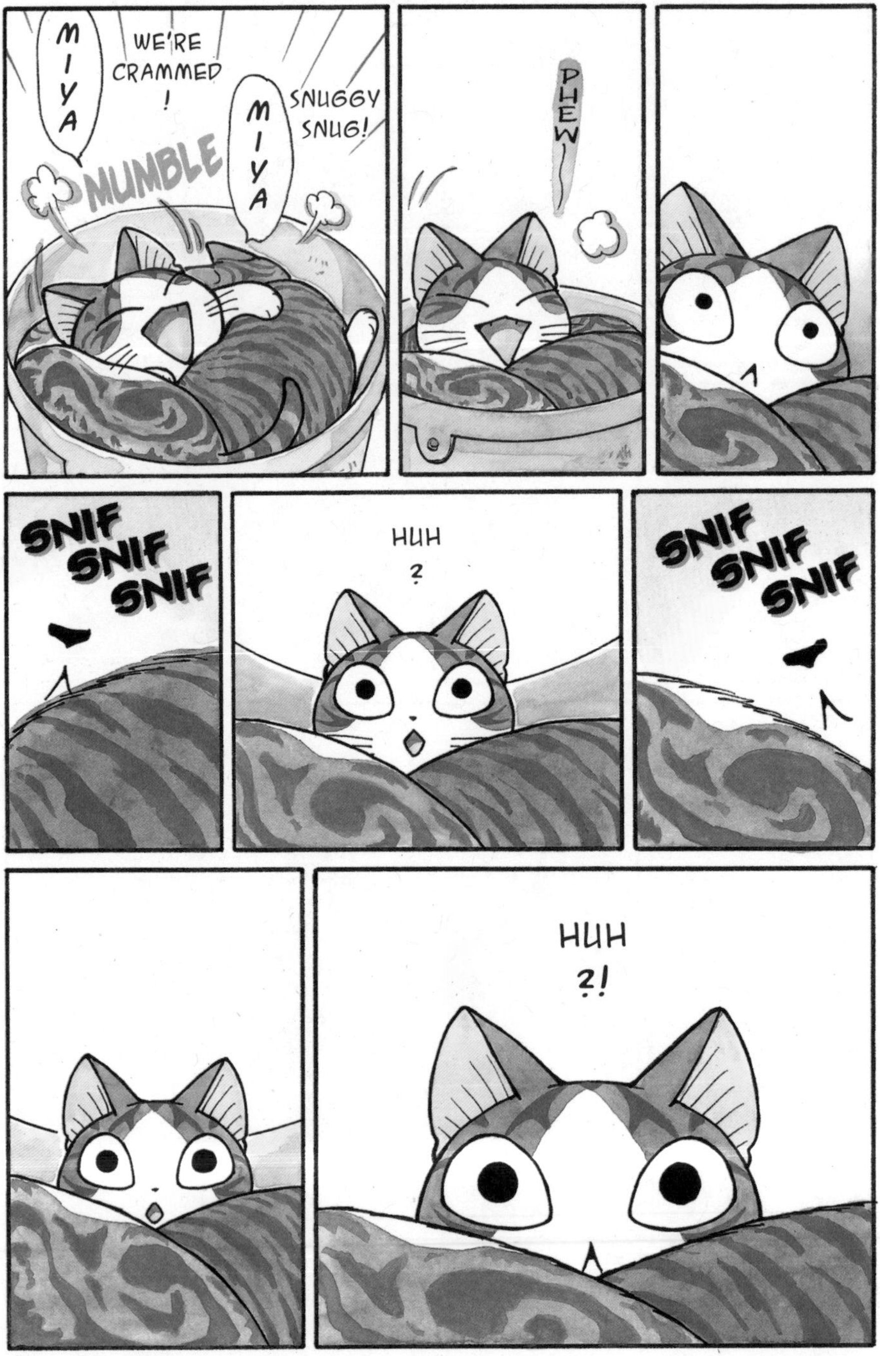
MIYA
WE'RE CRAMMED!
MIYA
SNUGGY SNUG!
MUMBLE
PHEW
SNIF SNIF SNIF
HUH?
SNIF SNIF SNIF
HUH?!

HAVE
I...

DONE
THIS
BEFORE?

RIGHT,

BACK
THEN.

REACH

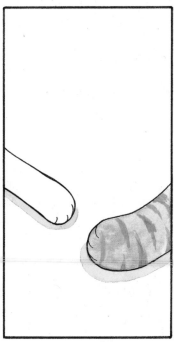

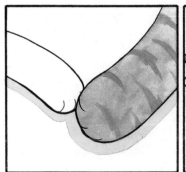

WHAT WAS THAT?

IT WAS ...

KLUNK

SPLAT

MYA

MRR!

I FOUND CHI!

76

the end

homemade 174: a cat ponders

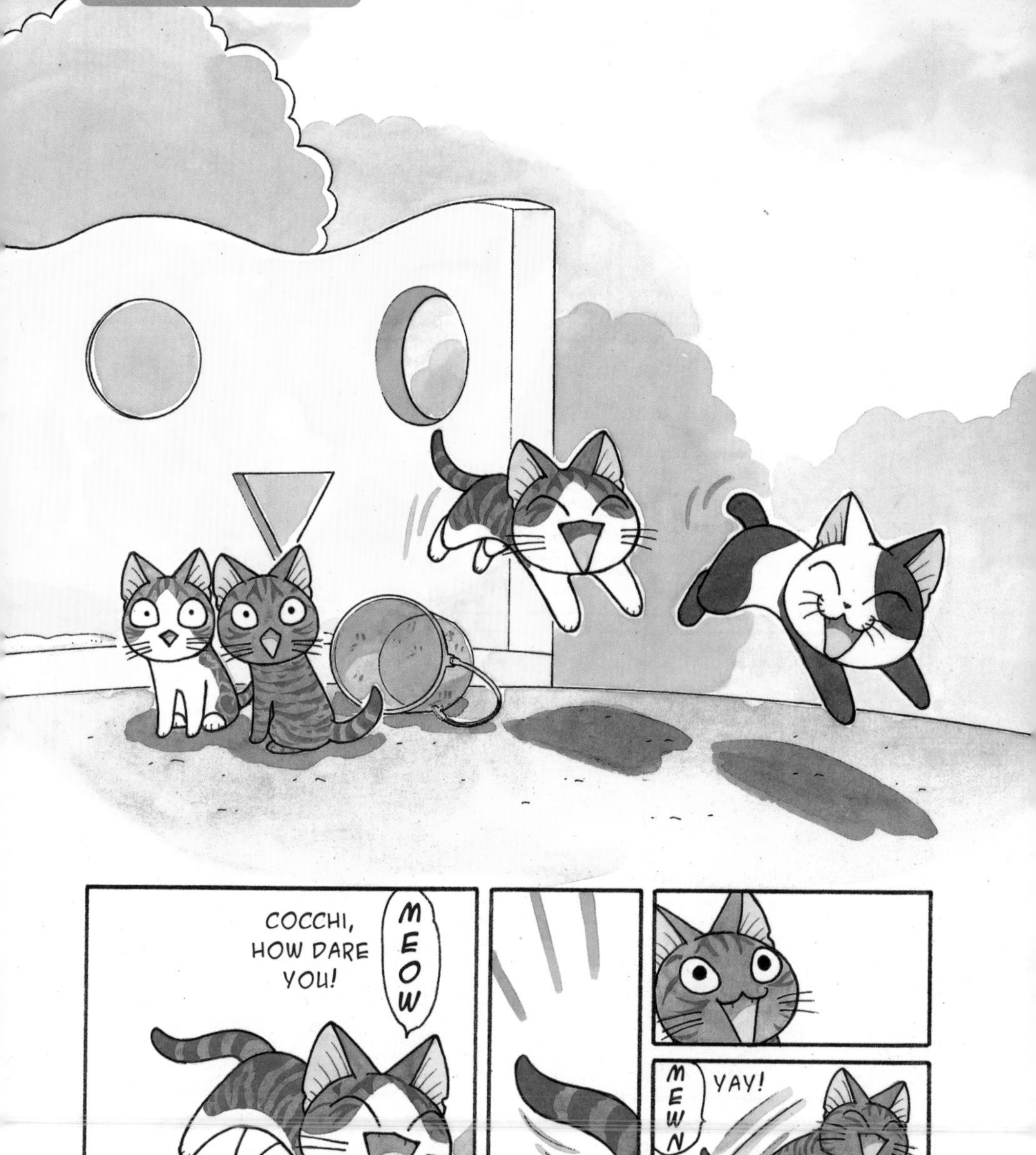
COCCHI, HOW DARE YOU!
MEOW
MEWN
YAY!
BOUND

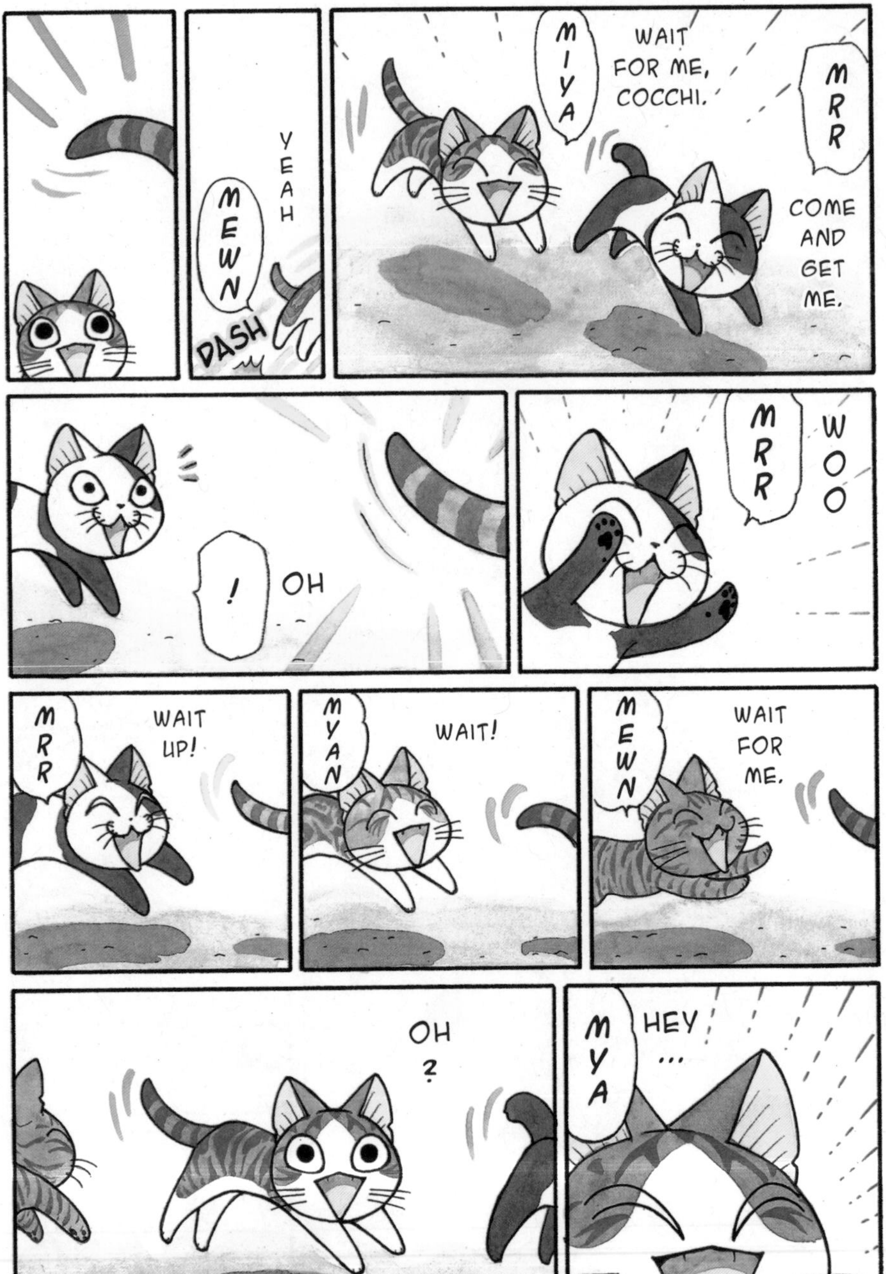
MEWN
YEAH
DASH
MIYA
WAIT FOR ME, COCCHI.
MRR
COME AND GET ME.
!
OH
MRR
WOO
MRR
WAIT UP!
MYAN
WAIT!
MEWN
WAIT FOR ME.
OH ?
MYA
HEY ...

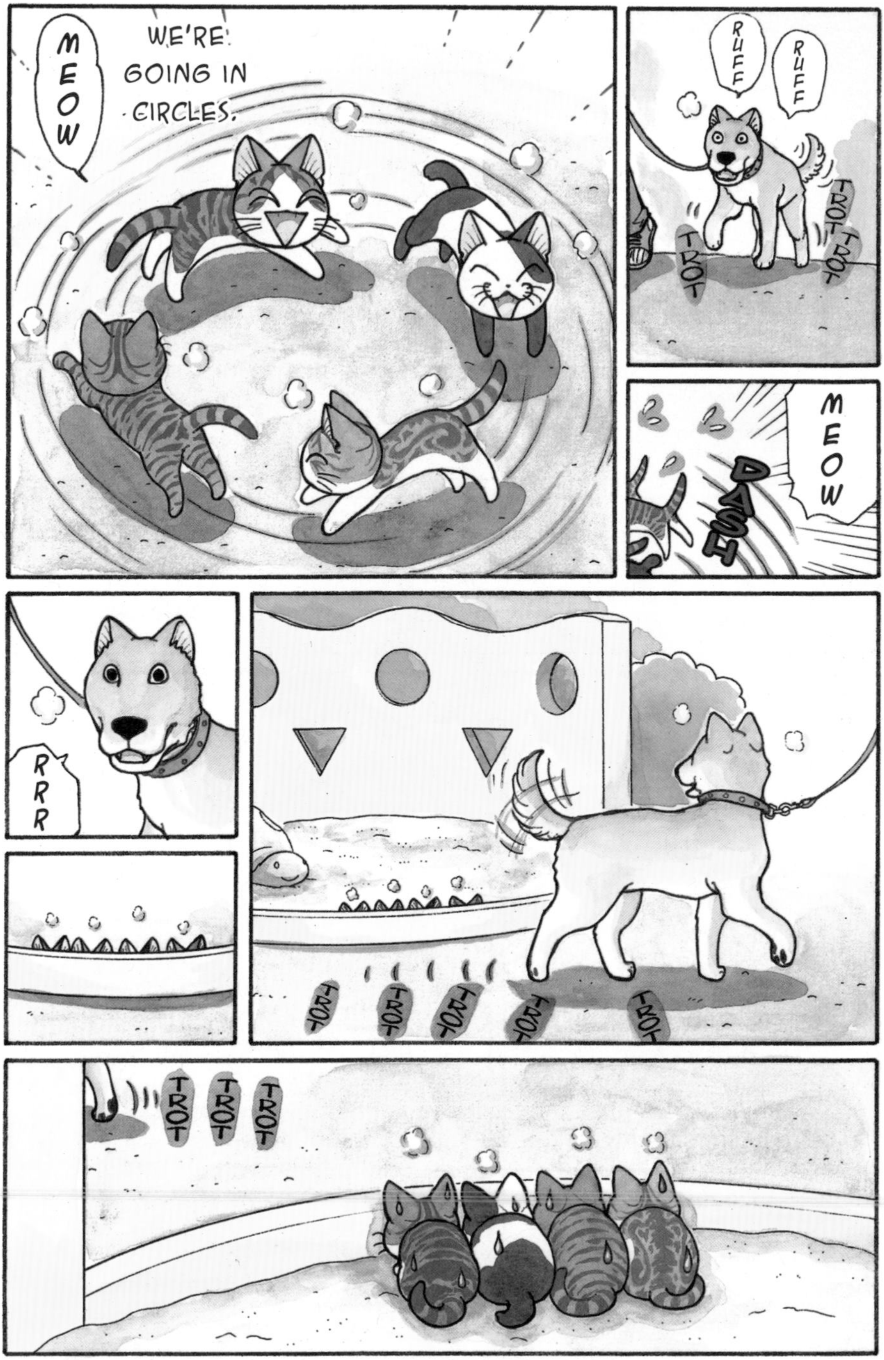
MEOW
WE'RE GOING IN CIRCLES.
RUFF
RUFF
TROT TROT
TROT TROT
MEOW
DASH
RRR
TROT TROT TROT TROT TROT
TROT TROT TROT

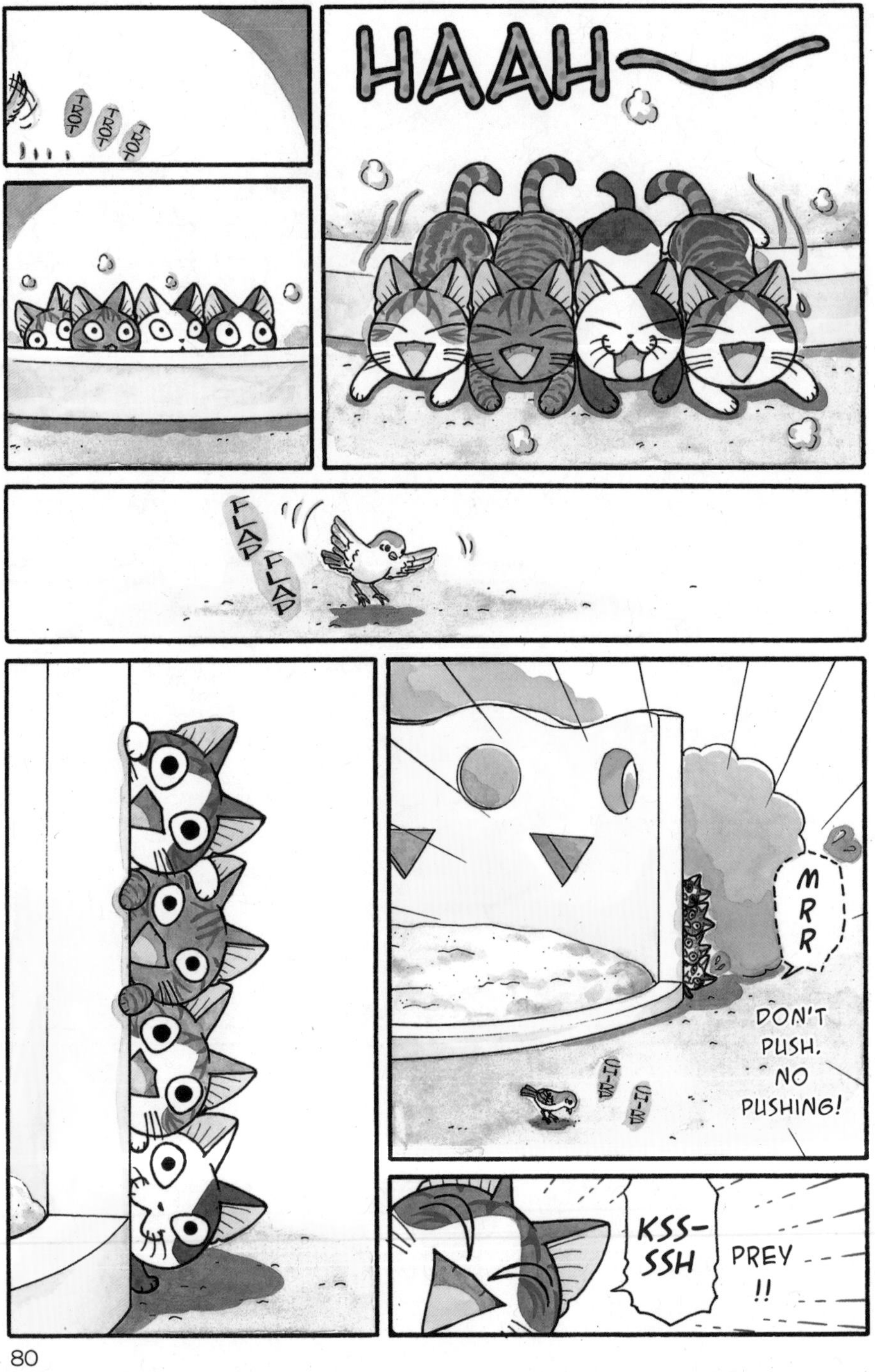
TROT TROT TROT
HAAH~
FLAP FLAP
MRR
DON'T PUSH. NO PUSHING!
CHIRP CHIRP
KSS-SSH
PREY !!

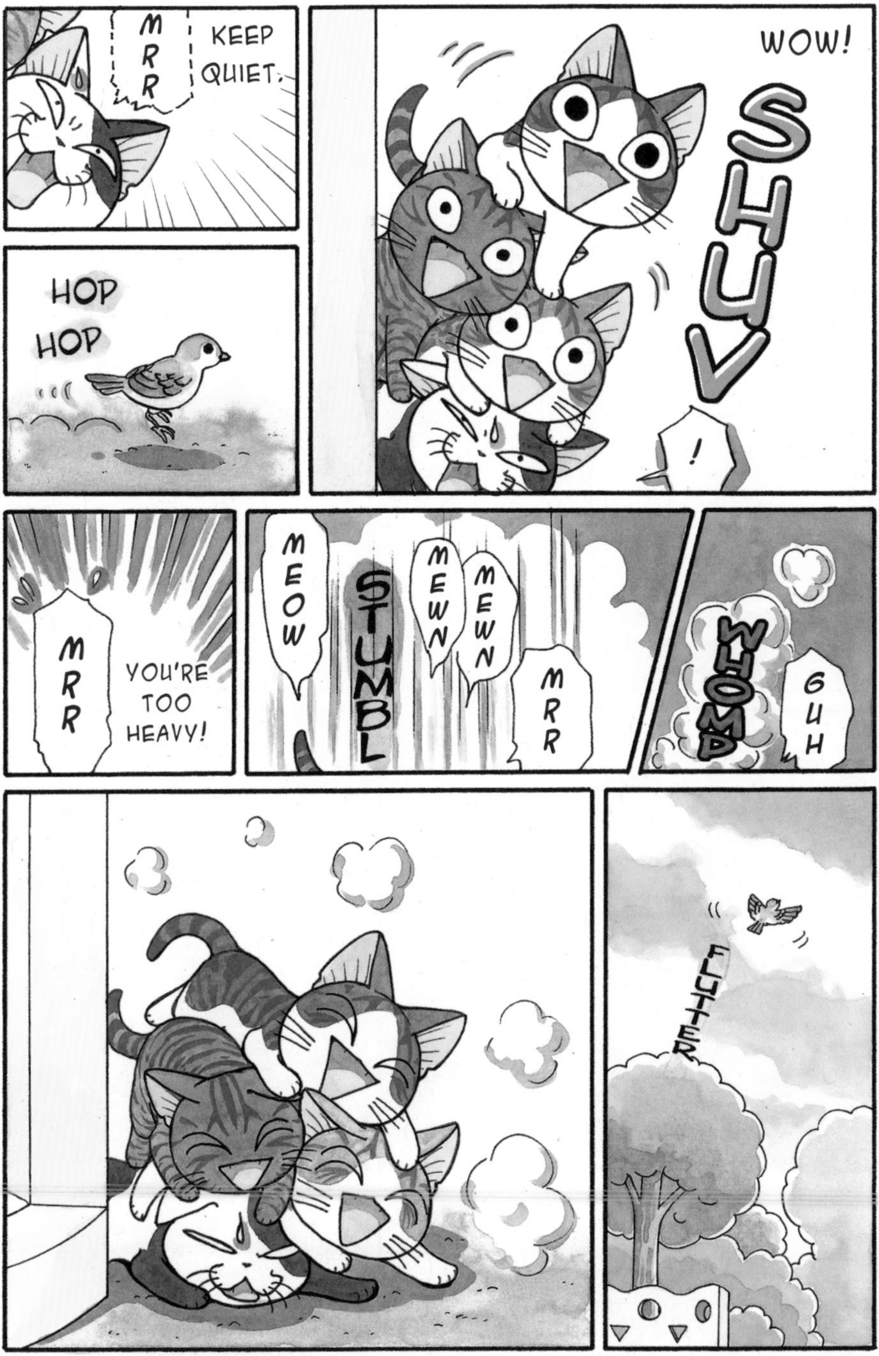
MRR
KEEP QUIET.
HOP
HOP
WOW!
SHUV
!
MRR
YOU'RE TOO HEAVY!
MEOW
STUMBL
MEWN
MEWN
MRR
WHOMP
GUH
FLUTTER

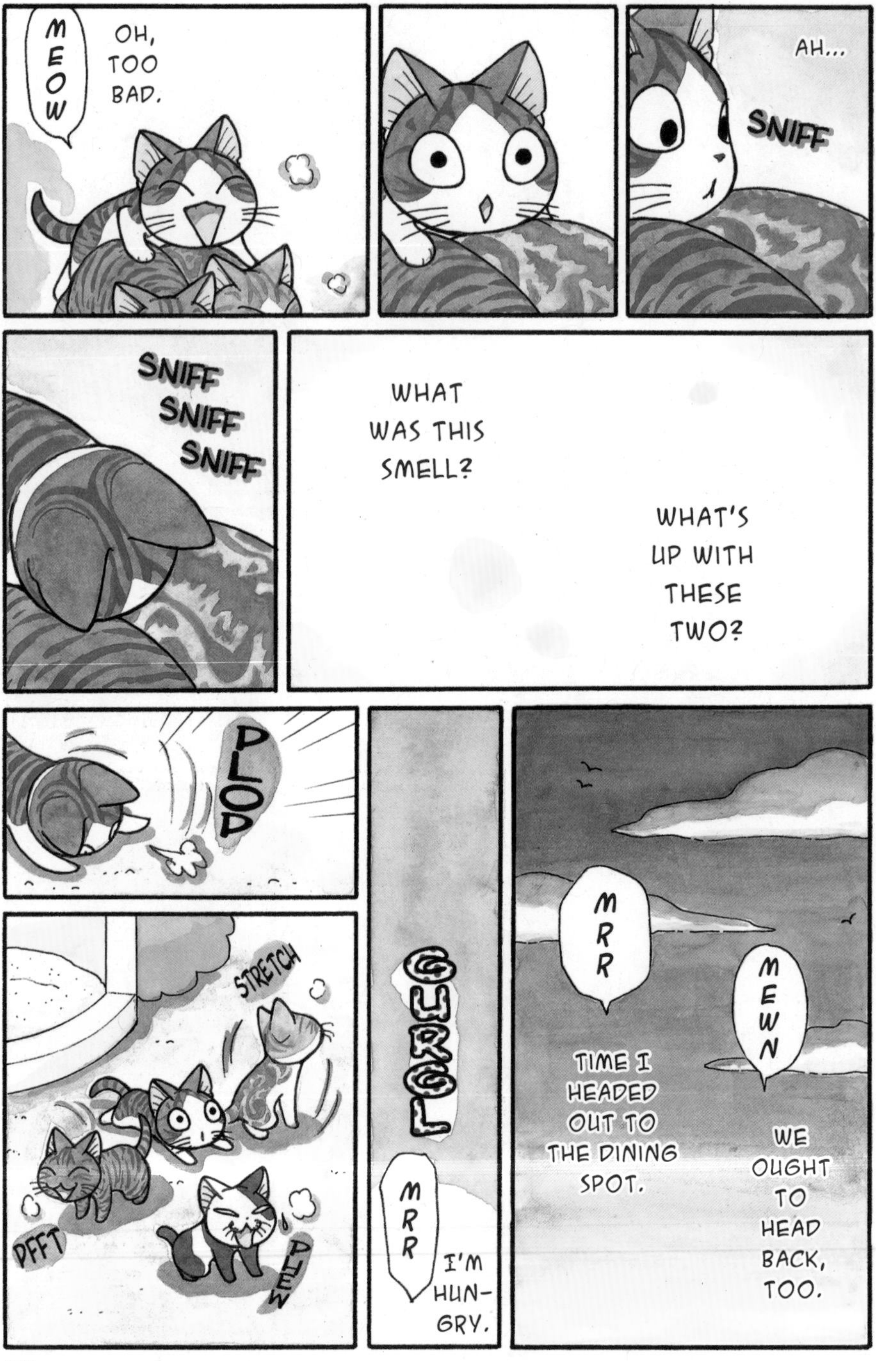
MEOW
OH, TOO BAD.
AH...
SNIFF
SNIFF SNIFF SNIFF
WHAT WAS THIS SMELL?
WHAT'S UP WITH THESE TWO?
PLOP
STRETCH
DFFT
PHEW
GURGL
MRR
I'M HUN-GRY.
MRR
MEWN
TIME I HEADED OUT TO THE DINING SPOT.
WE OUGHT TO HEAD BACK, TOO.

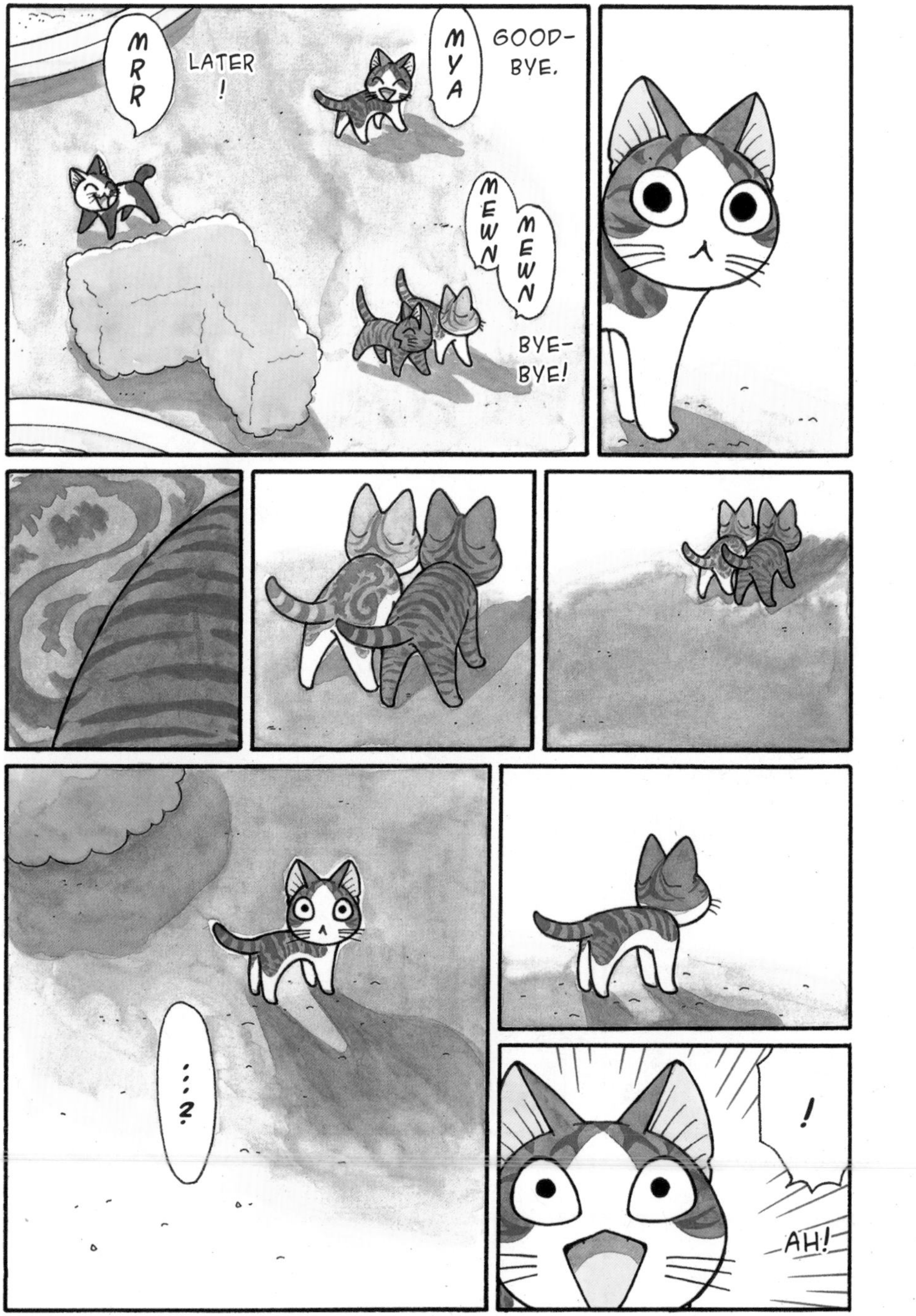
MRR
LATER!
MYA
GOOD-BYE.
MEWN
MEWN
BYE-BYE!
...?
!
AH!

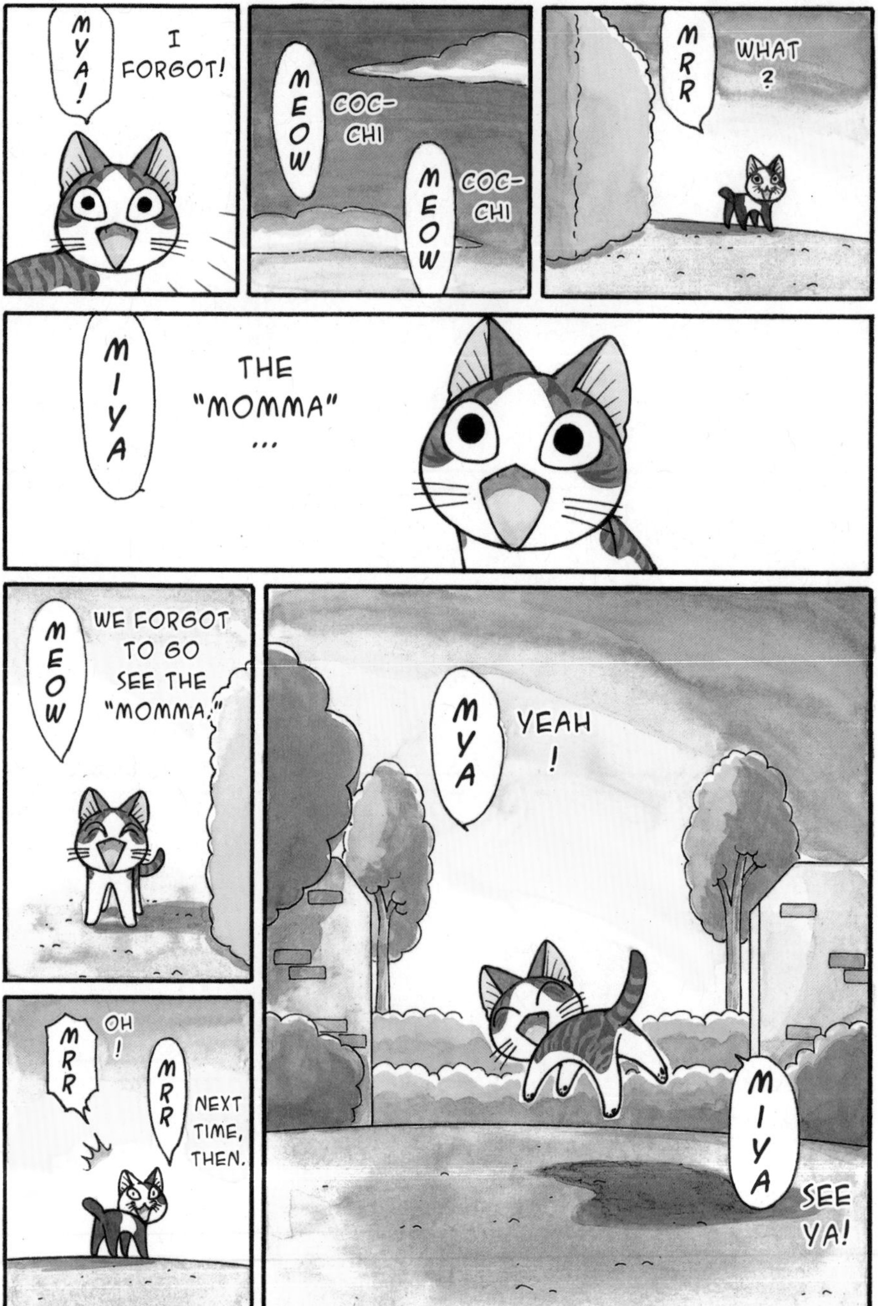
MYA!
I FORGOT!
MEOW
COC-CHI
MEOW
COC-CHI
MRR
WHAT?
MIYA
THE "MOMMA"...
MEOW
WE FORGOT TO GO SEE THE "MOMMA."
MRR
OH!
MRR
NEXT TIME, THEN.
MYA
YEAH!
MIYA
SEE YA!

the end

homemade 175: a-cat realizes

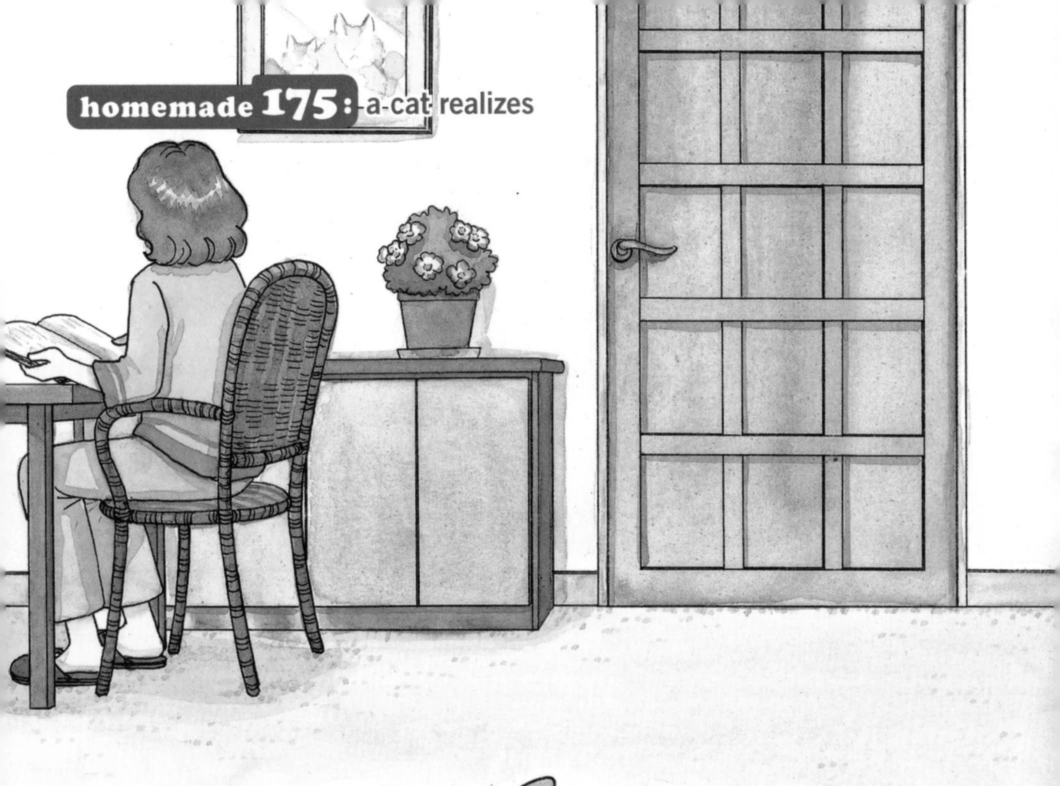

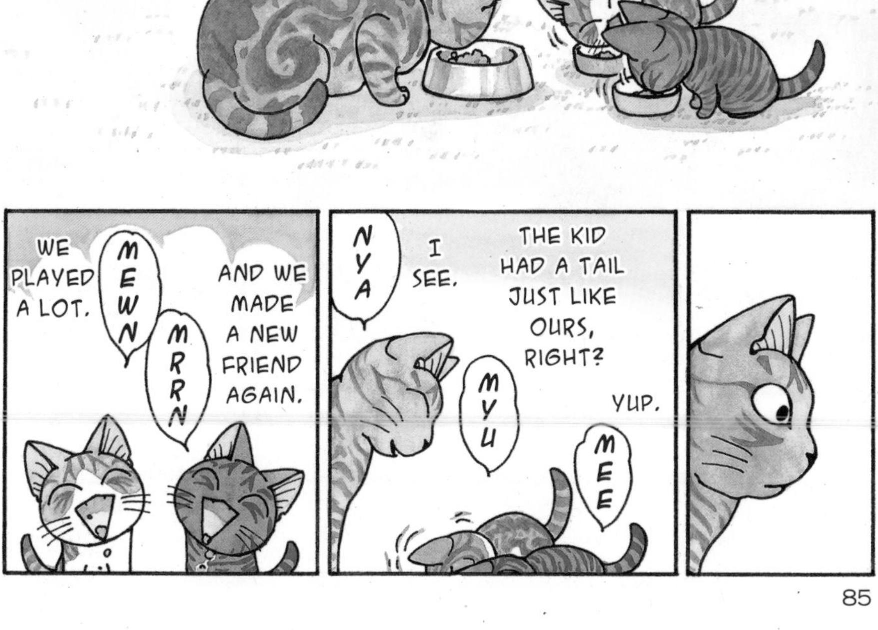

WE PLAYED A LOT.
MEWN
MRRN
AND WE MADE A NEW FRIEND AGAIN.
NYA
I SEE.
THE KID HAD A TAIL JUST LIKE OURS, RIGHT?
MYU
YUP.
MEE

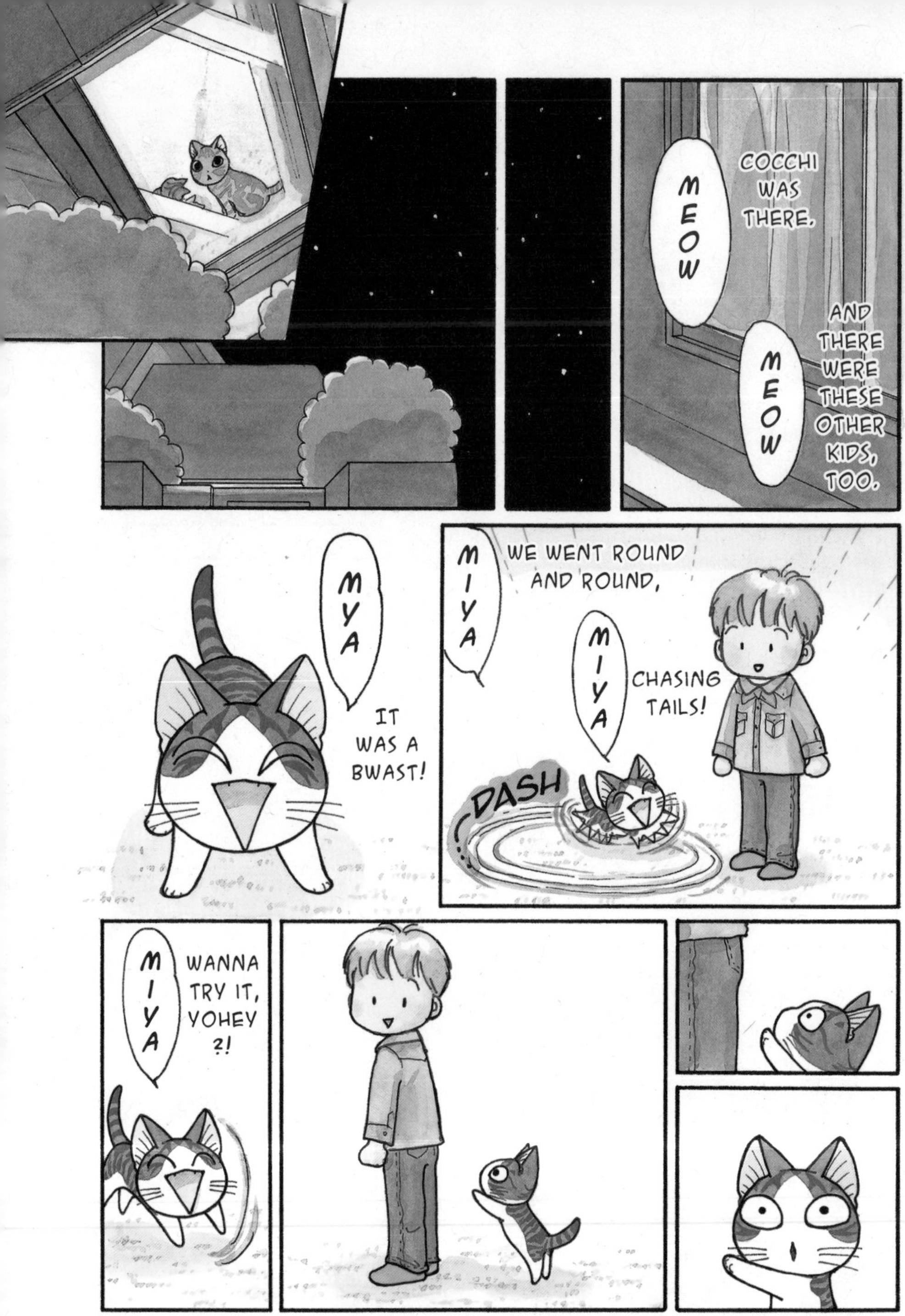

MEOW
COCCHI WAS THERE.
MEOW
AND THERE WERE THESE OTHER KIDS, TOO.
MYA
IT WAS A BWAST!
MIYA
WE WENT ROUND AND ROUND,
MIYA
CHASING TAILS!
DASH
MIYA
WANNA TRY IT, YOHEY ?!

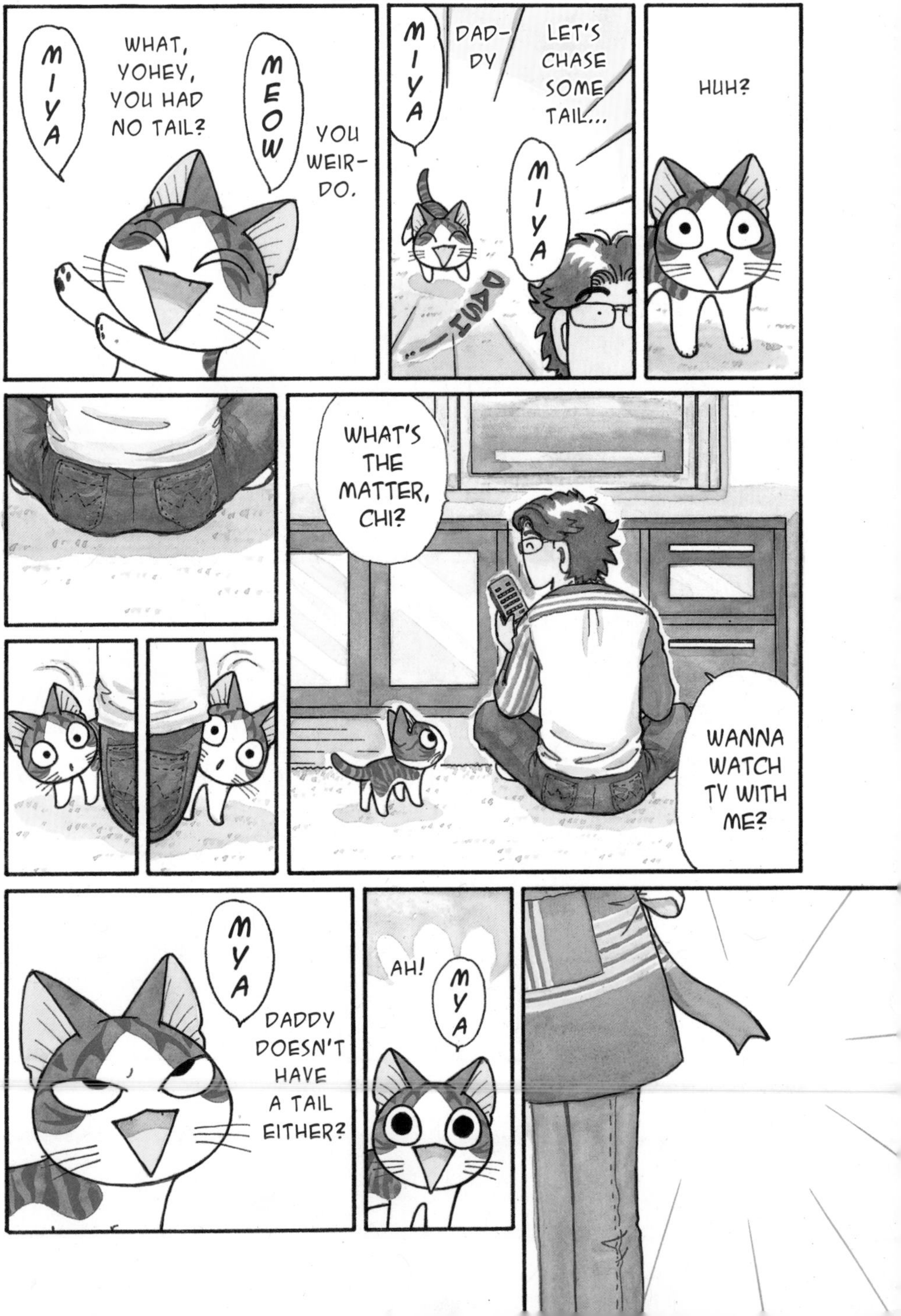
MIYA
WHAT, YOHEY, YOU HAD NO TAIL?
MEOW
YOU WEIR-DO.
MIYA
DAD-DY
LET'S CHASE SOME TAIL...
MIYA
HUH?
WHAT'S THE MATTER, CHI?
WANNA WATCH TV WITH ME?
MYA
DADDY DOESN'T HAVE A TAIL EITHER?
AH!
MYA

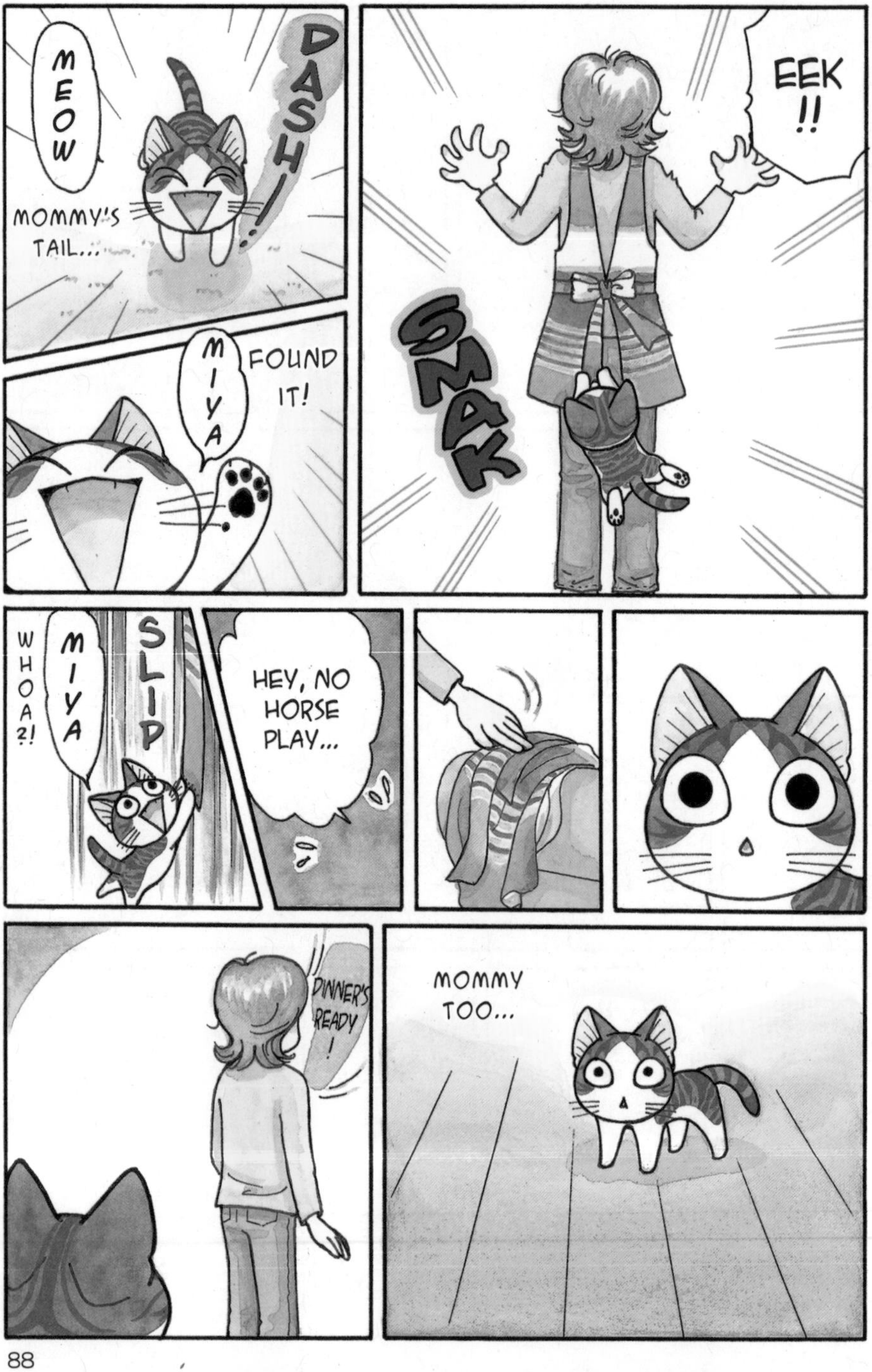
MEOW
DASH!
MOMMY'S TAIL...
MIYA
FOUND IT!
EEK !!
SMAK
WHOA?!
MIYA
SLIP
HEY, NO HORSE PLAY...
DINNER'S READY!
MOMMY TOO...

I MADE CHICKEN BREAST FOR DINNER.

WE'LL HAVE IT FRIED.

I LOVE THAT!

AH-HAH.

CHI'S IS BOILED.

WHAT SHOULD WE HAVE IT WITH? ANY SAUCE?

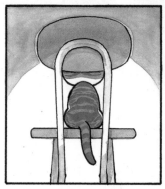

CHI'S THE ONLY ONE WITH A TAIL.

IT HAS SALT AND PEPPER ON IT.

MINE TOO?

DON'T WORRY, IT'S NOT SPICY.

SOME LEMON MIGHT BE GOOD.

I DON'T UNDER-STAND THEM.

CHI'S THE ONLY ONE WHO DOESN'T UNDERSTAND.

WHAT ARE THEY SAYING?

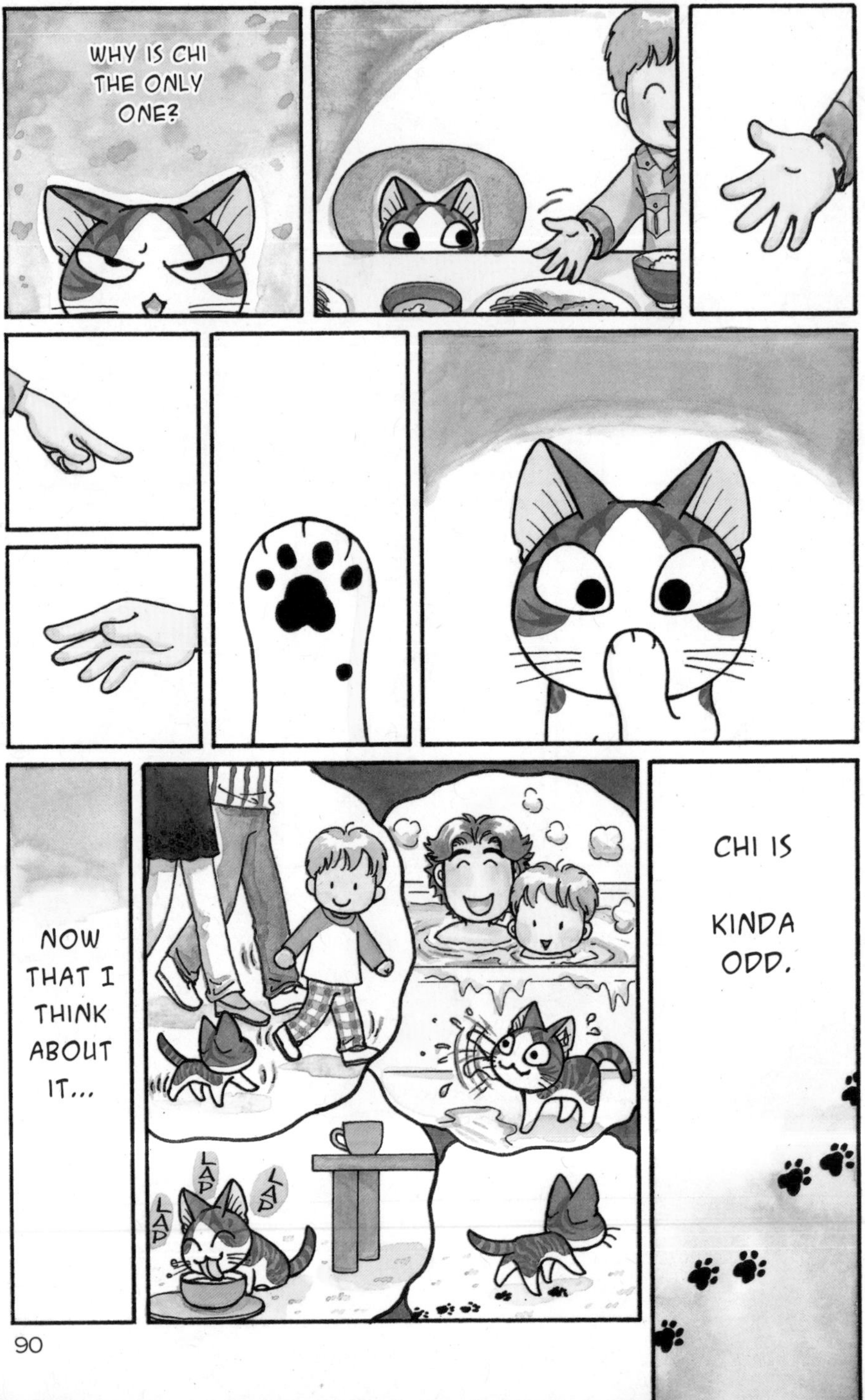
WHY IS CHI THE ONLY ONE?
NOW THAT I THINK ABOUT IT...
LAP
LAP
LAP
CHI IS
KINDA ODD.

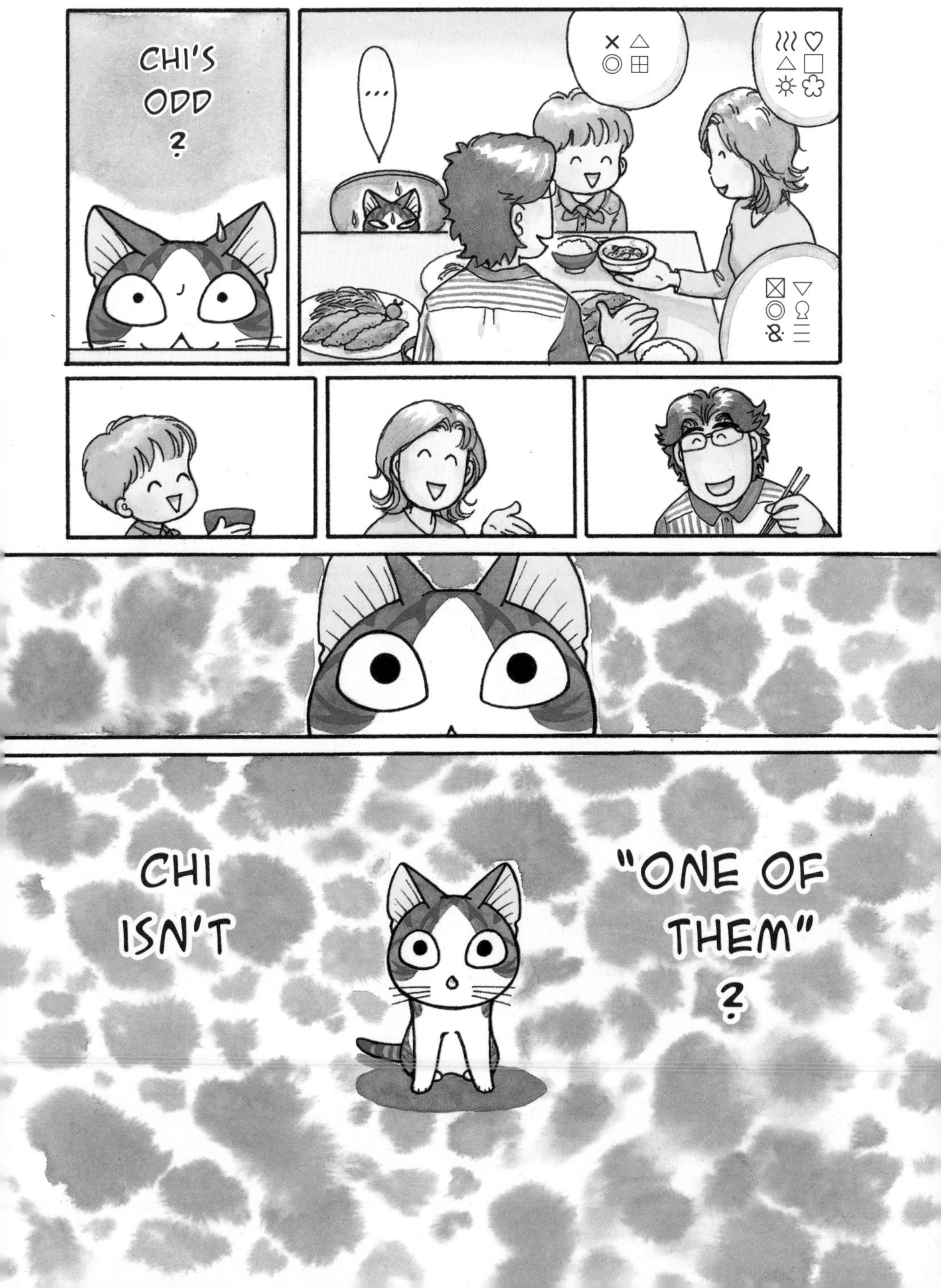
CHI'S ODD ?
...
CHI ISN'T "ONE OF THEM" ?

ARRIVED A LITTLE LATE, HUH, TINY.

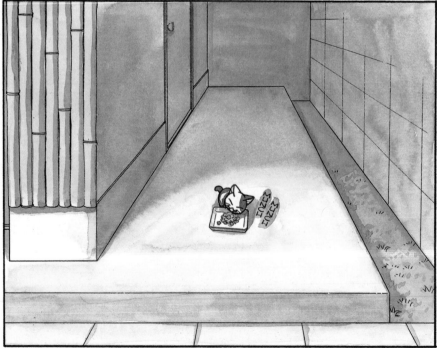

the end

homemade 176: a cat queries

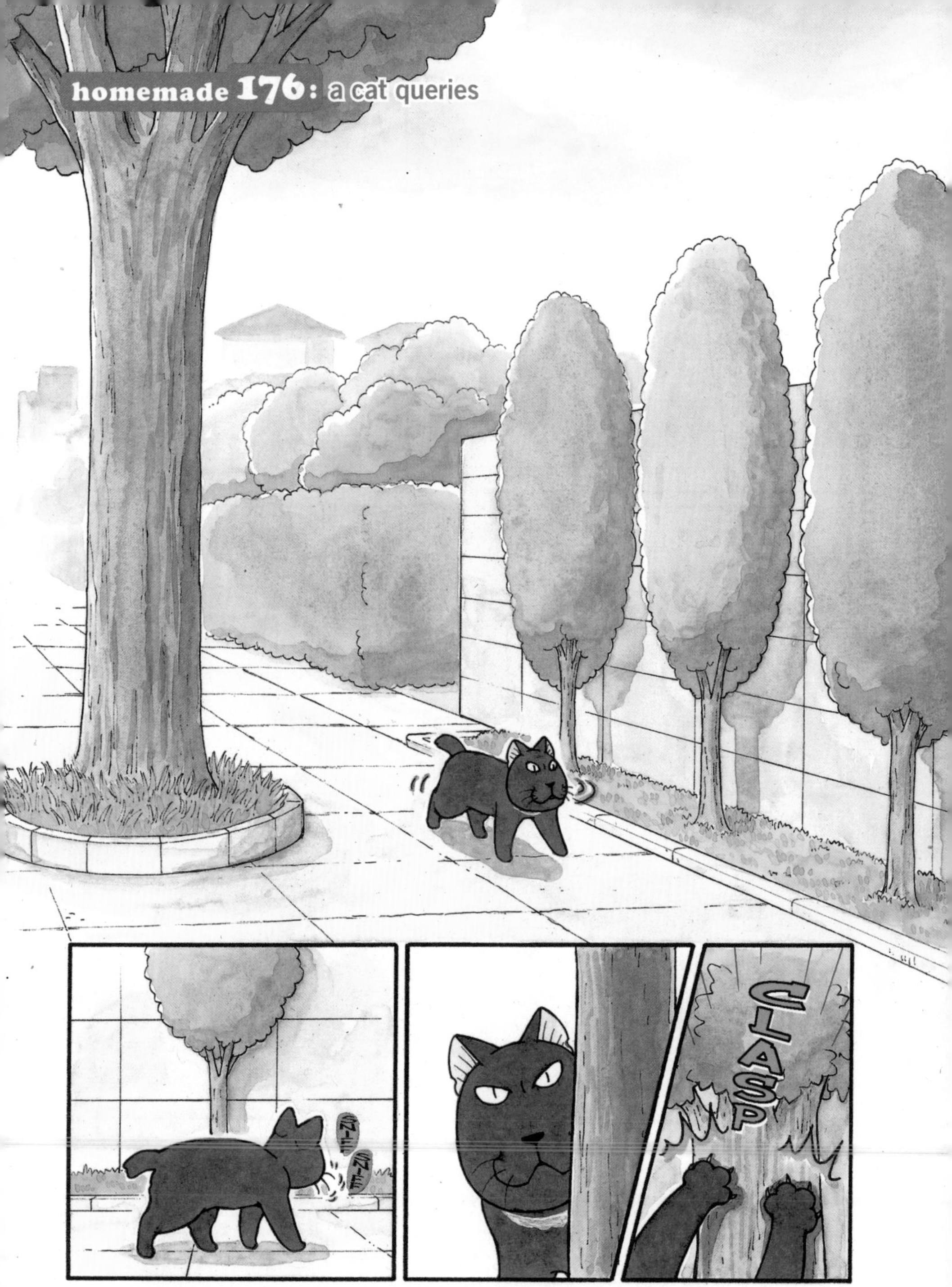
SNIF
SNIF
CLASP

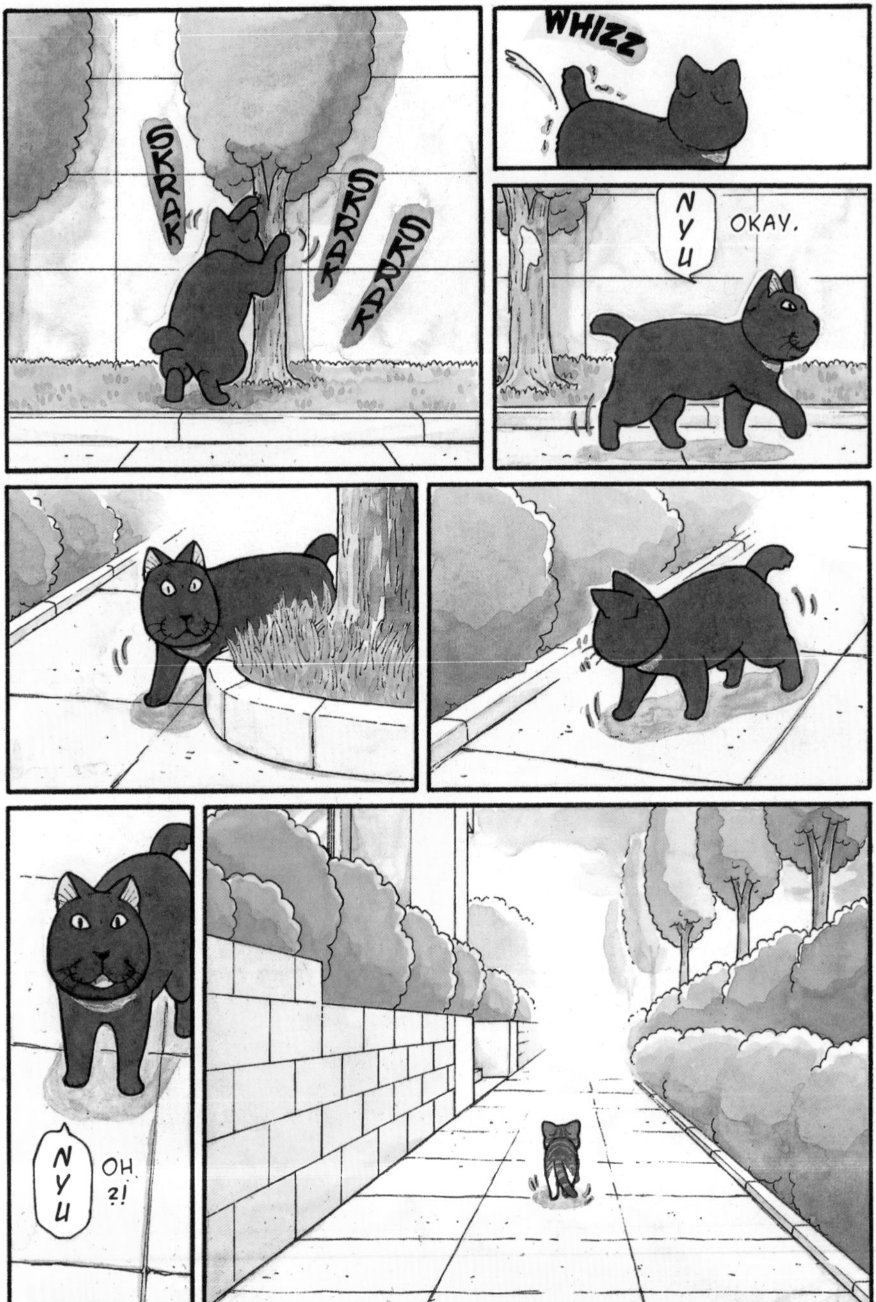
SKRAK
SKRAK
SKRAK
WHIZZ
NYU
OKAY.
NYU
OH ?!

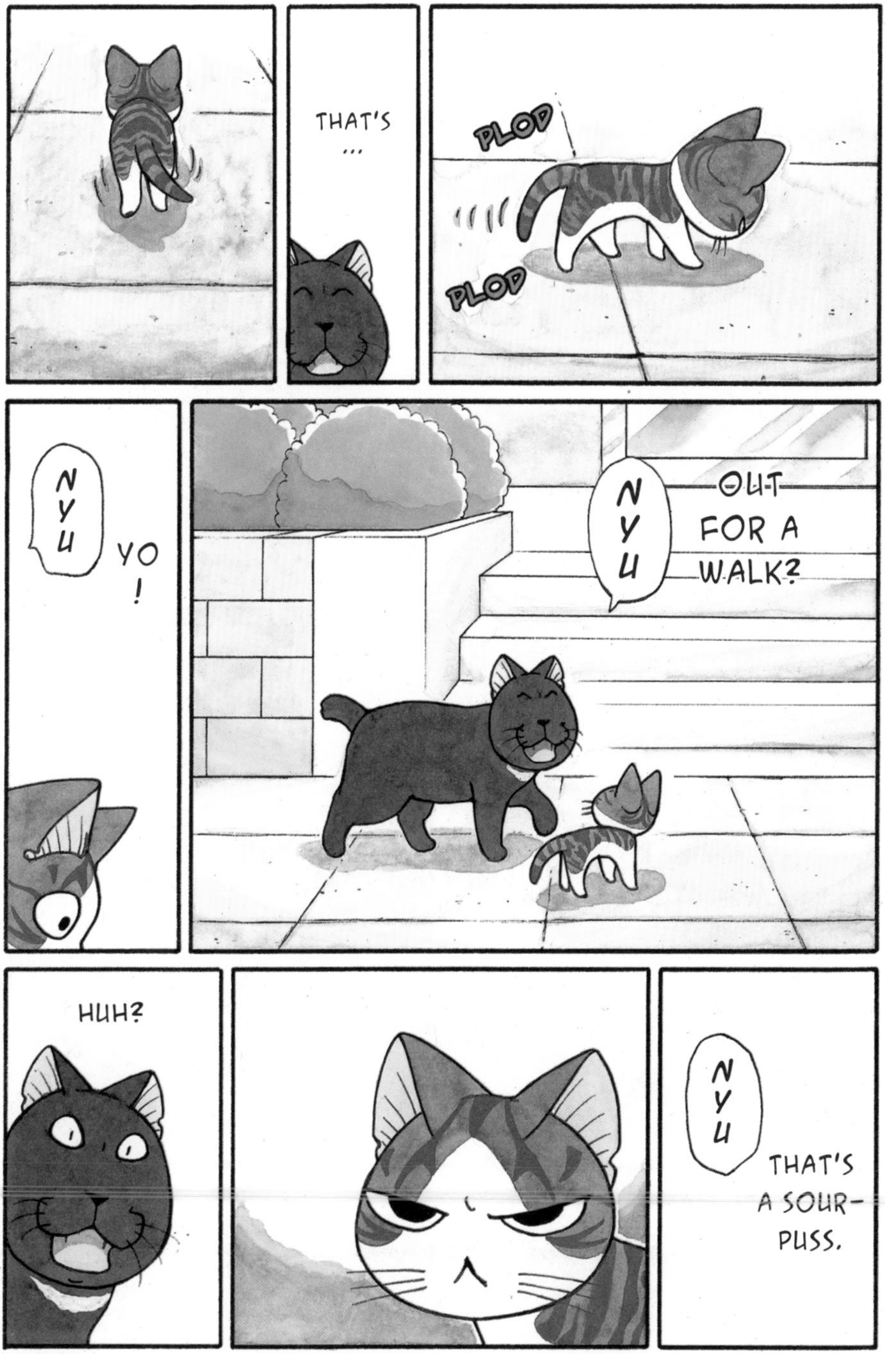
THAT'S ...
PLOD
PLOD
NYU
YO!
NYU
OUT FOR A WALK?
HUH?
NYU
THAT'S A SOUR-PUSS.

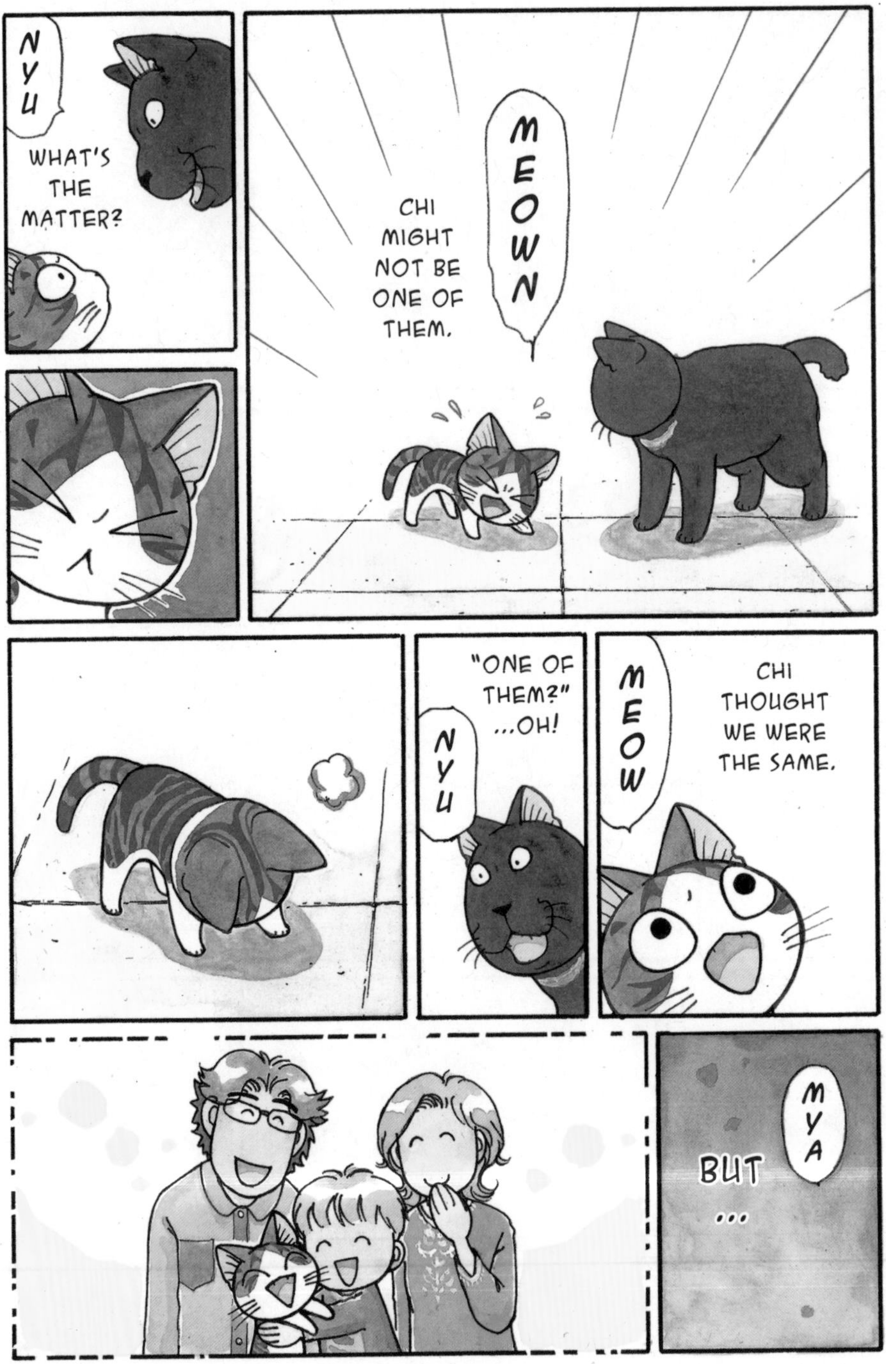
NYU
WHAT'S THE MATTER?
CHI MIGHT NOT BE ONE OF THEM.
MEOWN
"ONE OF THEM?" ...OH!
NYU
MEOW
CHI THOUGHT WE WERE THE SAME.
BUT ...
MYA

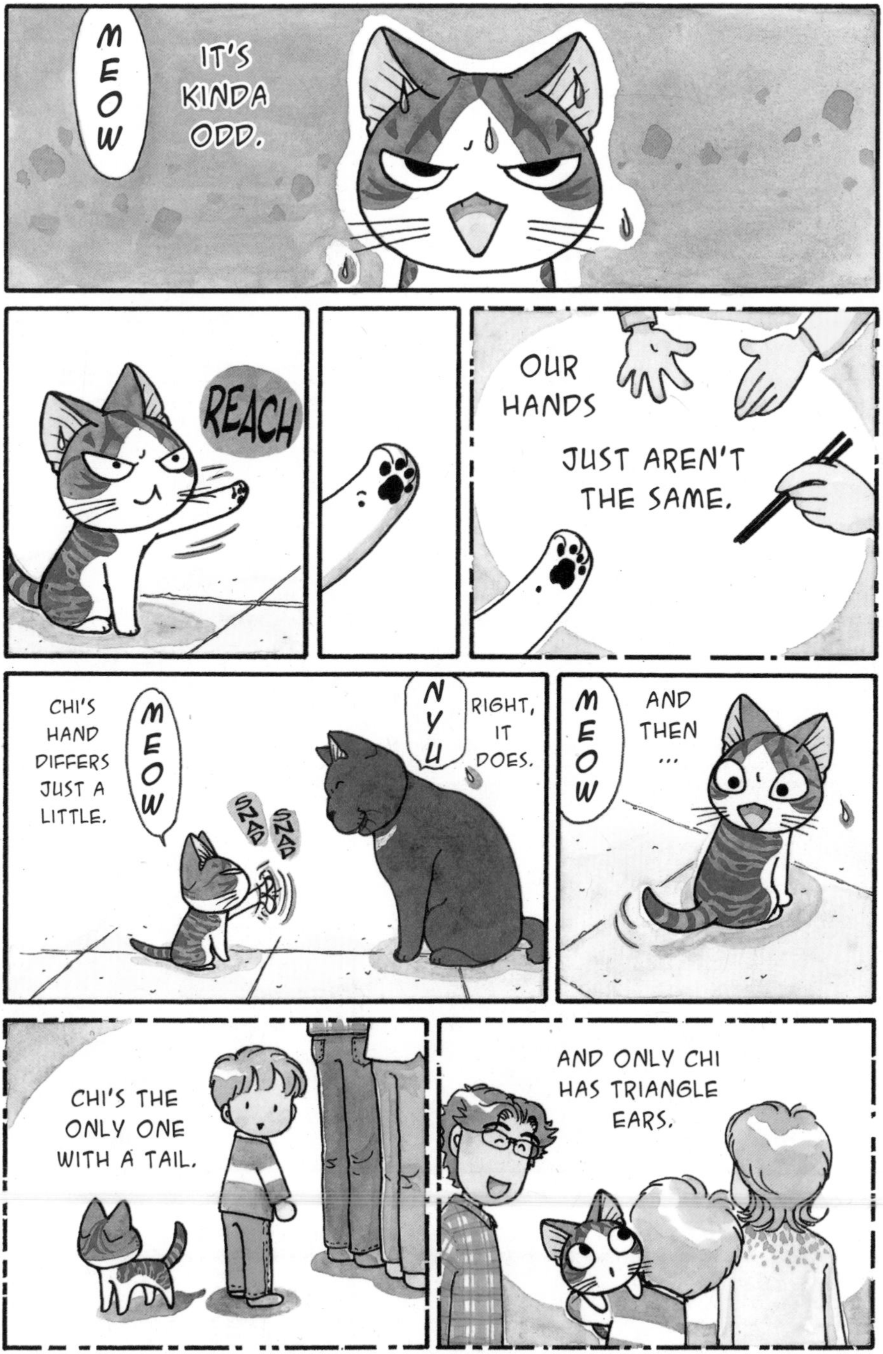
MEOW
IT'S KINDA ODD.
REACH
OUR HANDS
JUST AREN'T THE SAME.
CHI'S HAND DIFFERS JUST A LITTLE.
MEOW
SNAP SNAP
NYU
RIGHT, IT DOES.
MEOW
AND THEN ...
CHI'S THE ONLY ONE WITH A TAIL.
AND ONLY CHI HAS TRIANGLE EARS.

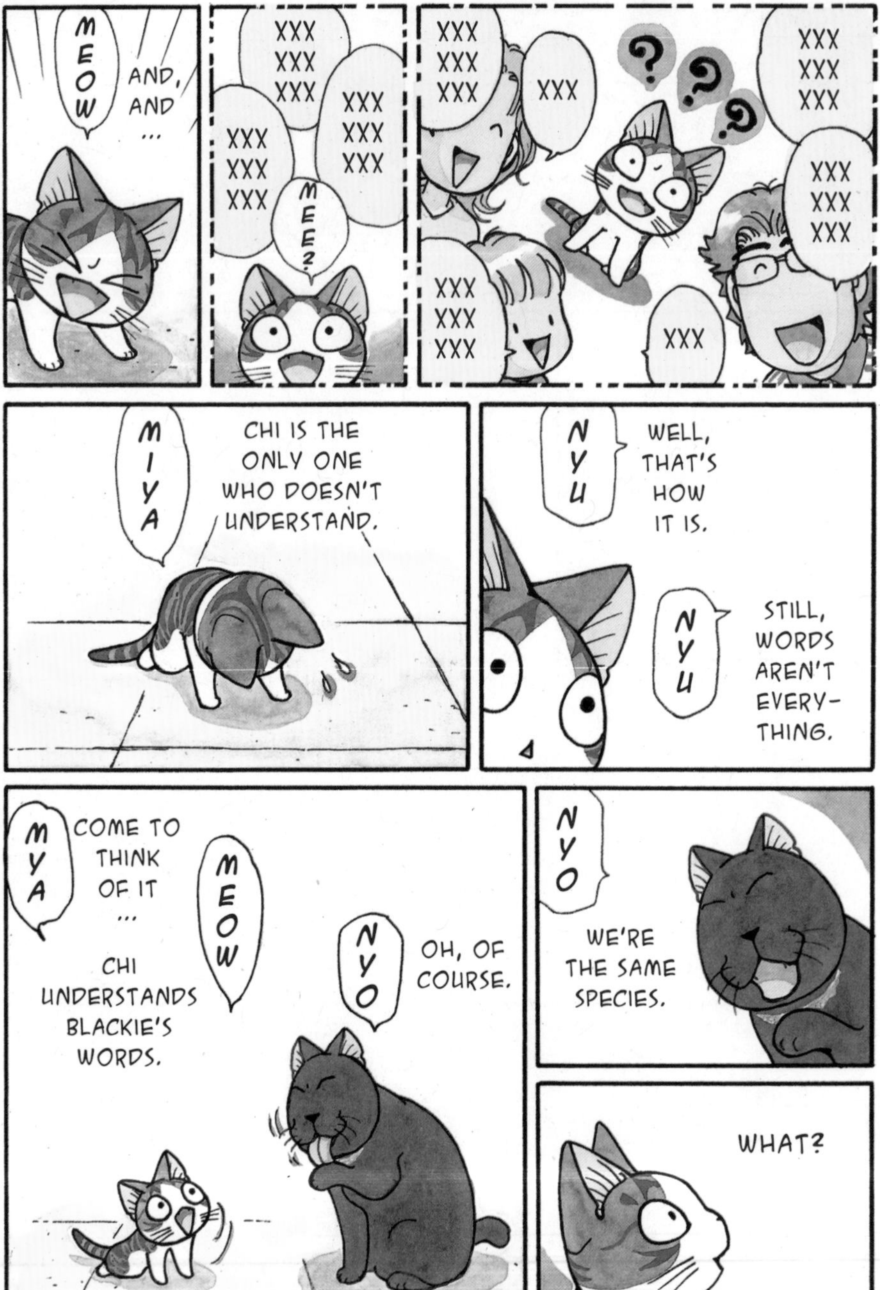
MEOW
AND, AND ...
XXX XXX XXX
XXX XXX XXX
XXX XXX XXX
MEE?
XXX XXX XXX
XXX
? ? ?
XXX XXX XXX
XXX XXX XXX
XXX XXX XXX
XXX
XXX XXX XXX
MIYA
CHI IS THE ONLY ONE WHO DOESN'T UNDERSTAND.
NYU
WELL, THAT'S HOW IT IS.
NYU
STILL, WORDS AREN'T EVERY-THING.
MYA
COME TO THINK OF IT ...
CHI UNDERSTANDS BLACKIE'S WORDS.
MEOW
NYO
OH, OF COURSE.
NYO
WE'RE THE SAME SPECIES.
WHAT?

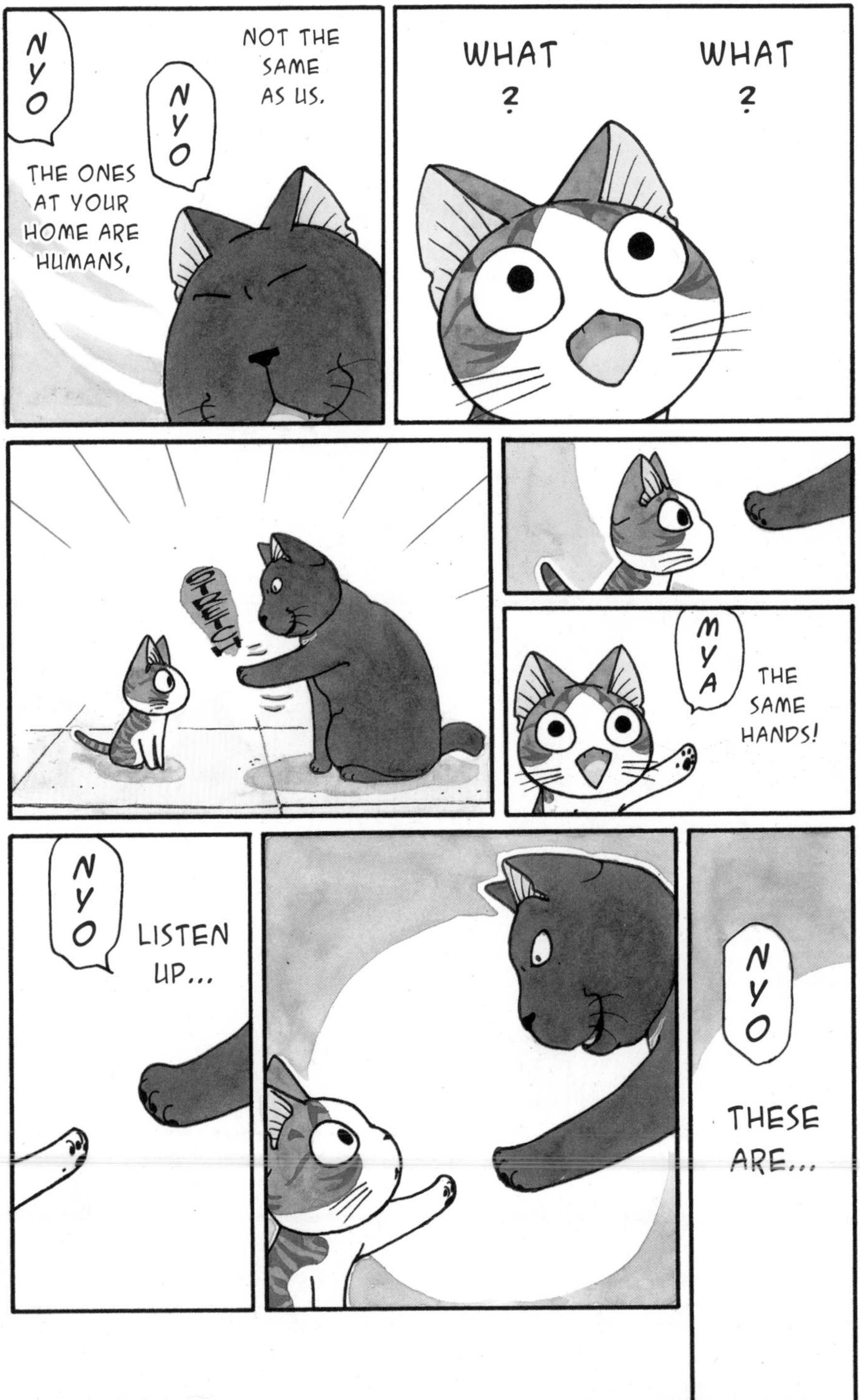
NYO
NYO
THE ONES AT YOUR HOME ARE HUMANS,
NOT THE SAME AS US.
WHAT?
WHAT?
STRETCH
MYA
THE SAME HANDS!
NYO
LISTEN UP...
NYO
THESE ARE...

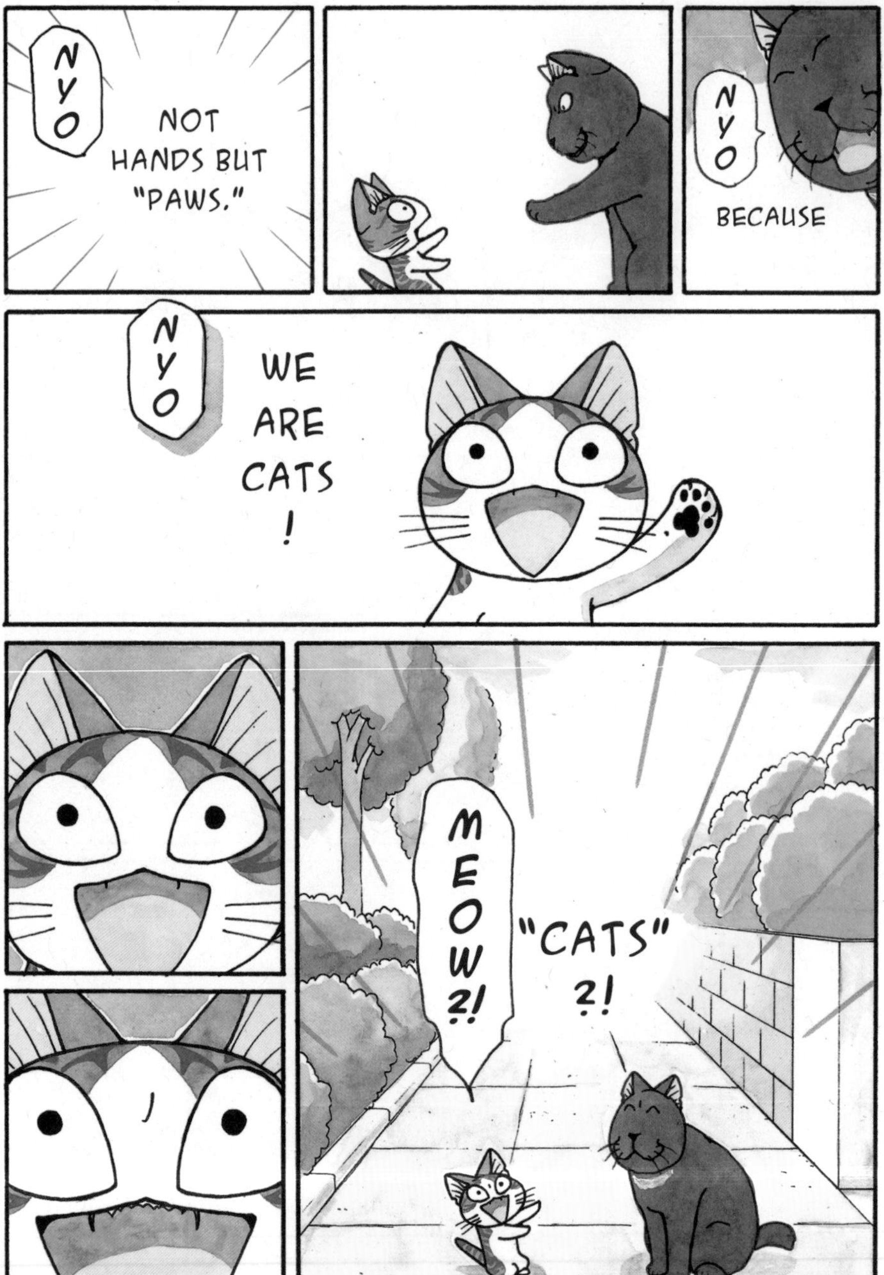
NYO
NOT HANDS BUT "PAWS."
NYO
BECAUSE
NYO
WE ARE CATS!
MEOW?!
"CATS"?!

the end

homemade 177: a cat is briefed

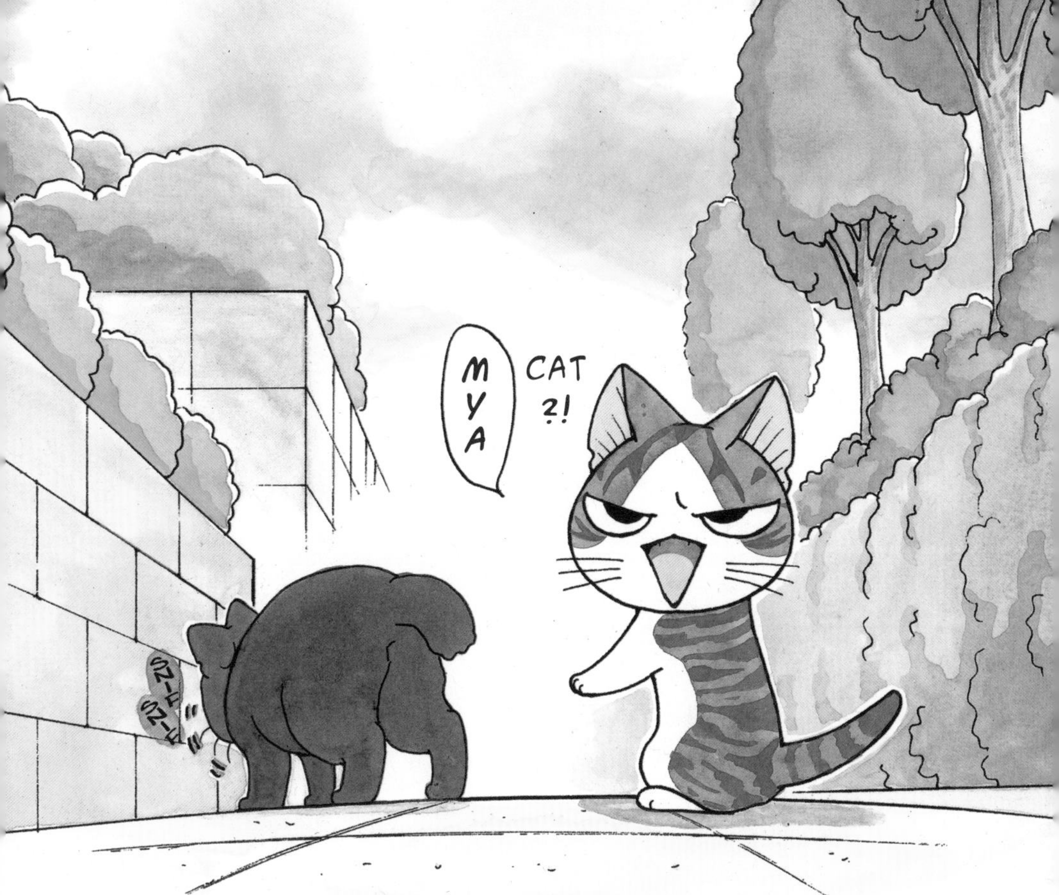
MYA
CAT?!
SNIF
SNIF

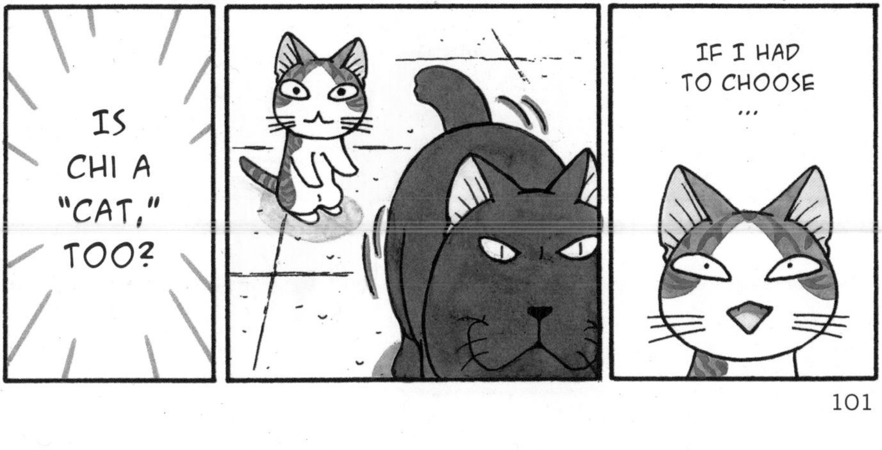
IS CHI A "CAT," TOO?
IF I HAD TO CHOOSE ...

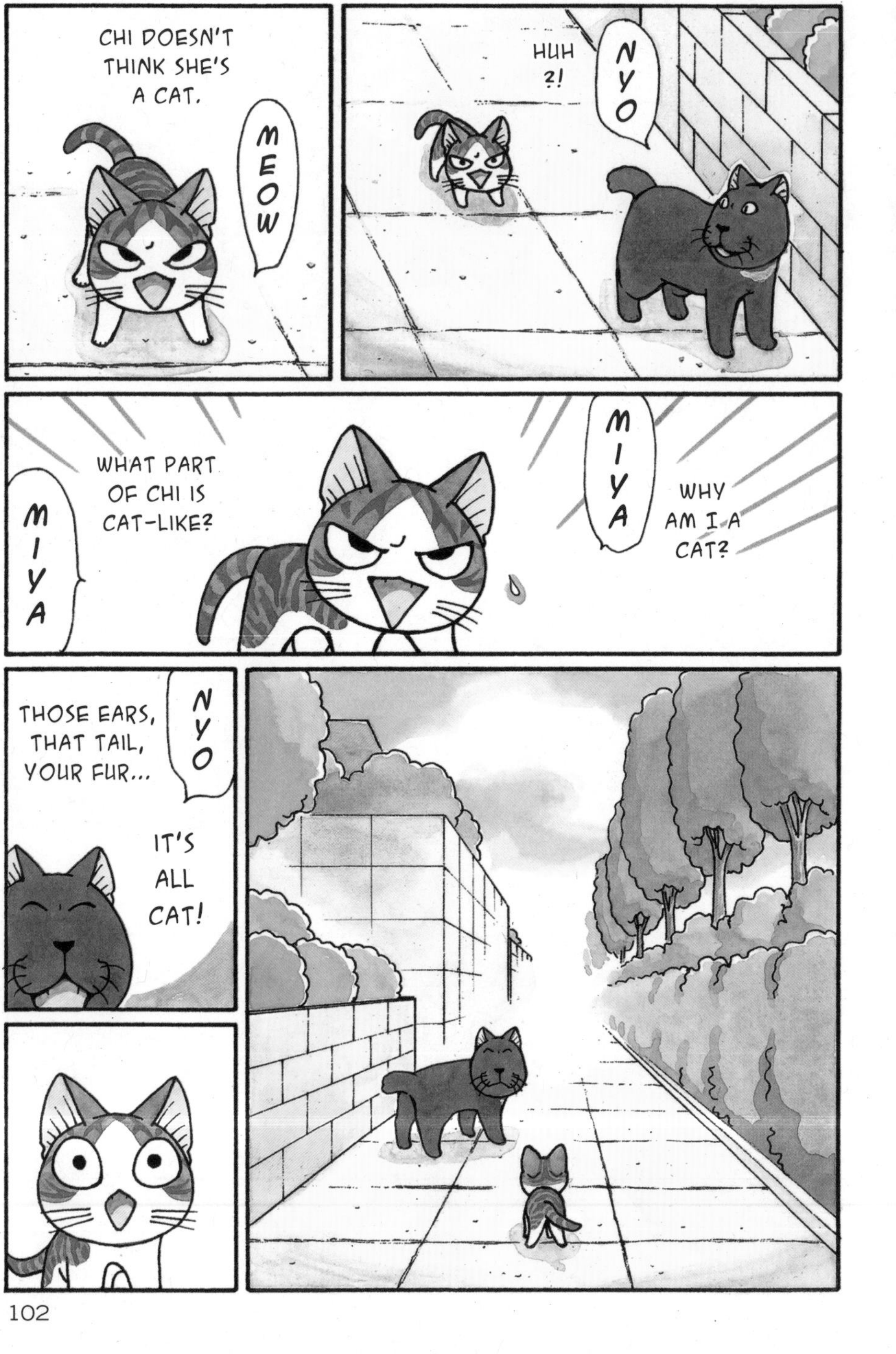
CHI DOESN'T THINK SHE'S A CAT.
MEOW
HUH ?!
NYO
MIYA
WHAT PART OF CHI IS CAT-LIKE?
MIYA
WHY AM I A CAT?
THOSE EARS, THAT TAIL, YOUR FUR...
NYO
IT'S ALL CAT!

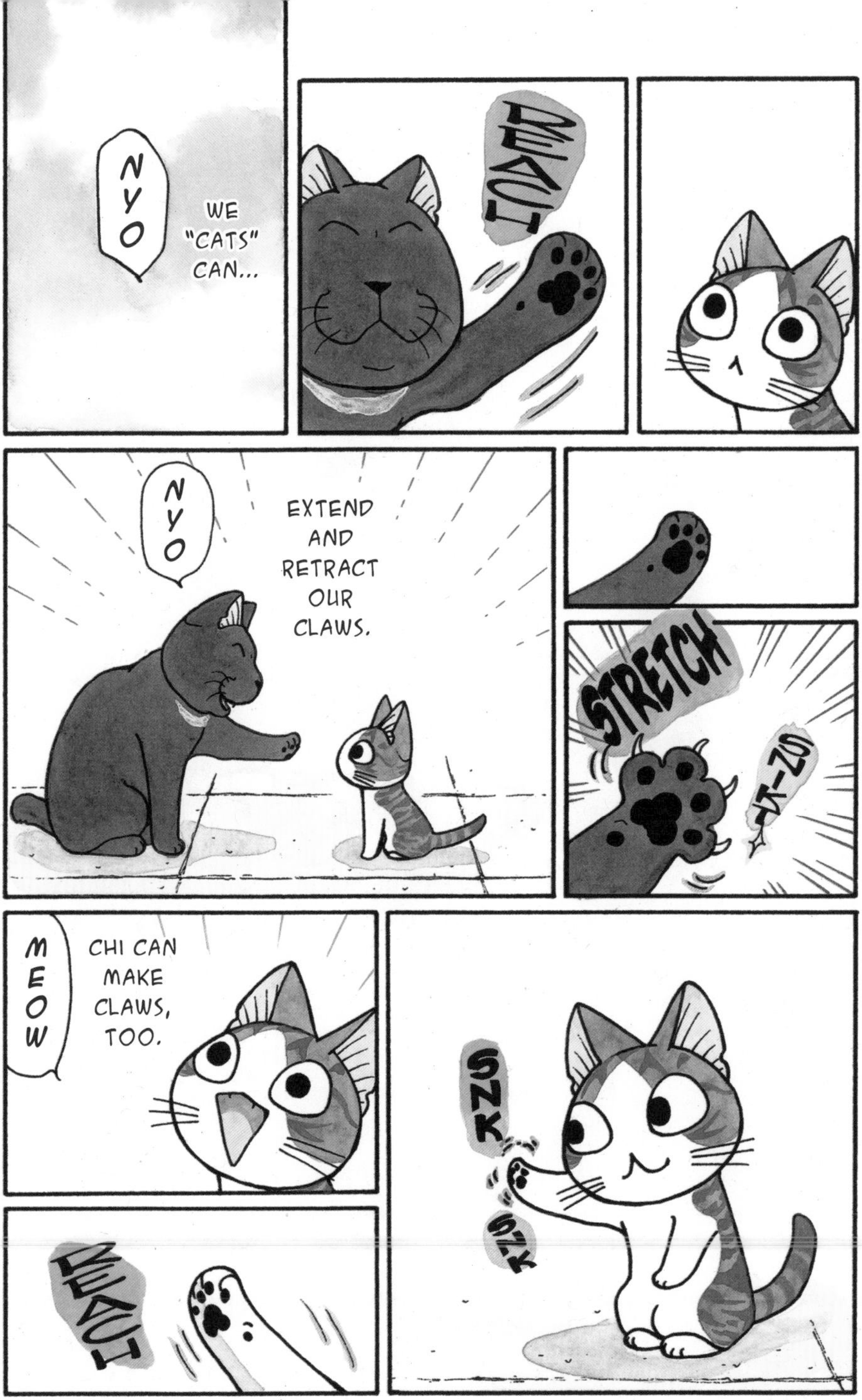
NYO
WE "CATS" CAN...
REACH
NYO
EXTEND AND RETRACT OUR CLAWS.
STRETCH
MEOW
CHI CAN MAKE CLAWS, TOO.
REACH
SNK
SNK

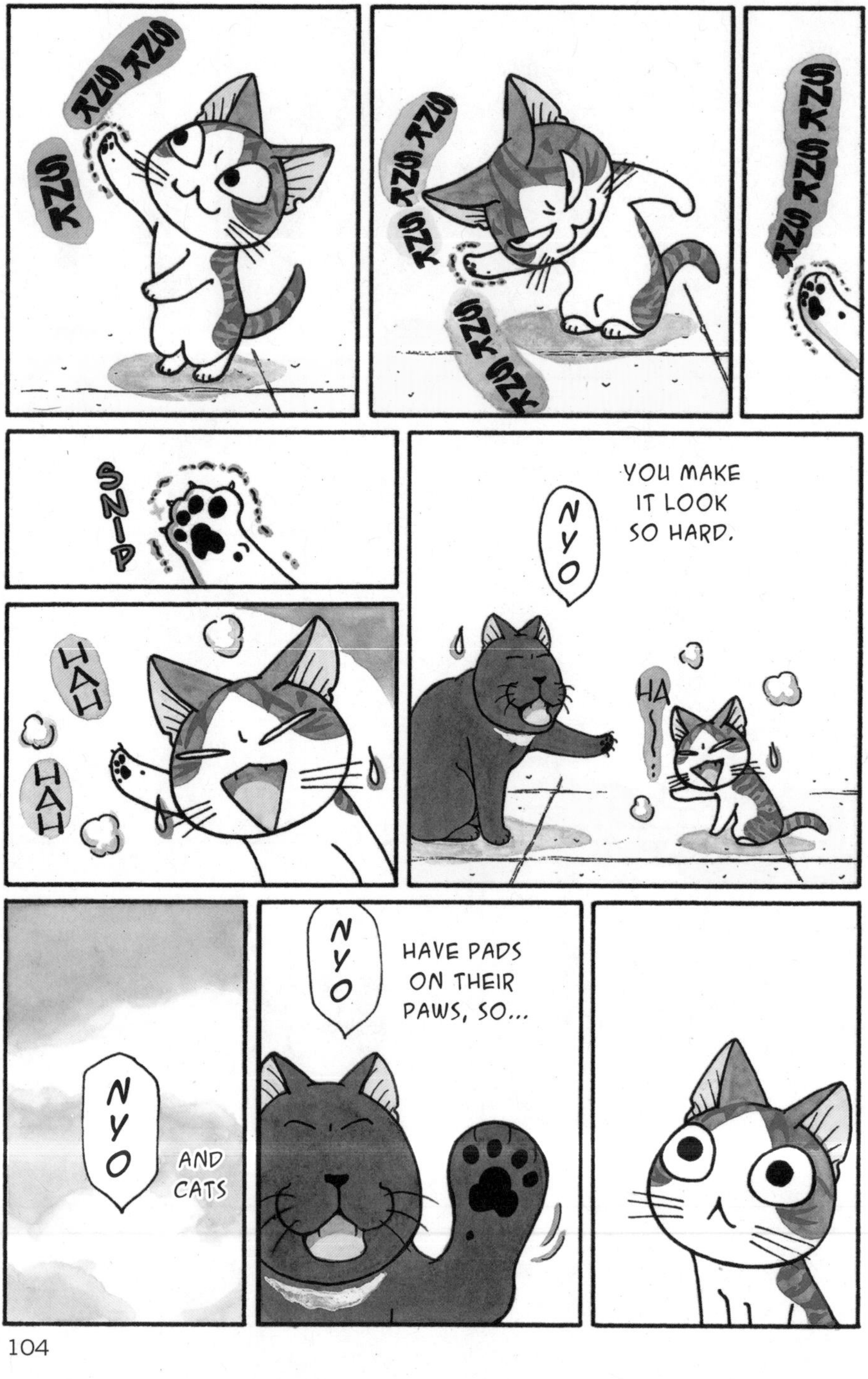
SNK SNK SNK
SNK SNK
SNK SNK
SNK SNK SNK SNK
SNIP
HAH HAH
YOU MAKE IT LOOK SO HARD.
NYO
HA
NYO
AND CATS
NYO
HAVE PADS ON THEIR PAWS, SO...

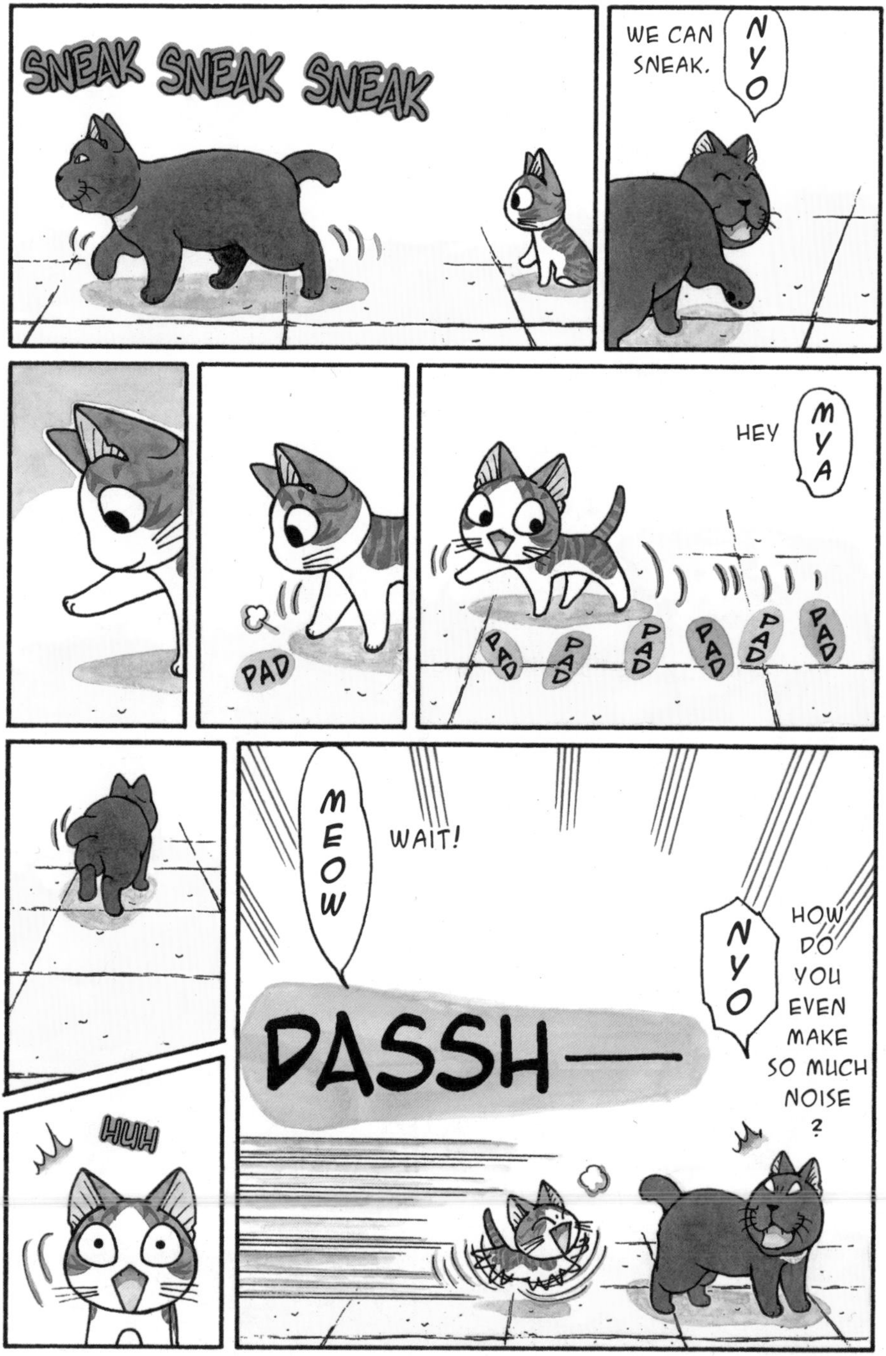
SNEAK SNEAK SNEAK
WE CAN SNEAK.
NYO
HEY
MYA
PAD
PAD PAD PAD PAD PAD PAD
HUH
MEOW
WAIT!
DASSH—
NYO
HOW DO YOU EVEN MAKE SO MUCH NOISE?

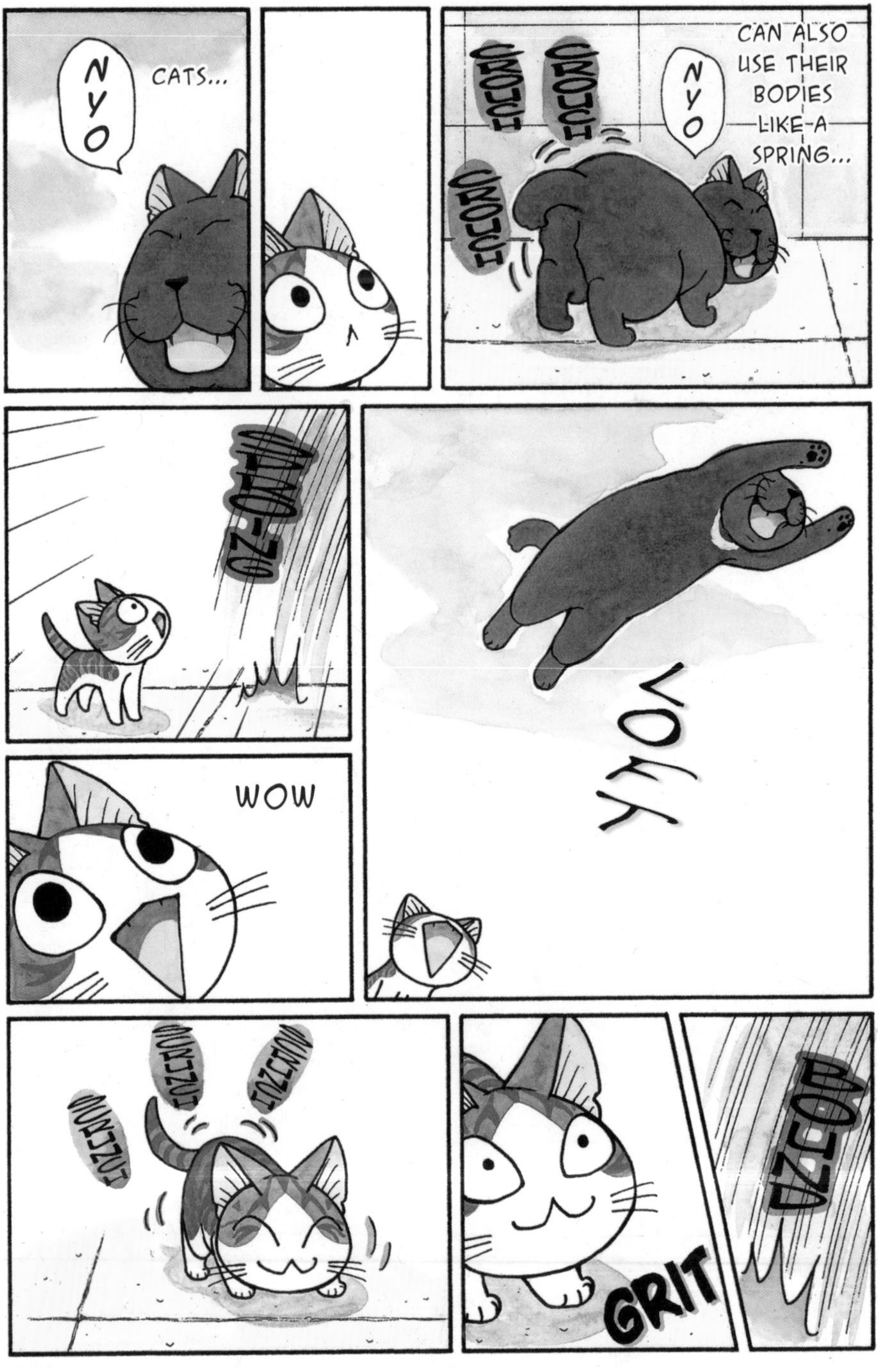
NYO
CATS...
CROUCH
CROUCH
CROUCH
NYO
CAN ALSO USE THEIR BODIES LIKE A SPRING...
WOW
GRIT

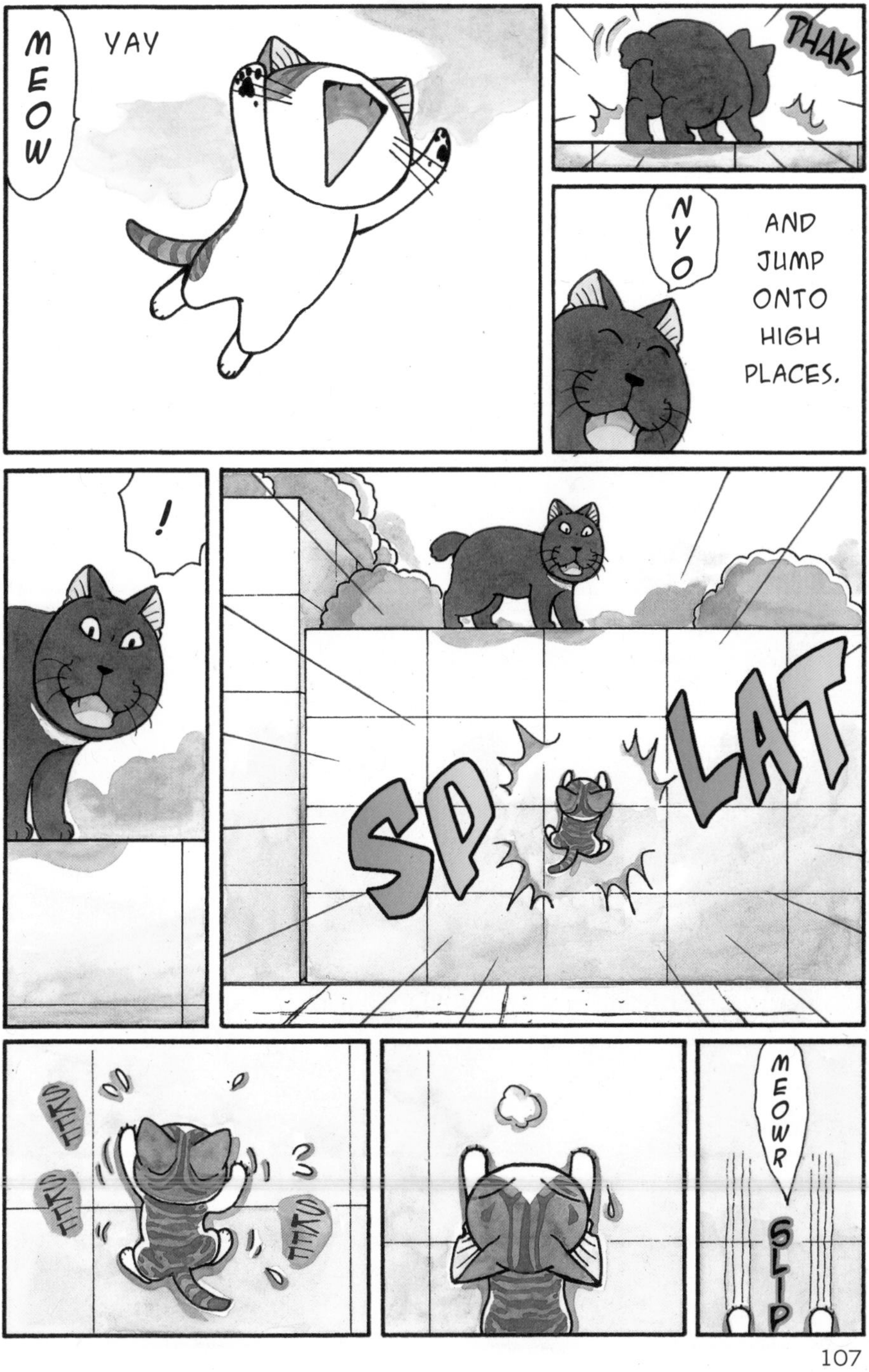
MEOW
YAY
THAK
NYO
AND JUMP ONTO HIGH PLACES.
!
SP
LAT
SKEE
SKEE
SKEE
MEOWR
SLIP

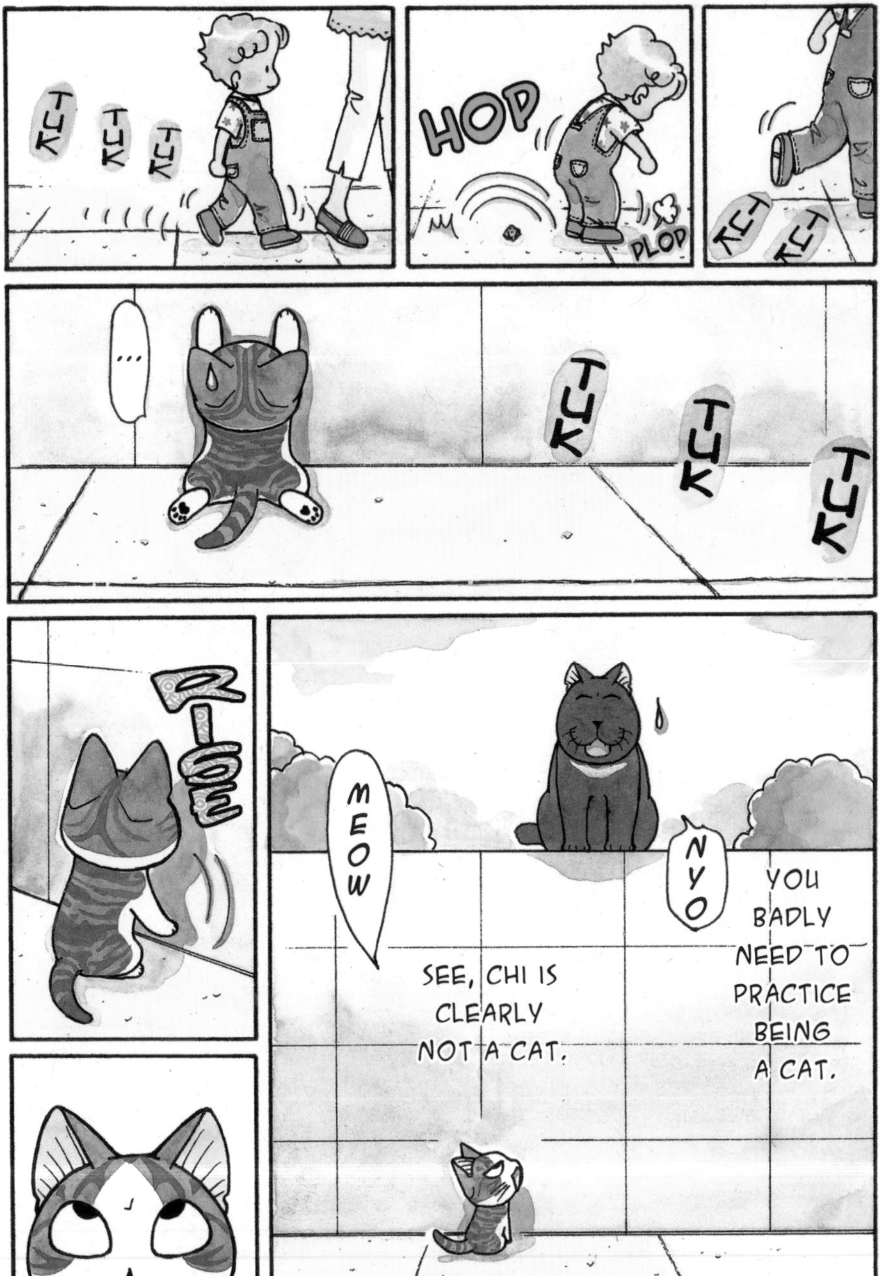
TUK
TUK
TUK
HOP
PLOP
TUK
TUK
...
TUK
TUK
TUK
RISE
MEOW
NYO
SEE, CHI IS CLEARLY NOT A CAT.
YOU BADLY NEED TO PRACTICE BEING A CAT.

the end

homemade 178: a cat trains

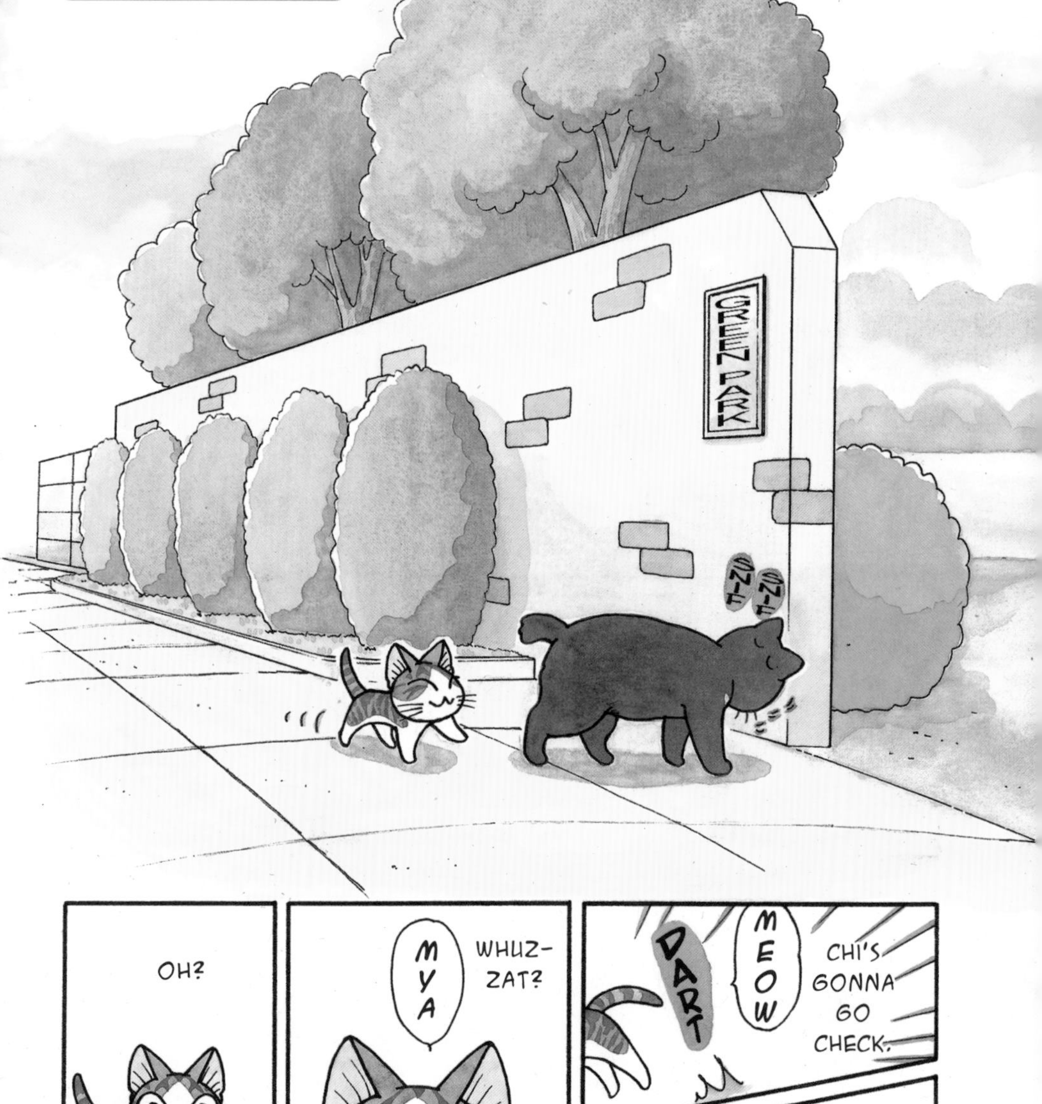
GREEN PARK
SNIF SNIF

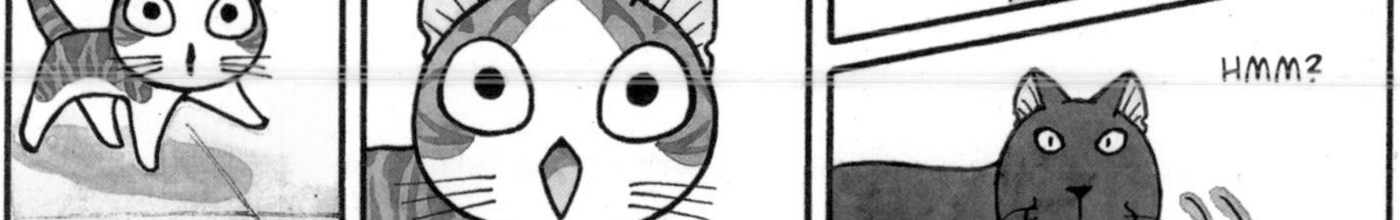
OH?
MYA
WHUZ-ZAT?
DART
MEOW
CHI'S GONNA GO CHECK.
HMM?

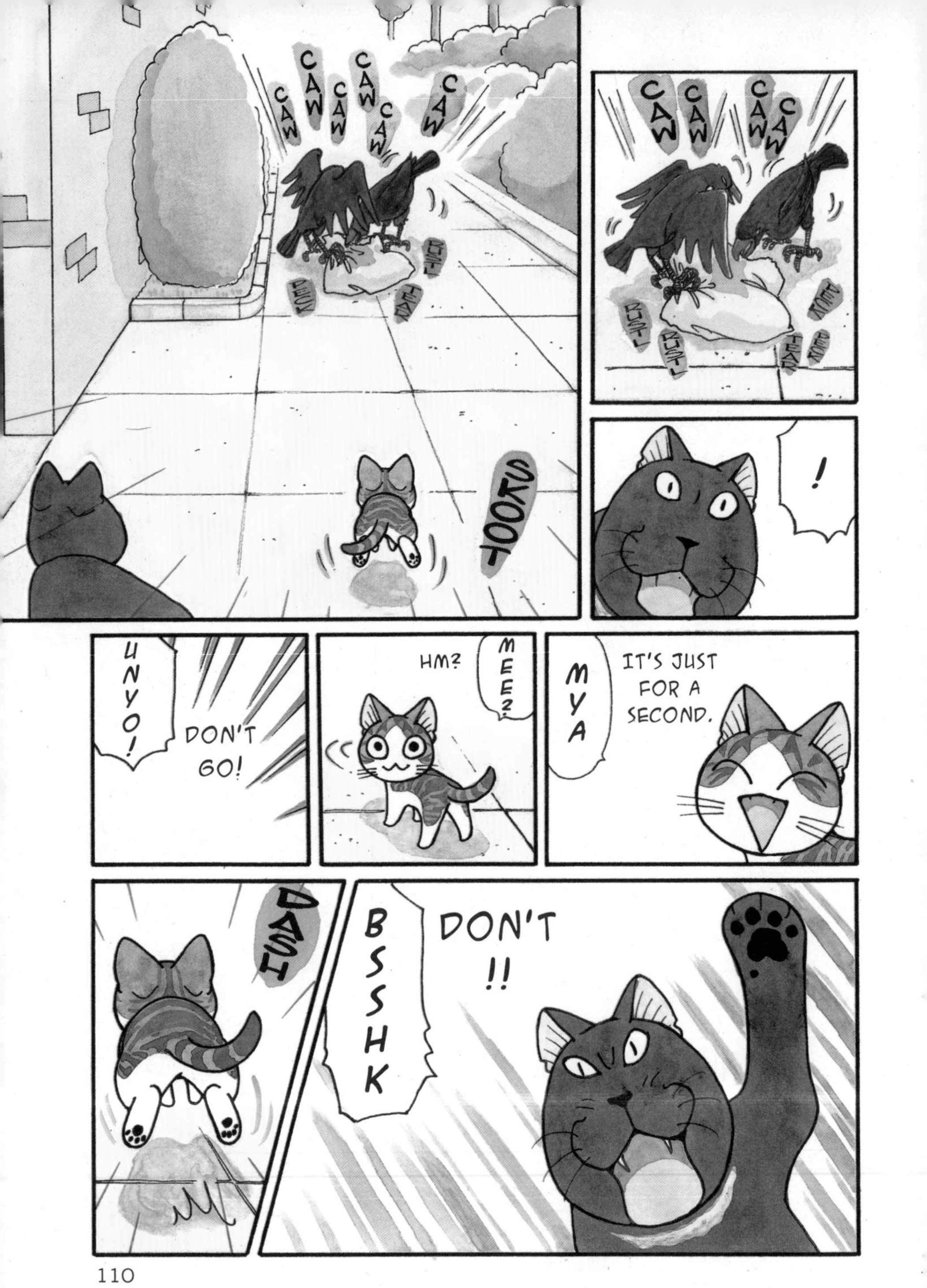
CAW
CAW
CAW
CAW
CAW
RUSTL
PECK
TEAR
SKOOT
CAW
CAW
CAW
CAW
PECK
RUSTL
RUSTL
TEAR
PECK
!
UNYO!
DON'T GO!
HM?
MEE?
MYA
IT'S JUST FOR A SECOND.
DASH
BSSHK
DON'T !!

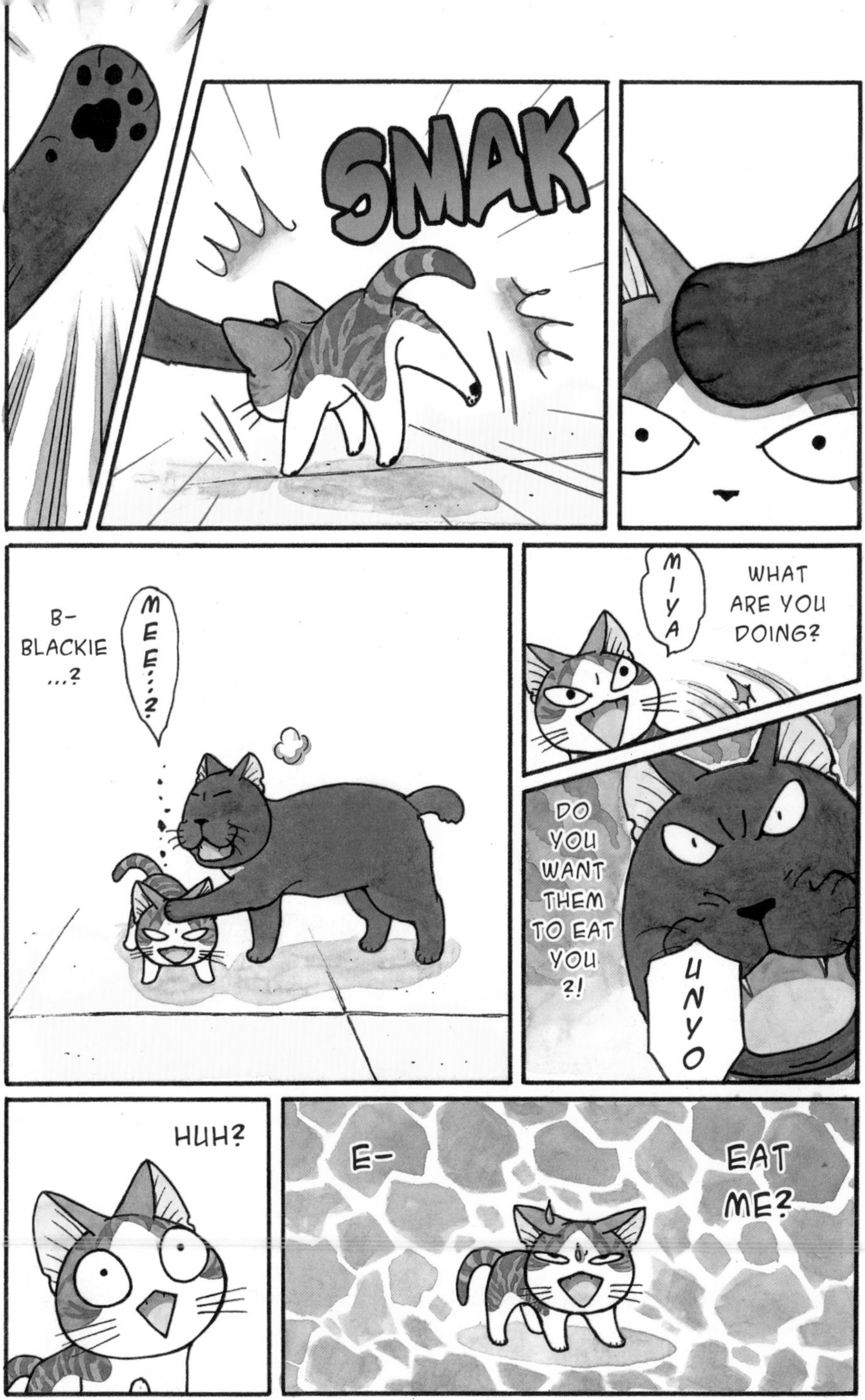
SMAK
B- BLACKIE ...?
MEE...?
MIYA
WHAT ARE YOU DOING?
DO YOU WANT THEM TO EAT YOU?!
UNYO
HUH?
E-
EAT ME?

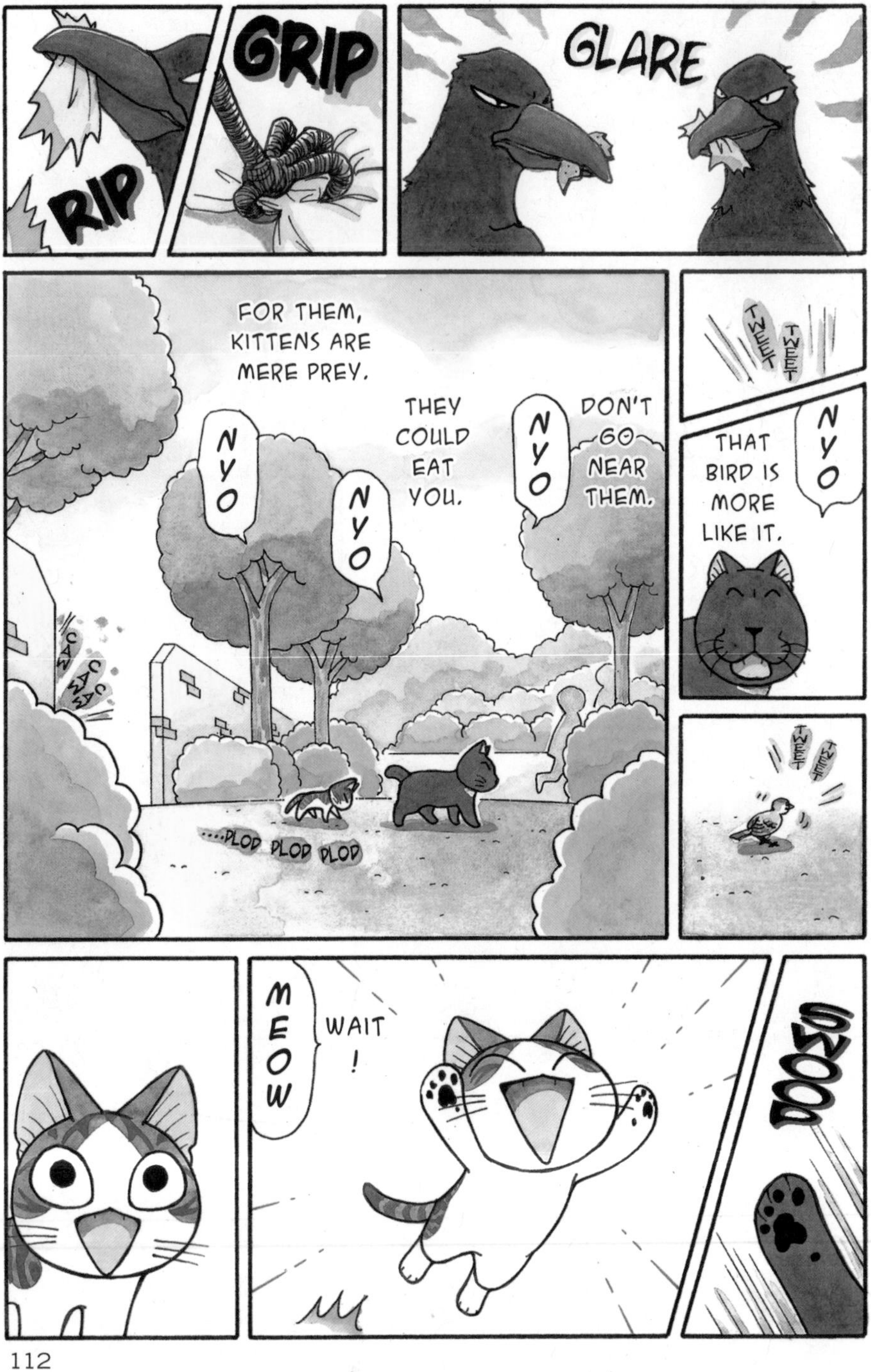
RIP
GRIP
GLARE
FOR THEM, KITTENS ARE MERE PREY.
NYO
NYO
THEY COULD EAT YOU.
NYO
DON'T GO NEAR THEM.
CAW CAW
....PLOD PLOD PLOD
TWEET TWEET
THAT BIRD IS MORE LIKE IT.
NYO
TWEET TWEET
MEOW
WAIT!
SWOOP

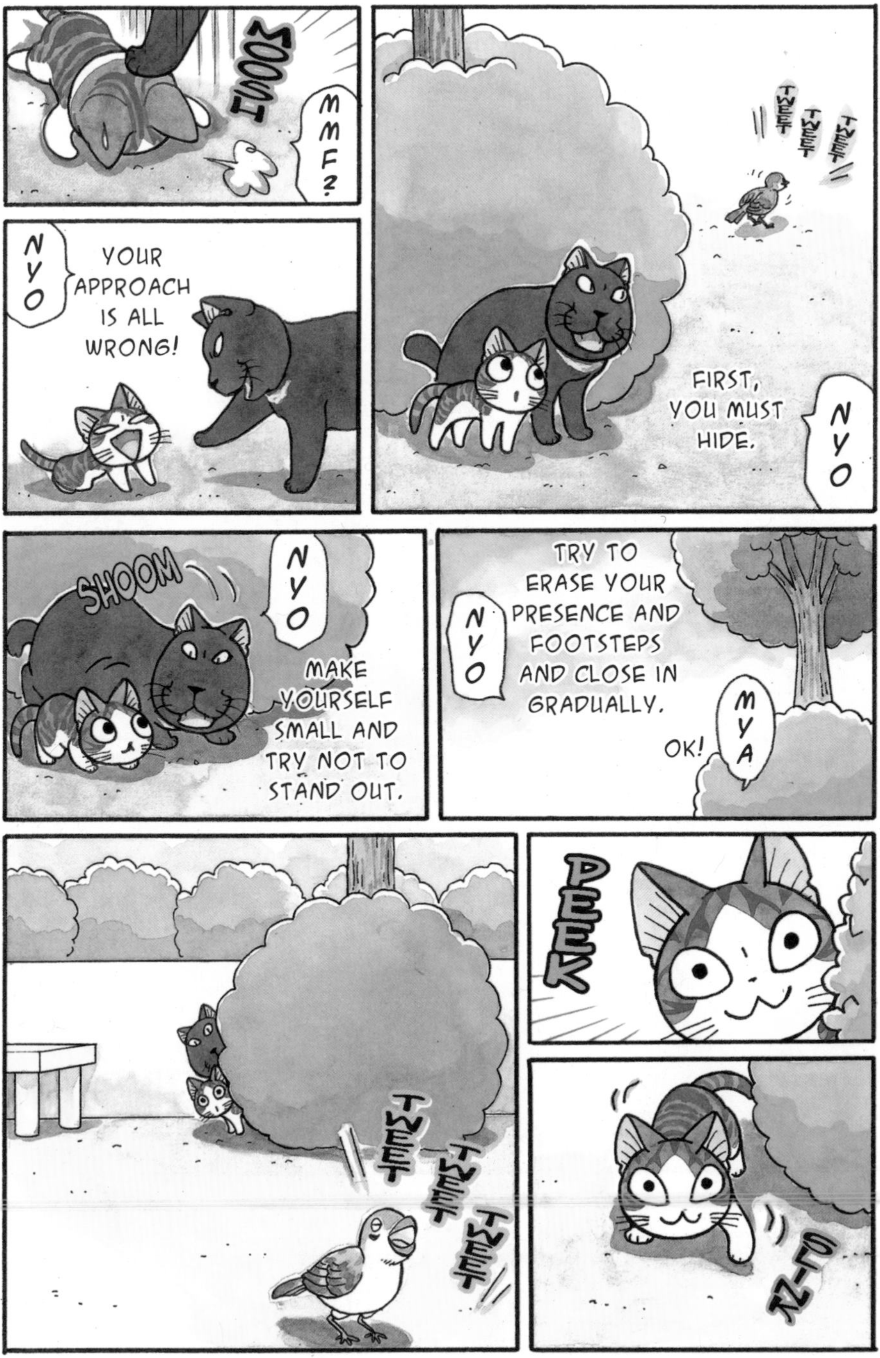
MOOSH
MMF?
NYO
YOUR APPROACH IS ALL WRONG!
TWEET TWEET TWEET
FIRST, YOU MUST HIDE.
NYO
SHOOM
NYO
MAKE YOURSELF SMALL AND TRY NOT TO STAND OUT.
NYO
TRY TO ERASE YOUR PRESENCE AND FOOTSTEPS AND CLOSE IN GRADUALLY.
MYA
OK!
TWEET TWEET TWEET
PEEK
SLINK

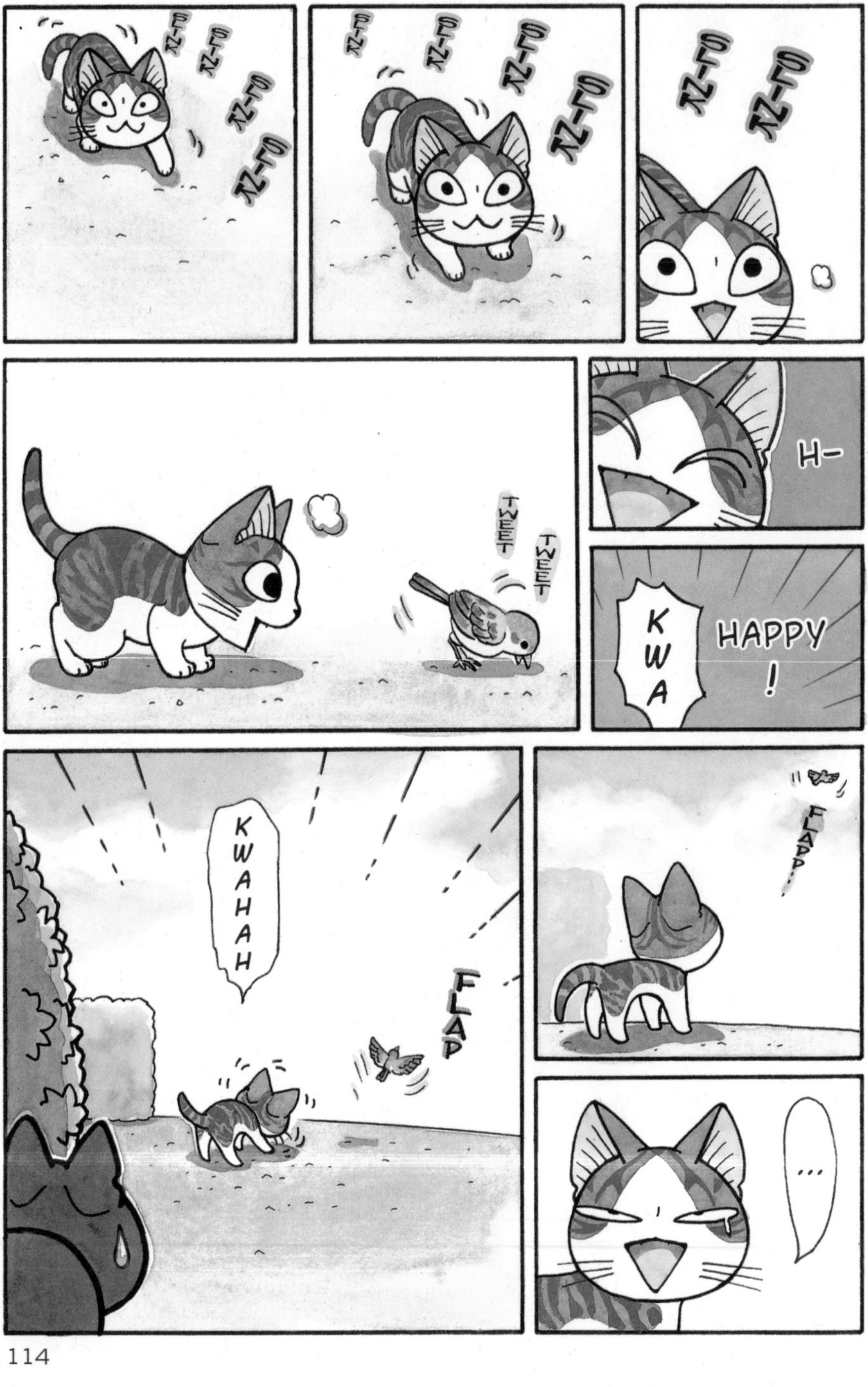
SLINK
SLINK
SLINK
SLINK
SLINK
SLINK
SLINK
SLINK
SLINK
SLINK
TWEET
TWEET
H-
KWA
HAPPY !
KWAHAHAH
FLAP
FLAP...
...

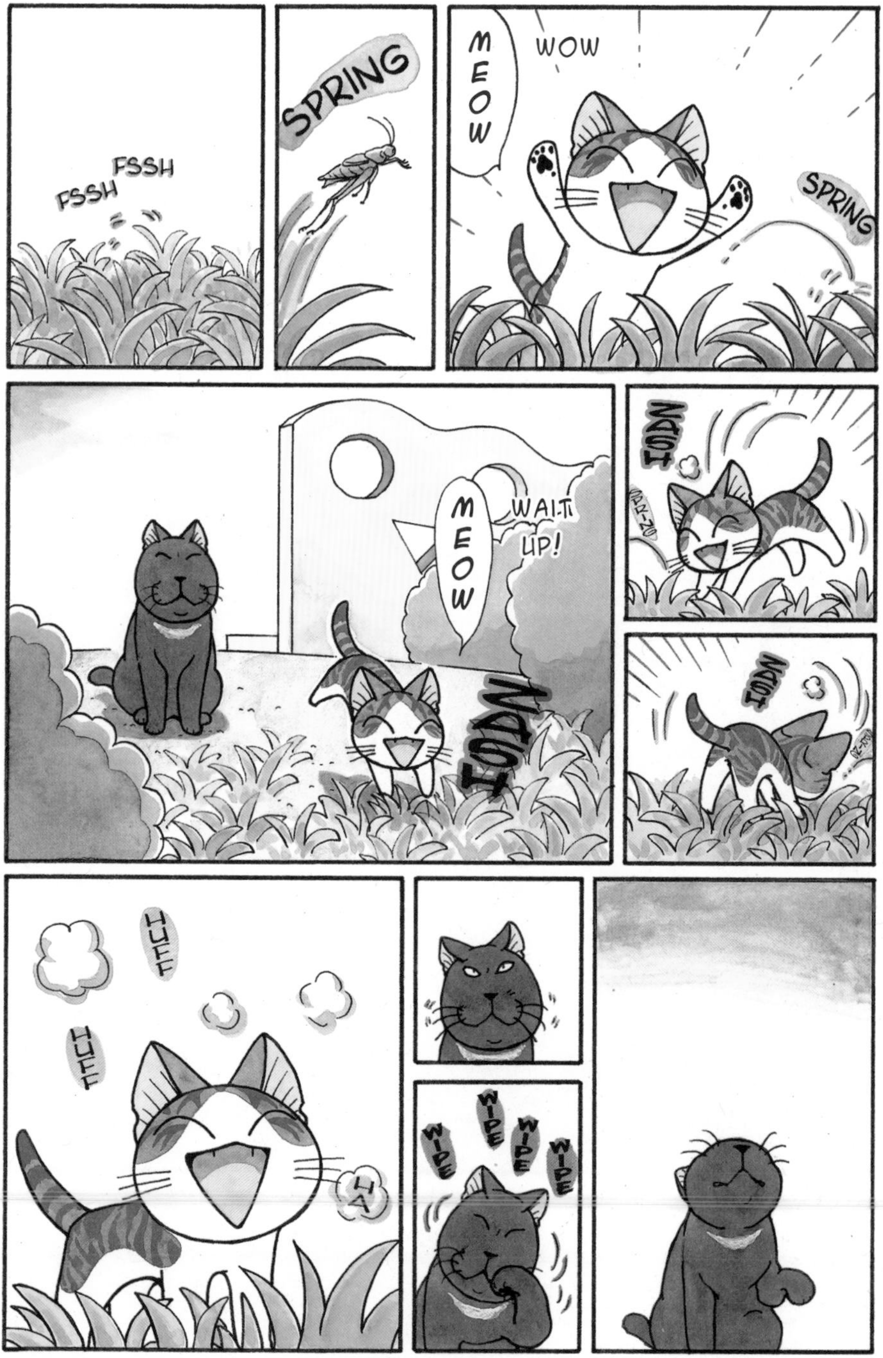
MEOW
WOW
SPRING
SPRING
FSSH
FSSH
ZASH
SPRING
ZASH
MEOW
WAIT UP!
ZASH
WIPE
WIPE
WIPE
WIPE
HUFF
HUFF
HA

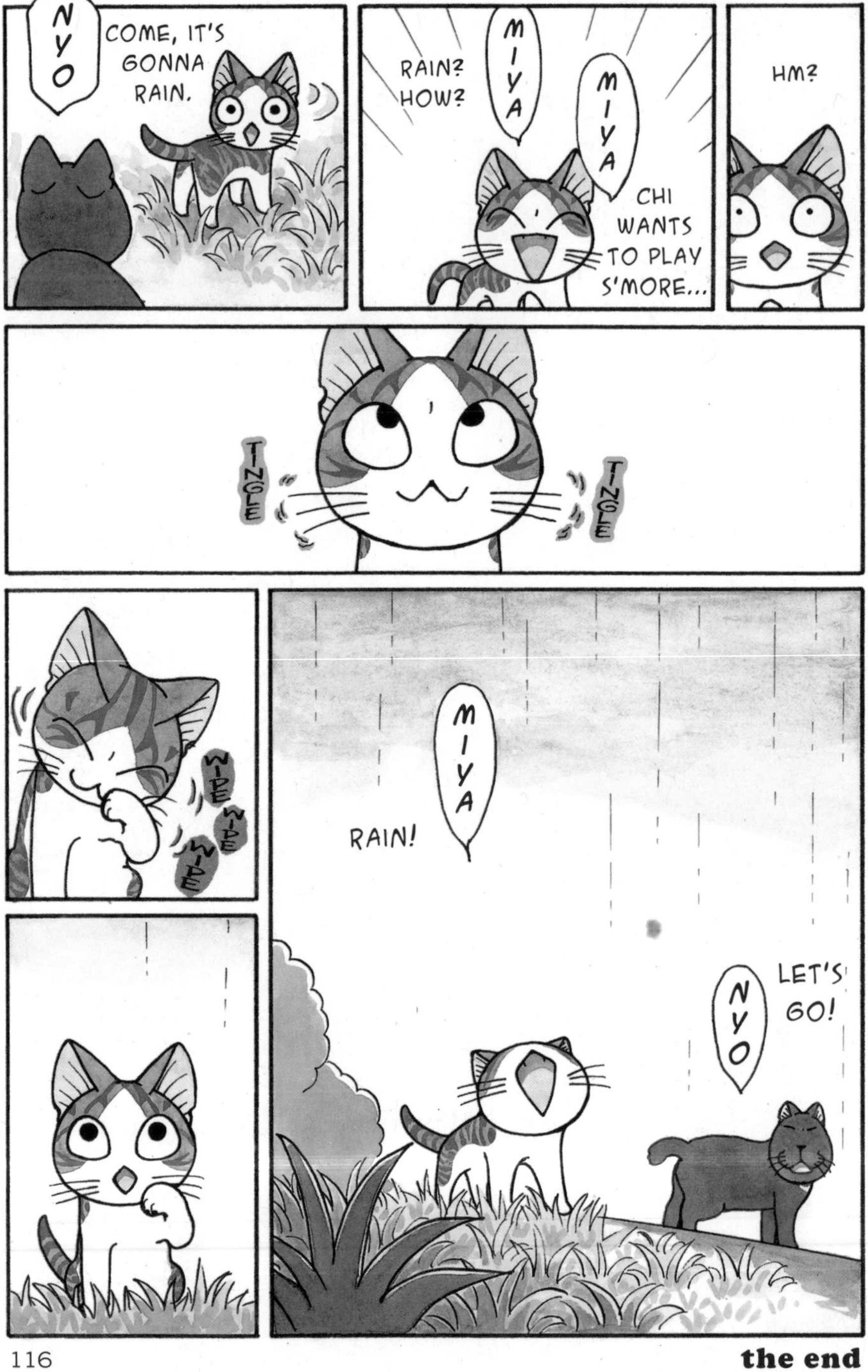
NYO
COME, IT'S GONNA RAIN.
RAIN? HOW?
MIYA
MIYA
CHI WANTS TO PLAY S'MORE...
HM?
TINGLE
TINGLE
WIPE WIPE WIPE
RAIN!
MIYA
NYO
LET'S GO!

the end

homemade 179: a cat holds

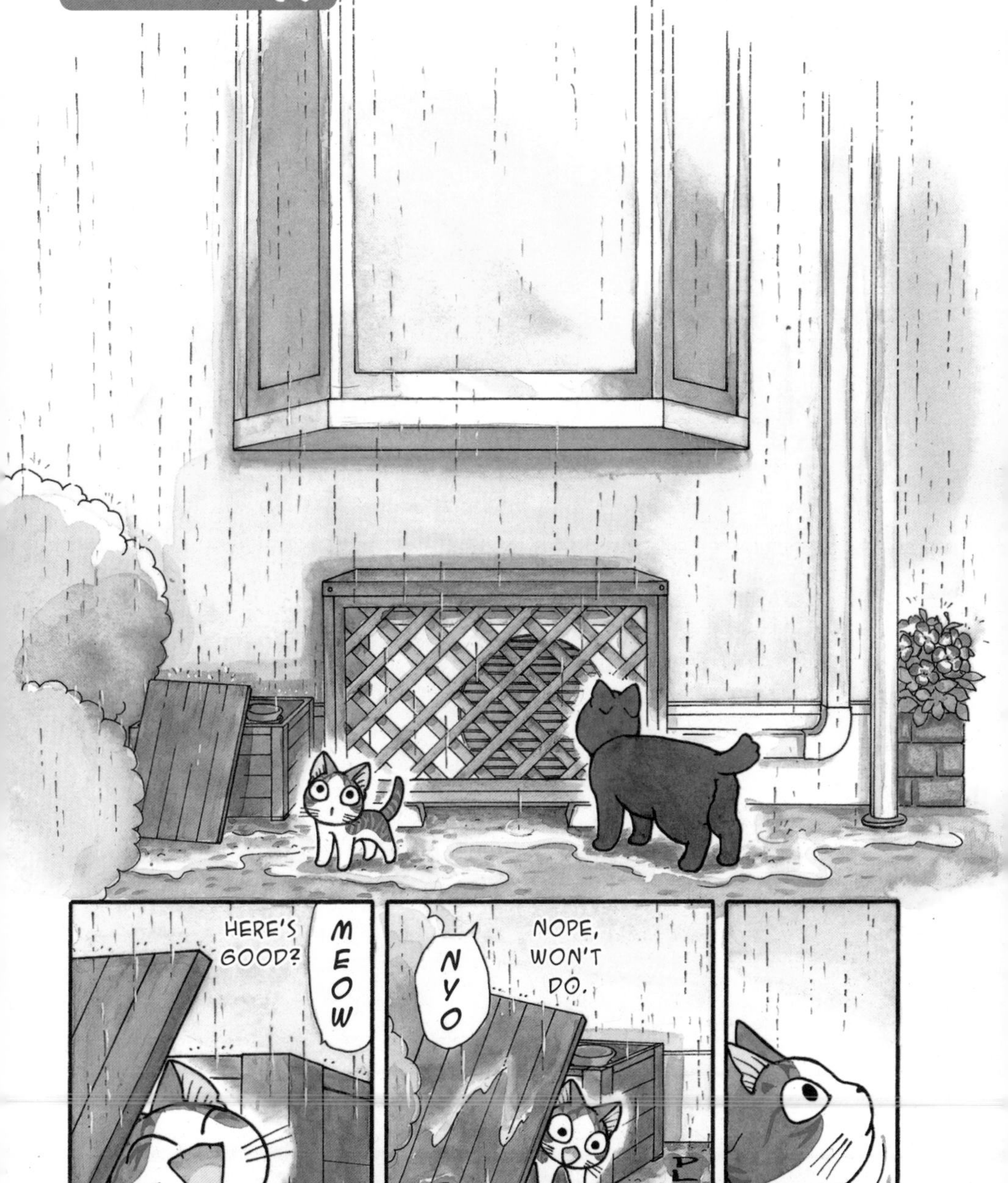
HERE'S GOOD?
MEOW
NYO
NOPE, WON'T DO.
PLIP
PLIP
PLIP

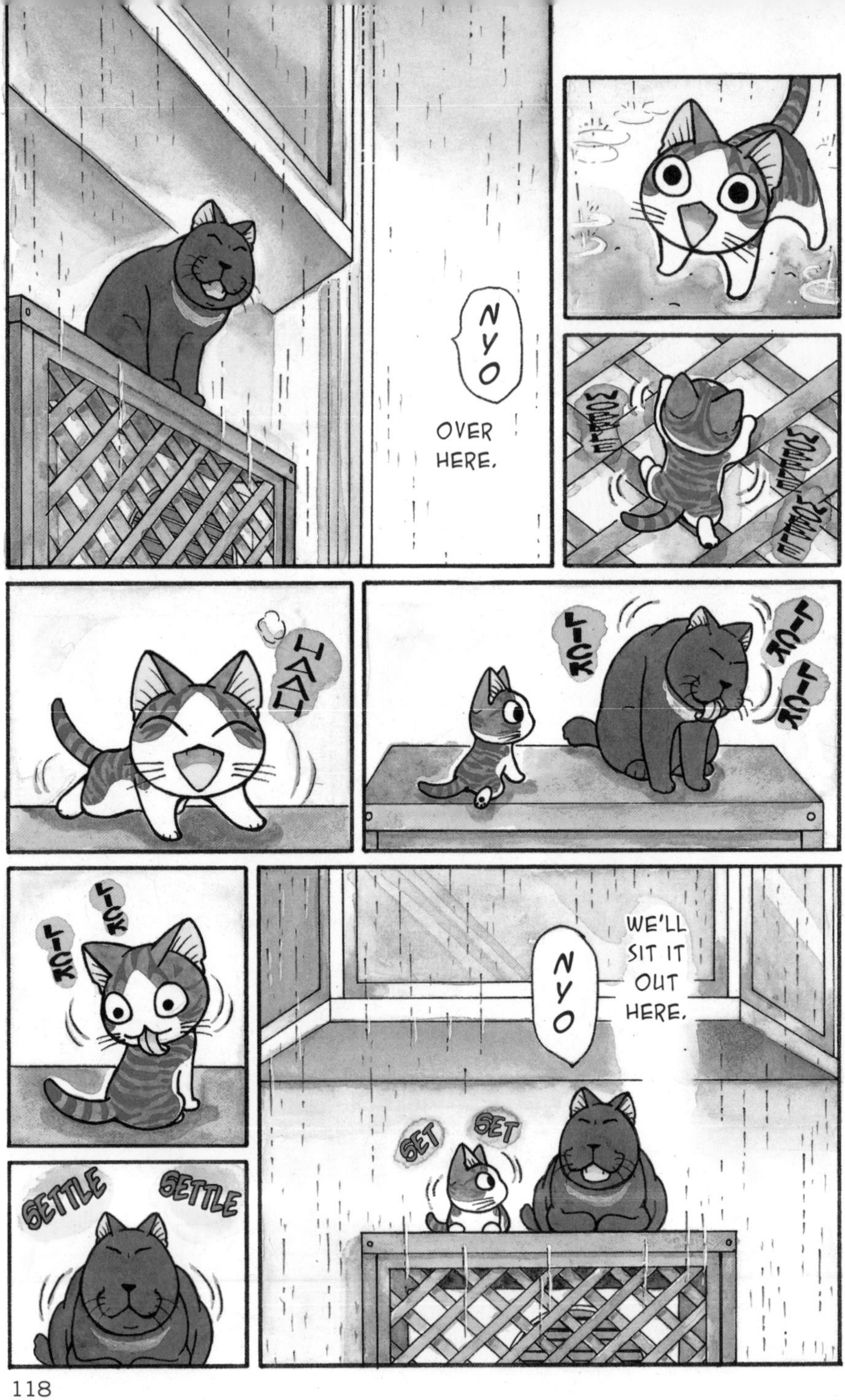
NYO
OVER HERE.
WOBBLE
WOBBLE
WOBBLE
HAAH
LICK
LICK
LICK
LICK
LICK
SETTLE
SETTLE
NYO
WE'LL SIT IT OUT HERE.
SET
SET

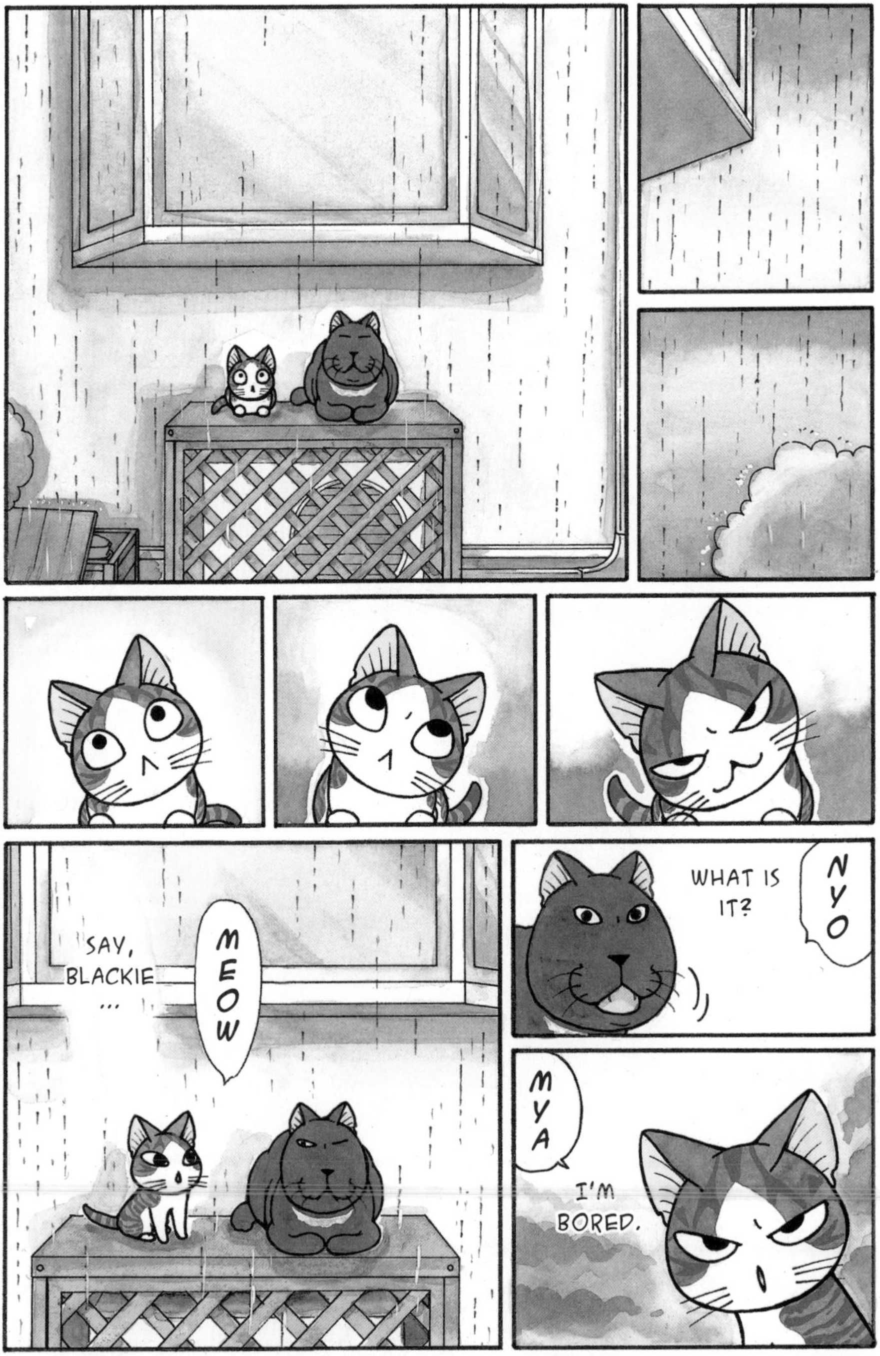
SAY, BLACKIE ...
MEOW
WHAT IS IT?
NYO
MYA
I'M BORED.

YOU CAN'T HUNT OR PLAY NOW.

NYO

NYO

REST WELL.

NYO

DROWSE DROWSE

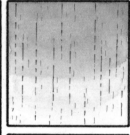

MYA

HEY, BLACKIE—

MEOW

LET'S PLAY!

NYO

GET SOME SLEEP.

DONE
DONE
MEOW
BUT CHI WANTS TO PLAY.
WHAP
MEOW
WHEE!
MEOWR

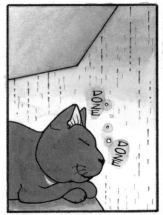

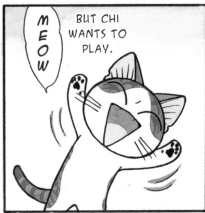

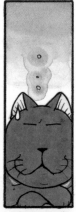

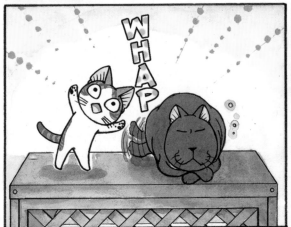

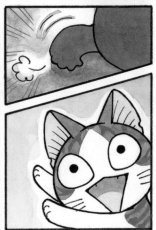

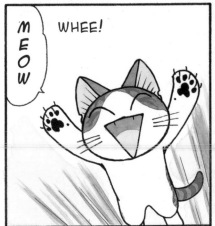

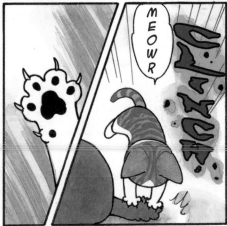

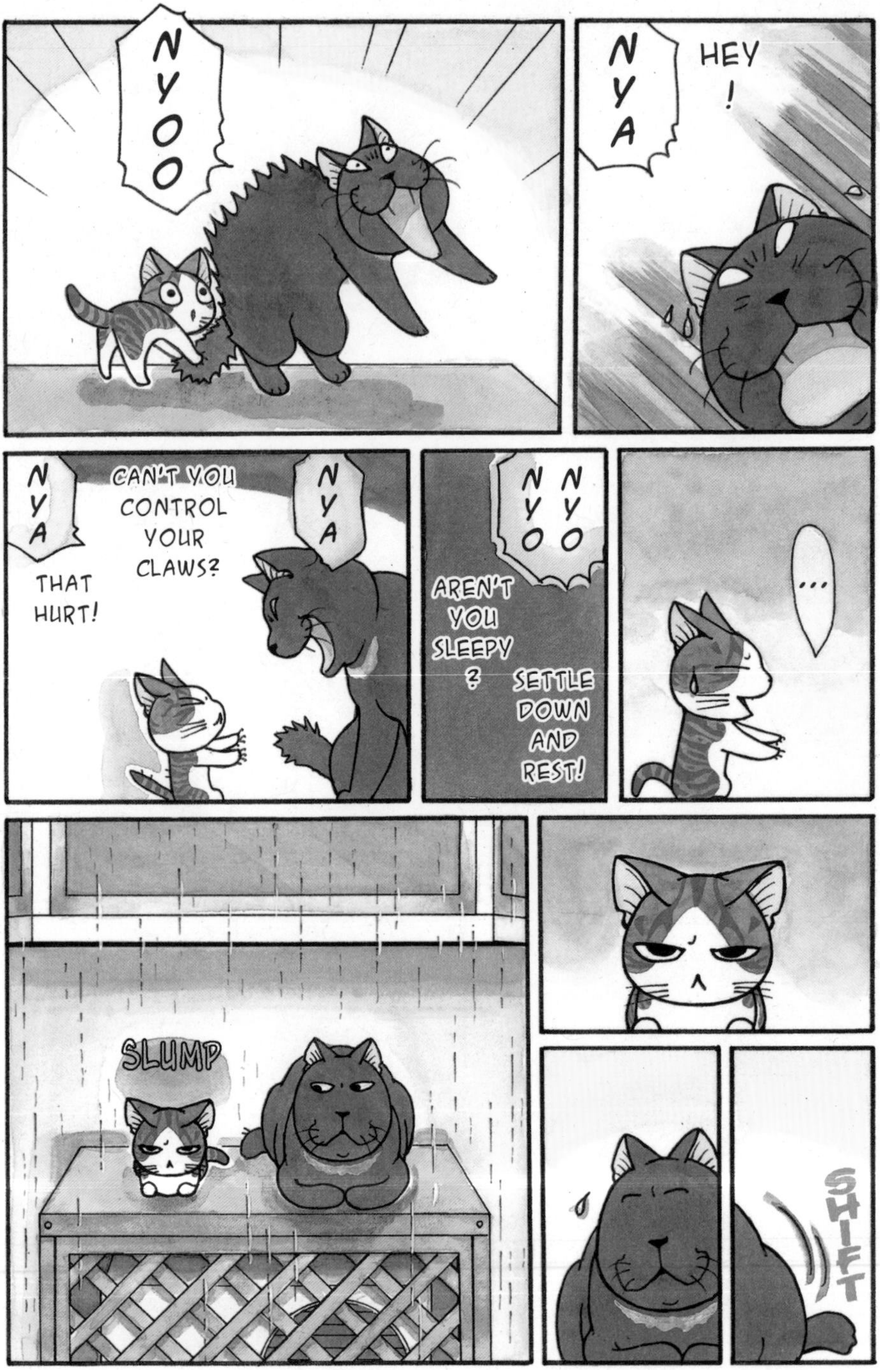
NYOO
NYA
HEY!
NYA
THAT HURT!
CAN'T YOU CONTROL YOUR CLAWS?
NYA
NYO NYO
AREN'T YOU SLEEPY?
SETTLE DOWN AND REST!
...
SLUMP
SHIFT

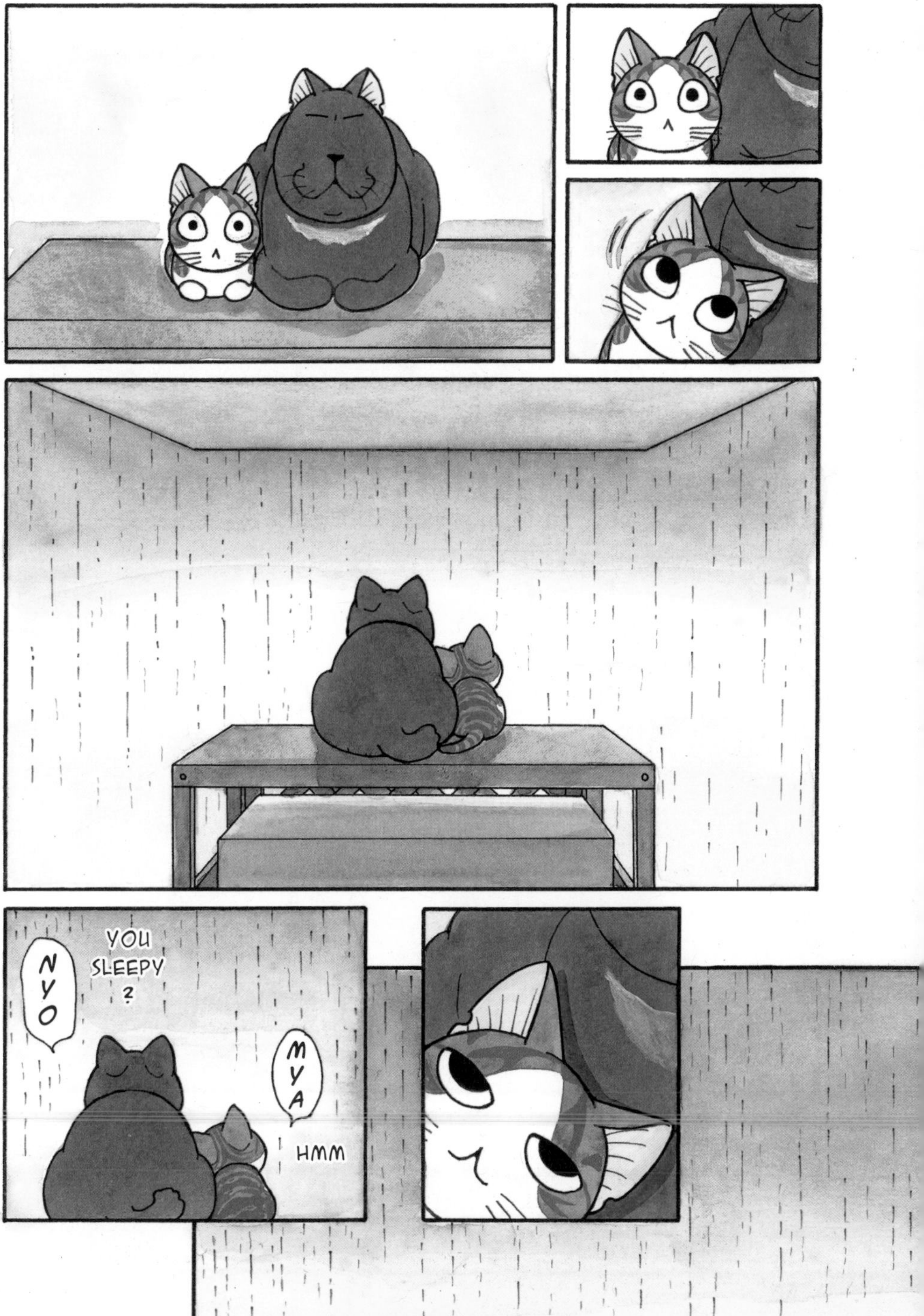
NYO
YOU SLEEPY ?
MYA
HMM

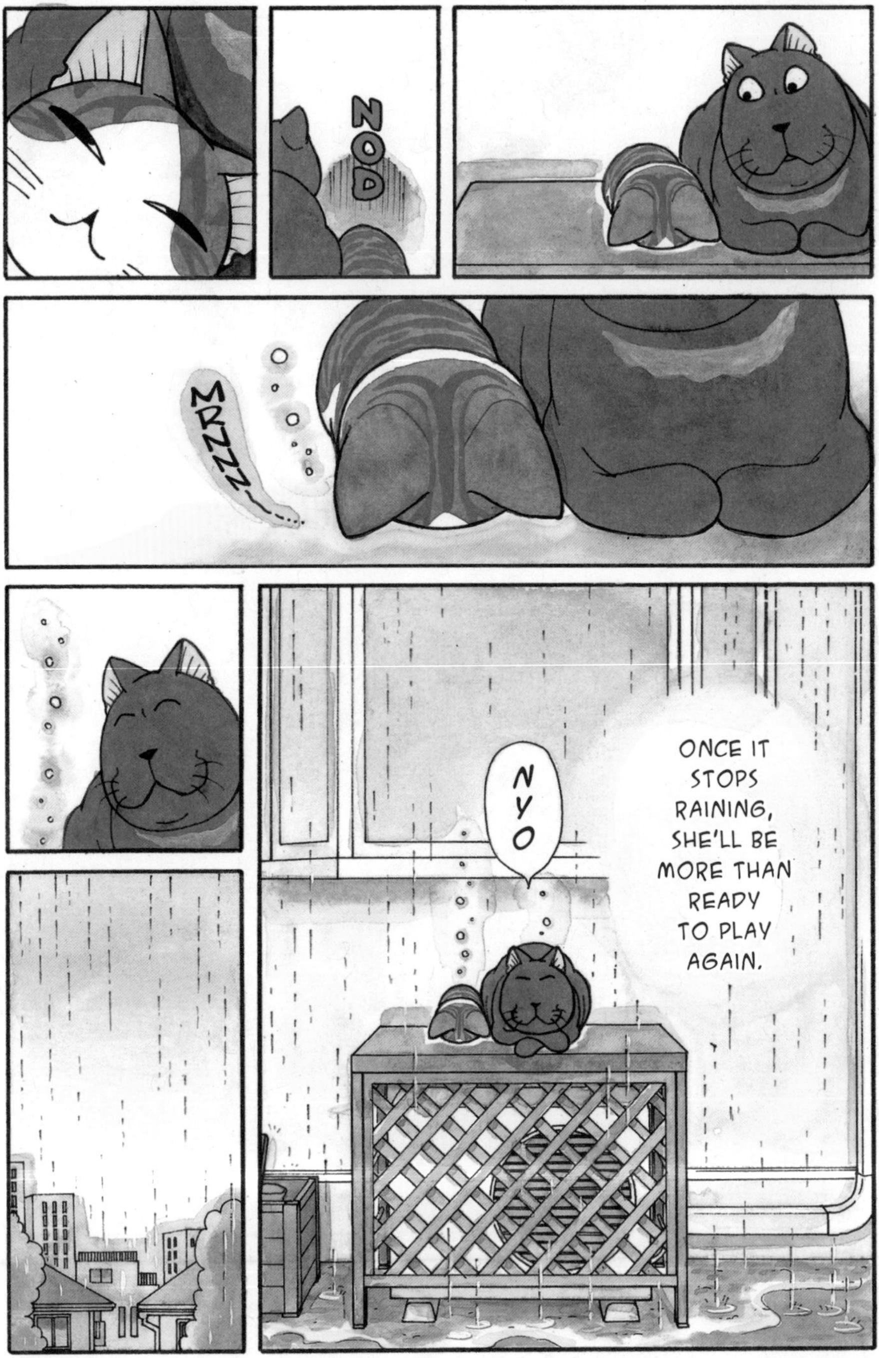
NOD
MRZZZ—...
NYO
ONCE IT STOPS RAINING, SHE'LL BE MORE THAN READY TO PLAY AGAIN.

the end

homemade 180: a cat masters

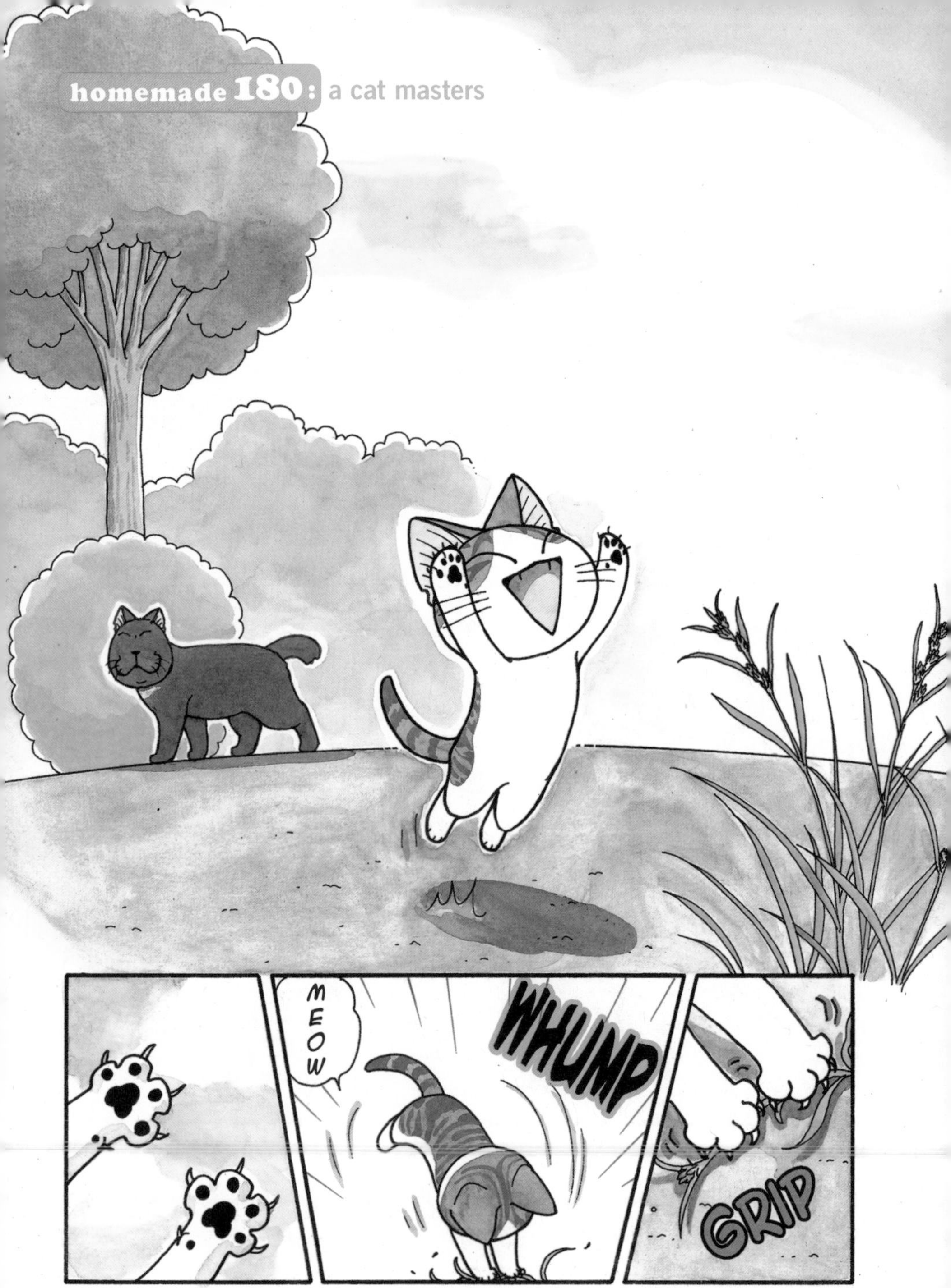
MEOW
WHUMP
GRIP

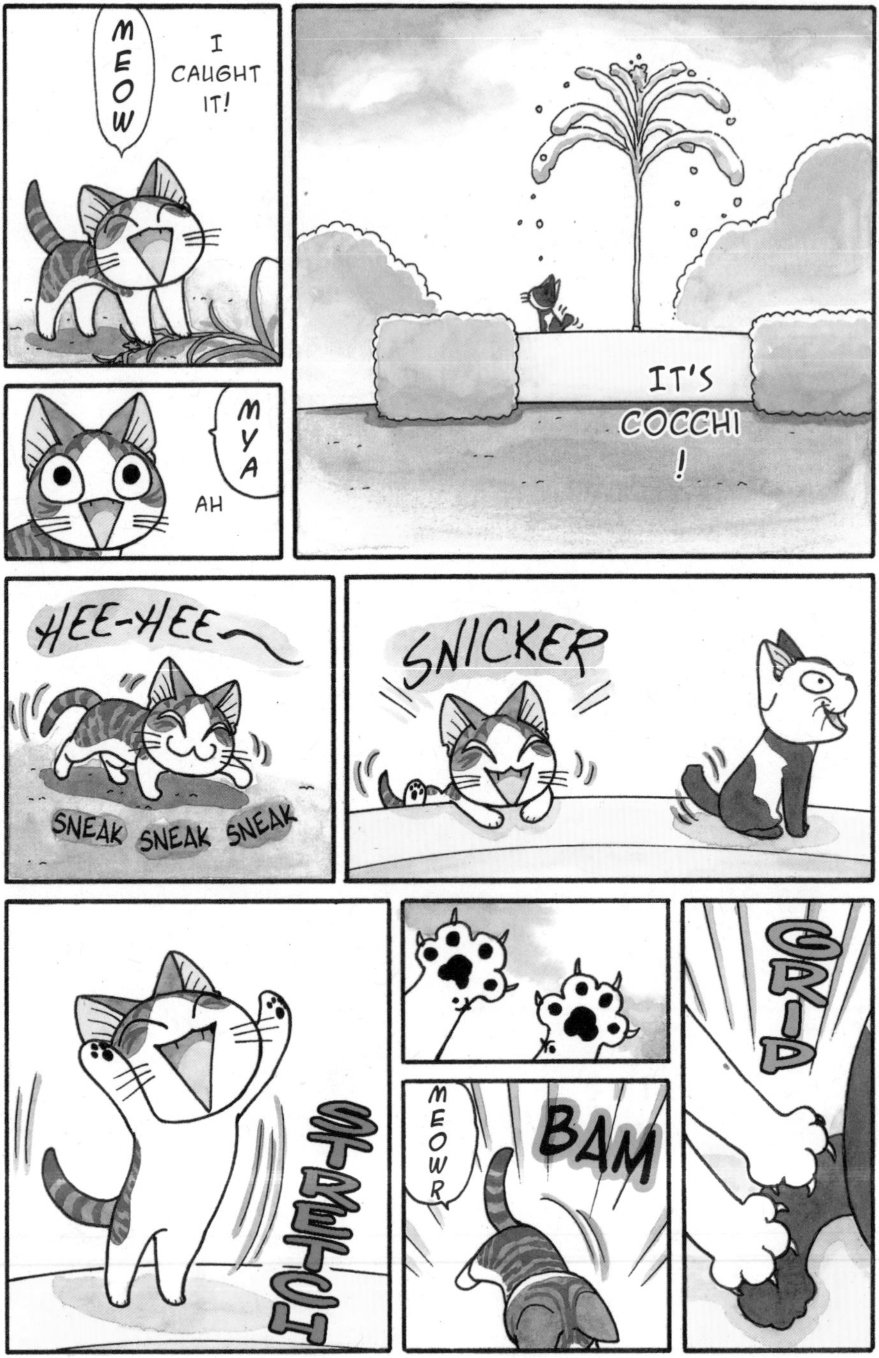
MEOW
I CAUGHT IT!
MYA
AH
IT'S COCCHI!
HEE-HEE~
SNEAK SNEAK SNEAK
SNICKER
STRETCH
MEOWR
BAM
GRID

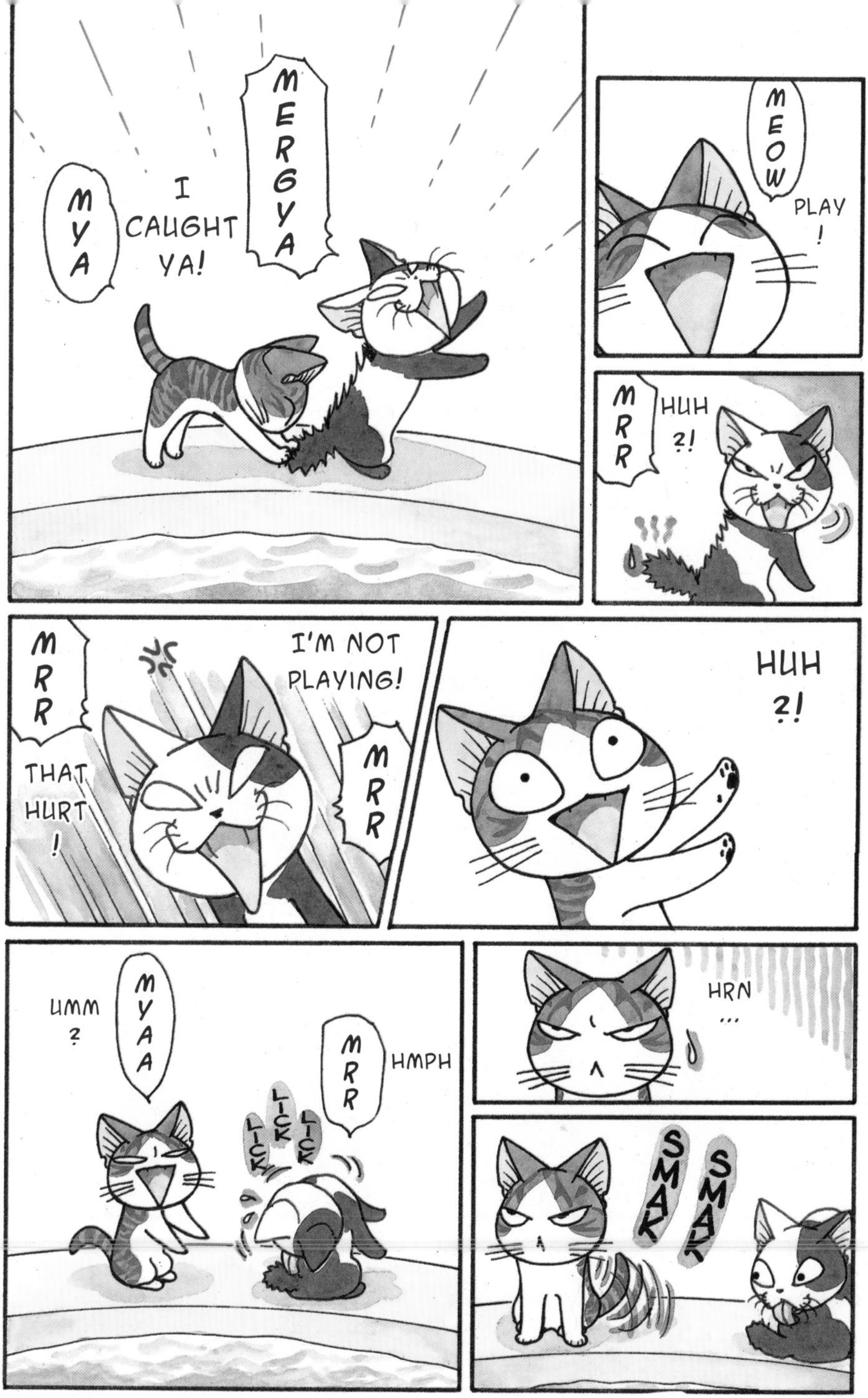

MYA
I CAUGHT YA!
MERGYA
MEOW
PLAY!
MRR
HUH ?!
MRR
I'M NOT PLAYING!
THAT HURT!
MRR
HUH ?!
UMM ?
MYAA
MRR
HMPH
LICK LICK LICK
HRN ...
SMAK SMAK

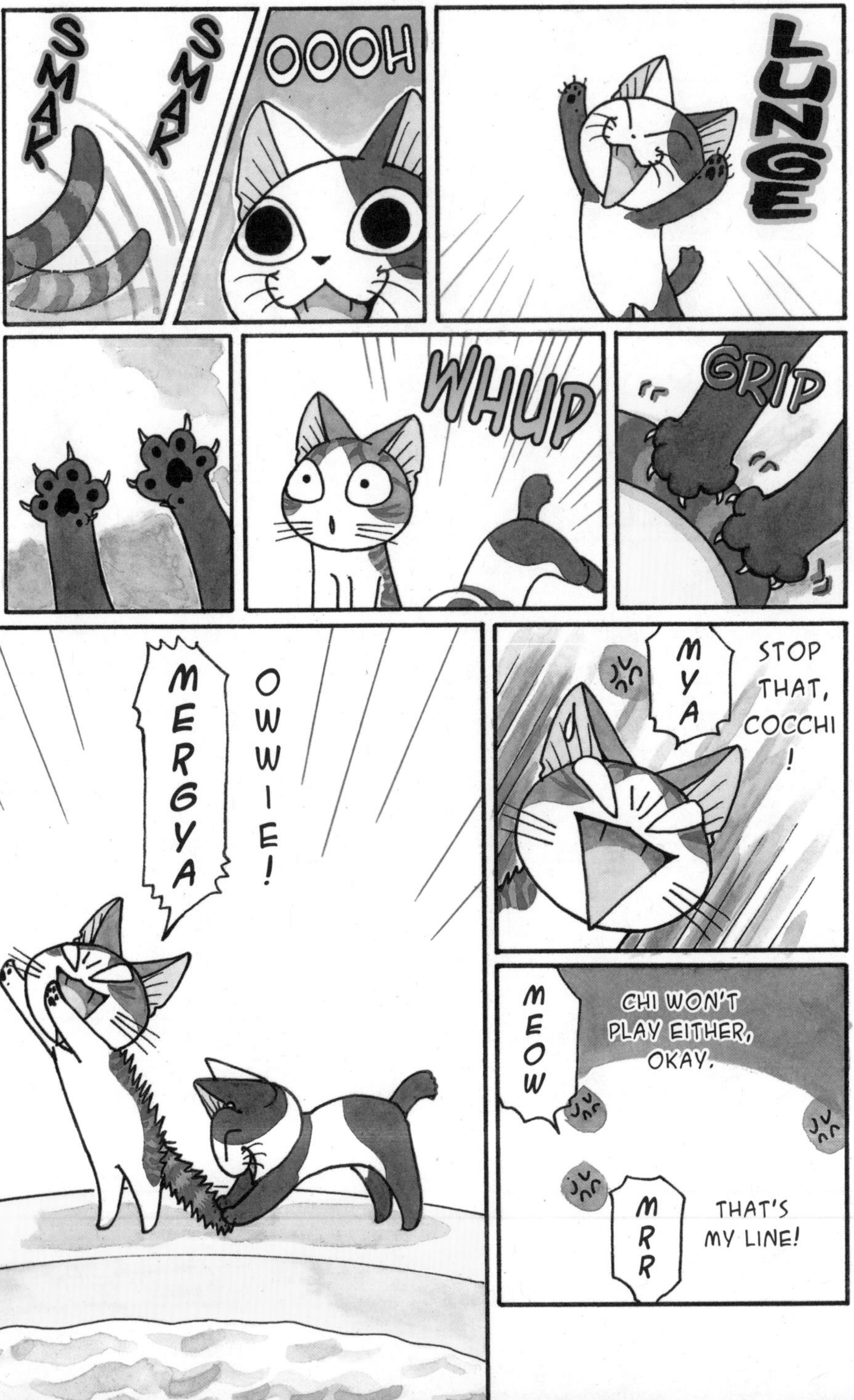
SMAK
SMAK
OOOH
LUNGE
WHUD
GRIP
MERGYA
OWWIE!
MYA
STOP THAT, COCCHI!
MEOW
CHI WON'T PLAY EITHER, OKAY.
MRR
THAT'S MY LINE!

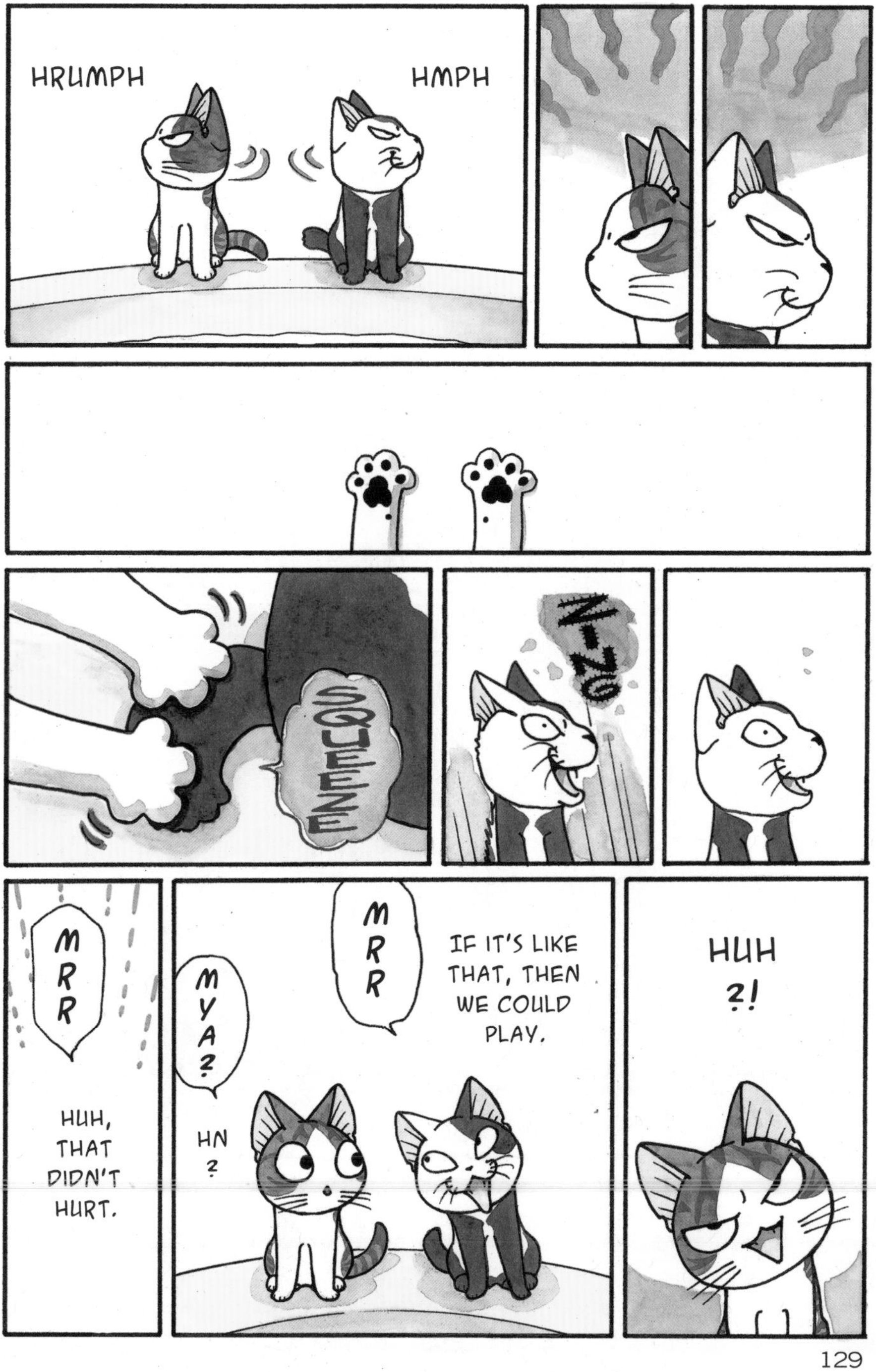
HRUMPH
HMPH
SQUEEZE
NNG
MRR
HUH, THAT DIDN'T HURT.
MRR
MYA?
HN?
IF IT'S LIKE THAT, THEN WE COULD PLAY.
HUH ?!

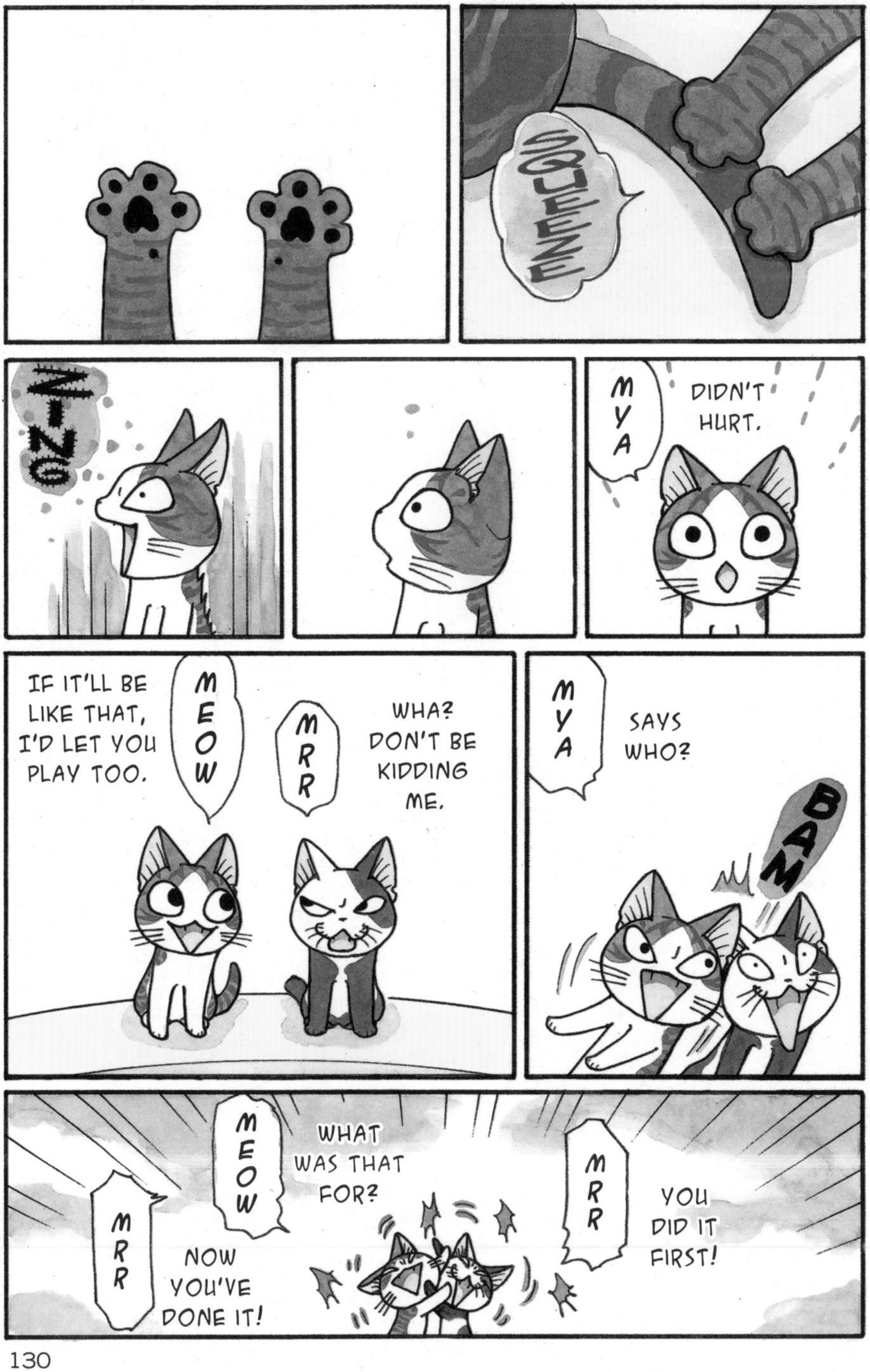

SQUEEZE
ZING
MYA
DIDN'T HURT.
IF IT'LL BE LIKE THAT, I'D LET YOU PLAY TOO.
MEOW
MRR
WHA? DON'T BE KIDDING ME.
MYA
SAYS WHO?
BAM
MRR
NOW YOU'VE DONE IT!
MEOW
WHAT WAS THAT FOR?
MRR
YOU DID IT FIRST!

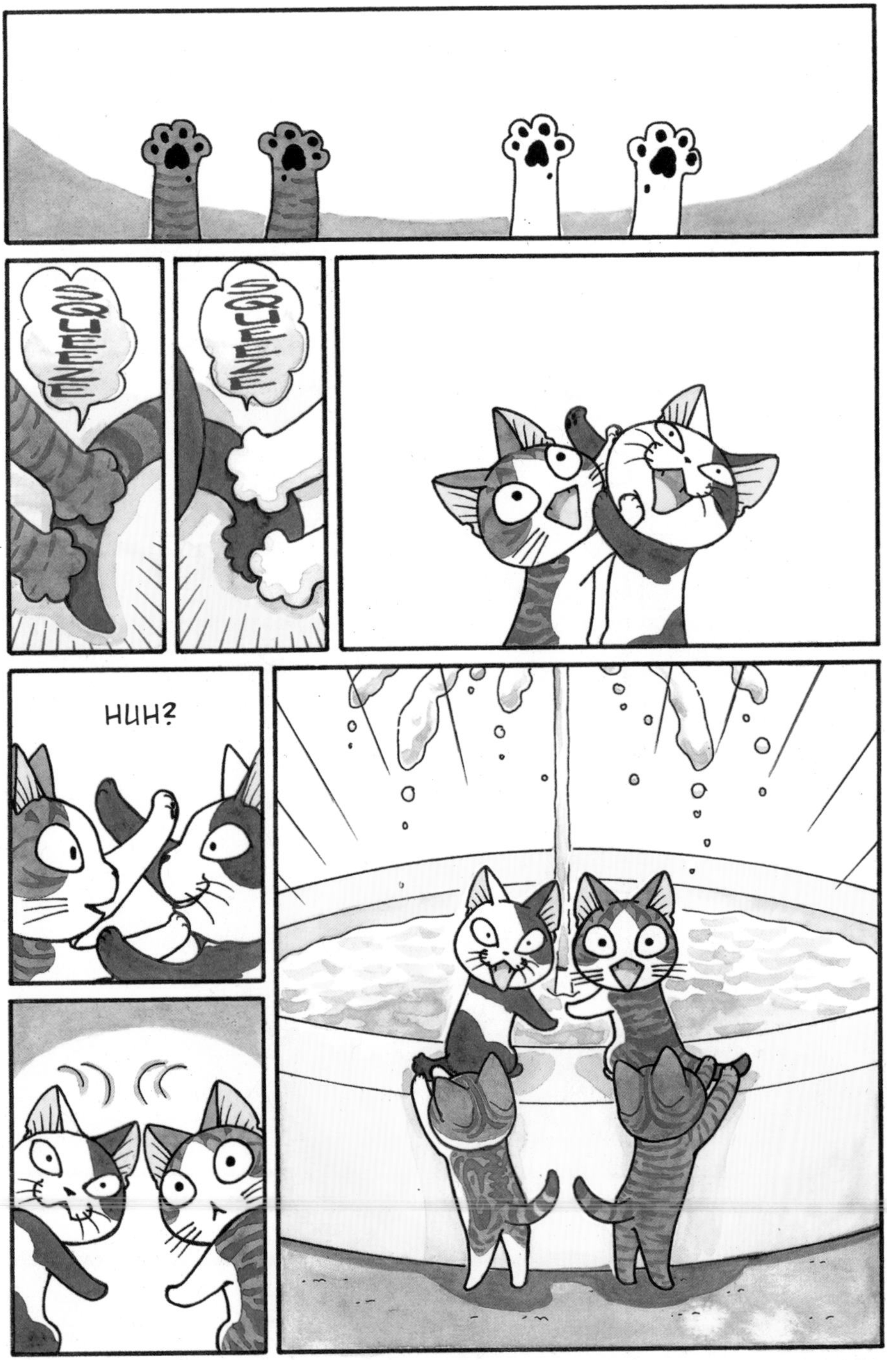
SQUEEZE
SQUEEZE
HUH?

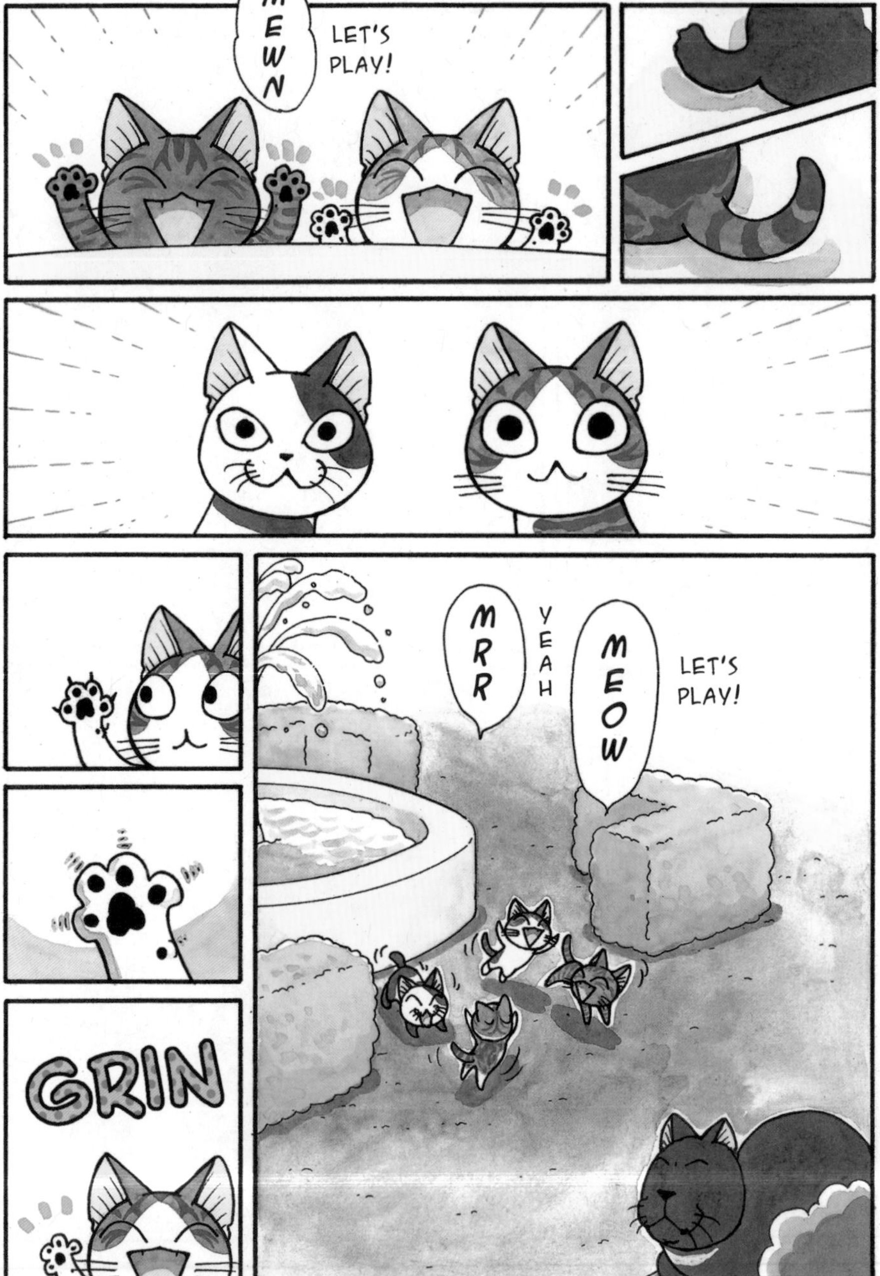
MEWN
LET'S PLAY!
MRR
YEAH
MEOW
LET'S PLAY!
GRIN

the end

homemade 181: a cat joins up

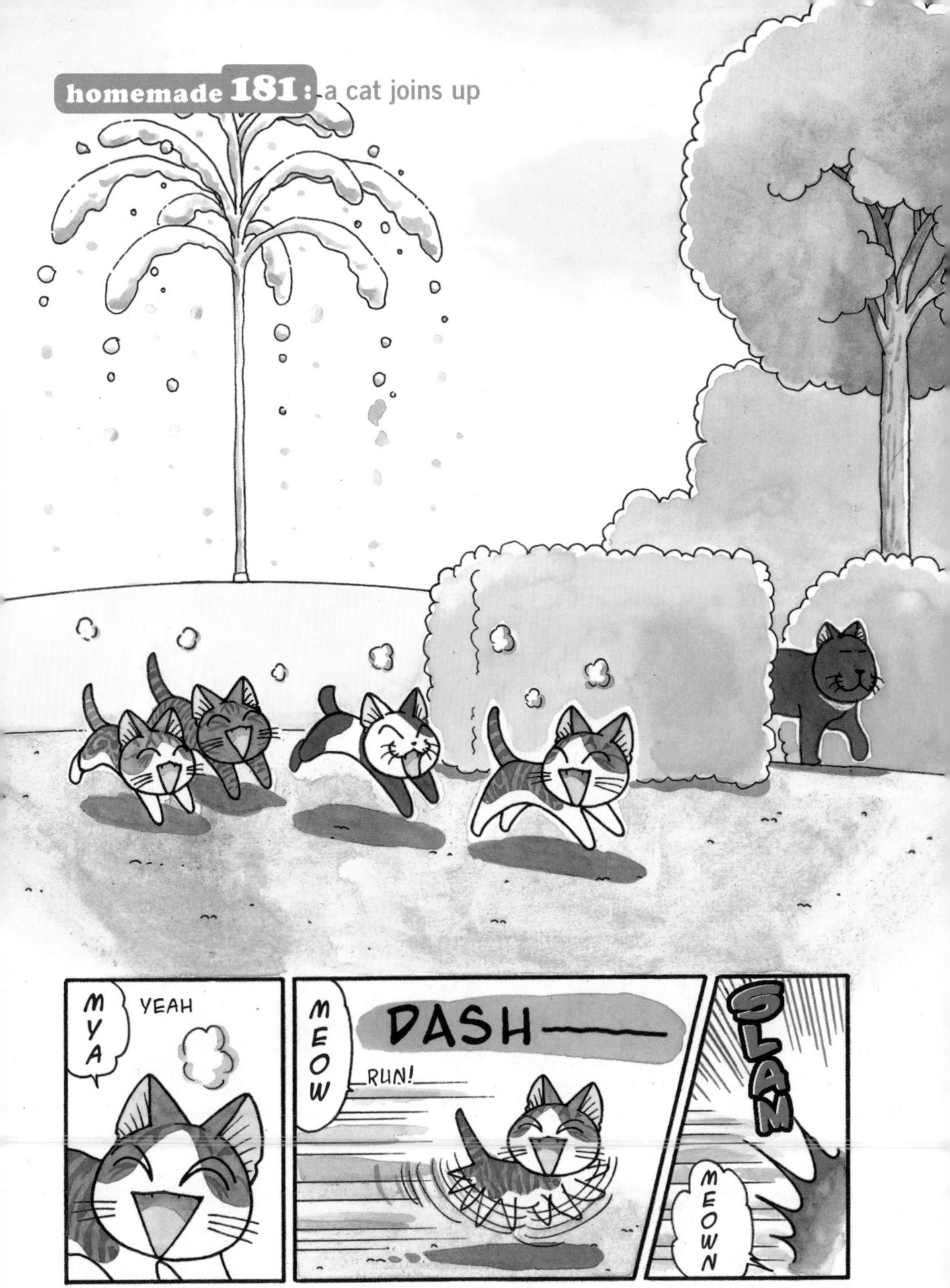
MYA
YEAH
MEOW
DASH——
RUN!
SLAM
MEOWN

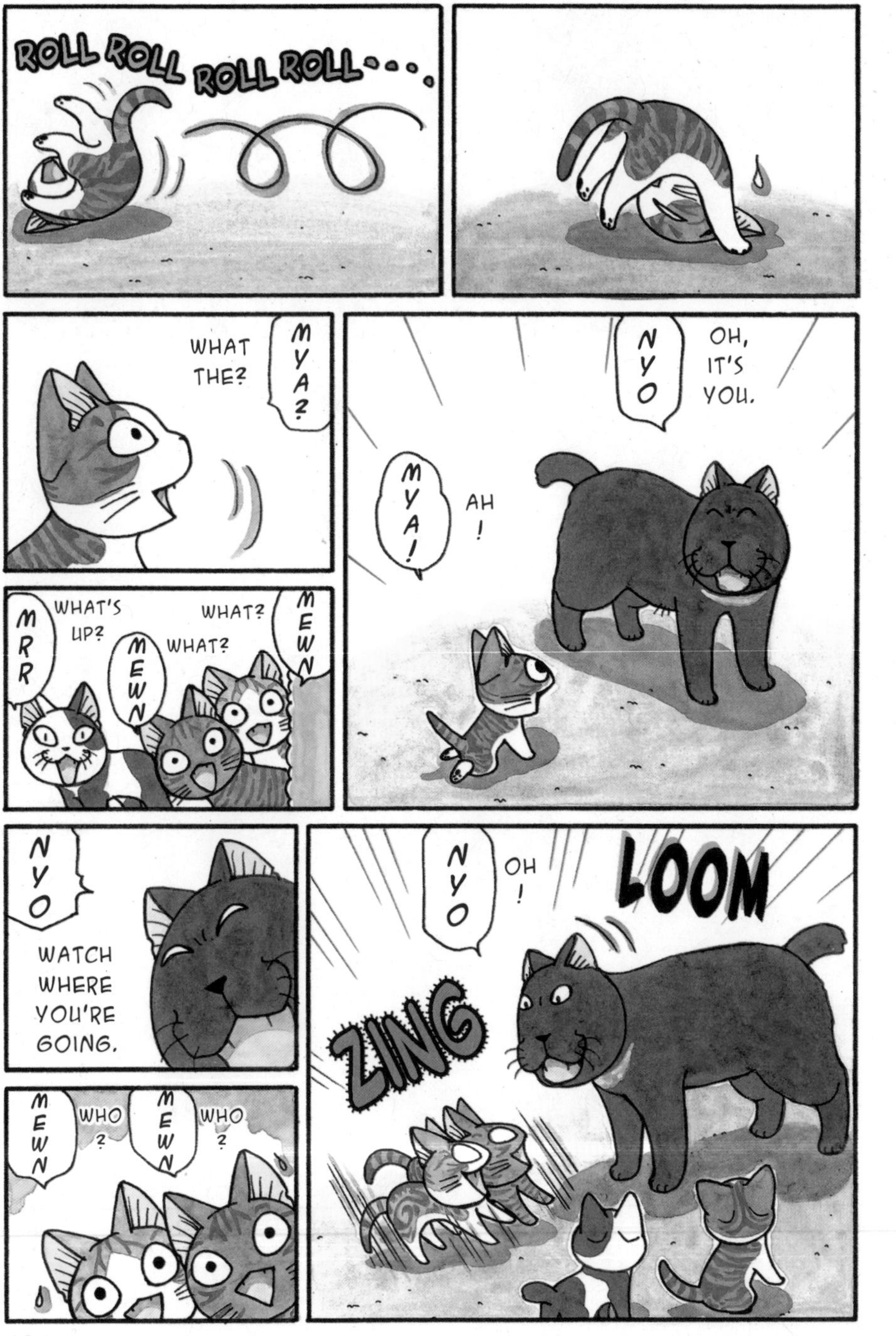
ROLL ROLL ROLL ROLL...
WHAT THE?
MYA?
MRR
WHAT'S UP?
MEWN
WHAT?
WHAT?
MEWN
NYO
OH, IT'S YOU.
MYA!
AH!
NYO
WATCH WHERE YOU'RE GOING.
MEWN
WHO?
MEWN
WHO?
NYO
OH!
LOOM
ZING

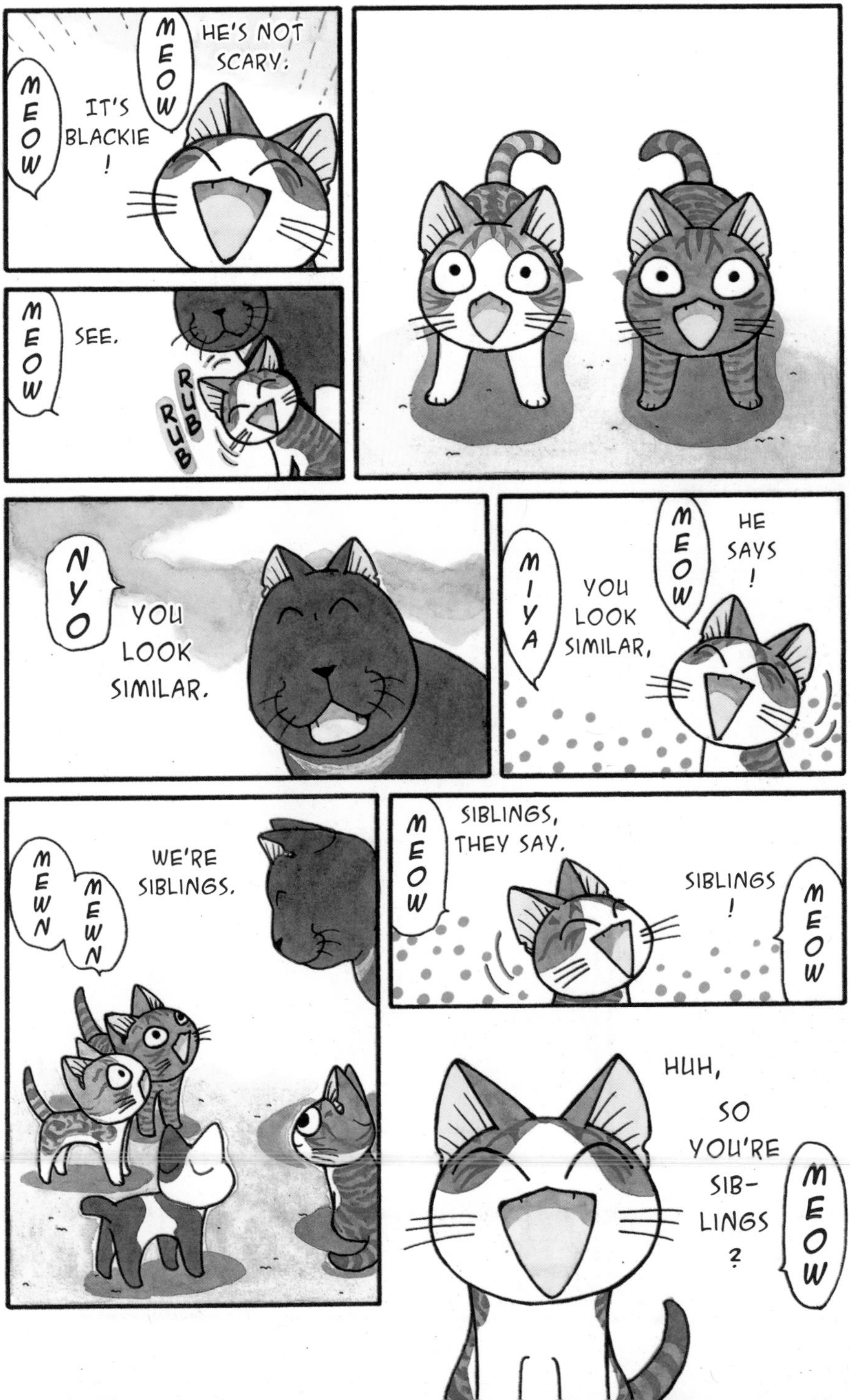
MEOW
IT'S BLACKIE!
MEOW
HE'S NOT SCARY.
MEOW
SEE.
RUB RUB
NYO
YOU LOOK SIMILAR.
MIYA
YOU LOOK SIMILAR,
MEOW
HE SAYS!
MEWN
MEWN
WE'RE SIBLINGS.
MEOW
SIBLINGS, THEY SAY.
SIBLINGS!
MEOW
HUH,
SO YOU'RE SIB-LINGS?
MEOW

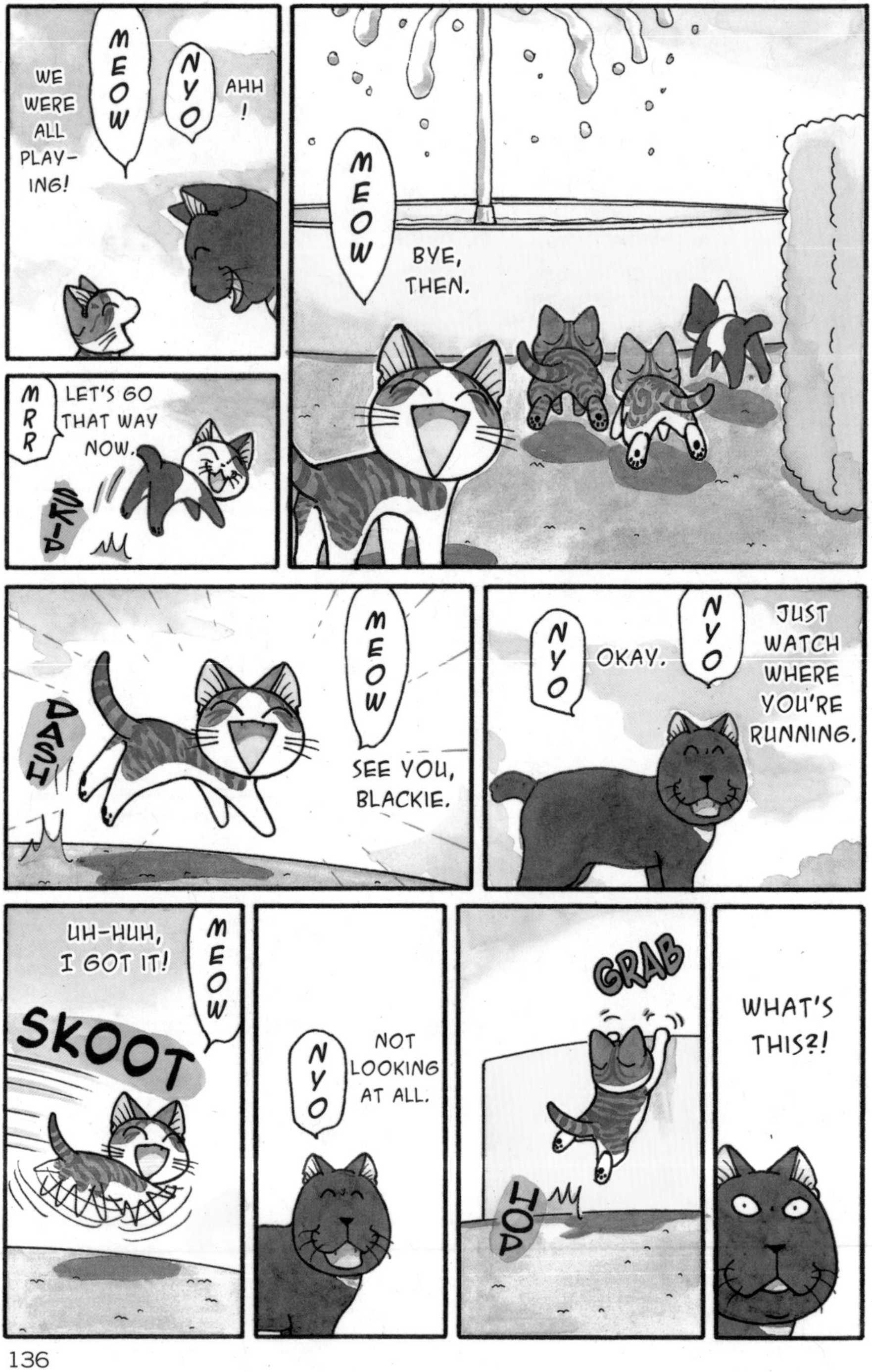
MEOW
WE WERE ALL PLAYING!
NYO
AHH!
MRR
LET'S GO THAT WAY NOW.
SKIP
MEOW
BYE, THEN.
DASH
MEOW
SEE YOU, BLACKIE.
NYO
OKAY.
NYO
JUST WATCH WHERE YOU'RE RUNNING.
UH-HUH, I GOT IT!
MEOW
SKOOT
NYO
NOT LOOKING AT ALL.
GRAB
HOP
WHAT'S THIS?!

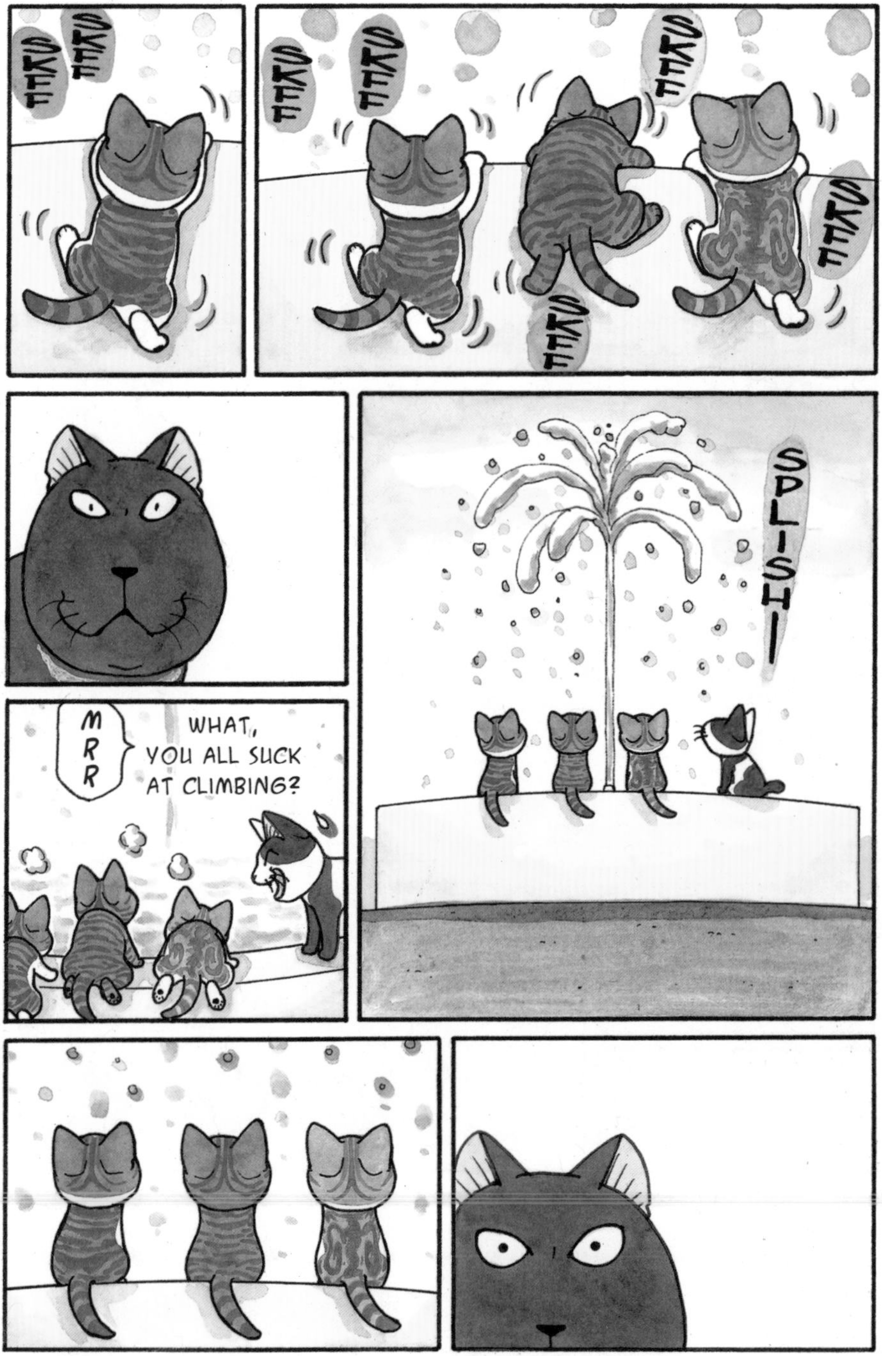
SKEE
SKEE
SKEE
SKEE
SKEE
SKEE
SKEE
MRR
WHAT, YOU ALL SUCK AT CLIMBING?
SPLISH

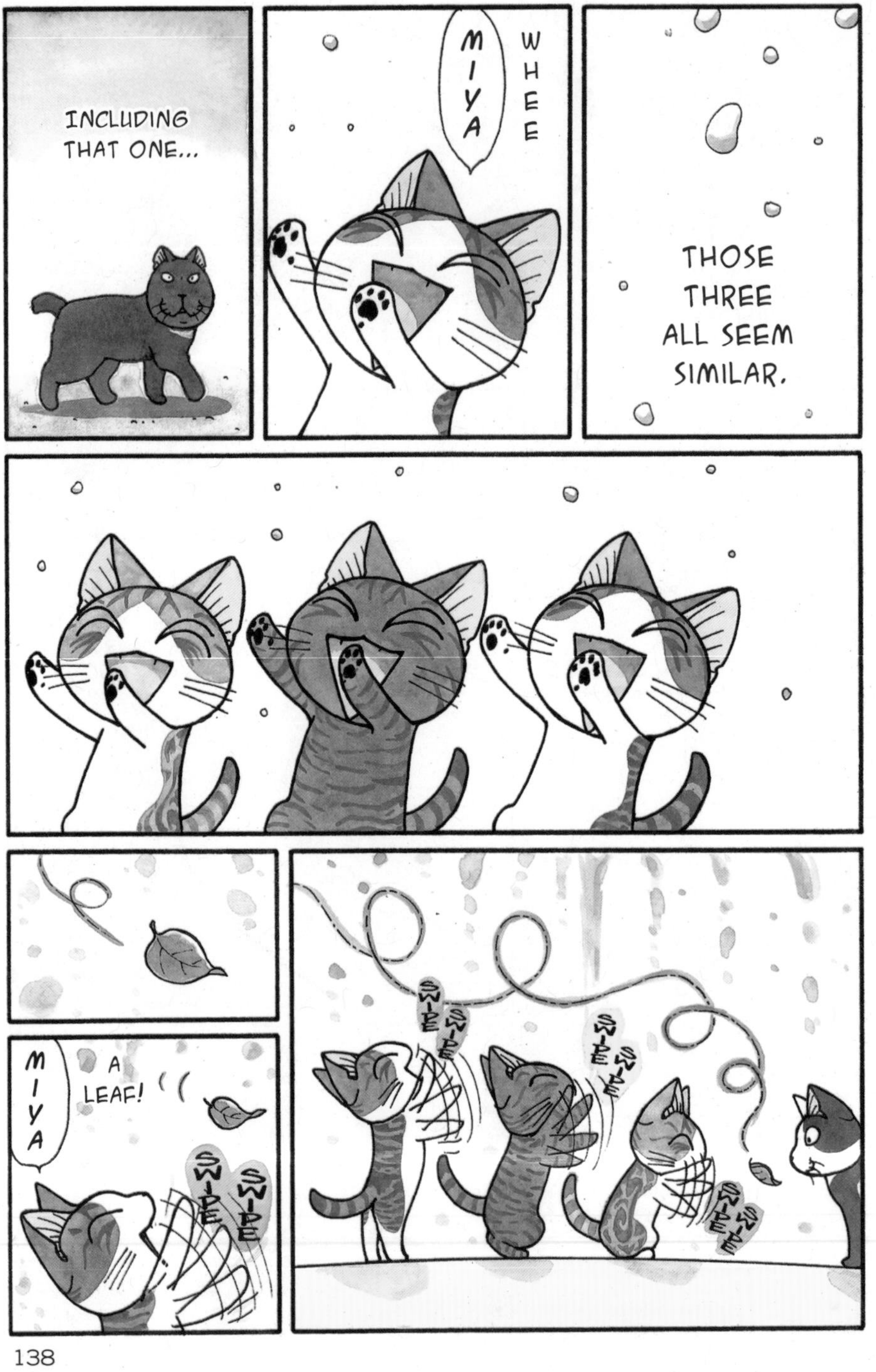
INCLUDING THAT ONE...
MIYA
WHEE
THOSE THREE ALL SEEM SIMILAR.
MIYA
A LEAF!
SWIPE
SWIPE
SWIPE
SWIPE
SWIPE
SWIPE
SWIPE
SWIPE

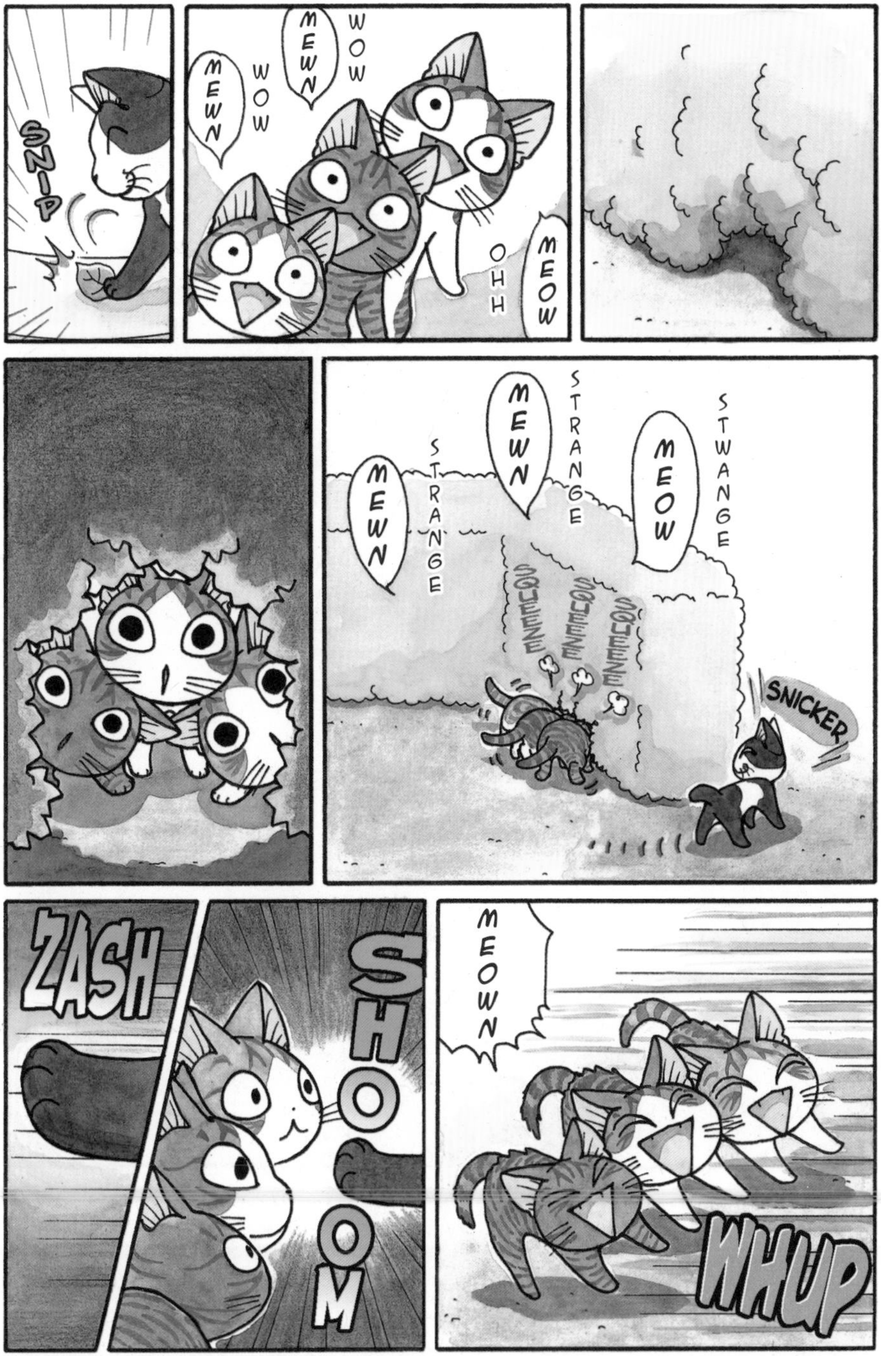
SNIP
MEWN
WOW
MEWN
WOW
OHH
MEOW
MEWN
STRANGE
MEWN
STRANGE
MEOW
STWANGE
SQUEEZE
SQUEEZE
SQUEEZE
SNICKER
ZASH
SHOOOM
MEOWN
WHUP

THAT WAS ME!

MRR

MEOW

WHAT A SURPRISE, HUH!

A SURPRISE.

MYA

MYA

A SURPRISE!

MRR

YOU GUYS ARE LIKE "PEAS IN A POD."

MEOW

WEIRD!

MEOW

WHAT'RE "PEAS IN A POD"?

140

the end

homemade 182: a cat begins to change

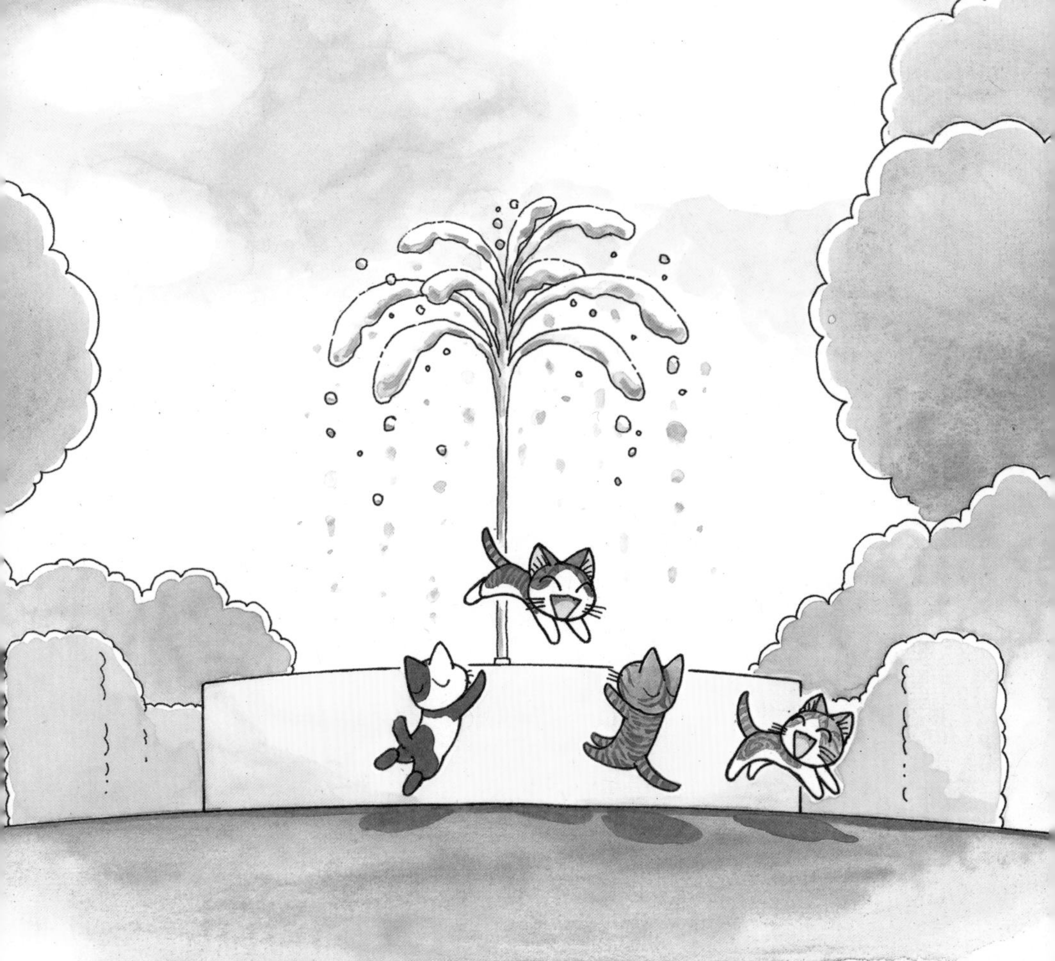

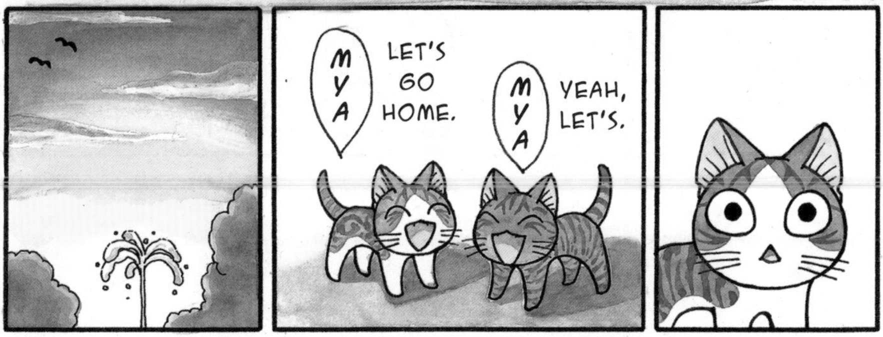
MYA
LET'S GO HOME.
MYA
YEAH, LET'S.

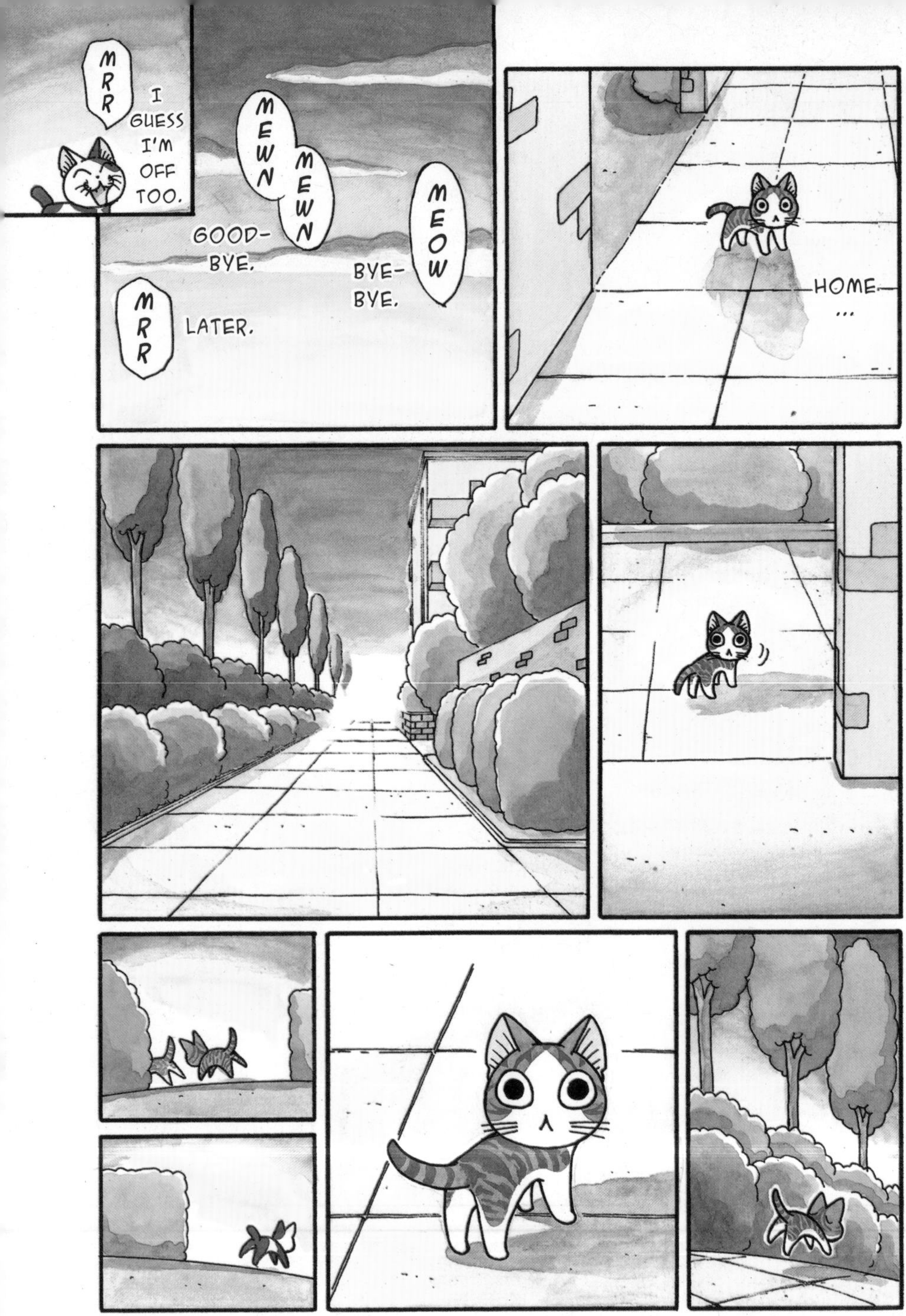
MRR
I GUESS I'M OFF TOO.
MEWN
MEWN
GOOD-BYE.
MRR
LATER.
MEOW
BYE-BYE.
HOME...

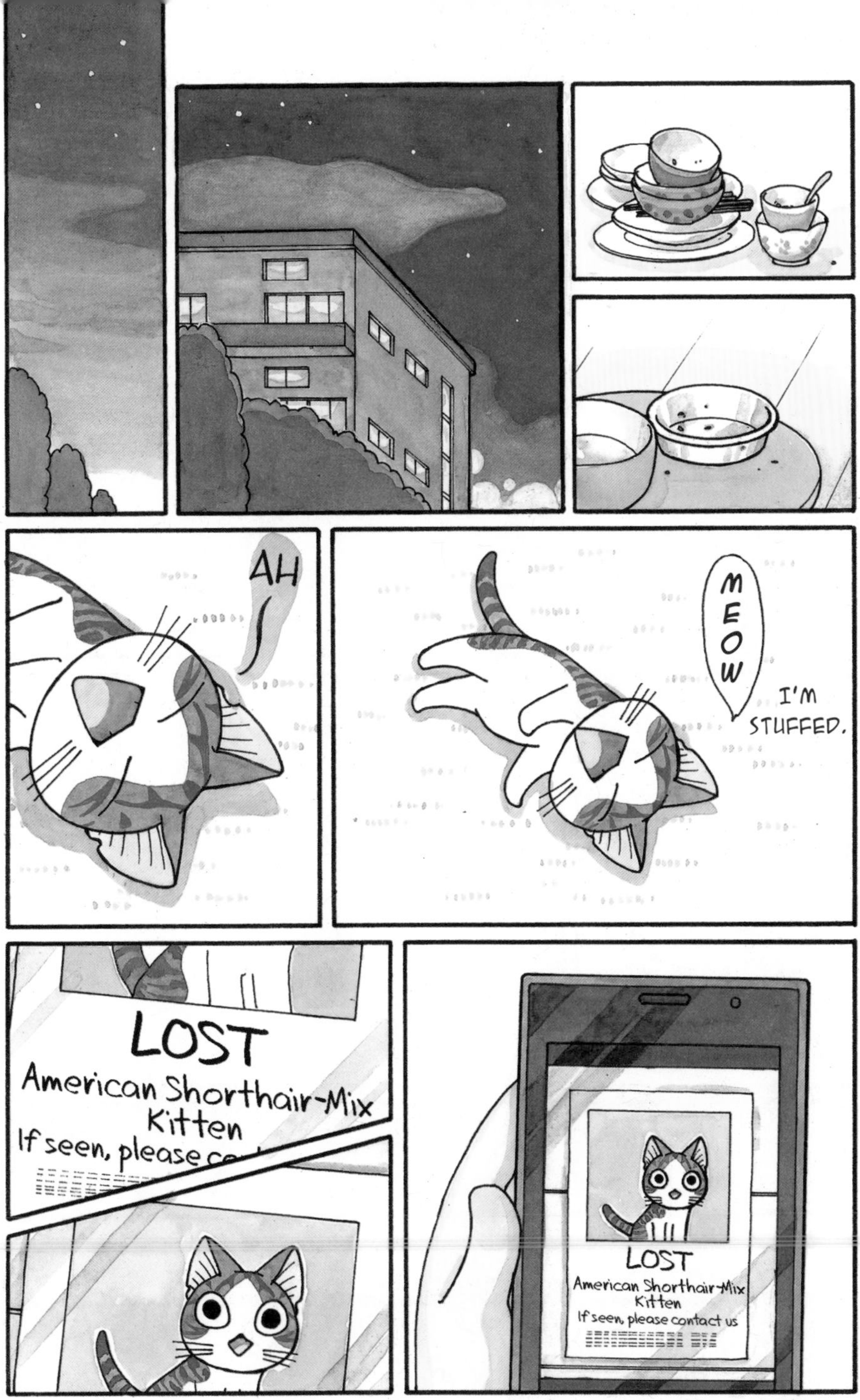
AH
MEOW
I'M STUFFED.
LOST
American Shorthair-Mix Kitten
If seen, please
LOST
American Shorthair-Mix Kitten
If seen, please contact us

ZASH

WHAT TO DO?

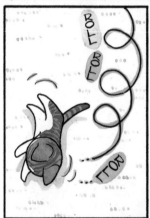

ROLL ROLL ROLL

BONK

WE'VE GOT TO DO SOME-THING.

WHAT ARE YOU PLANNING TO DO WITH OUR CHI?

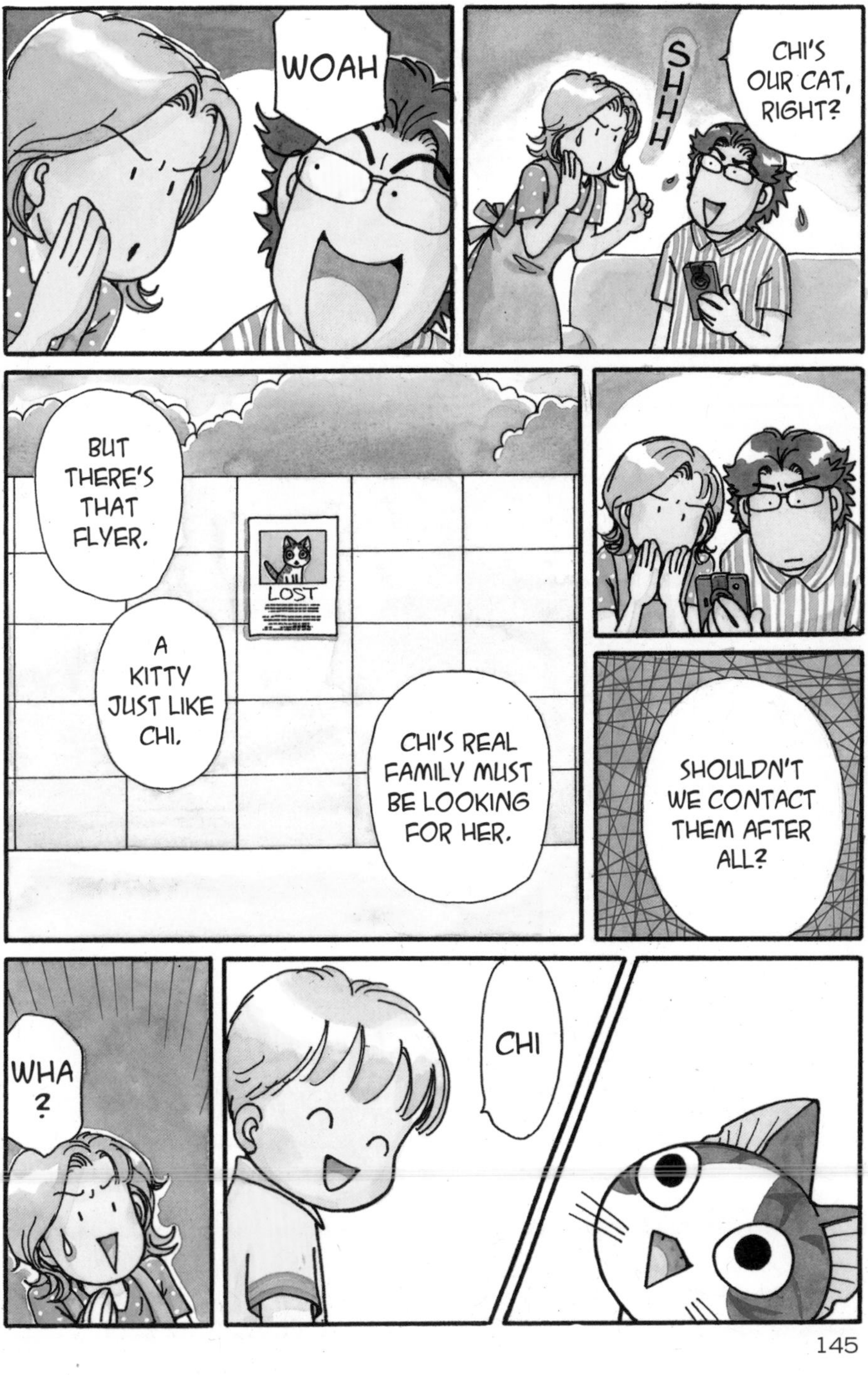
WOAH
SHHH
CHI'S OUR CAT, RIGHT?
BUT THERE'S THAT FLYER.
LOST
A KITTY JUST LIKE CHI.
CHI'S REAL FAMILY MUST BE LOOKING FOR HER.
SHOULDN'T WE CONTACT THEM AFTER ALL?
WHA ?
CHI

MEOW

UM, UM...

GLOMP

MEOW

TODAY, CHI...

AND THEN WHAT WILL HAPPEN TO HER?

AND WHAT ABOUT YOHEI...

UHH...

MEOW

WE PLAYED A LOT.

MEE

AND THEN...

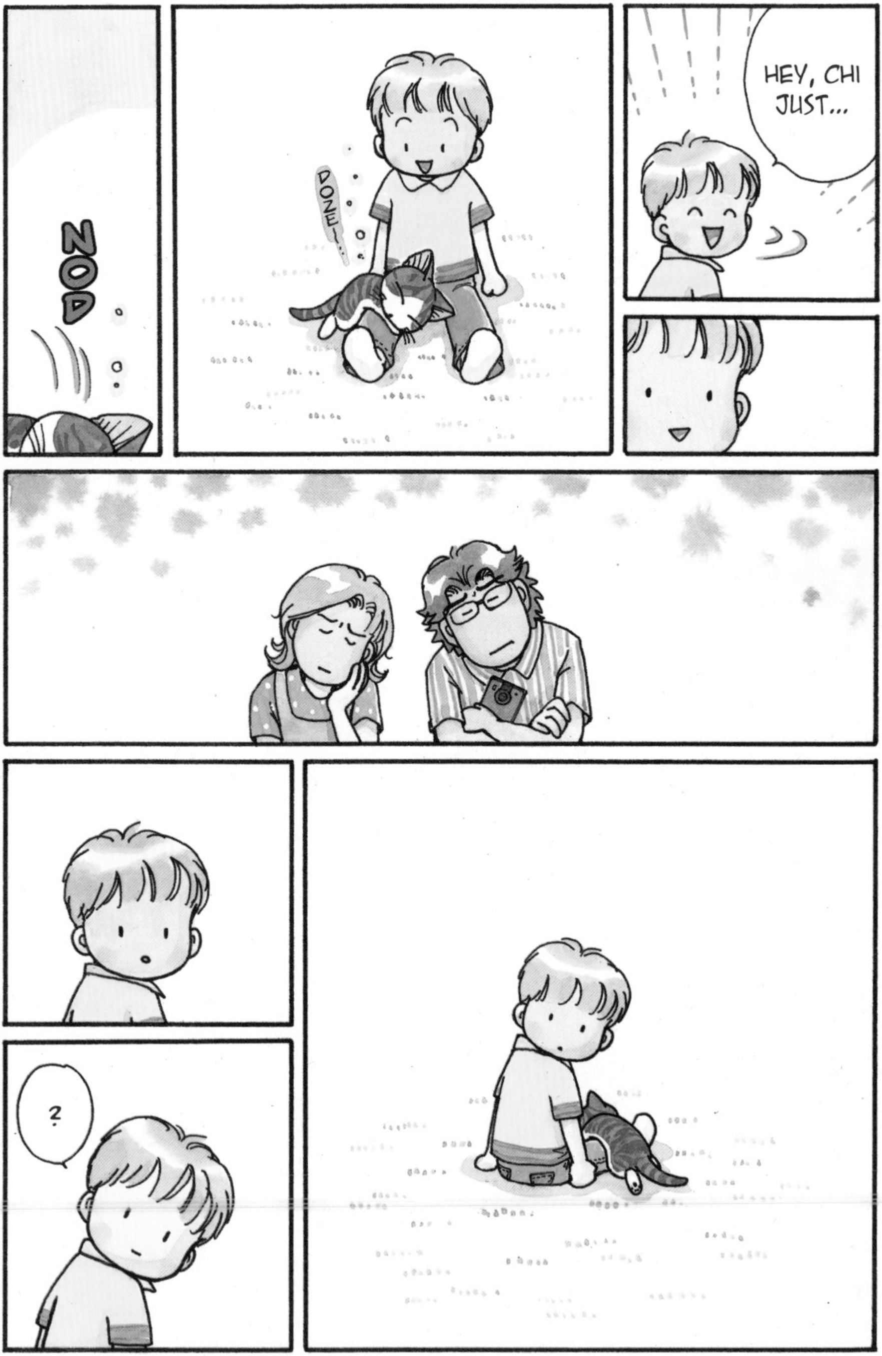
NOD
DOZE…
HEY, CHI JUST...
?

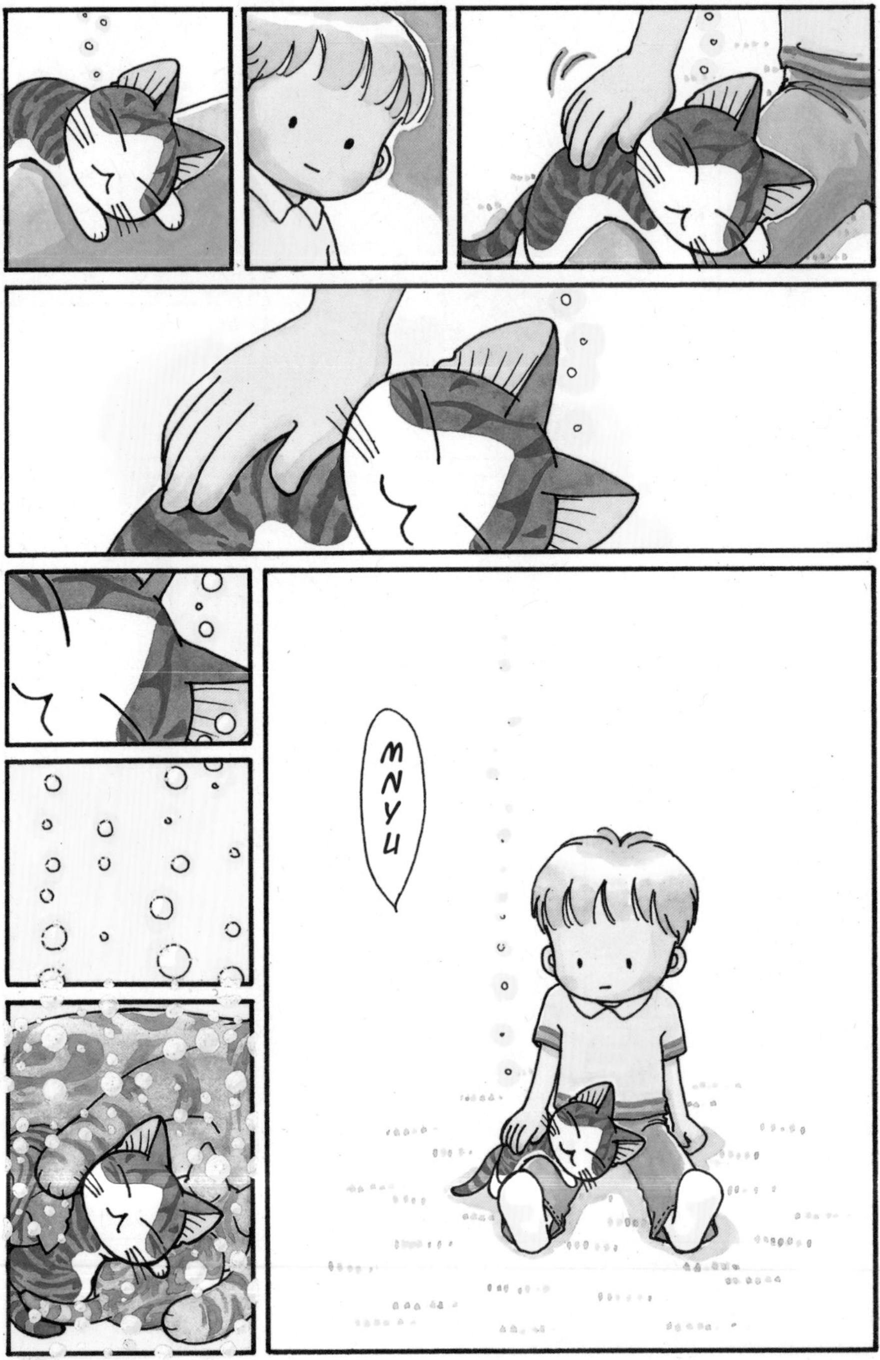
MNYU

the end

homemade 183: a cat calls

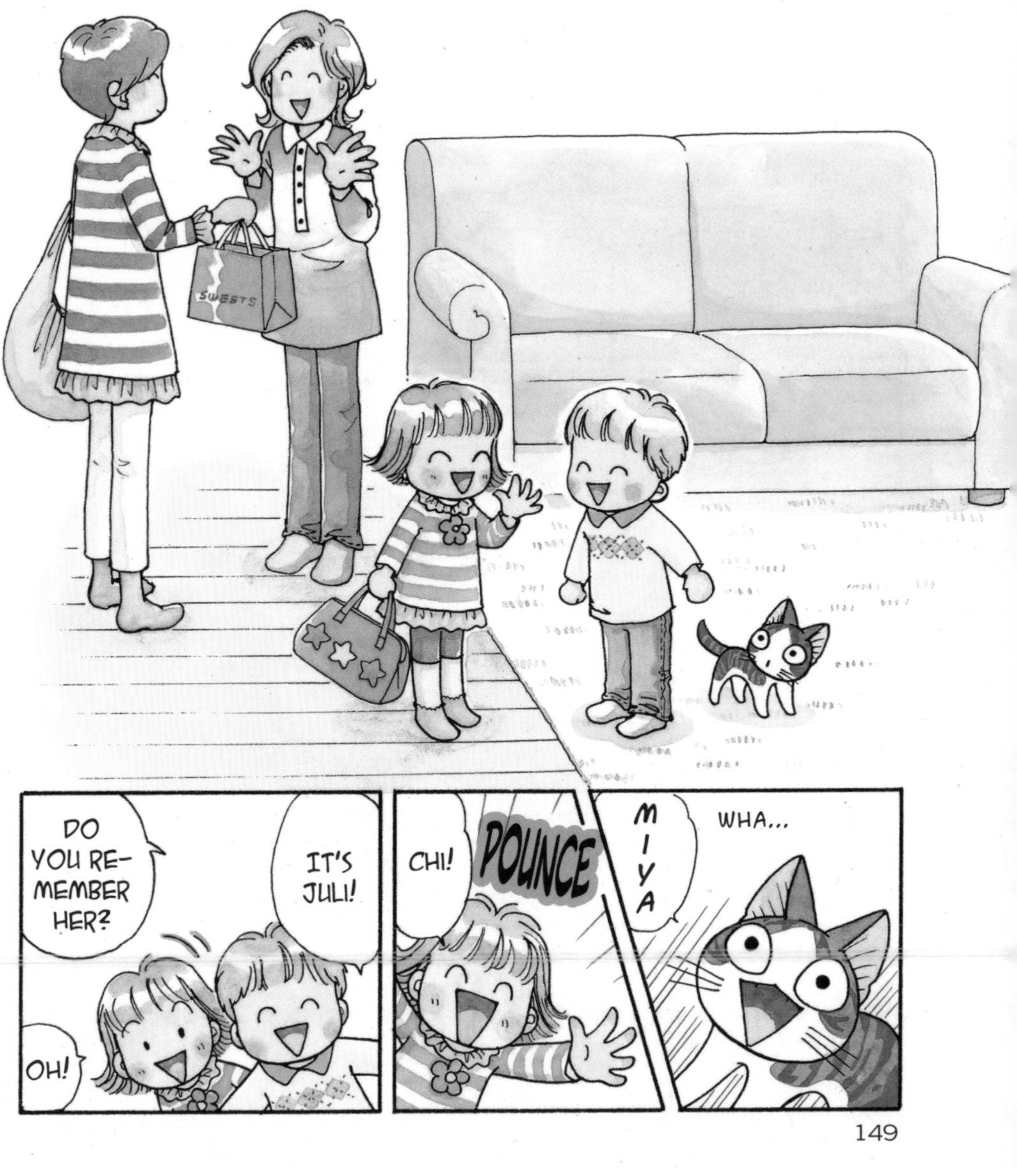

SWEETS
DO YOU RE-MEMBER HER?
OH!
IT'S JULI!
CHI!
POUNCE
MIYA
WHA...

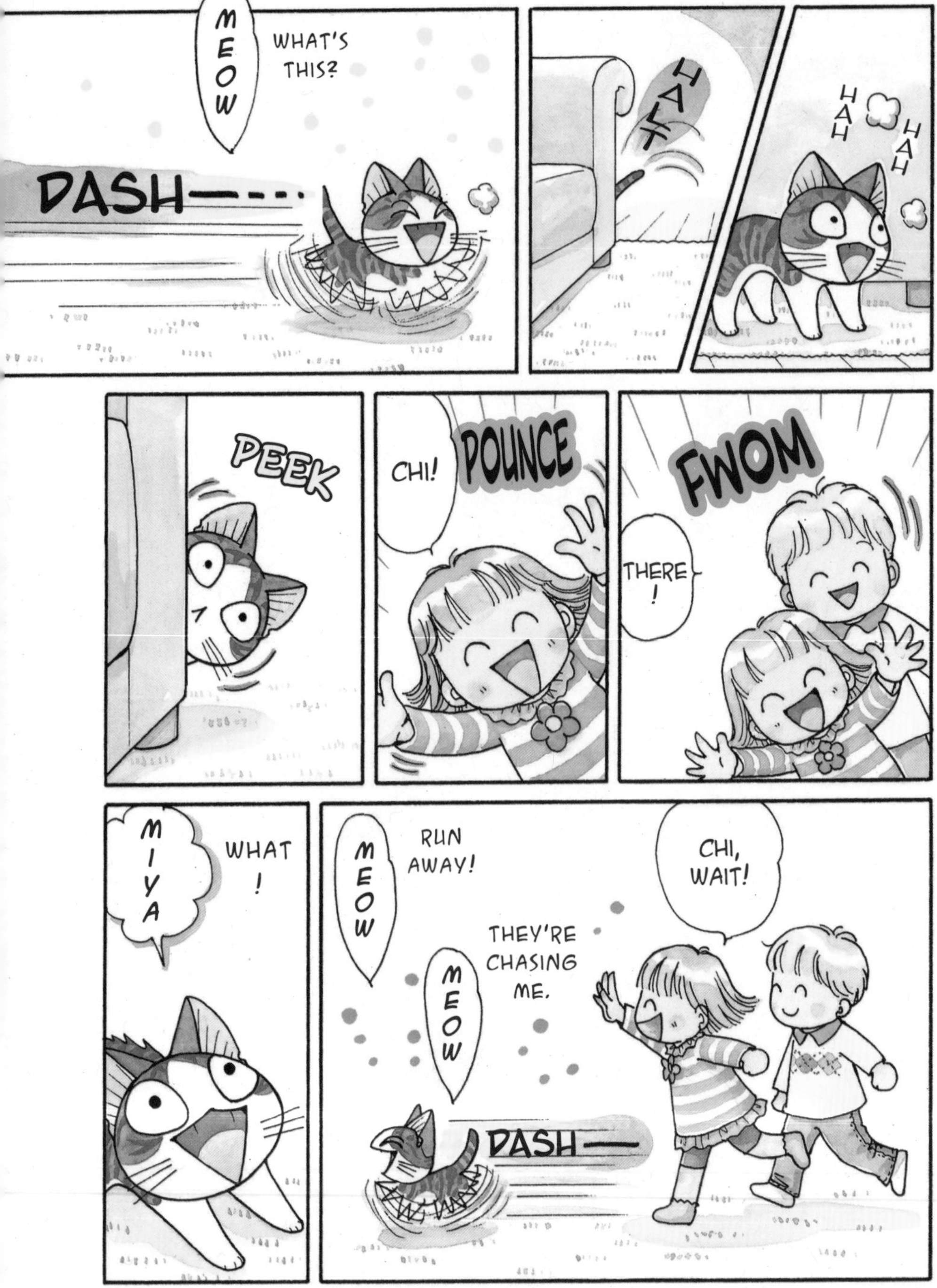
MEOW
WHAT'S THIS?
DASH
HALT
HAH HAH
PEEK
CHI!
POUNCE
FWOM
THERE!
MIYA
WHAT!
MEOW
RUN AWAY!
CHI, WAIT!
THEY'RE CHASING ME.
MEOW
DASH

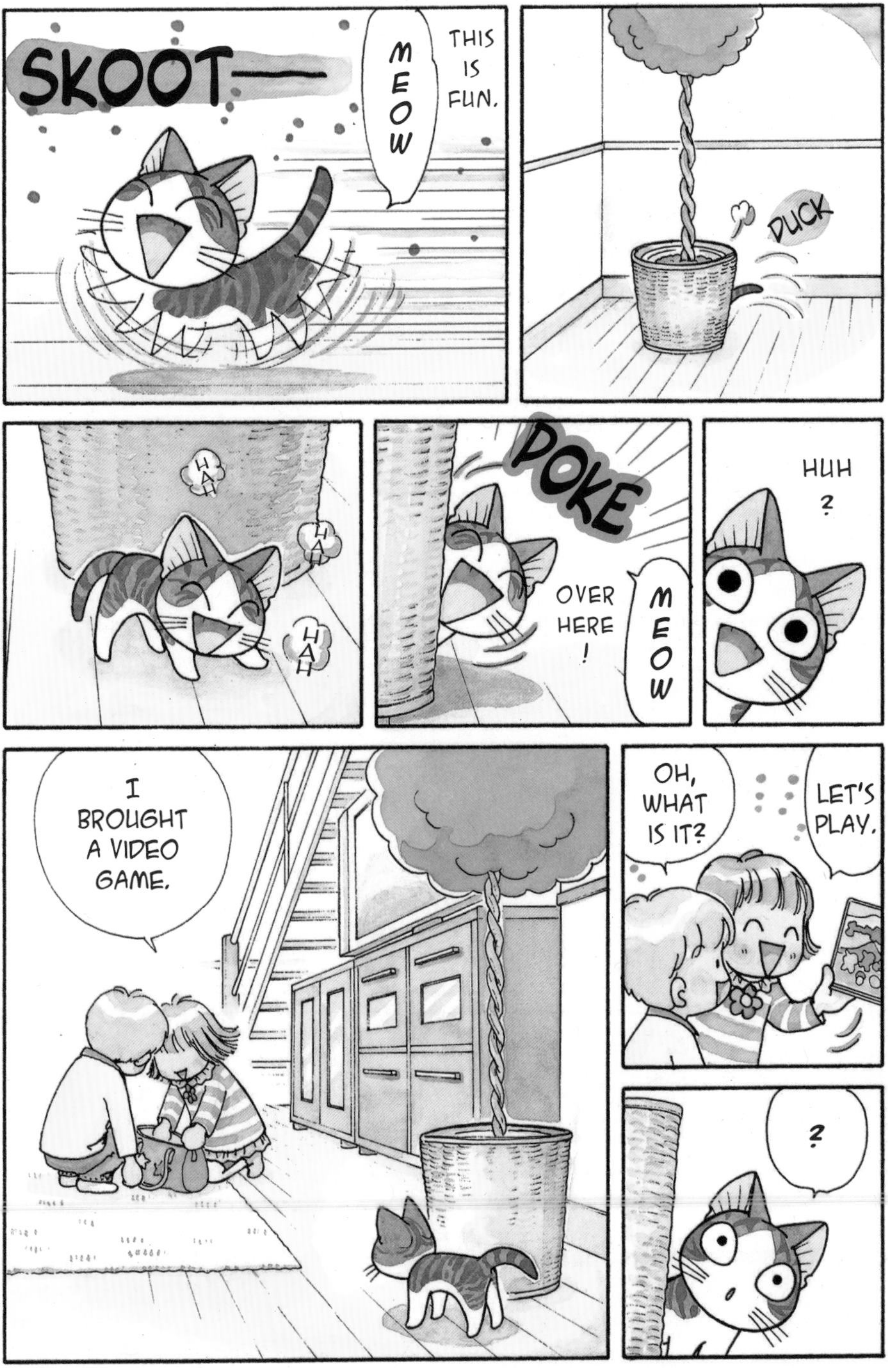
SKOOT——
MEOW
THIS IS FUN.
DUCK
HAH
HAH
HAH
DOKE
OVER HERE!
MEOW
HUH?
I BROUGHT A VIDEO GAME.
OH, WHAT IS IT?
LET'S PLAY.
?

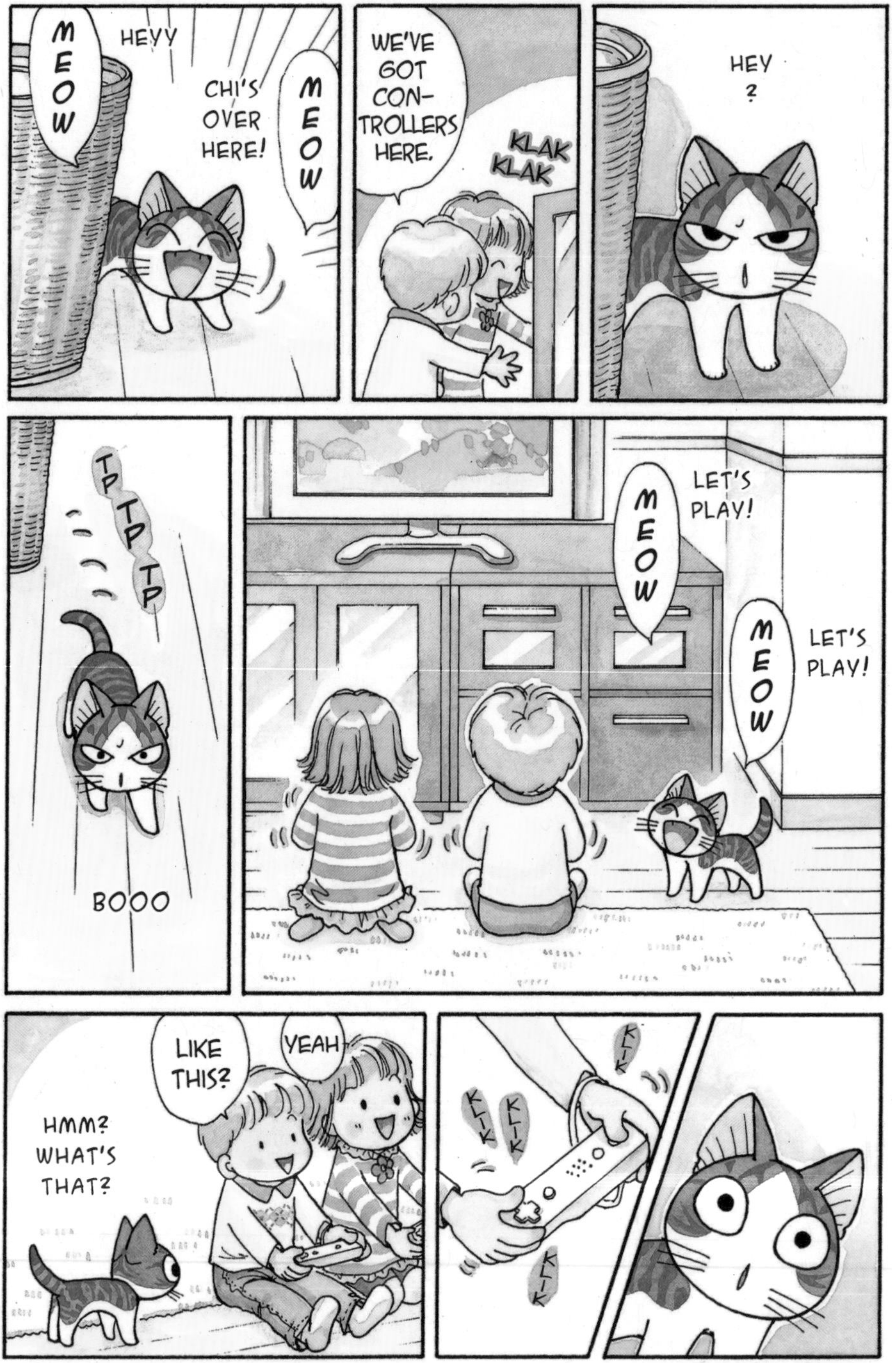
MEOW
HEYY
CHI'S OVER HERE!
MEOW
WE'VE GOT CON-TROLLERS HERE.
KLAK KLAK
HEY ?
TP TP TP TP
BOOO
MEOW
LET'S PLAY!
MEOW
LET'S PLAY!
LIKE THIS?
YEAH
HMM? WHAT'S THAT?
KLIK
KLIK
KLIK
KLIK

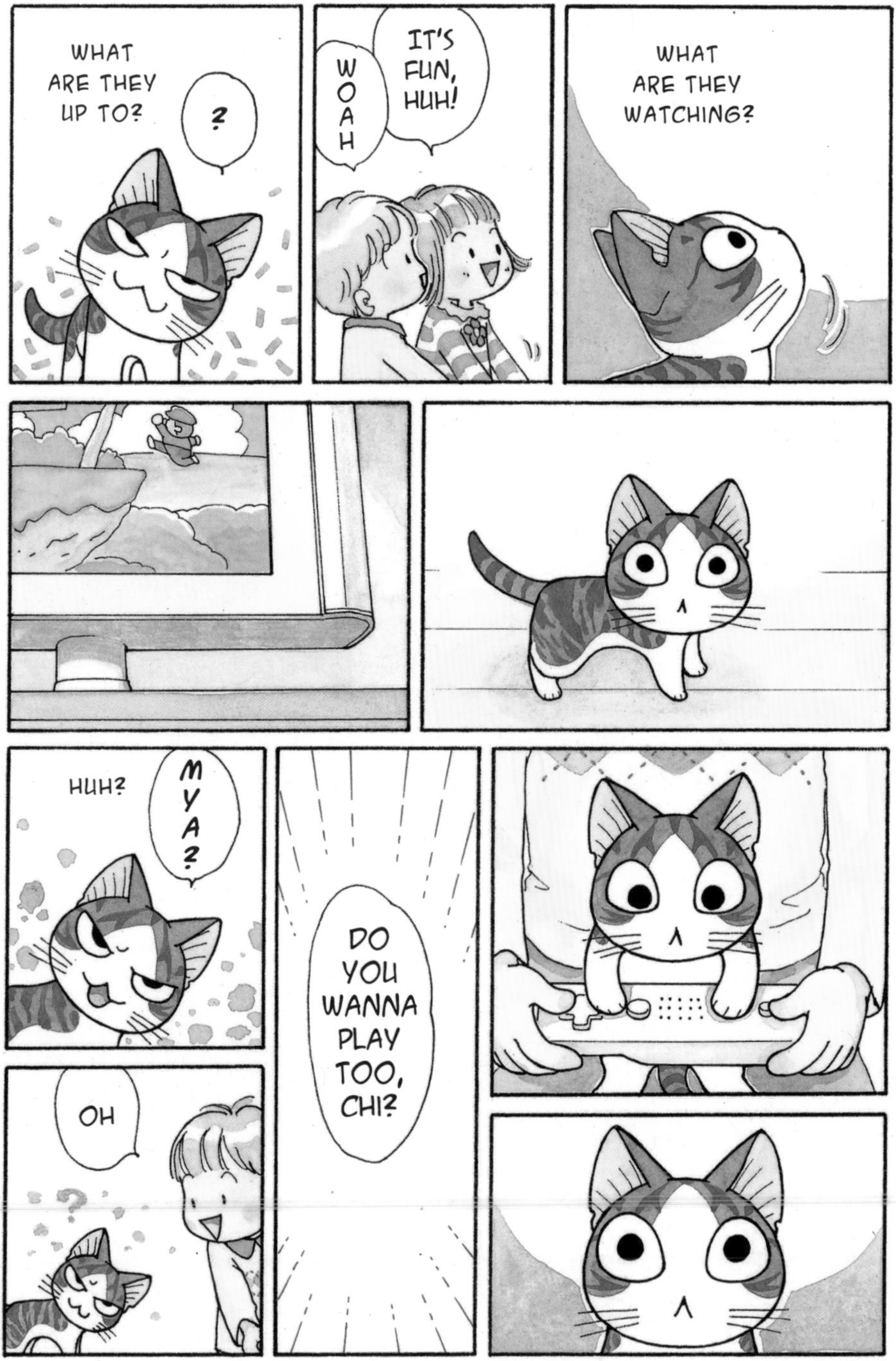
WHAT ARE THEY UP TO?
?
WOAH
IT'S FUN, HUH!
WHAT ARE THEY WATCHING?
HUH?
MYA?
DO YOU WANNA PLAY TOO, CHI?
OH

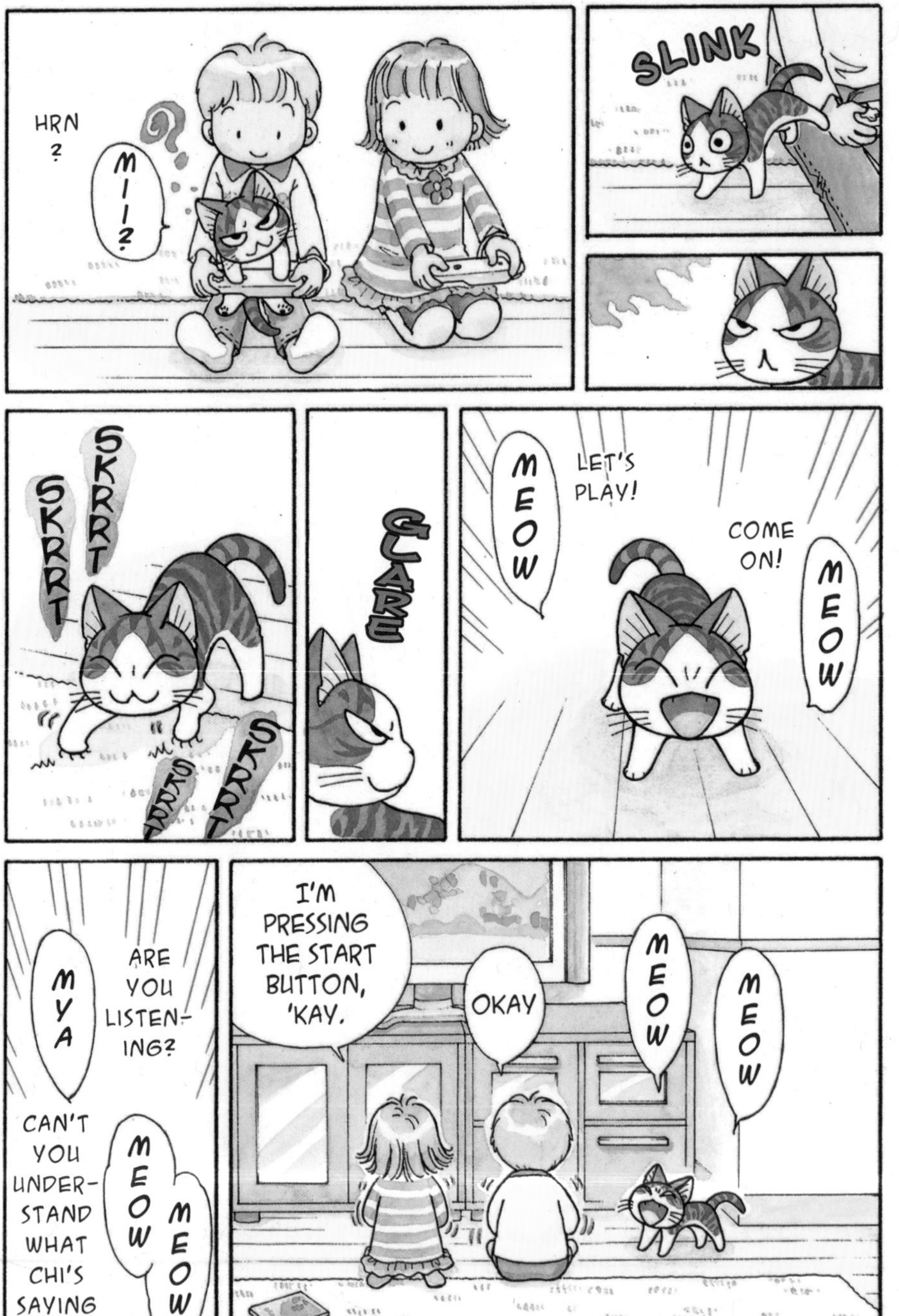
HRN ?
MII?
SLINK
SKRRT
SKRRT
SKRRT
SKRRT
GLARE
MEOW
LET'S PLAY!
COME ON!
MEOW
MYA
ARE YOU LISTEN-ING?
CAN'T YOU UNDER-STAND WHAT CHI'S SAYING ?
MEOW
MEOW
I'M PRESSING THE START BUTTON, 'KAY.
OKAY
MEOW
MEOW

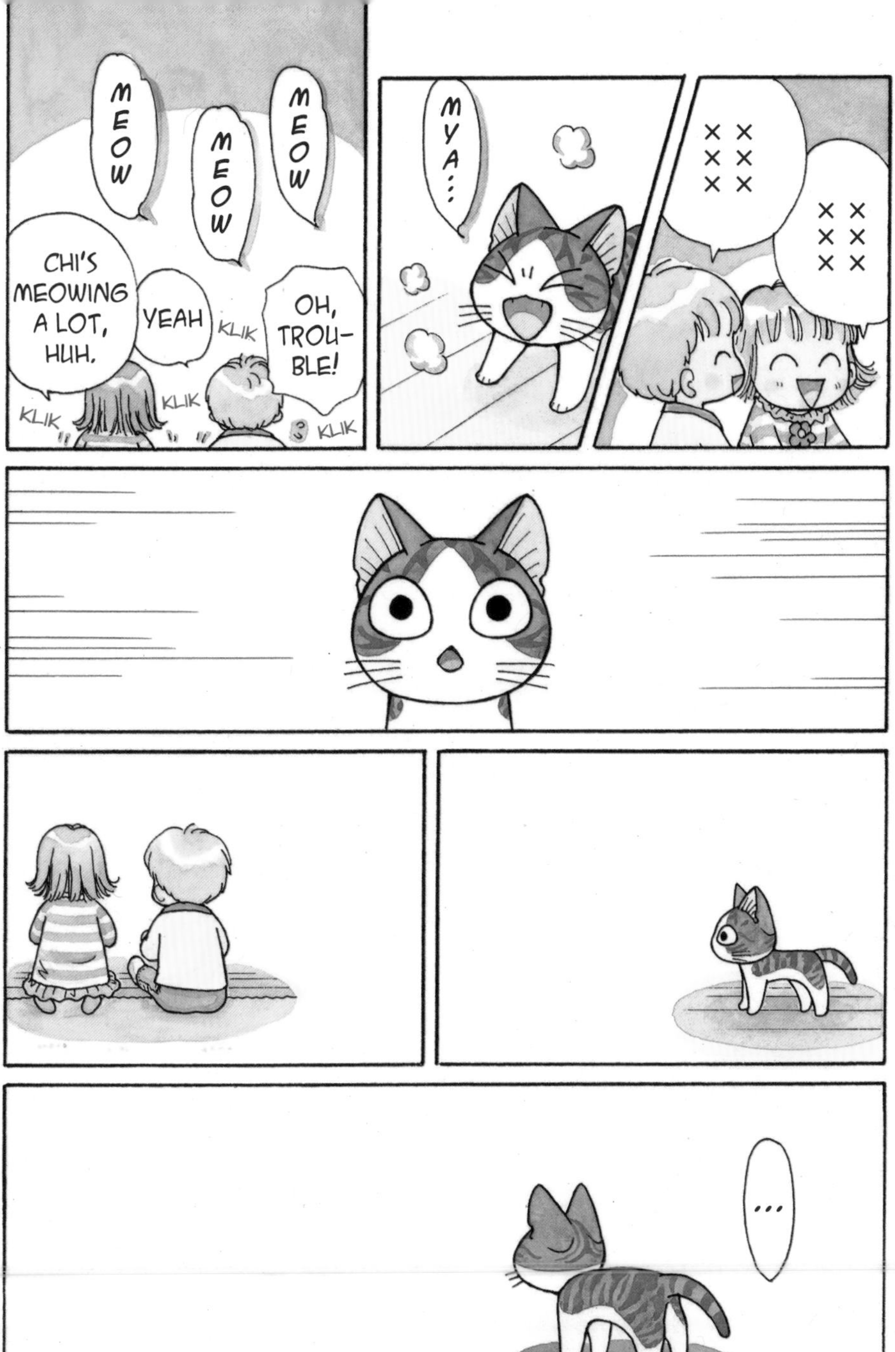
MEOW
MEOW
MEOW
CHI'S MEOWING A LOT, HUH.
YEAH
KLIK
KLIK
KLIK
OH, TROUBLE!
KLIK
MYA...
...

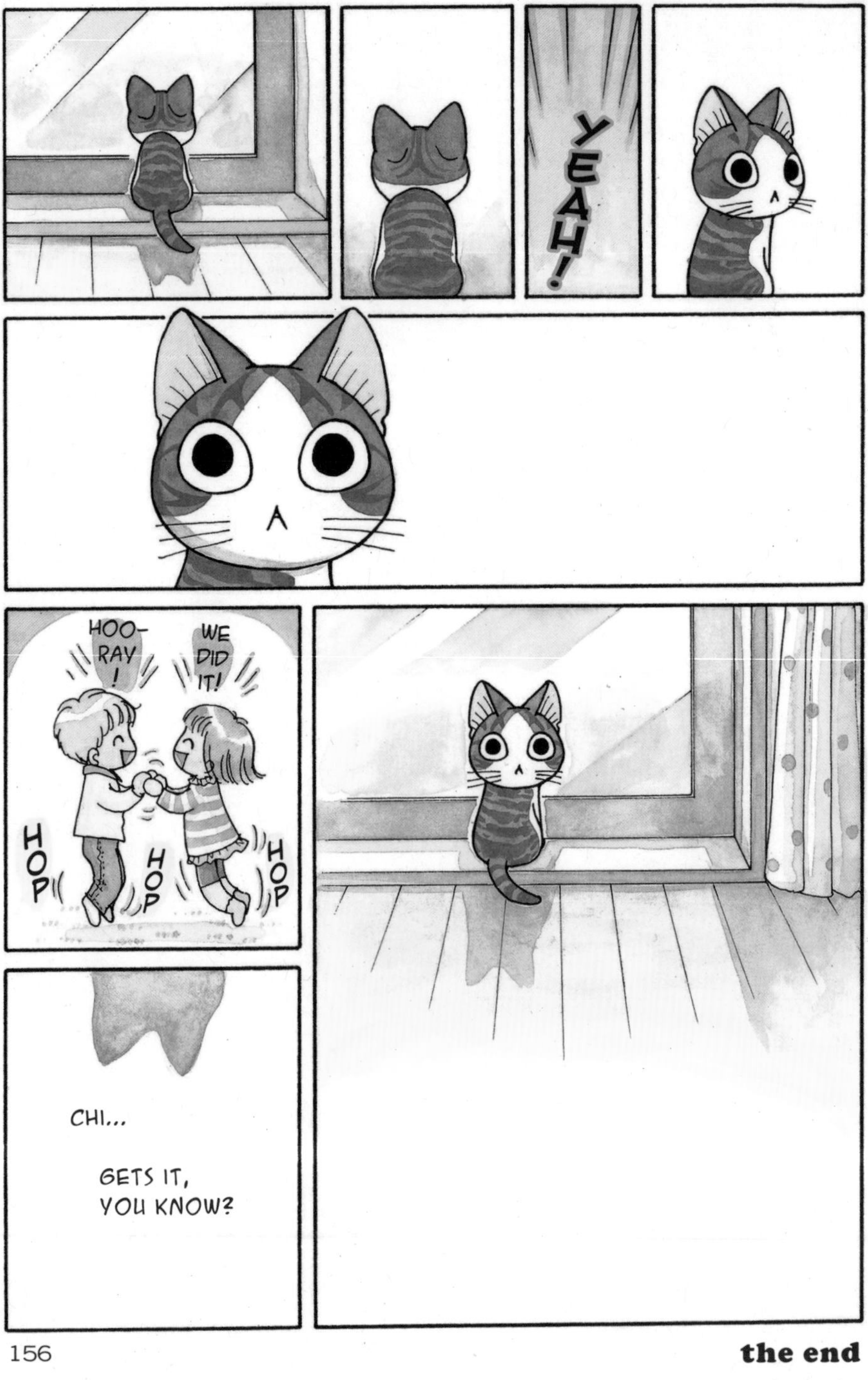
YEAH!
HOO-RAY!
WE DID IT!
HOP
HOP
HOP
HOP
CHI...
GETS IT, YOU KNOW?

the end

homemade 184: a cat is distressed

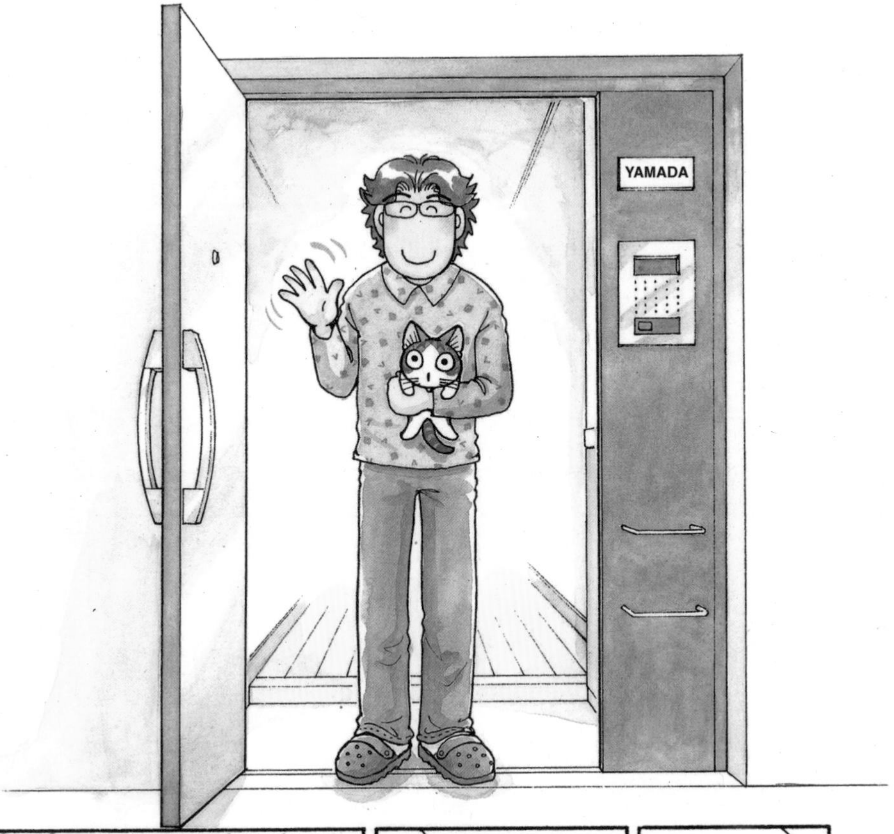
YAMADA

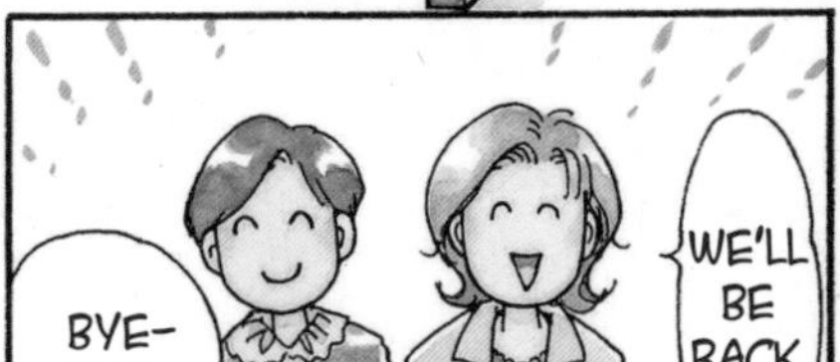
BYE-BYE, UNCLE!
WE'LL BE BACK.

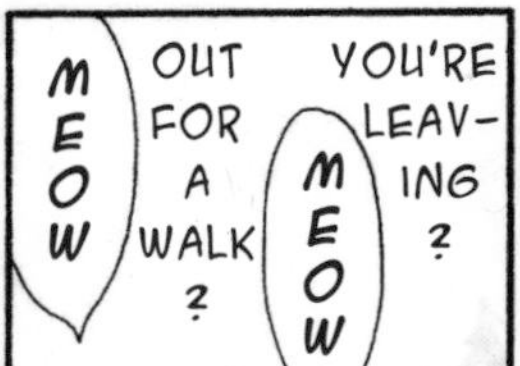
MEOW
OUT FOR A WALK?
MEOW
YOU'RE LEAVING?

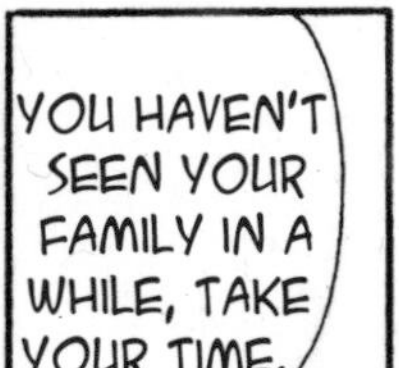
YOU HAVEN'T SEEN YOUR FAMILY IN A WHILE, TAKE YOUR TIME.

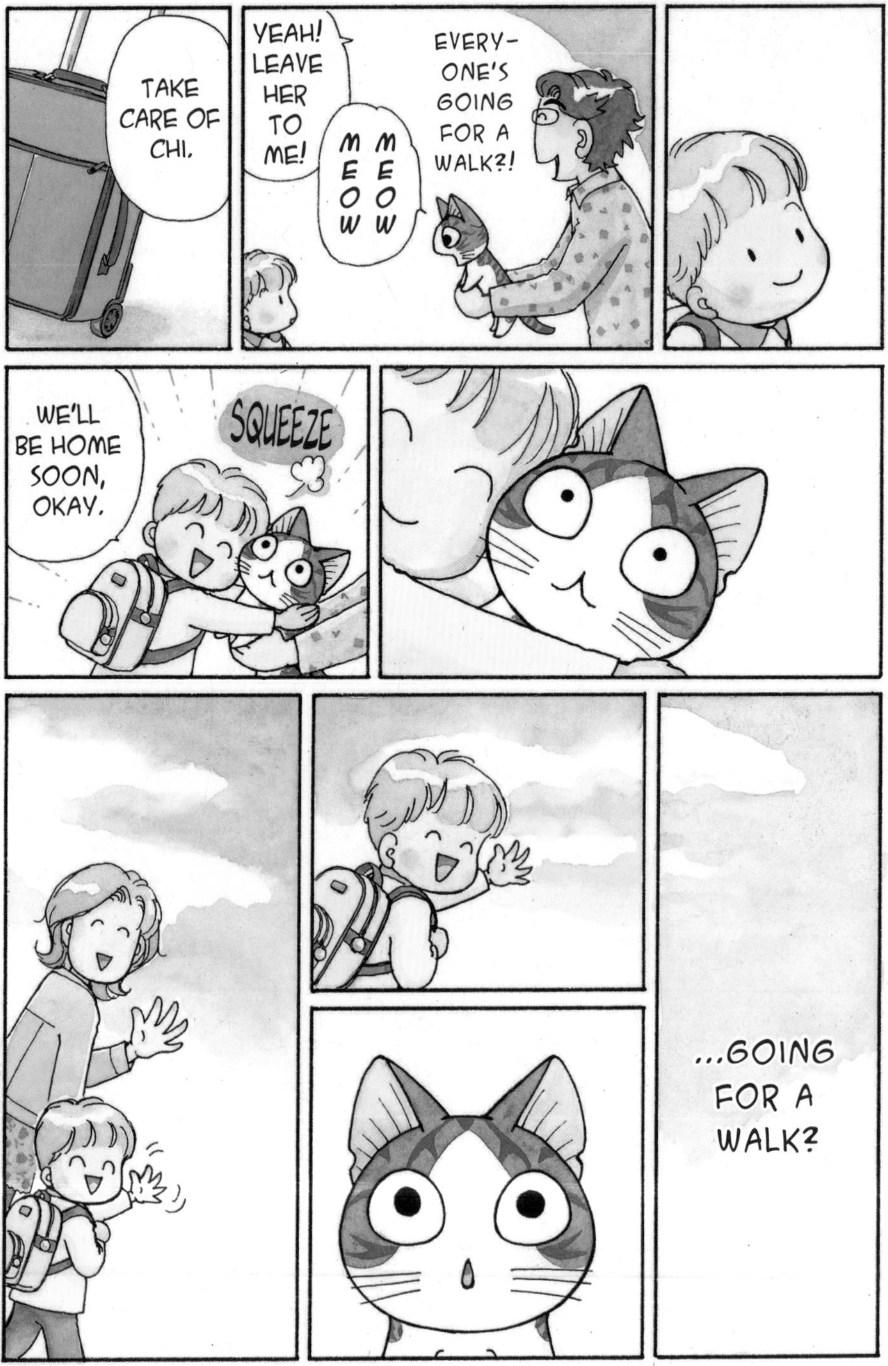
TAKE CARE OF CHI.
YEAH! LEAVE HER TO ME!
MEOW MEOW
EVERY-ONE'S GOING FOR A WALK?!
WE'LL BE HOME SOON, OKAY.
SQUEEZE
...GOING FOR A WALK?

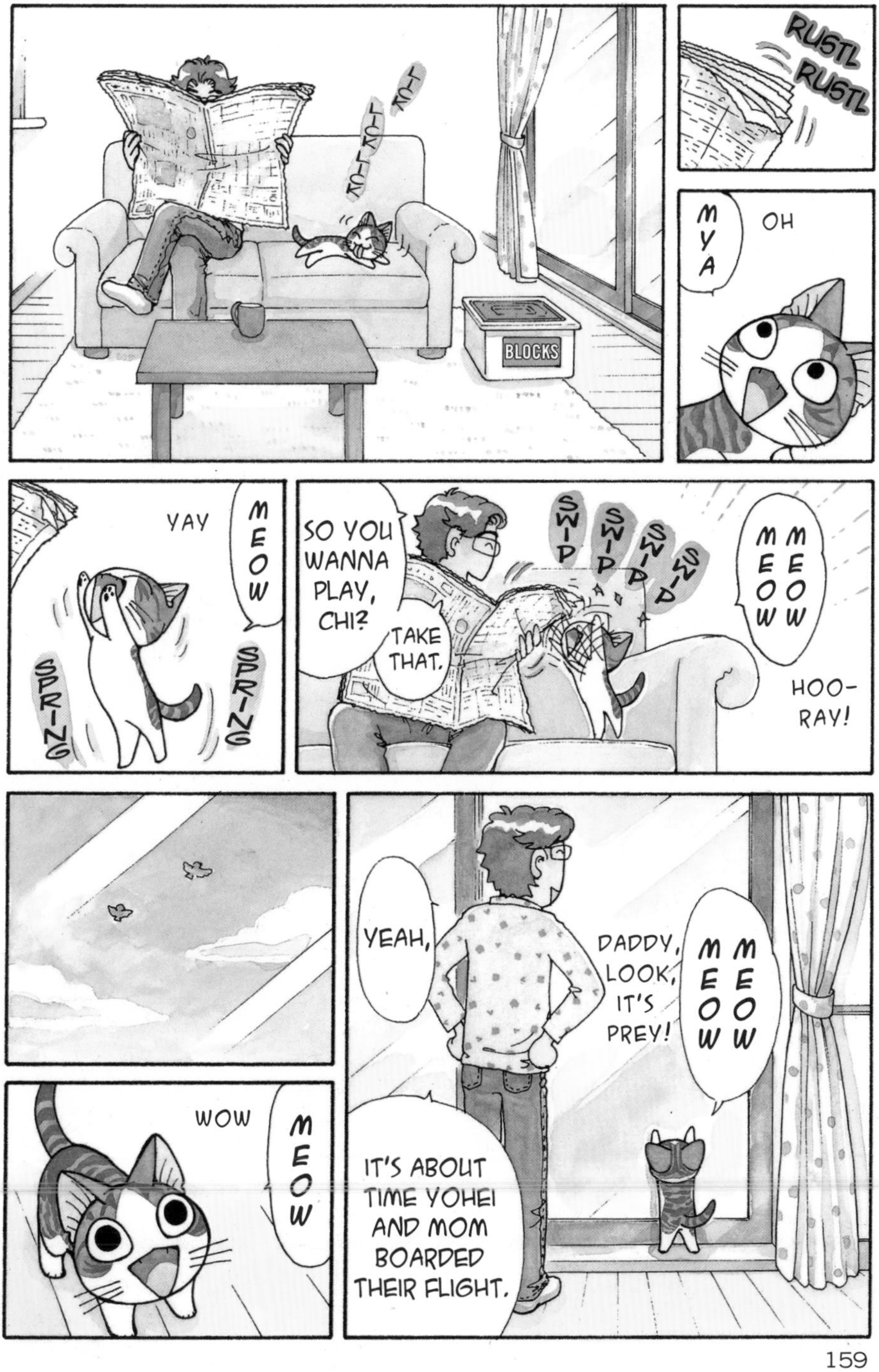
LICK LICK LICK
RUSTL RUSTL
MYA
OH
YAY
MEOW
SPRING SPRING
SO YOU WANNA PLAY, CHI?
TAKE THAT.
SWIP SWIP SWIP SWIP
MEOW MEOW
HOO-RAY!
WOW
MEOW
YEAH,
DADDY, LOOK, IT'S PREY!
MEOW MEOW
IT'S ABOUT TIME YOHEI AND MOM BOARDED THEIR FLIGHT.

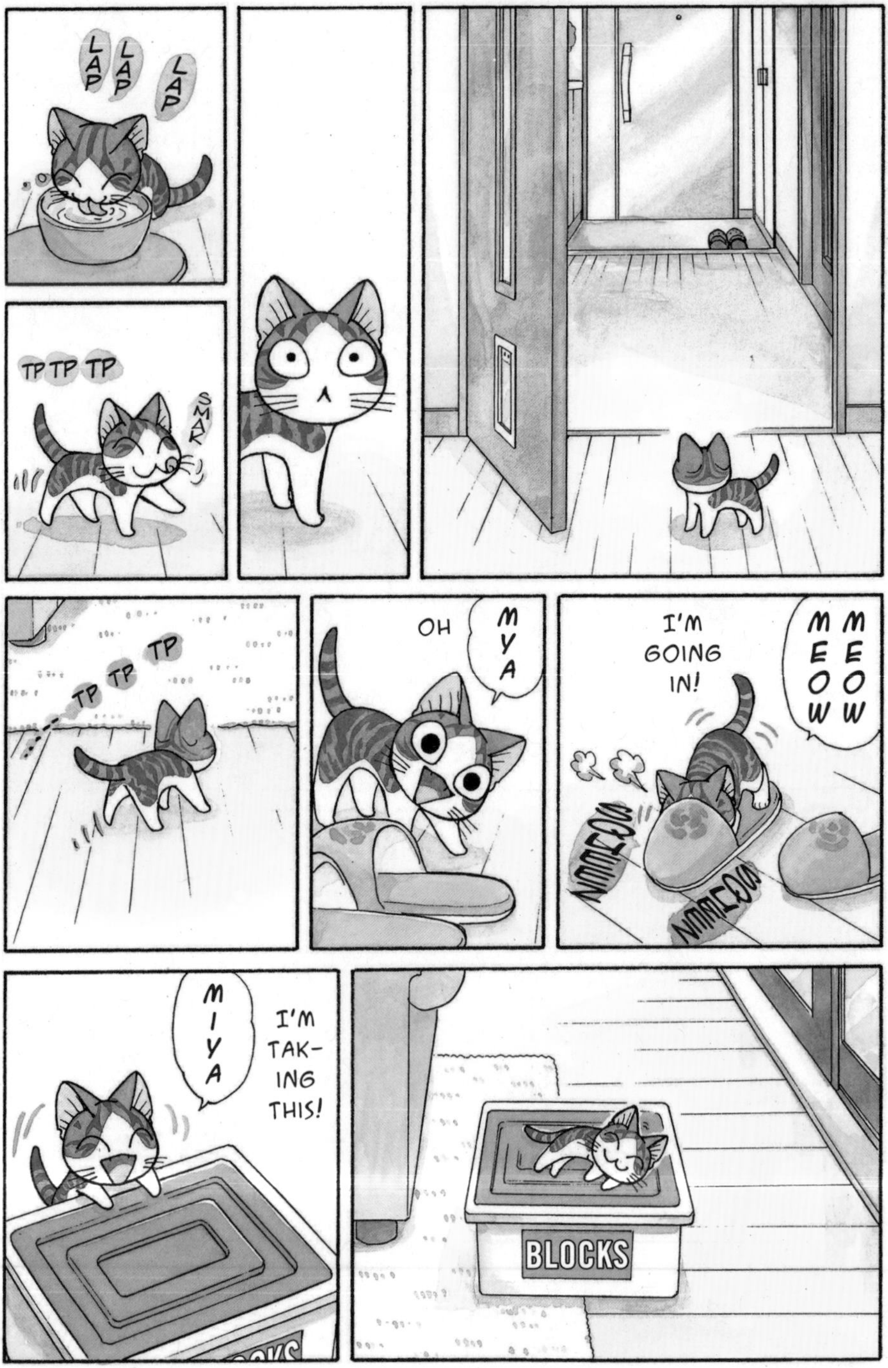
LAP
LAP
LAP
TP TP TP
SMAK
TP
TP
TP
TP
OH
MYA
I'M GOING IN!
MEOW
MEOW
MIYA
I'M TAKING THIS!
BLOCKS

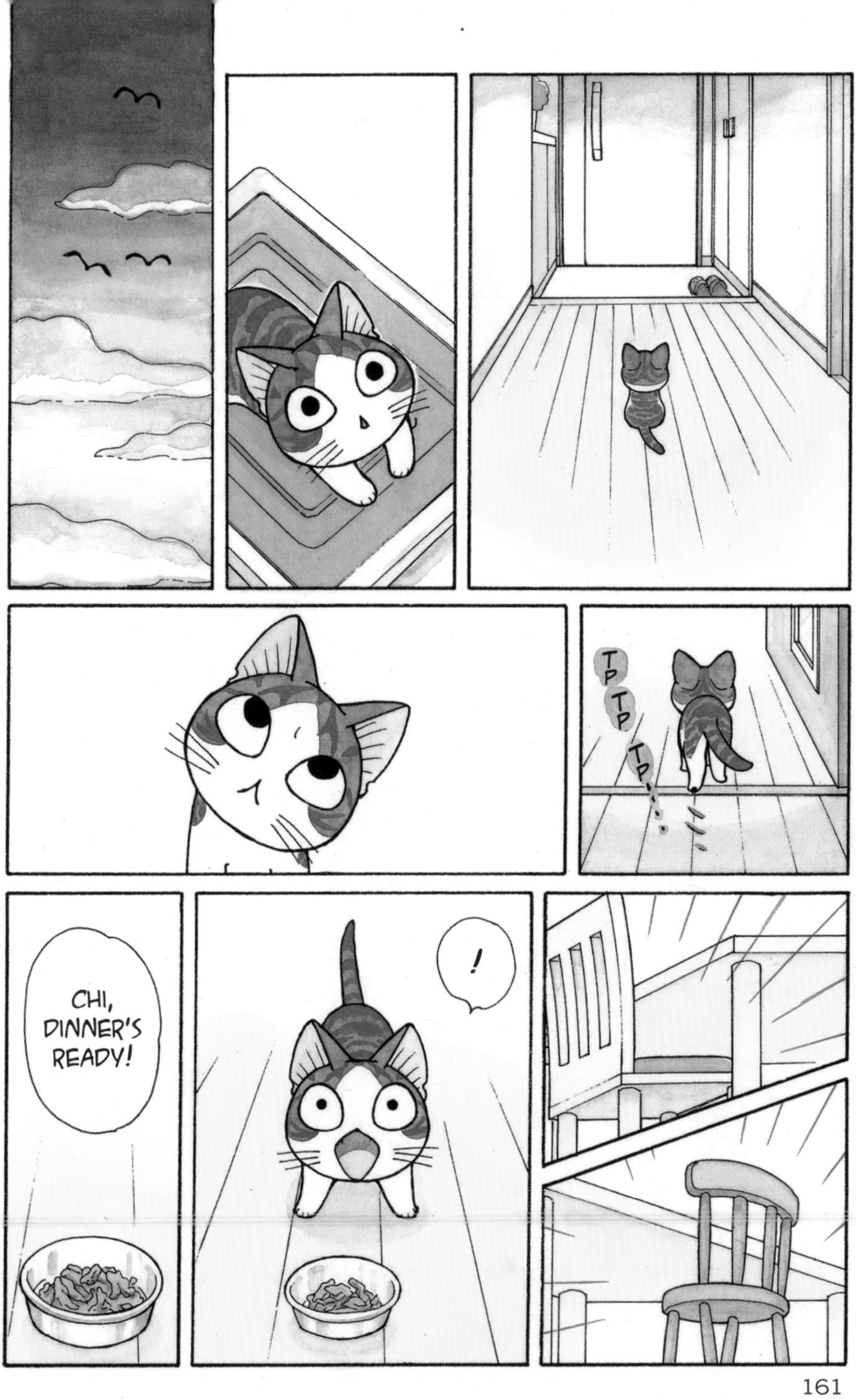
TP TP TP...
CHI, DINNER'S READY!
!

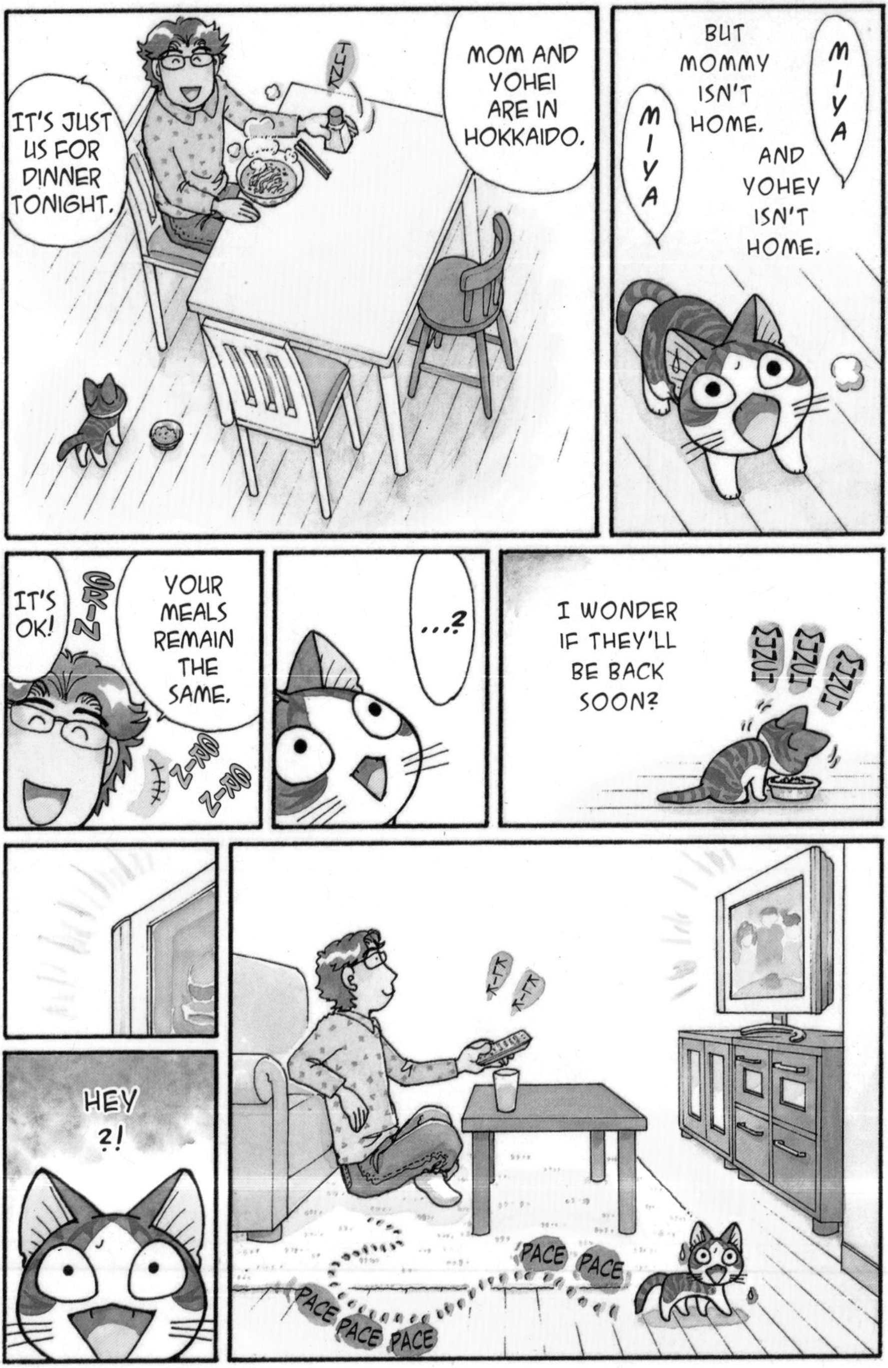
IT'S JUST US FOR DINNER TONIGHT.
TUNK
MOM AND YOHEI ARE IN HOKKAIDO.
BUT MOMMY ISN'T HOME.
MIYA
MIYA
AND YOHEY ISN'T HOME.
IT'S OK!
GRIN
YOUR MEALS REMAIN THE SAME.
Z-RO Z-RO
...?
I WONDER IF THEY'LL BE BACK SOON?
MUNCH MUNCH MUNCH
HEY ?!
KLIK KLIK
PACE PACE
PACE PACE PACE

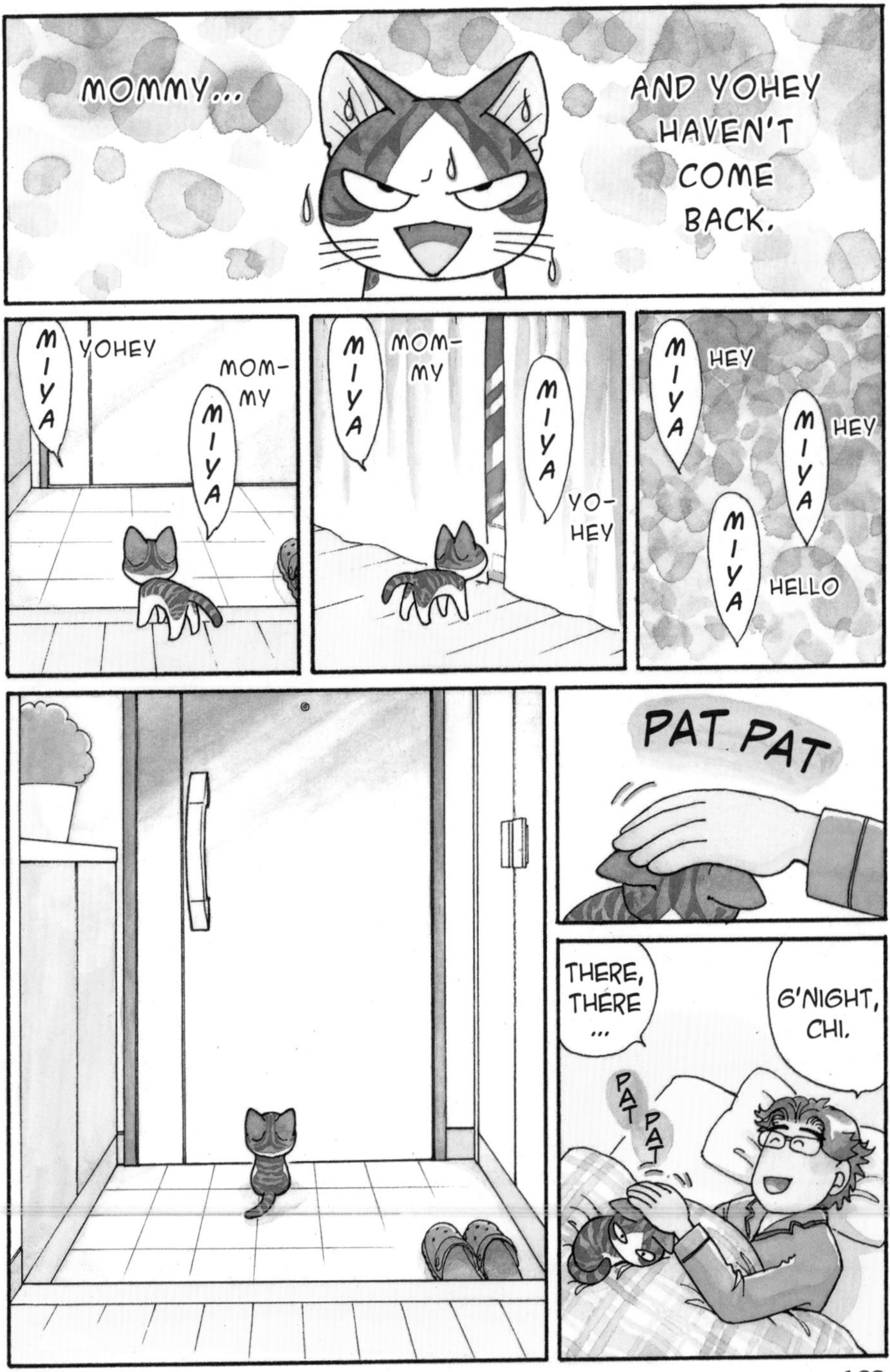
MOMMY...
AND YOHEY HAVEN'T COME BACK.
MIYA
YOHEY
MOM-MY
MIYA
MIYA
MOM-MY
MIYA
YO-HEY
MIYA
HEY
MIYA
HEY
MIYA
HELLO
PAT PAT
THERE, THERE ...
G'NIGHT, CHI.
PAT PAT

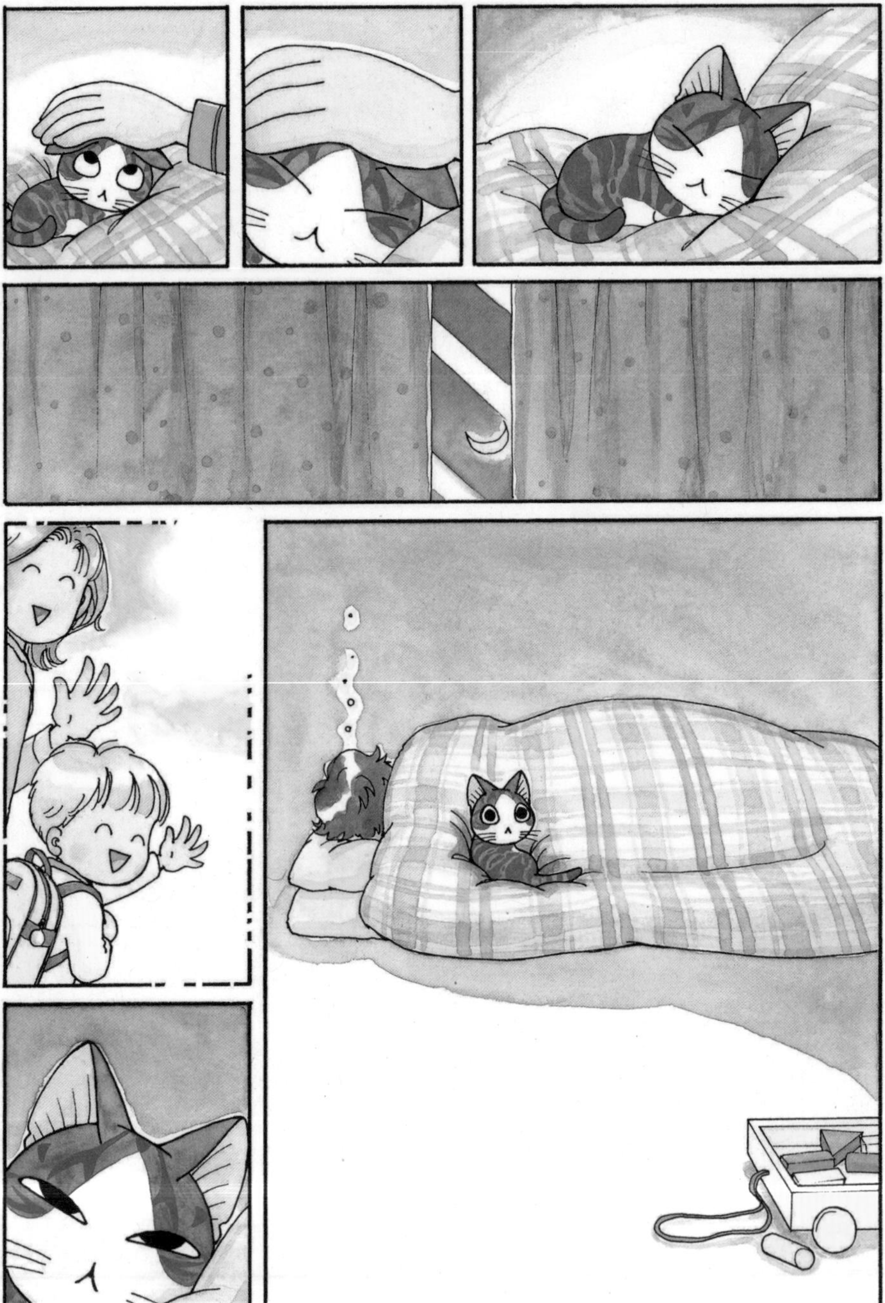

the end

homemade 185: a cat is feeling gloomy

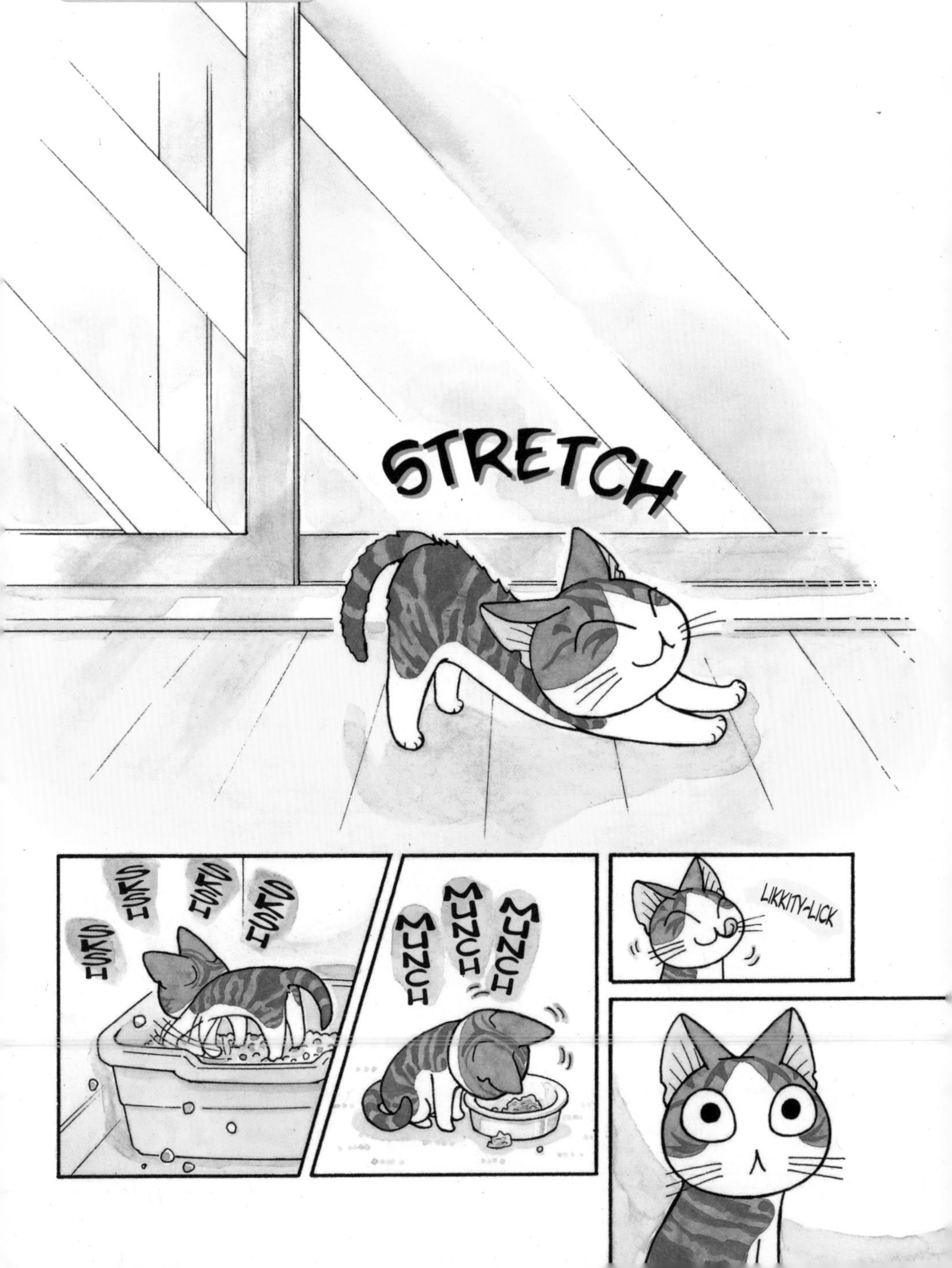
STRETCH
SKSH
SKSH
SKSH
SKSH
MUNCH
MUNCH
MUNCH
LIKKITY-LICK

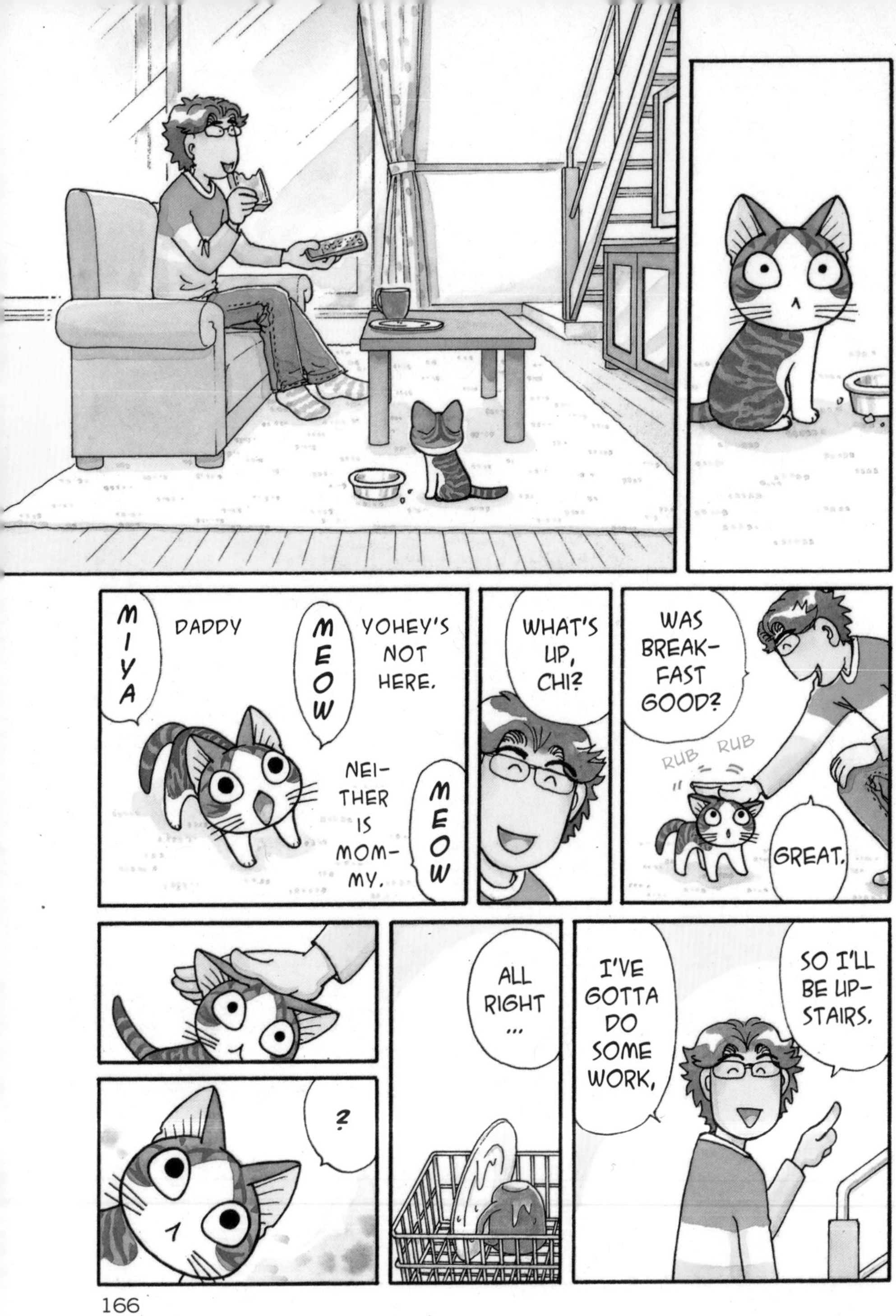
MIYA
DADDY
MEOW
YOHEY'S NOT HERE.
NEI-THER IS MOM-MY.
MEOW
WHAT'S UP, CHI?
WAS BREAK-FAST GOOD?
RUB RUB
GREAT.
?
ALL RIGHT ...
I'VE GOTTA DO SOME WORK,
SO I'LL BE UP-STAIRS.

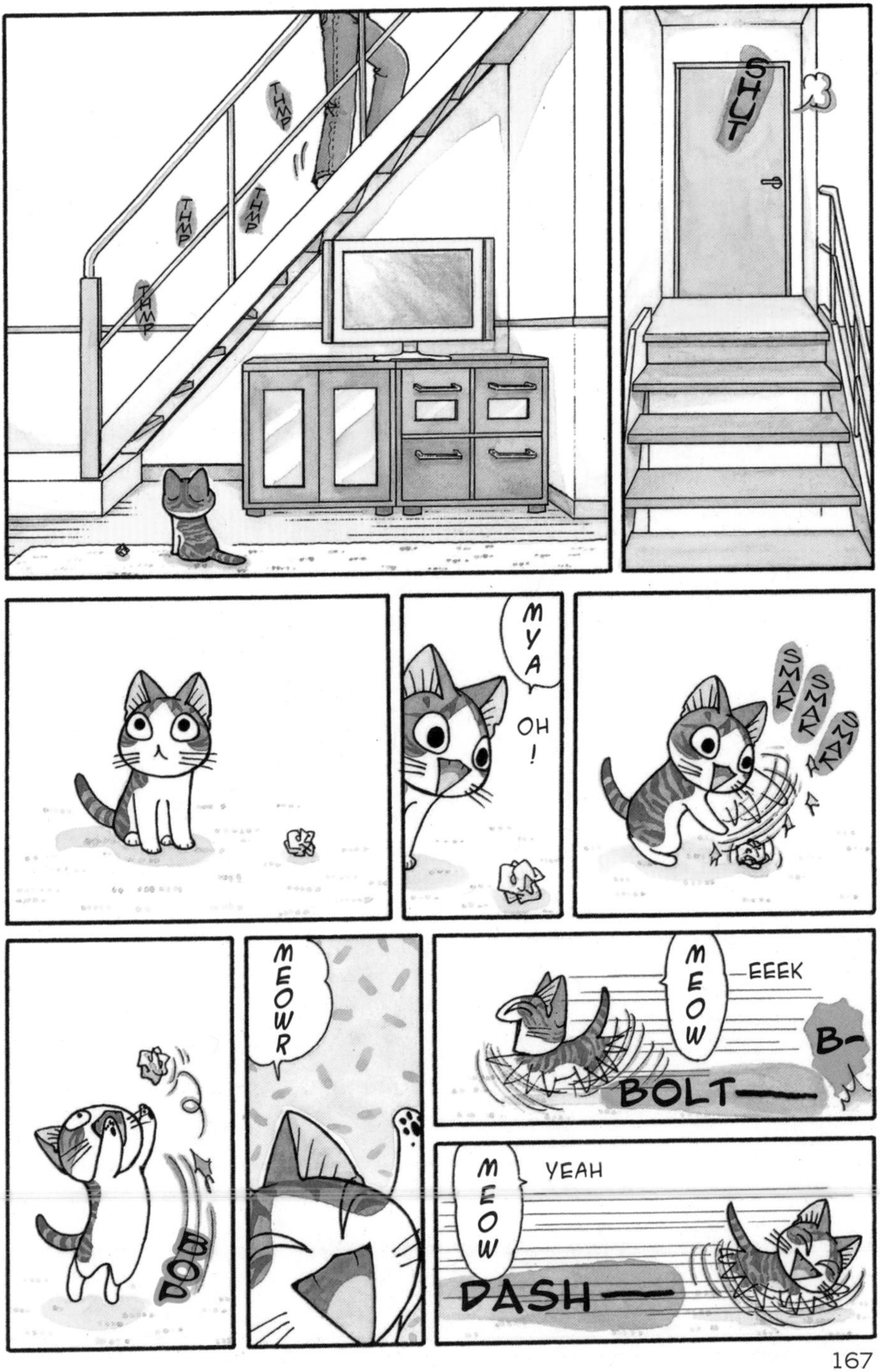
THMP
THMP
THMP
THMP
SHUT
MYA
OH!
SMAK
SMAK
SMAK
BOP
MEOWR
MEOW
EEEK
B-
BOLT——
MEOW
YEAH
DASH——

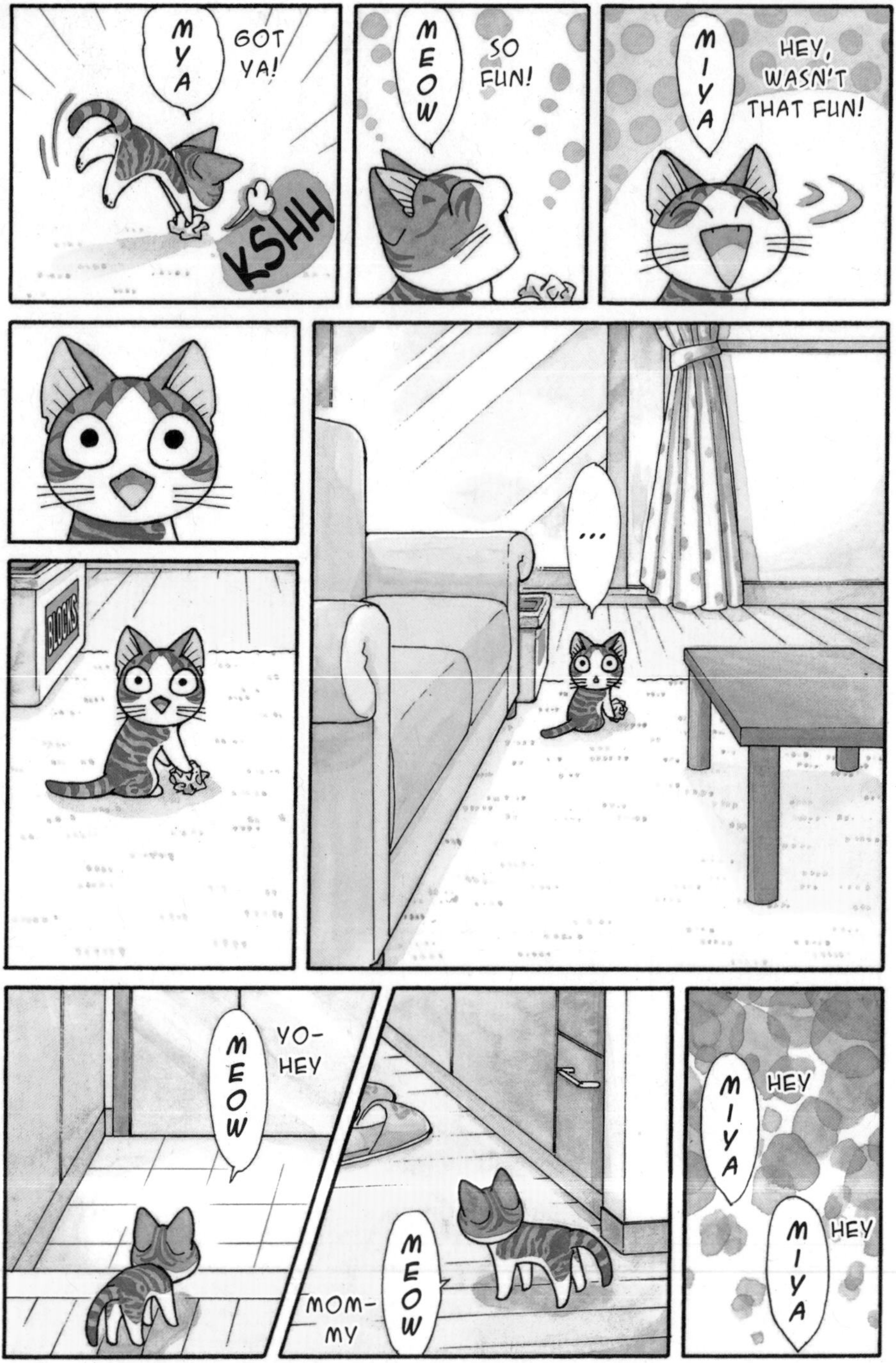

MYA
GOT YA!
KSHH
MEOW
SO FUN!
MIYA
HEY, WASN'T THAT FUN!
BLOCKS
...
MEOW
YO-HEY
MEOW
MOM-MY
MIYA
HEY
MIYA
HEY

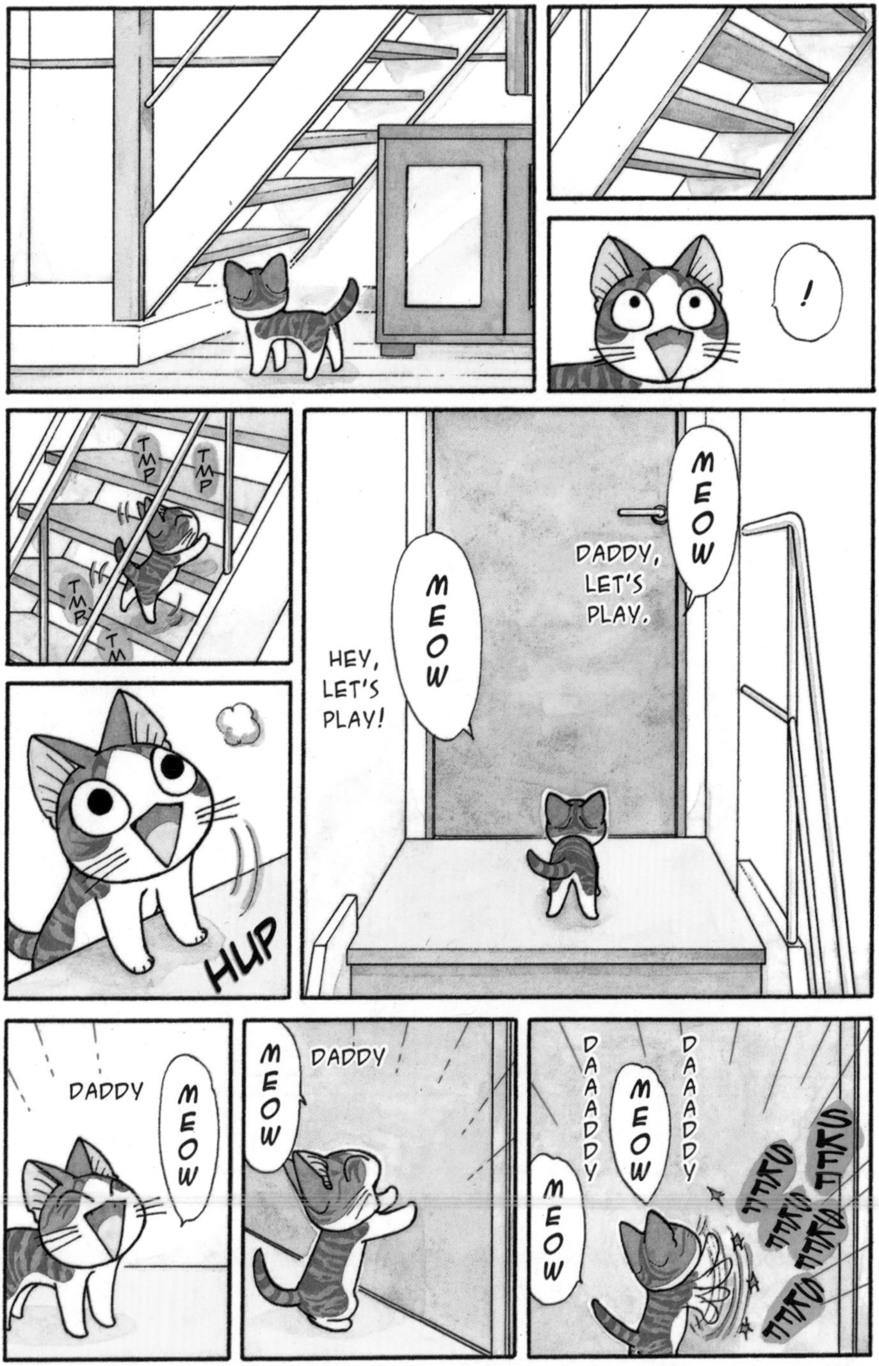
!
TMP
TMP
TMR
TM
HUP
MEOW
DADDY, LET'S PLAY.
MEOW
HEY, LET'S PLAY!
DADDY
MEOW
MEOW
DADDY
DAAAADDY
MEOW
MEOW
DAAAADDY

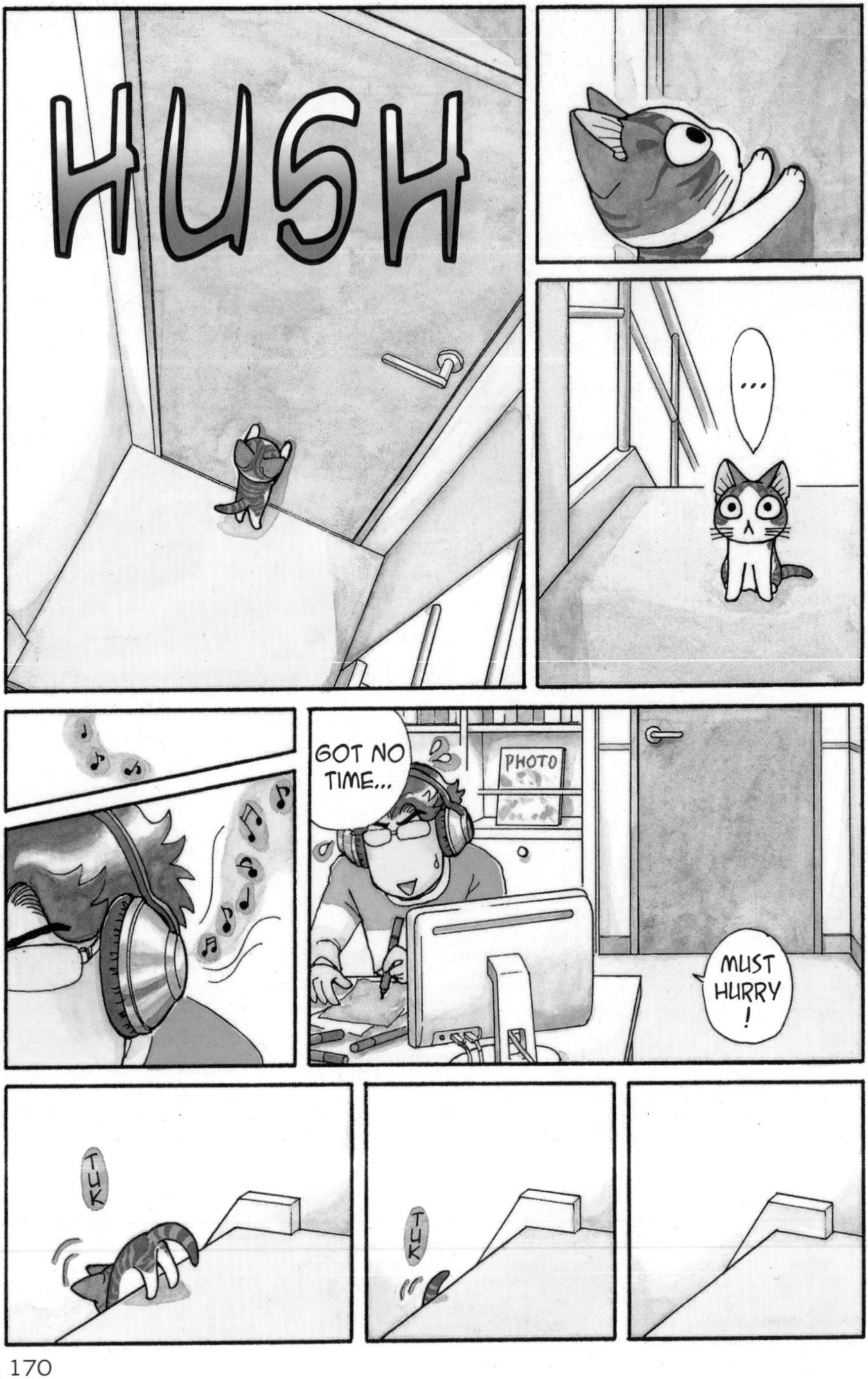
HUSH
...
GOT NO TIME...
MUST HURRY!
TUK
TUK

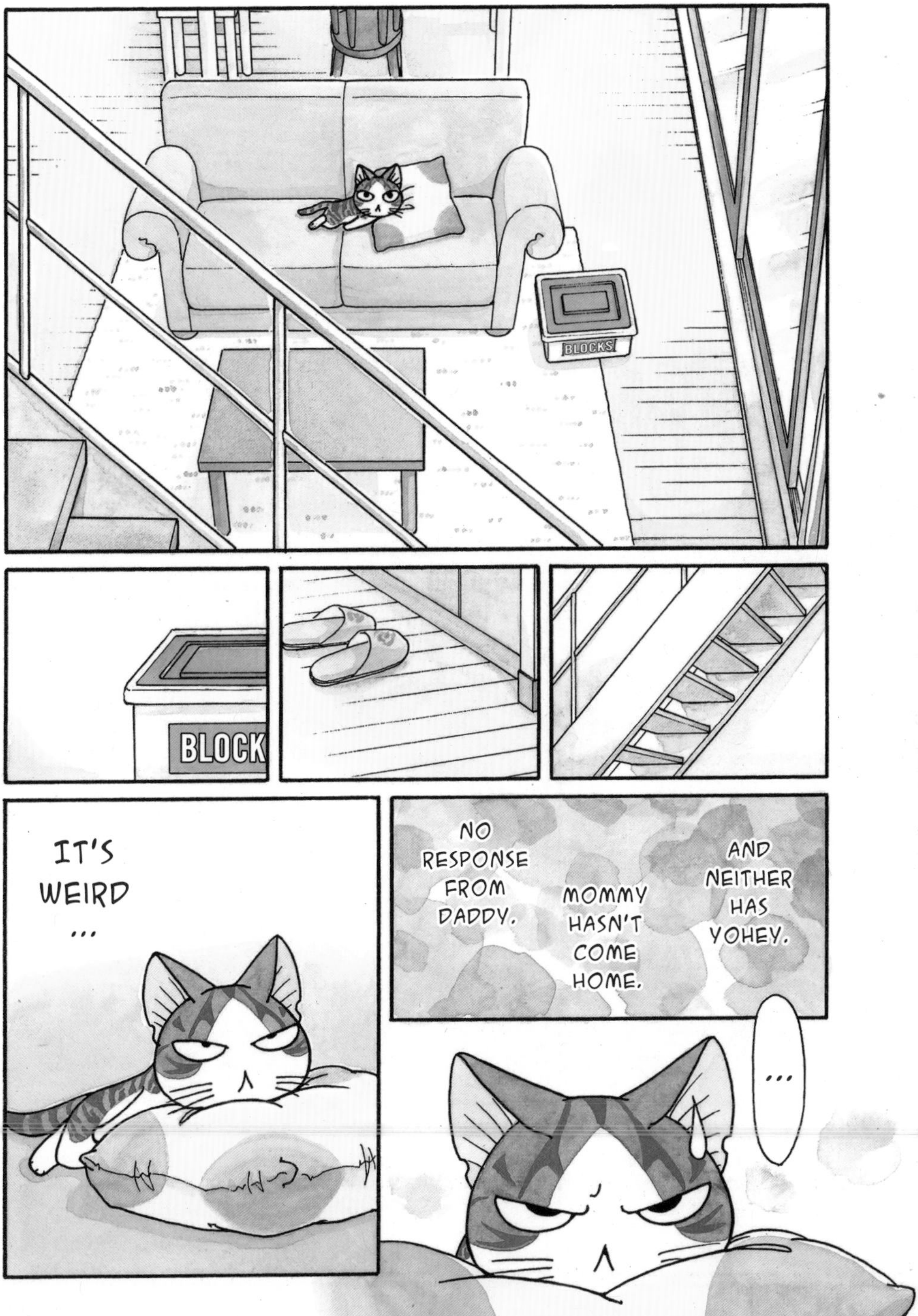
BLOCKS
BLOCK
IT'S WEIRD ...
NO RESPONSE FROM DADDY.
MOMMY HASN'T COME HOME.
AND NEITHER HAS YOHEY.
...

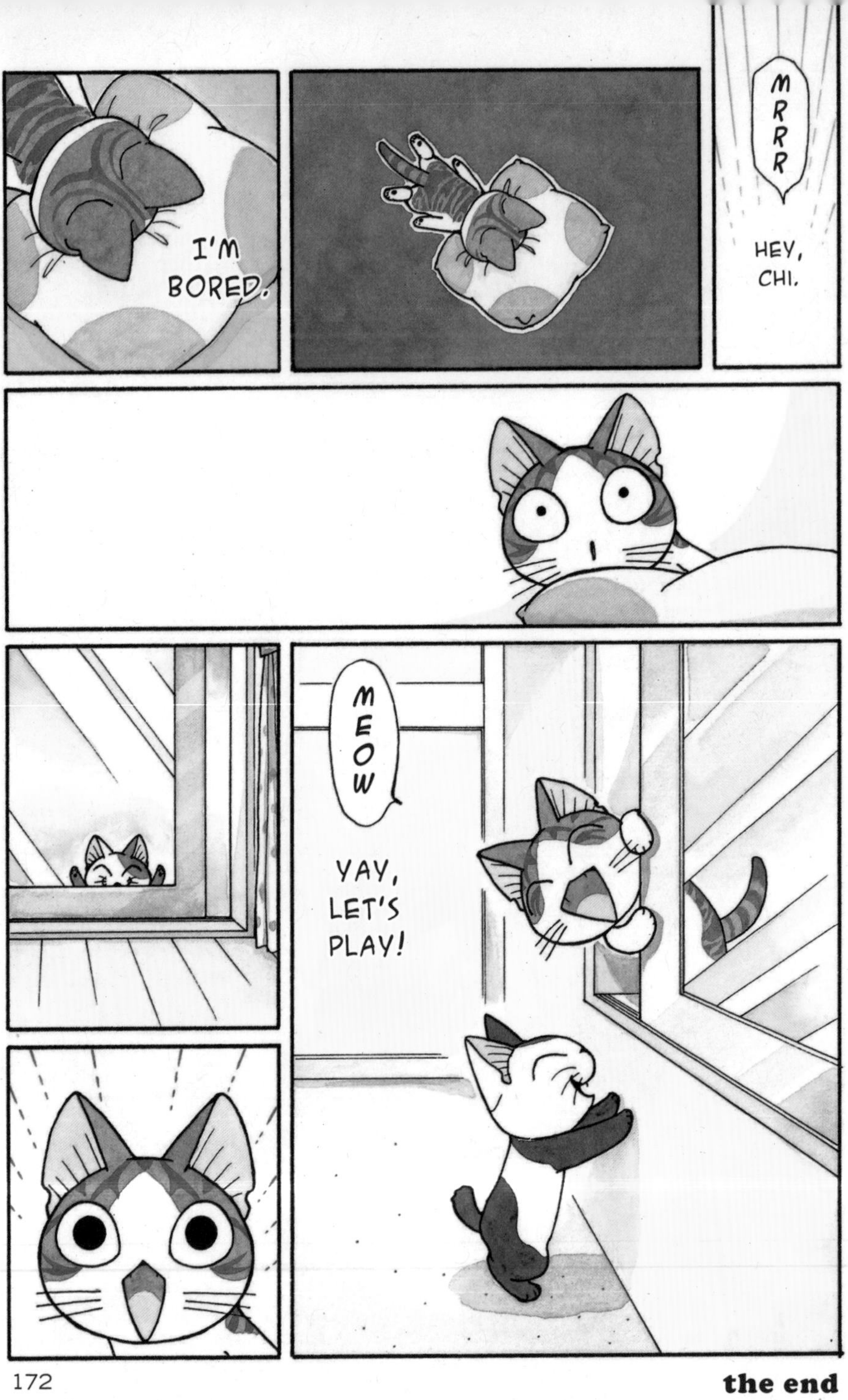
I'M BORED.
MRRR
HEY, CHI.
MEOW
YAY, LET'S PLAY!

the end

homemade 186: a cat receives a shock

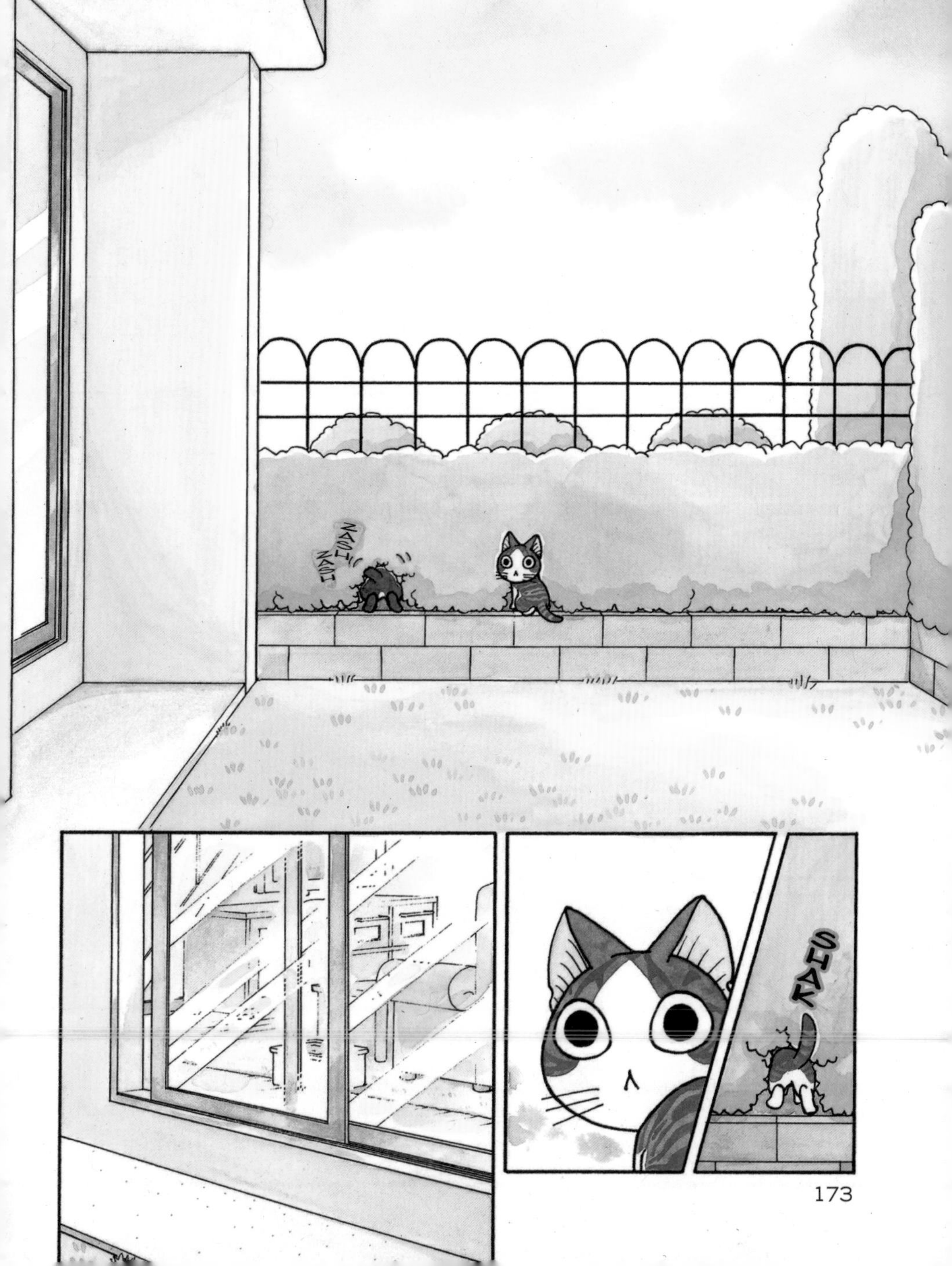
ZASH
ZASH
SHAK

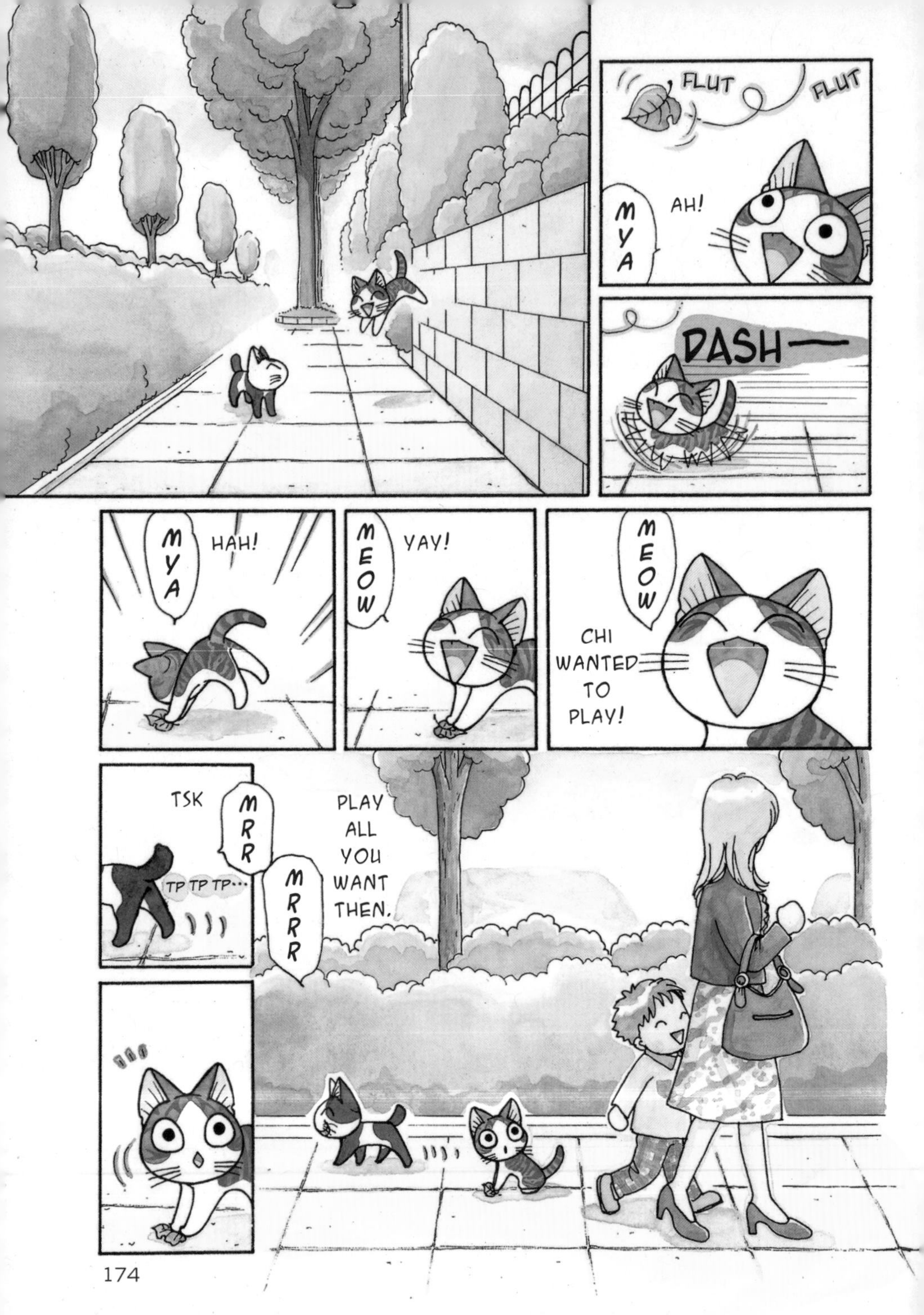
FLUT
FLUT
MYA
AH!
DASH—
MYA
HAH!
MEOW
YAY!
MEOW
CHI WANTED TO PLAY!
TSK
MRR
TP TP TP...
MRRR
PLAY ALL YOU WANT THEN.

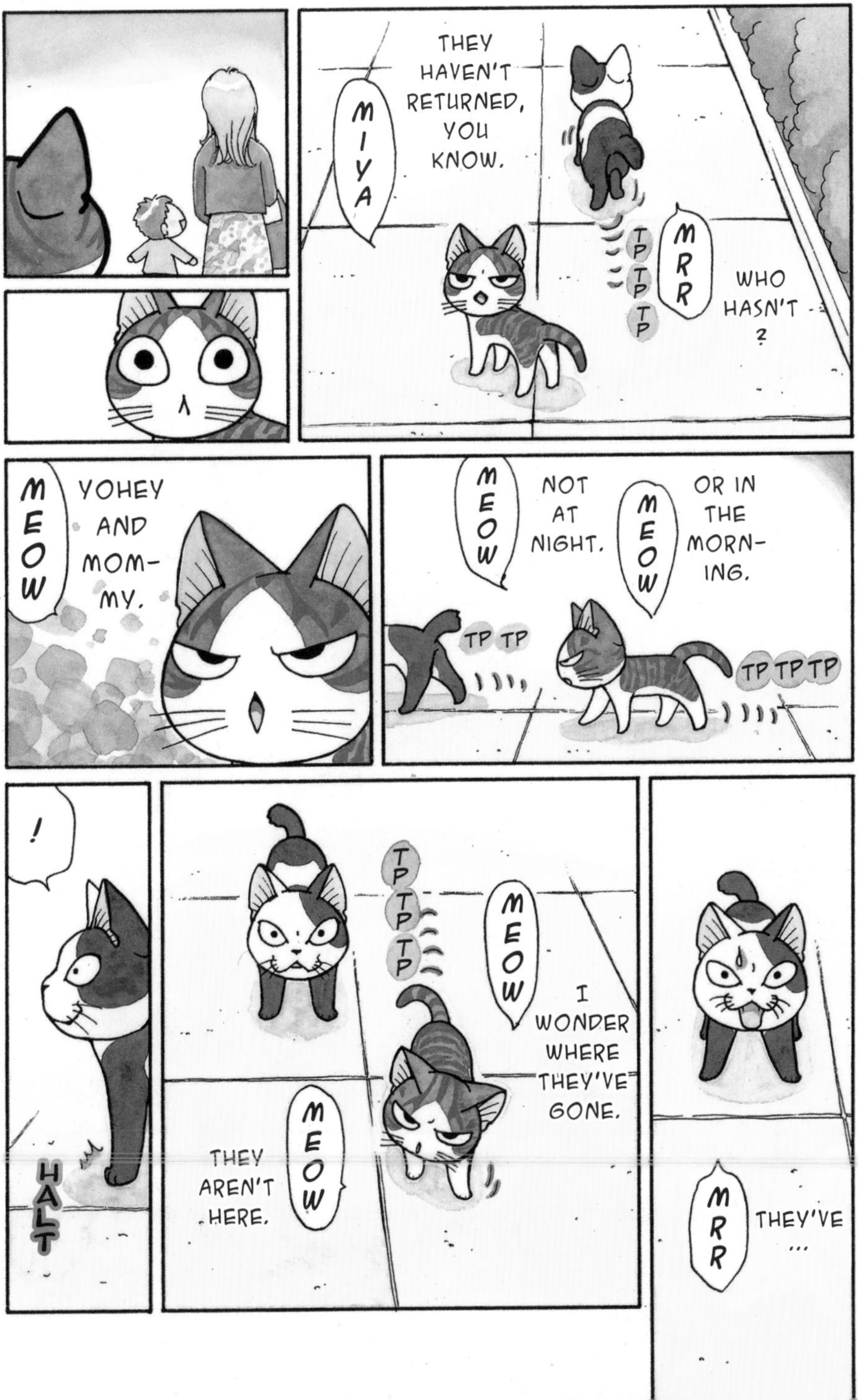
MIYA
THEY HAVEN'T RETURNED, YOU KNOW.
TP TP TP TP
MRR
WHO HASN'T?
MEOW
YOHEY AND MOM-MY.
MEOW
NOT AT NIGHT.
MEOW
OR IN THE MORN-ING.
TP TP
TP TP TP
!
HALT
TP TP TP TP
MEOW
I WONDER WHERE THEY'VE GONE.
MEOW
THEY AREN'T HERE.
MRR
THEY'VE ...

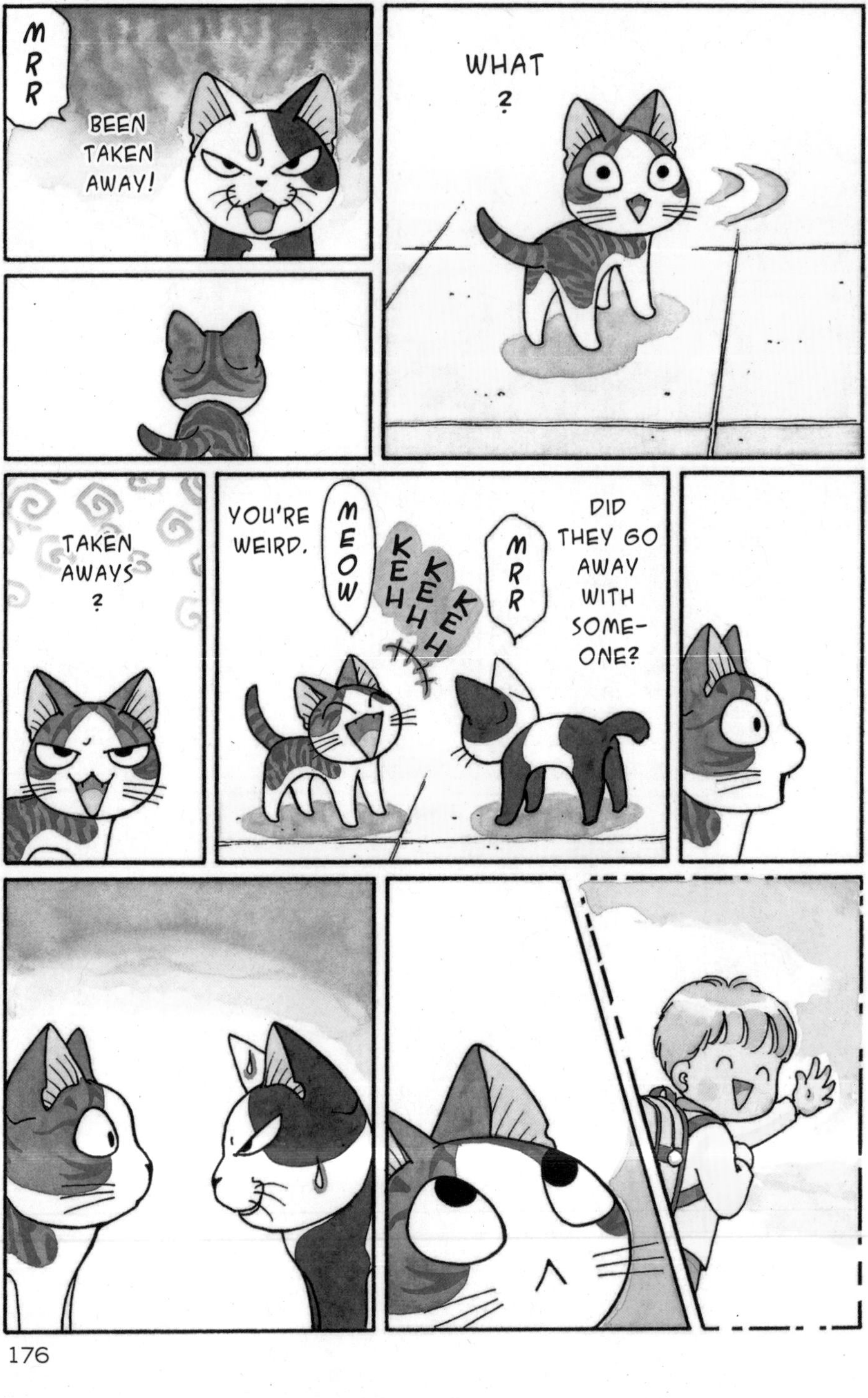
MRR
BEEN TAKEN AWAY!
WHAT?
TAKEN AWAYS?
YOU'RE WEIRD.
MEOW
KEH KEH KEH
MRR
DID THEY GO AWAY WITH SOME-ONE?

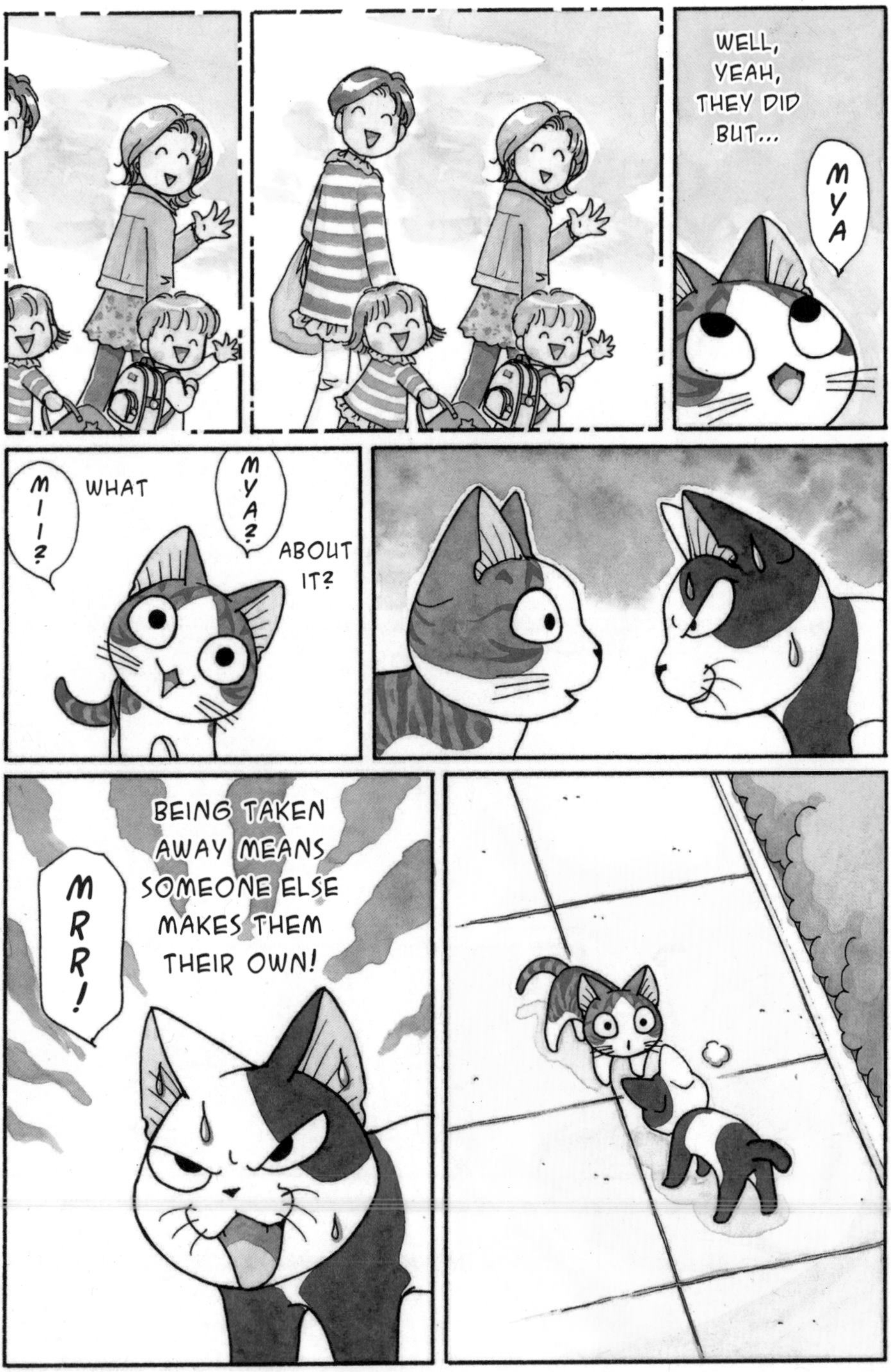
WELL, YEAH, THEY DID BUT...
MYA
MII?
WHAT
MYA?
ABOUT IT?
BEING TAKEN AWAY MEANS SOMEONE ELSE MAKES THEM THEIR OWN!
MRR!

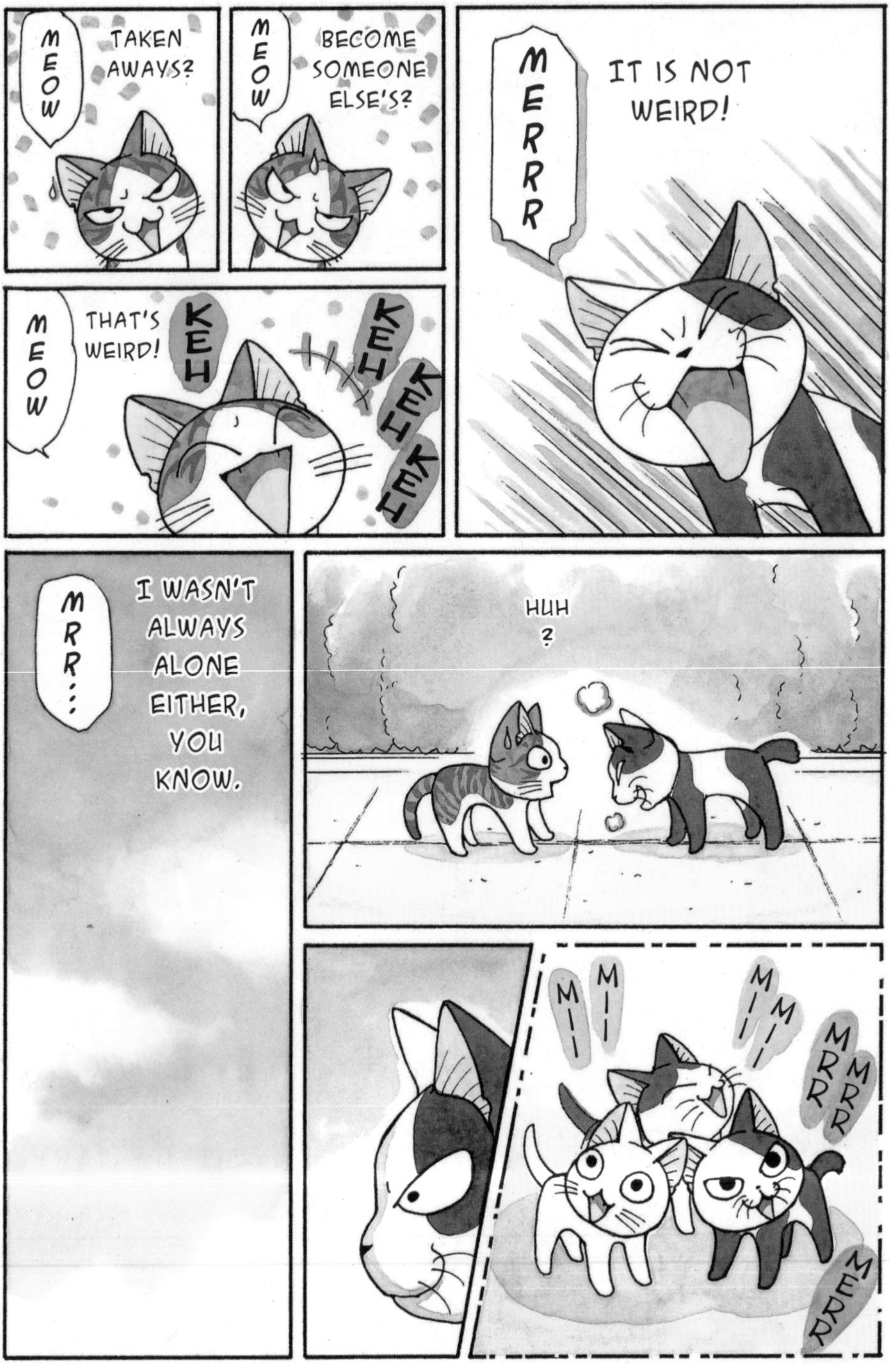
MEOW
TAKEN AWAYS?
MEOW
BECOME SOMEONE ELSE'S?
MERRR
IT IS NOT WEIRD!
MEOW
THAT'S WEIRD!
KEH KEH KEH KEH
MRR...
I WASN'T ALWAYS ALONE EITHER, YOU KNOW.
HUH?
MI MI
MI MI
MRR MRR
MERR

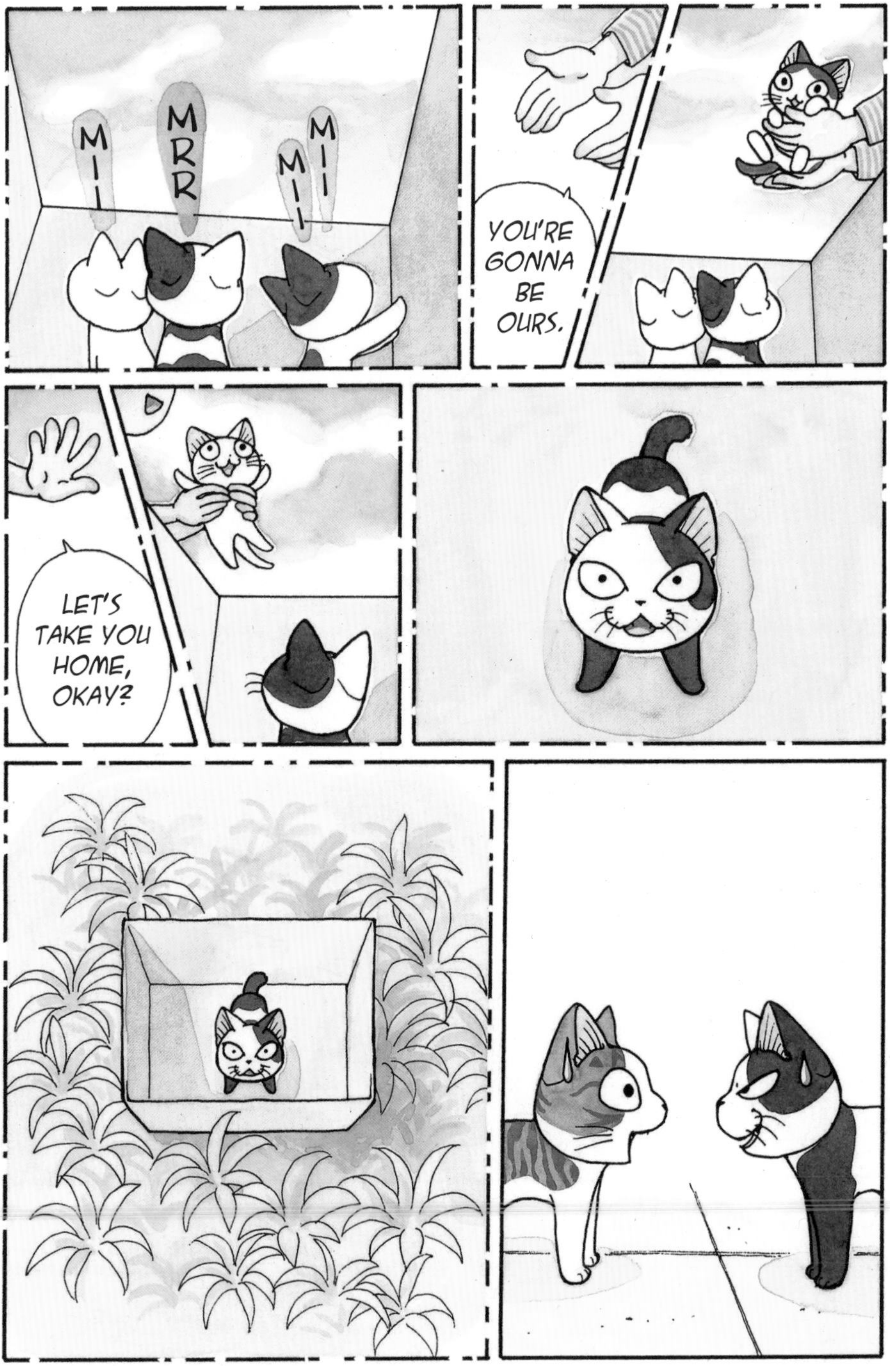
MI
MRR
MI
MI
YOU'RE GONNA BE OURS.
LET'S TAKE YOU HOME, OKAY?

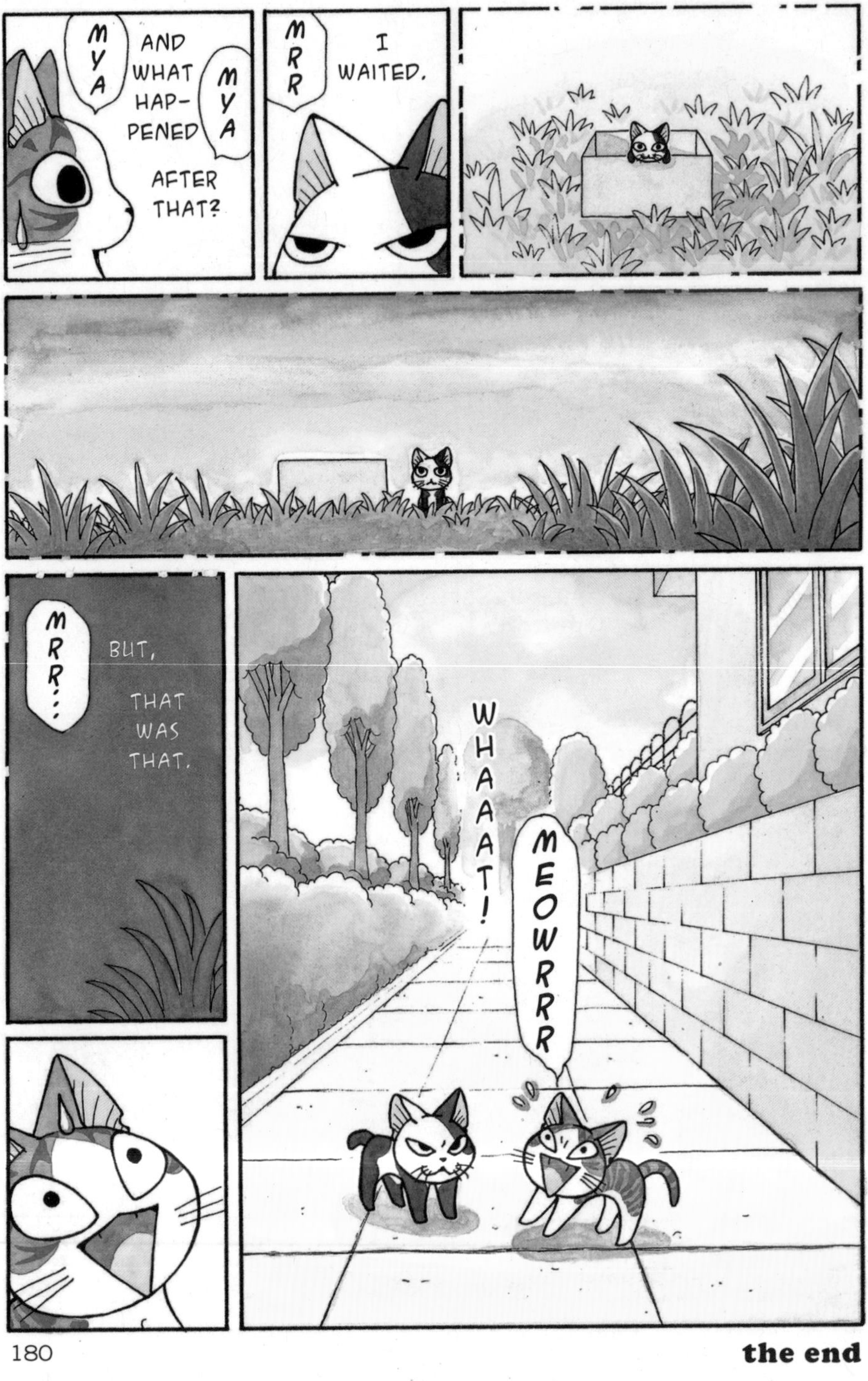
MYA
AND WHAT HAP-PENED AFTER THAT?
MYA
MRR
I WAITED.
MRR...
BUT, THAT WAS THAT.
WHAAAAT!
MEOWRRR

the end

homemade 187: a cat is in denial

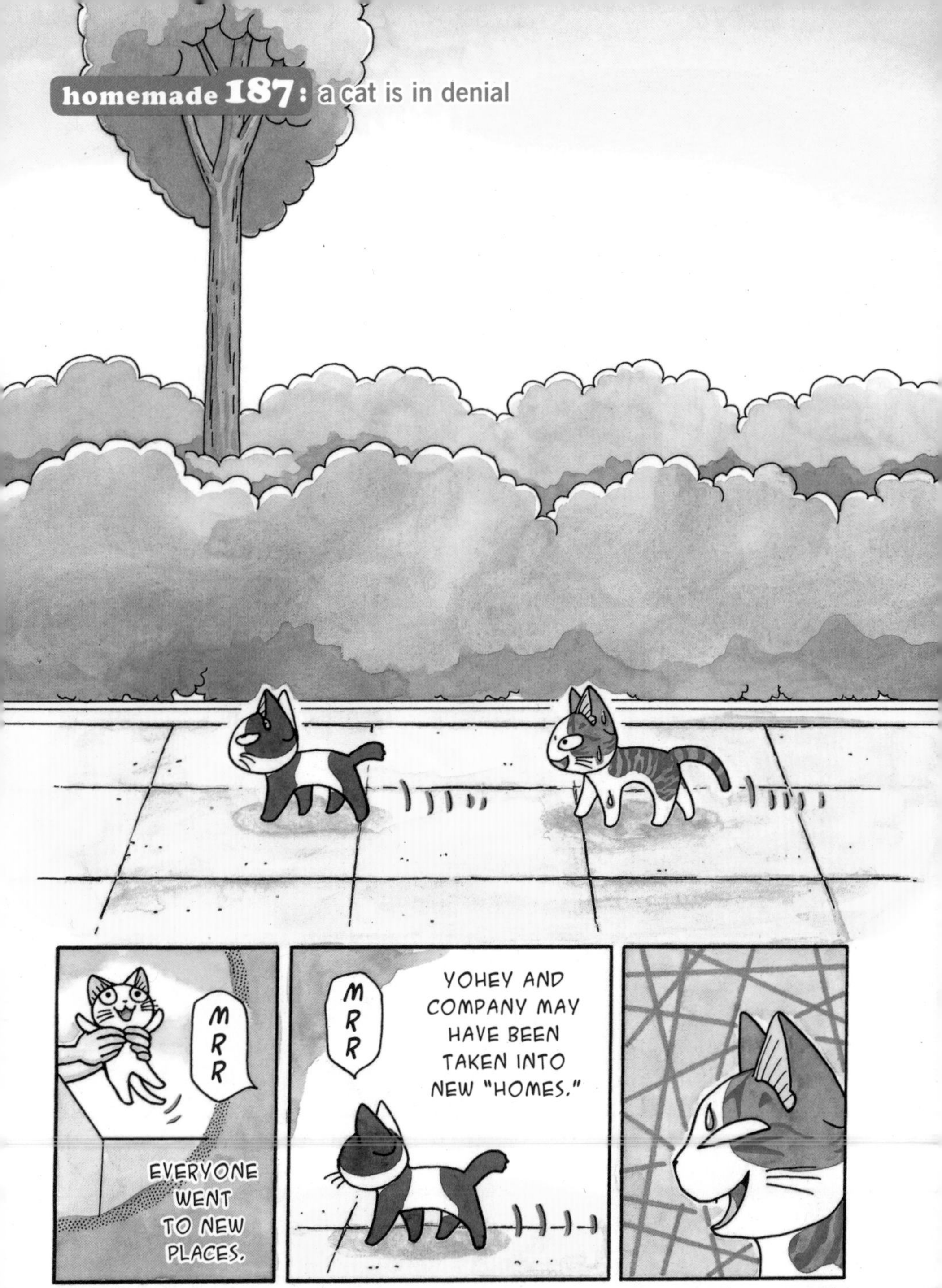

MRR
EVERYONE WENT TO NEW PLACES.
MRR
YOHEY AND COMPANY MAY HAVE BEEN TAKEN INTO NEW "HOMES."

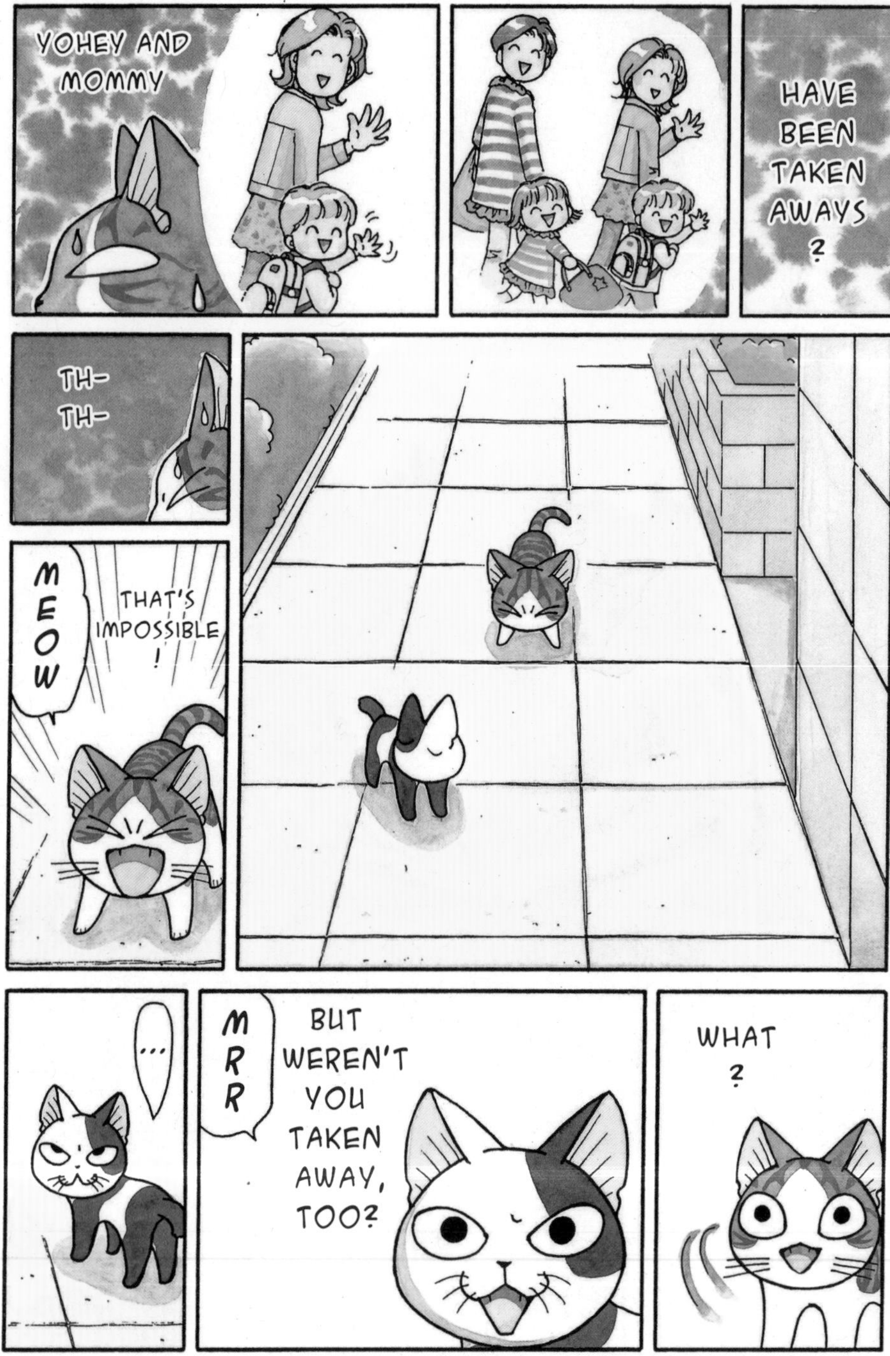
YOHEY AND MOMMY
HAVE BEEN TAKEN AWAYS?
TH- TH-
MEOW
THAT'S IMPOSSIBLE!
...
MRR
BUT WEREN'T YOU TAKEN AWAY, TOO?
WHAT?

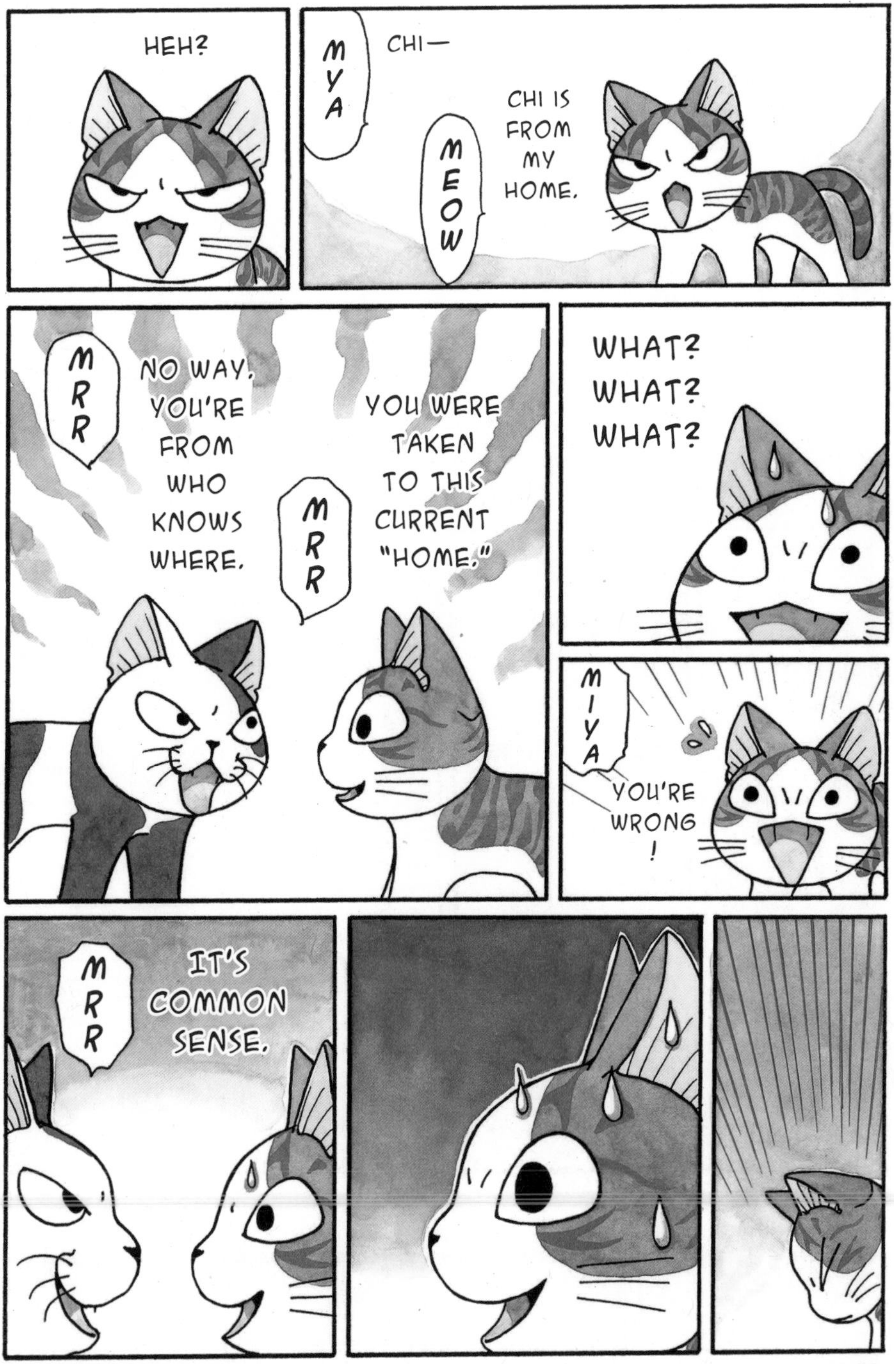
HEH?
MYA
CHI—
MEOW
CHI IS FROM MY HOME.
MRR
NO WAY. YOU'RE FROM WHO KNOWS WHERE.
MRR
YOU WERE TAKEN TO THIS CURRENT "HOME."
WHAT? WHAT? WHAT?
MIYA
YOU'RE WRONG!
MRR
IT'S COMMON SENSE.

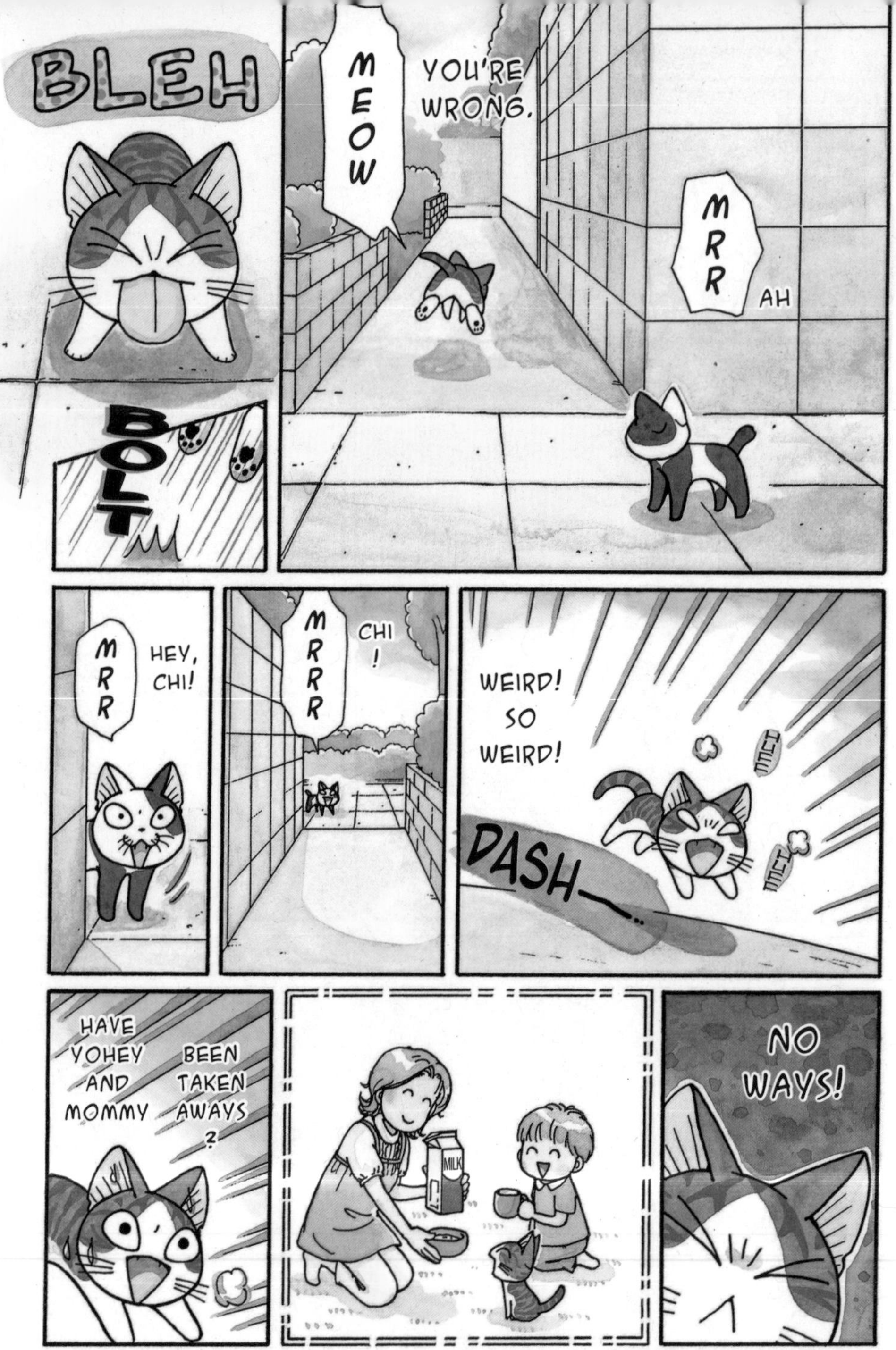
BLEH
BOLT
MEOW
YOU'RE WRONG.
MRR
AH
MRR
HEY, CHI!
MRRR
CHI!
WEIRD! SO WEIRD!
DASH
HAVE YOHEY AND MOMMY BEEN TAKEN AWAYS?
MILK
NO WAYS!

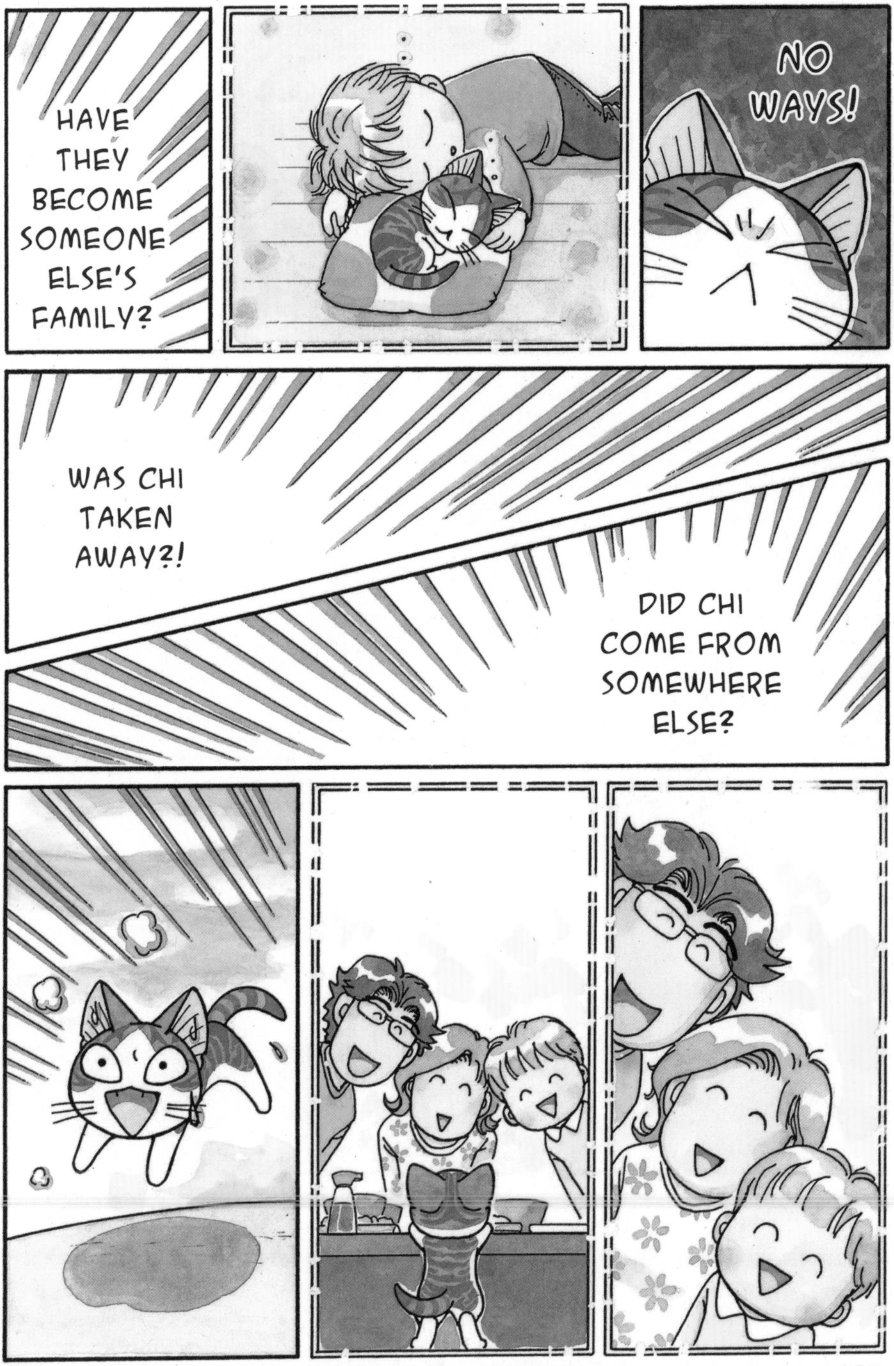
HAVE THEY BECOME SOMEONE ELSE'S FAMILY?
NO WAYS!
WAS CHI TAKEN AWAY?!
DID CHI COME FROM SOMEWHERE ELSE?

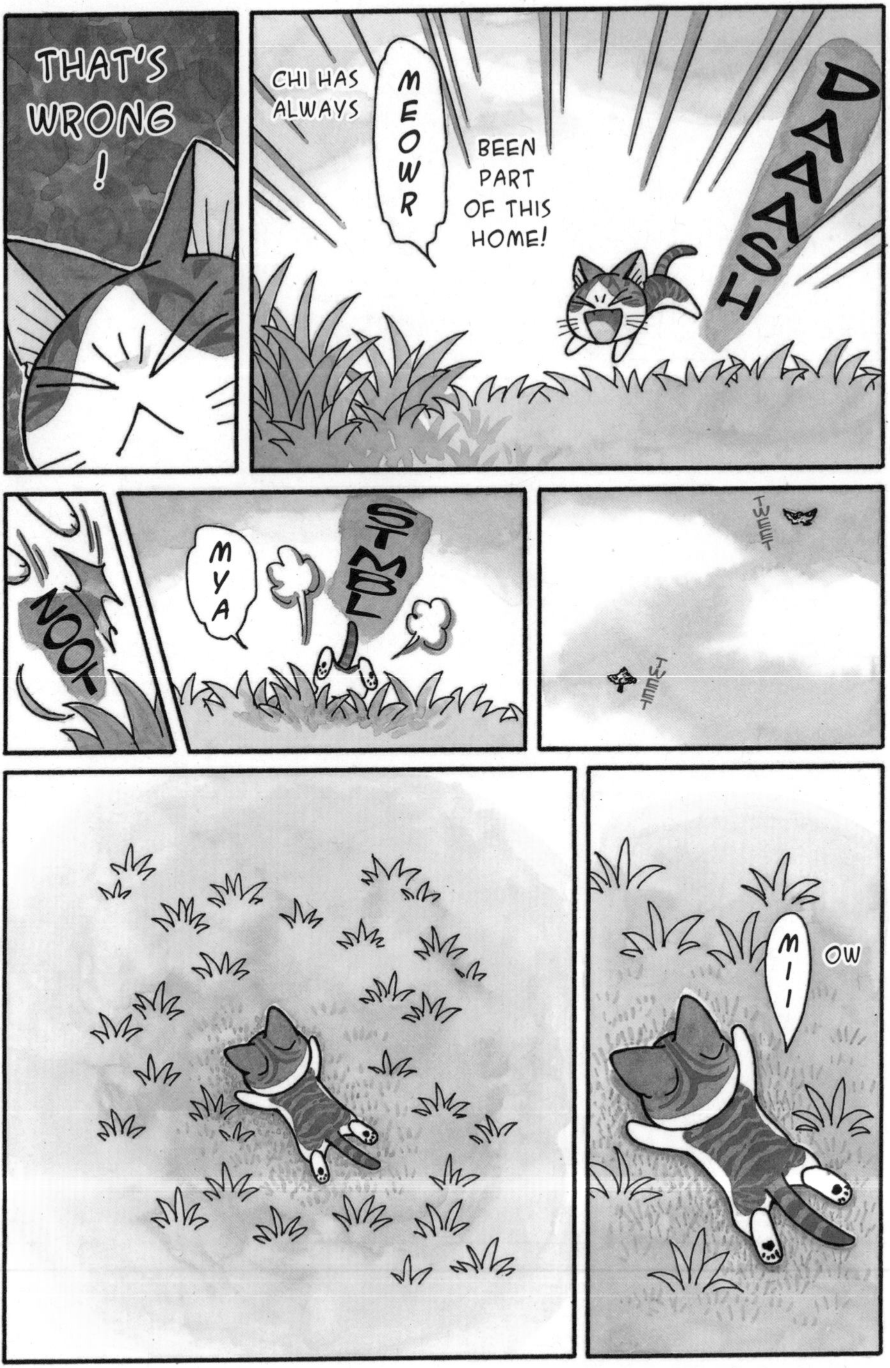
THAT'S WRONG!
CHI HAS ALWAYS
MEOWR
BEEN PART OF THIS HOME!
DAAASH
NOOK
MYA
STMBL
TWEET
TWEET
MII
OW

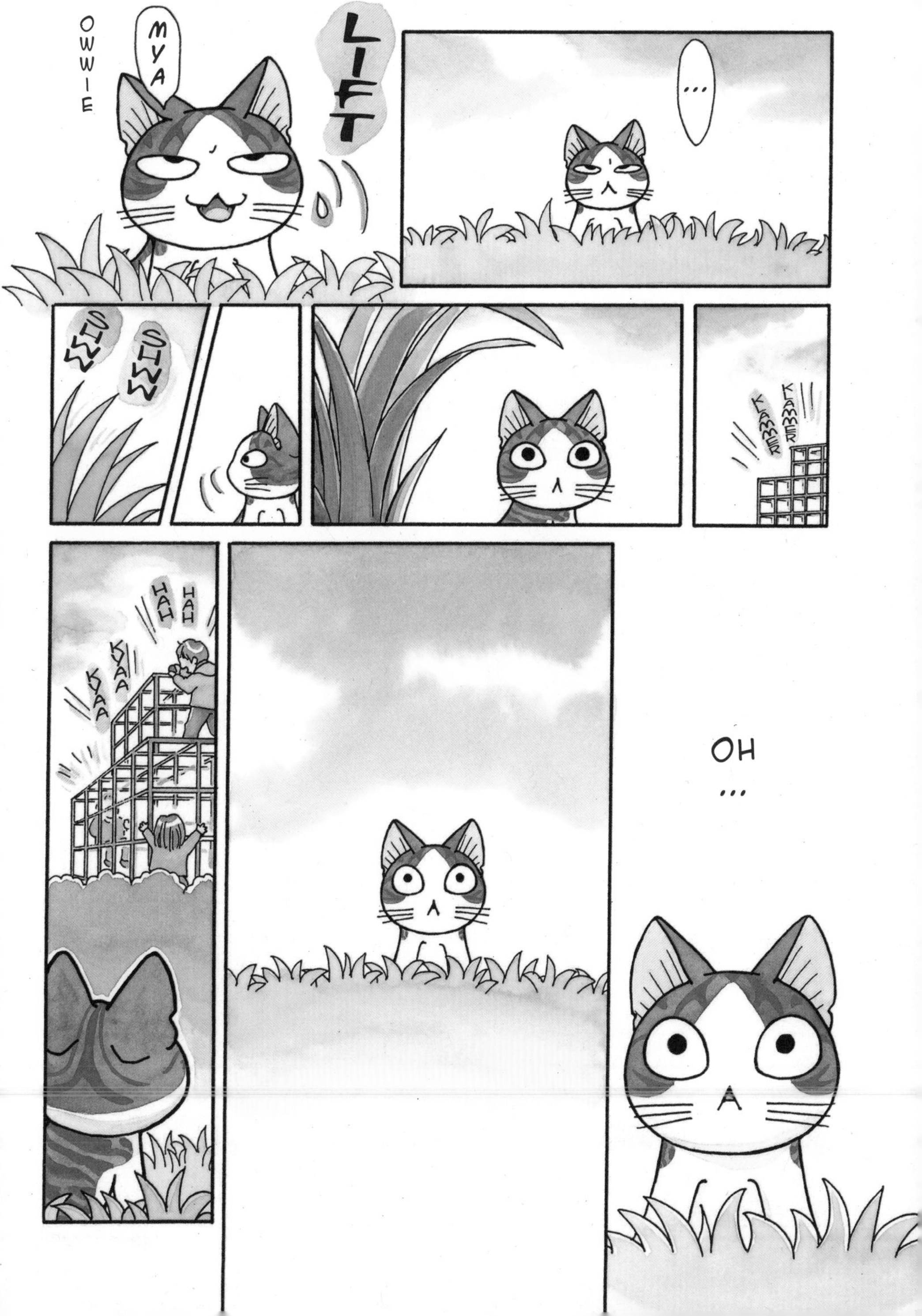
OWWIE
MYA
LIFT
...
SHWW SHWW
KLAMMER KLAMMER
HAH HAH
KYAA KYAA
OH
...

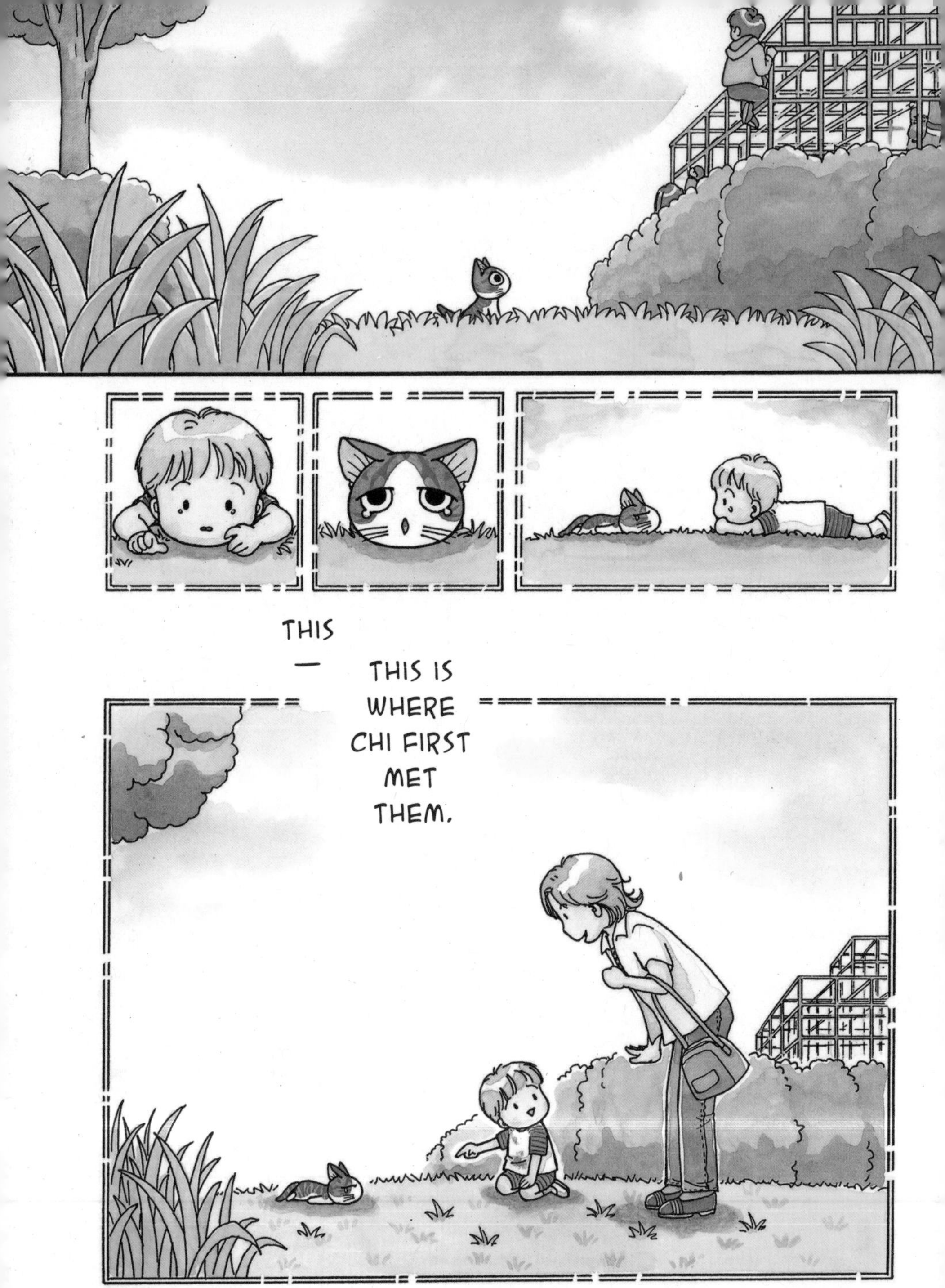
THIS
— THIS IS WHERE CHI FIRST MET THEM.

the end

homemade 188: a cat notices

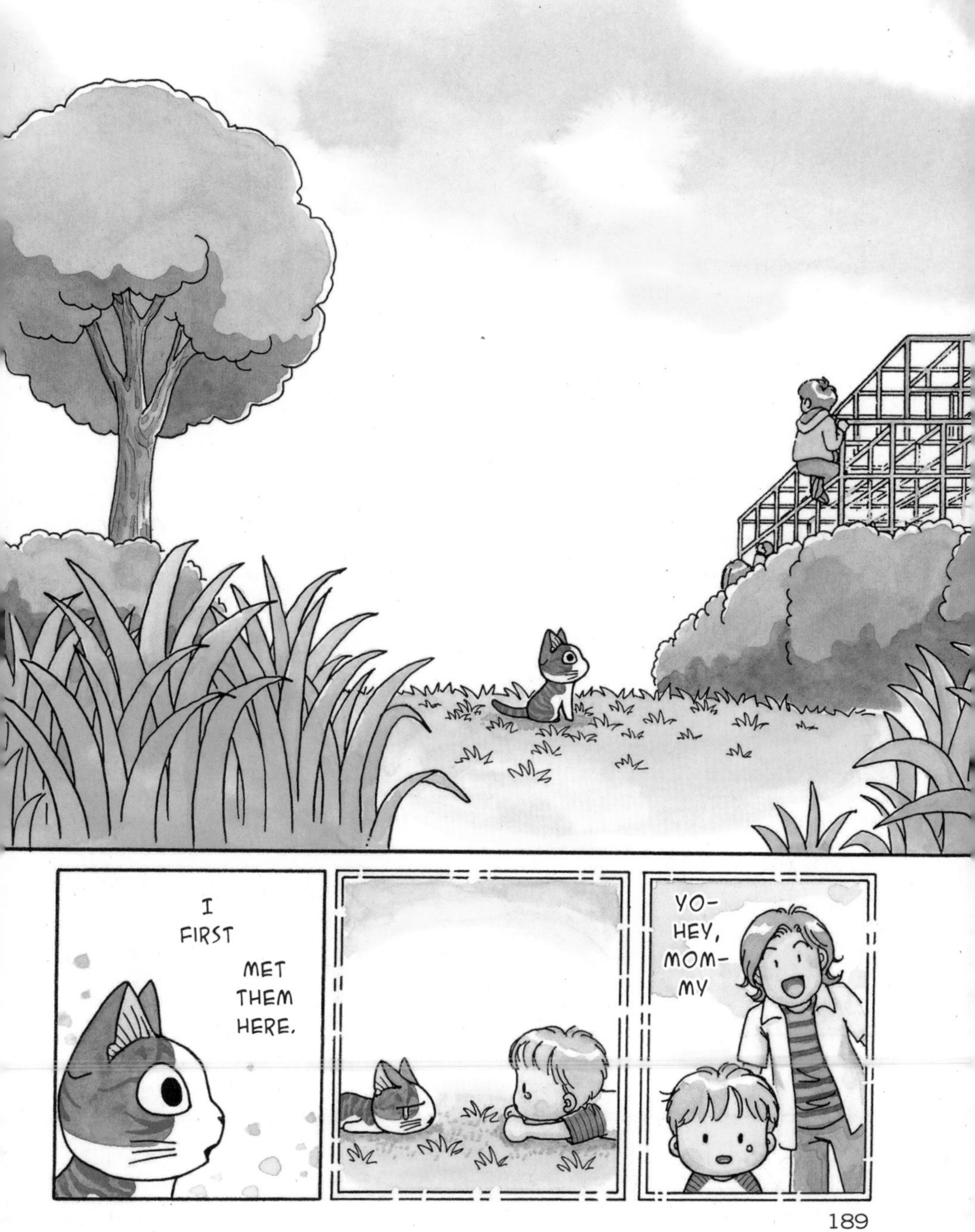
I FIRST MET THEM HERE.
YO-HEY, MOM-MY

CHI BECAME "A PART OF THEIR HOME"

BACK THEN!

JUST LIKE COCCHI SAID.

MEOW

!

WHICH MEANS...

YOHEY AND COMPANY,

MAY HAVE BEEN TAKEN

INTO NEW "HOMES."

MRR

MOMMY AND YOHEY,

MYA...

HAVE REALLY BEEN TAKEN AWAY!

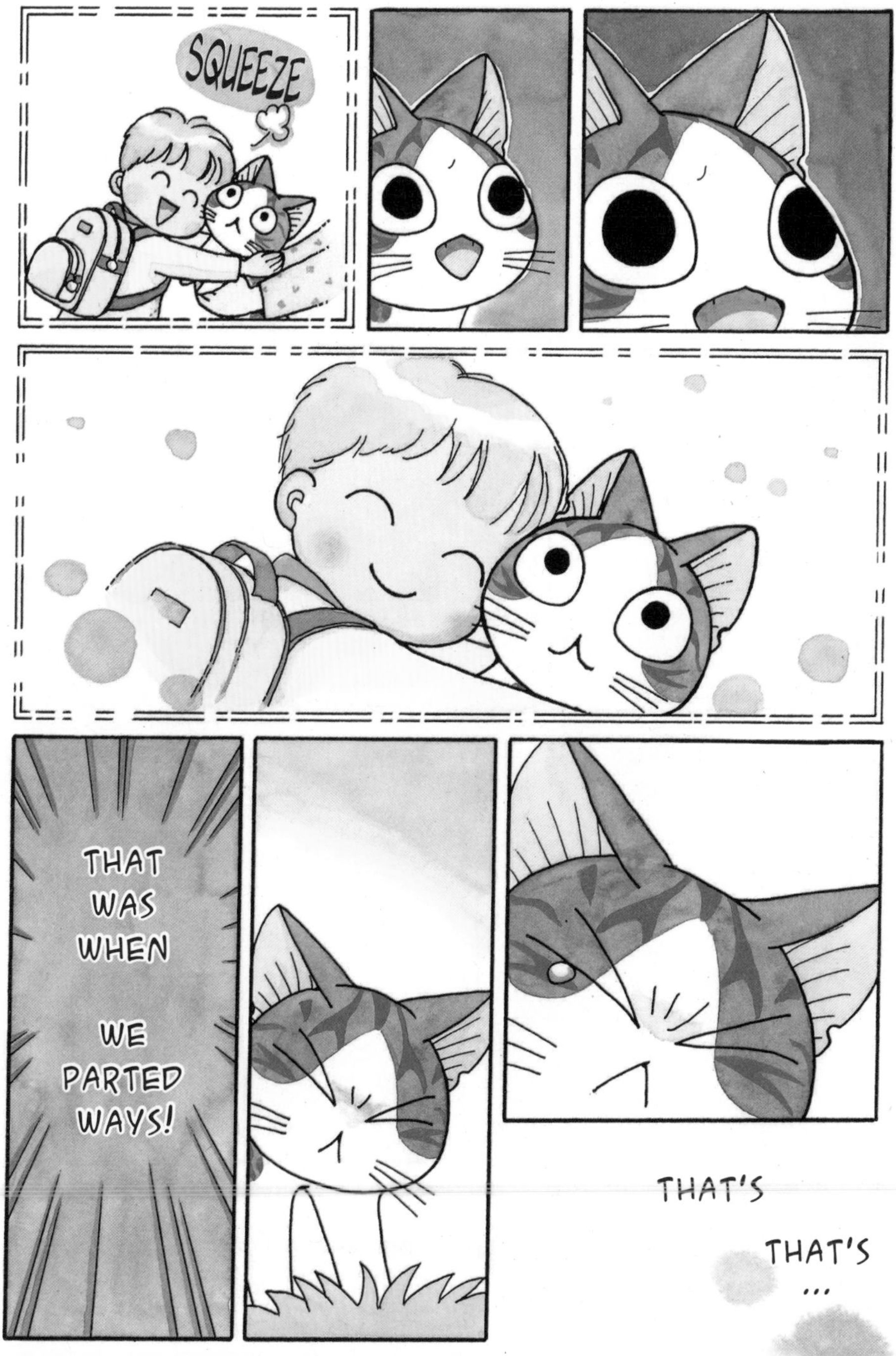
SQUEEZE
THAT WAS WHEN WE PARTED WAYS!
THAT'S
THAT'S ...

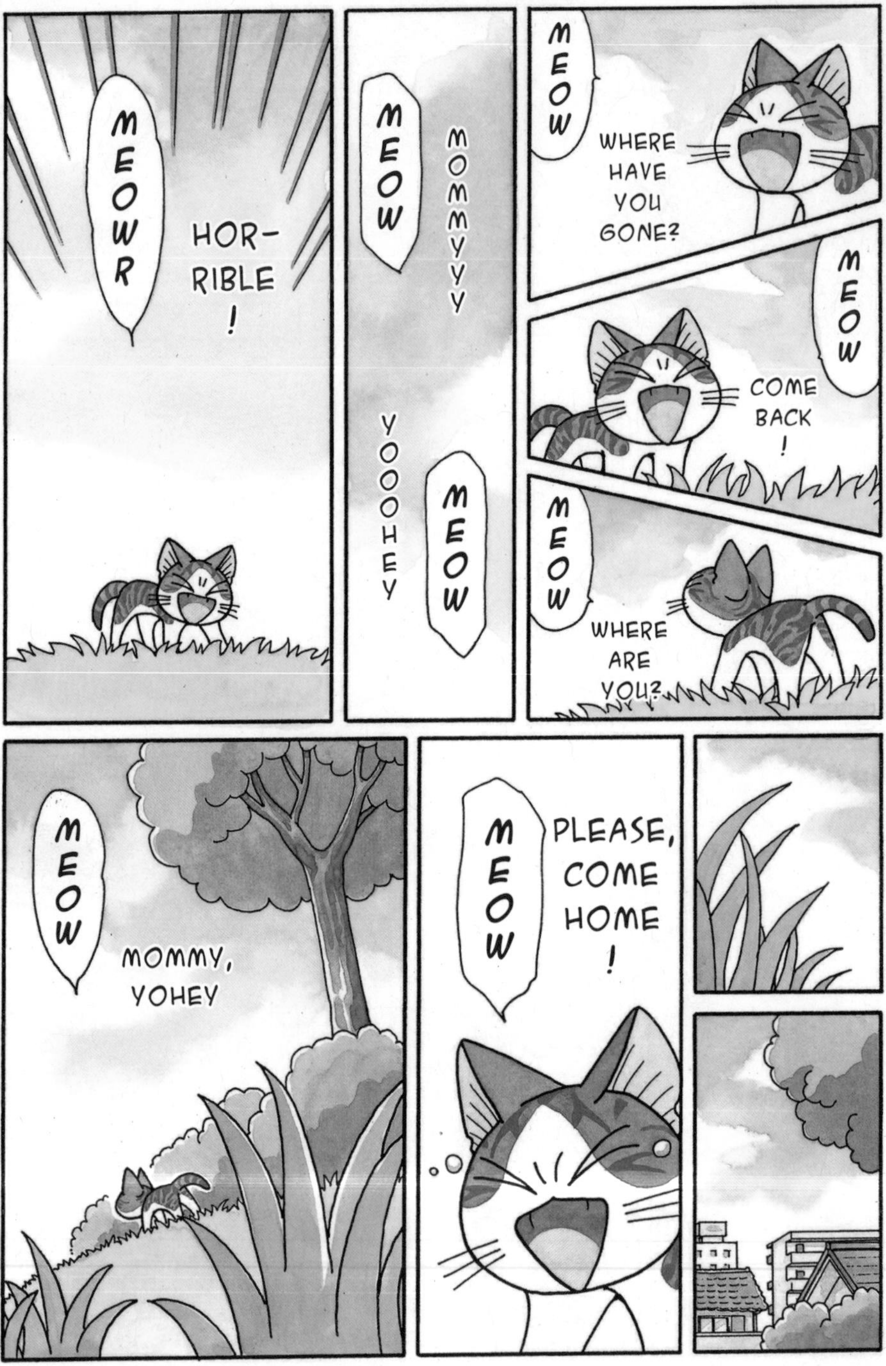
MEOWR
HOR-RIBLE!
MEOW
MOMMYYY
YOOOOHEY
MEOW
MEOW
WHERE HAVE YOU GONE?
MEOW
COME BACK!
MEOW
WHERE ARE YOU?
MEOW
MOMMY, YOHEY
MEOW
PLEASE, COME HOME!

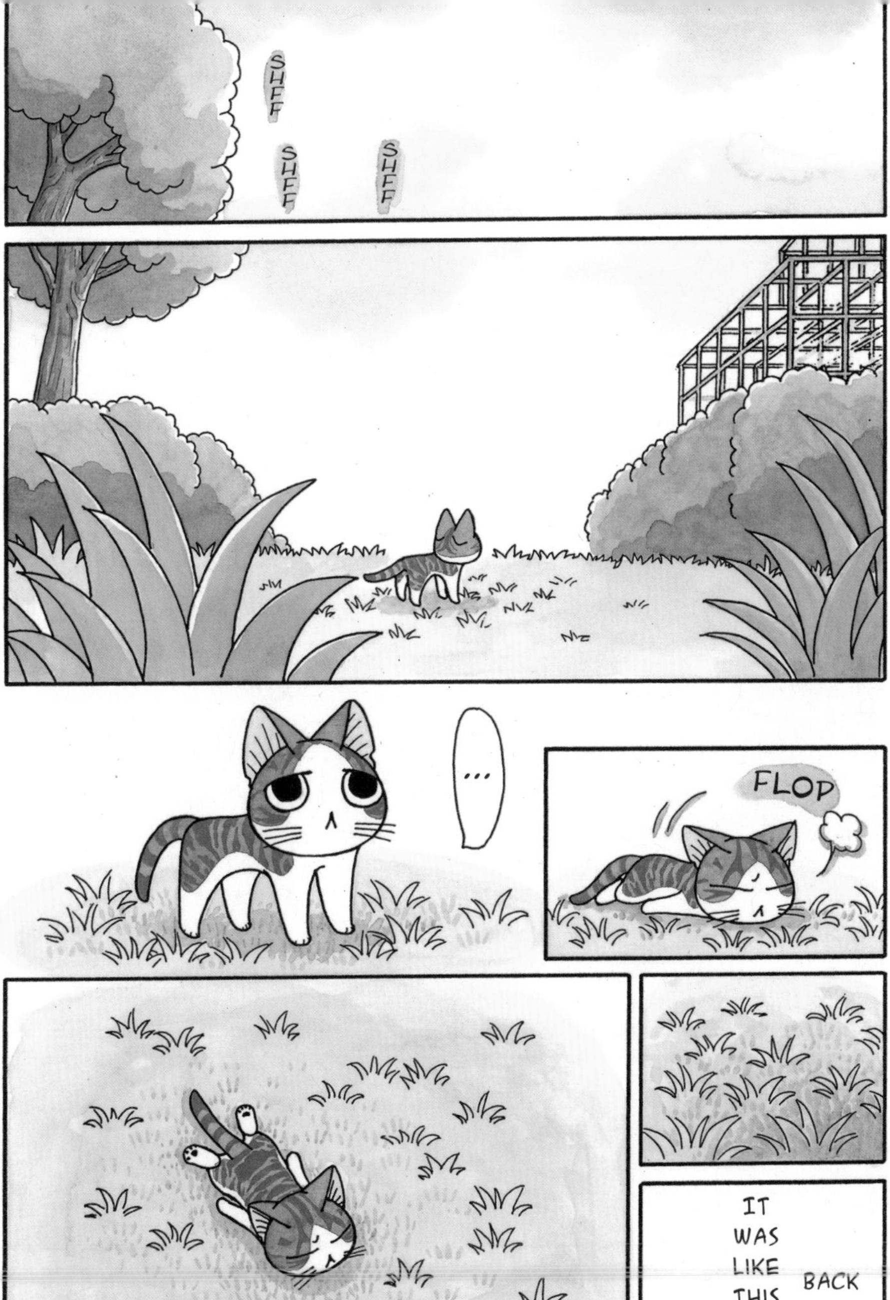
SHFF
SHFF
SHFF
...
FLOP
IT WAS LIKE THIS BACK THEN TOO.

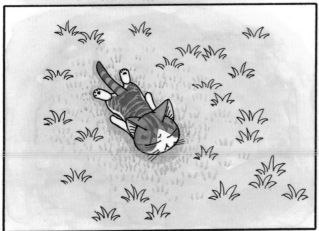

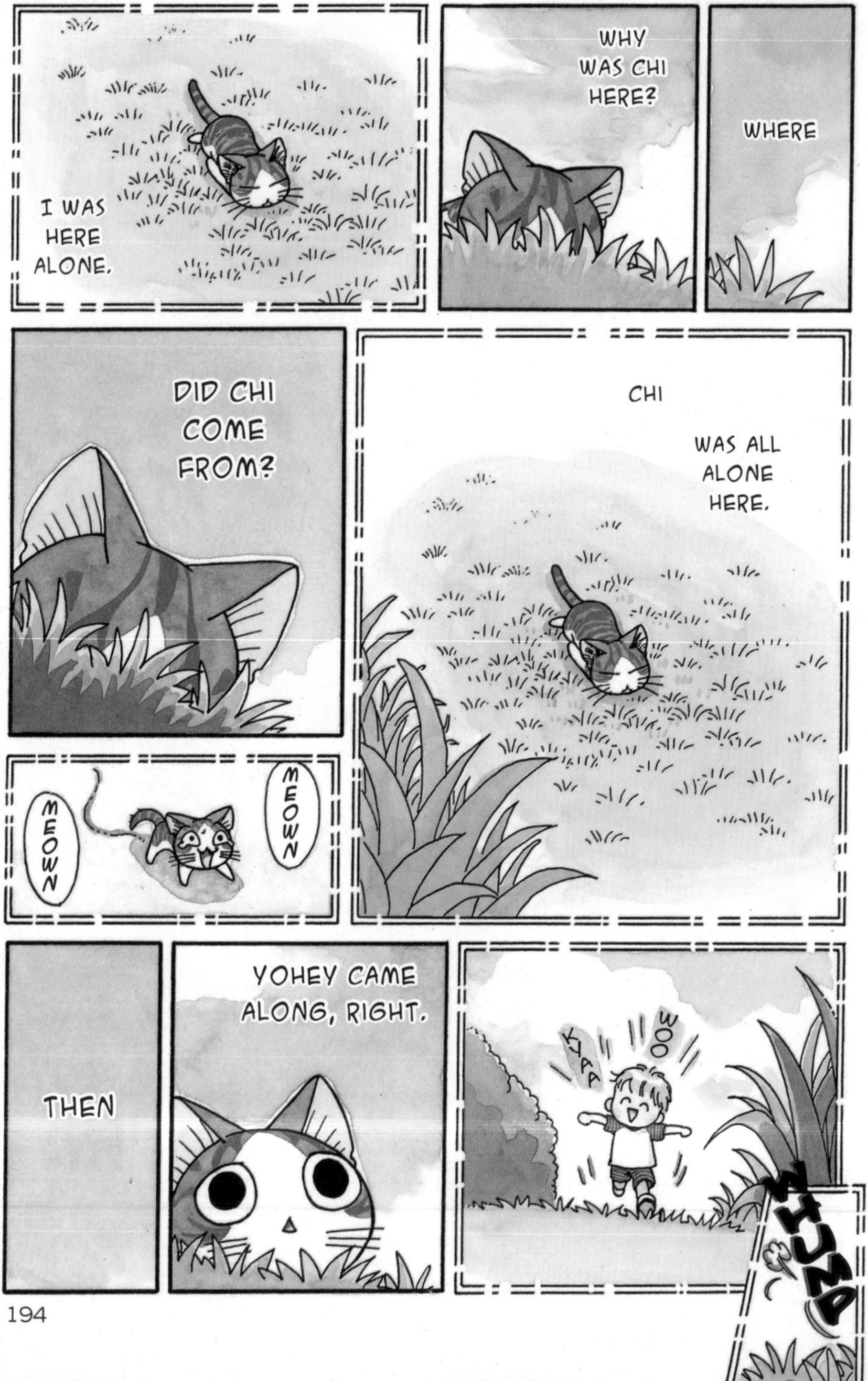
I WAS HERE ALONE.
WHY WAS CHI HERE?
WHERE
DID CHI COME FROM?
MEOWN
MEOWN
CHI
WAS ALL ALONE HERE.
THEN
YOHEY CAME ALONG, RIGHT.
KYAA
WOO
THUMP

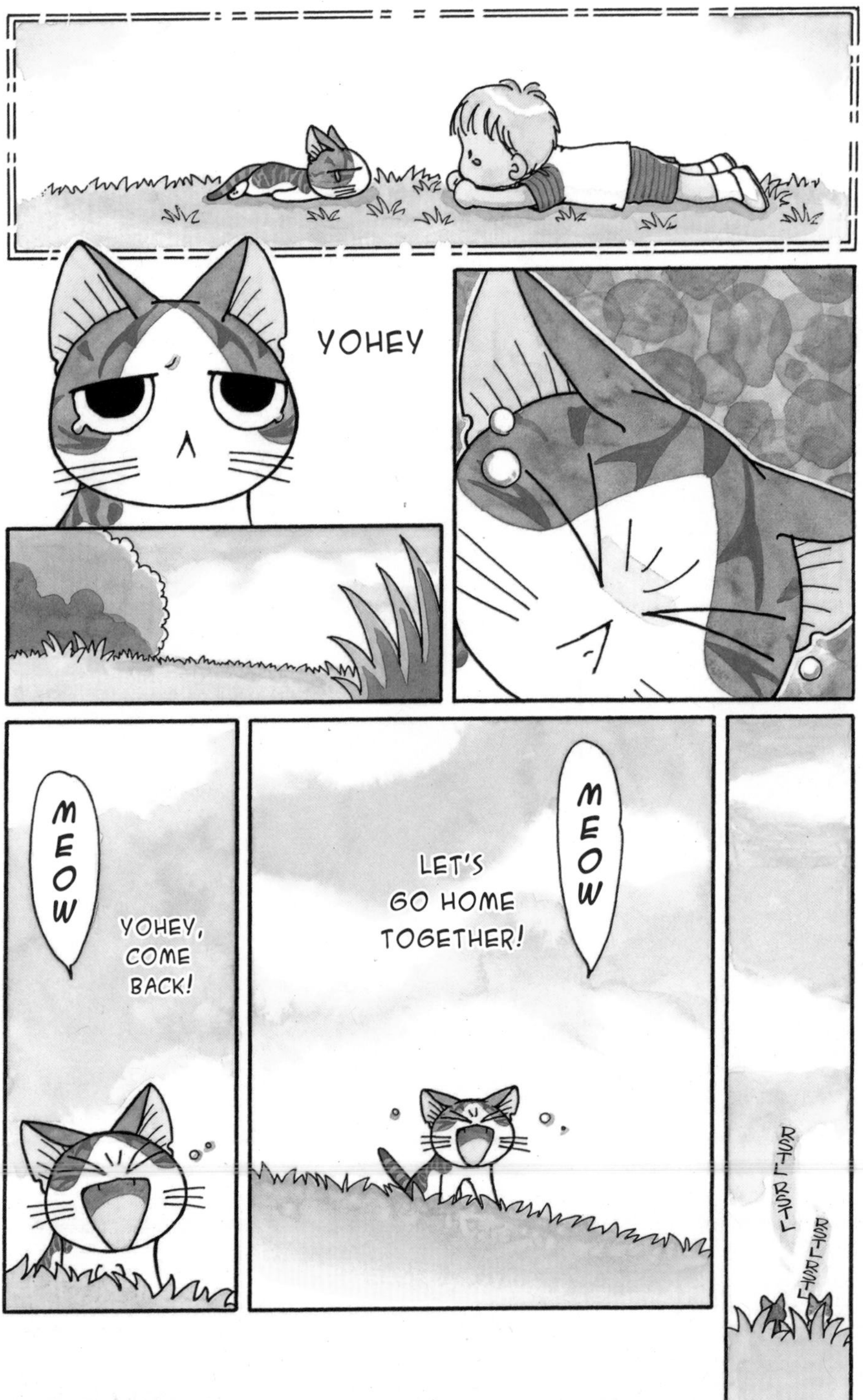
YOHEY
MEOW
YOHEY, COME BACK!
MEOW
LET'S GO HOME TOGETHER!
RSTL RSTL
RSTL RSTL

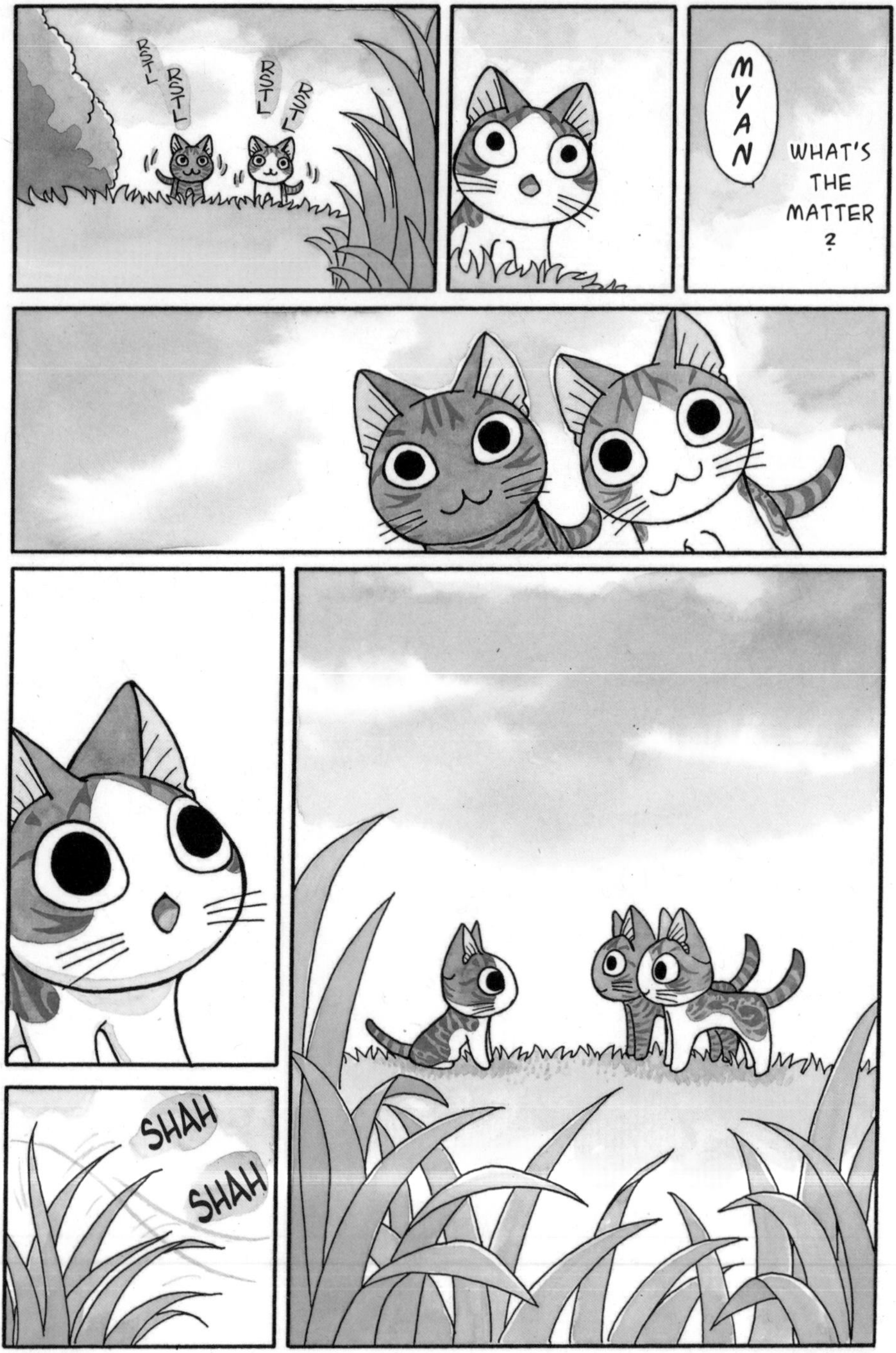
RSTL
RSTL
RSTL
RSTL
MYAN
WHAT'S THE MATTER ?
SHAH
SHAH

the end

homemade 189: a cat hangs her head

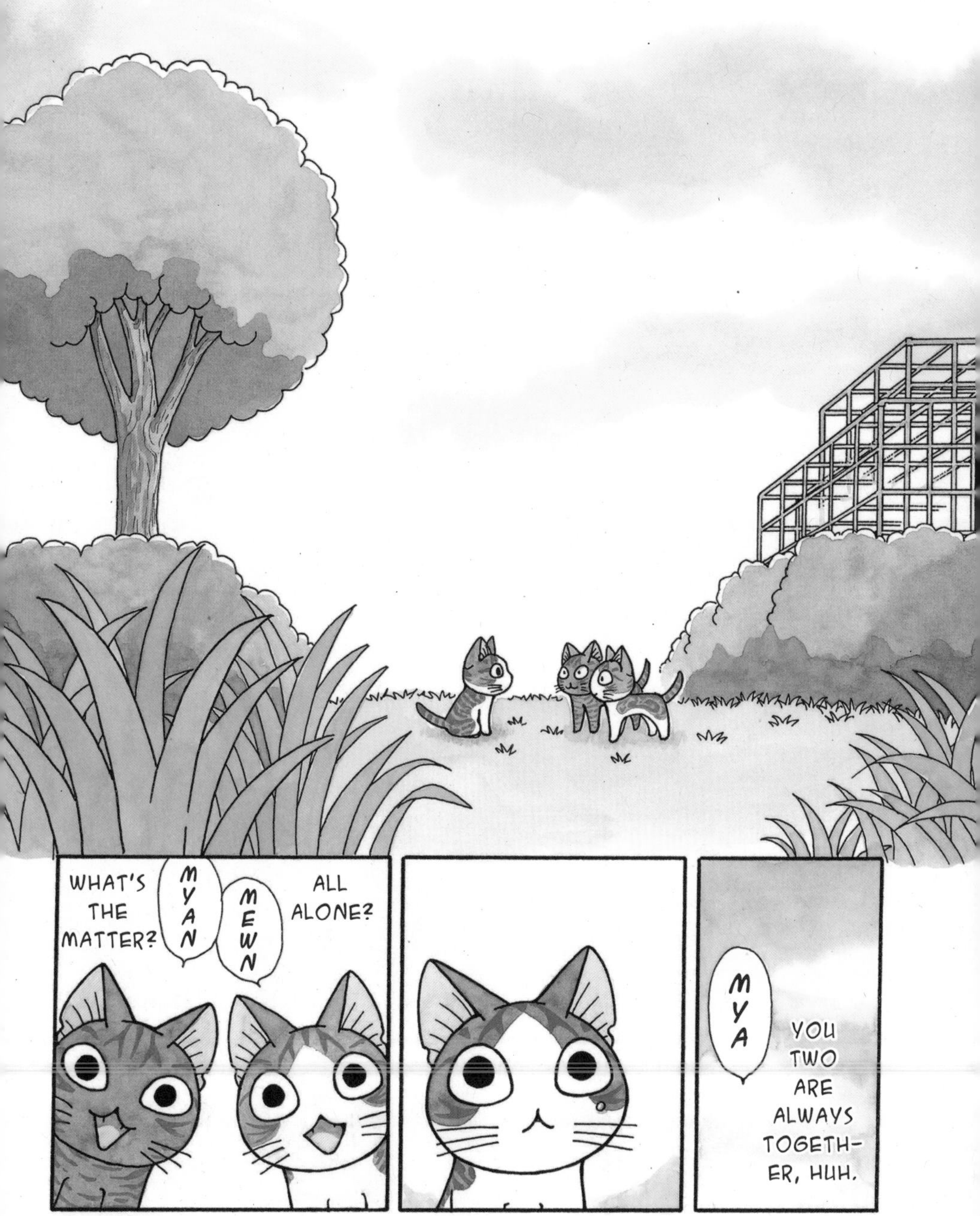
WHAT'S THE MATTER?
MYAN
MEWN
ALL ALONE?
MYA
YOU TWO ARE ALWAYS TOGETH-ER, HUH.

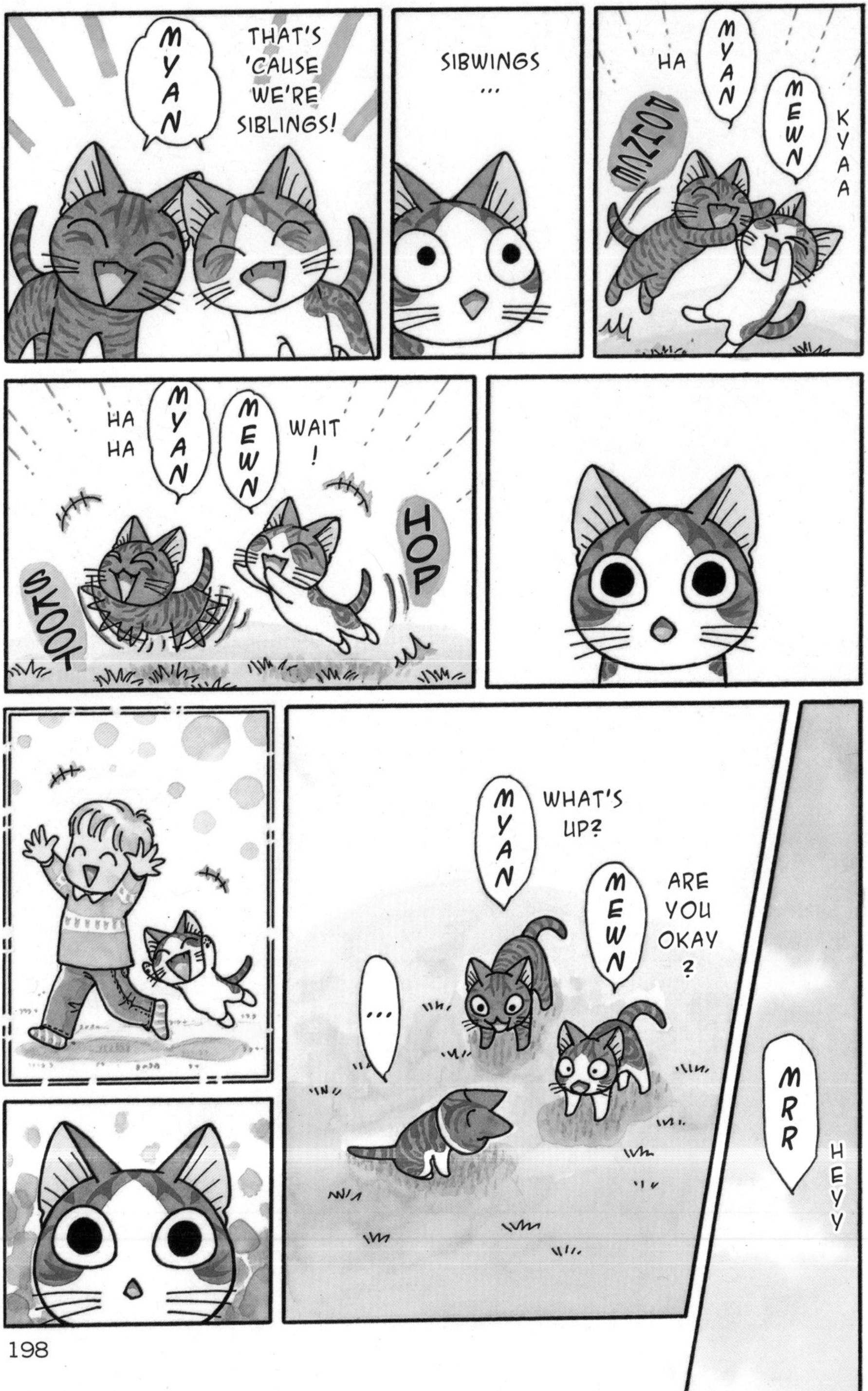
MYAN
THAT'S 'CAUSE WE'RE SIBLINGS!
SIBWINGS ...
HA
MYAN
MEWN
KYAA
POUNCE
HA HA
MYAN
MEWN
WAIT!
SKOOT
HOP
MYAN
WHAT'S UP?
MEWN
ARE YOU OKAY?
...
MRR
HEYY

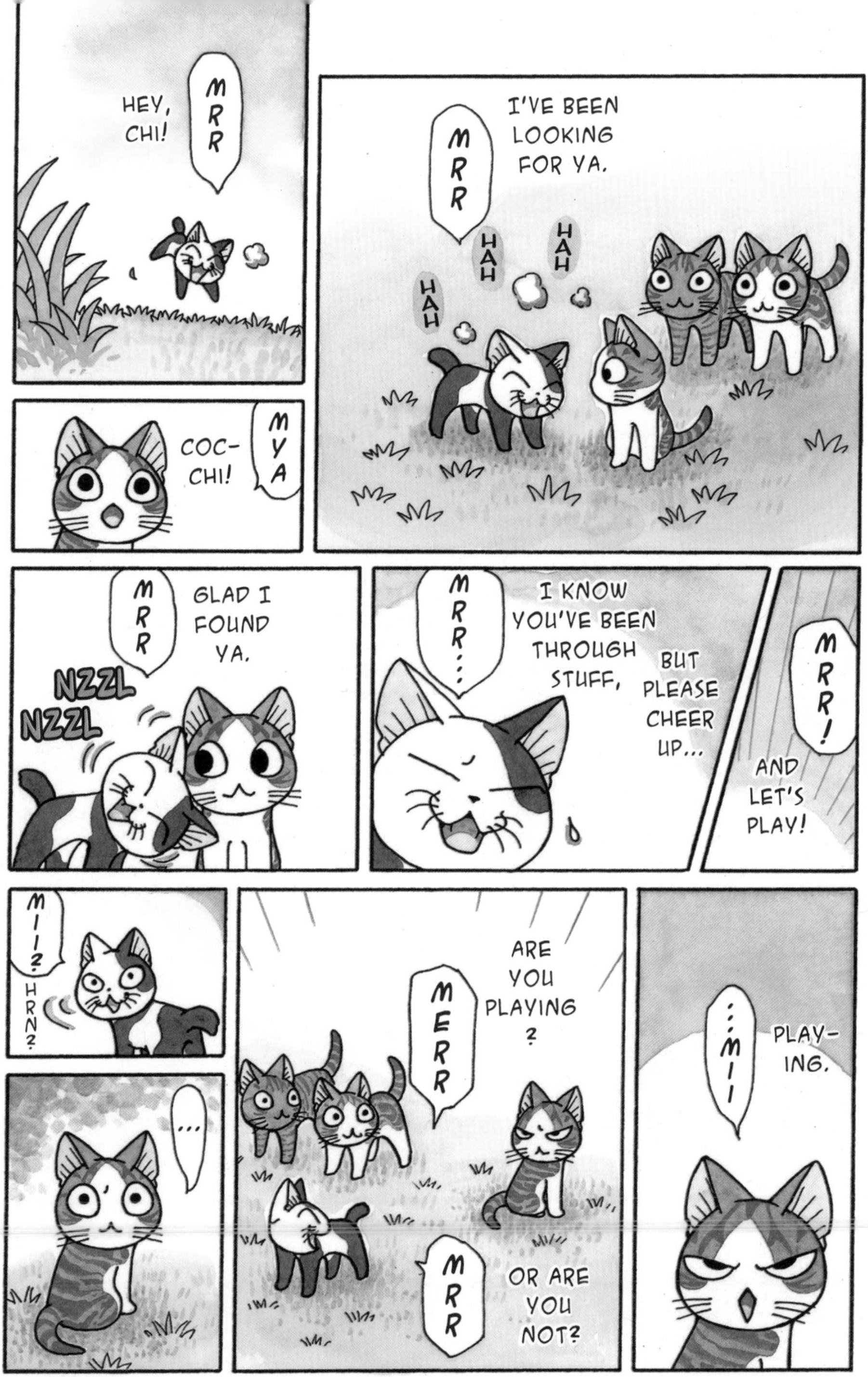
HEY, CHI!
MRR
COC-CHI!
MYA
I'VE BEEN LOOKING FOR YA.
MRR
HAH
HAH
HAH
MRR
GLAD I FOUND YA.
NZZL NZZL
MRR...
I KNOW YOU'VE BEEN THROUGH STUFF,
BUT PLEASE CHEER UP...
MRR!
AND LET'S PLAY!
MII?
HRN?
...
ARE YOU PLAYING?
MERR
OR ARE YOU NOT?
MRR
...MII
PLAY-ING.

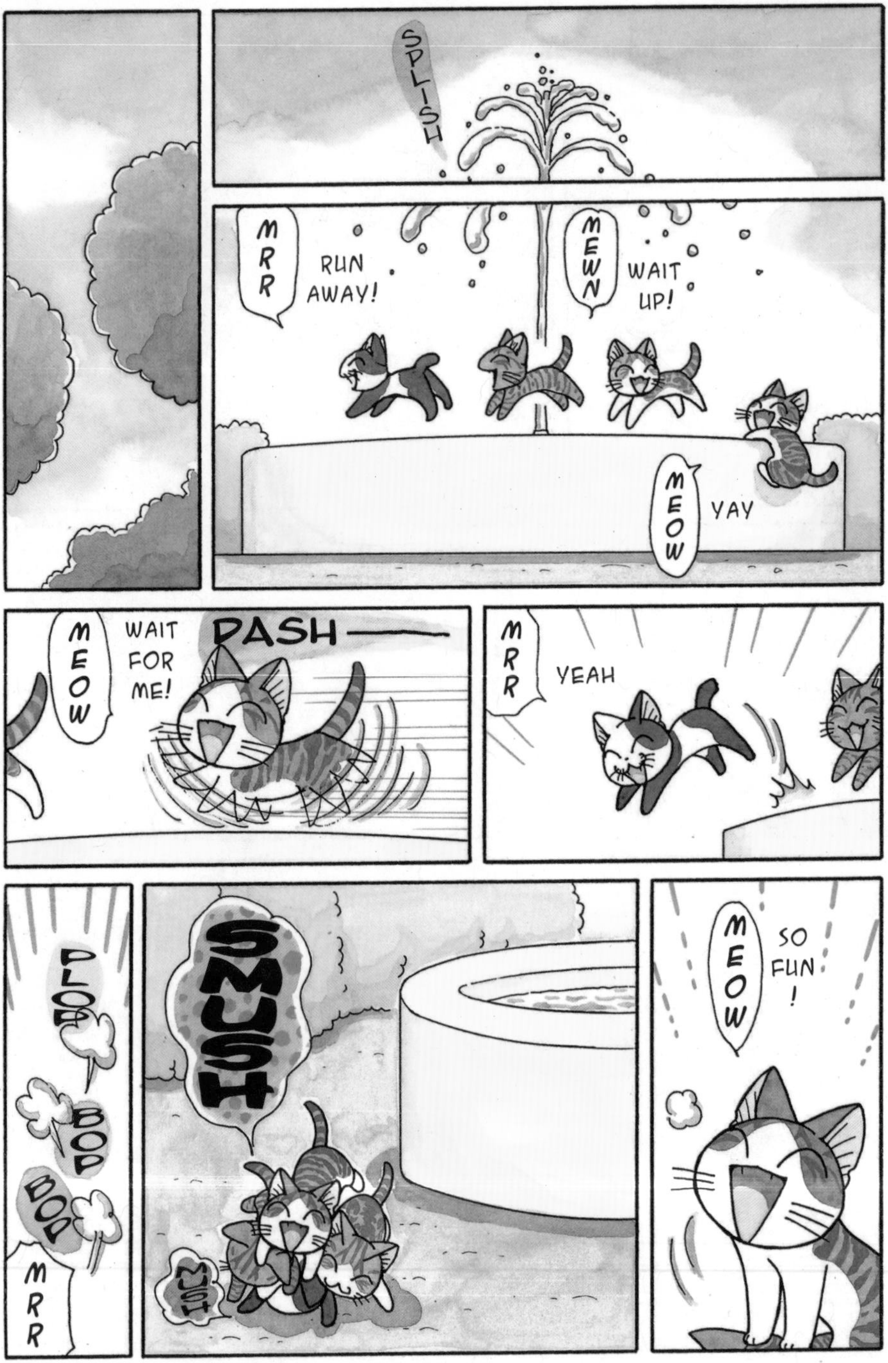
SPLISH
MRR
RUN AWAY!
MEWN
WAIT UP!
MEOW
YAY
MEOW
WAIT FOR ME!
DASH
MRR
YEAH
PLOP
BOP
BOP
MRR
SMUSH
MUSH
MEOW
SO FUN!

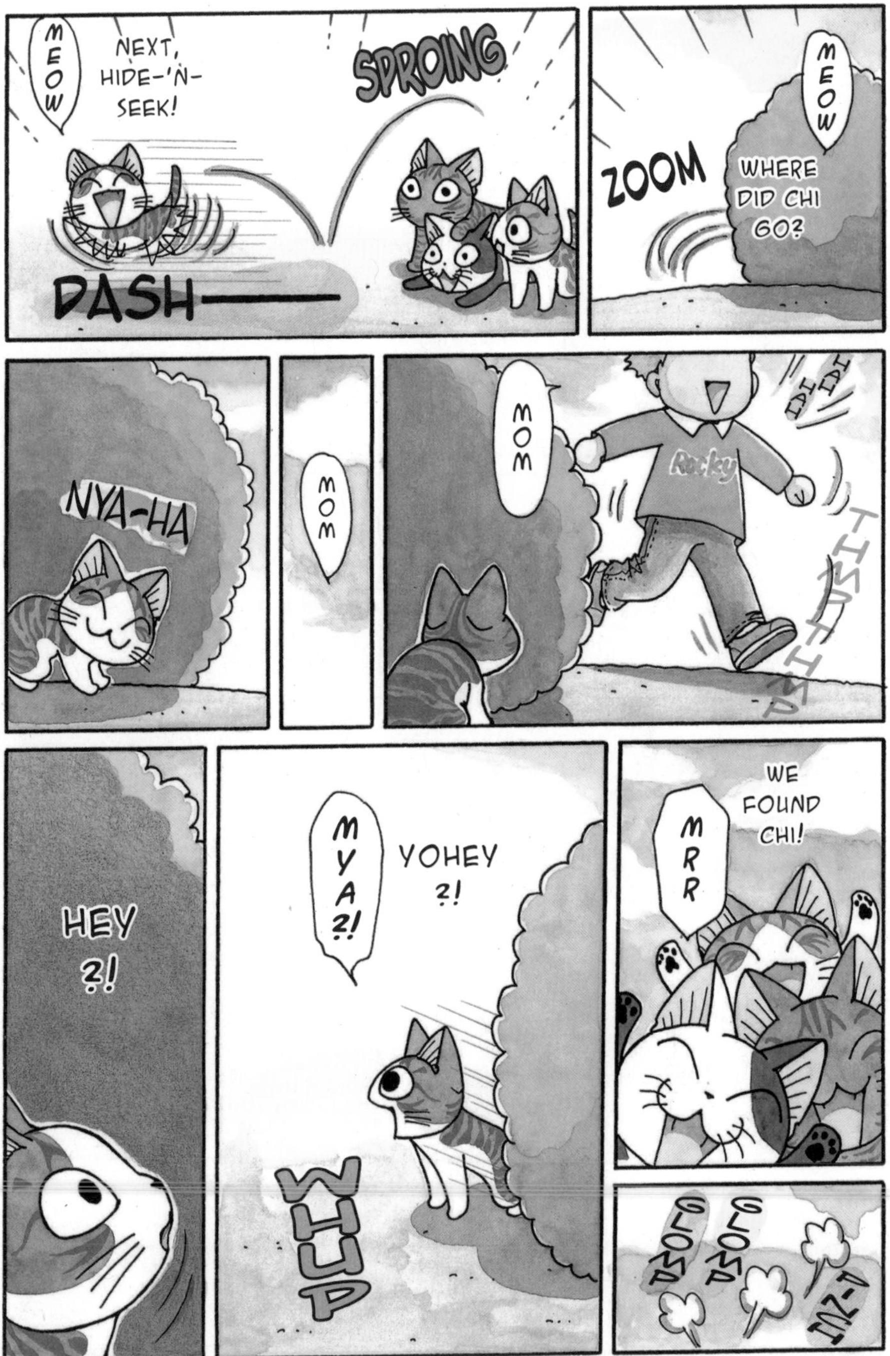
MEOW
NEXT, HIDE-'N-SEEK!
SPROING
DASH——
MEOW
ZOOM
WHERE DID CHI GO?
NYA-HA
MOM
MOM
THMP THMP
HEY ?!
MYA?!
YOHEY ?!
WHUP
WE FOUND CHI!
MRR
GLOMP
GLOMP

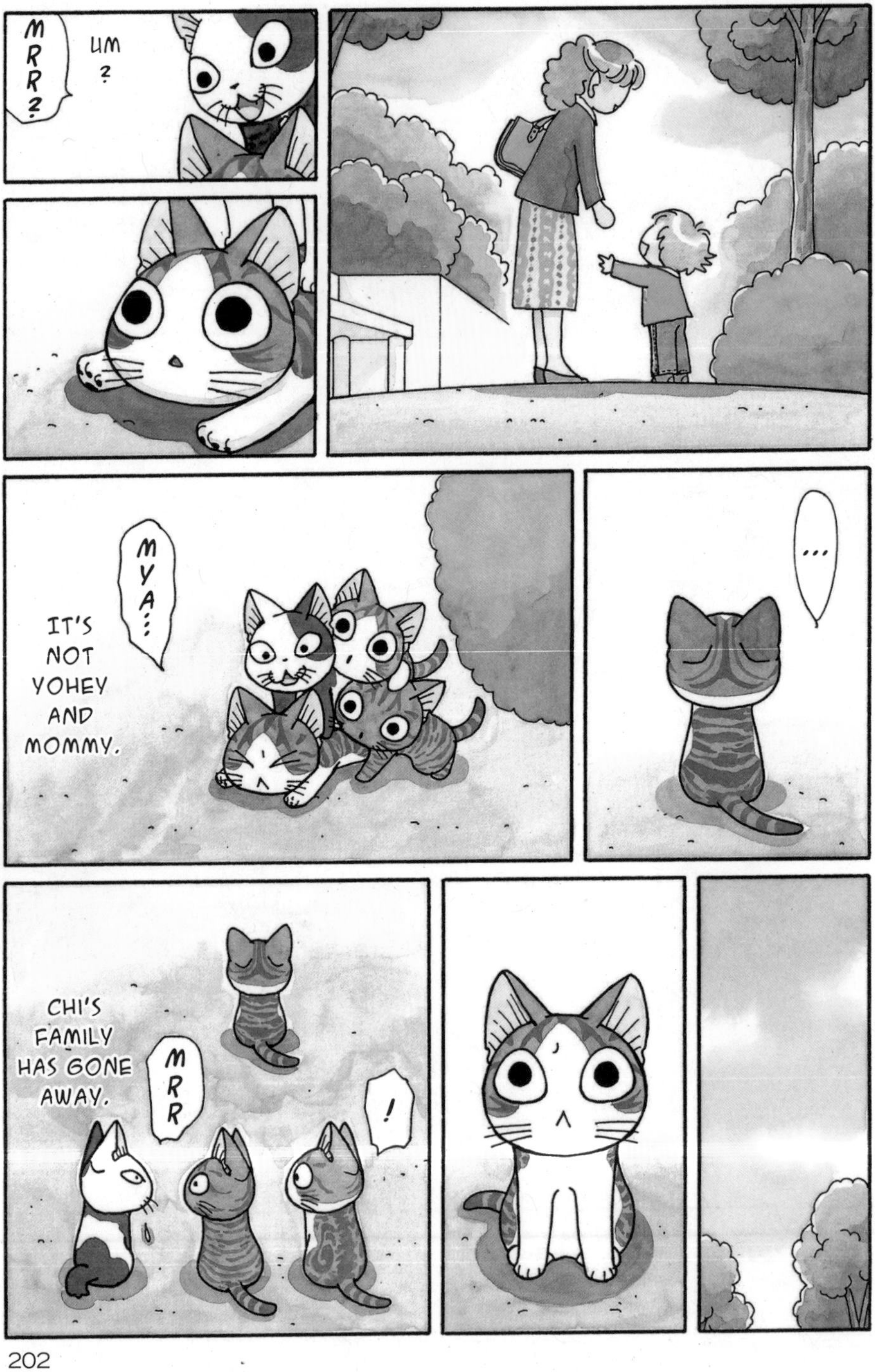
MRR?
UM?
MYA...
IT'S NOT YOHEY AND MOMMY.
...
CHI'S FAMILY HAS GONE AWAY.
MRR
!

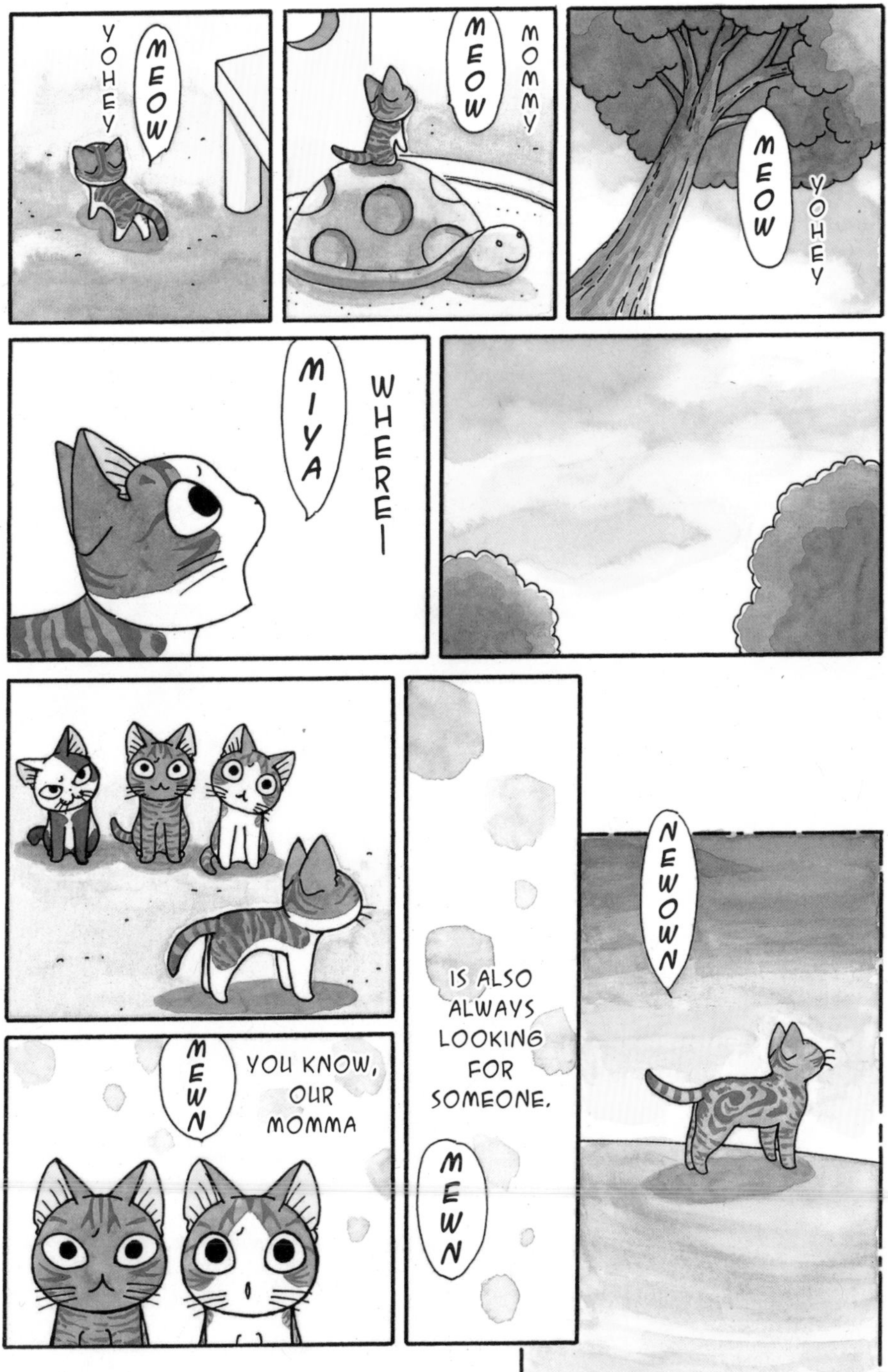
YOHEY
MEOW
MEOW
MOMMY
MEOW
YOHEY
MIYA
WHERE!
MEWN
YOU KNOW, OUR MOMMA
IS ALSO ALWAYS LOOKING FOR SOMEONE.
MEWN
NEWOWN

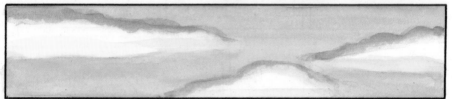

NYAN

MEWN

MYAN

OH,
IT'S
MOM-
MA.

OK,
BYE!

MRR

LAT-
ER

"MOMMA"
?

204

the end

homemade 190: a cat is called upon

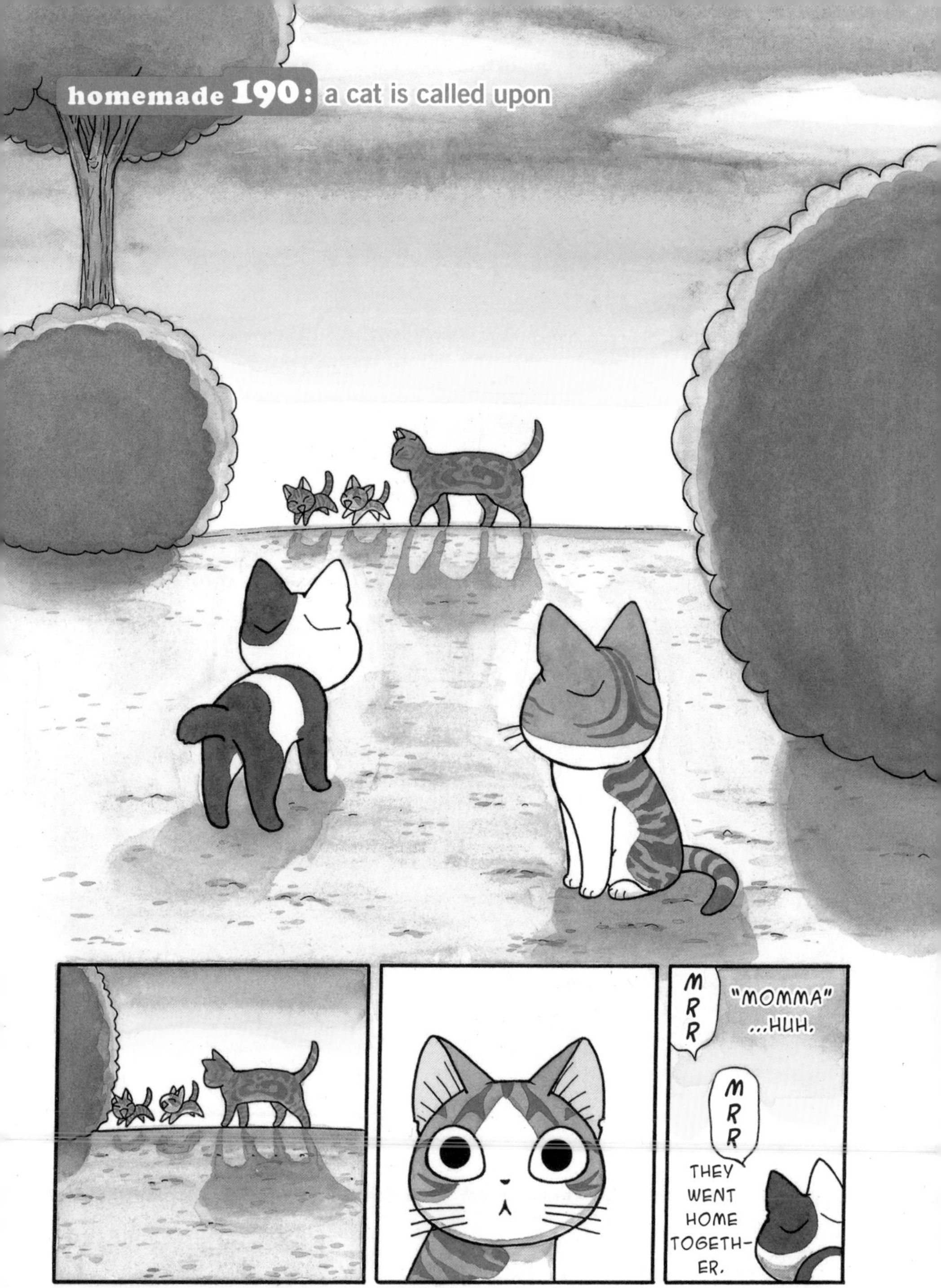
MRR
"MOMMA" ...HUH.
MRR
THEY WENT HOME TOGETH-ER.

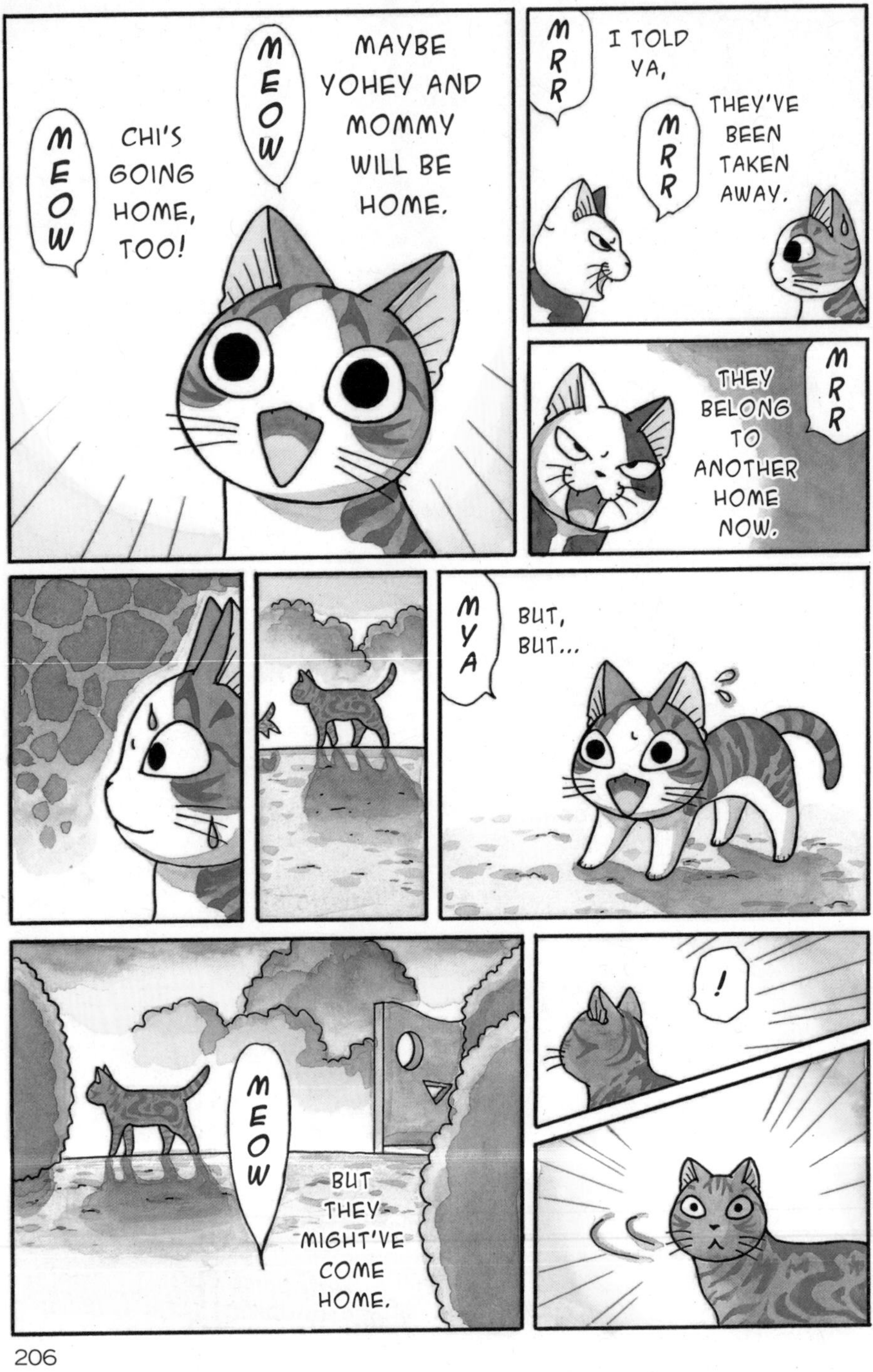
MEOW
CHI'S GOING HOME, TOO!
MEOW
MAYBE YOHEY AND MOMMY WILL BE HOME.
MRR
I TOLD YA,
MRR
THEY'VE BEEN TAKEN AWAY.
THEY BELONG TO ANOTHER HOME NOW.
MRR
MYA
BUT, BUT...
MEOW
BUT THEY MIGHT'VE COME HOME.
!

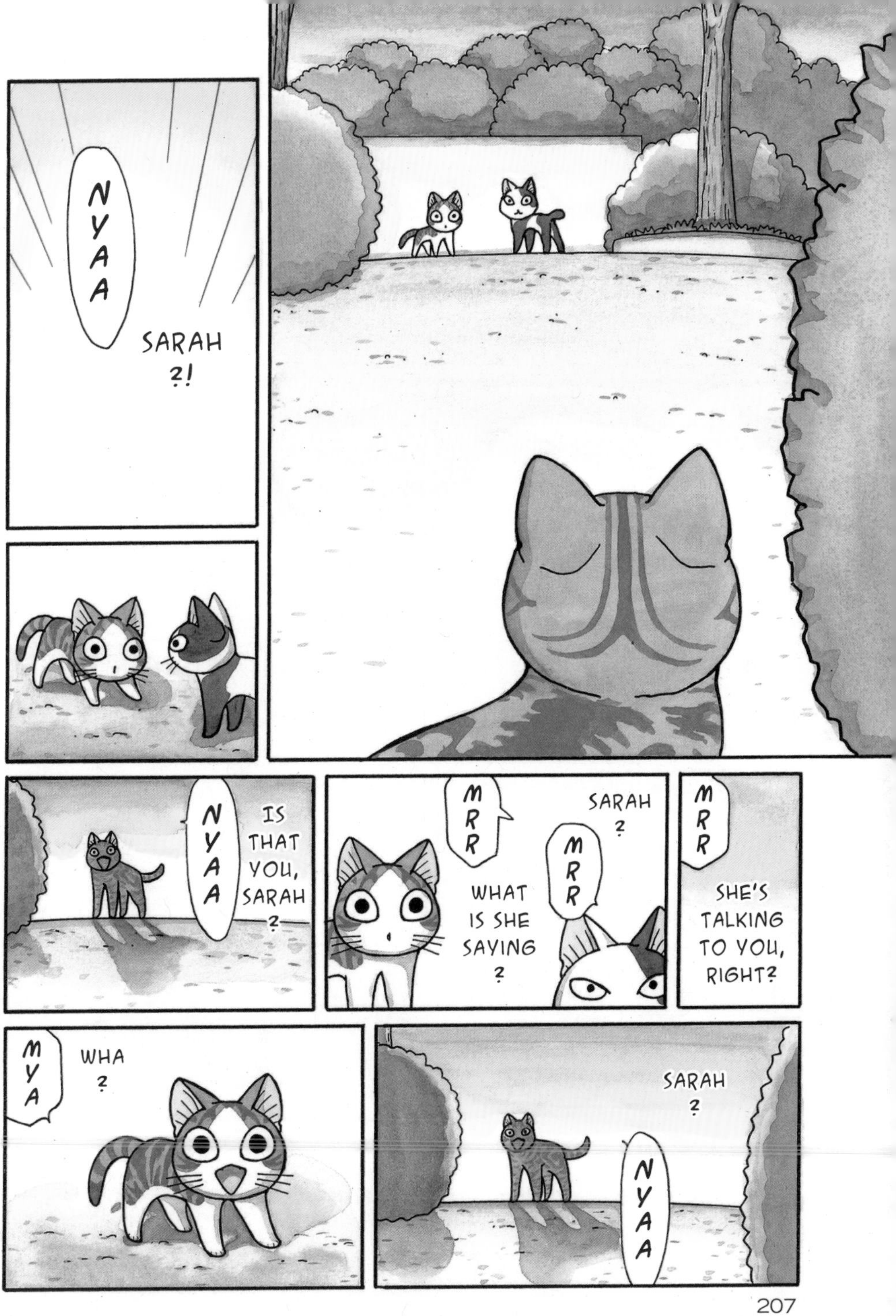
NYAA
SARAH?!
NYAA
IS THAT YOU, SARAH?
MRR
SARAH?
MRR
WHAT IS SHE SAYING?
MRR
SHE'S TALKING TO YOU, RIGHT?
MYA
WHA?
SARAH?
NYAA

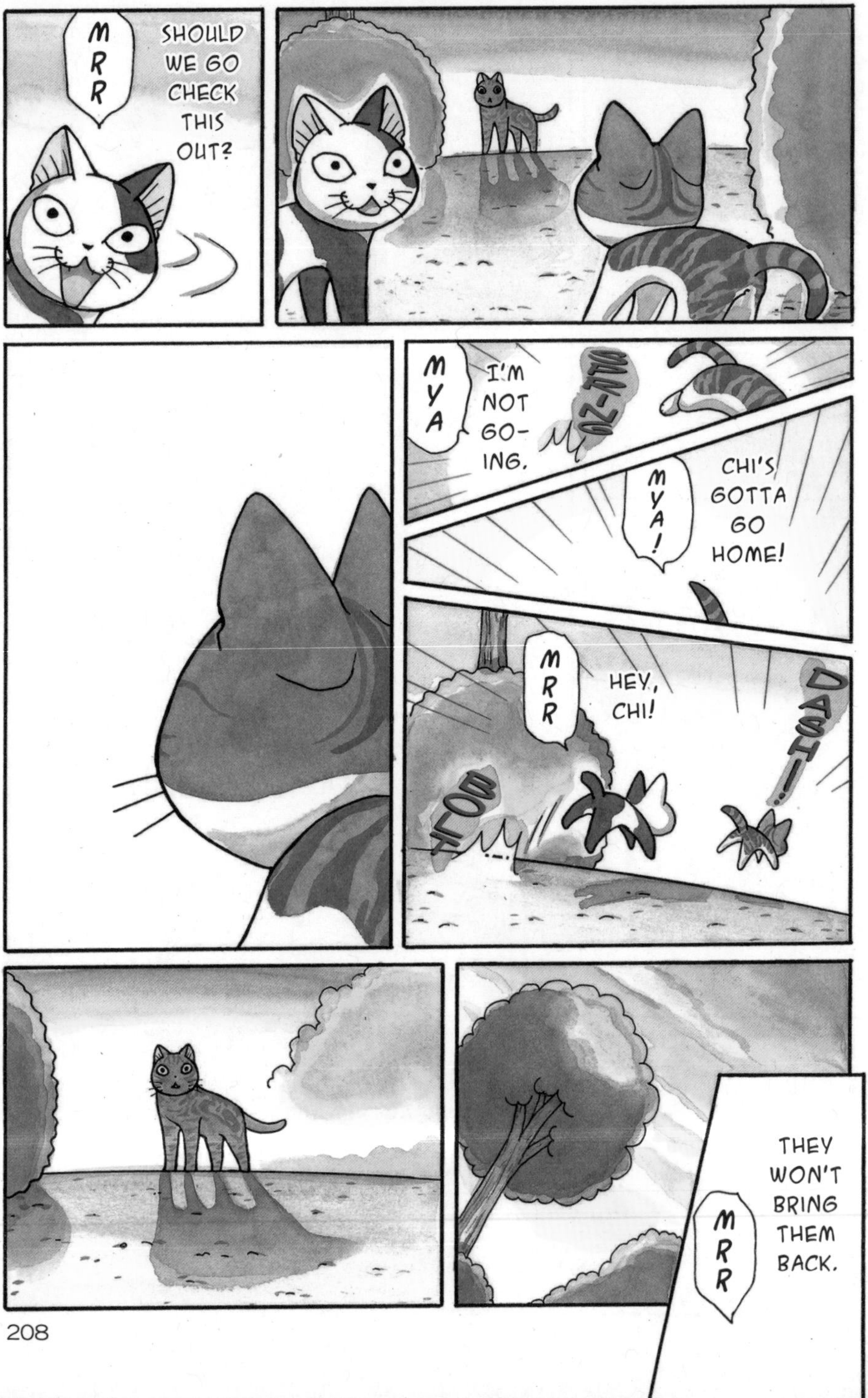
MRR
SHOULD WE GO CHECK THIS OUT?
MYA
I'M NOT GOING.
SPRING
MYA!
CHI'S GOTTA GO HOME!
MRR
HEY, CHI!
BOLT
DASH!
MRR
THEY WON'T BRING THEM BACK.

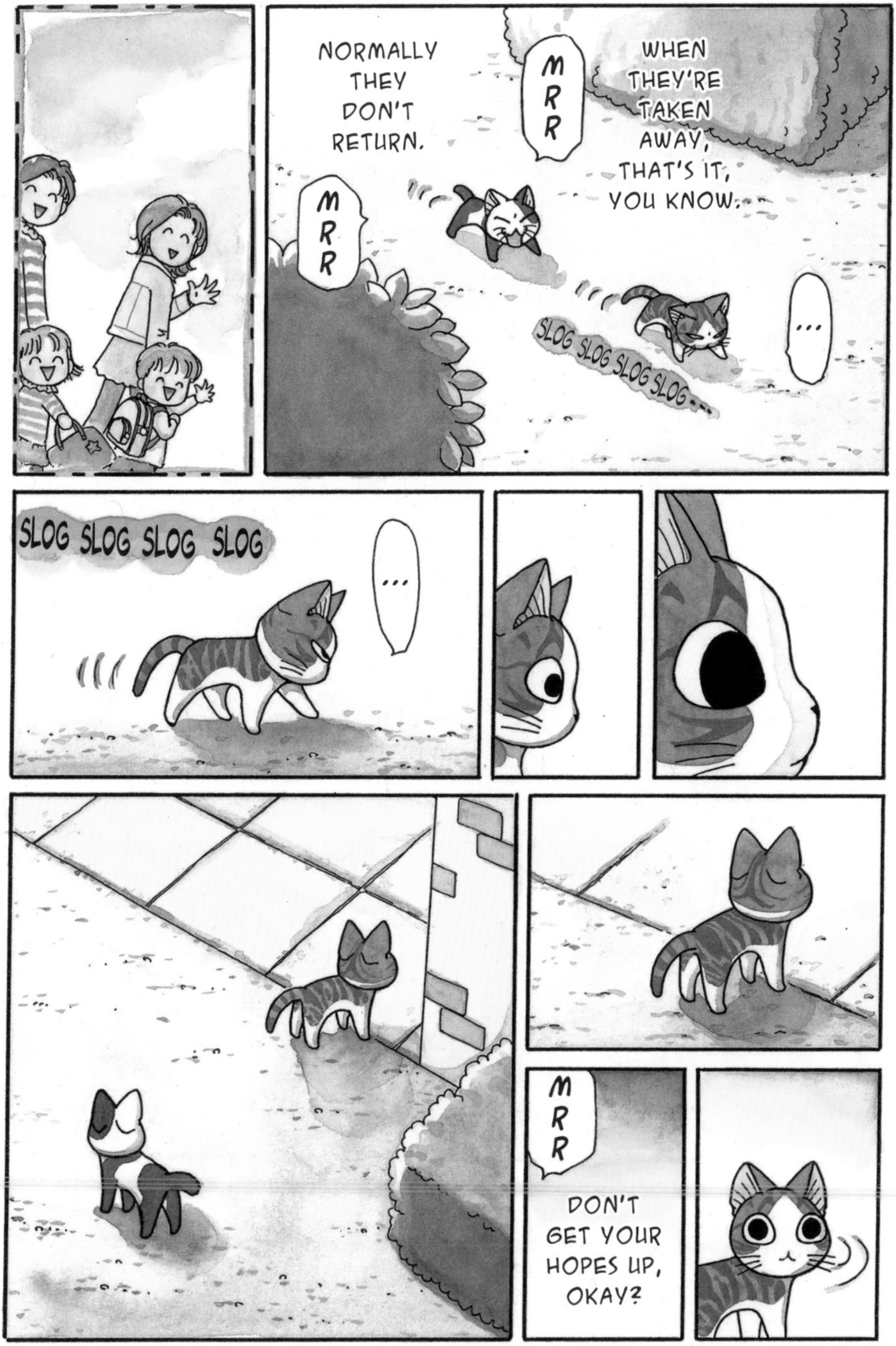
NORMALLY THEY DON'T RETURN.
MRR
WHEN THEY'RE TAKEN AWAY, THAT'S IT, YOU KNOW.
MRR
SLOG SLOG SLOG SLOG...
...
SLOG SLOG SLOG SLOG
...
MRR
DON'T GET YOUR HOPES UP, OKAY?

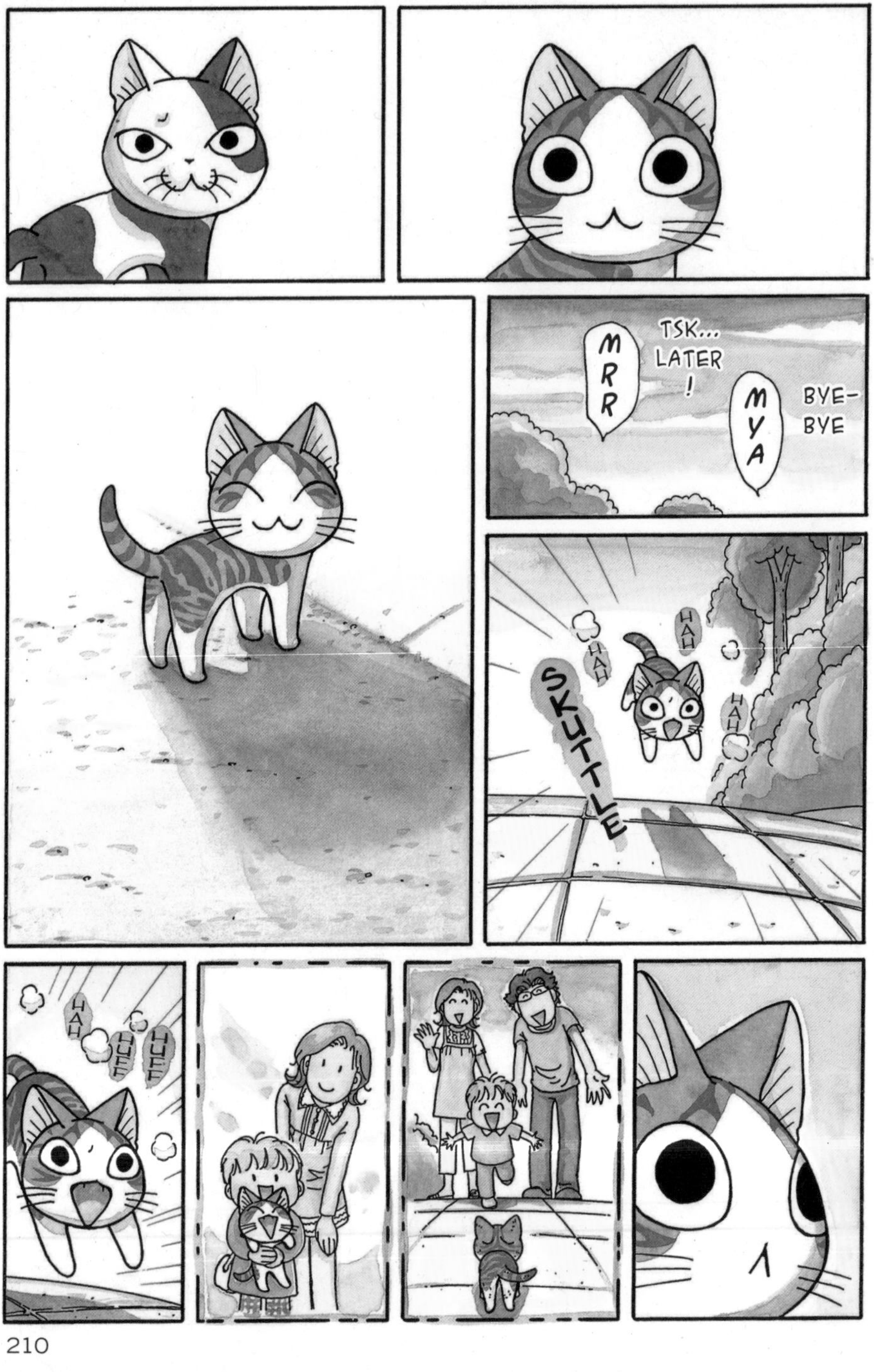
MRR
TSK... LATER!
MYA
BYE-BYE
HAH
HAH
SKUTTLE
HAH
HAH
HUFF
HUFF

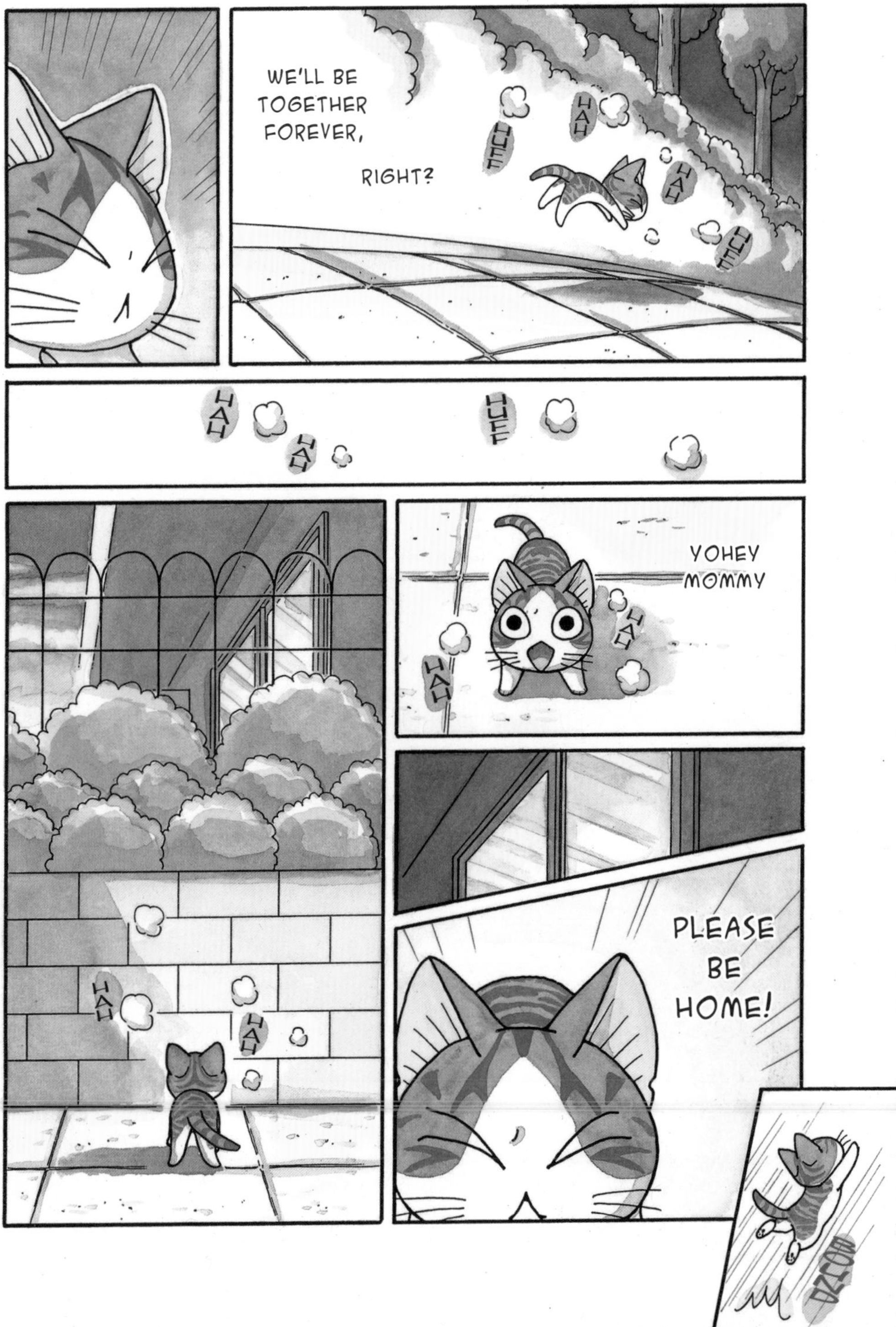
WE'LL BE TOGETHER FOREVER,
RIGHT?
HUFF
HAH
HAH
HUFF
HAH
HAH
HUFF
HAH
HAH
YOHEY MOMMY
HAH
HAH
PLEASE BE HOME!
DZOOM

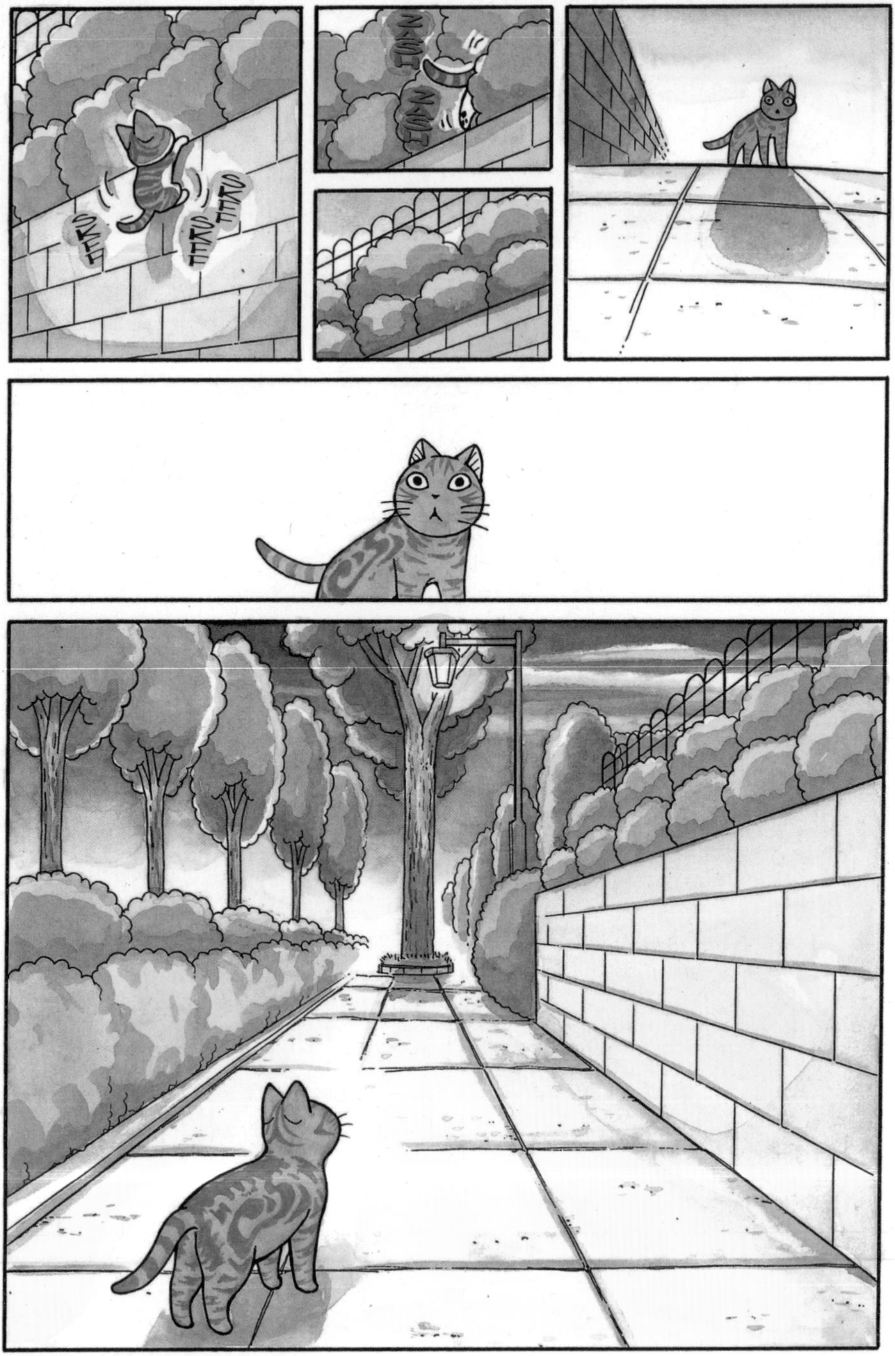
SKFF
SKFF
SKFF
ZISH
ZISH

the end

homemade 191: a cat becomes sensitive

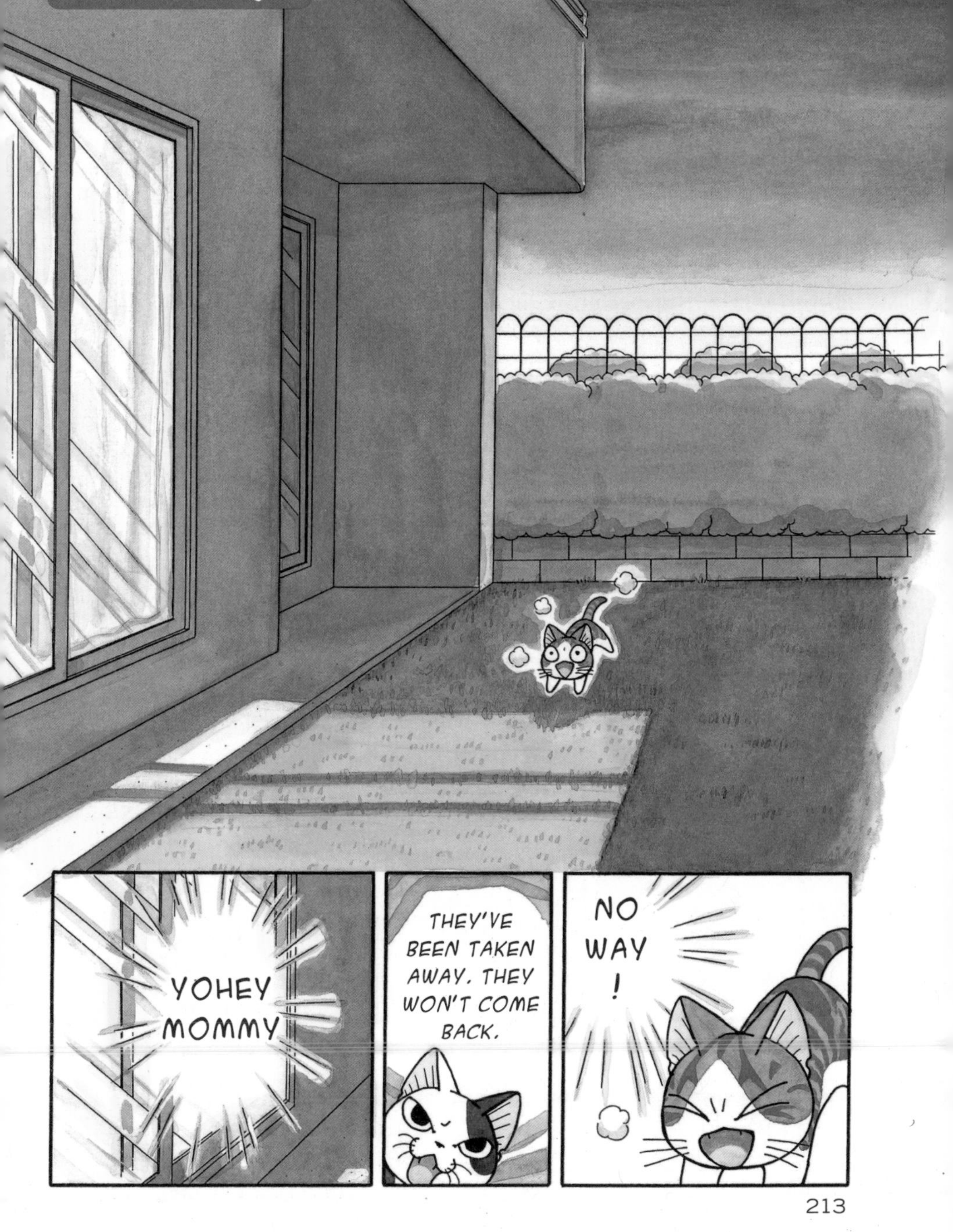
YOHEY MOMMY
THEY'VE BEEN TAKEN AWAY. THEY WON'T COME BACK.
NO WAY!

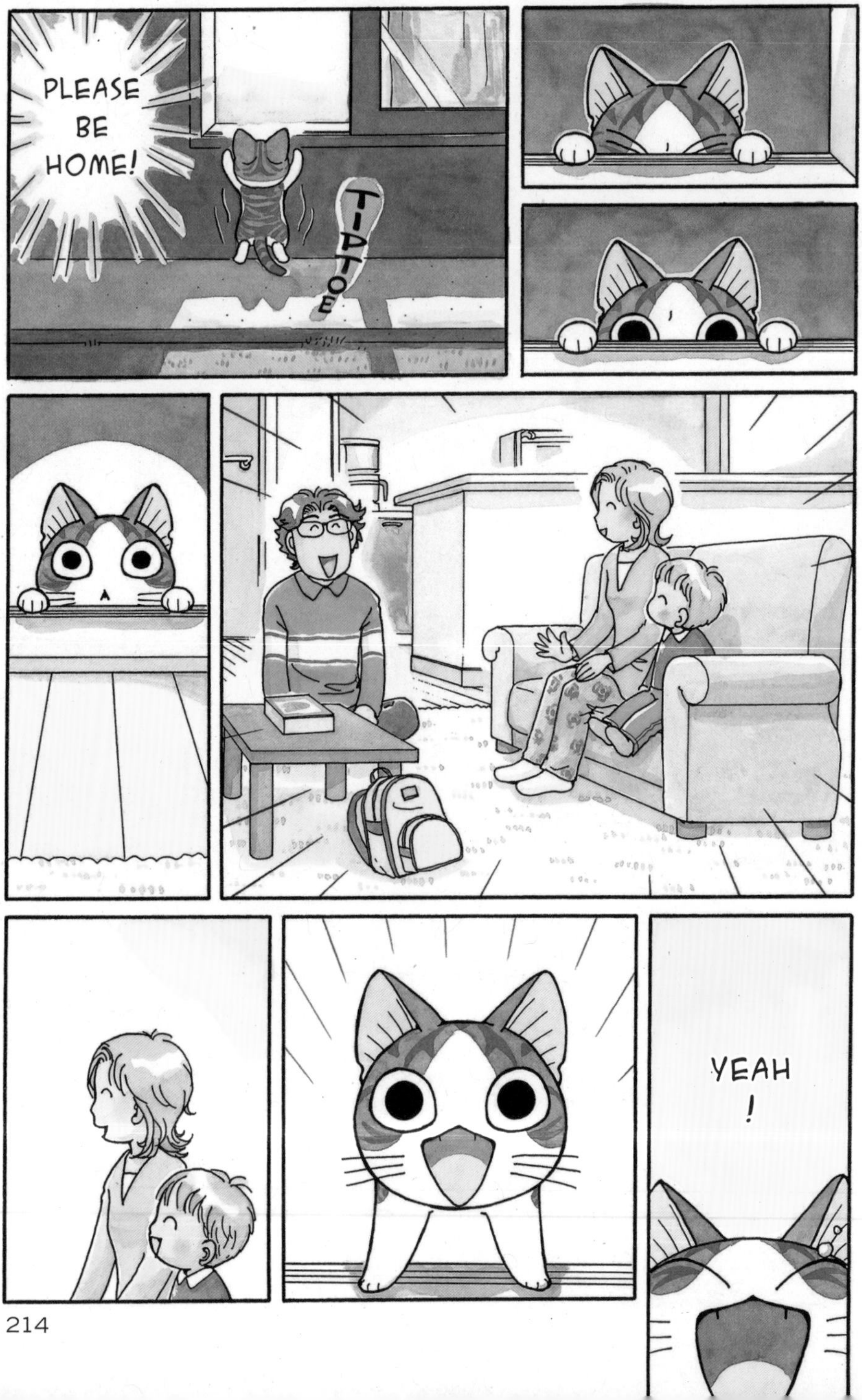
PLEASE BE HOME!
TIPTOE
YEAH!

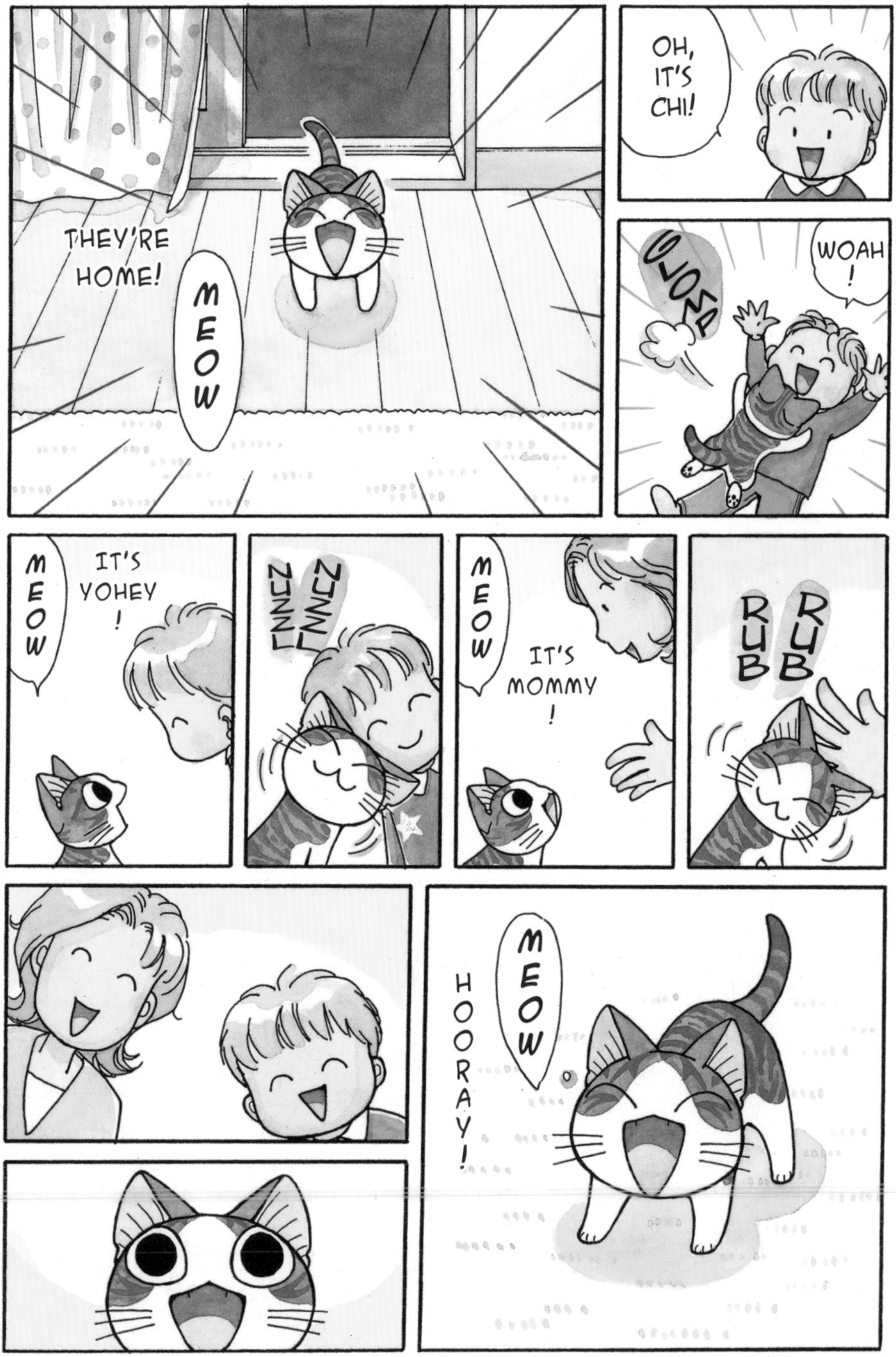
THEY'RE HOME!
MEOW
OH, IT'S CHI!
GLOMP
WOAH!
MEOW
IT'S YOHEY!
NUZZLE NUZZLE
MEOW
IT'S MOMMY!
RUB RUB
MEOW
HOORAY!

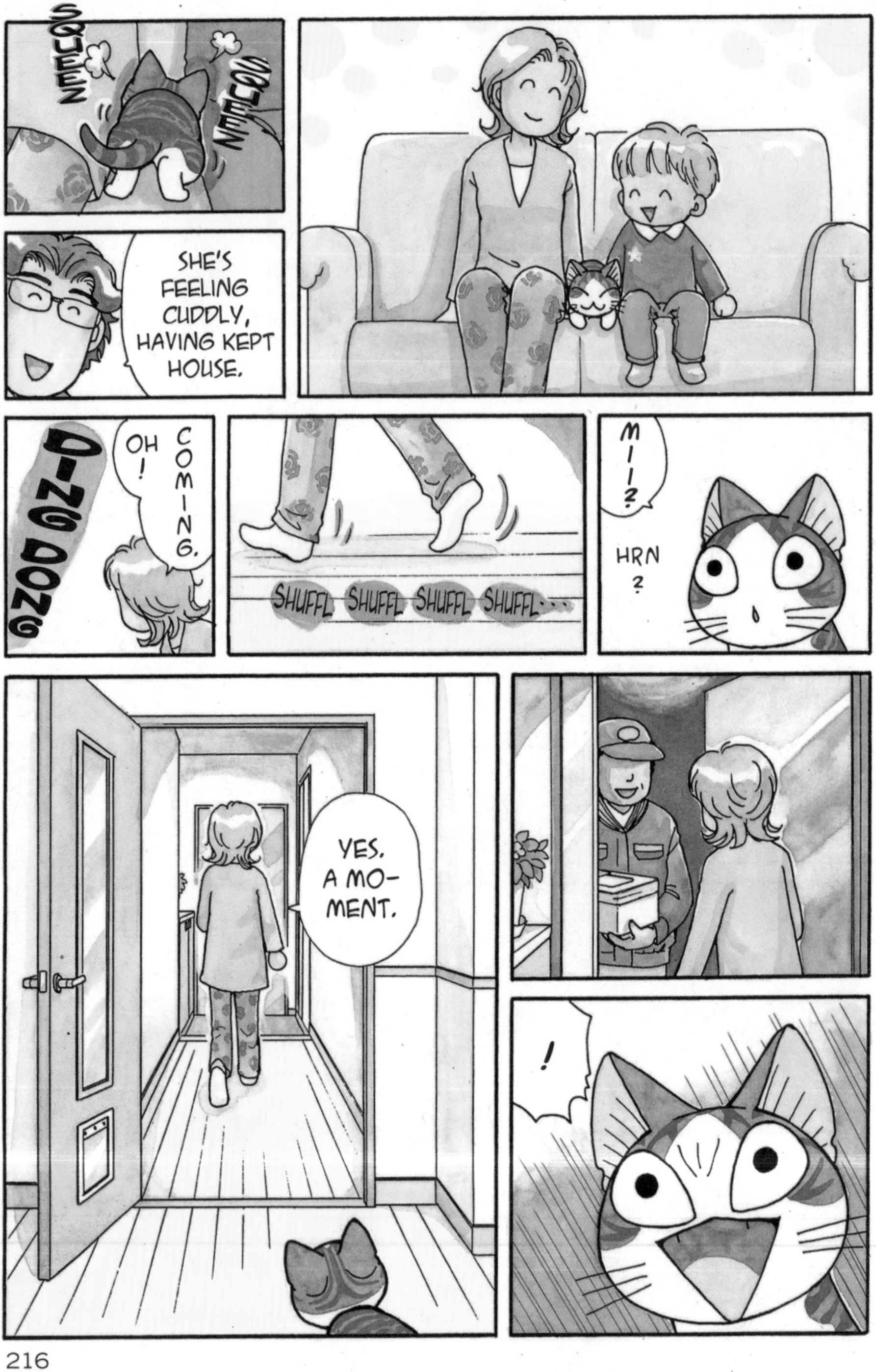
SQUEEN
SQUEEN
SHE'S FEELING CUDDLY, HAVING KEPT HOUSE.
DING DONG
OH! COMING.
SHUFFL SHUFFL SHUFFL SHUFFL...
MII?
HRN?
YES. A MO-MENT.
!

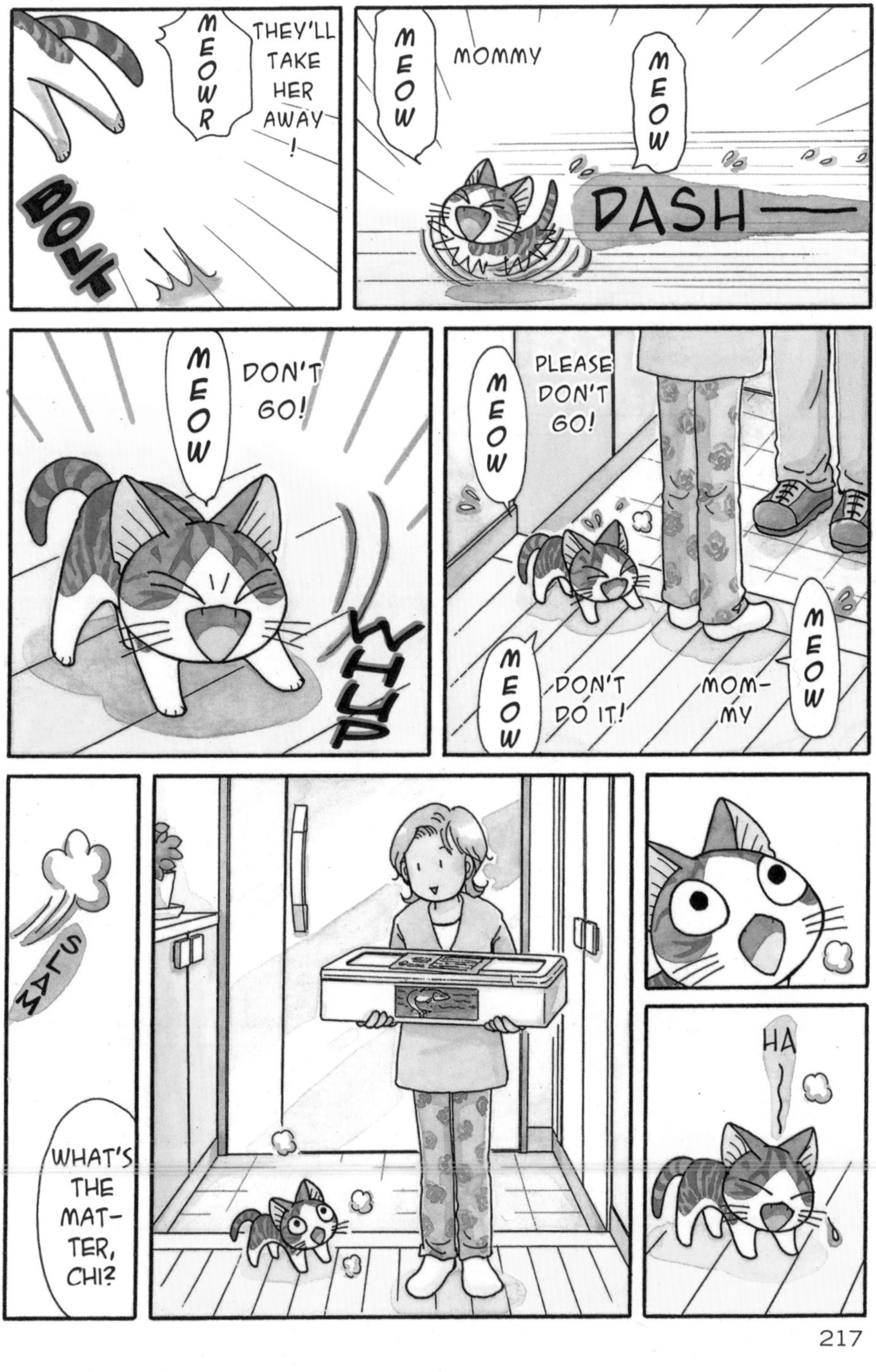
MEOWR
THEY'LL TAKE HER AWAY!
BOLT
MEOW
MOMMY
MEOW
DASH—
MEOW
DON'T GO!
WHUP
MEOW
PLEASE DON'T GO!
MEOW
DON'T DO IT!
MOM-MY
MEOW
SLAM
WHAT'S THE MAT-TER, CHI?
HA

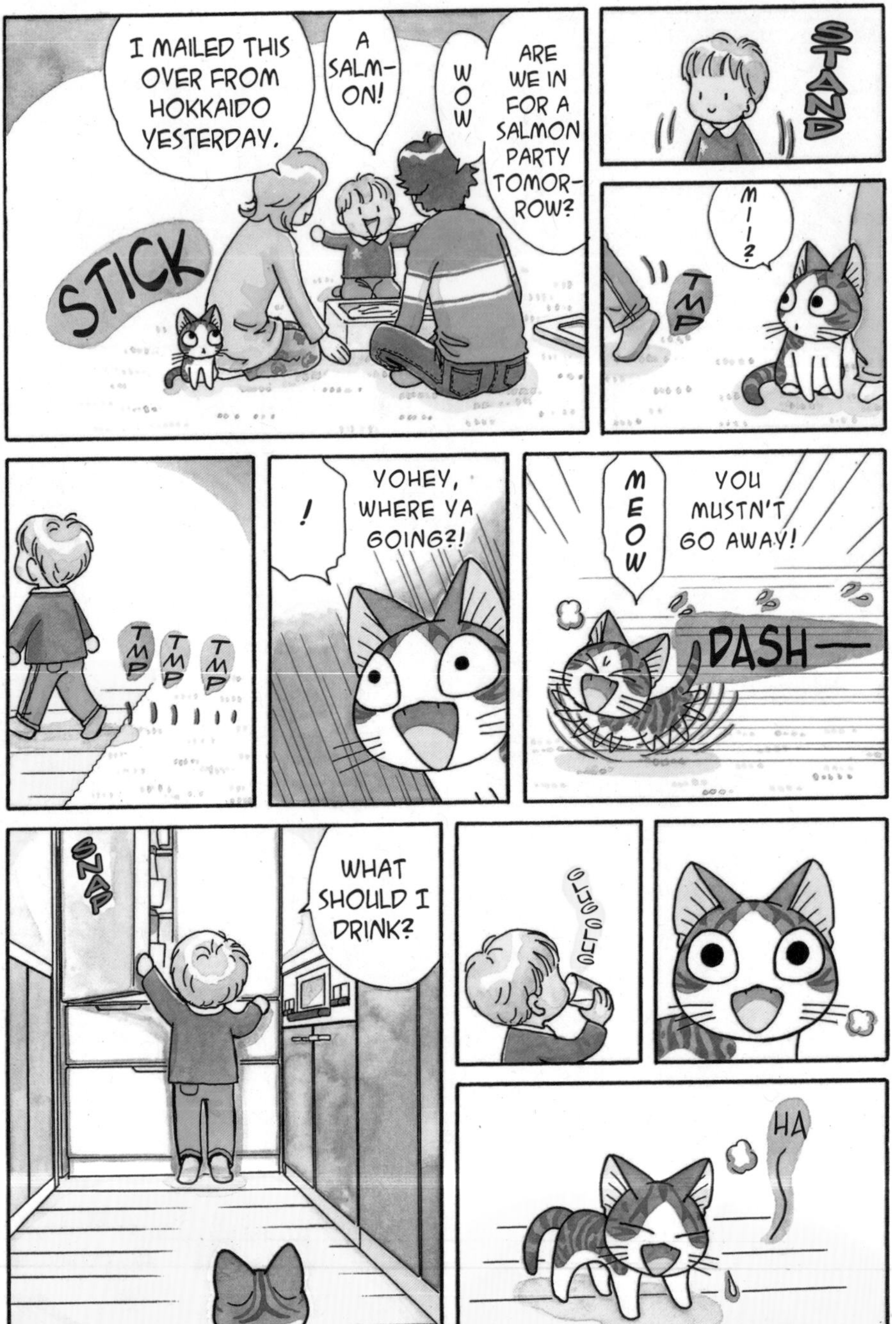

I MAILED THIS OVER FROM HOKKAIDO YESTERDAY.
A SALMON!
WOW
ARE WE IN FOR A SALMON PARTY TOMORROW?
STICK
STAND
MII?
TMP
TMP TMP TMP
!
YOHEY, WHERE YA GOING?!
MEOW
YOU MUSTN'T GO AWAY!
DASH—
SNAP
WHAT SHOULD I DRINK?
GLUG GLUG
HA

STM STM STM

S-L-I-N-K

TMP TMP TMP

TP TP TP TP

TP TP TP TP

HALT

HMM?

MEOW TOGETHER.

MEOW CHI THINKS IT'S BEST WHEN WE'RE ALL TOGETHER.

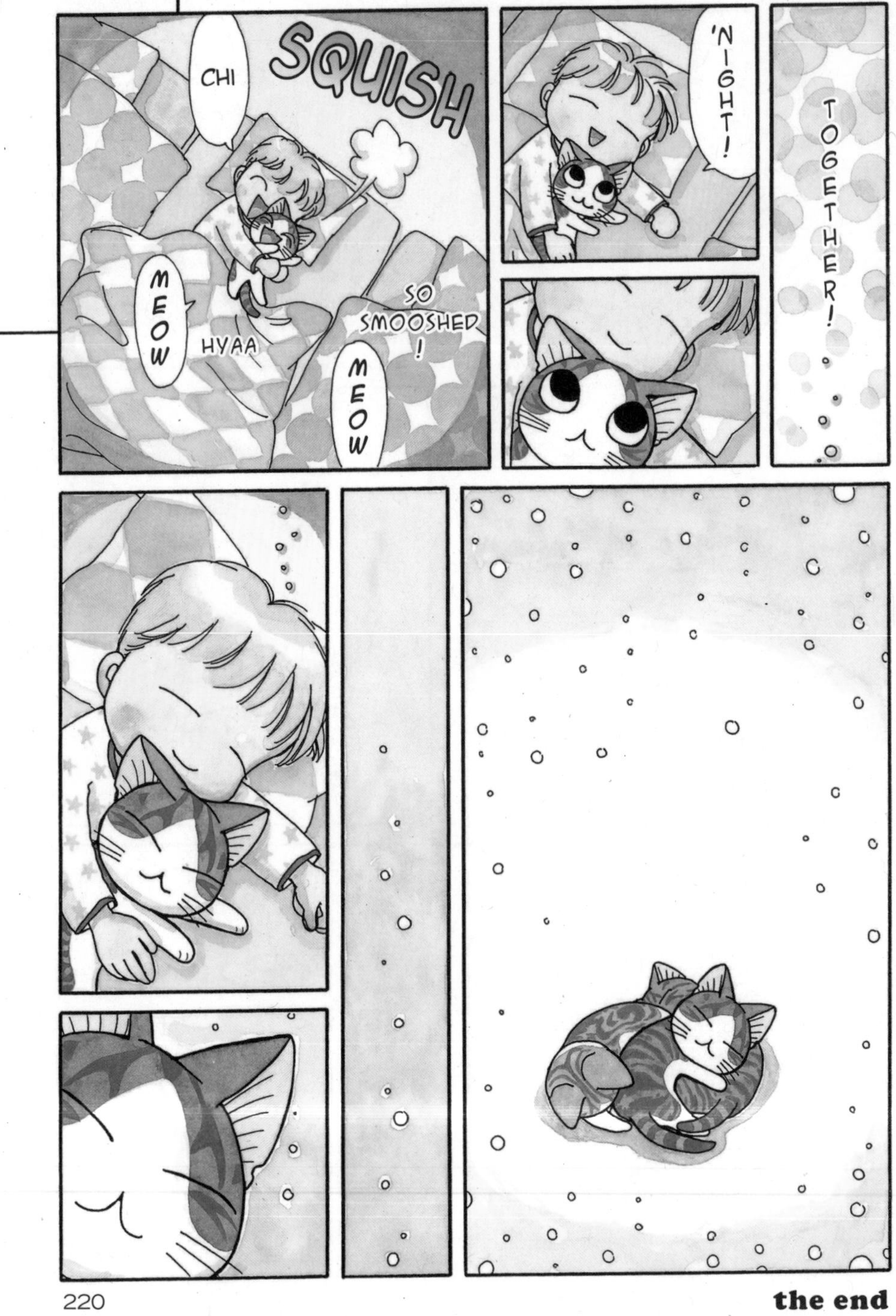
CHI
SQUISH
MEOW
HYAA
SO SMOOSHED!
MEOW
'NIGHT!
TOGETHER!

the end

homemade 192: a cat communes

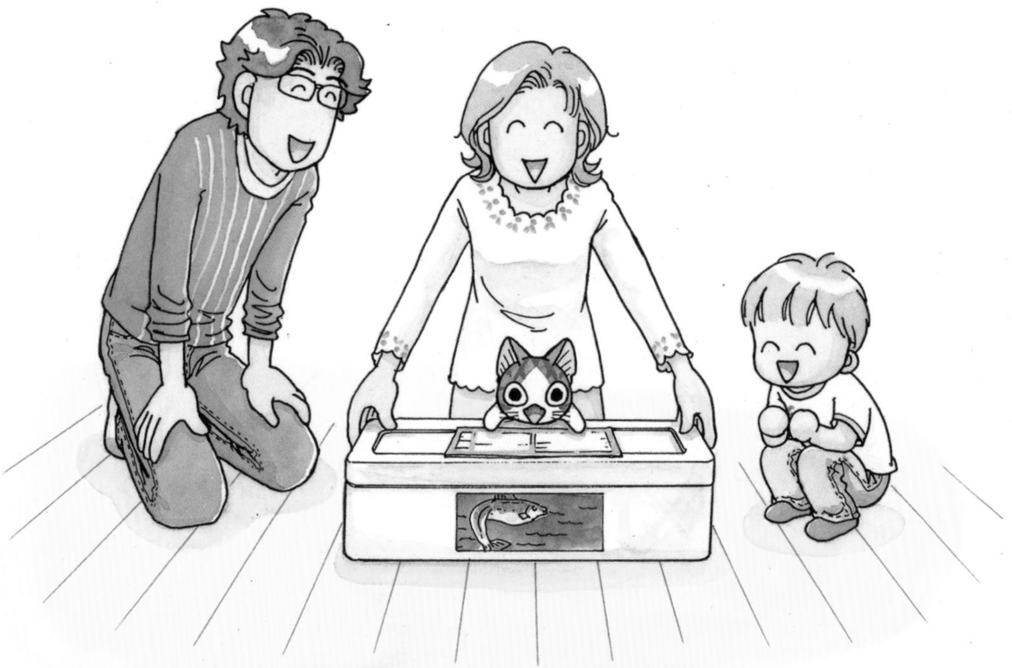

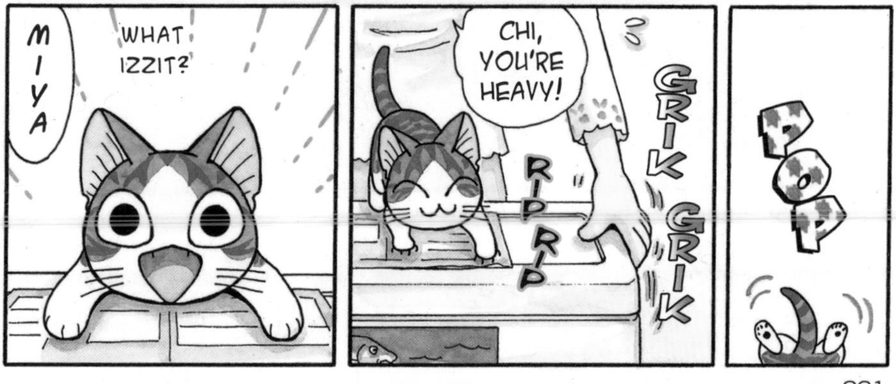
MIYA
WHAT IZZIT?
CHI, YOU'RE HEAVY!
RIP RIP
GRIK GRIK
POP

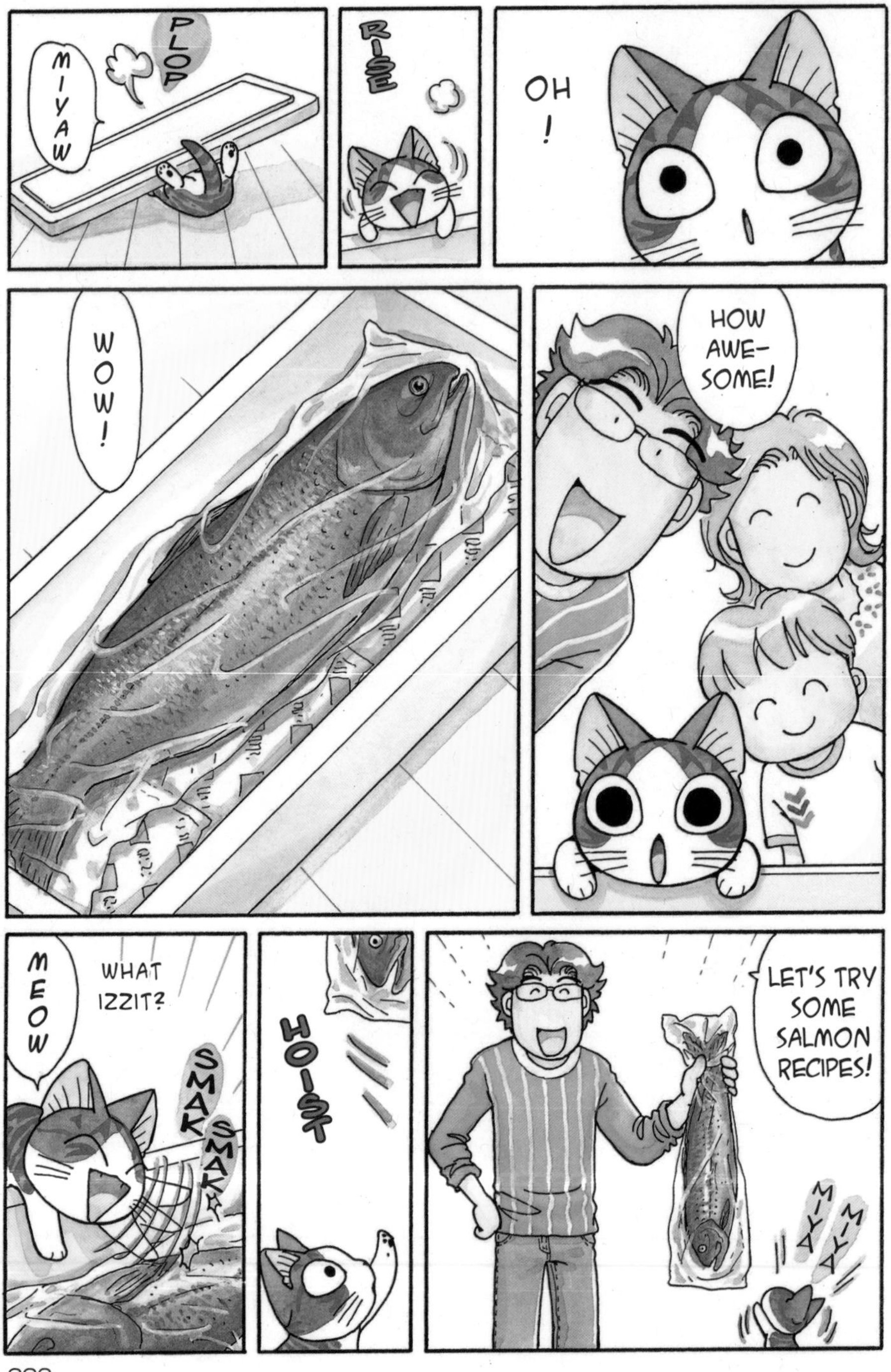
MIYAW
PLOP
RISE
OH!
WOW!
HOW AWE-SOME!
MEOW
WHAT IZZIT?
SMAK
SMAK
HOIST
LET'S TRY SOME SALMON RECIPES!
MIYA
MIYA

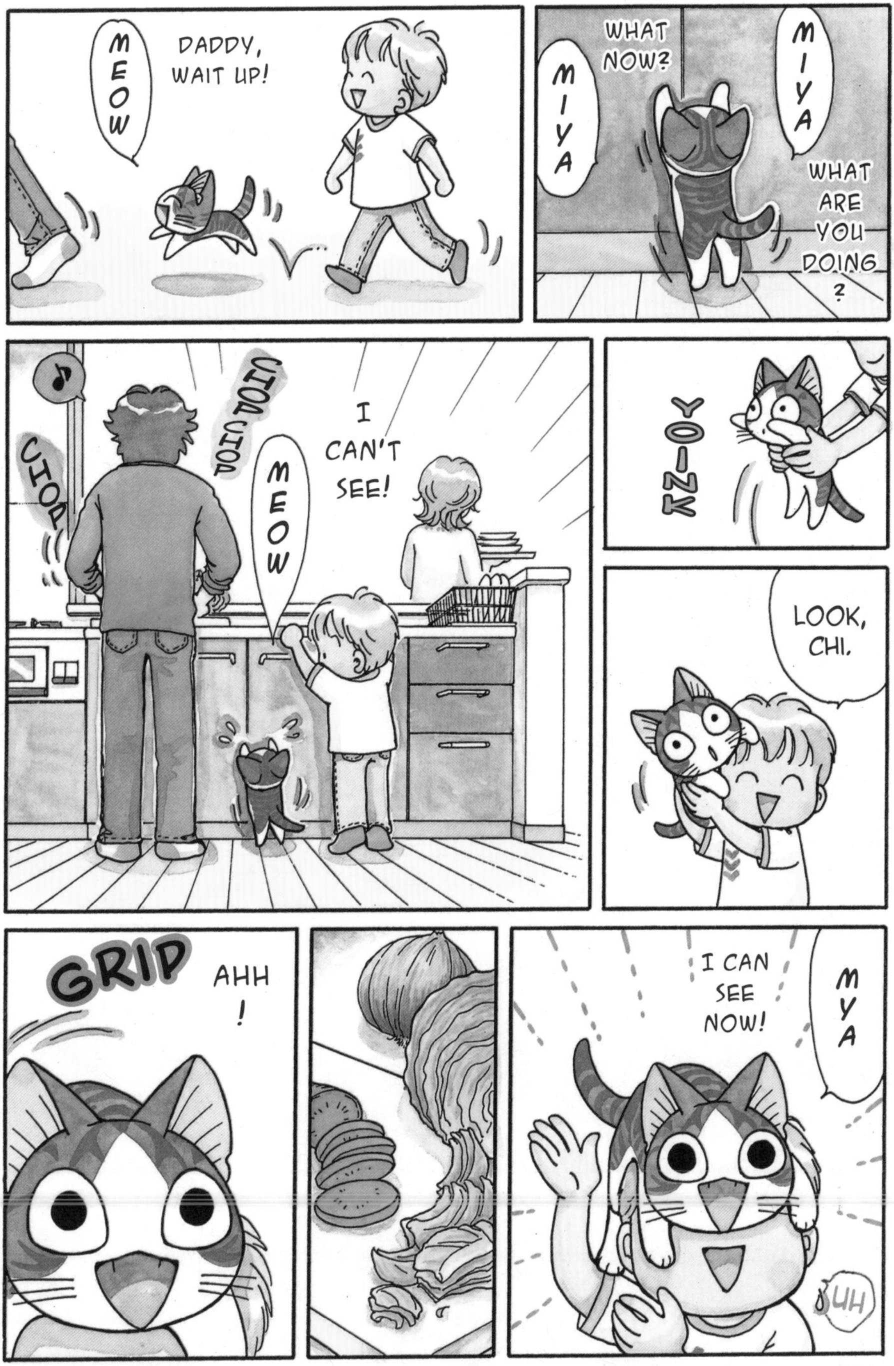
MEOW
DADDY, WAIT UP!
MIYA
WHAT NOW?
MIYA
WHAT ARE YOU DOING?
CHOP
CHOP CHOP
MEOW
I CAN'T SEE!
YOINK
LOOK, CHI.
GRIP
AHH!
I CAN SEE NOW!
MYA
UH

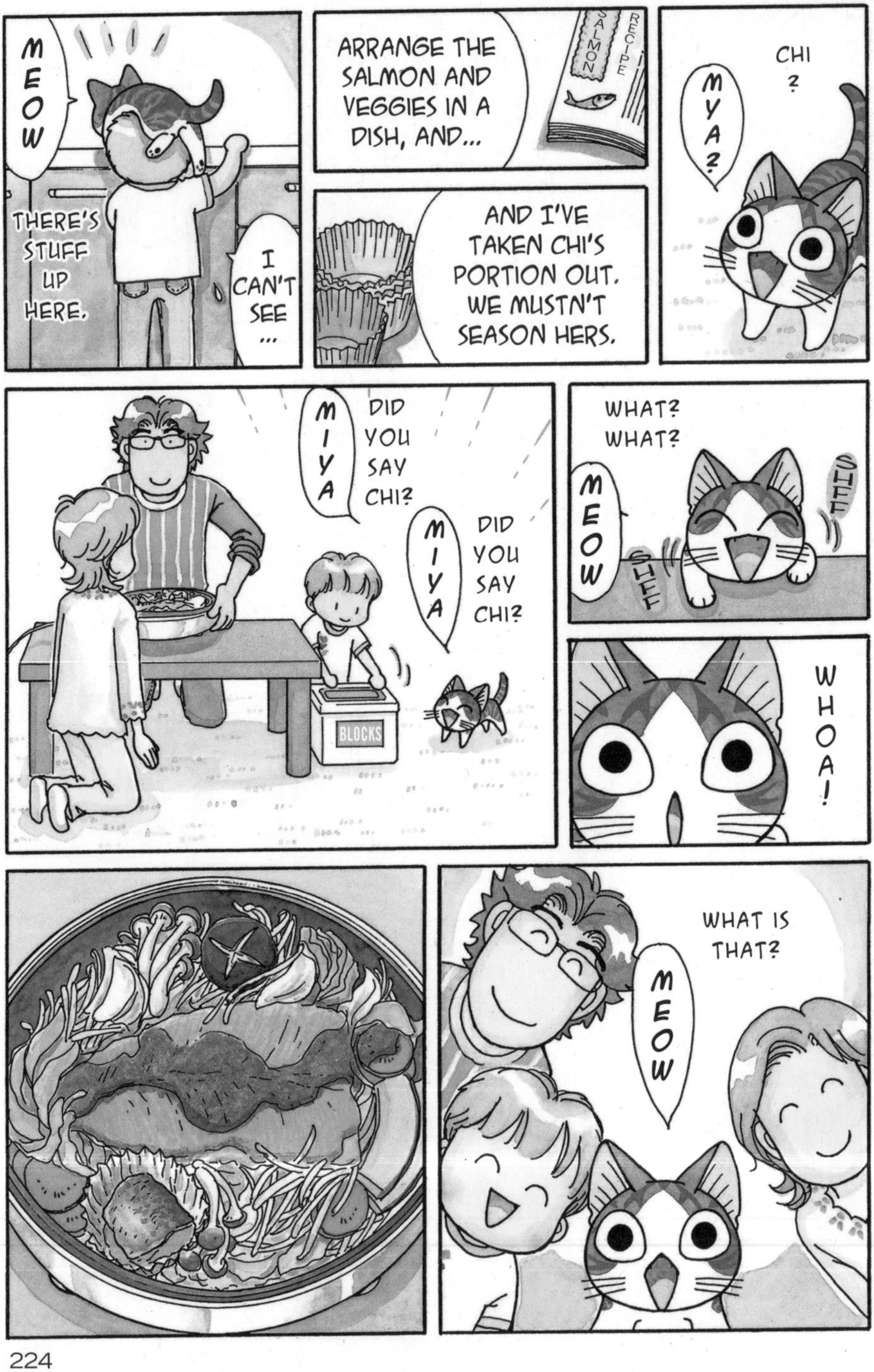
MEOW
THERE'S STUFF UP HERE.
I CAN'T SEE ...
ARRANGE THE SALMON AND VEGGIES IN A DISH, AND...
RECIPE
SALMON
AND I'VE TAKEN CHI'S PORTION OUT. WE MUSTN'T SEASON HERS.
MYA?
CHI?
MIYA
DID YOU SAY CHI?
MIYA
DID YOU SAY CHI?
BLOCKS
MEOW
WHAT? WHAT?
SHUFF
SHUFF
WHOA!
MEOW
WHAT IS THAT?

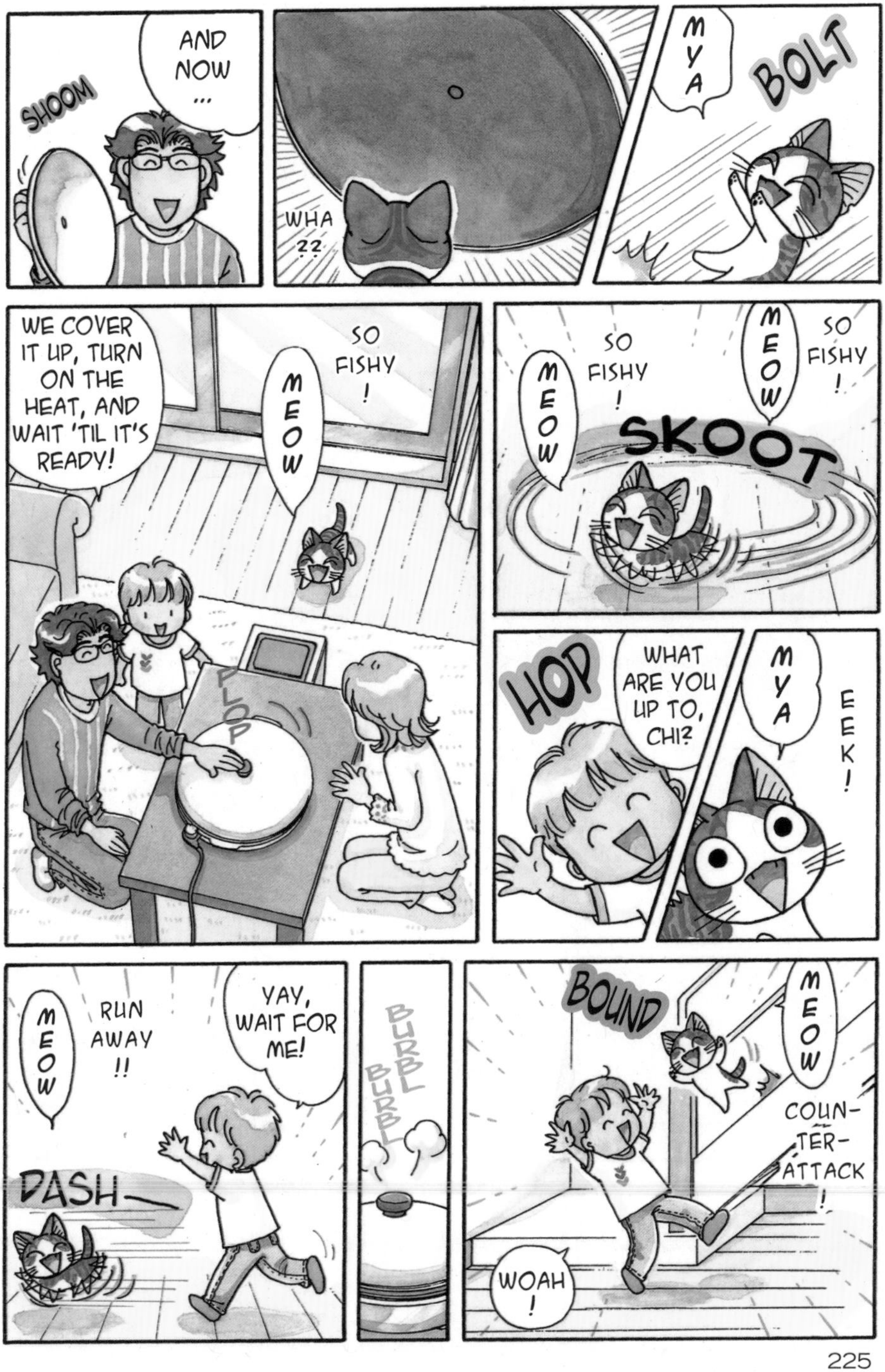
SHOOM
AND NOW ...
WHA ??
MYA
BOLT
WE COVER IT UP, TURN ON THE HEAT, AND WAIT 'TIL IT'S READY!
SO FISHY!
MEOW
PLOP
MEOW
SO FISHY!
MEOW
SO FISHY!
SKOOT
HOP
WHAT ARE YOU UP TO, CHI?
MYA
EEK!
MEOW
RUN AWAY!!
YAY, WAIT FOR ME!
DASH
BURBL
BURBL
BOUND
MEOW
COUNTER-ATTACK!
WOAH!

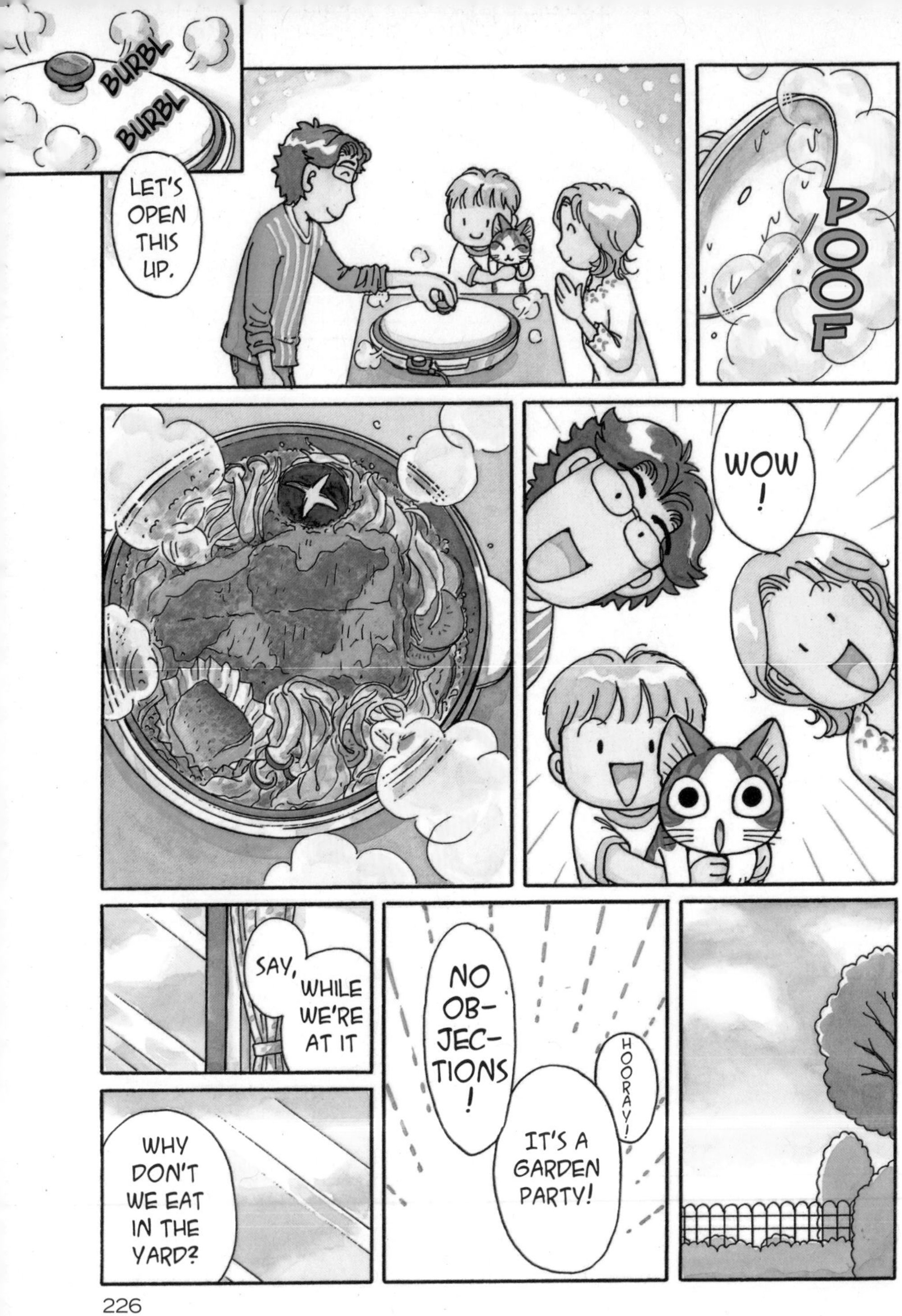
BURBL
BURBL
LET'S OPEN THIS UP.
POOF
WOW!
SAY, WHILE WE'RE AT IT
WHY DON'T WE EAT IN THE YARD?
NO OBJECTIONS!
HOORAY!
IT'S A GARDEN PARTY!

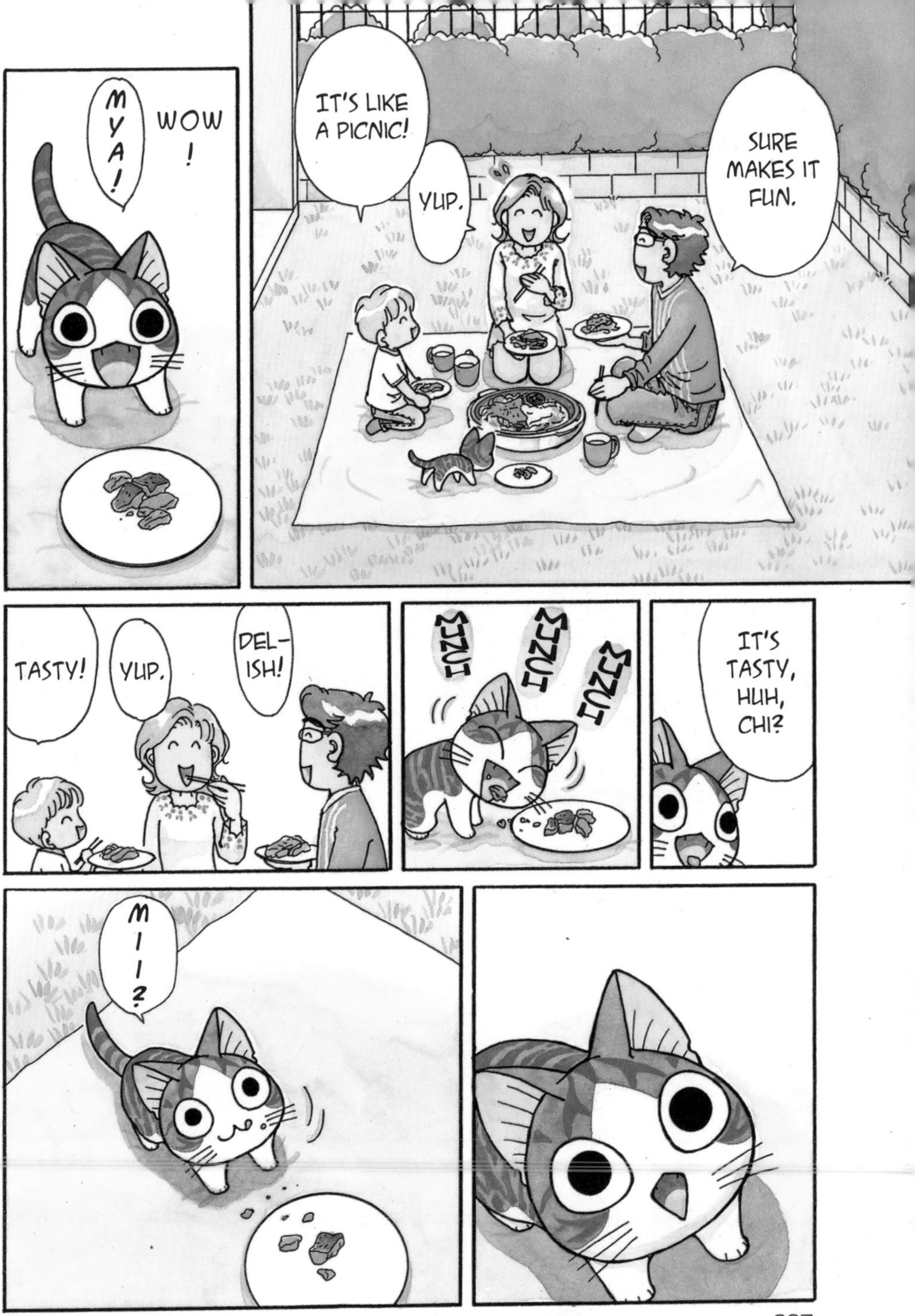
MYA!
WOW!
IT'S LIKE A PICNIC!
YUP.
SURE MAKES IT FUN.
TASTY!
YUP.
DEL-ISH!
MUNCH
MUNCH
MUNCH
IT'S TASTY, HUH, CHI?
MII?

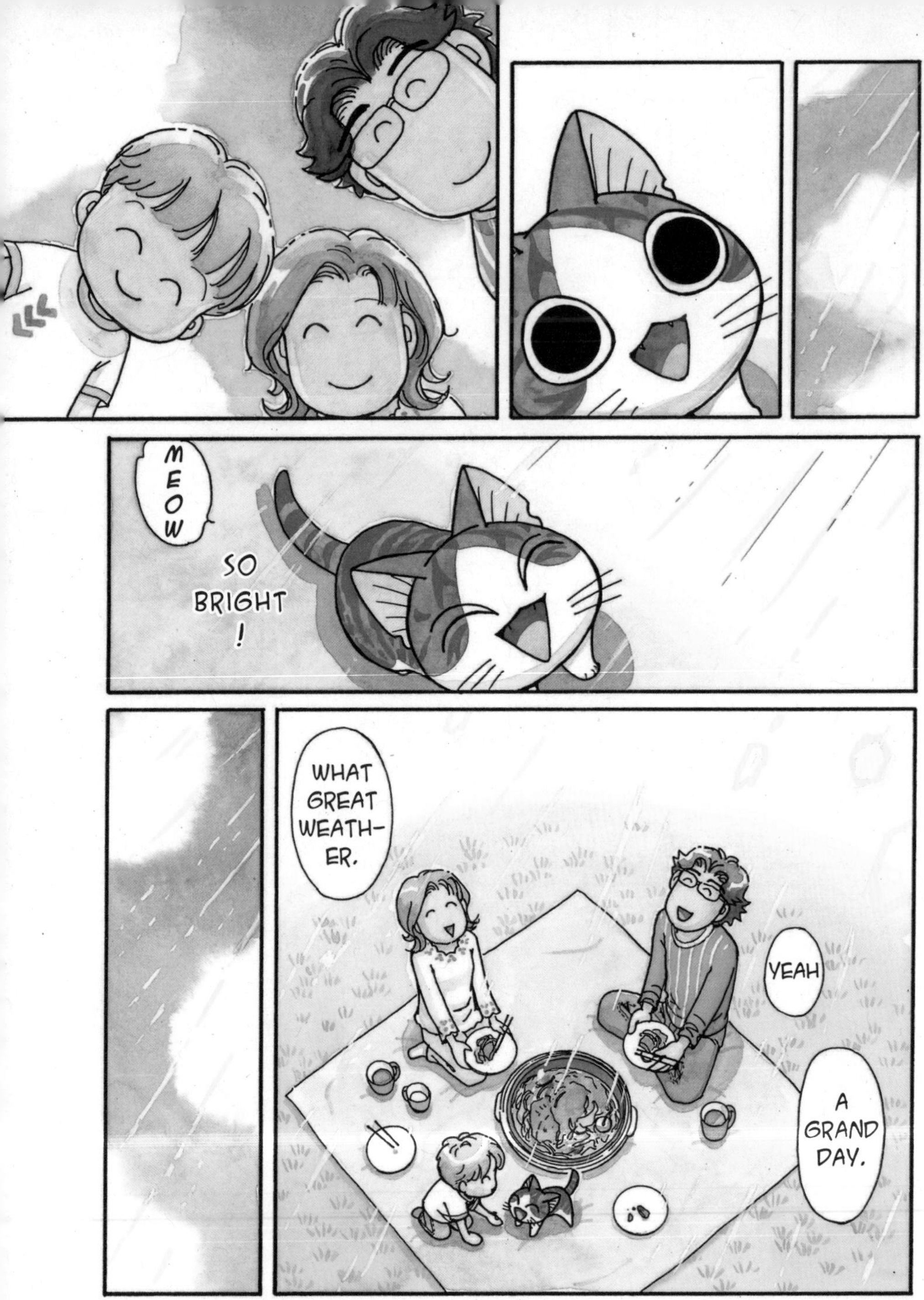
MEOW
SO BRIGHT!
WHAT GREAT WEATHER.
YEAH
A GRAND DAY.

the end

homemade 193: a cat is surprised

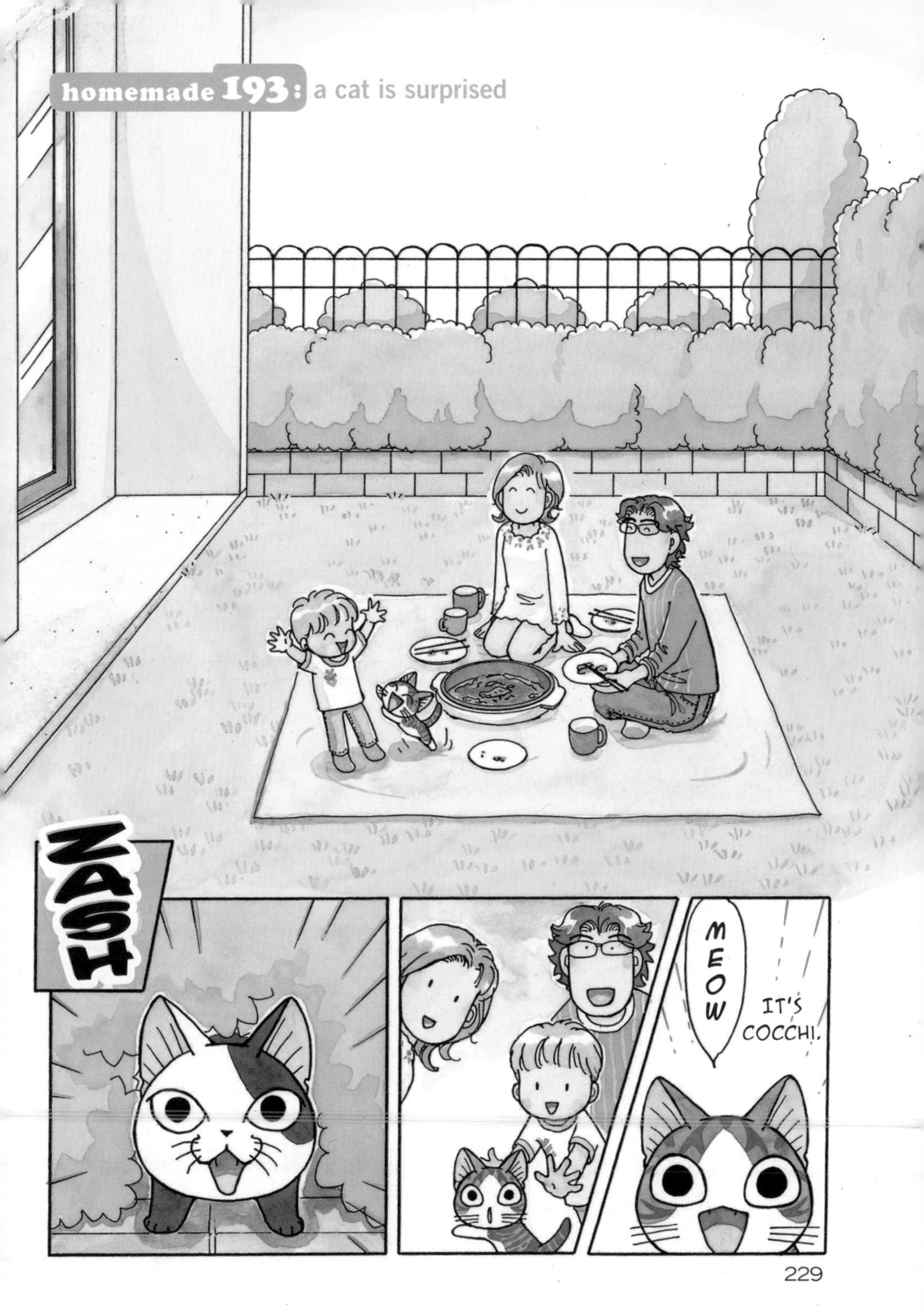
ZASH
MEOW
IT'S COCCHI.

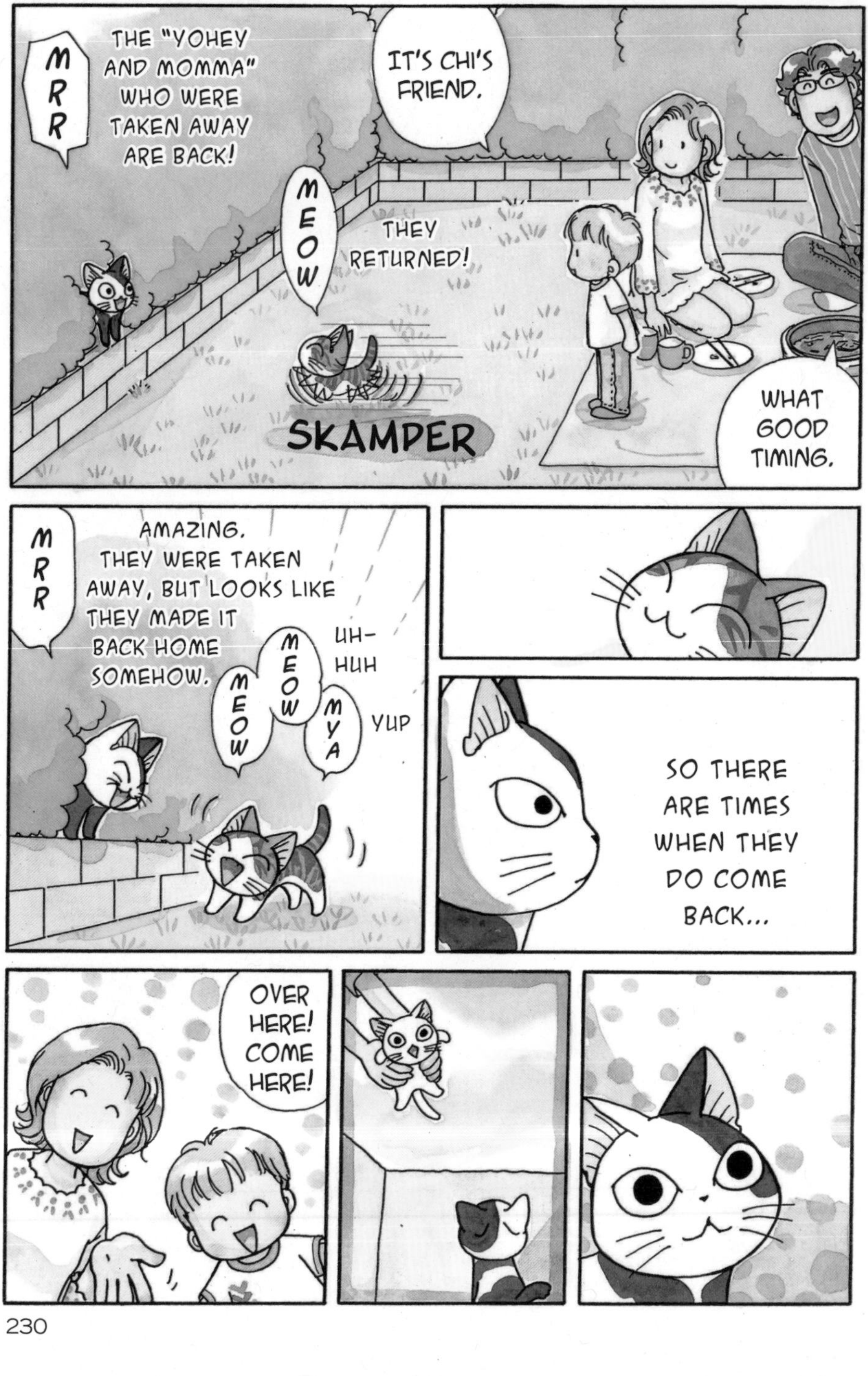
MRR
THE "YOHEY AND MOMMA" WHO WERE TAKEN AWAY ARE BACK!
IT'S CHI'S FRIEND.
MEOW
THEY RETURNED!
SKAMPER
WHAT GOOD TIMING.
MRR
AMAZING. THEY WERE TAKEN AWAY, BUT LOOKS LIKE THEY MADE IT BACK HOME SOMEHOW.
MEOW
UH-HUH
MEOW
MYA
YUP
SO THERE ARE TIMES WHEN THEY DO COME BACK...
OVER HERE! COME HERE!

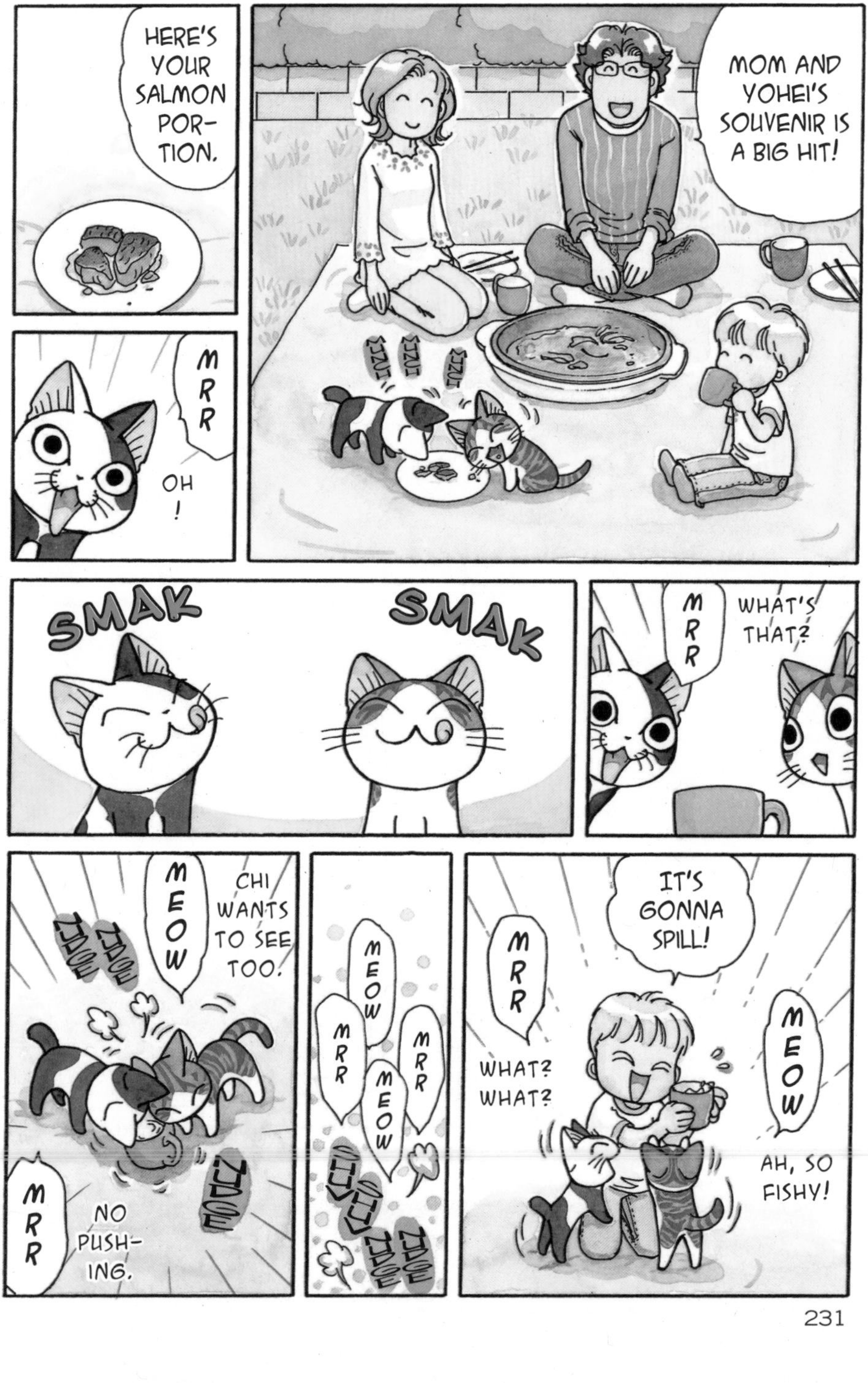
HERE'S YOUR SALMON POR-TION.
MRR
OH!
MOM AND YOHEI'S SOUVENIR IS A BIG HIT!
SMAK
SMAK
MRR
WHAT'S THAT?
MEOW
CHI WANTS TO SEE TOO.
NUDGE
NUDGE
MRR
NO PUSH-ING.
NUDGE
MEOW
MRR
MRR
MEOW
NUDGE
NUDGE
IT'S GONNA SPILL!
MRR
WHAT? WHAT?
MEOW
AH, SO FISHY!

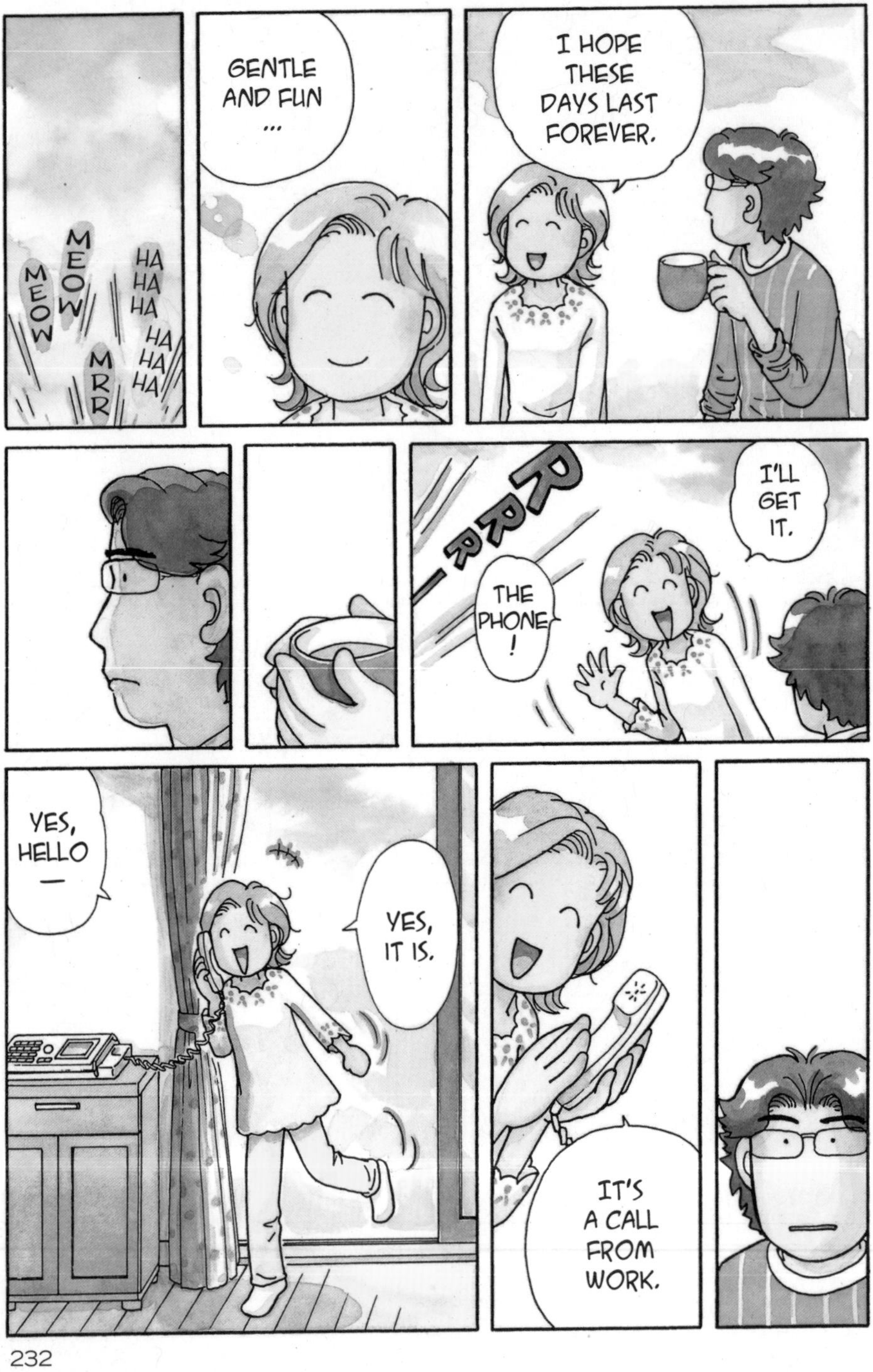
MEOW
MEOW
MRR
HA HA HA
HA HA HA
GENTLE AND FUN ...
I HOPE THESE DAYS LAST FOREVER.
RRRR—
THE PHONE!
I'LL GET IT.
YES, HELLO —
YES, IT IS.
IT'S A CALL FROM WORK.

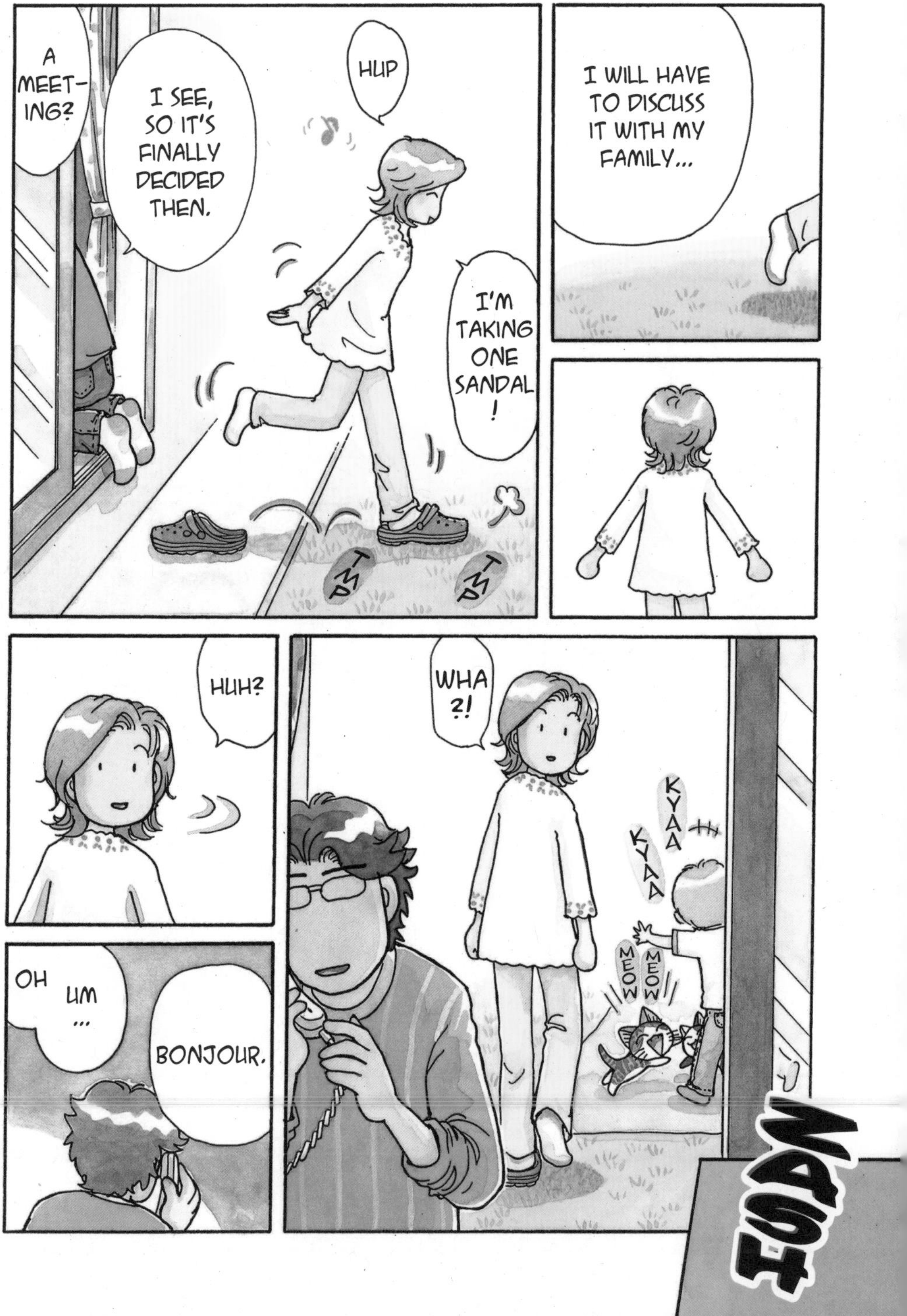
A MEET-ING?
I SEE, SO IT'S FINALLY DECIDED THEN.
HUP
I'M TAKING ONE SANDAL!
TMP
TMP
I WILL HAVE TO DISCUSS IT WITH MY FAMILY...
HUH?
OH
UM ...
BONJOUR.
WHA ?!
KYAA
KYAA
MEOW
MEOW

SARAH!

NYA

SARAH!

NYA

!

IT'S AN ADULT STRIPEY CAT!

IT'S THE MOMMA OF THOSE TWO WE MET AT THE PARK.

MRR

SHE'S STILL SAYING "SARAH" TO CHI?

NYA

YOU ARE SARAH, RIGHT?

NYA

HAVE YOU FORGOTTEN, SARAH?

MYA

FOR-GOTTEN WHAT?

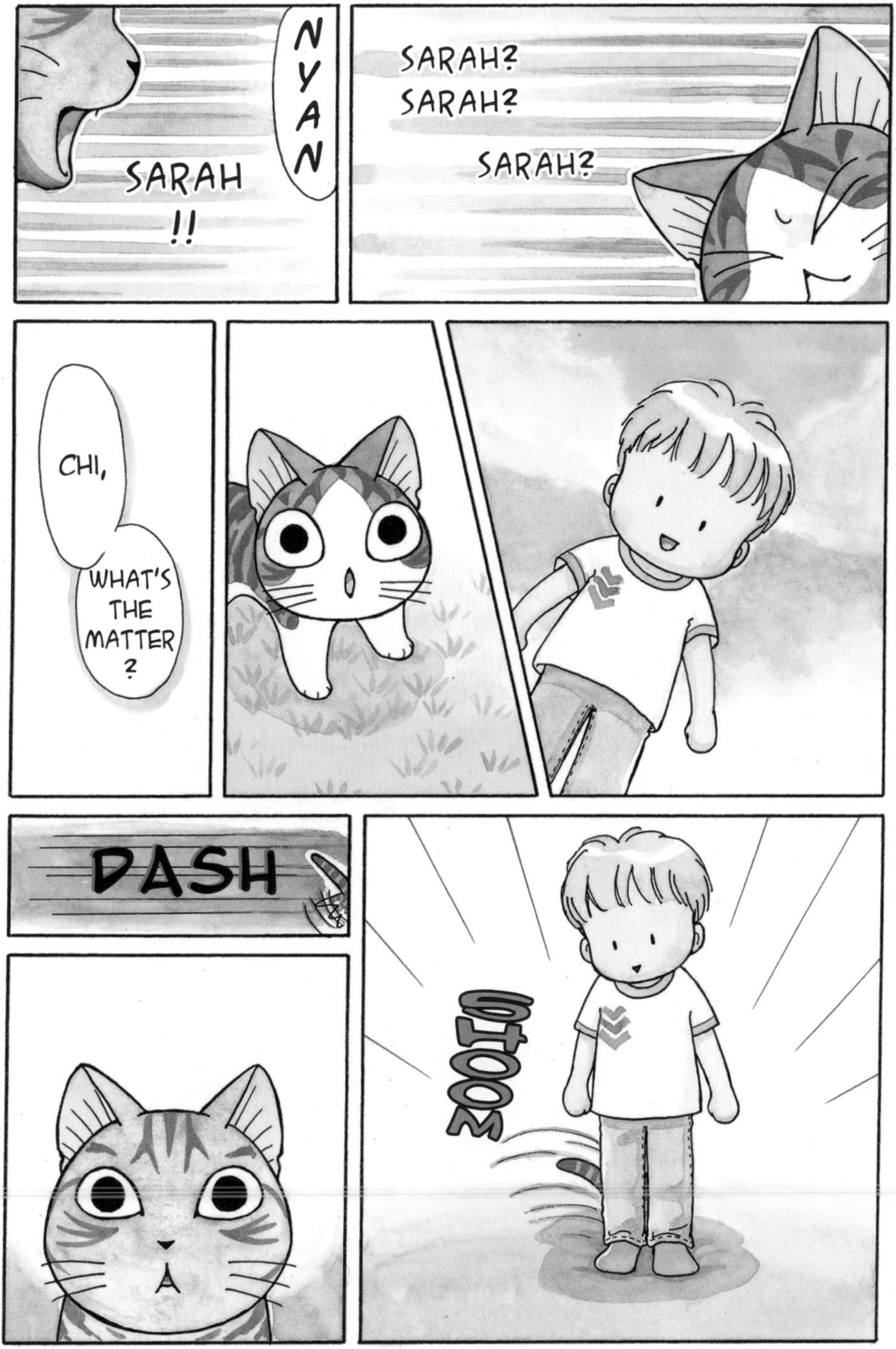
SARAH !!
NYAN
SARAH?
SARAH?
SARAH?
CHI,
WHAT'S THE MATTER?
DASH
SHOOM

RUSTLE
RUSTLE

the end

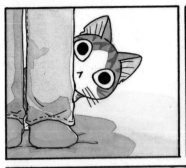

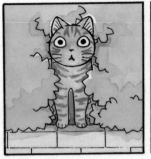

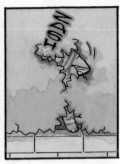

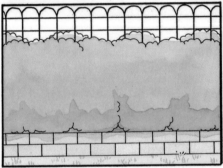

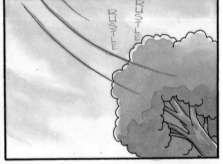

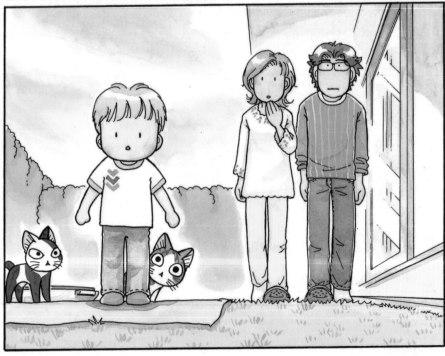

homemade 194: a cat is compelled

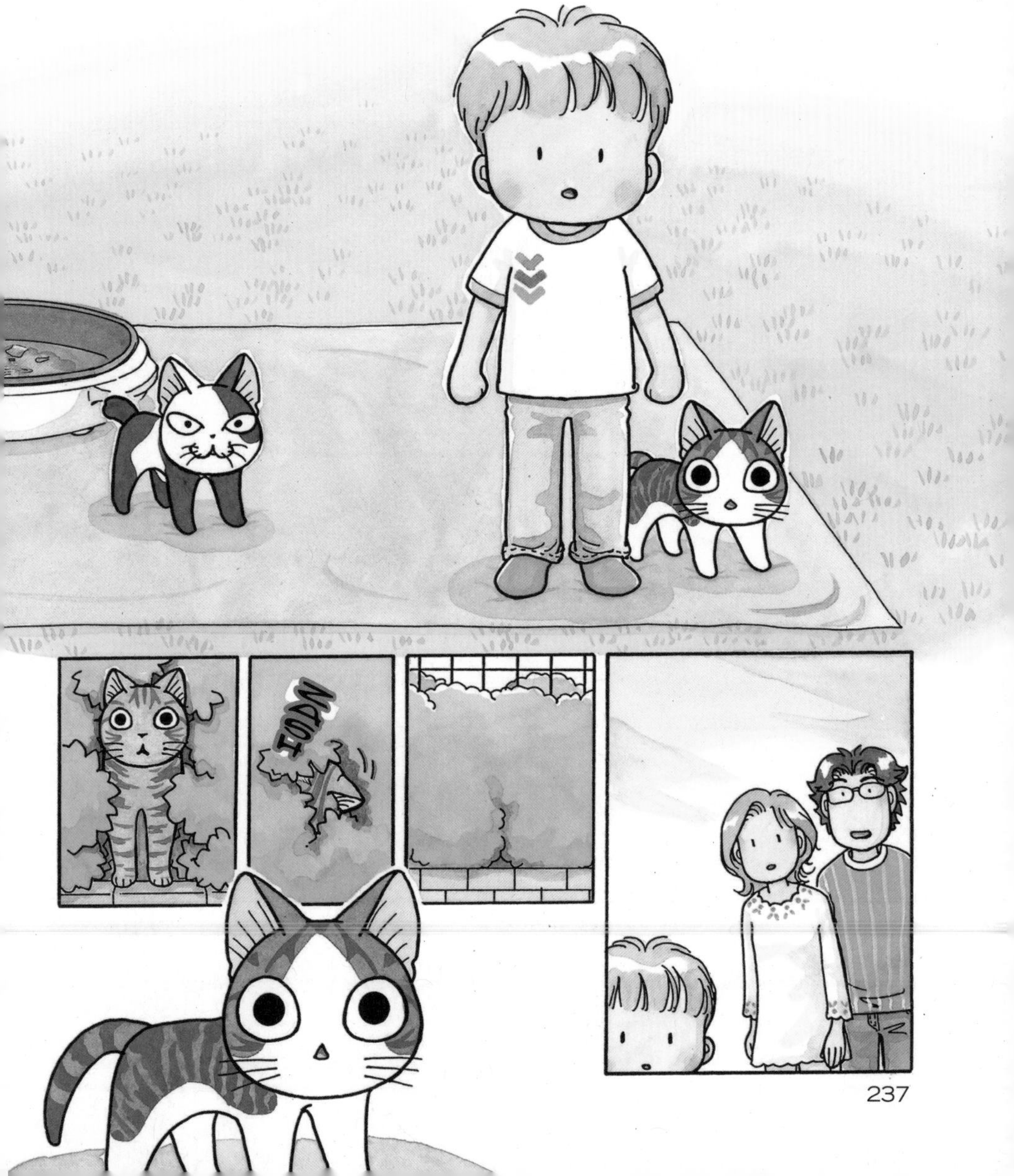

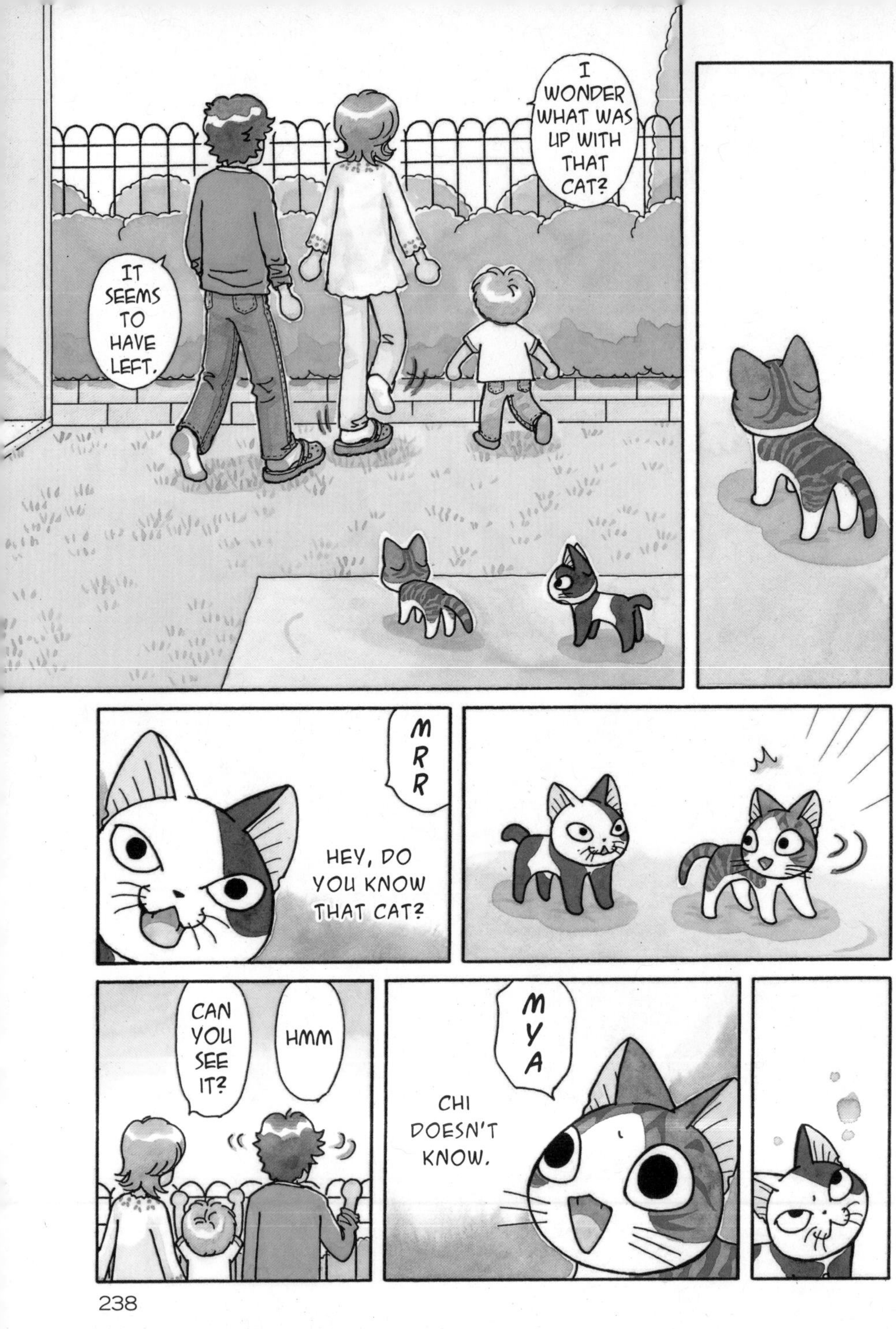
I WONDER WHAT WAS UP WITH THAT CAT?
IT SEEMS TO HAVE LEFT.
MRR
HEY, DO YOU KNOW THAT CAT?
CAN YOU SEE IT?
HMM
MYA
CHI DOESN'T KNOW.

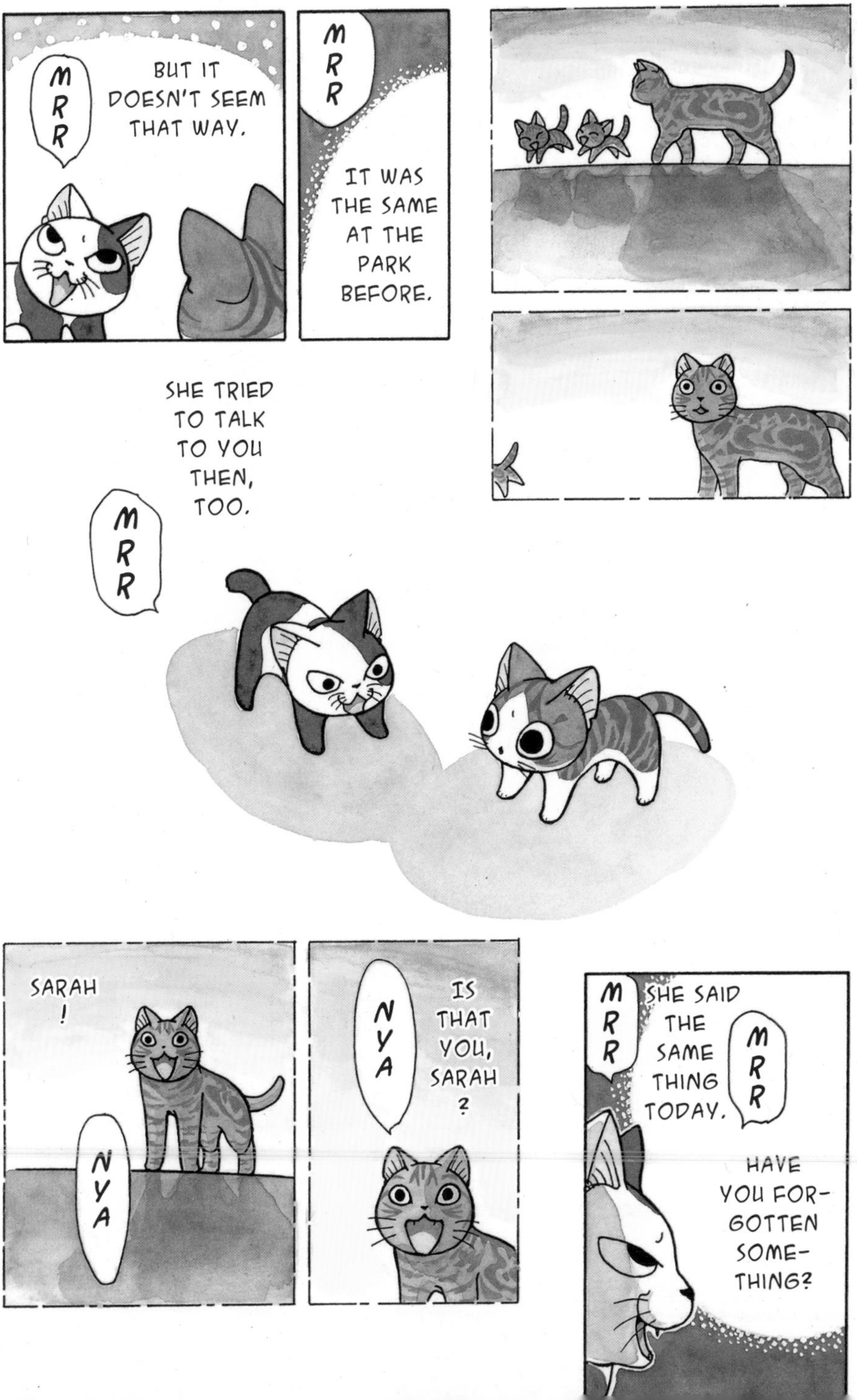
MRR
BUT IT DOESN'T SEEM THAT WAY.
MRR
IT WAS THE SAME AT THE PARK BEFORE.
SHE TRIED TO TALK TO YOU THEN, TOO.
MRR
SARAH!
NYA
NYA
IS THAT YOU, SARAH?
MRR
SHE SAID THE SAME THING TODAY.
MRR
HAVE YOU FORGOTTEN SOMETHING?

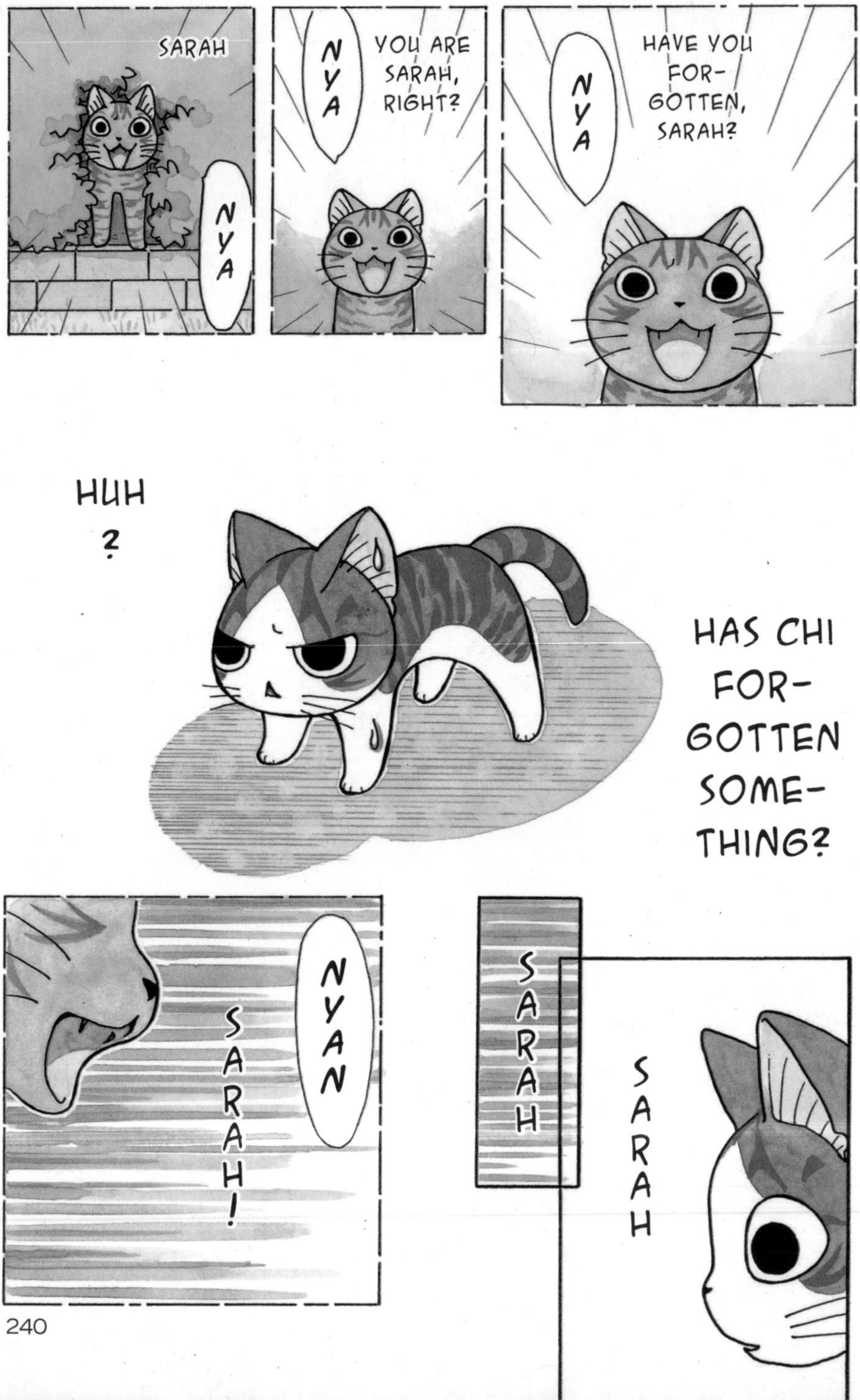
SARAH
NYA
NYA
YOU ARE SARAH, RIGHT?
NYA
HAVE YOU FOR-GOTTEN, SARAH?
HUH?
HAS CHI FOR-GOTTEN SOME-THING?
NYAN
SARAH!
SARAH
SARAH

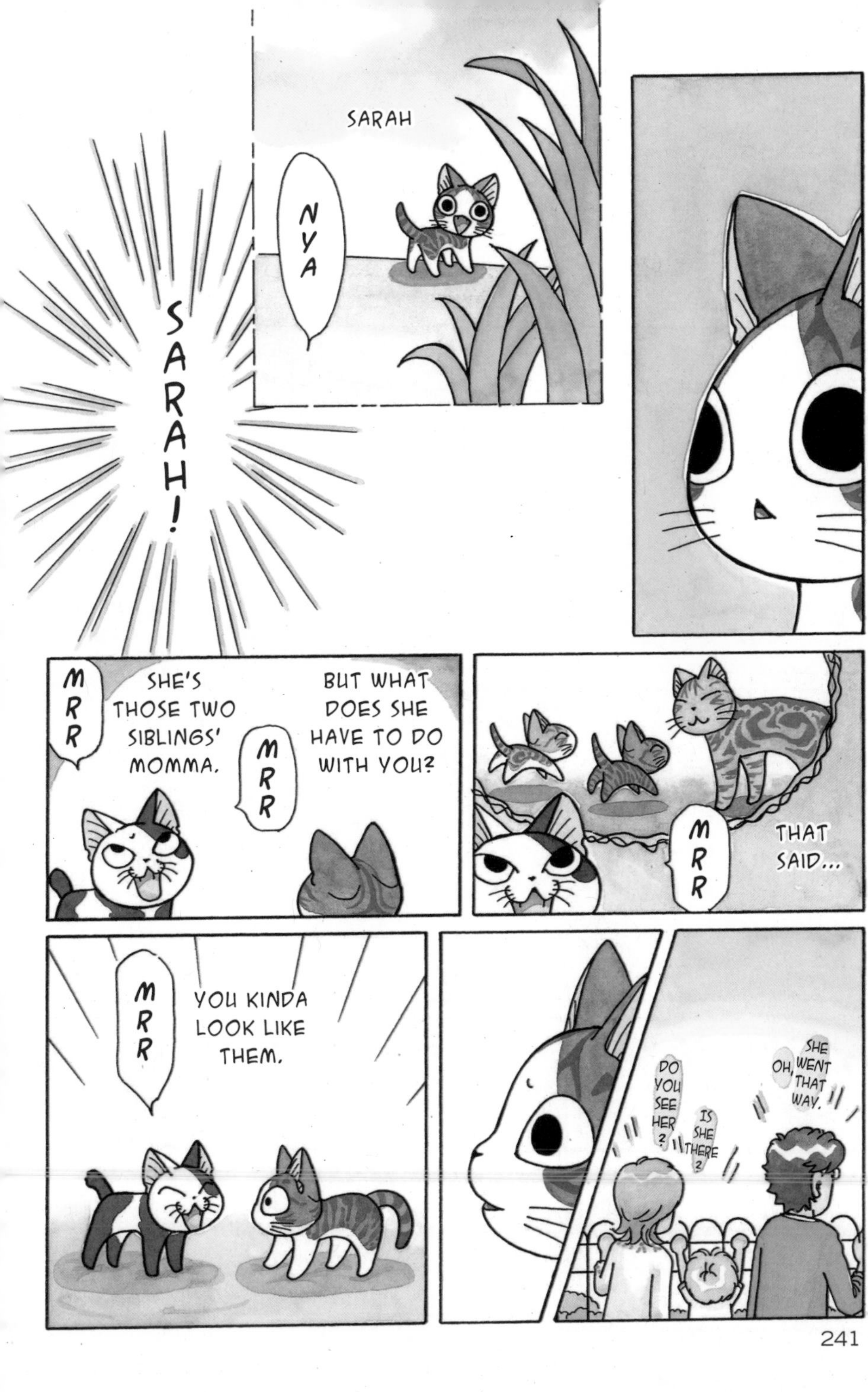
SARAH!
SARAH
NYA
MRR
SHE'S THOSE TWO SIBLINGS' MOMMA.
MRR
BUT WHAT DOES SHE HAVE TO DO WITH YOU?
MRR
THAT SAID...
MRR
YOU KINDA LOOK LIKE THEM.
DO YOU SEE HER?
IS SHE THERE?
OH, SHE WENT THAT WAY.

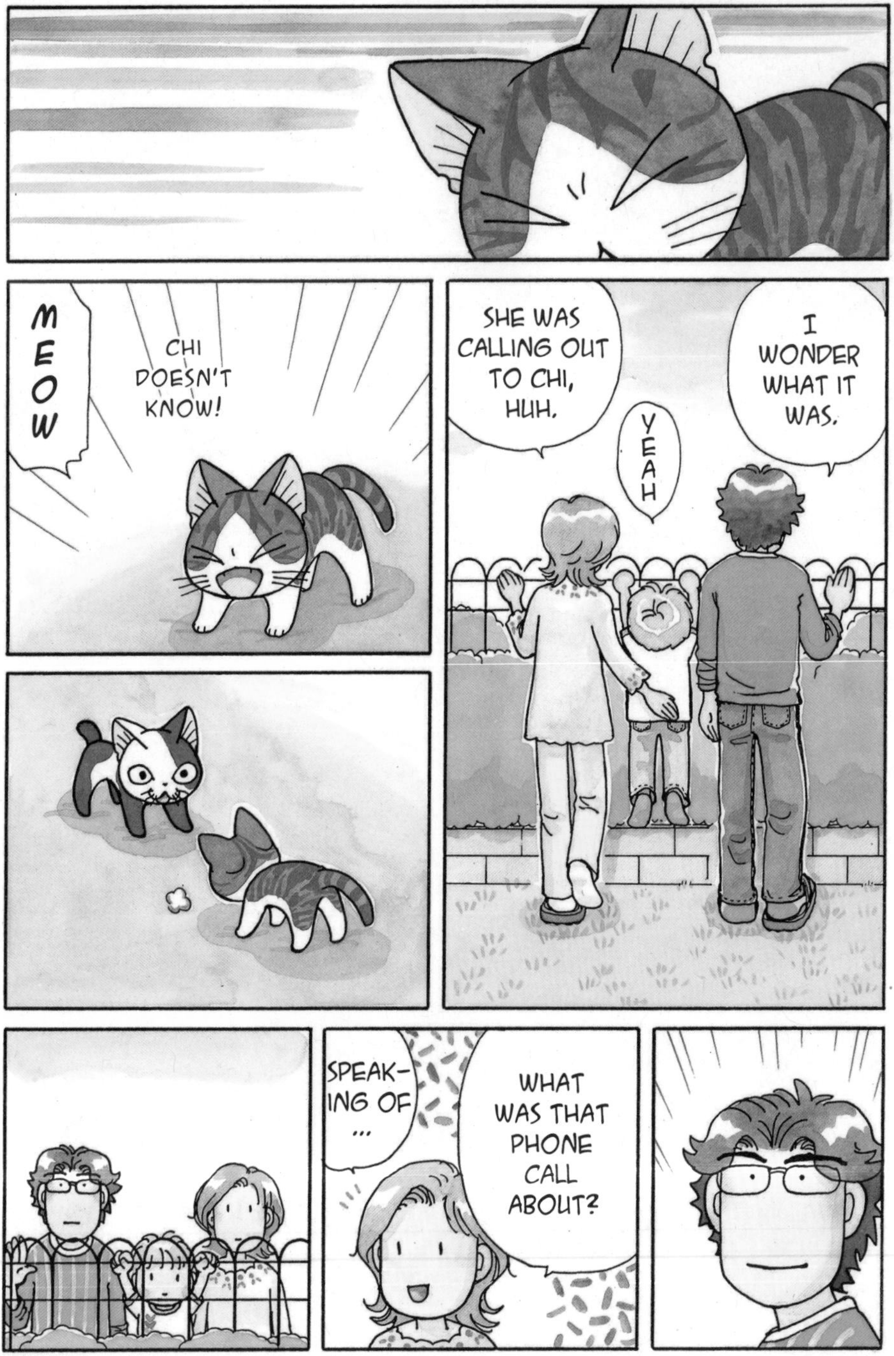
MEOW
CHI DOESN'T KNOW!
SHE WAS CALLING OUT TO CHI, HUH.
YEAH
I WONDER WHAT IT WAS.
SPEAK-ING OF ...
WHAT WAS THAT PHONE CALL ABOUT?

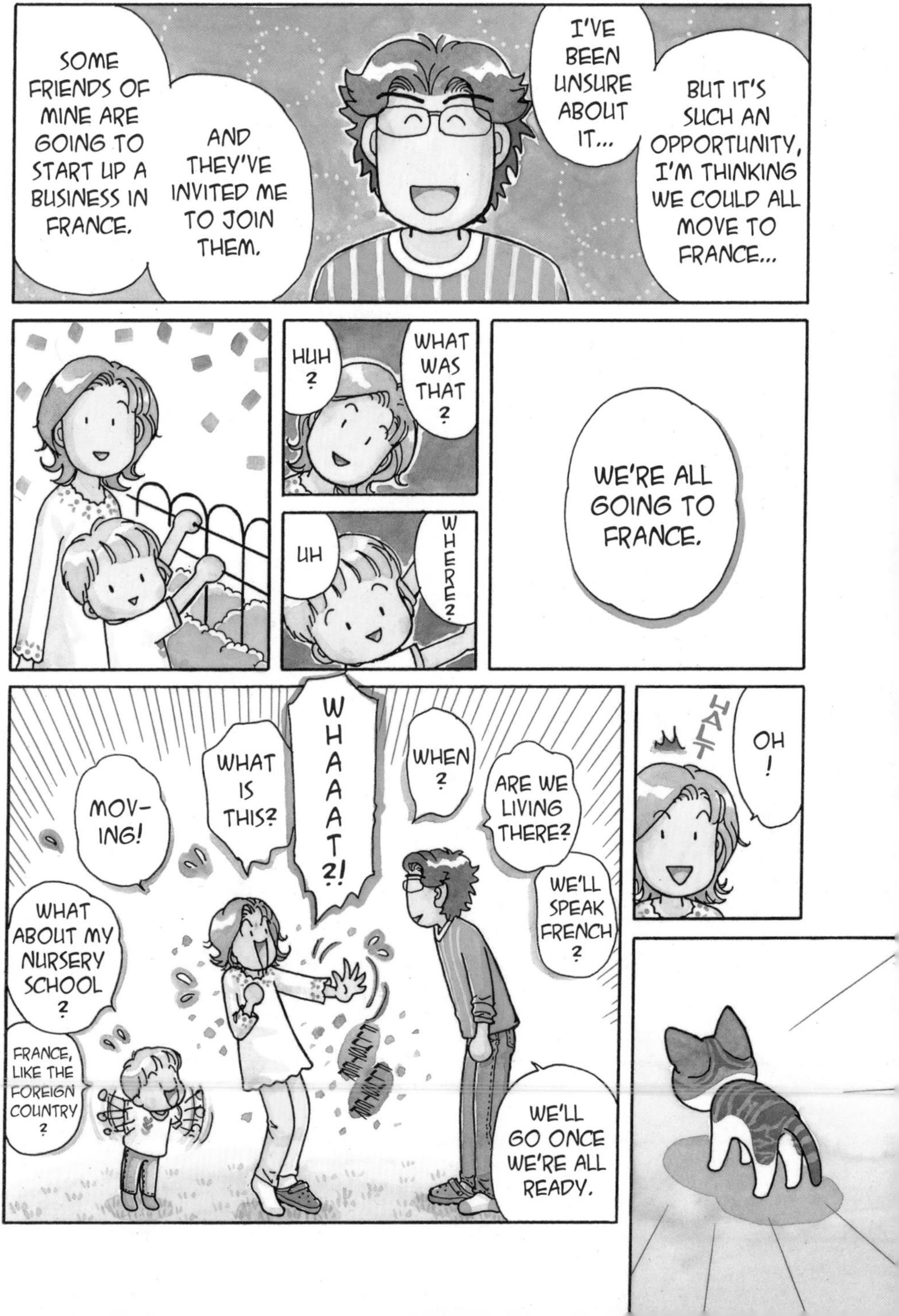
SOME FRIENDS OF MINE ARE GOING TO START UP A BUSINESS IN FRANCE.
AND THEY'VE INVITED ME TO JOIN THEM.
I'VE BEEN UNSURE ABOUT IT...
BUT IT'S SUCH AN OPPORTUNITY, I'M THINKING WE COULD ALL MOVE TO FRANCE...
HUH?
WHAT WAS THAT?
UH
WHERE?
WE'RE ALL GOING TO FRANCE.
MOV-ING!
WHAT IS THIS?
WHAAAAT?!
WHEN?
ARE WE LIVING THERE?
WHAT ABOUT MY NURSERY SCHOOL?
WE'LL SPEAK FRENCH?
FRANCE, LIKE THE FOREIGN COUNTRY?
WE'LL GO ONCE WE'RE ALL READY.
HALT
OH!

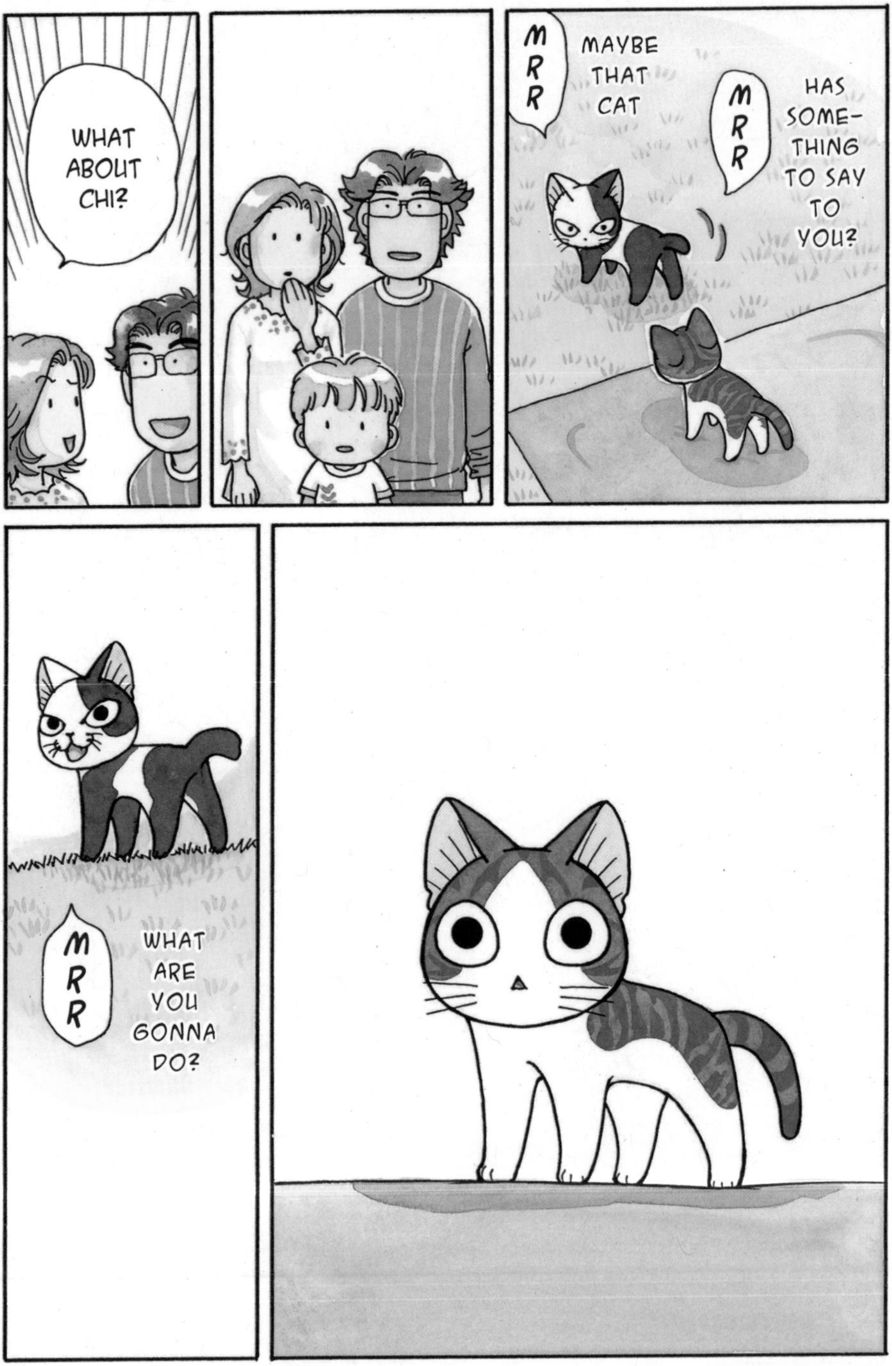
WHAT ABOUT CHI?
MRR
MAYBE THAT CAT
MRR
HAS SOME-THING TO SAY TO YOU?
MRR
WHAT ARE YOU GONNA DO?

the end

homemade 195: a cat recalls

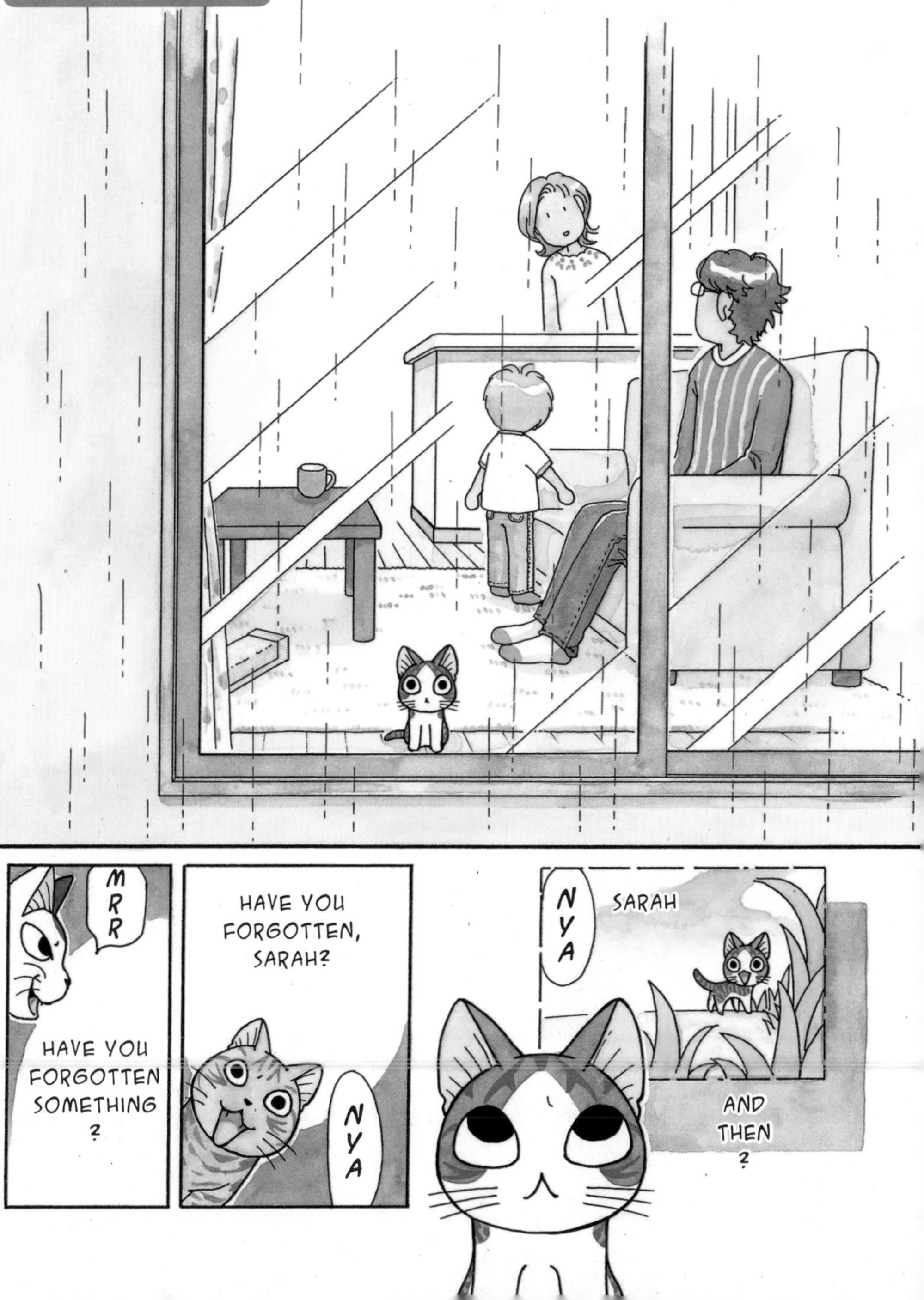
MRR
HAVE YOU FORGOTTEN SOMETHING?
HAVE YOU FORGOTTEN, SARAH?
NYA
NYA
SARAH
AND THEN?

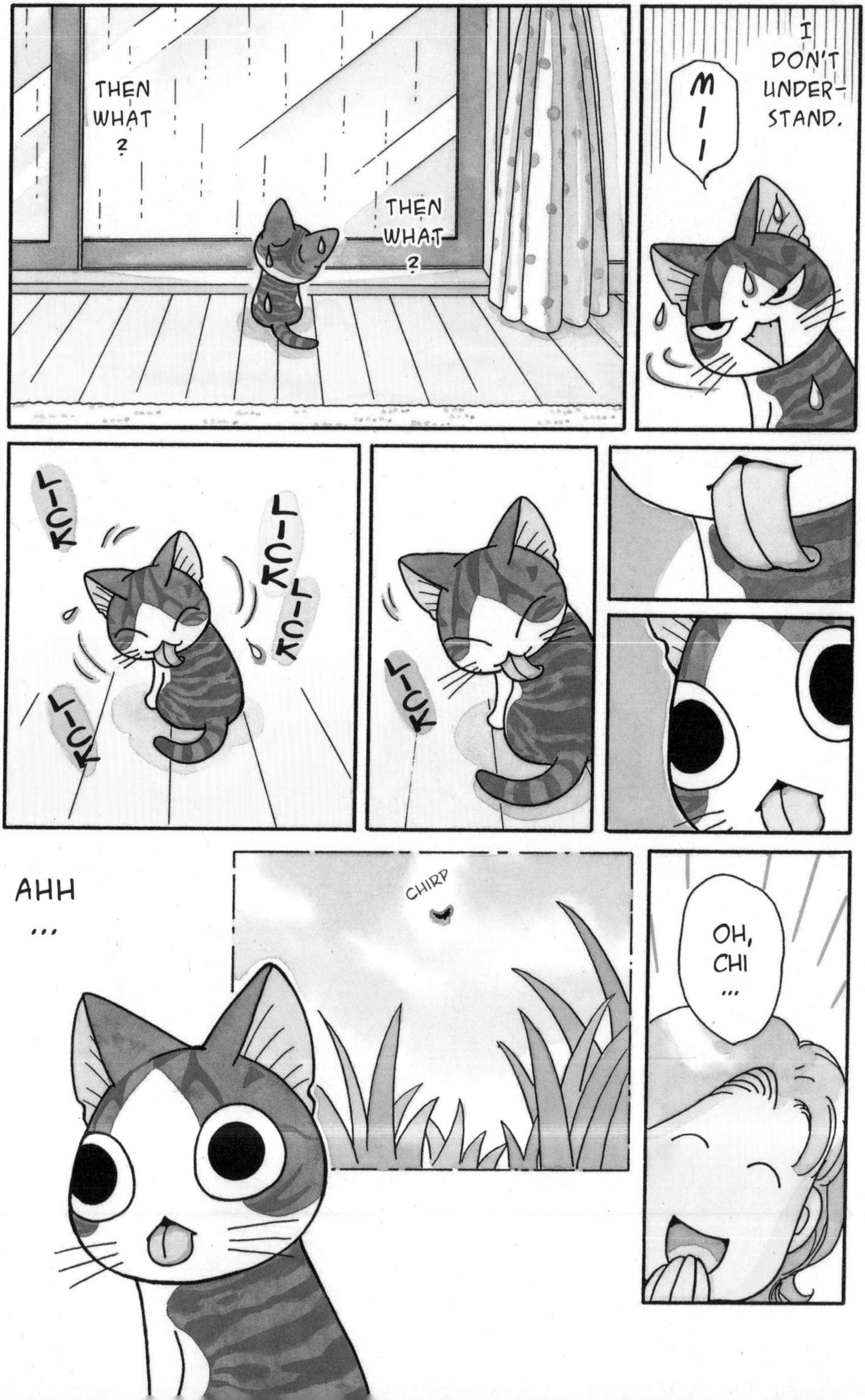
THEN WHAT ?
THEN WHAT ?
MI I
I DON'T UNDER-STAND.
LICK
LICK LICK
LICK
LICK
AHH ...
CHIRP
OH, CHI ...

LOOK AT THAT TONGUE HANGING OUT.

PAT PAT

MII?

PURR PURR PURR

HMM ?!

WHAT WAS I...

...?

SKFF SKFF SKFF

SKFF SKFF

SKFF

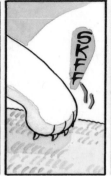

OH...

HEY, CHI...

SHOOM

MAYBE WE SHOULD TRIM YOUR CLAWS.

LET'S SEE.

MYA

248

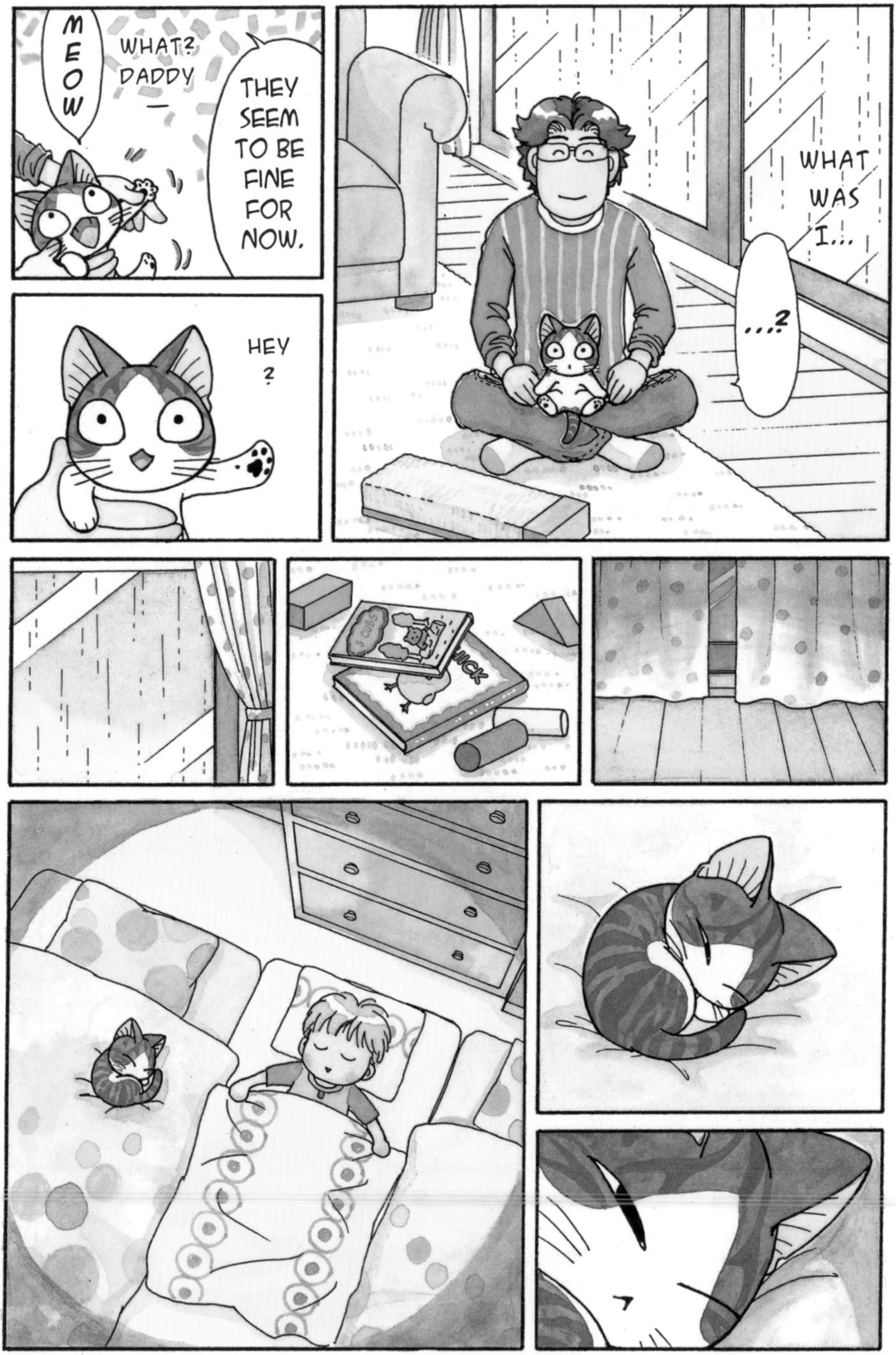
MEOW
WHAT? DADDY —
THEY SEEM TO BE FINE FOR NOW.
HEY ?
WHAT WAS I...
...?

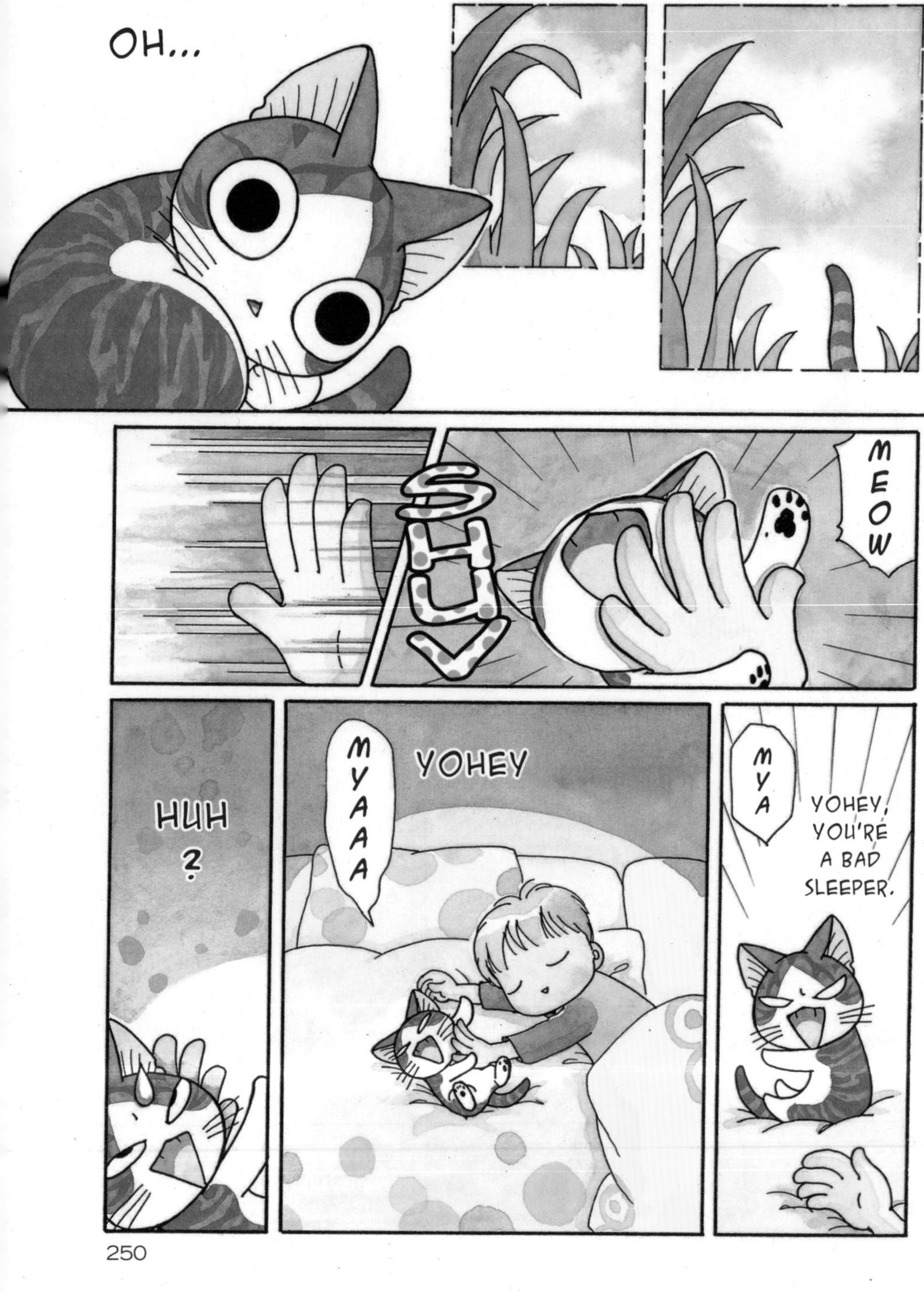
OH...
SHU
MEOW
HUH ?
MYAAAA
YOHEY
MYA
YOHEY, YOU'RE A BAD SLEEPER.

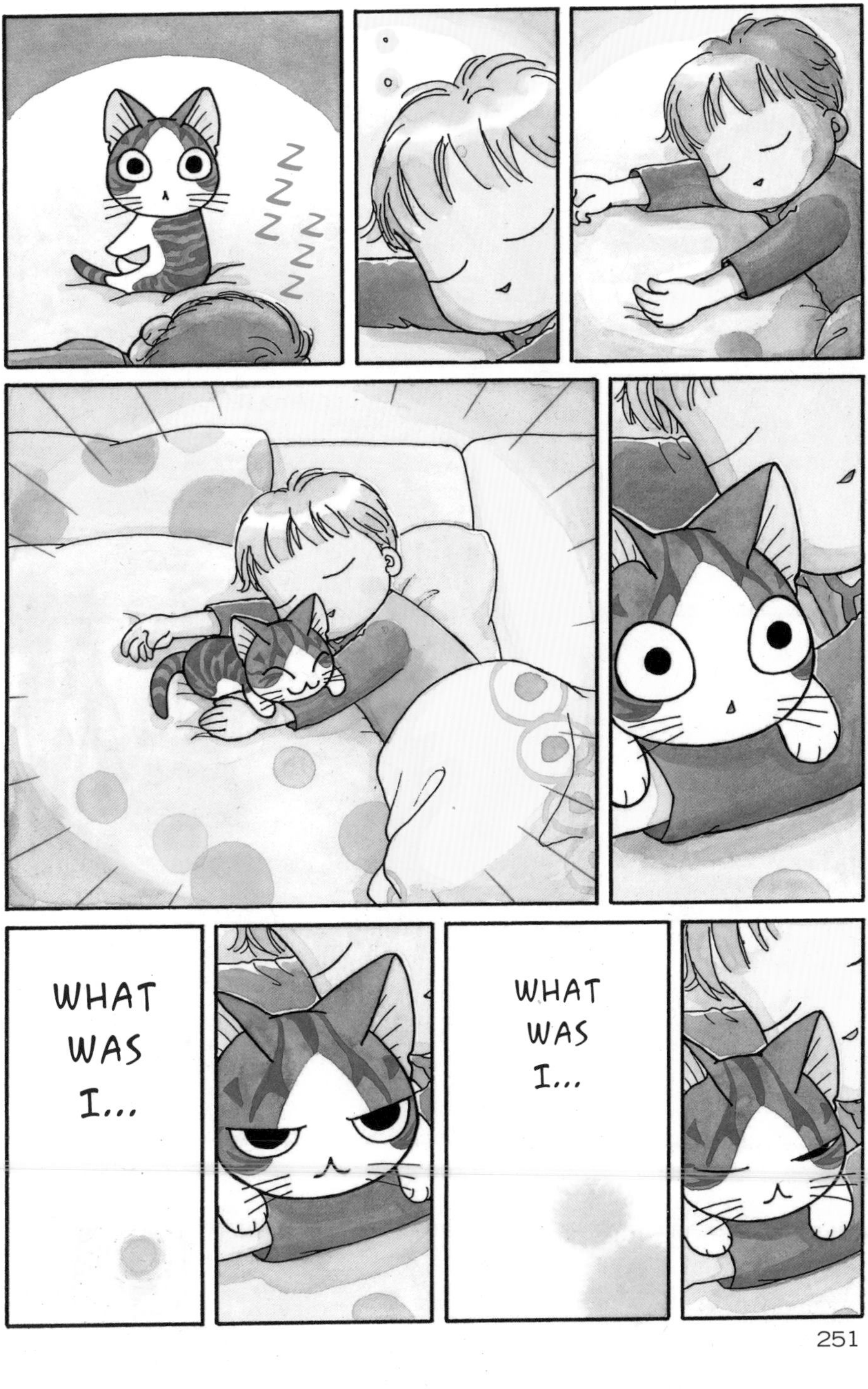
Z Z Z Z Z Z Z
WHAT WAS I...
WHAT WAS I...

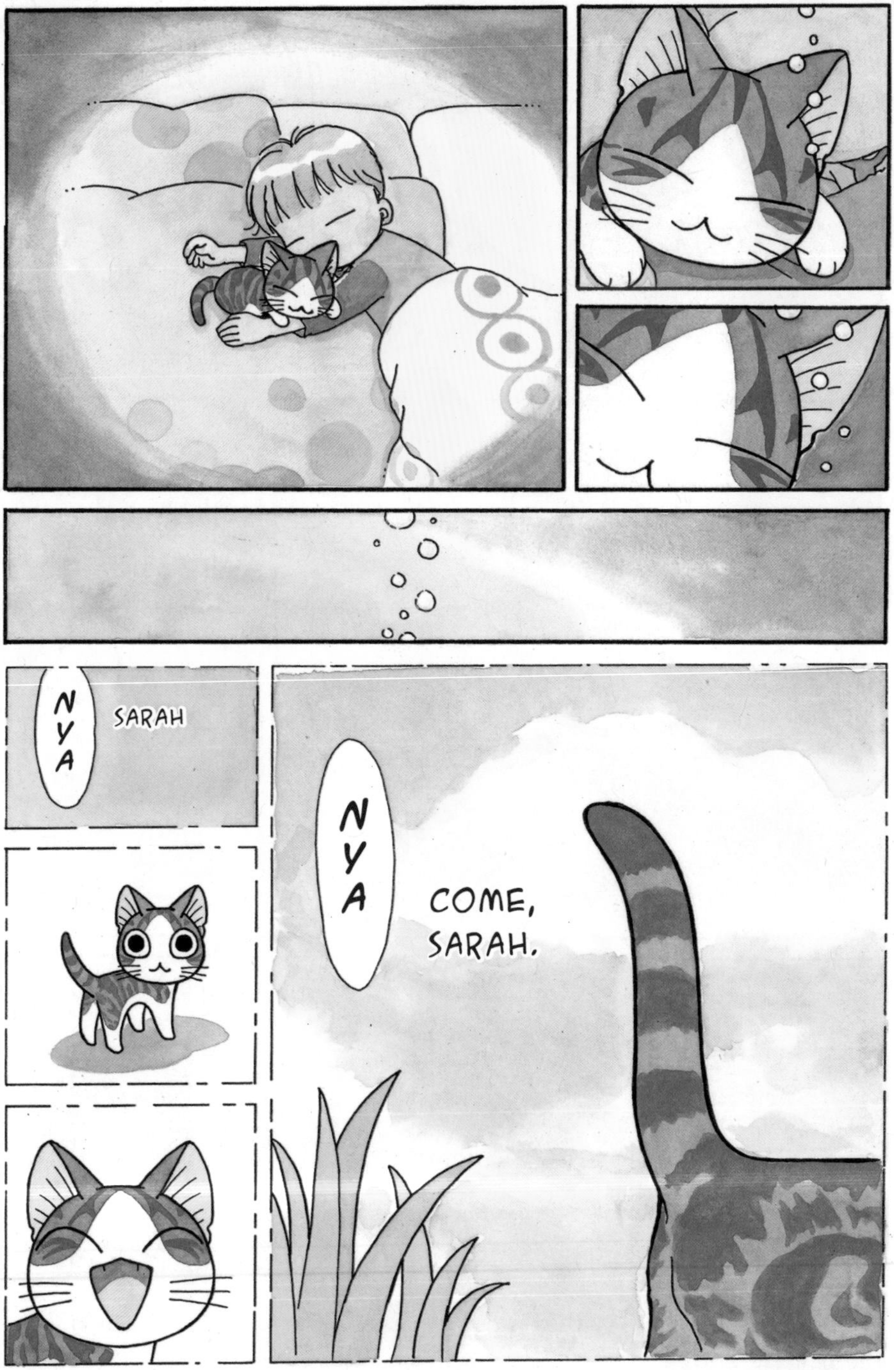
NYA
SARAH
NYA
COME, SARAH.

the end

homemade 196: a cat is lost in thought

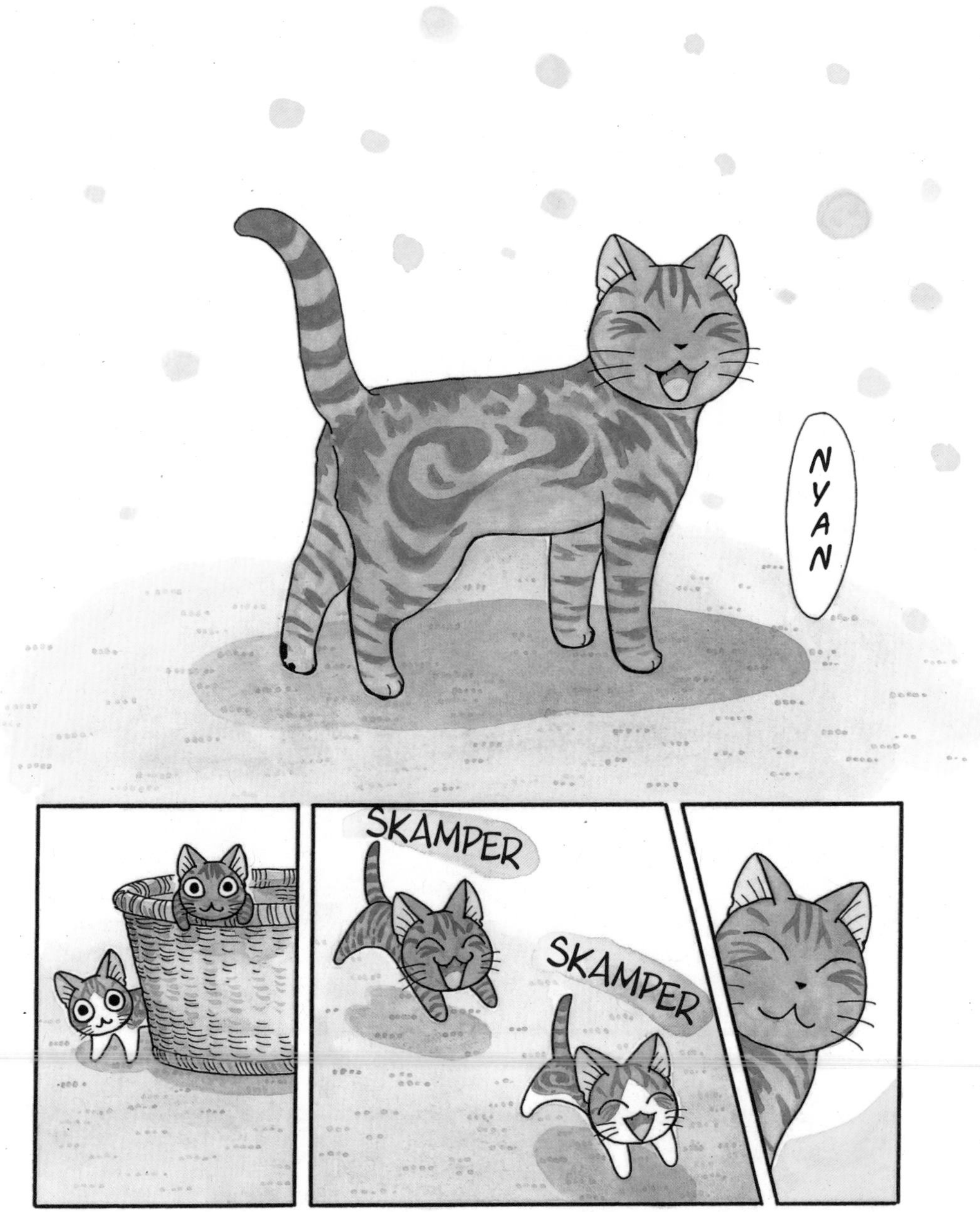
NYAN
SKAMPER
SKAMPER

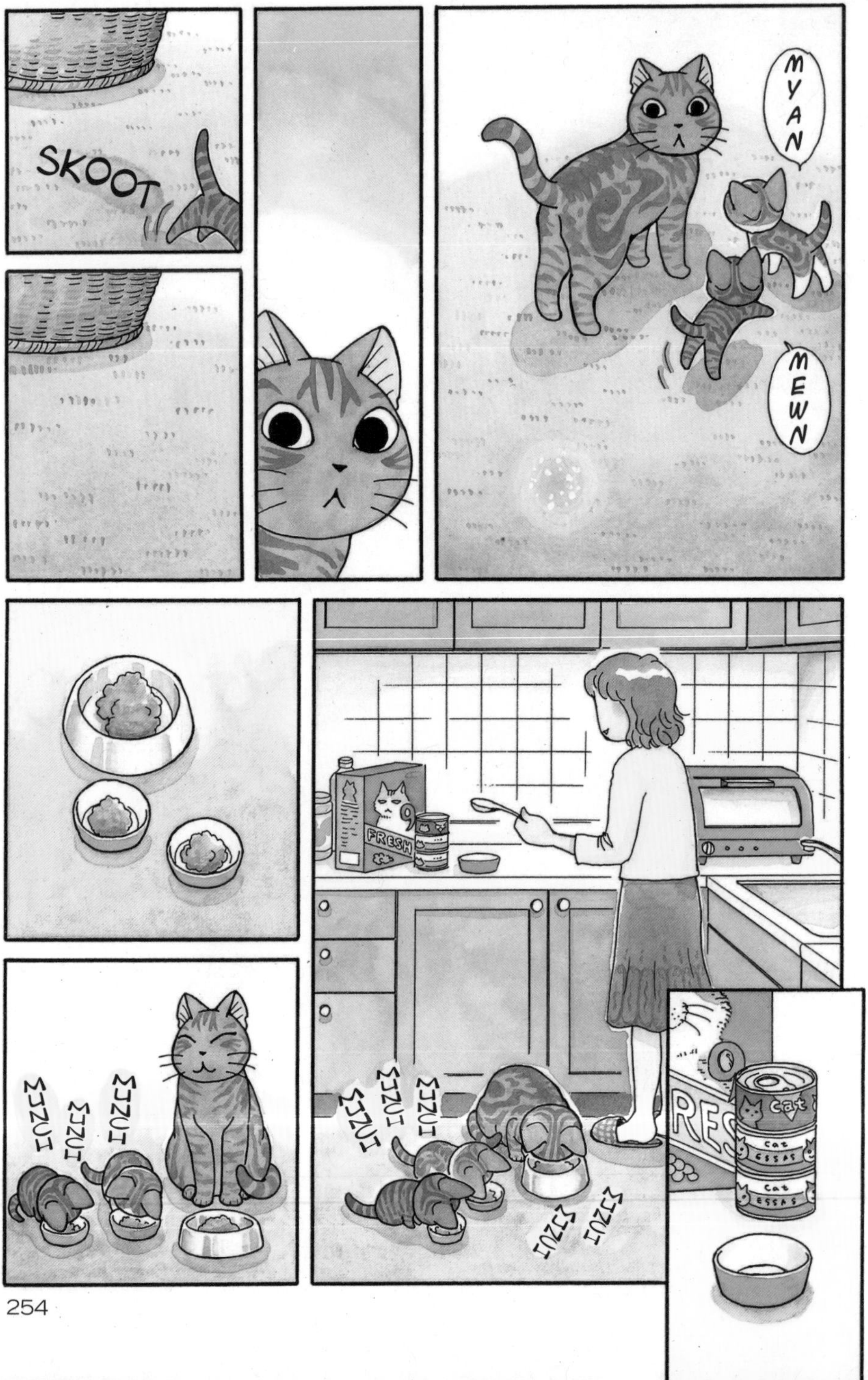
SKOOT
MYAN
MEWN
FRESH
MUNCH
MUNCH
MUNCH
MUNCH
MUNCH
MUNCH
MUNCH
MUNCH
Cat

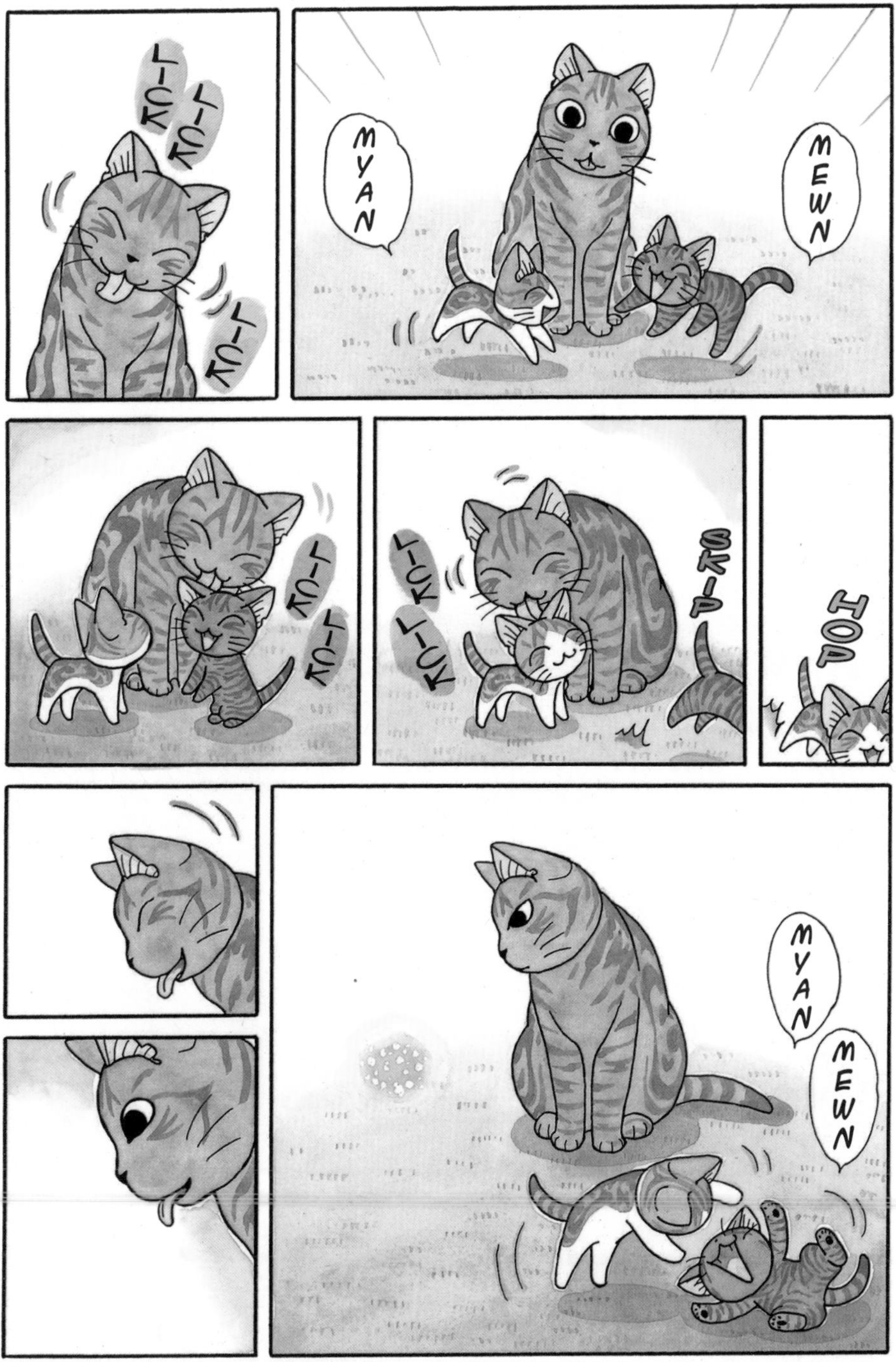
LICK LICK
LICK
MYAN
MEWN
LICK
LICK
LICK LICK
SKIP
HOP
MYAN
MEWN

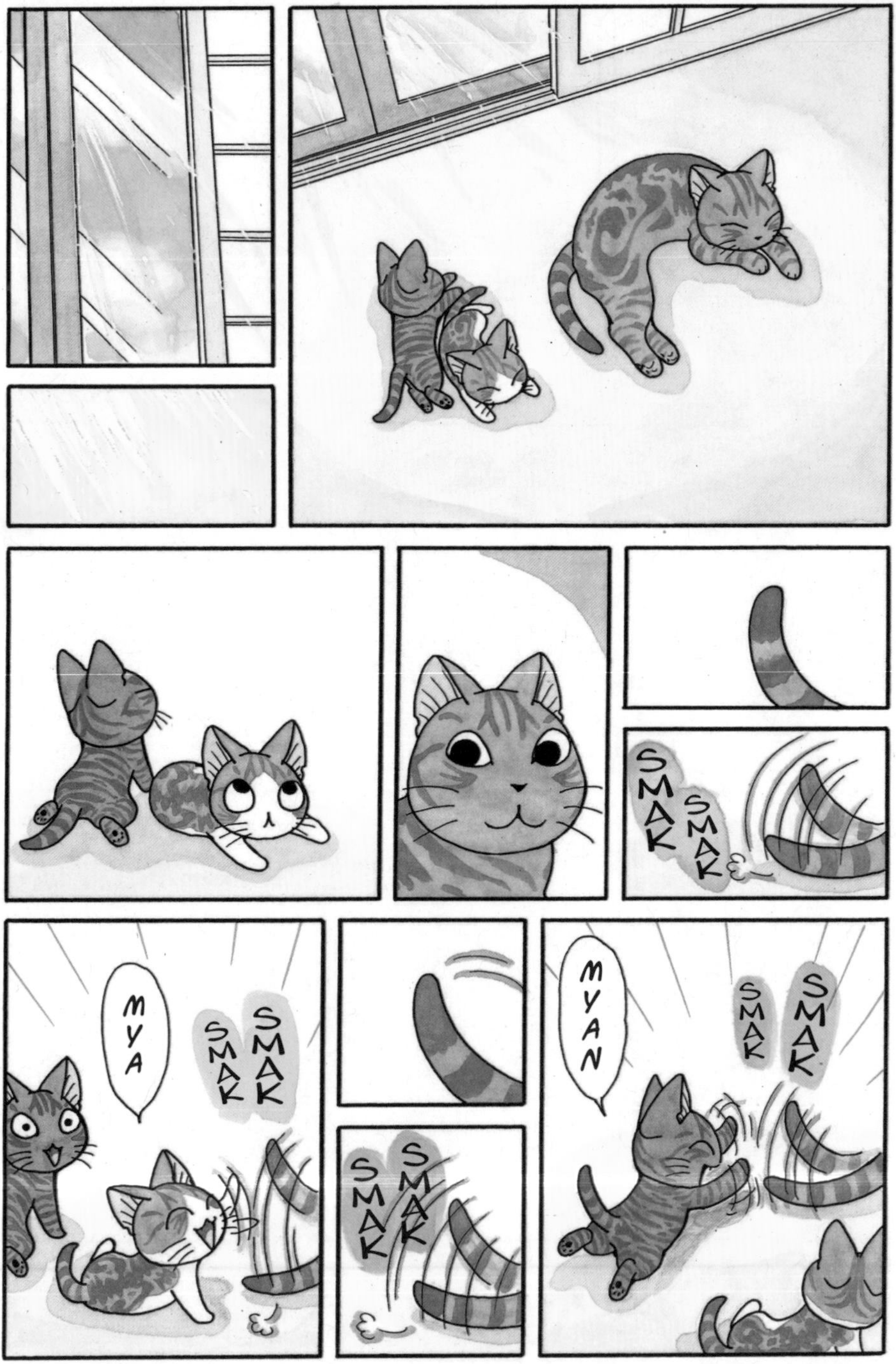
SMAK
SMAK
MYA
SMAK
SMAK
SMAK
SMAK
MYAN
SMAK
SMAK

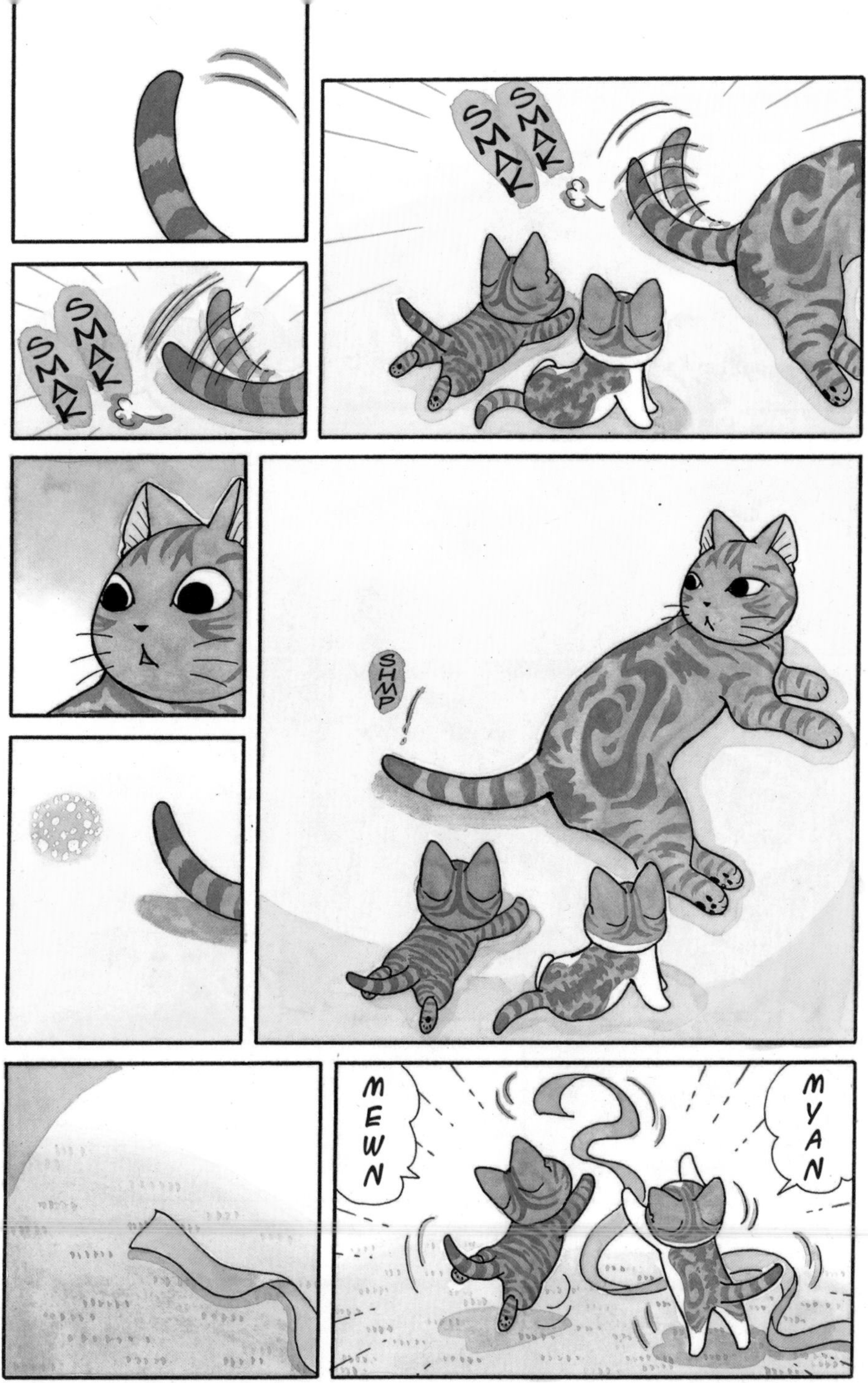
SMAK
SMAK
SMAK
SMAK
SHMP
MEWN
MYAN

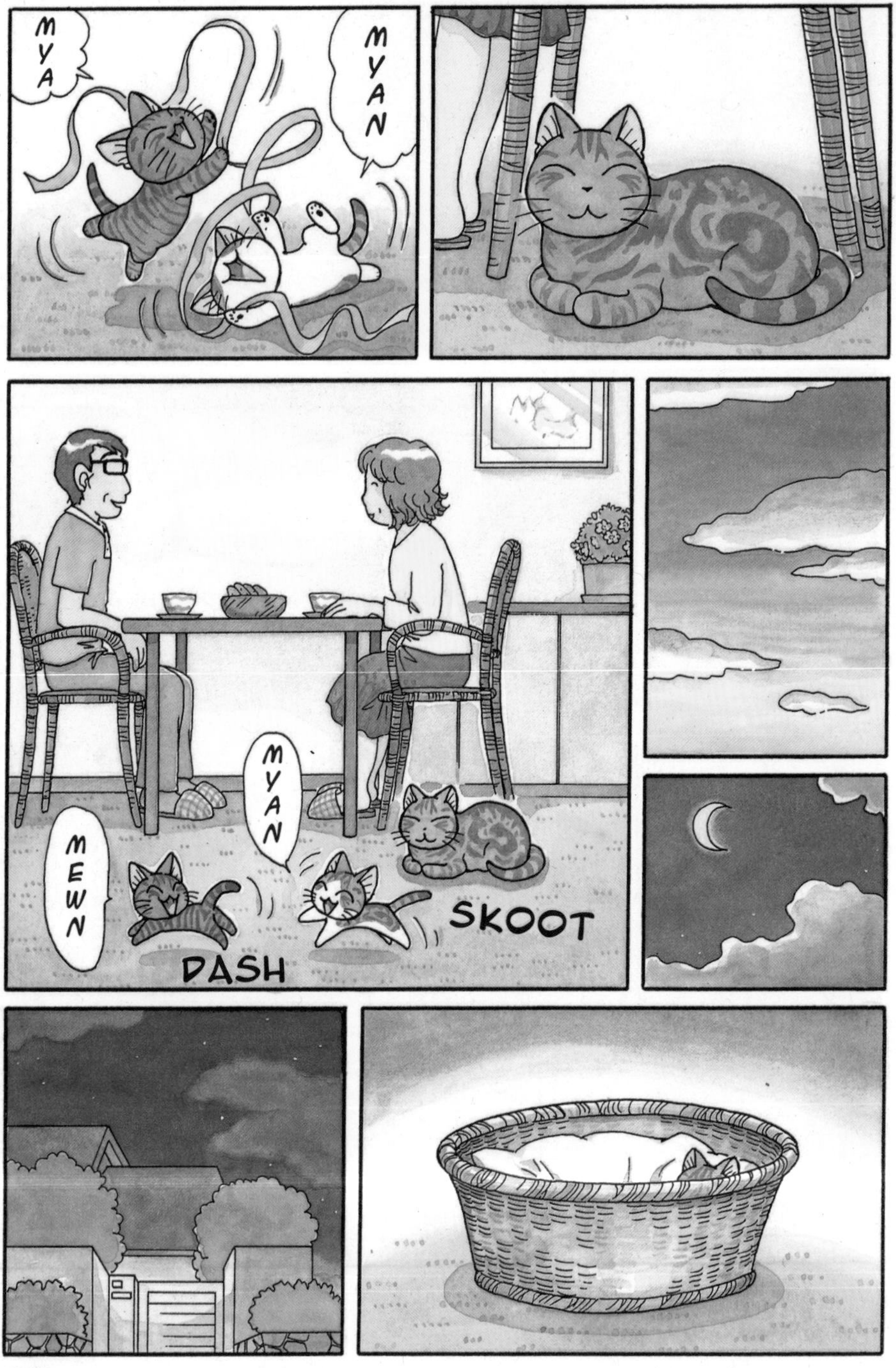
MYA
MYAN
MYAN
MEWN
SKOOT
DASH

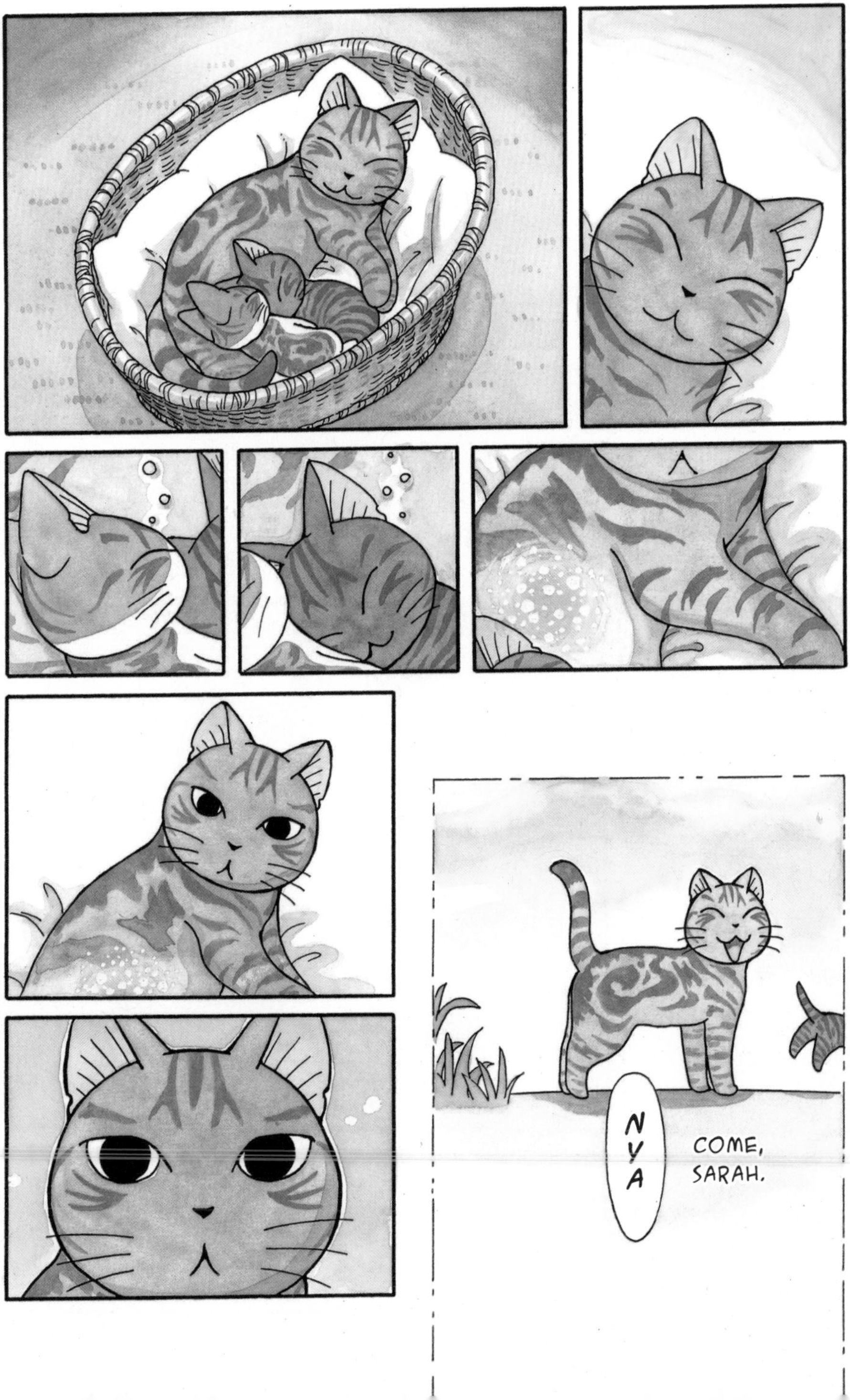
NYA
COME, SARAH.

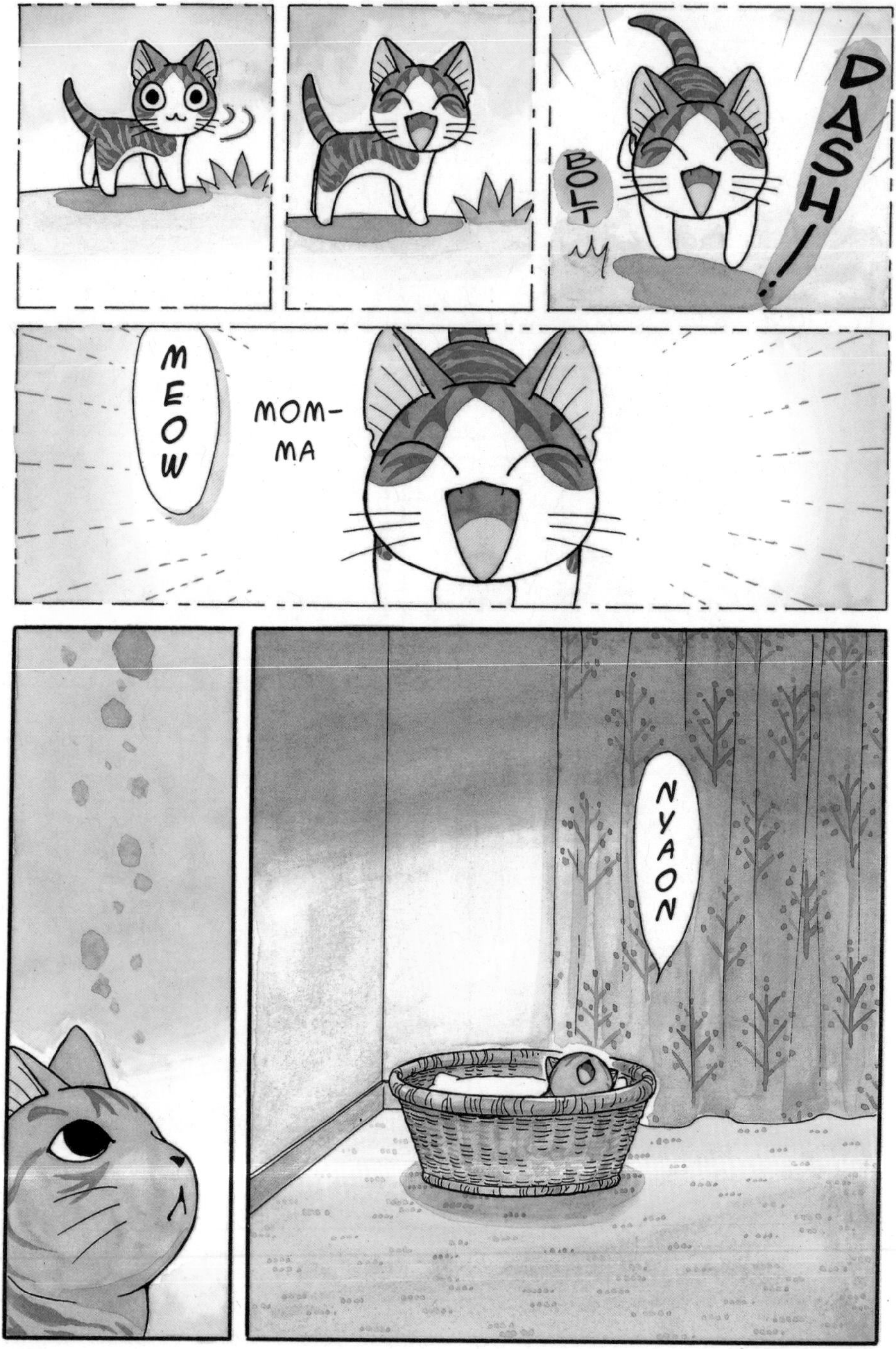
BOLT
DASH!!
MEOW
MOM-MA
NYAON

the end

homemade 197: a cat is looked for

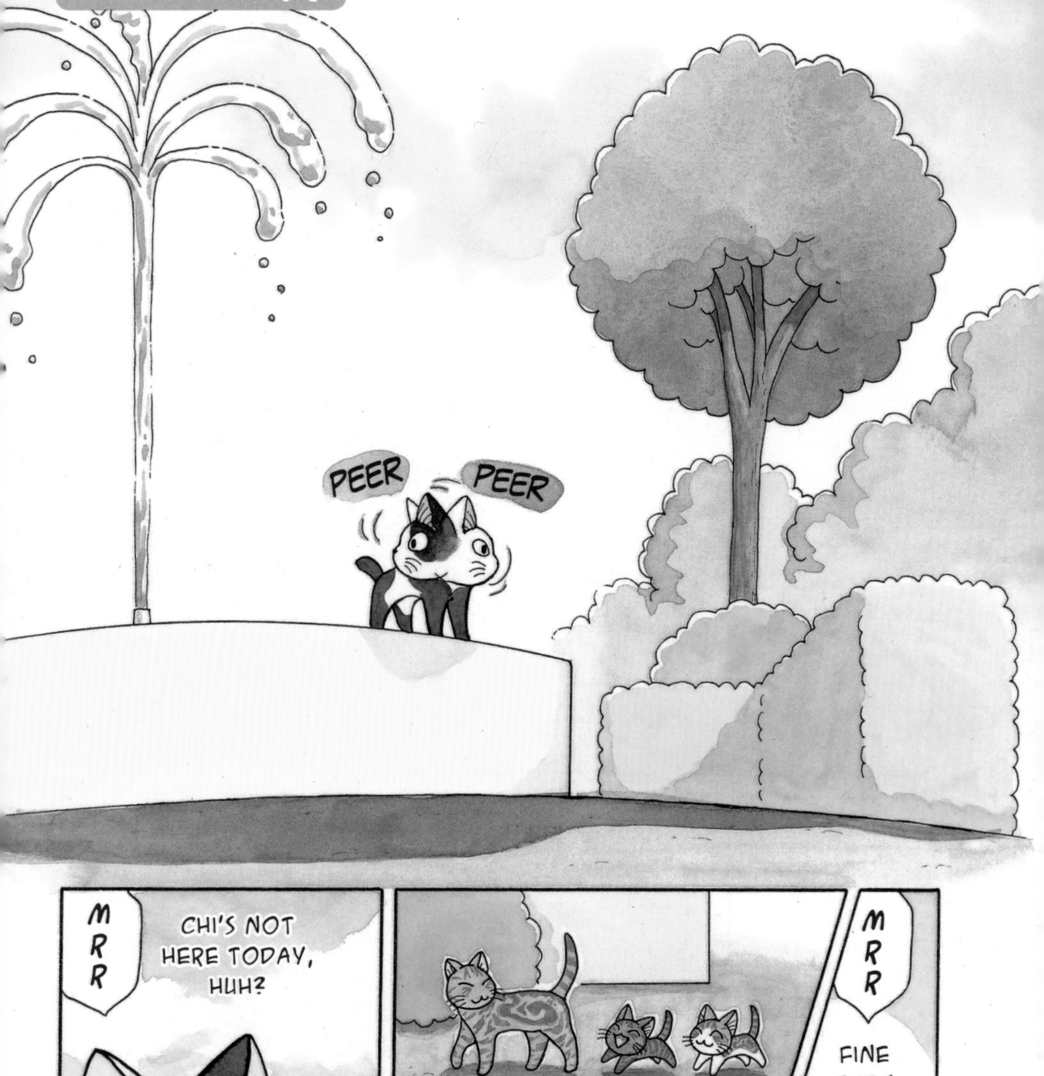
PEER
PEER
MRR
CHI'S NOT HERE TODAY, HUH?
MRR
OH!
MRR
FINE THEN ...

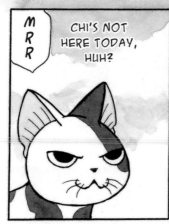

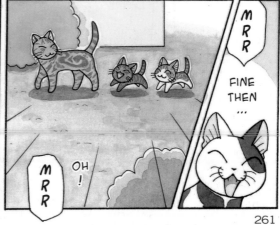

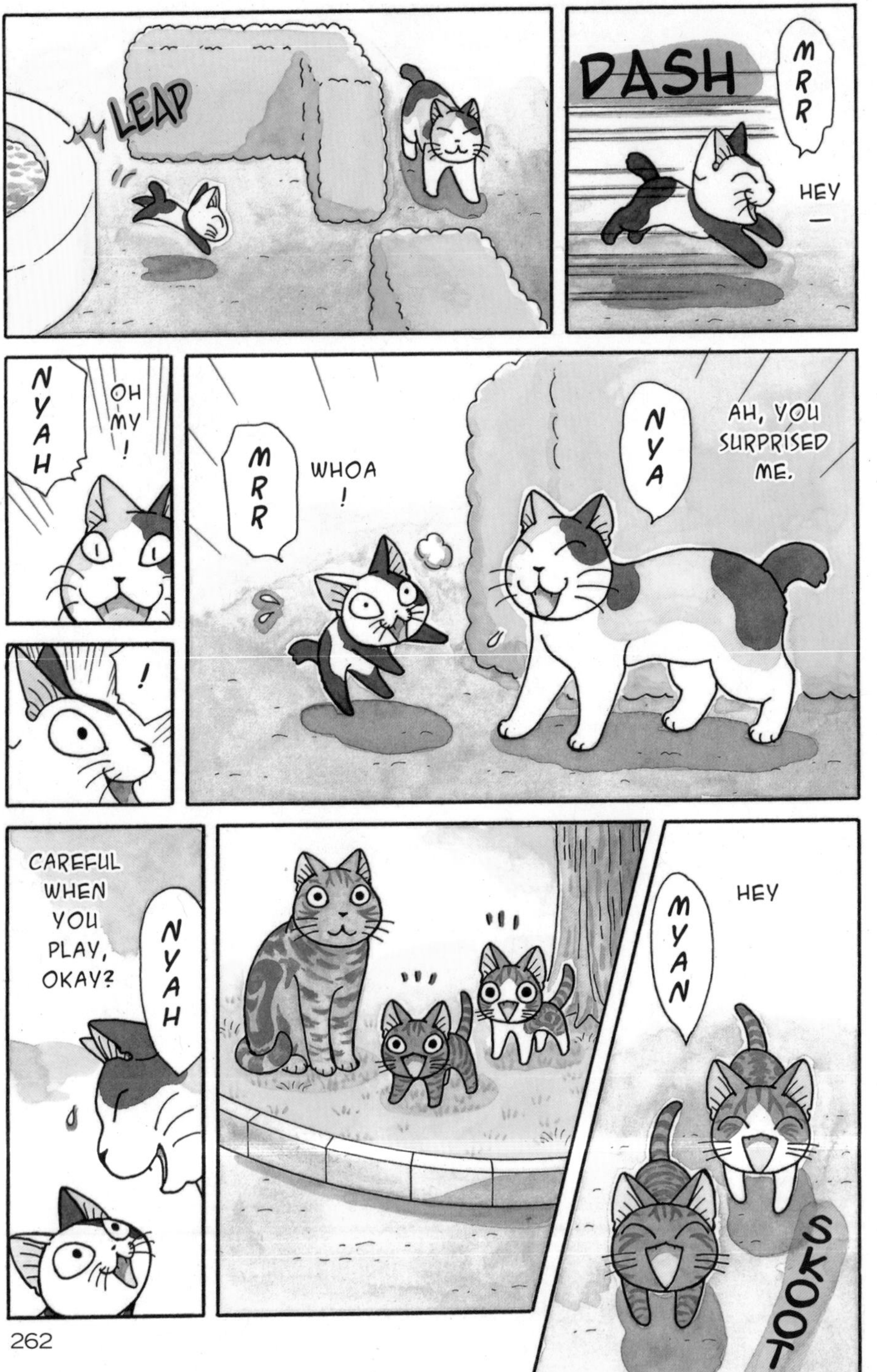
LEAP
DASH
MRR
HEY —
NYAH
OH MY!
!
MRR
WHOA!
NYA
AH, YOU SURPRISED ME.
CAREFUL WHEN YOU PLAY, OKAY?
NYAH
MYAN
HEY
SKOOT

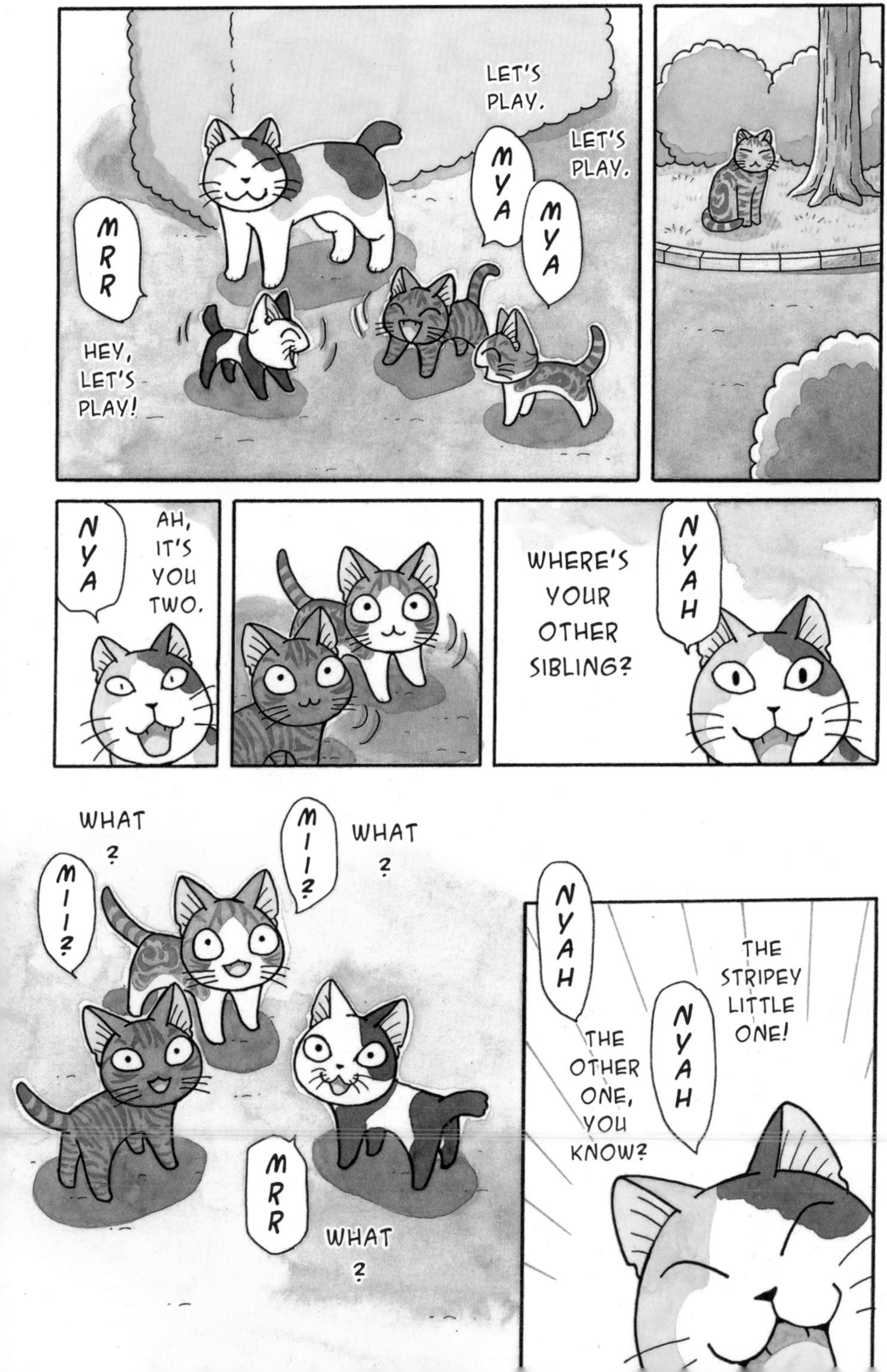
LET'S PLAY.
MYA
LET'S PLAY.
MYA
MRR
HEY, LET'S PLAY!
NYA
AH, IT'S YOU TWO.
WHERE'S YOUR OTHER SIBLING?
NYAH
WHAT ?
MII?
MII?
WHAT ?
MRR
WHAT ?
NYAH
THE OTHER ONE, YOU KNOW?
NYAH
THE STRIPEY LITTLE ONE!

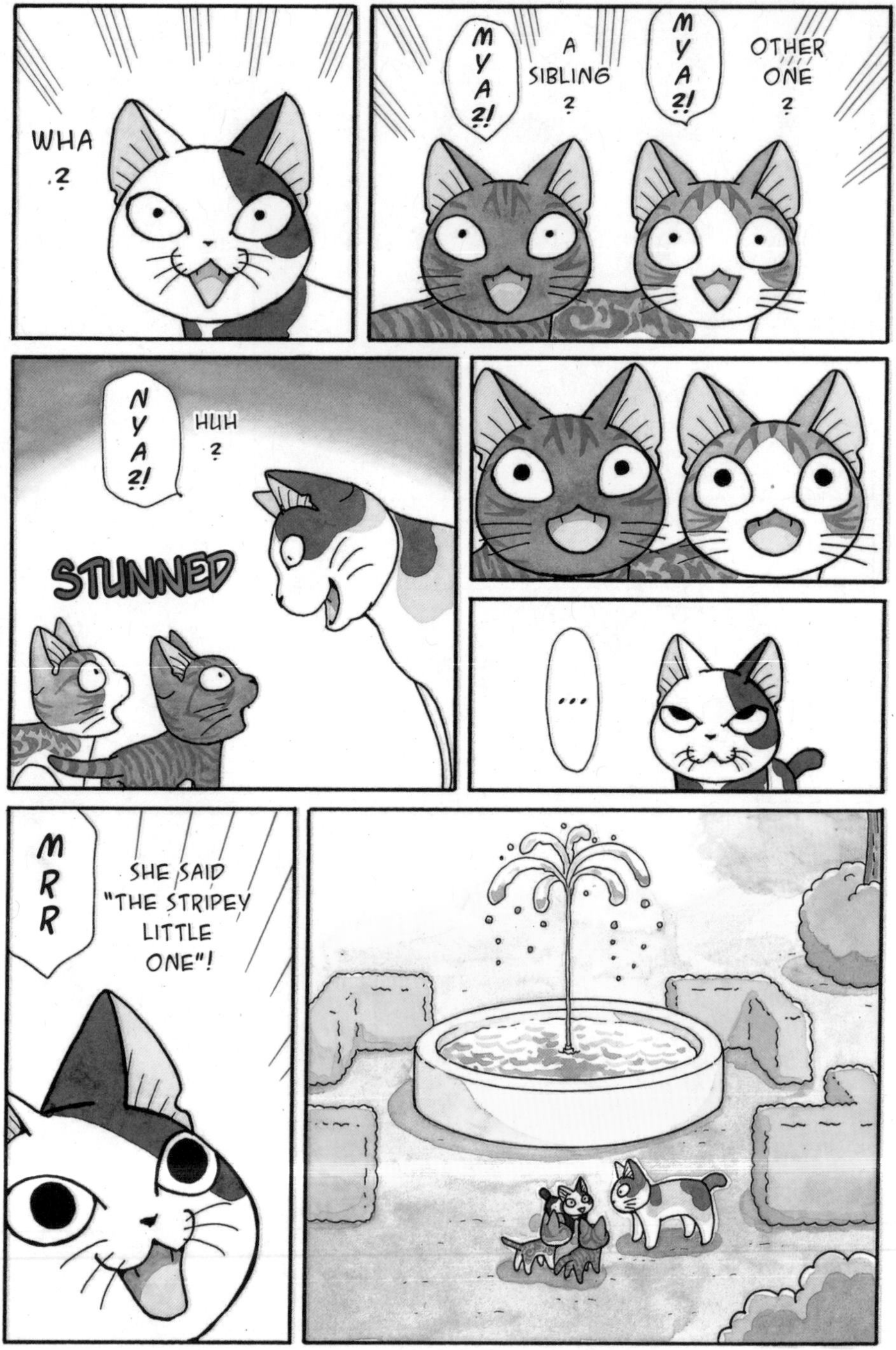
WHA?
MYA?!
A SIBLING?
MYA?!
OTHER ONE?
NYA?!
HUH?
STUNNED
...
MRR
SHE SAID "THE STRIPEY LITTLE ONE"!

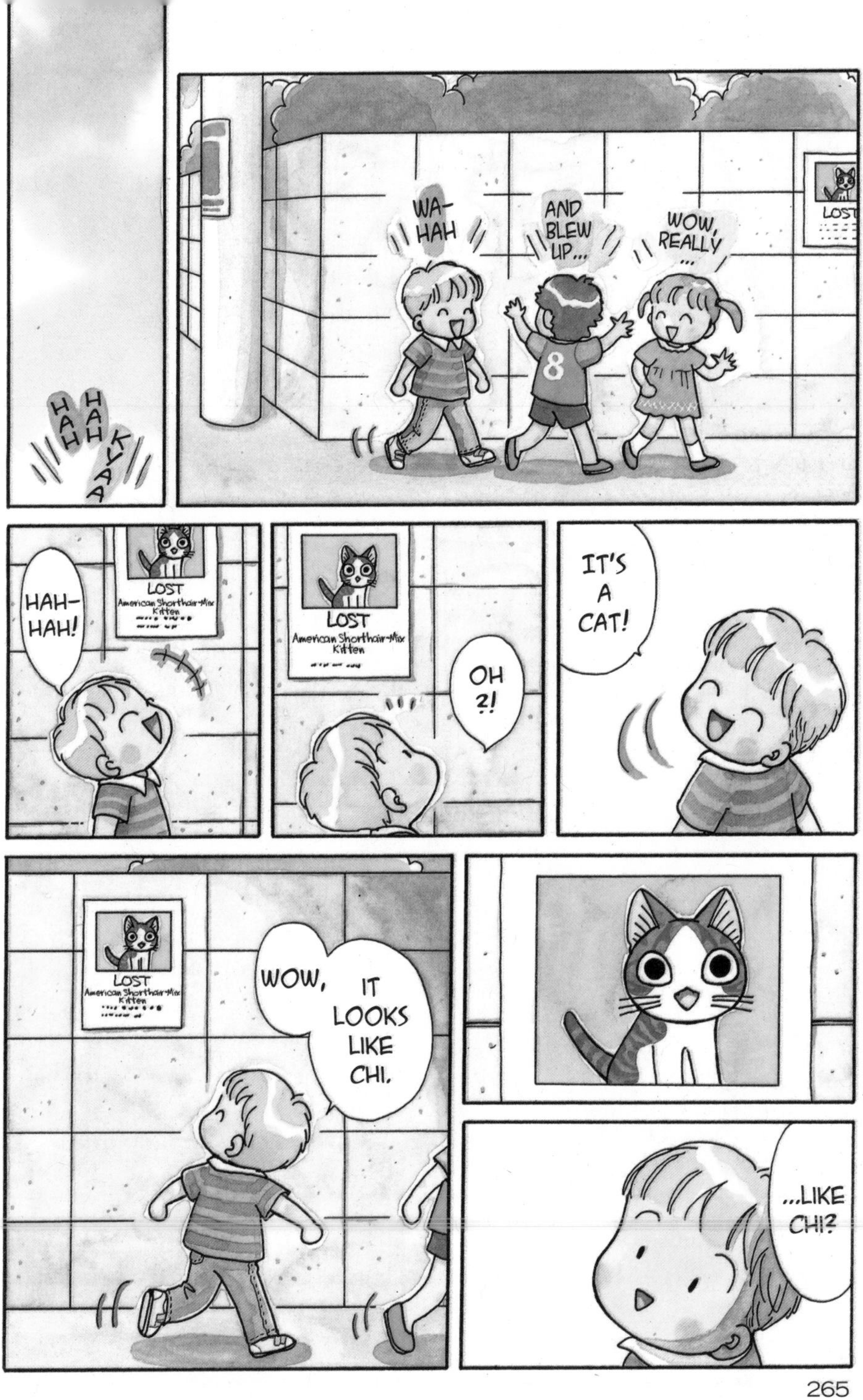

HAH HAH KYAA
WA-HAH
AND BLEW UP...
WOW, REALLY...
LOST
LOST
American Shorthair-Mix Kitten
HAH-HAH!
LOST
American Shorthair-Mix Kitten
OH?!
IT'S A CAT!
LOST
American Shorthair-Mix Kitten
WOW, IT LOOKS LIKE CHI.
...LIKE CHI?

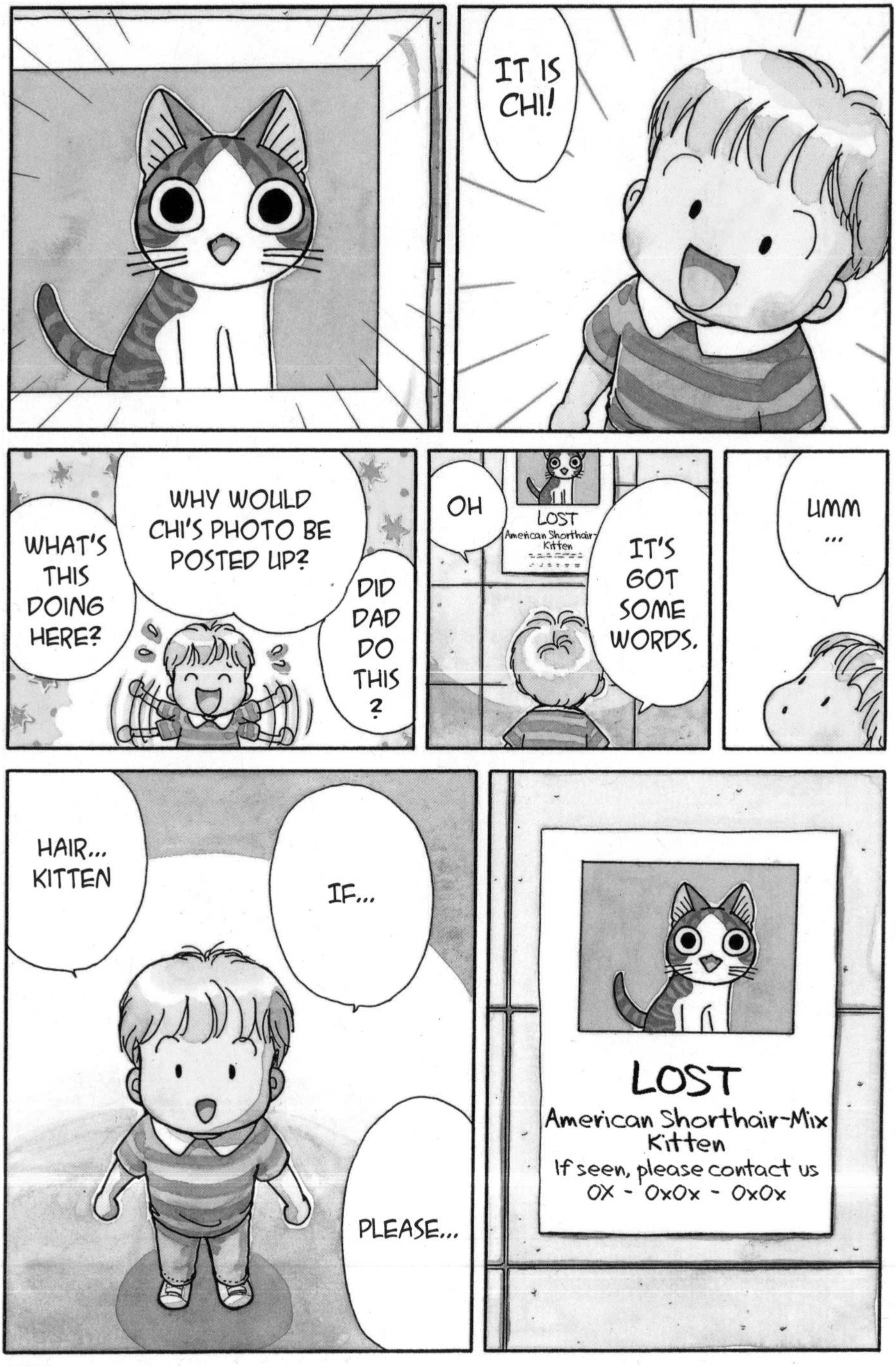
IT IS CHI!
WHAT'S THIS DOING HERE?
WHY WOULD CHI'S PHOTO BE POSTED UP?
DID DAD DO THIS?
OH
LOST
American Shorthair-
Kitten
IT'S GOT SOME WORDS.
UMM ...
HAIR... KITTEN
IF...
PLEASE...
LOST
American Shorthair-Mix Kitten
If seen, please contact us
OX - OxOx - OxOx

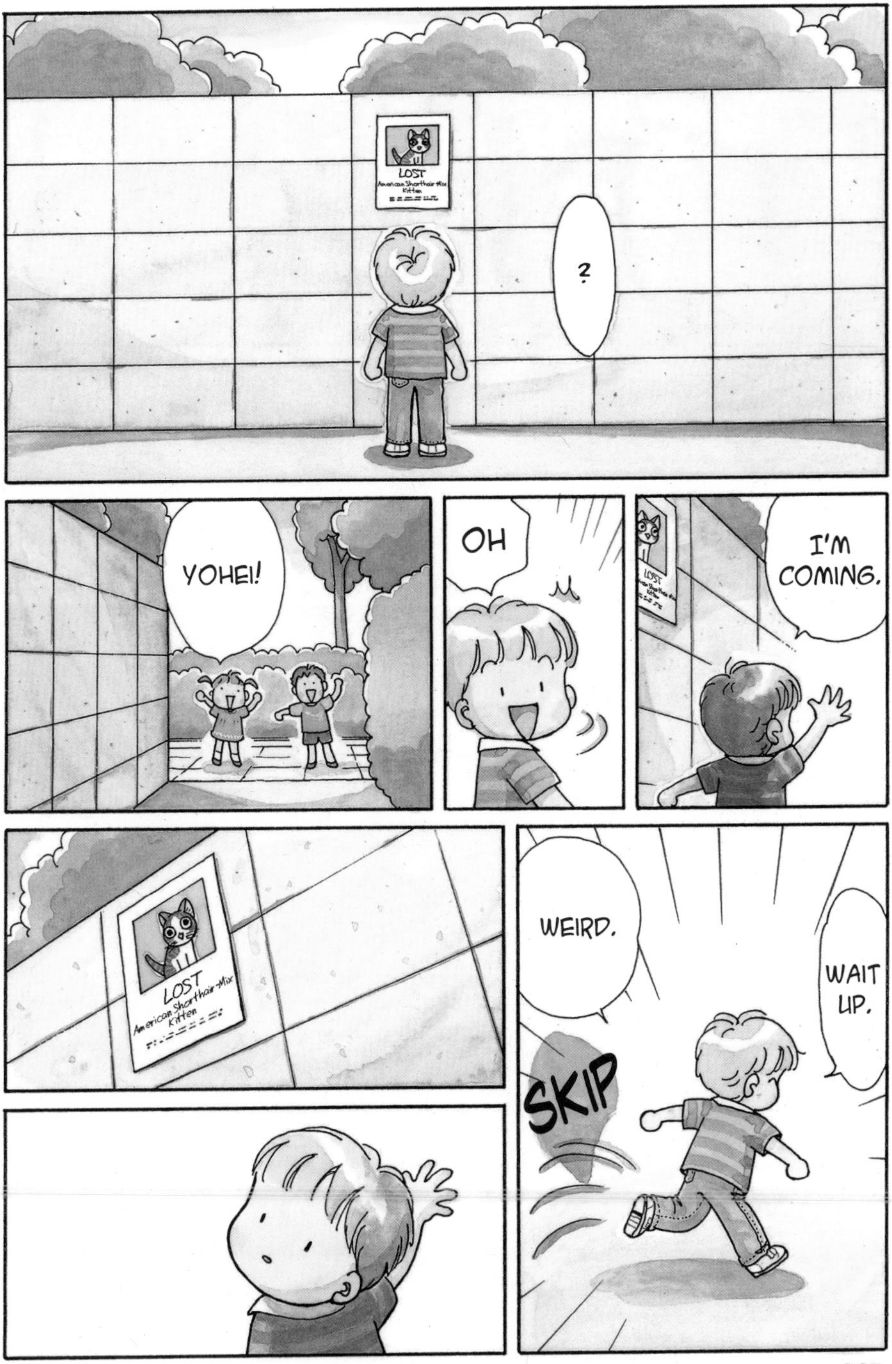
LOST
American Shorthair Mix
Kitten
?
YOHEI!
OH
I'M COMING.
LOST
American Shorthair Mix
Kitten
WEIRD.
WAIT UP.
SKIP

the end

homemade 198: a cat is rejected

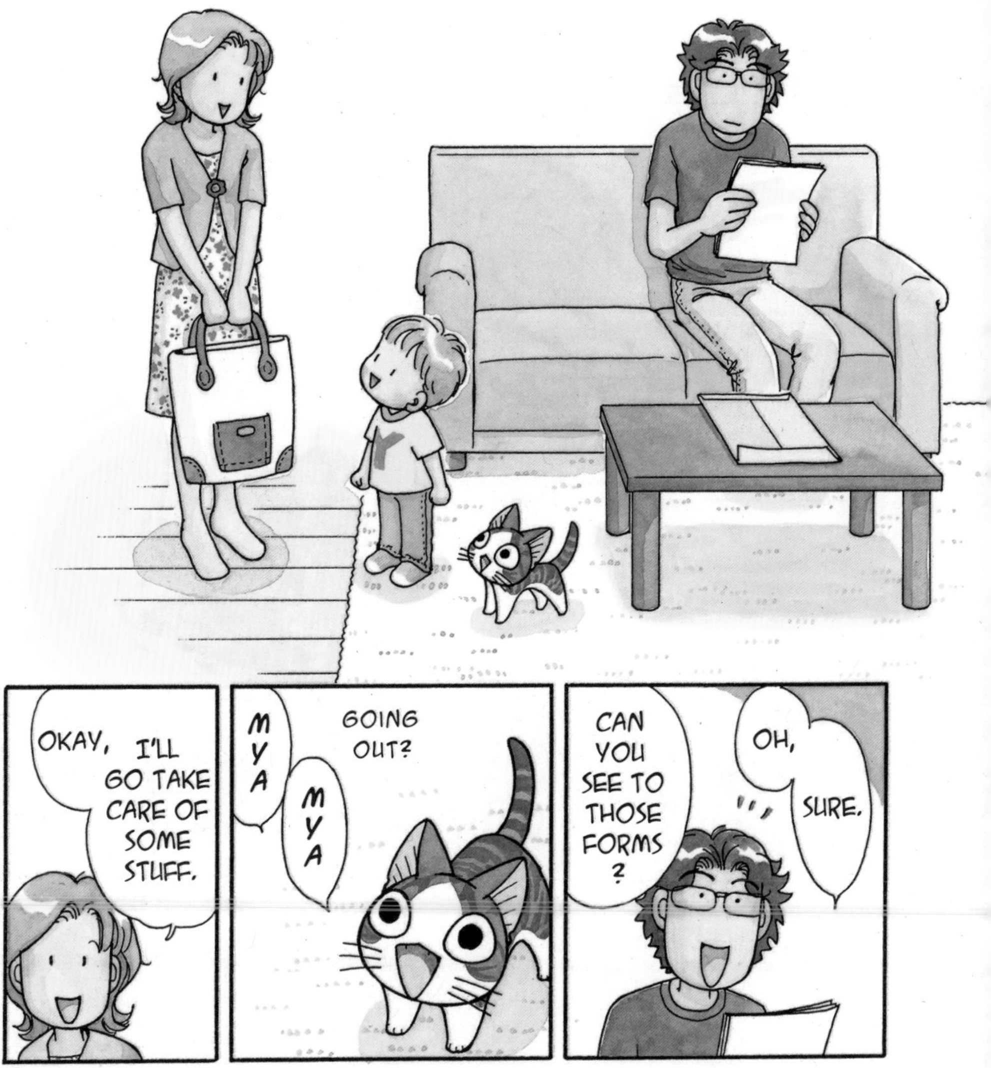

OKAY, I'LL GO TAKE CARE OF SOME STUFF.
MYA
GOING OUT?
MYA
CAN YOU SEE TO THOSE FORMS?
OH, SURE.

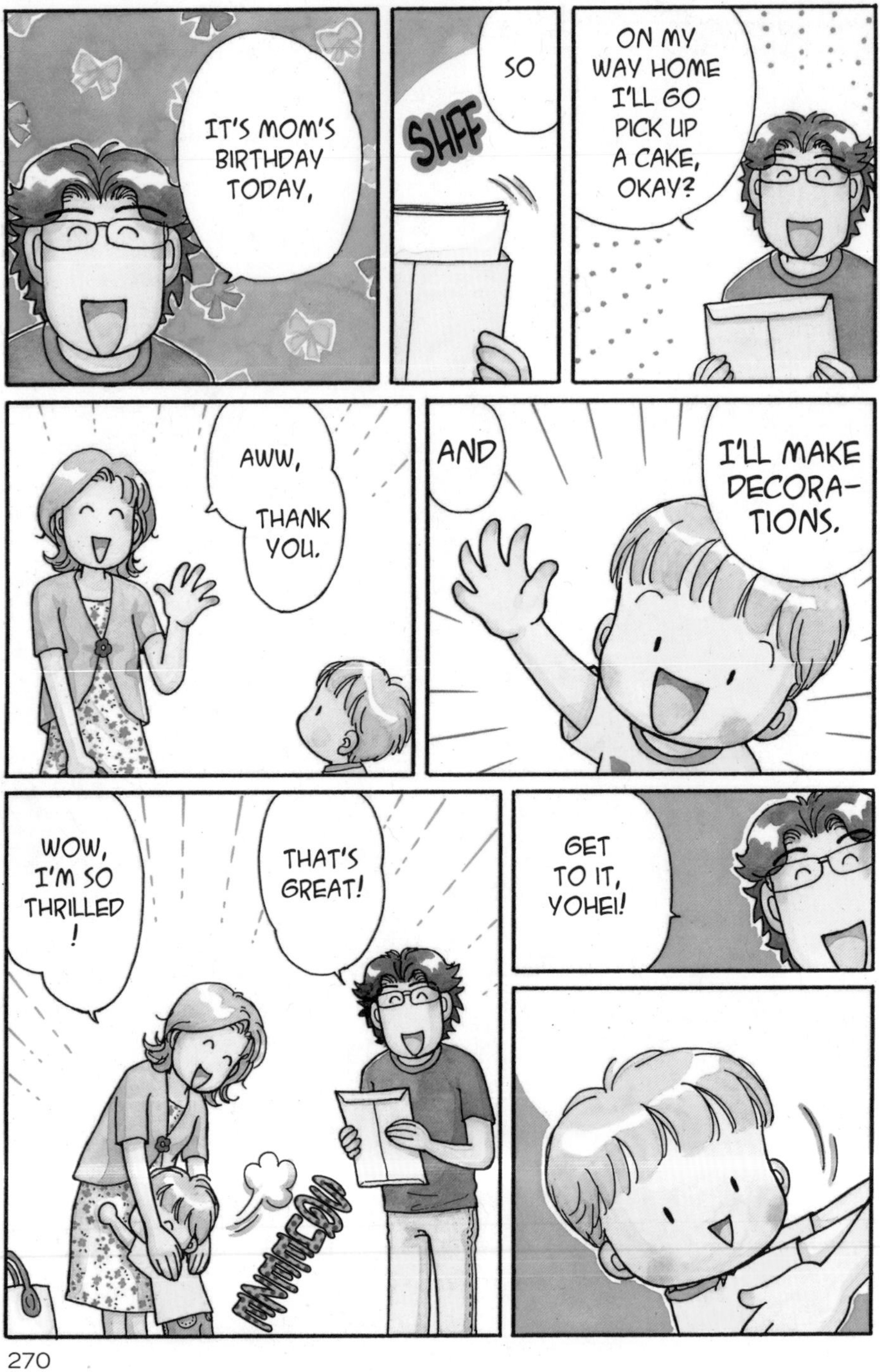
IT'S MOM'S BIRTHDAY TODAY,
SO
SHFF
ON MY WAY HOME I'LL GO PICK UP A CAKE, OKAY?
AWW,
THANK YOU.
AND
I'LL MAKE DECORA-TIONS.
WOW, I'M SO THRILLED!
THAT'S GREAT!
GET TO IT, YOHEI!

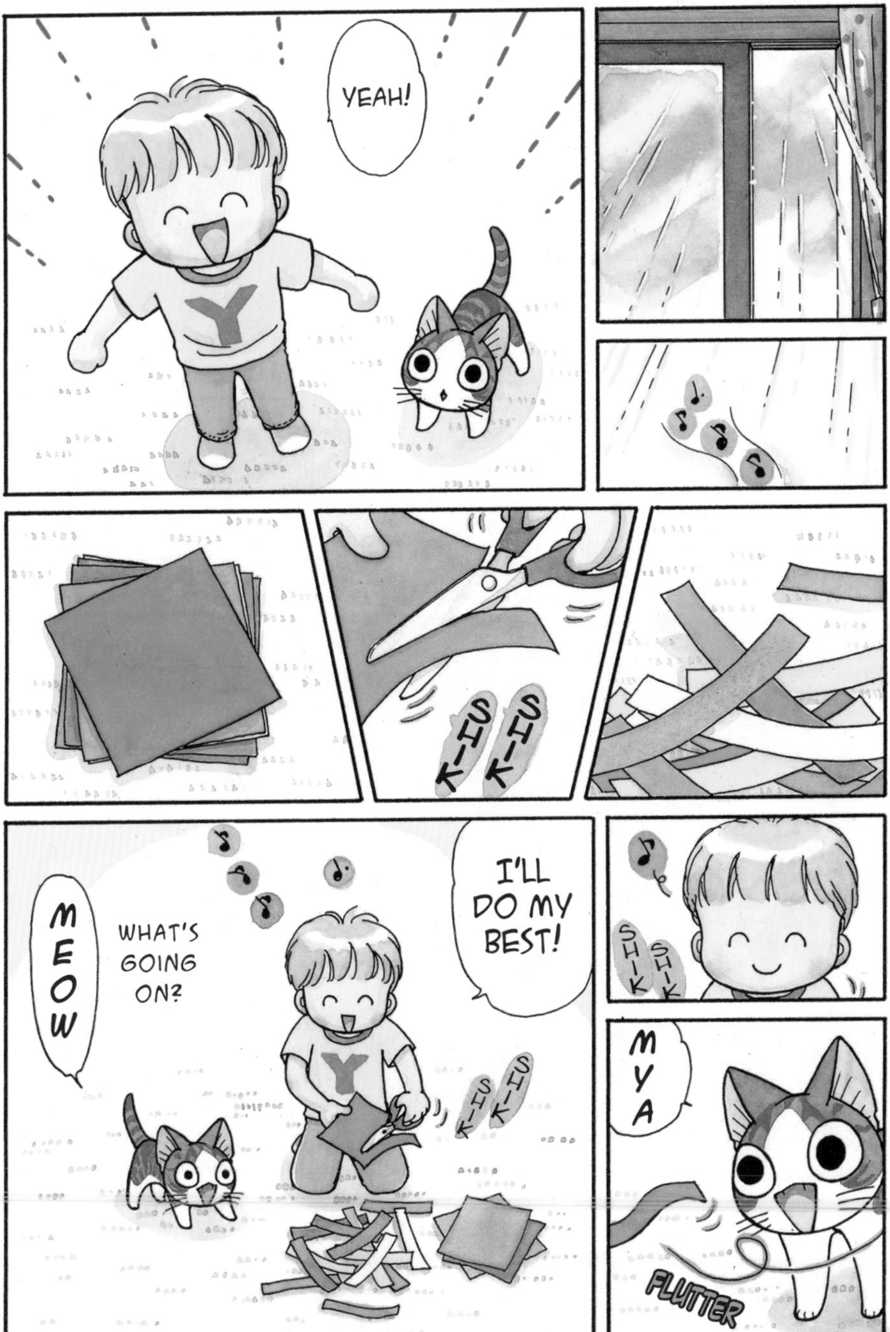
YEAH!
SHIK SHIK
MEOW
WHAT'S GOING ON?
I'LL DO MY BEST!
SHIK SHIK
SHIK SHIK
MYA
FLUTTER

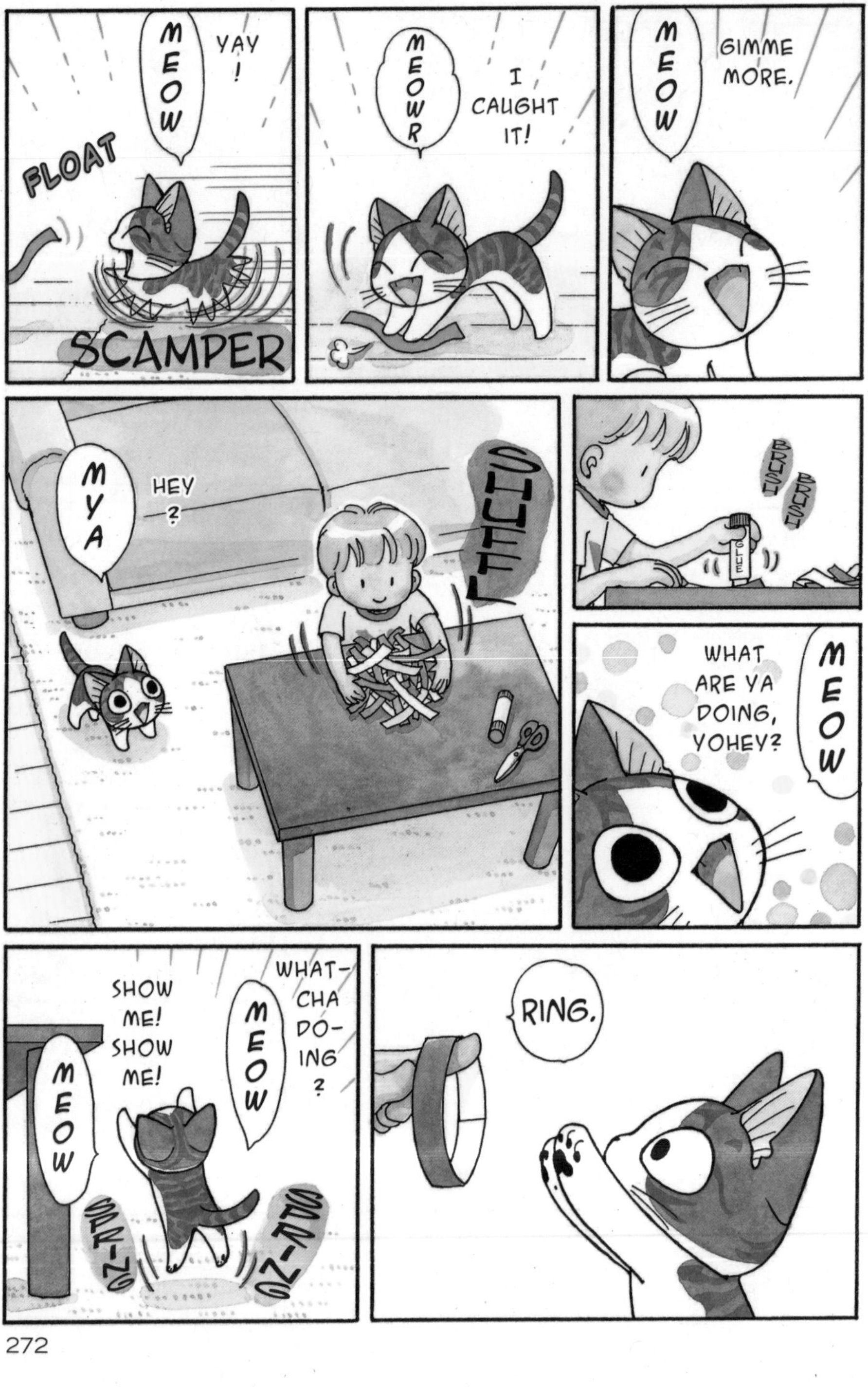
MEOW
YAY!
FLOAT
SCAMPER
MEOWR
I CAUGHT IT!
MEOW
GIMME MORE.
MYA
HEY?
SHUFFL
BRUSH BRUSH
GLUE
MEOW
WHAT ARE YA DOING, YOHEY?
SHOW ME! SHOW ME!
MEOW
MEOW
WHAT-CHA DO-ING?
SPRING
SPRING
RING.

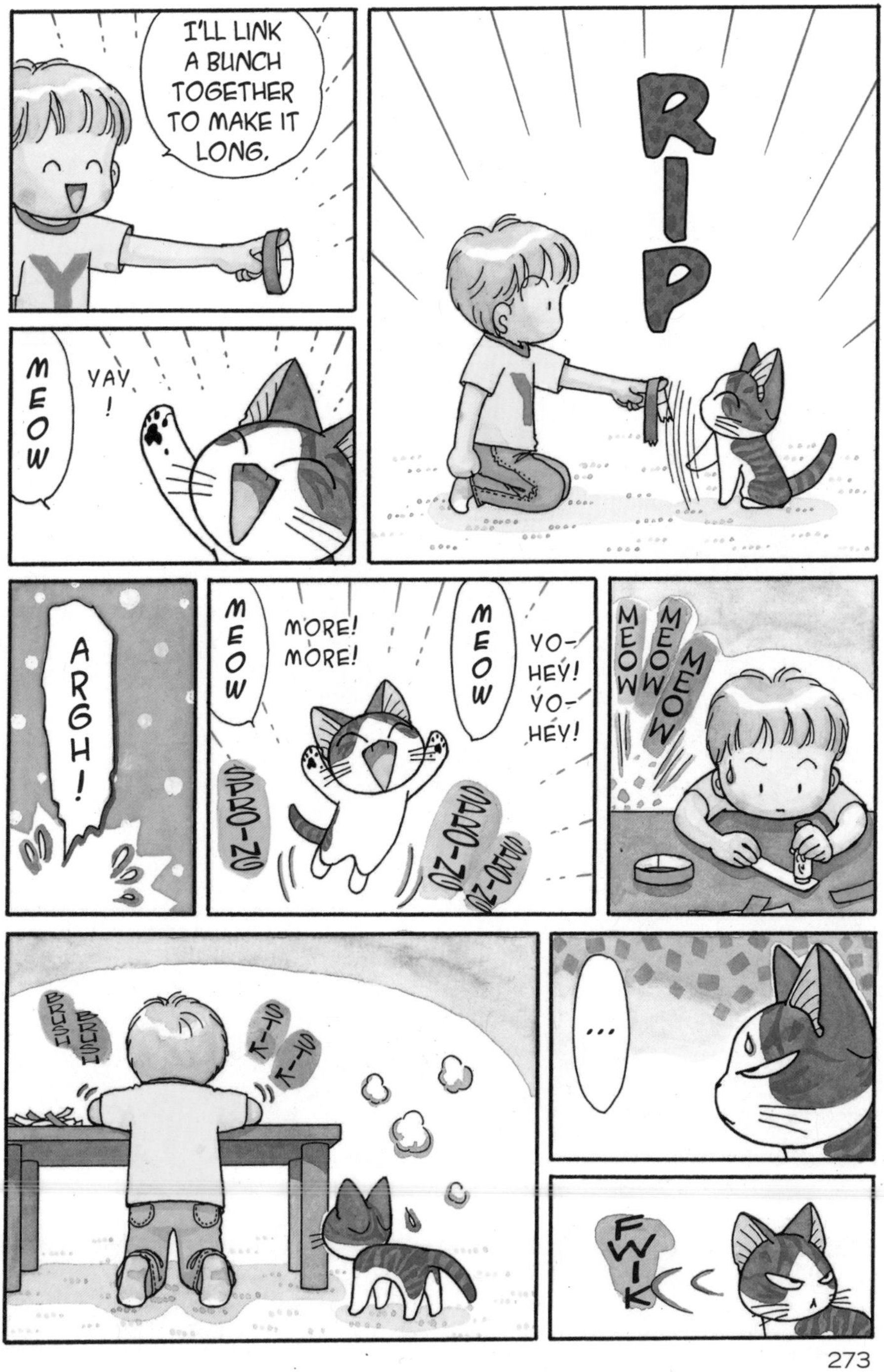
I'LL LINK A BUNCH TOGETHER TO MAKE IT LONG.
RIP
MEOW
YAY!
ARGH!
MEOW
MORE! MORE!
MEOW
YO-HEY! YO-HEY!
SPROING
SPROING
SPROING
MEOW
MEOW
MEOW
BRUSH BRUSH
STIK STIK
...
FWIK

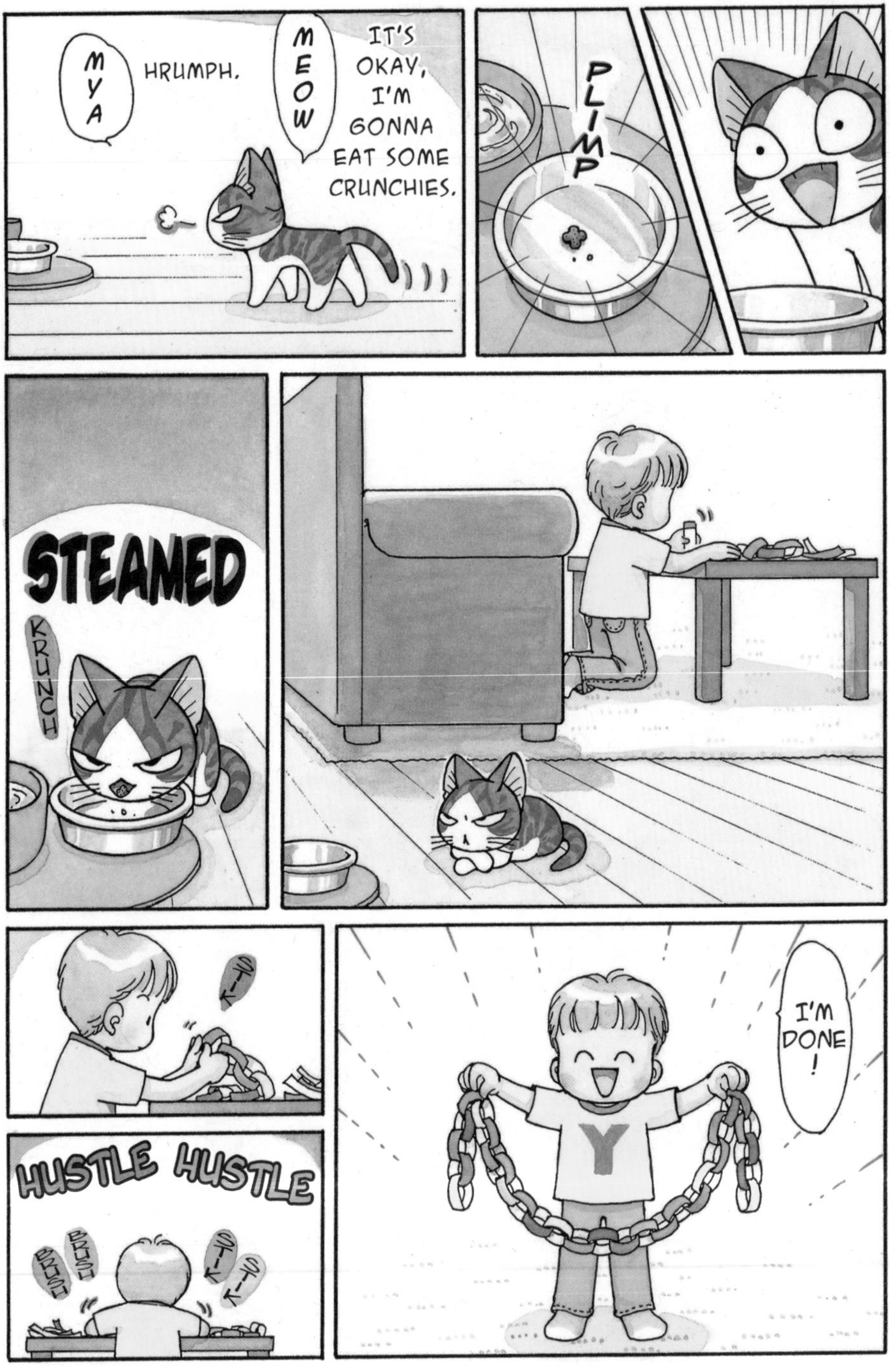
MYA
HRUMPH.
MEOW
IT'S OKAY, I'M GONNA EAT SOME CRUNCHIES.
PLIMP
STEAMED
KRUNCH
STIK
HUSTLE HUSTLE
BRUSH
BRUSH
STIK
STIK
I'M DONE!

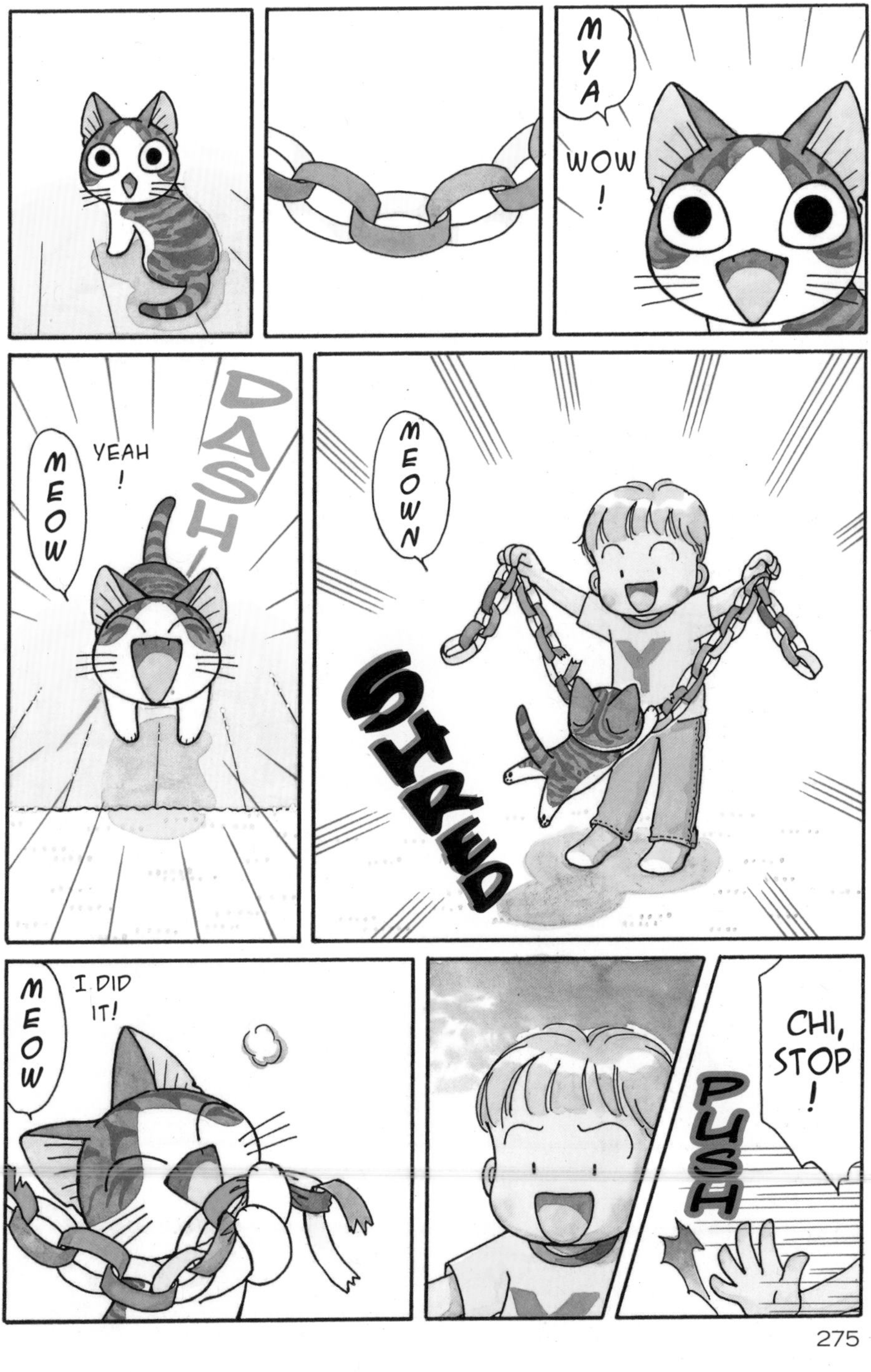
MYA
WOW!
MEOW
YEAH!
DASH
MEOWN
SHRED
MEOW
I DID IT!
CHI, STOP!
PUSH

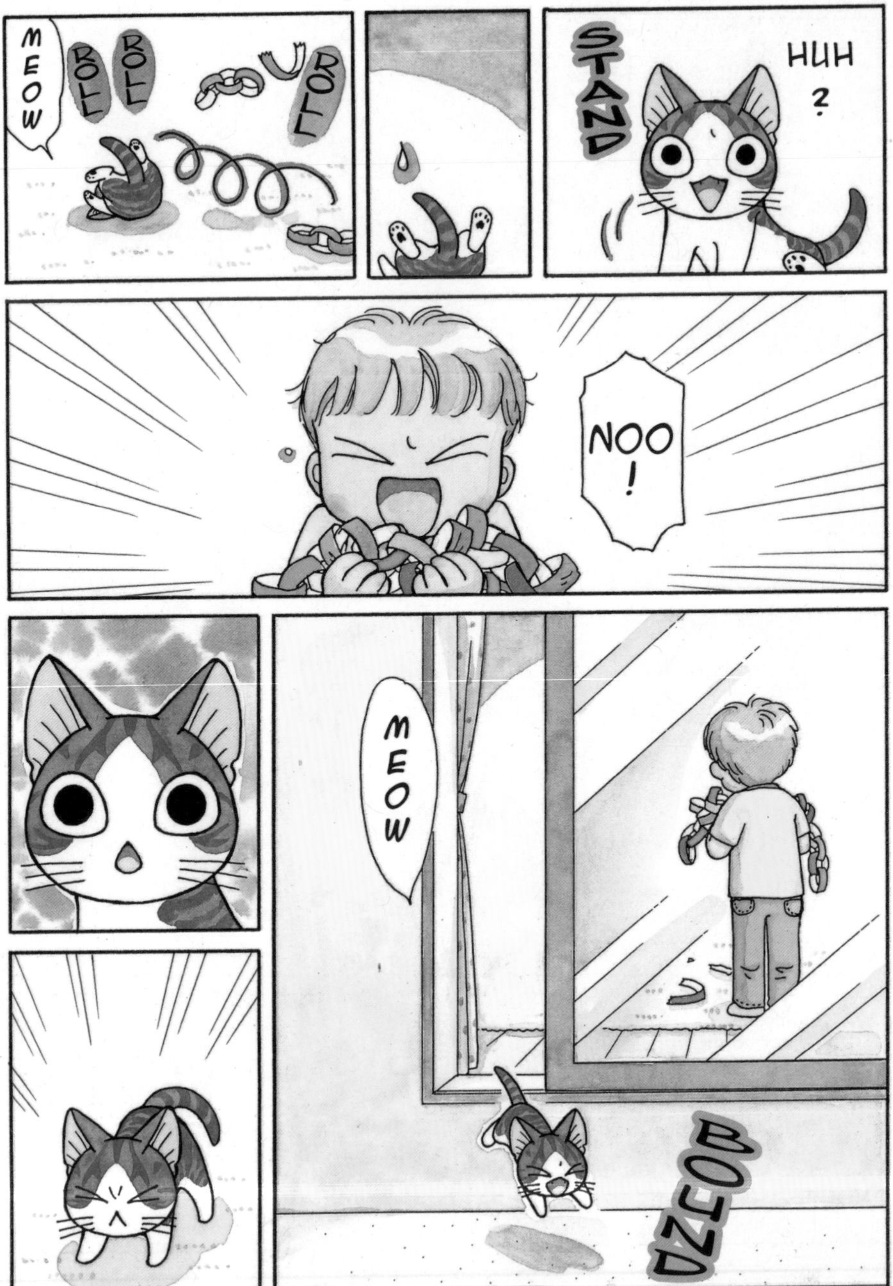
MEOW
ROLL
ROLL
ROLL
STAND
HUH?
NOO!
MEOW
BOUND

the end

homemade 199: a cat is irritable

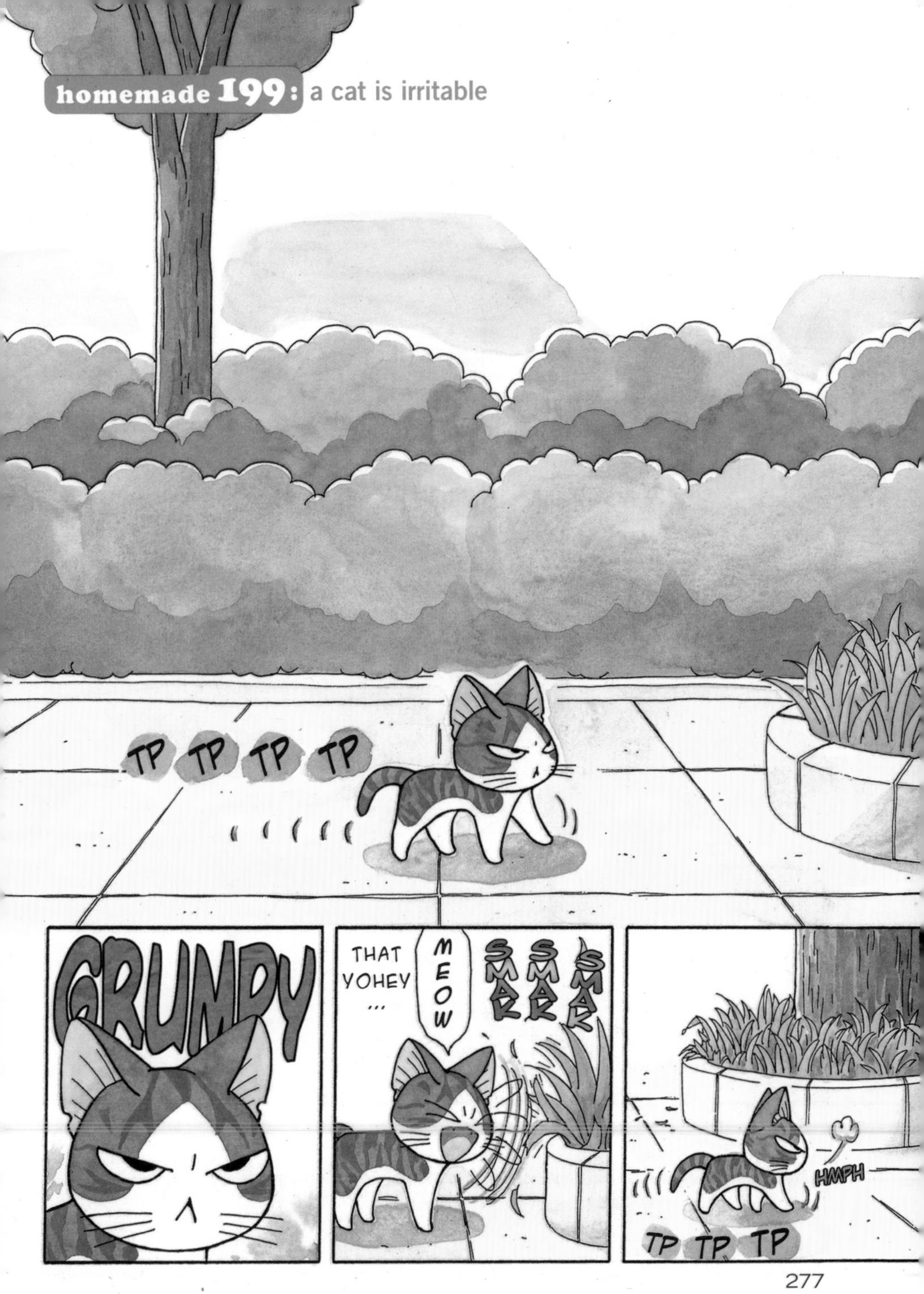
TP TP TP TP
GRUMPY
THAT YOHEY ...
MEOW
SMAK SMAK SMAK
HMPH
TP TP TP

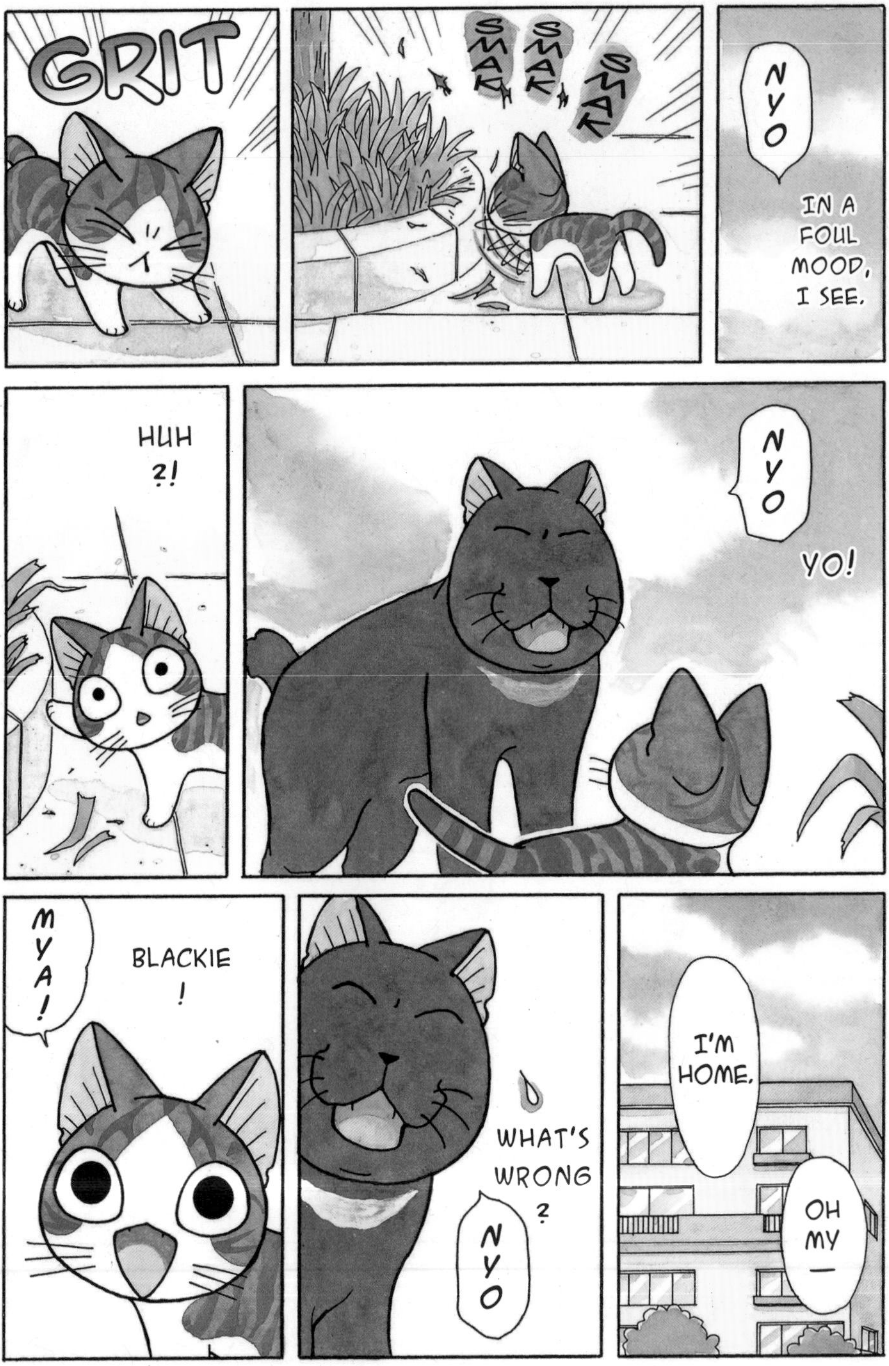
GRIT
SMAK SMAK SMAK
NYO
IN A FOUL MOOD, I SEE.
HUH ?!
NYO
YO!
MYA!
BLACKIE !
WHAT'S WRONG ?
NYO
I'M HOME.
OH MY —

WHAT'S THE MATTER?

CHI—

CHI DID...

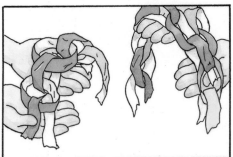

I SEE.

AND YOU TRIED SO HARD TO MAKE THESE.

WHAT CAN YOU DO, CHI'S A CAT.

BIRTHDAY CAKE

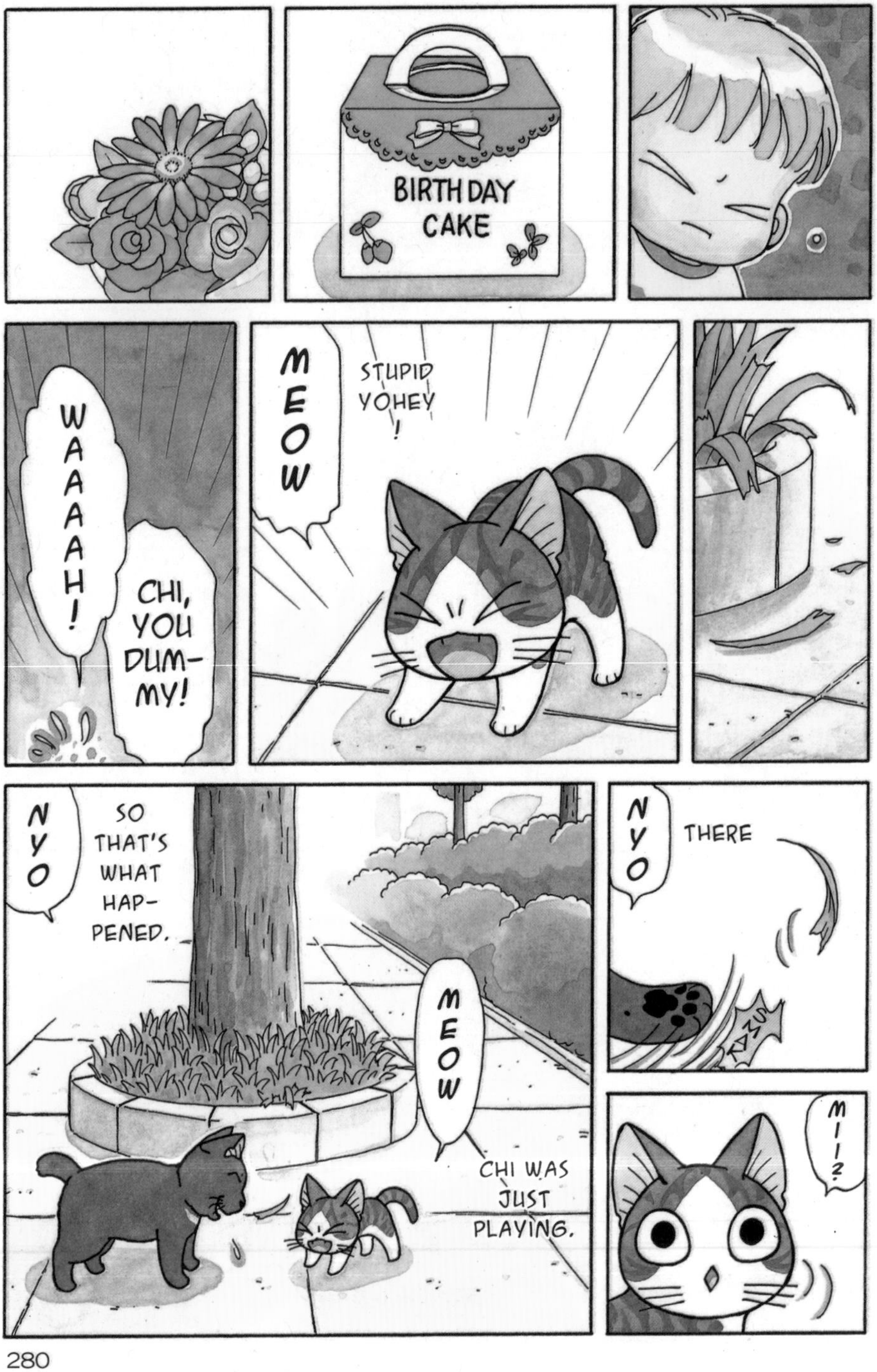
BIRTH DAY CAKE
WAAAAAH!
CHI, YOU DUM-MY!
MEOW
STUPID YOHEY!
NYO
SO THAT'S WHAT HAP-PENED.
MEOW
CHI WAS JUST PLAYING.
NYO
THERE
MII?

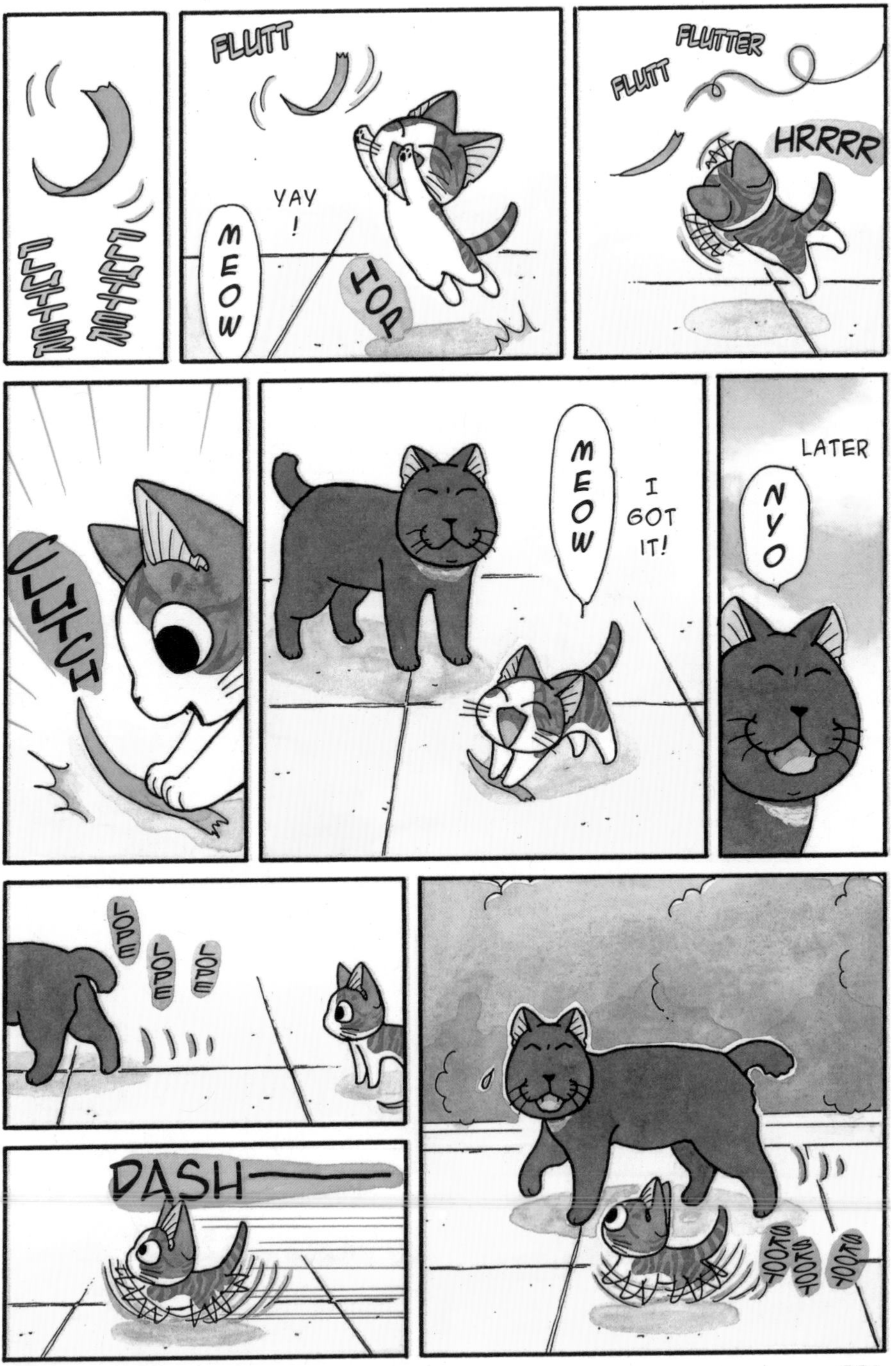

FLUTTER
FLUTTER
FLUTT
YAY!
MEOW
HOP
FLUTT
FLUTTER
HRRRR
CLUTCH
MEOW
I GOT IT!
LATER
NYO
LOPE
LOPE
LOPE
DASH
SKOOT
SKOOT
SKOOT

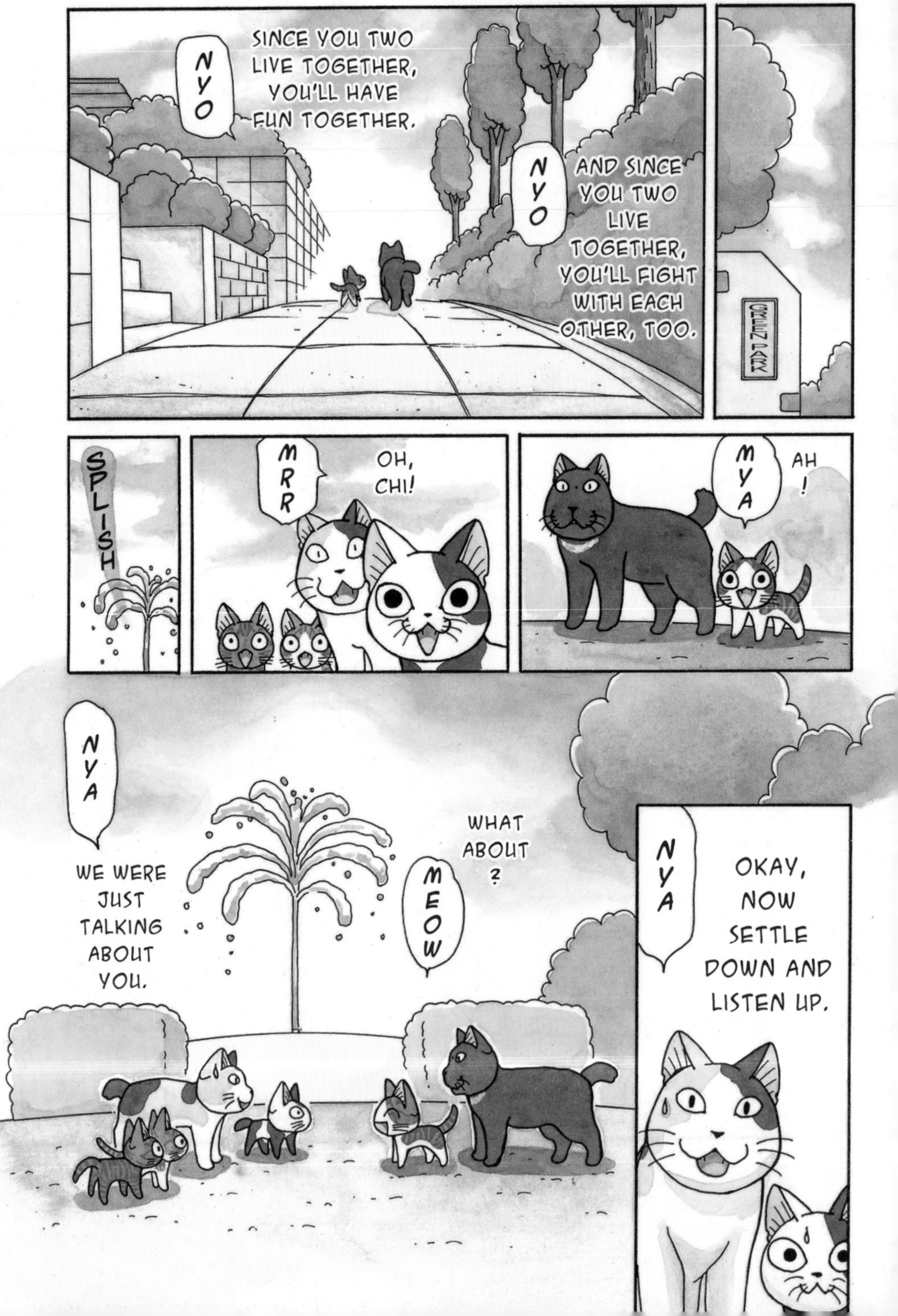
NYO
SINCE YOU TWO LIVE TOGETHER, YOU'LL HAVE FUN TOGETHER.
NYO
AND SINCE YOU TWO LIVE TOGETHER, YOU'LL FIGHT WITH EACH OTHER, TOO.
GREEN PARK
SPLISH
MRR
OH, CHI!
MYA
AH!
NYA
WE WERE JUST TALKING ABOUT YOU.
MEOW
WHAT ABOUT?
NYA
OKAY, NOW SETTLE DOWN AND LISTEN UP.

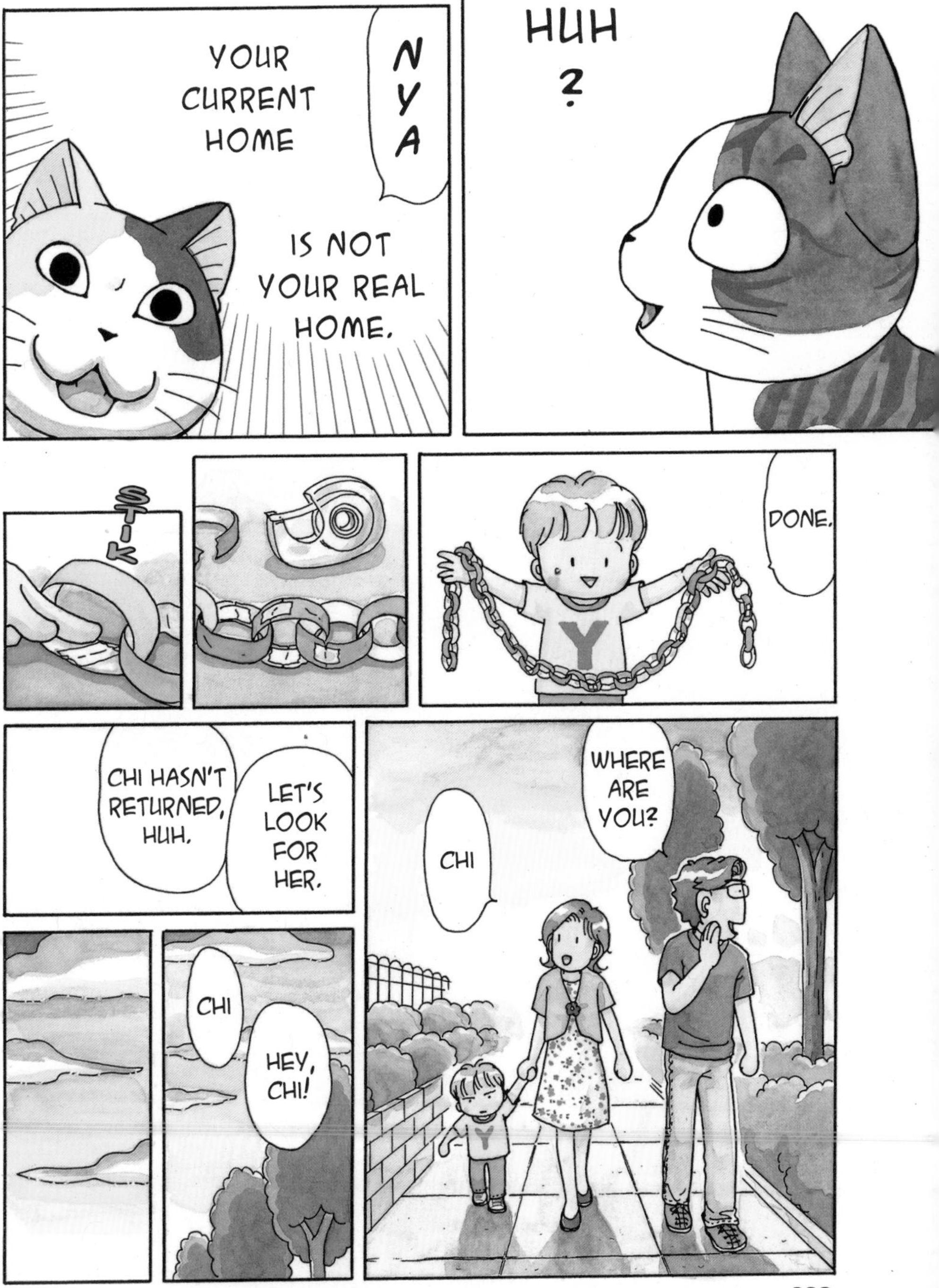
YOUR CURRENT HOME
NYA
IS NOT YOUR REAL HOME.
HUH ?
STIK
DONE.
CHI HASN'T RETURNED, HUH.
LET'S LOOK FOR HER.
WHERE ARE YOU?
CHI
CHI
HEY, CHI!

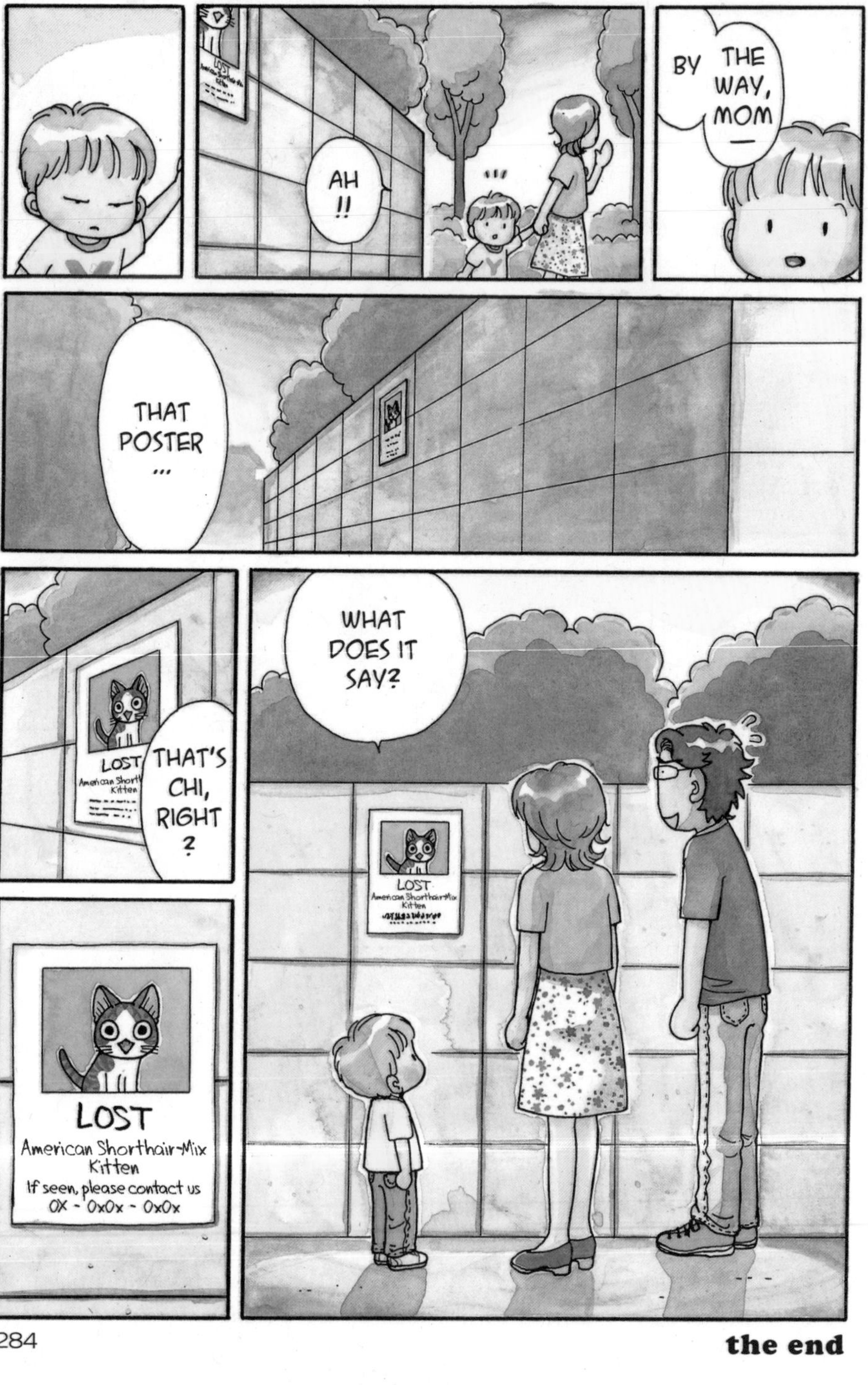
AH !!
BY THE WAY, MOM —
THAT POSTER ...
THAT'S CHI, RIGHT ?
LOST
American Shorthair-Mix Kitten
If seen, please contact us
0X - 0x0x - 0x0x
WHAT DOES IT SAY?
LOST
American Shorthair-Mix Kitten

the end

homemade 200: a cat has a chance meeting

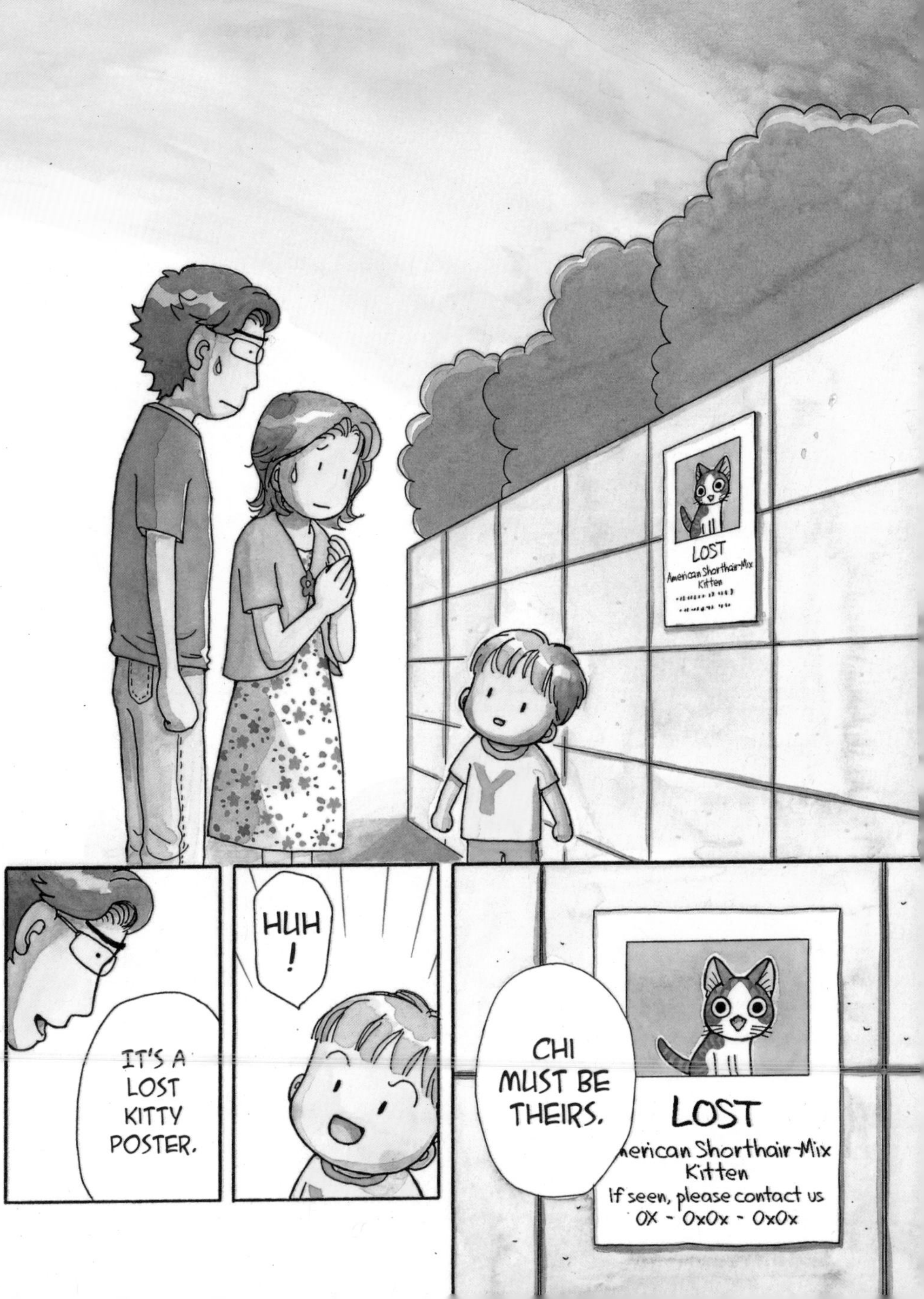
LOST
American Shorthair-Mix Kitten
IT'S A LOST KITTY POSTER.
HUH!
CHI MUST BE THEIRS.
LOST
merican Shorthair-Mix Kitten
If seen, please contact us
0X - 0x0x - 0x0x

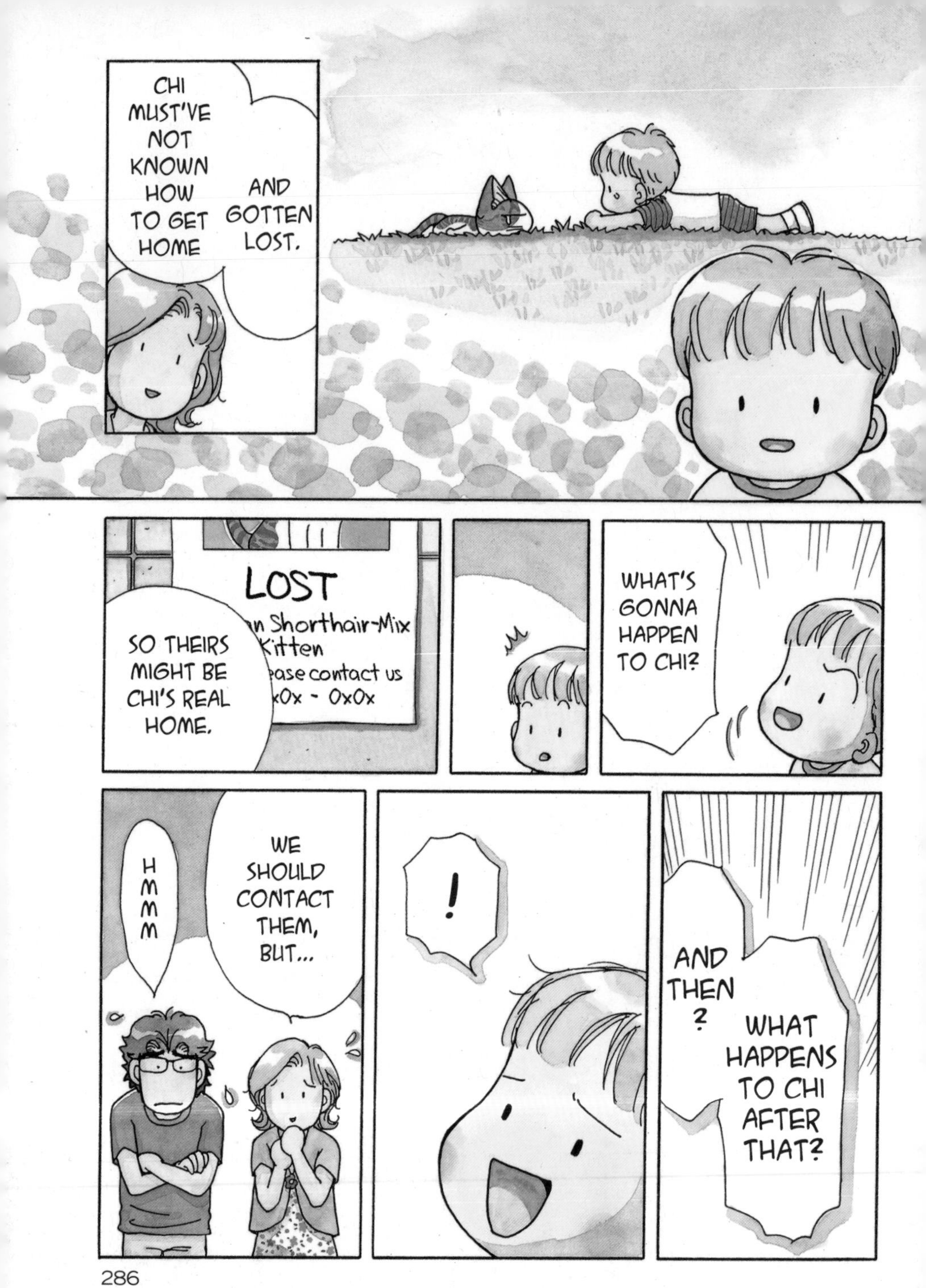
CHI MUST'VE NOT KNOWN HOW TO GET HOME
AND GOTTEN LOST.
LOST
n Shorthair-Mix
Kitten
ease contact us
x0x - 0x0x
SO THEIRS MIGHT BE CHI'S REAL HOME.
WHAT'S GONNA HAPPEN TO CHI?
HMMM
WE SHOULD CONTACT THEM, BUT...
!
AND THEN?
WHAT HAPPENS TO CHI AFTER THAT?

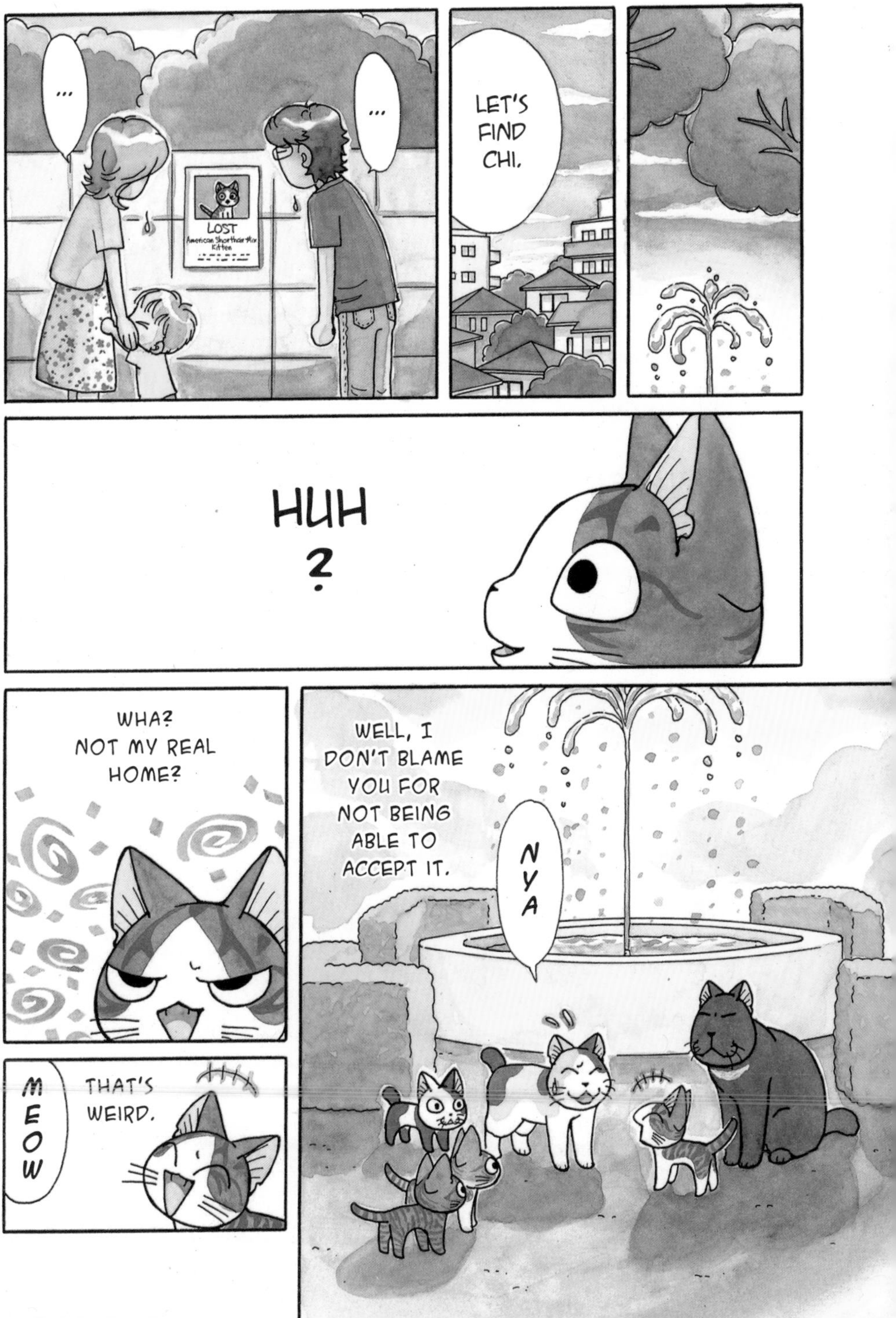
...
...
LOST
American Shorthair Mix Kitten
LET'S FIND CHI.
HUH ?
WHA? NOT MY REAL HOME?
MEOW
THAT'S WEIRD.
WELL, I DON'T BLAME YOU FOR NOT BEING ABLE TO ACCEPT IT.
NYA

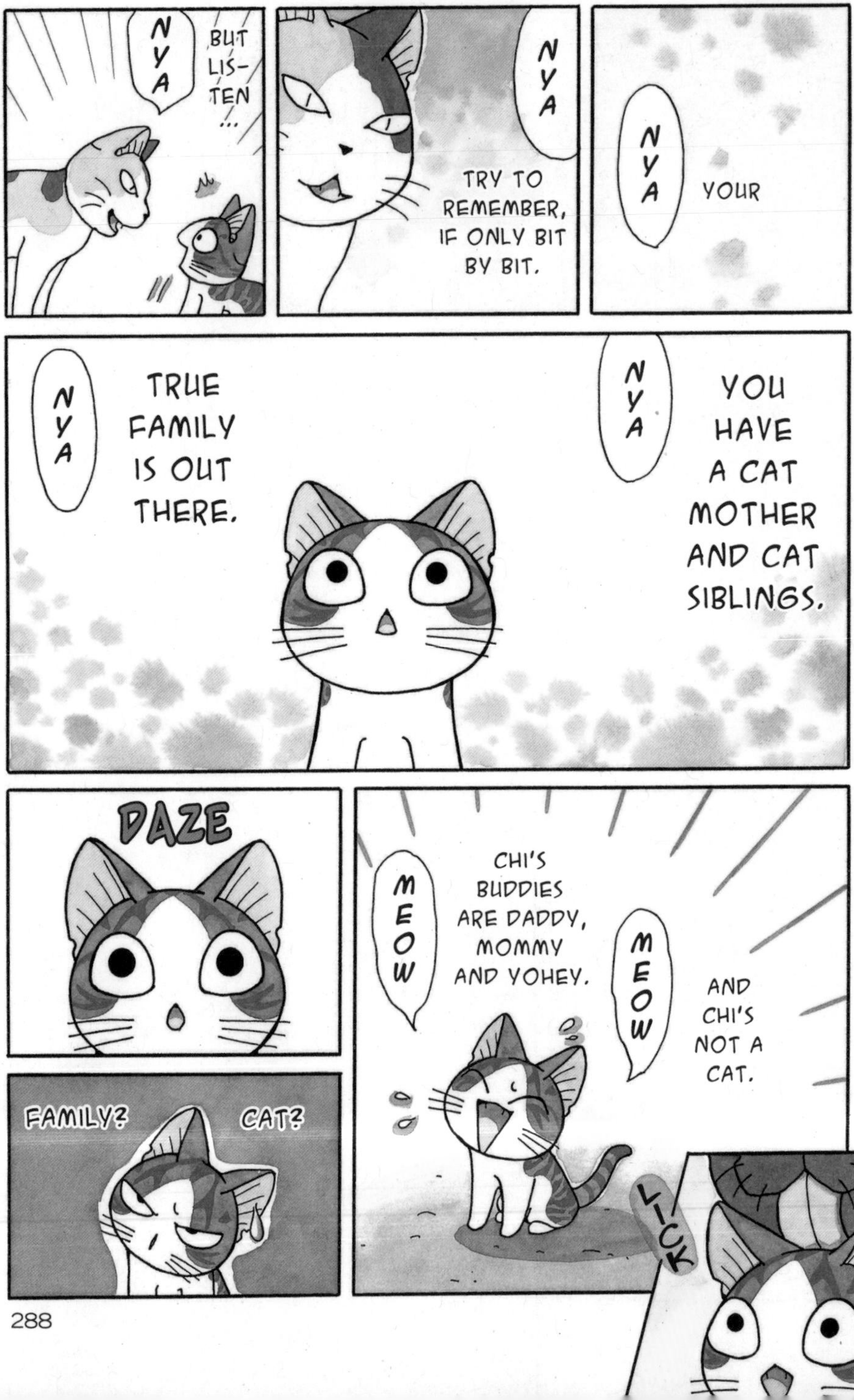
NYA
BUT LIS-TEN ...
NYA
TRY TO REMEMBER, IF ONLY BIT BY BIT.
NYA
YOUR
NYA
TRUE FAMILY IS OUT THERE.
NYA
YOU HAVE A CAT MOTHER AND CAT SIBLINGS.
DAZE
FAMILY?
CAT?
MEOW
CHI'S BUDDIES ARE DADDY, MOMMY AND YOHEY.
MEOW
AND CHI'S NOT A CAT.
LICK

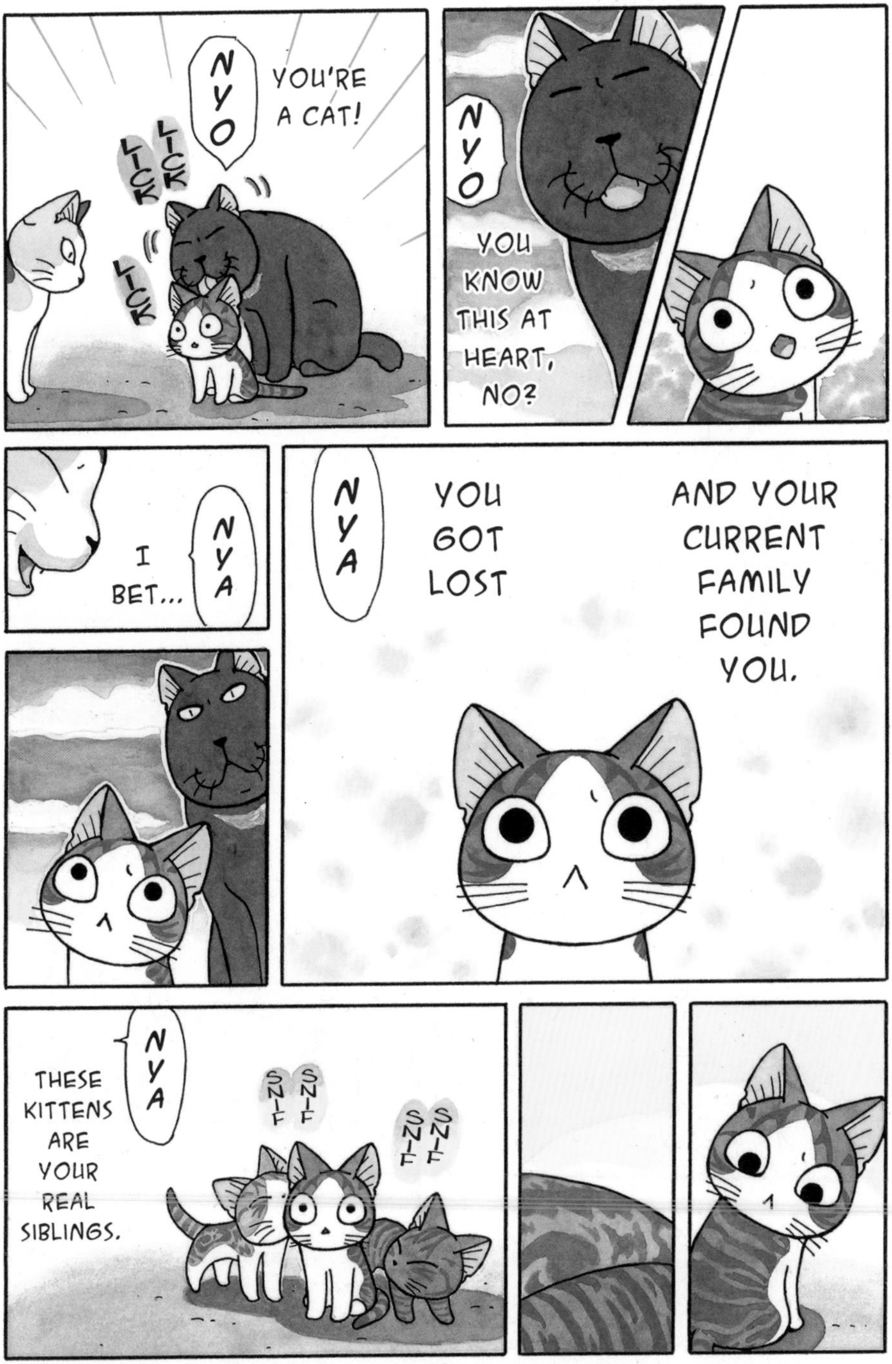
NYO
YOU'RE A CAT!
LICK LICK
LICK
NYO
YOU KNOW THIS AT HEART, NO?
I BET...
NYA
NYA
YOU GOT LOST
AND YOUR CURRENT FAMILY FOUND YOU.
NYA
THESE KITTENS ARE YOUR REAL SIBLINGS.
SNIF SNIF
SNIF SNIF

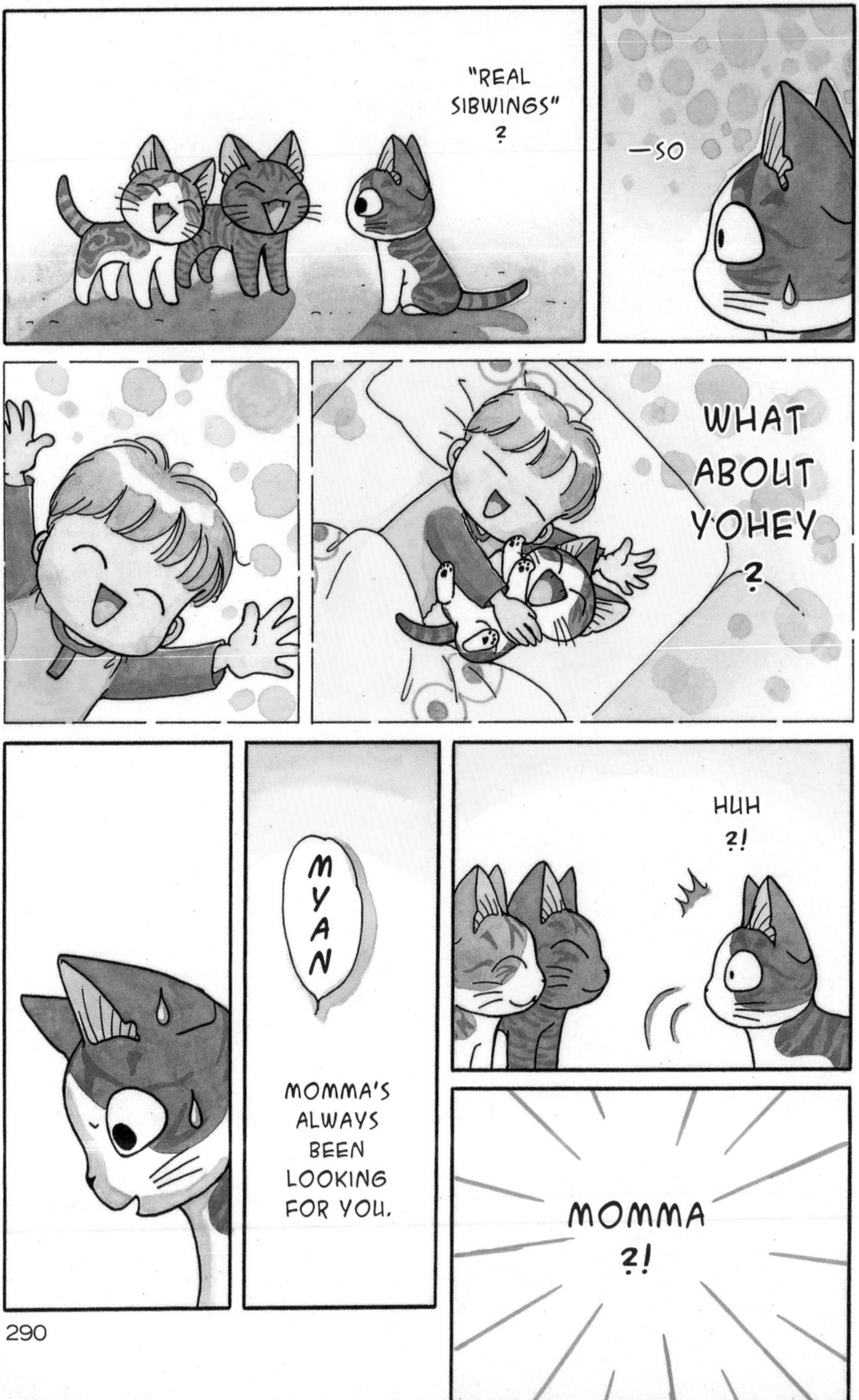
"REAL SIBWINGS" ?
—SO
WHAT ABOUT YOHEY ?
MYAN
MOMMA'S ALWAYS BEEN LOOKING FOR YOU.
HUH ?!
MOMMA ?!

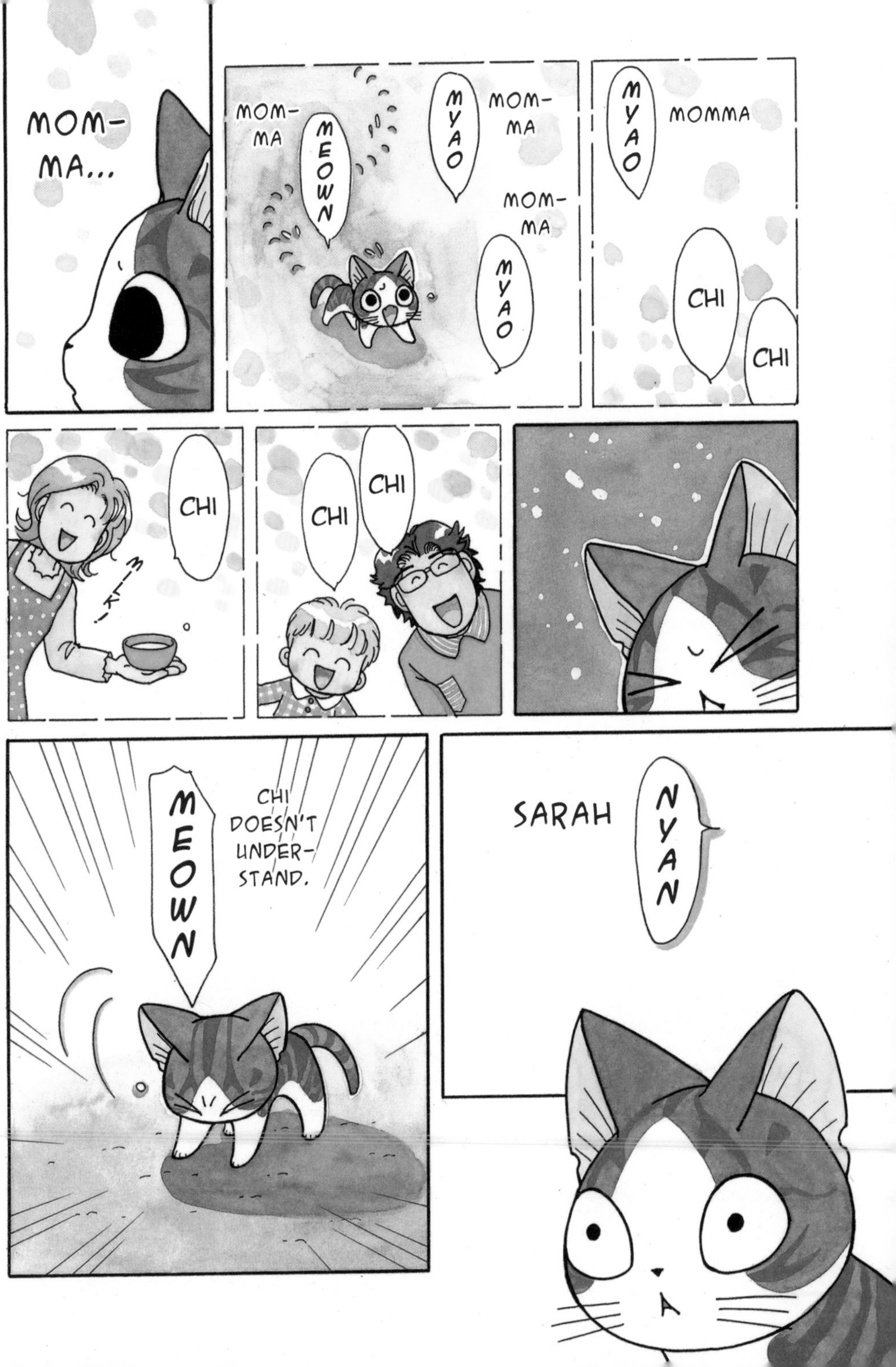
MOM-MA...
MOM-MA
MEOWN
MYAO
MOM-MA
MOM-MA
MYAO
MYAO
MOMMA
CHI
CHI
CHI
CHI
CHI
MEOWN
CHI DOESN'T UNDER-STAND.
SARAH
NYAN

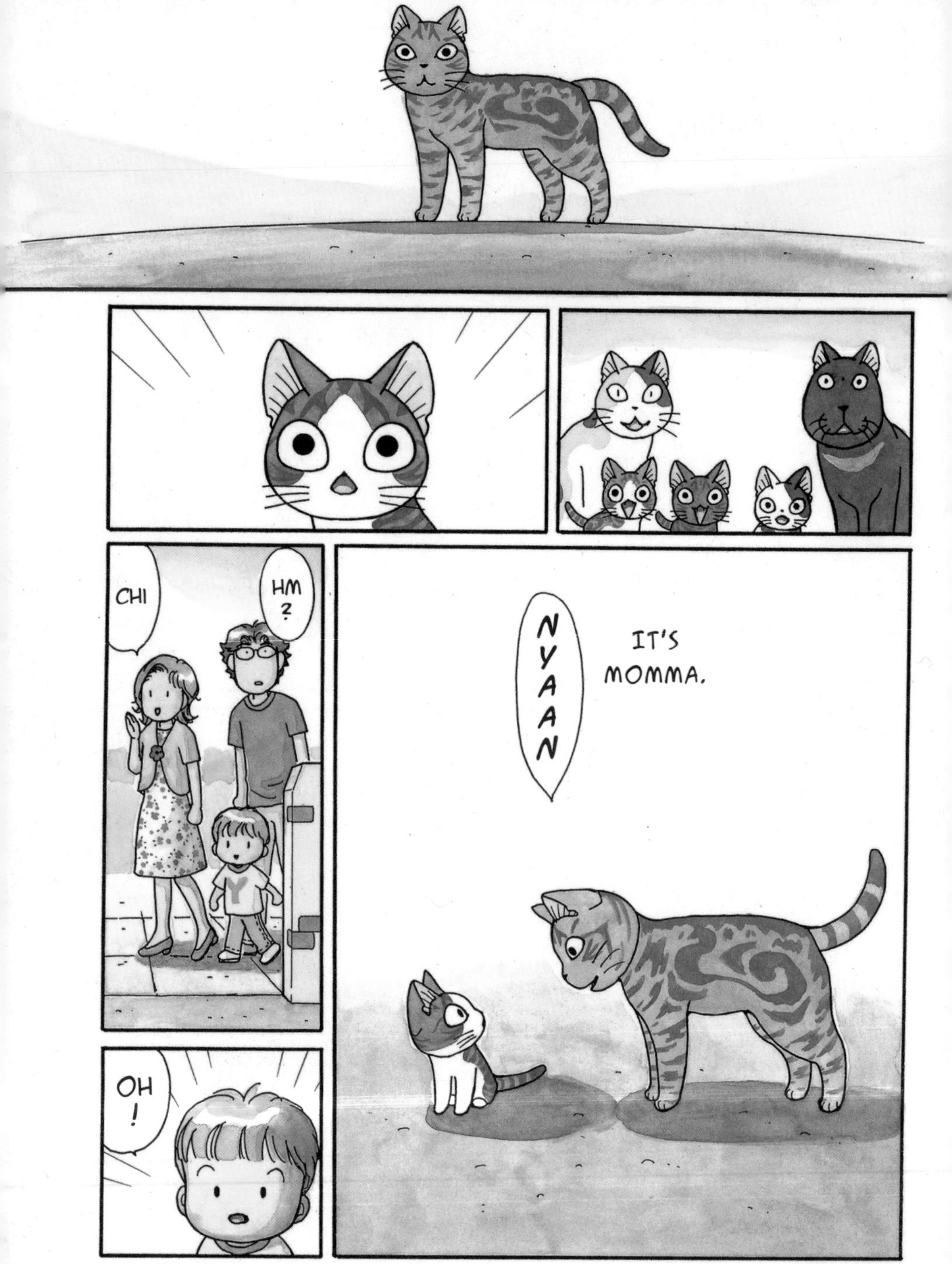
CHI
HM ?
OH !
NYAAN
IT'S MOMMA.

the end

homemade 201: a cat chases her memories

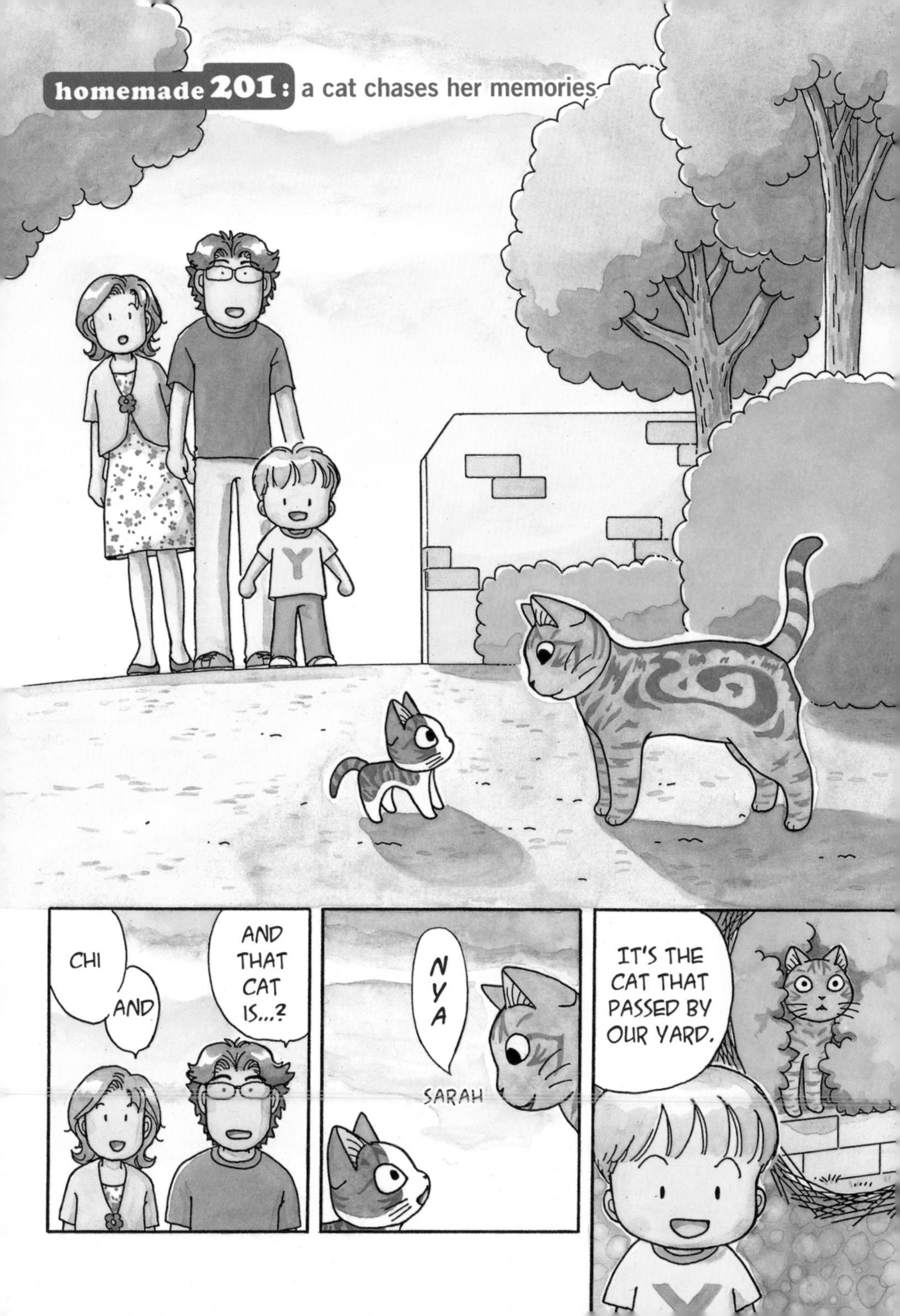
CHI
AND
AND THAT CAT IS...?
NYA
SARAH
IT'S THE CAT THAT PASSED BY OUR YARD.

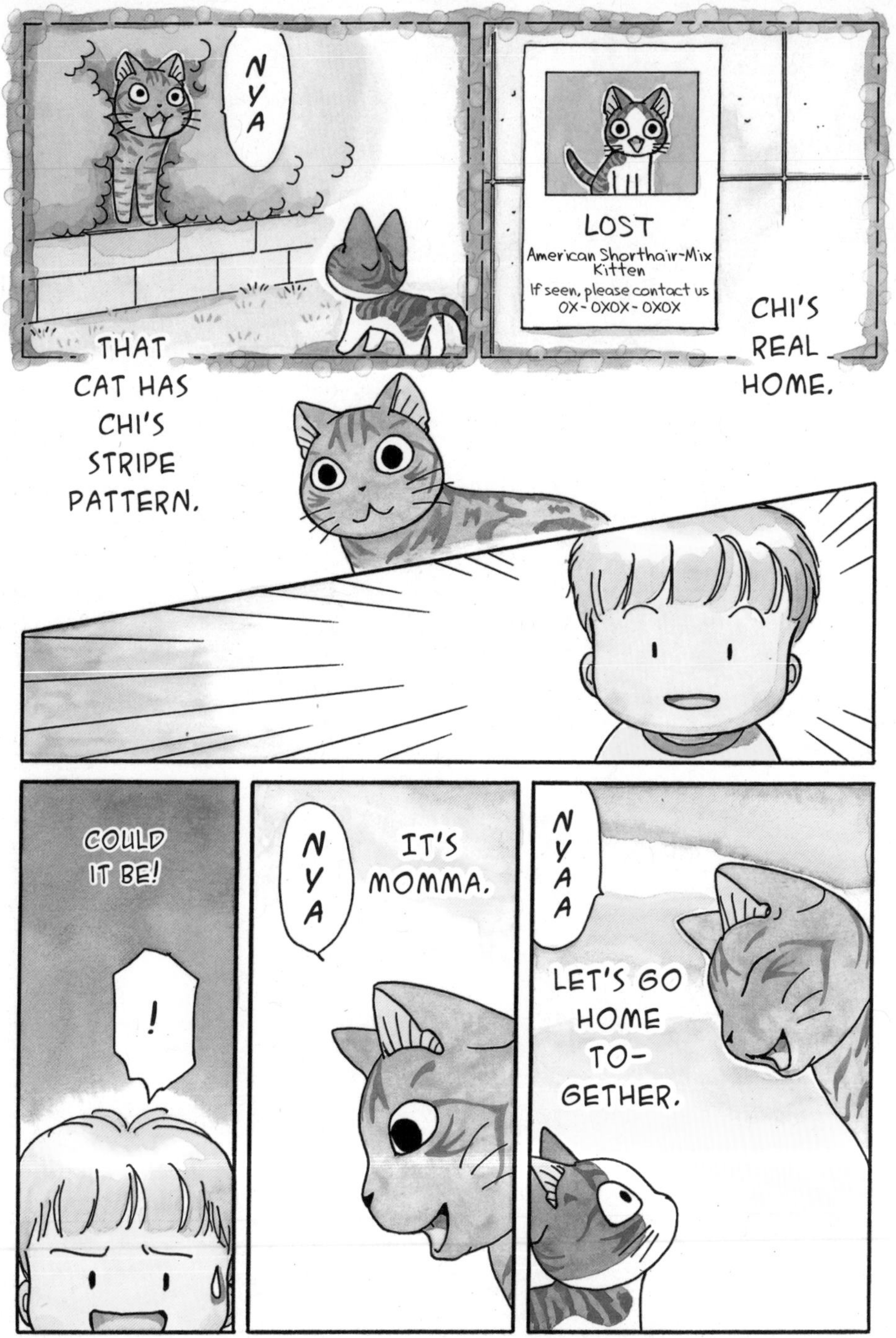
NYA
THAT CAT HAS CHI'S STRIPE PATTERN.
LOST
American Shorthair-Mix Kitten
If seen, please contact us
OX-OXOX-OXOX
CHI'S REAL HOME.
COULD IT BE!
!
NYA
IT'S MOMMA.
NYAA
LET'S GO HOME TO-GETHER.

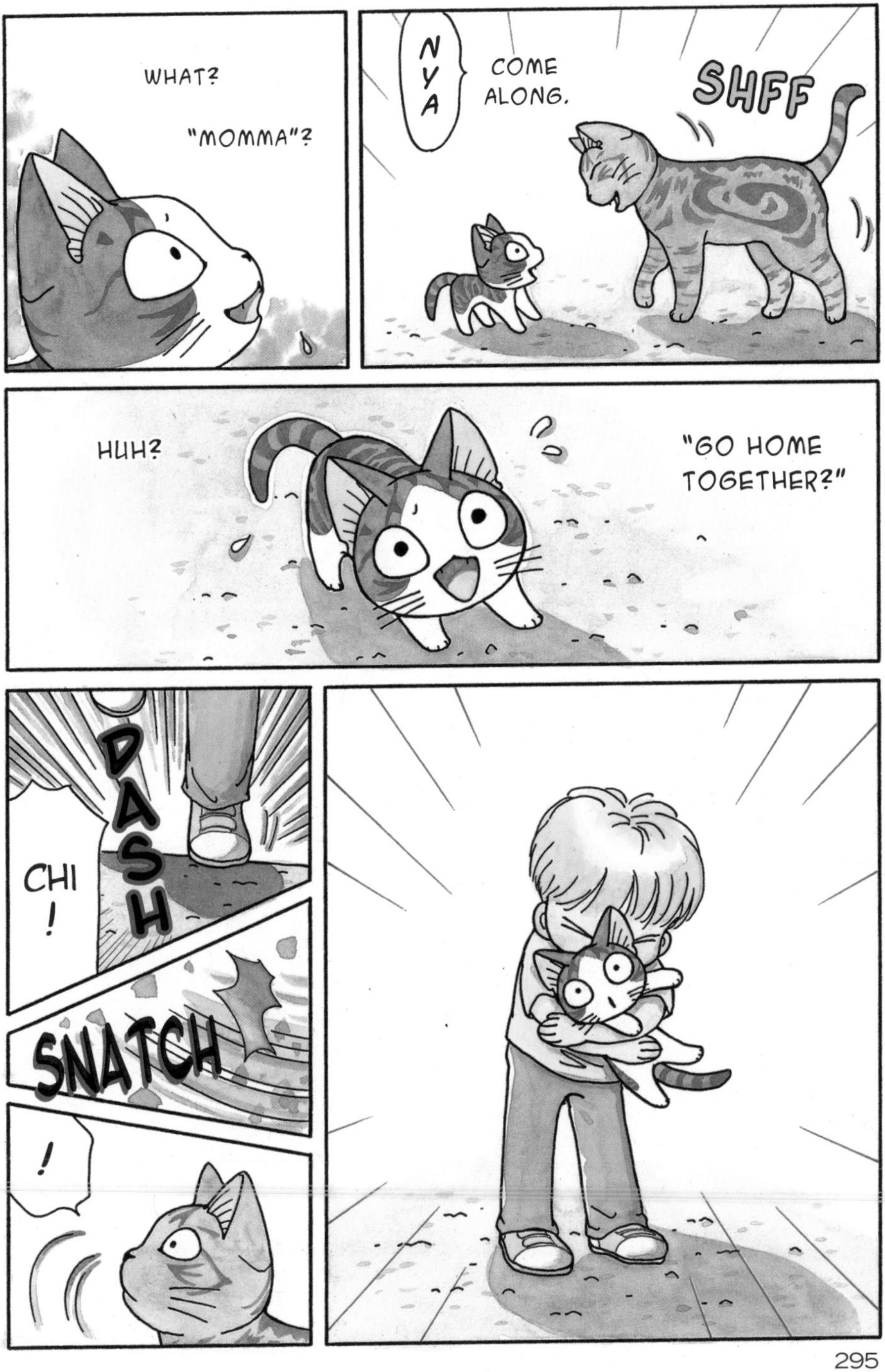
WHAT?
"MOMMA"?
NYA
COME ALONG.
SHFF
HUH?
"GO HOME TOGETHER?"
DASH
CHI!
SNATCH
!

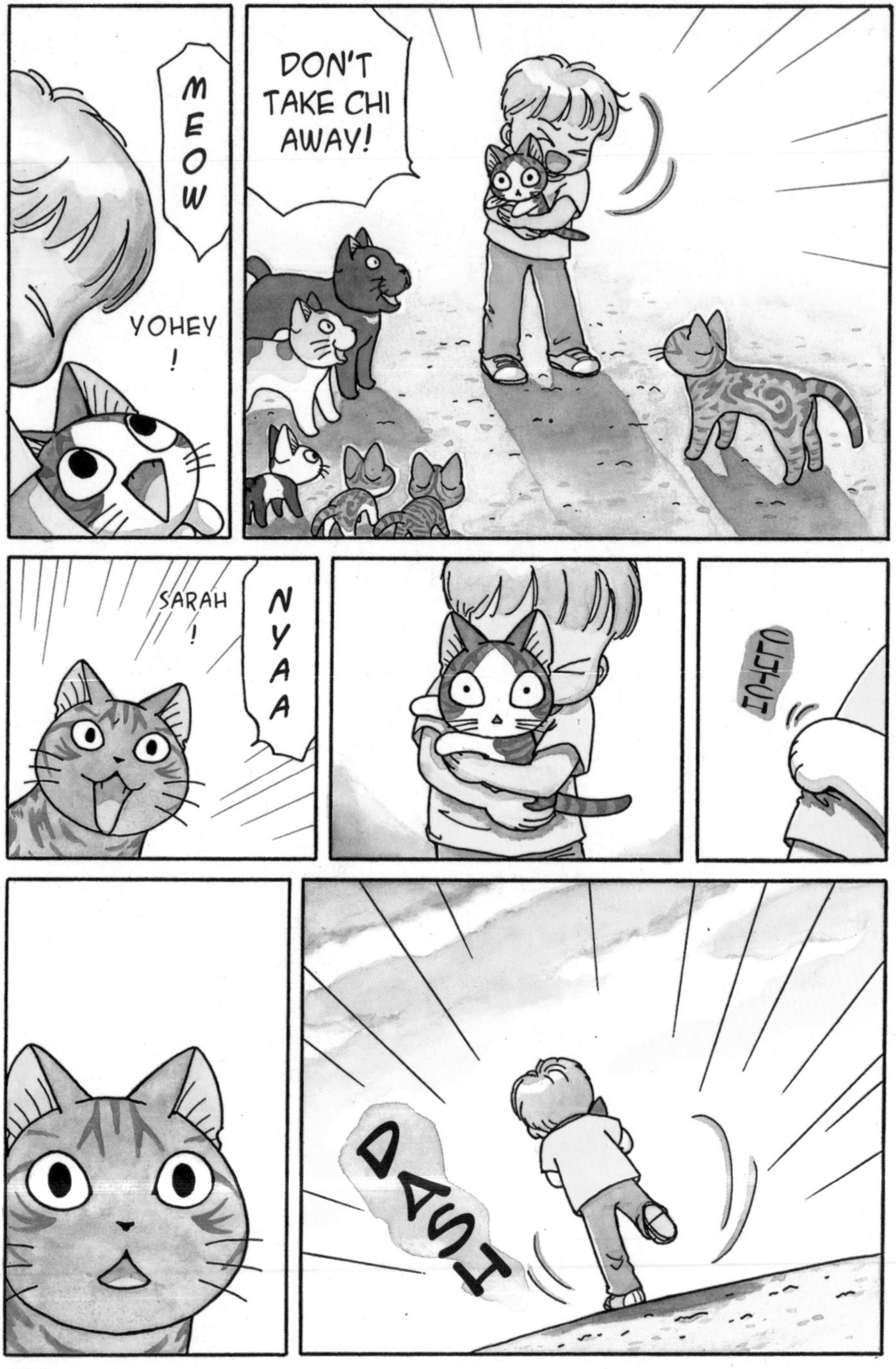
MEOW
YOHEY!
DON'T TAKE CHI AWAY!
SARAH!
NYAA
CLUTCH
DASH

COULD THAT CAT... BE CHI'S MOTHER?

IS HERE GOOD?

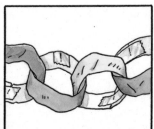

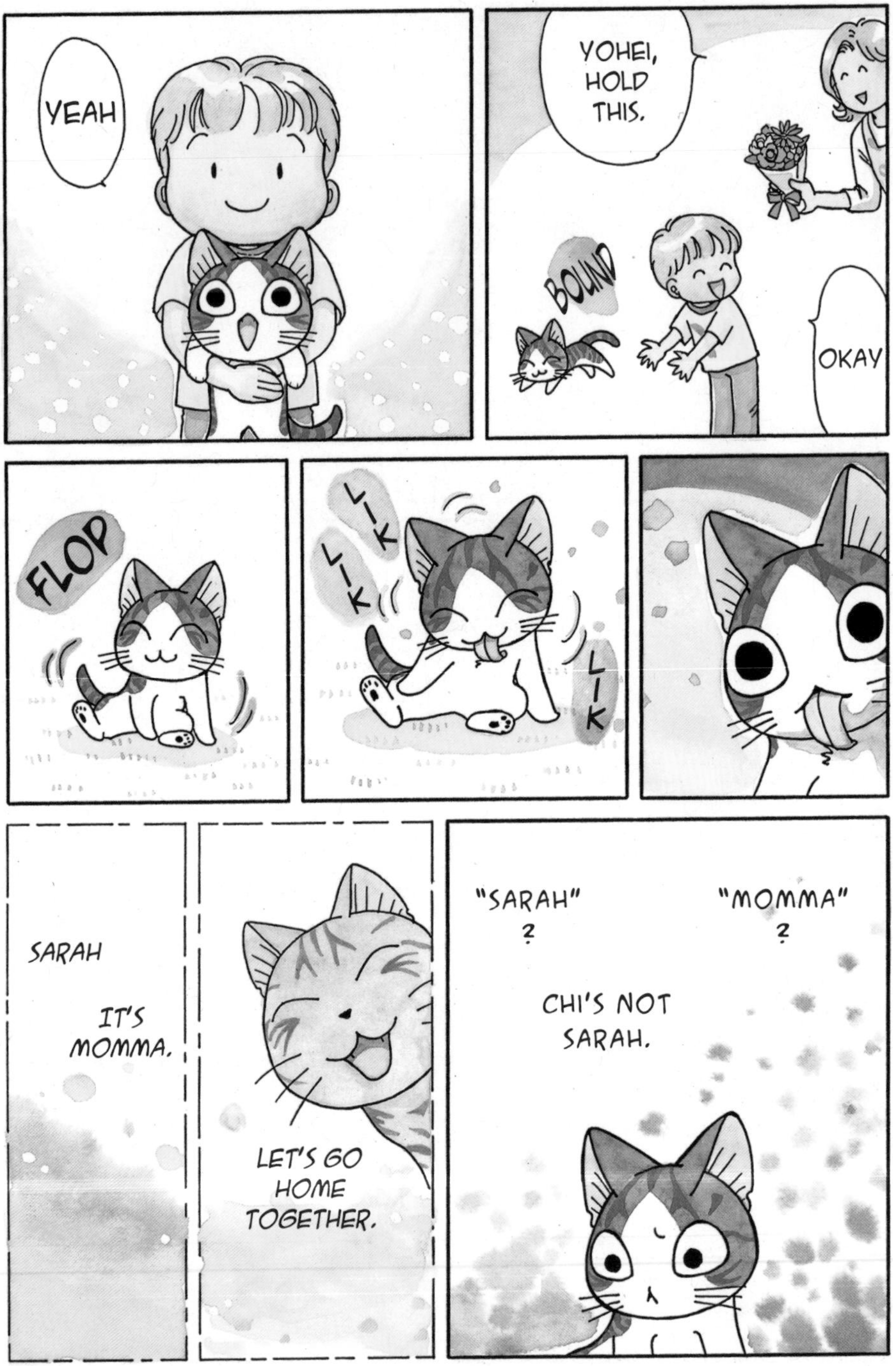
YEAH
YOHEI, HOLD THIS.
BOUND
OKAY
FLOP
LIK LIK
LIK
SARAH
IT'S MOMMA.
LET'S GO HOME TOGETHER.
"SARAH" ?
"MOMMA" ?
CHI'S NOT SARAH.

"HOME"
?

BUT THIS IS CHI'S HOME.

"LET'S GO"
?

!

MEOWN

MOMMA MOMMA

GOTTA GO HOME.

MEOWN

AH...?

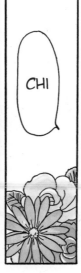

CHI

SNAP

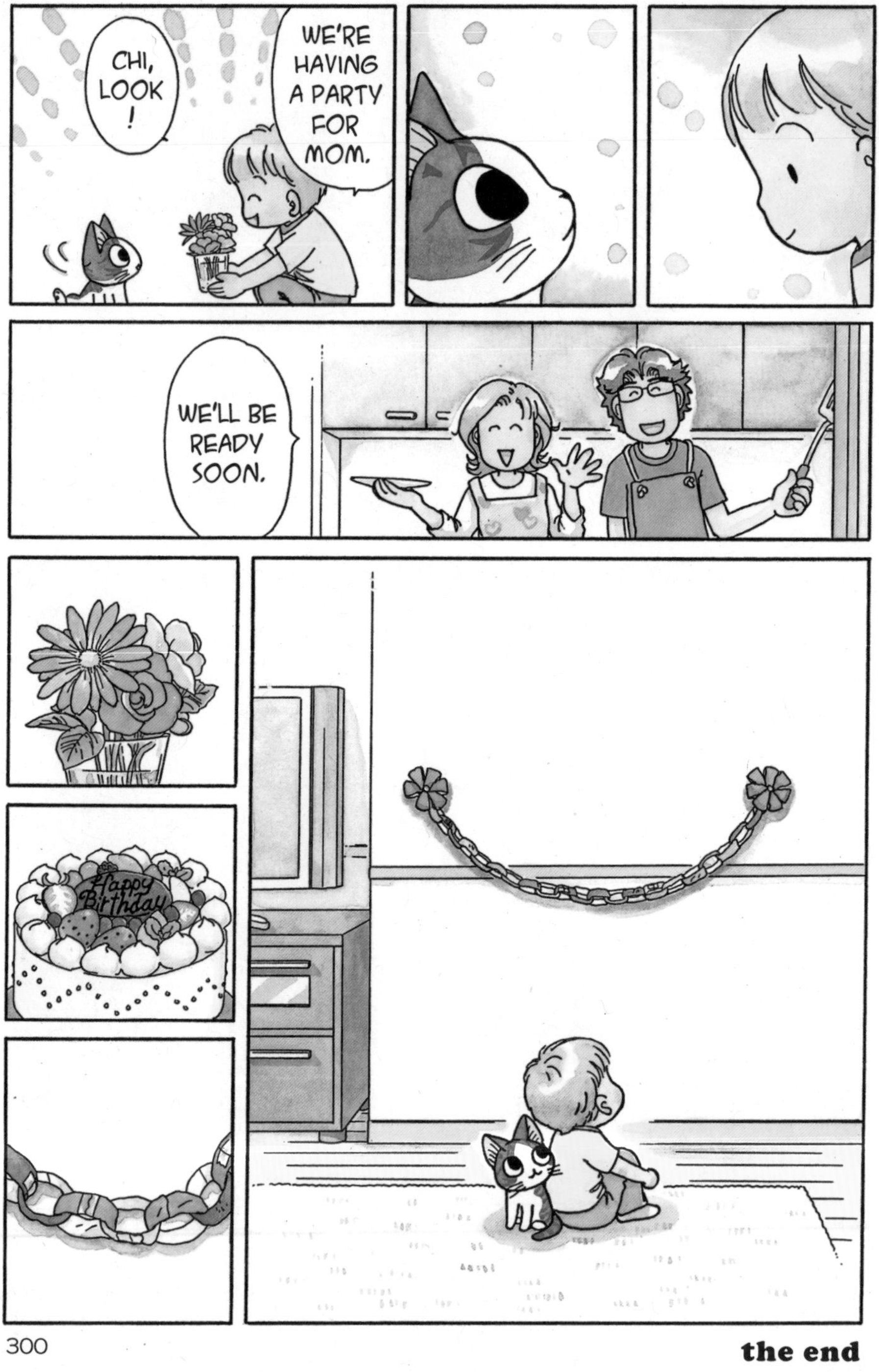
CHI, LOOK!
WE'RE HAVING A PARTY FOR MOM.
WE'LL BE READY SOON.
Happy Birthday

the end

homemade 202: a cat's spirits lift

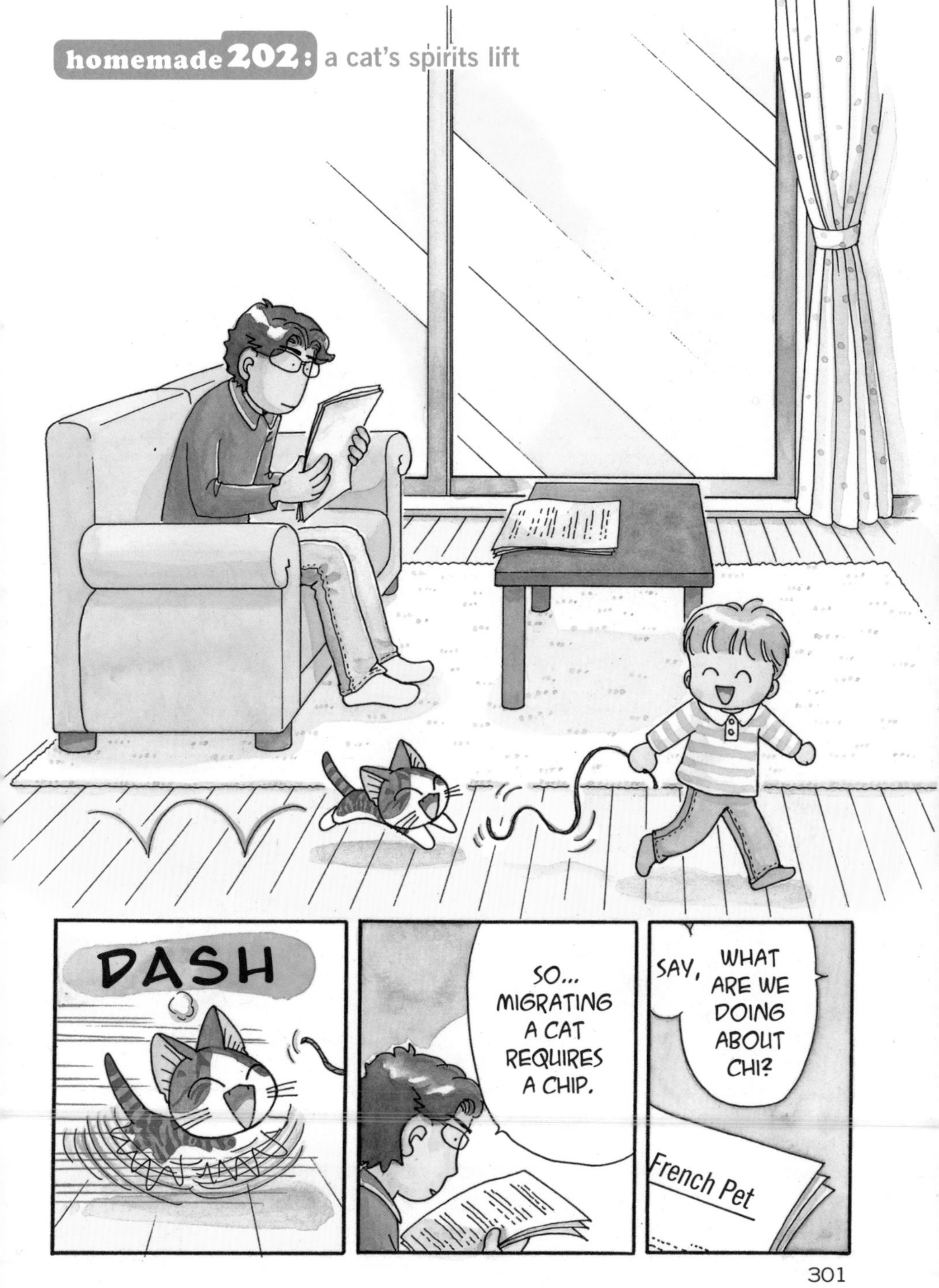
DASH
SO... MIGRATING A CAT REQUIRES A CHIP.
SAY, WHAT ARE WE DOING ABOUT CHI?
French Pet

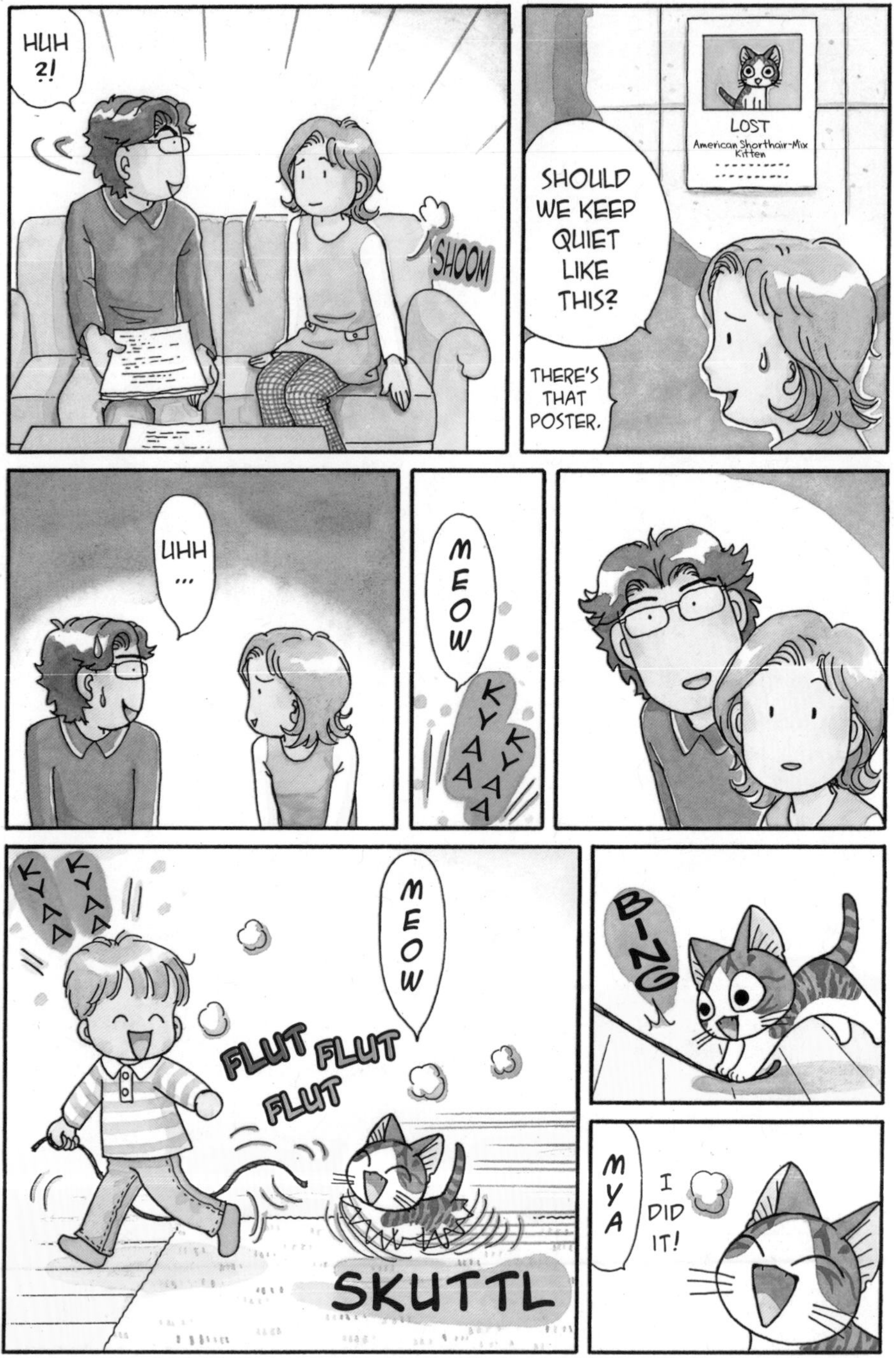
HUH ?!
SHOOM
SHOULD WE KEEP QUIET LIKE THIS?
LOST
American Shorthair-Mix Kitten
THERE'S THAT POSTER.
UHH ...
MEOW
KYAAA KYAAA
KYAA KYAA
MEOW
FLUT FLUT FLUT
SKUTTL
BING
MYA
I DID IT!

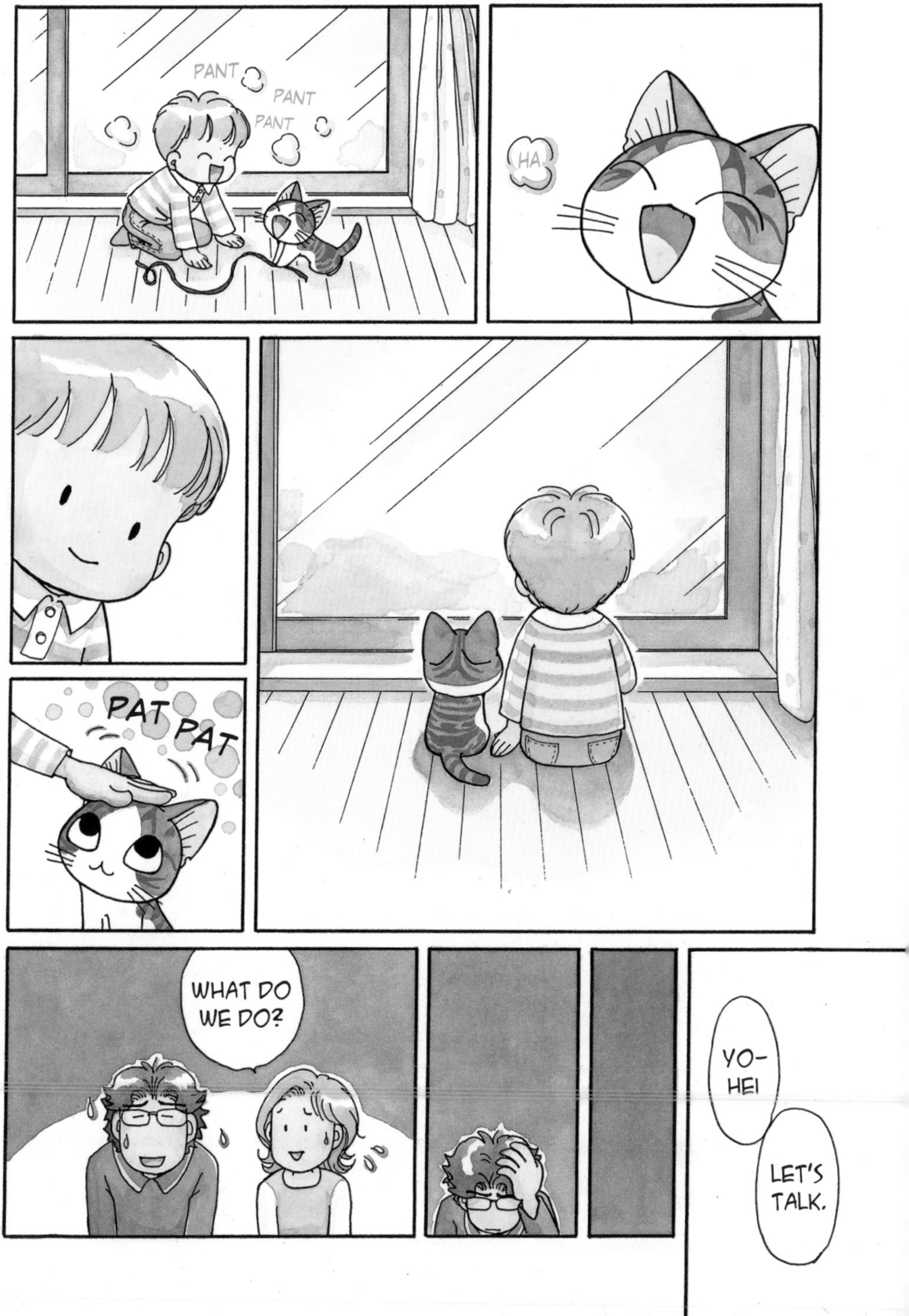
PANT
PANT
PANT
HA
PAT PAT
WHAT DO WE DO?
YO-HEI
LET'S TALK.

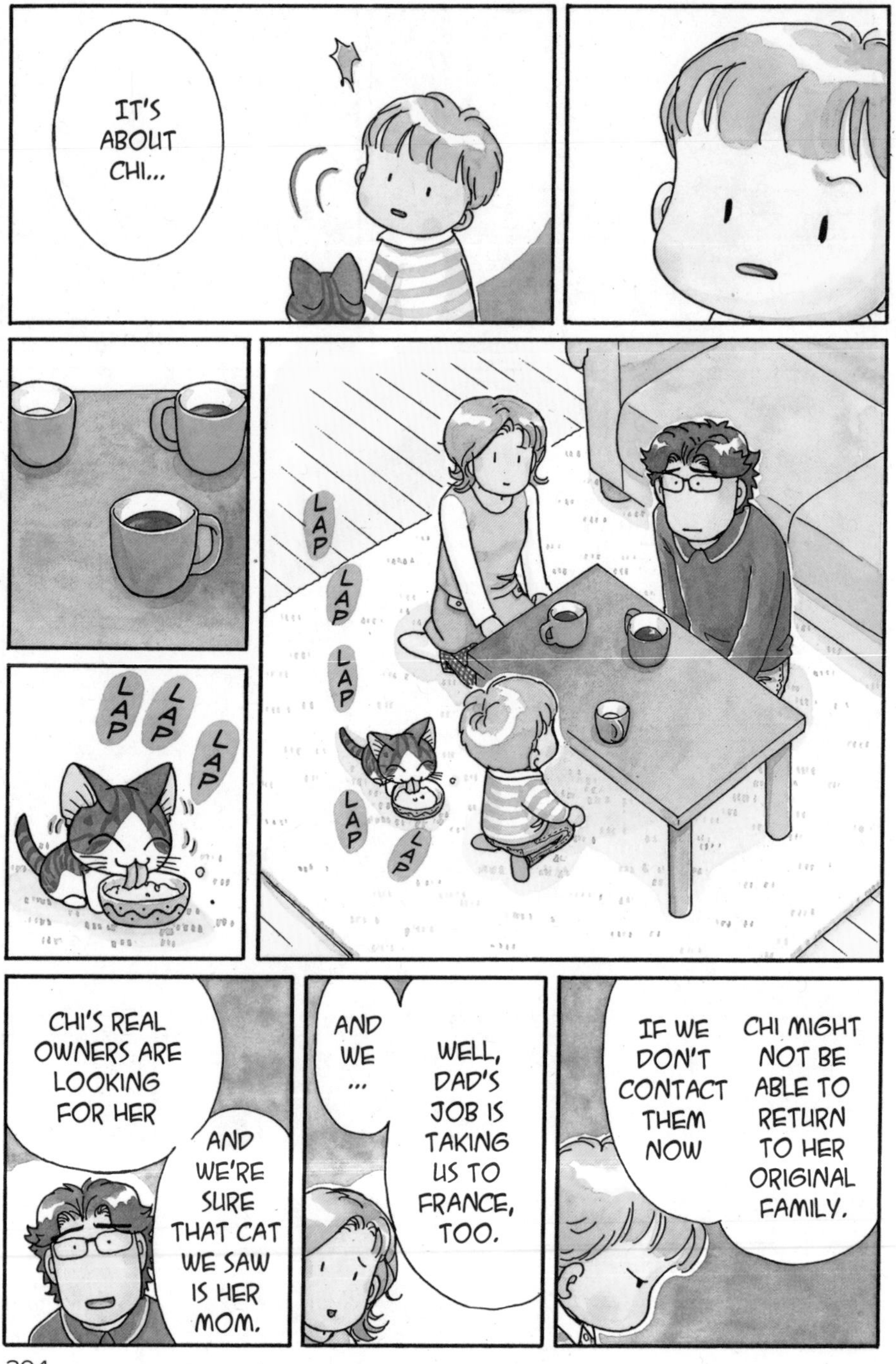
IT'S ABOUT CHI...
LAP LAP LAP
LAP LAP LAP LAP LAP
CHI'S REAL OWNERS ARE LOOKING FOR HER
AND WE'RE SURE THAT CAT WE SAW IS HER MOM.
AND WE ...
WELL, DAD'S JOB IS TAKING US TO FRANCE, TOO.
IF WE DON'T CONTACT THEM NOW
CHI MIGHT NOT BE ABLE TO RETURN TO HER ORIGINAL FAMILY.

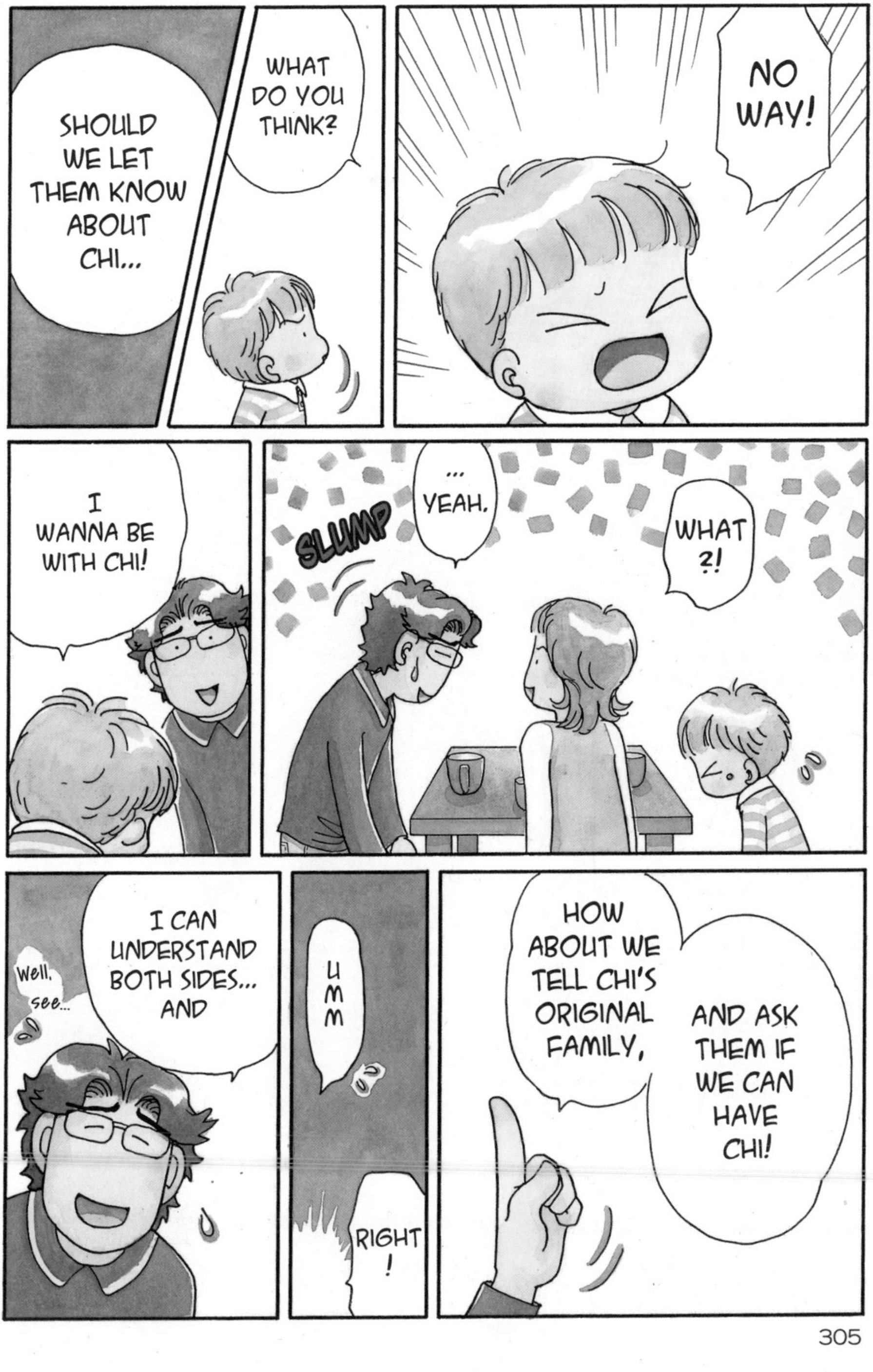
SHOULD WE LET THEM KNOW ABOUT CHI...
WHAT DO YOU THINK?
NO WAY!
I WANNA BE WITH CHI!
SLUMP
... YEAH.
WHAT?!
I CAN UNDERSTAND BOTH SIDES... AND
Well, see...
UMM
RIGHT!
HOW ABOUT WE TELL CHI'S ORIGINAL FAMILY,
AND ASK THEM IF WE CAN HAVE CHI!

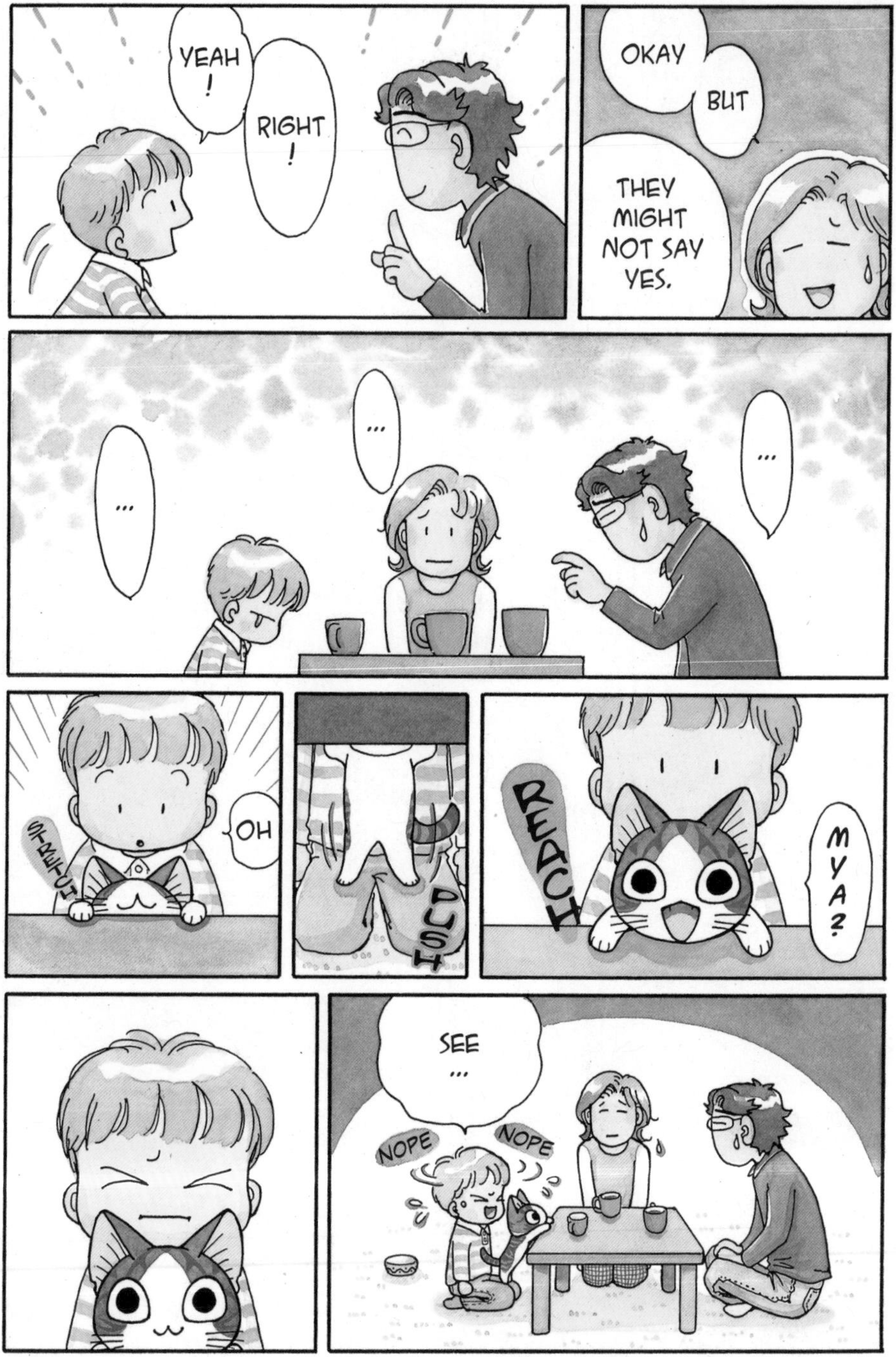
YEAH!
RIGHT!
OKAY
BUT
THEY MIGHT NOT SAY YES.
...
...
...
OH
STRETCH
PUSH
REACH
MYA?
SEE...
NOPE
NOPE

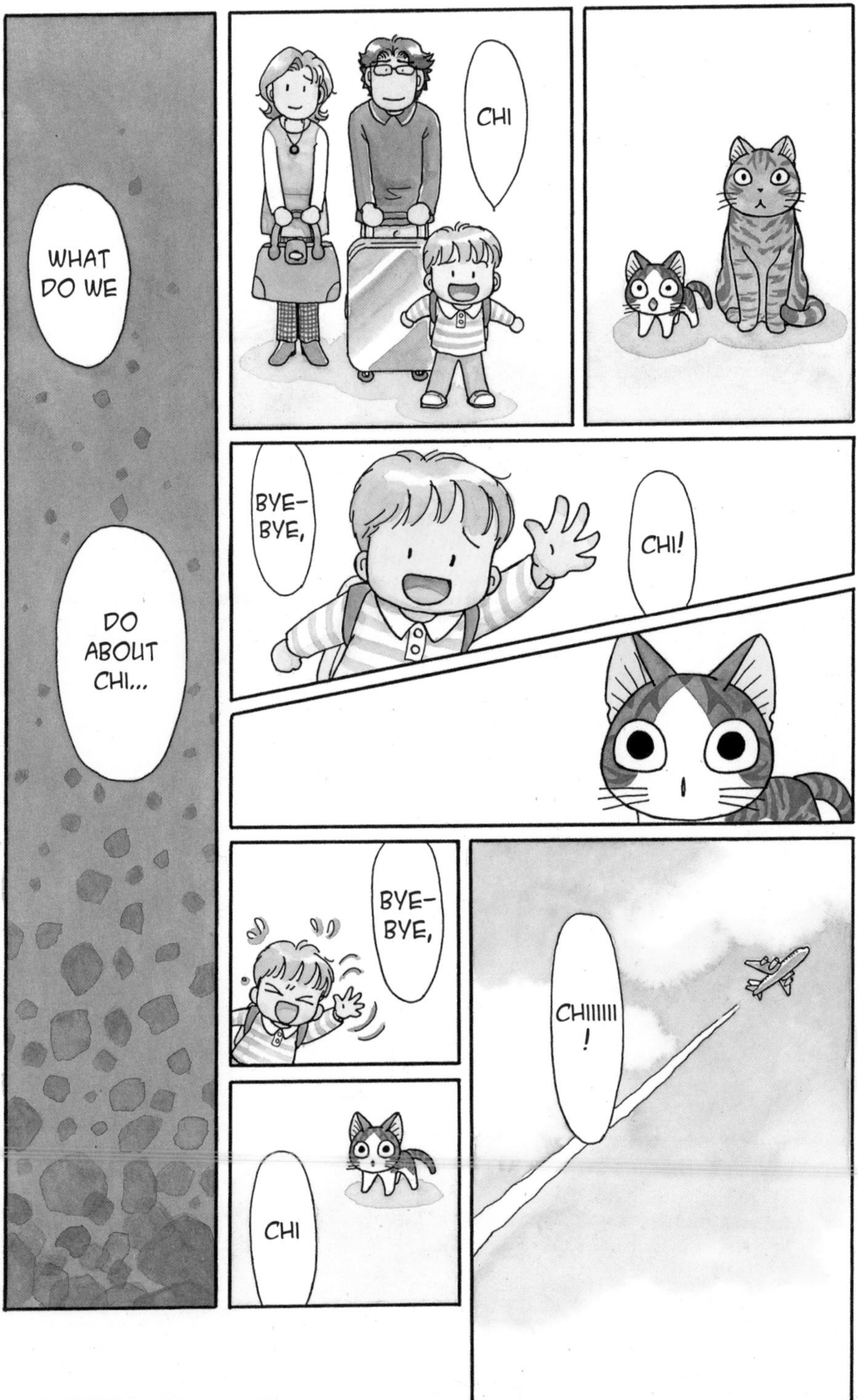
WHAT DO WE
DO ABOUT CHI...
CHI
BYE-BYE,
CHI!
BYE-BYE,
CHI
CHIIIIIII
!

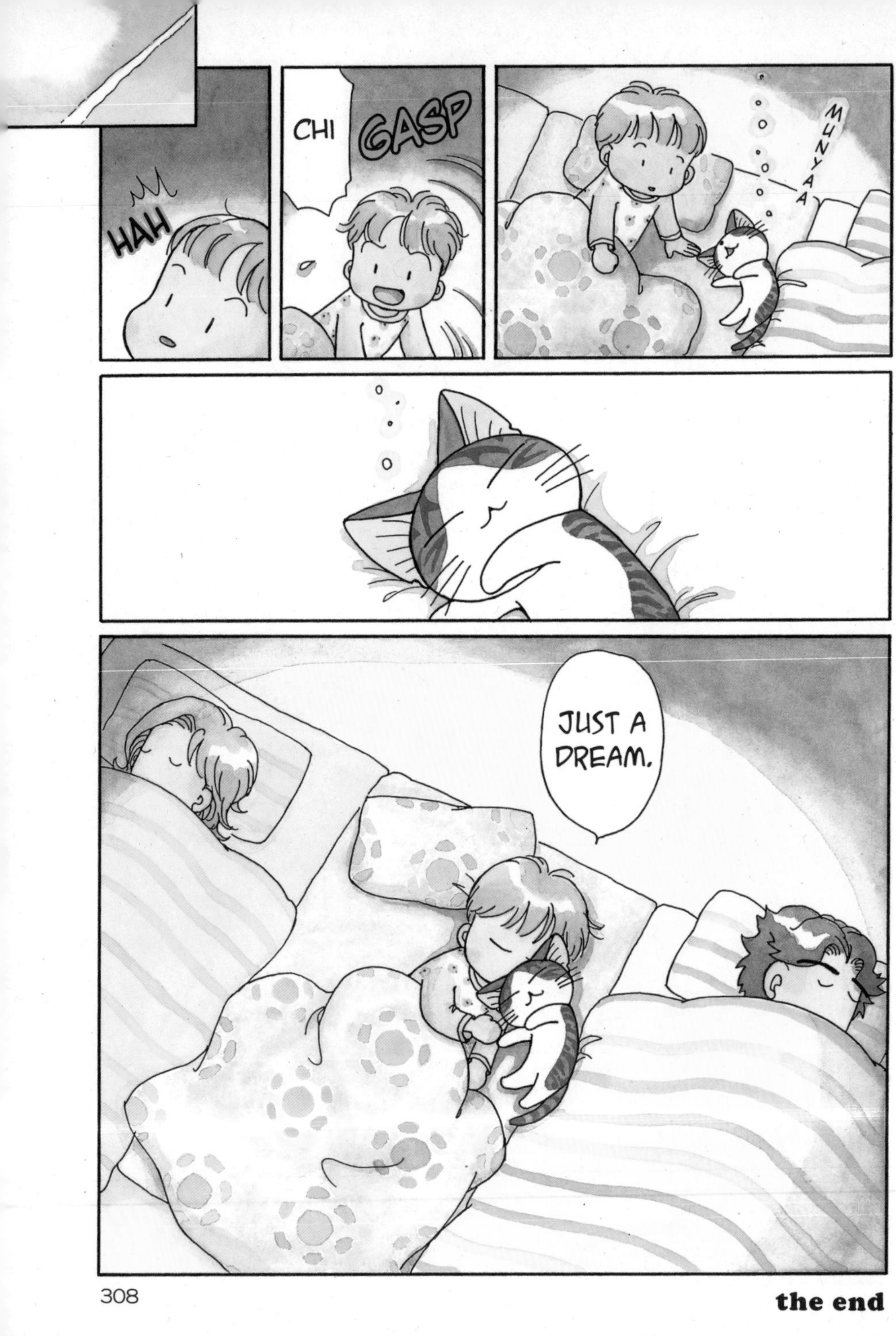
HAH
CHI
GASP
MUNYAA
JUST A DREAM.

the end

homemade 203: a cat meets trouble

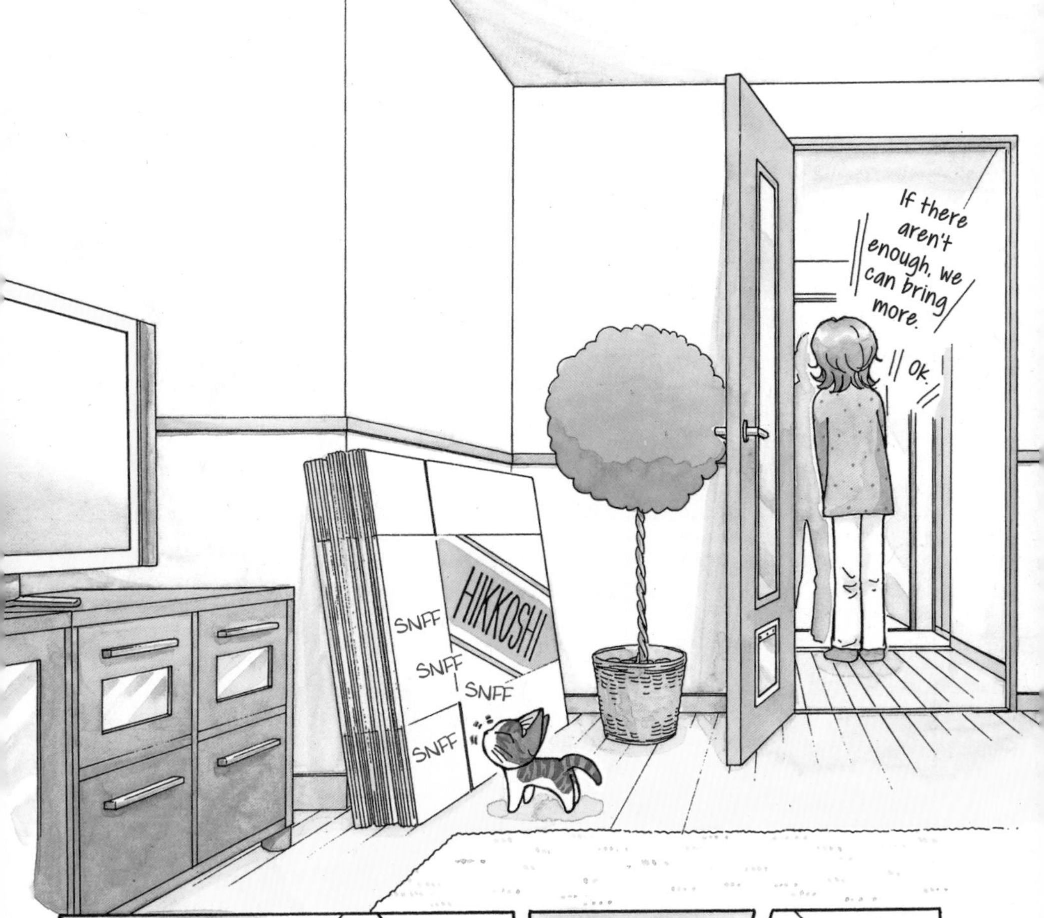
If there aren't enough, we can bring more.
OK.
SNFF
SNFF
SNFF
SNFF
HIKKOSHI

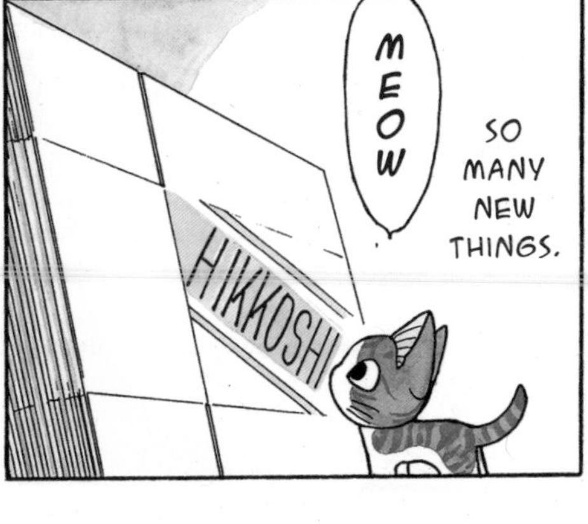
MEOW
SO MANY NEW THINGS.
HIKKOSHI

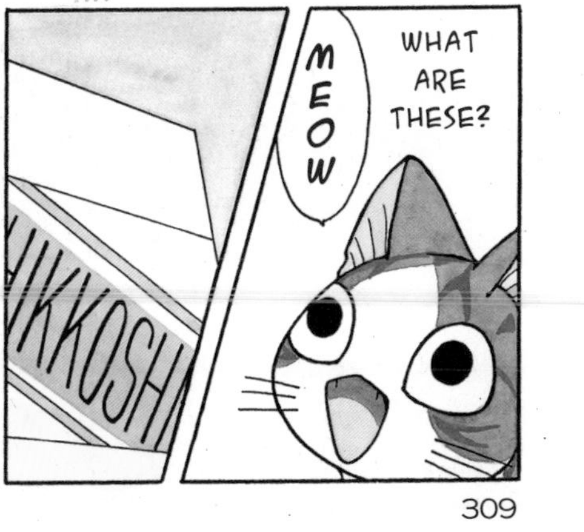
MEOW
WHAT ARE THESE?
HIKKOSHI

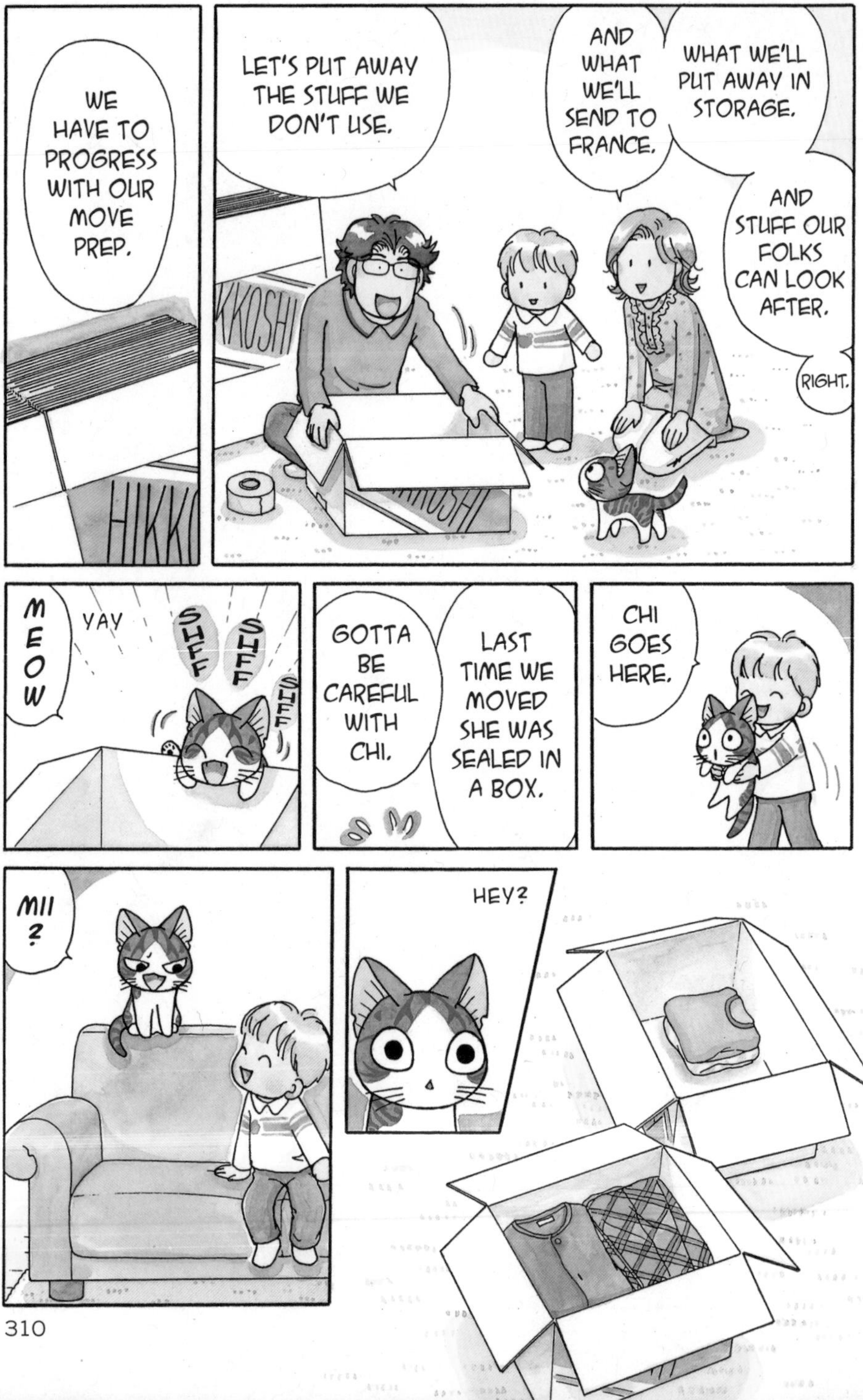
WE HAVE TO PROGRESS WITH OUR MOVE PREP.
HIKKO
LET'S PUT AWAY THE STUFF WE DON'T USE.
AND WHAT WE'LL SEND TO FRANCE.
WHAT WE'LL PUT AWAY IN STORAGE.
KKOSHI
AND STUFF OUR FOLKS CAN LOOK AFTER.
RIGHT.
MEOW
YAY
SHFF
SHFF
SHFF
GOTTA BE CAREFUL WITH CHI.
LAST TIME WE MOVED SHE WAS SEALED IN A BOX.
CHI GOES HERE.
MII?
HEY?

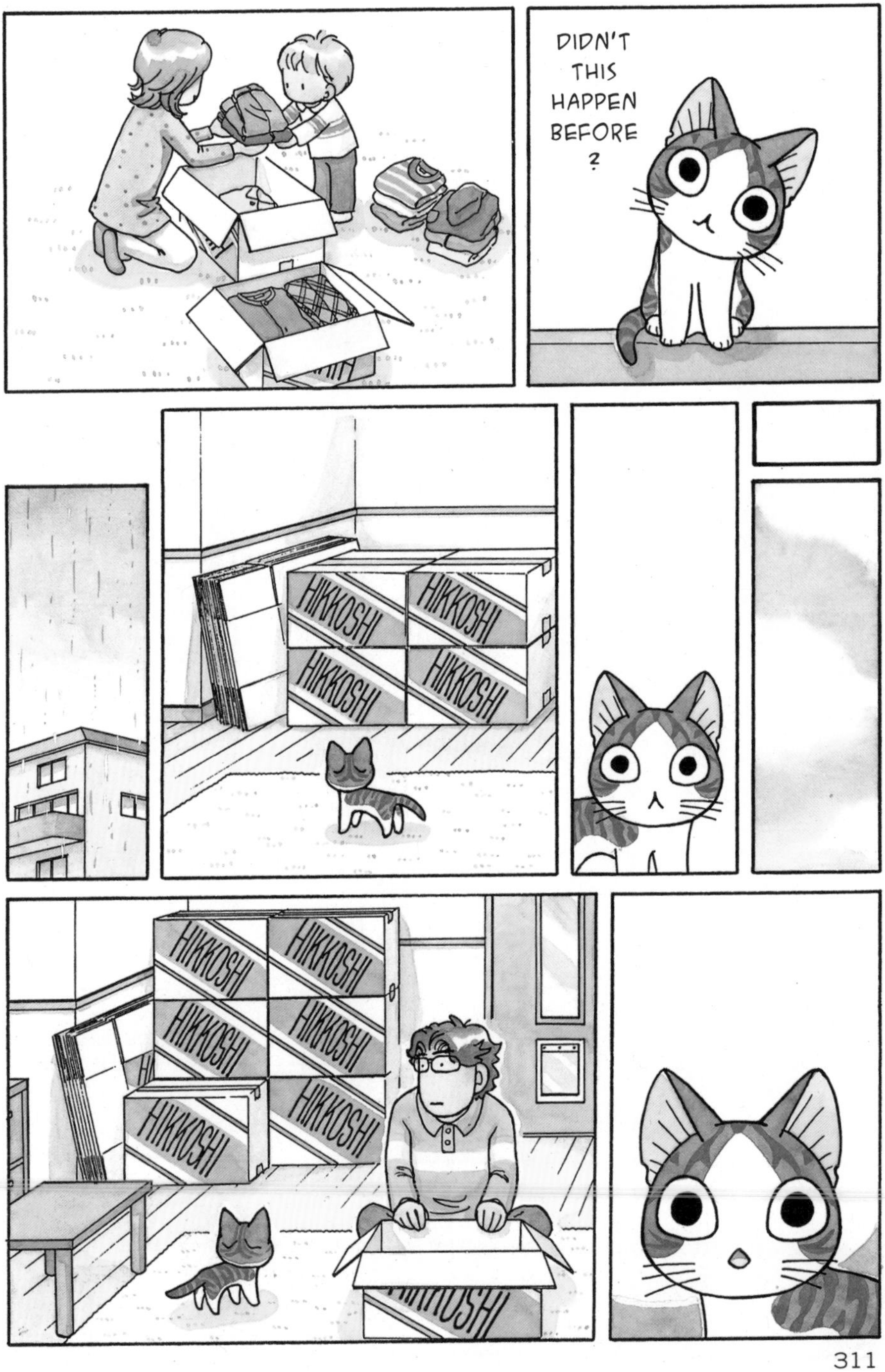
DIDN'T THIS HAPPEN BEFORE ?
HIKKOSHI
HIKKOSHI
HIKKOSHI
HIKKOSHI
HIKKOSHI
HIKKOSHI
HIKKOSHI
HIKKOSHI
HIKKOSHI
HIKKOSHI

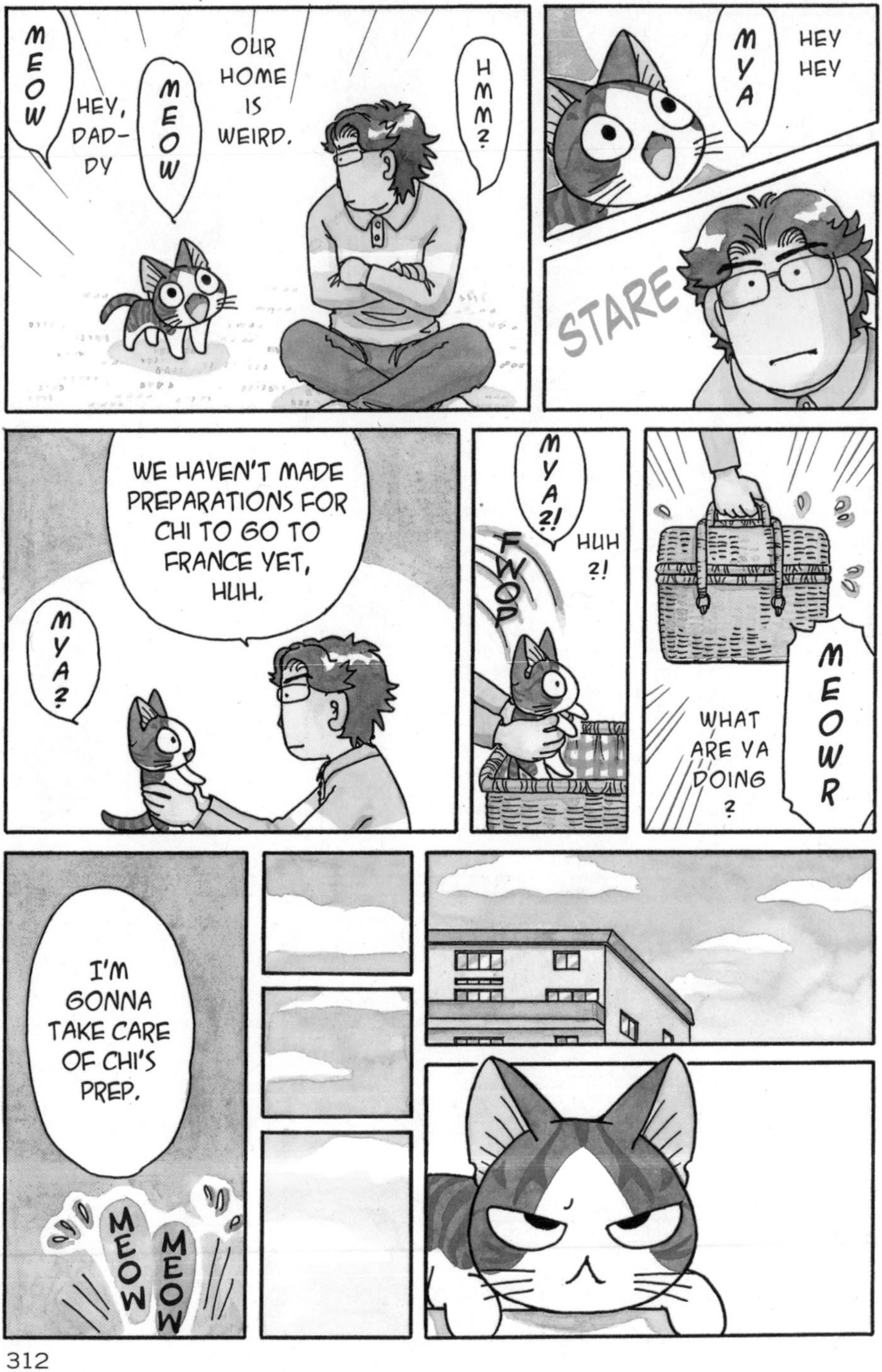
MEOW
HEY, DADDY
MEOW
OUR HOME IS WEIRD.
HMM?
MYA
HEY HEY
STARE
WE HAVEN'T MADE PREPARATIONS FOR CHI TO GO TO FRANCE YET, HUH.
MYA?
MYA?!
HUH?!
FWOP
WHAT ARE YA DOING?
MEOWR
I'M GONNA TAKE CARE OF CHI'S PREP.
MEOW MEOW
MEOW MEOW

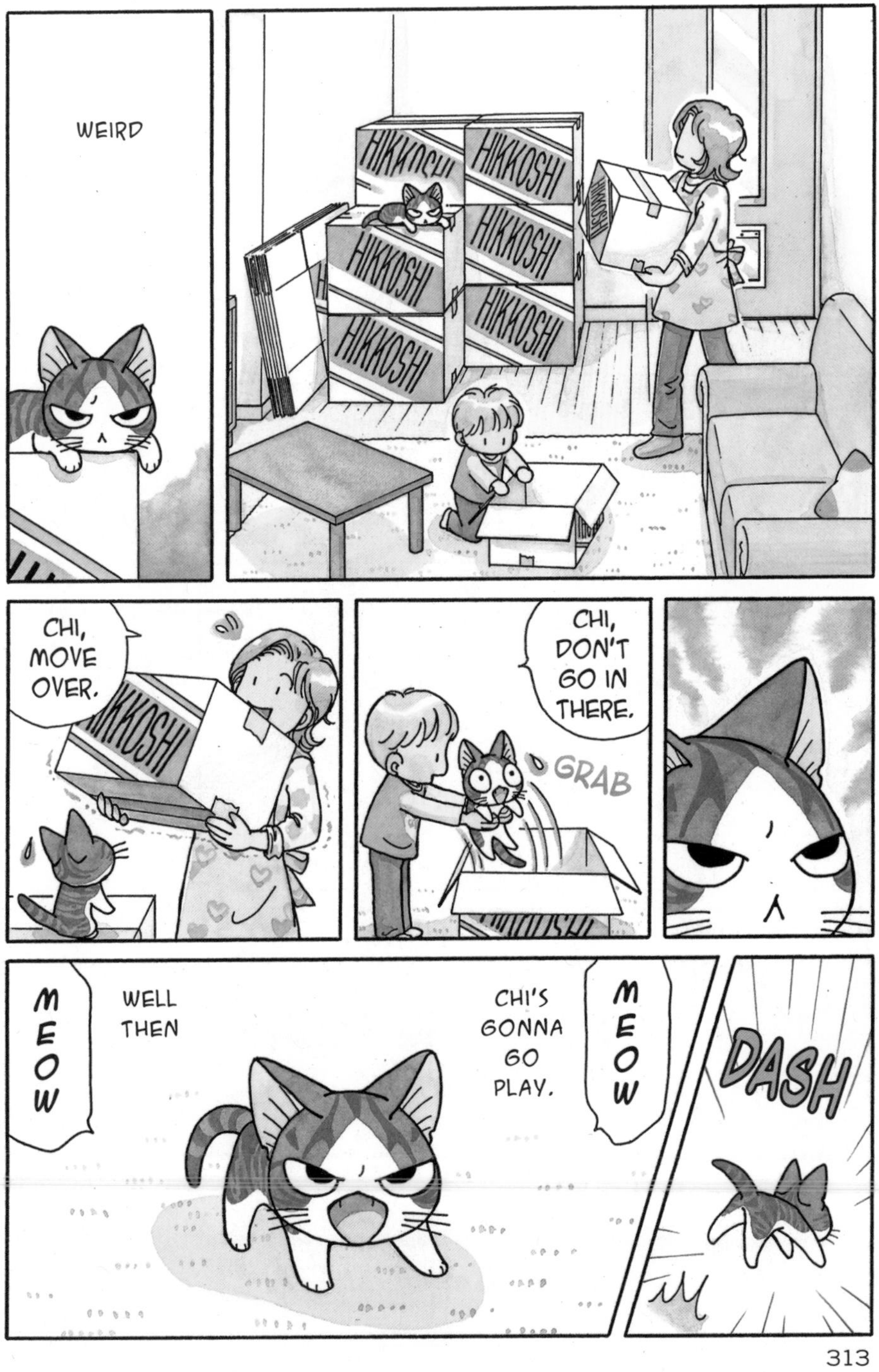
WEIRD
HIKKOSHI
HIKKOSHI
HIKKOSHI
HIKKOSHI
HIKKOSHI
HIKKOSHI
HIKKOSHI
HIKKOSHI
CHI, MOVE OVER.
HIKKOSHI
CHI, DON'T GO IN THERE.
GRAB
MEOW
WELL THEN
CHI'S GONNA GO PLAY.
MEOW
DASH

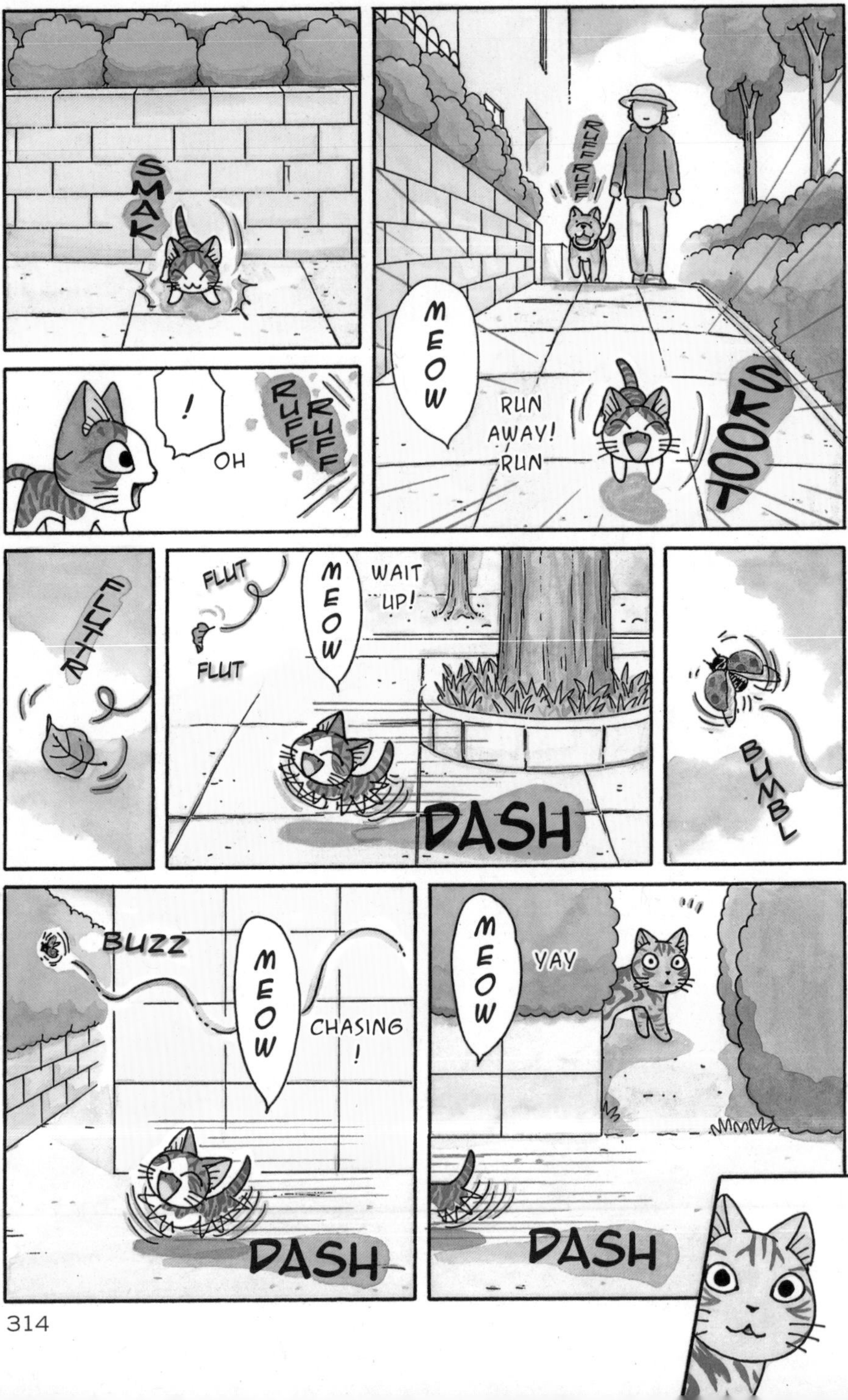
SMAK
!
OH
RUFF RUFF
RUFF RUFF
MEOW
RUN AWAY! RUN
SKOOT
FLUTTR
FLUT
FLUT
MEOW
WAIT UP!
DASH
BUMBL
BUZZ
MEOW
CHASING!
DASH
MEOW
YAY
DASH

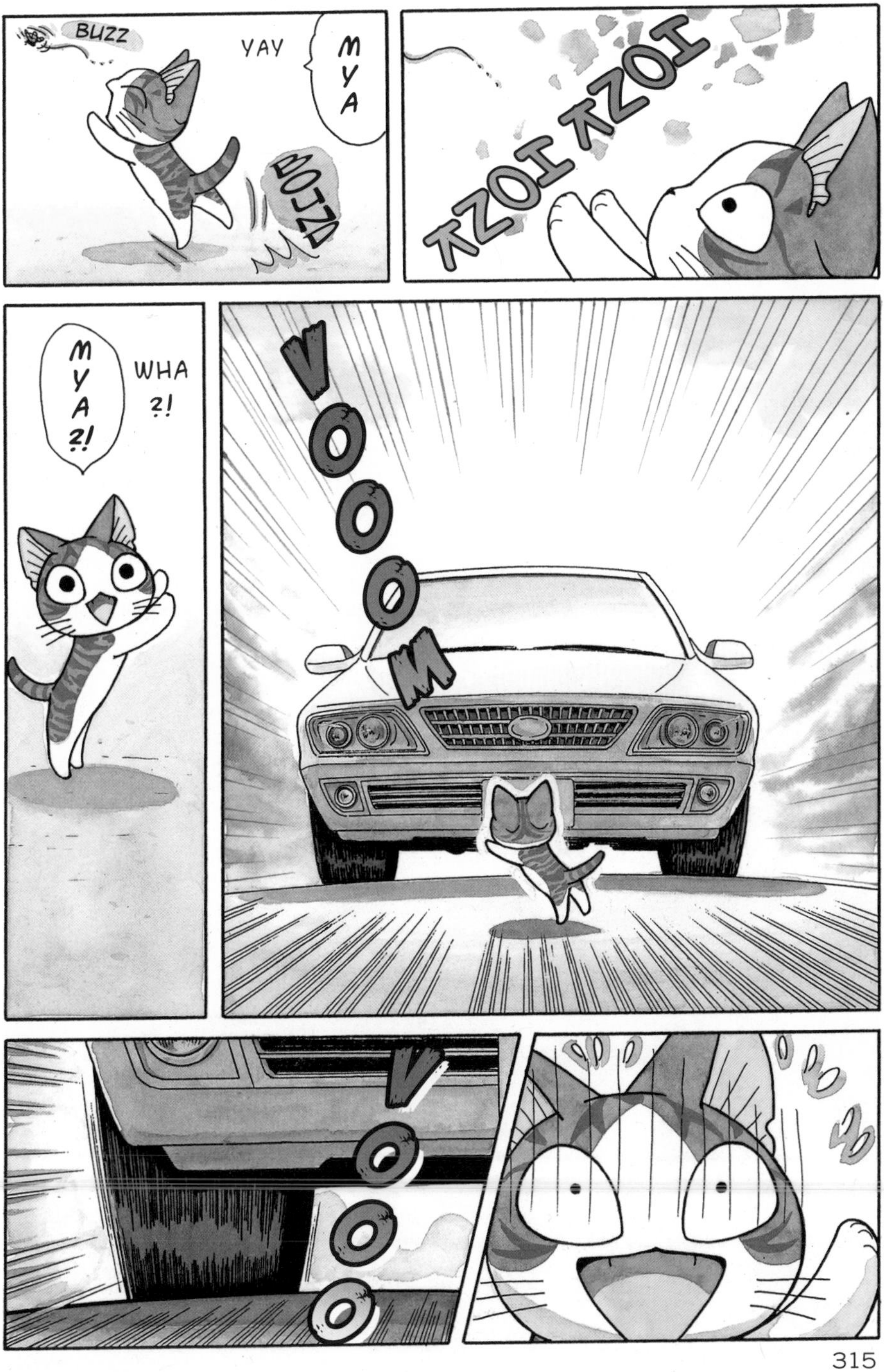
BUZZ
YAY
MYA
BOING
MYA?!
WHA?!
VOOOOM
VOOOO

VOOOOM
MEOW
NYA!
SARAH!
SHOOM

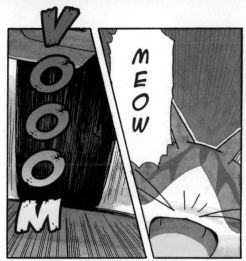

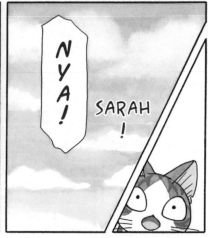

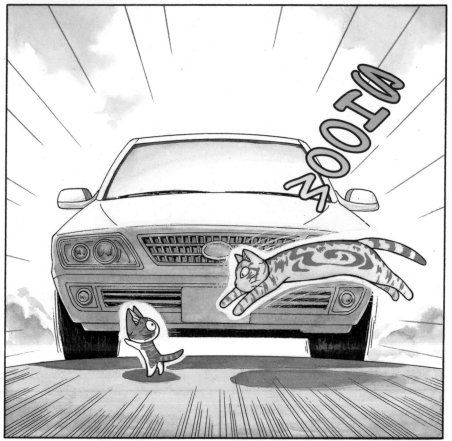

the end

homemade 204: a cat runs

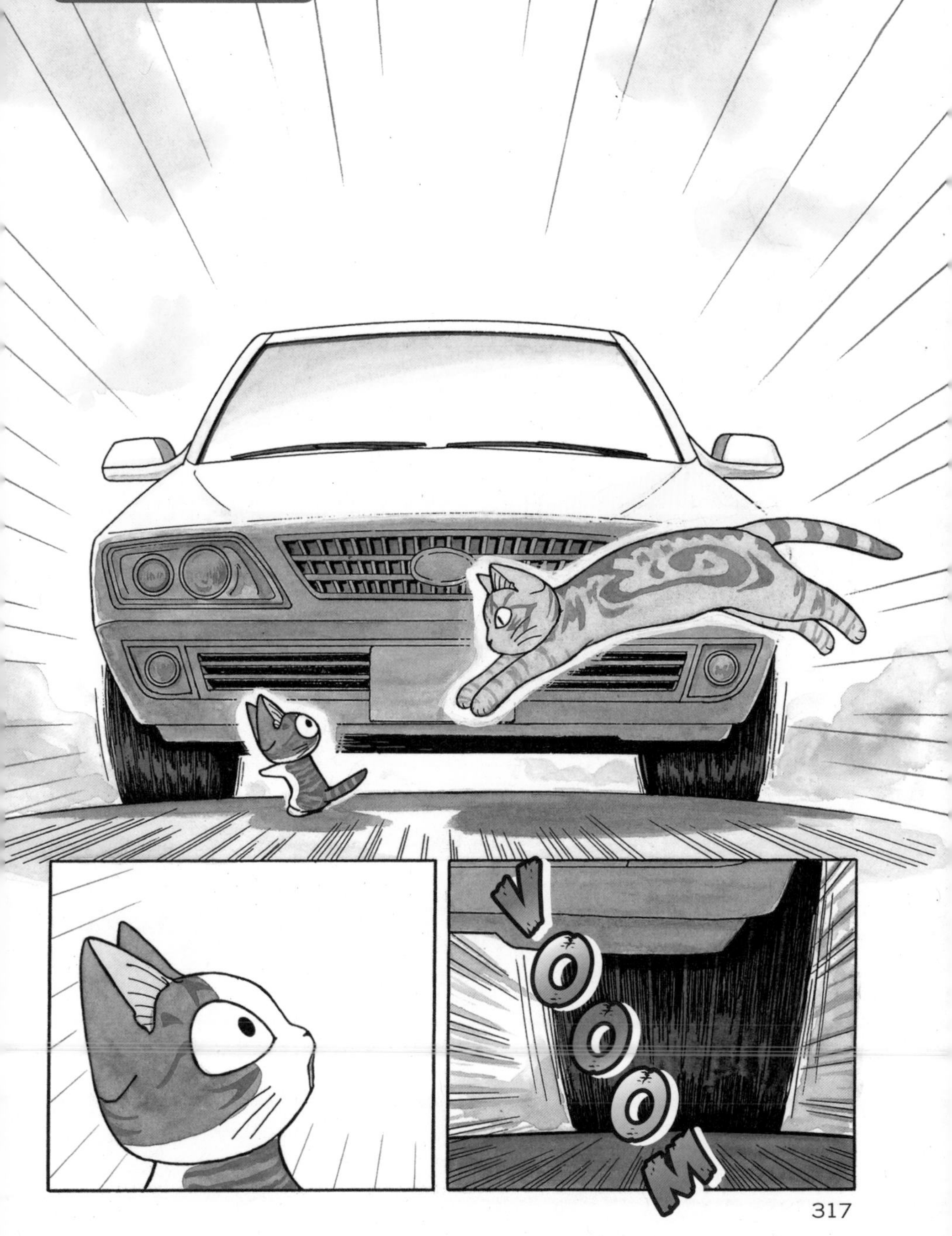
VOOOM

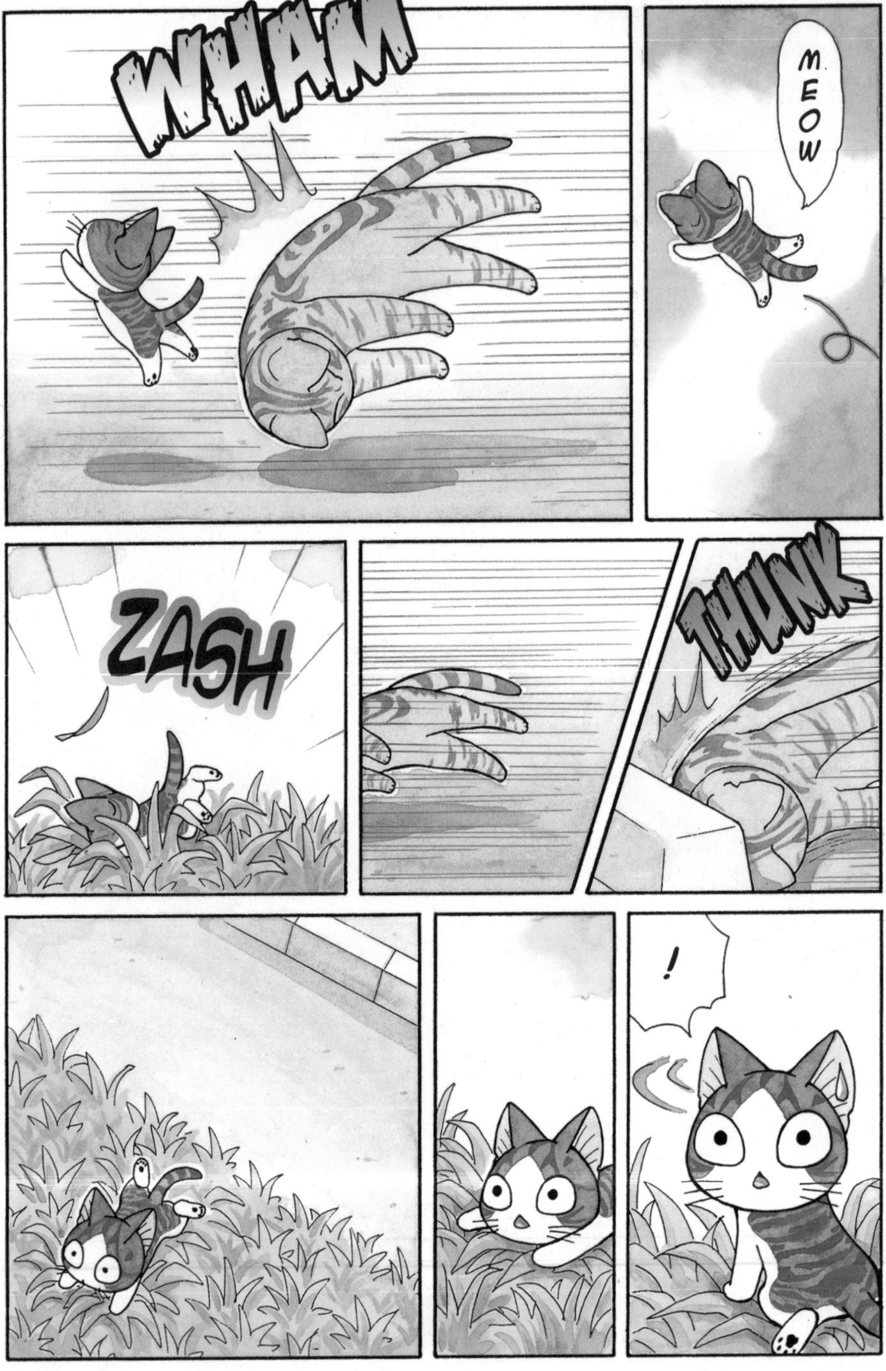
WHAM
MEOW
ZASH
THUNK
!

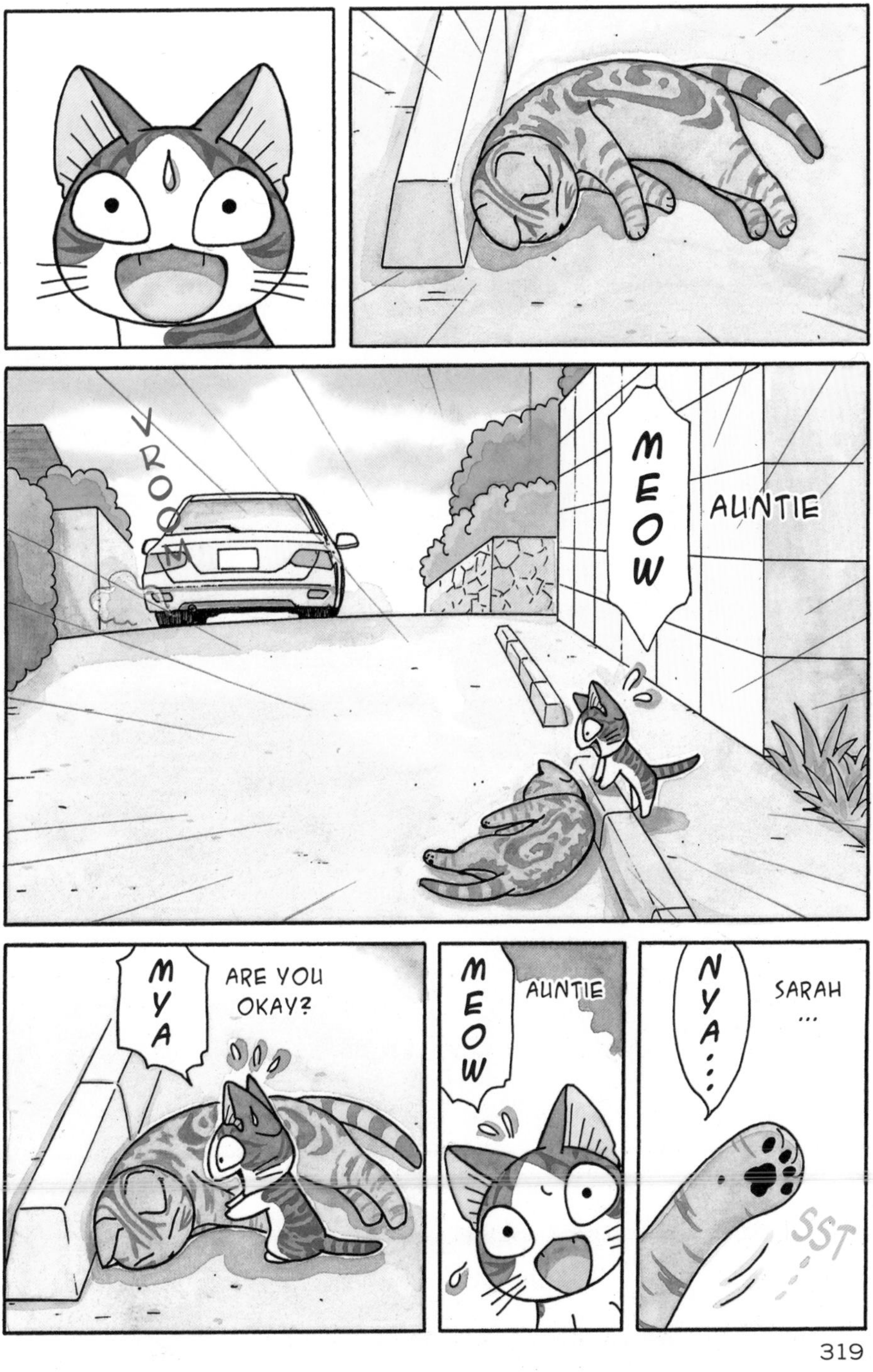
VROOM
MEOW
AUNTIE
MYA
ARE YOU OKAY?
MEOW
AUNTIE
NYA...
SARAH ...
SST

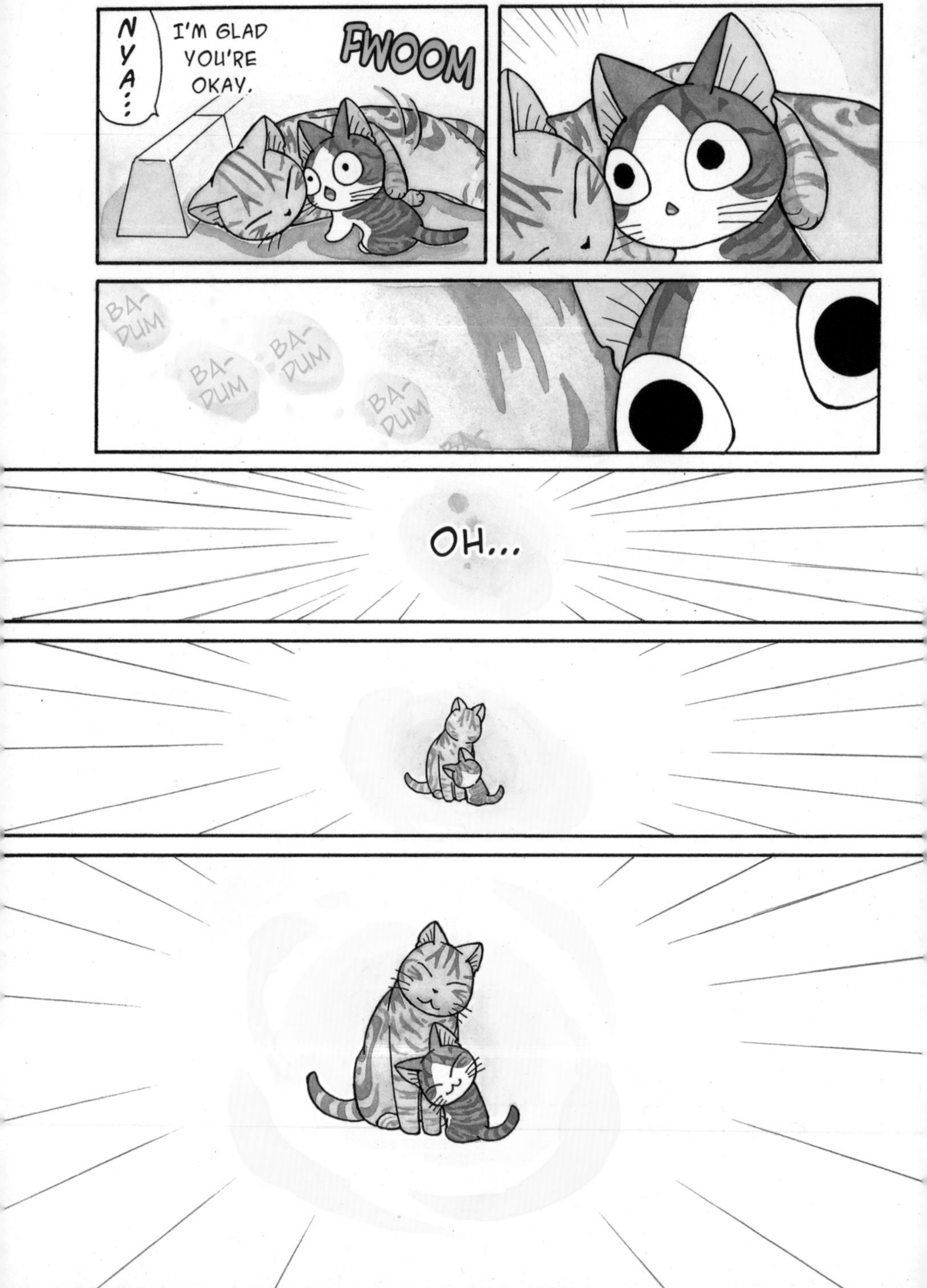
NYA...
I'M GLAD YOU'RE OKAY.
FWOOM
BA-DUM
BA-DUM
BA-DUM
BA-DUM
OH...

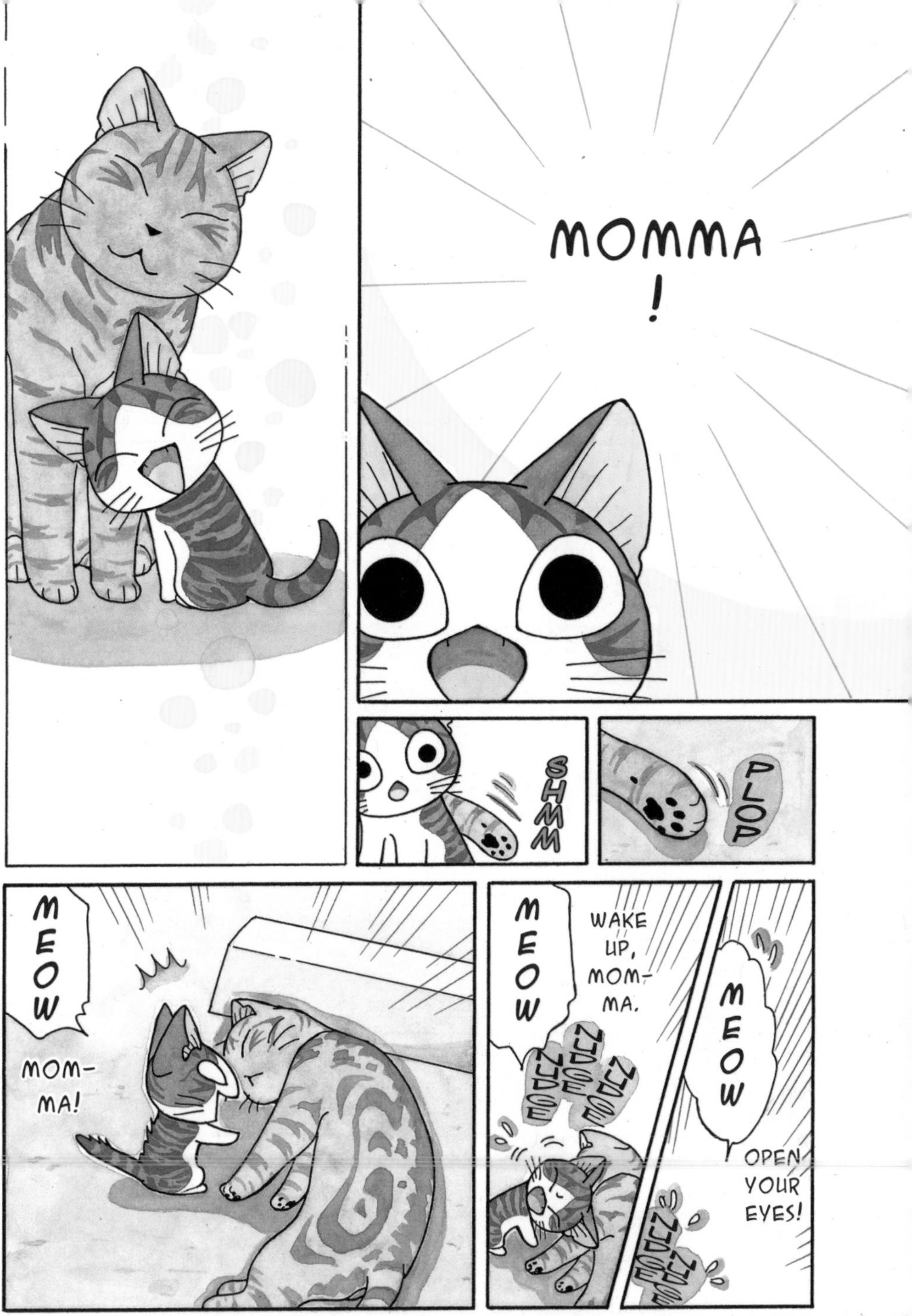
MOMMA!
SHMM
PLOP
MEOW
MOM-MA!
MEOW
WAKE UP, MOM-MA.
NUDGE NUDGE NUDGE NUDGE
MEOW
OPEN YOUR EYES!
NUDGE NUDGE

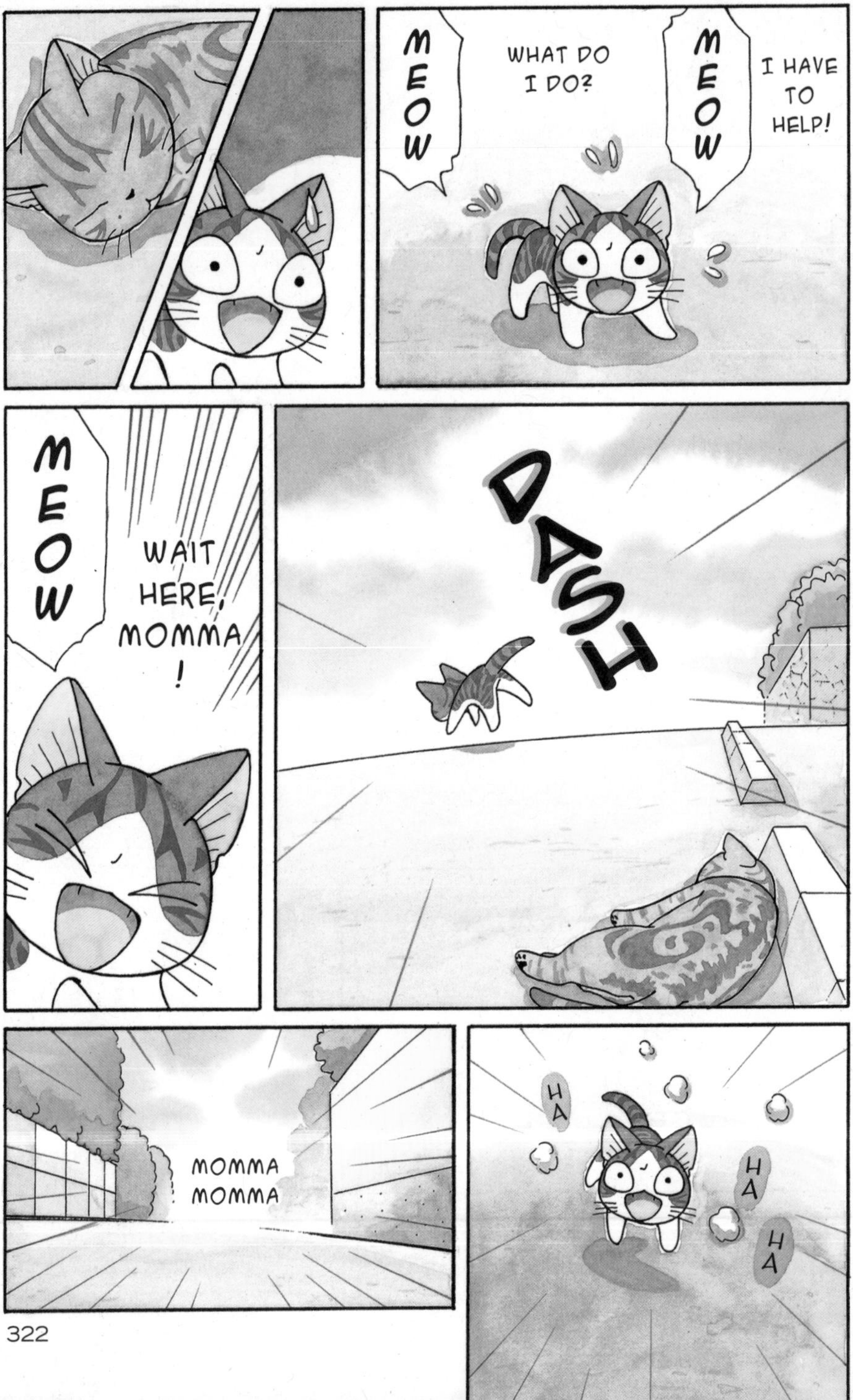
MEOW
WHAT DO I DO?
MEOW
I HAVE TO HELP!
MEOW
WAIT HERE, MOMMA!
DASH
MOMMA MOMMA
HA
HA
HA
HA

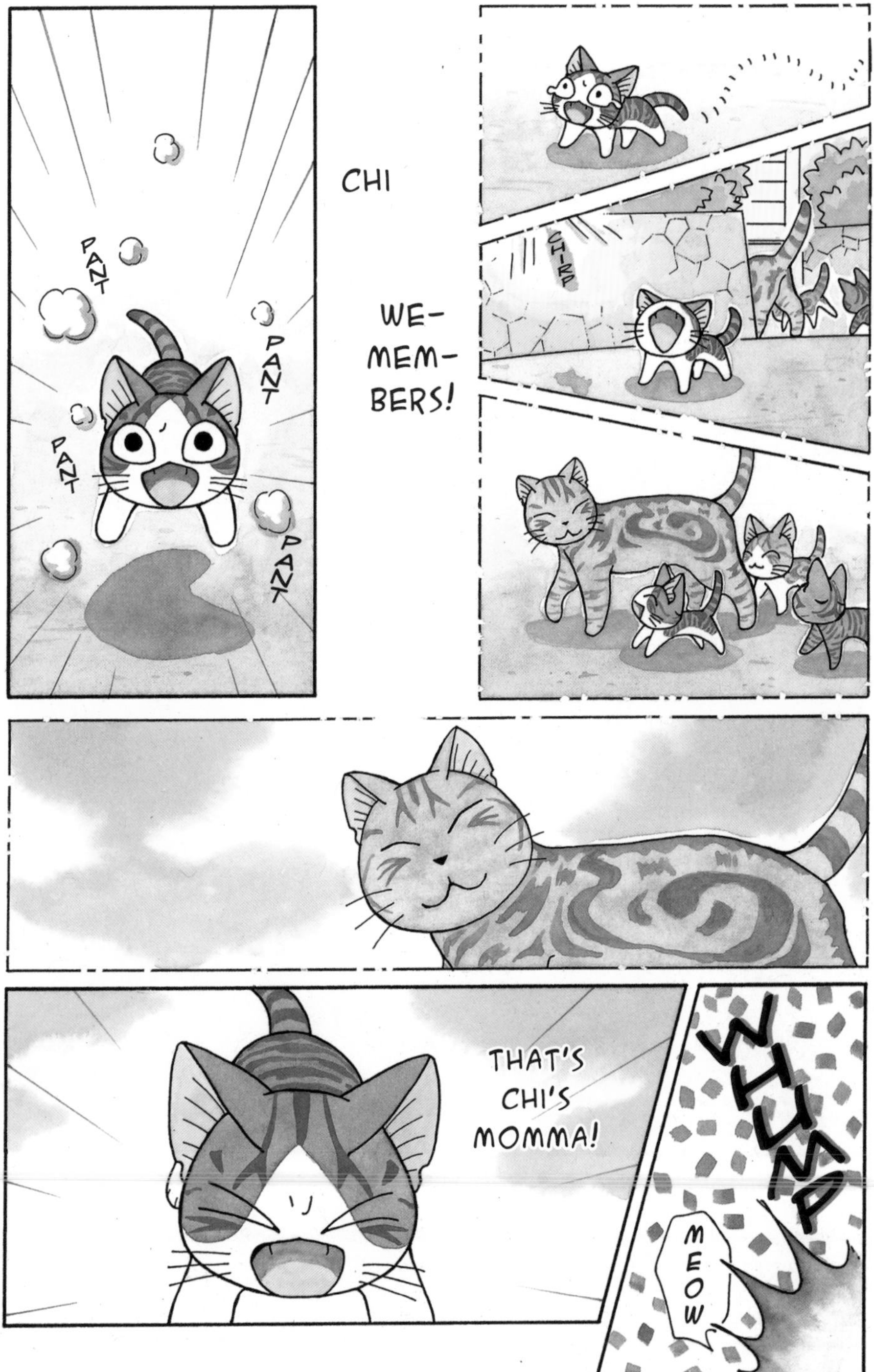
PANT
PANT
PANT
PANT
CHI
CHIRP
WE-MEMBERS!
THAT'S CHI'S MOMMA!
WHUMP
MEOW

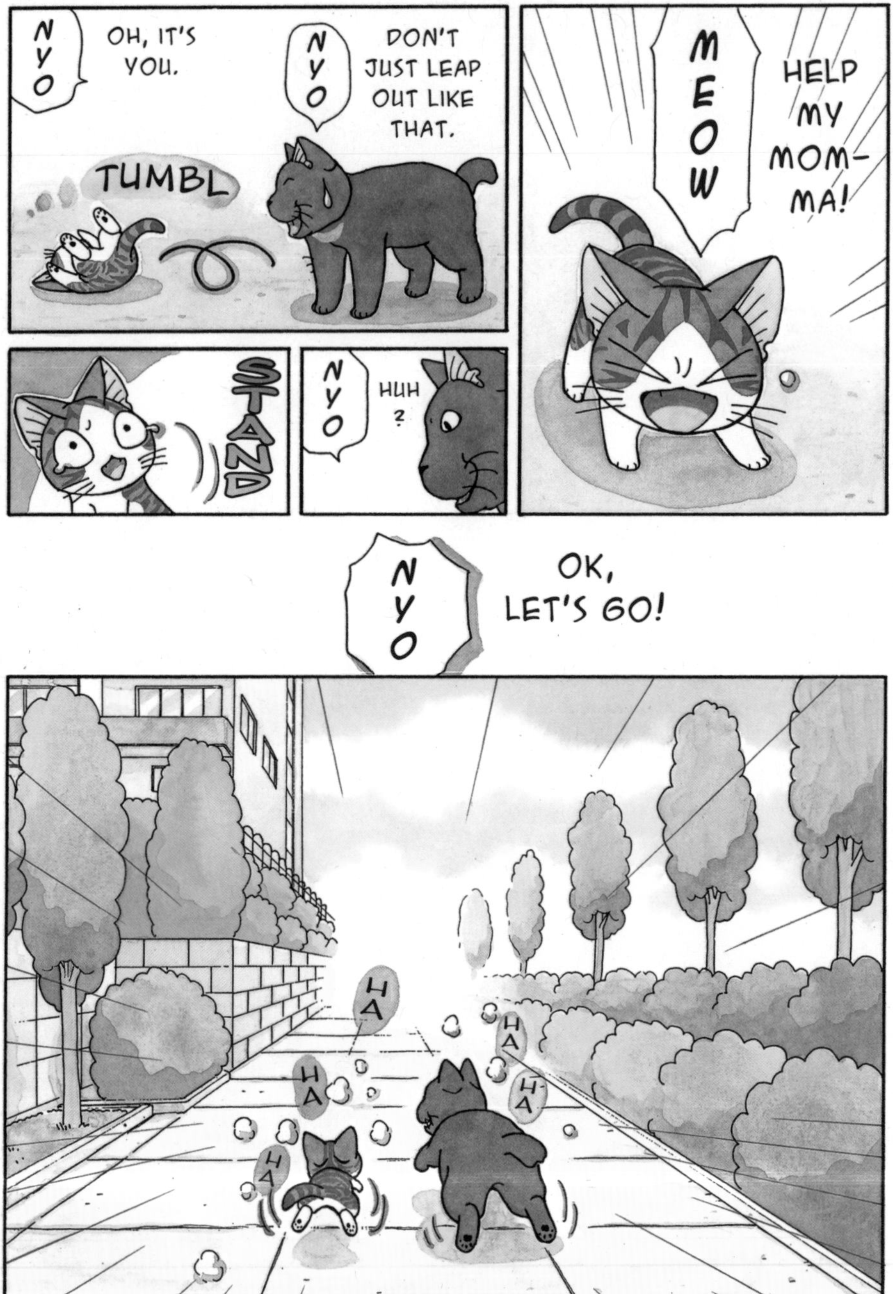
NYO
OH, IT'S YOU.
NYO
DON'T JUST LEAP OUT LIKE THAT.
TUMBL
STAND
NYO
HUH?
MEOW
HELP MY MOM-MA!
NYO
OK, LET'S GO!
HA
HA
HA
HA
HA
HA-HA

the end

homemade 205: a cat helps

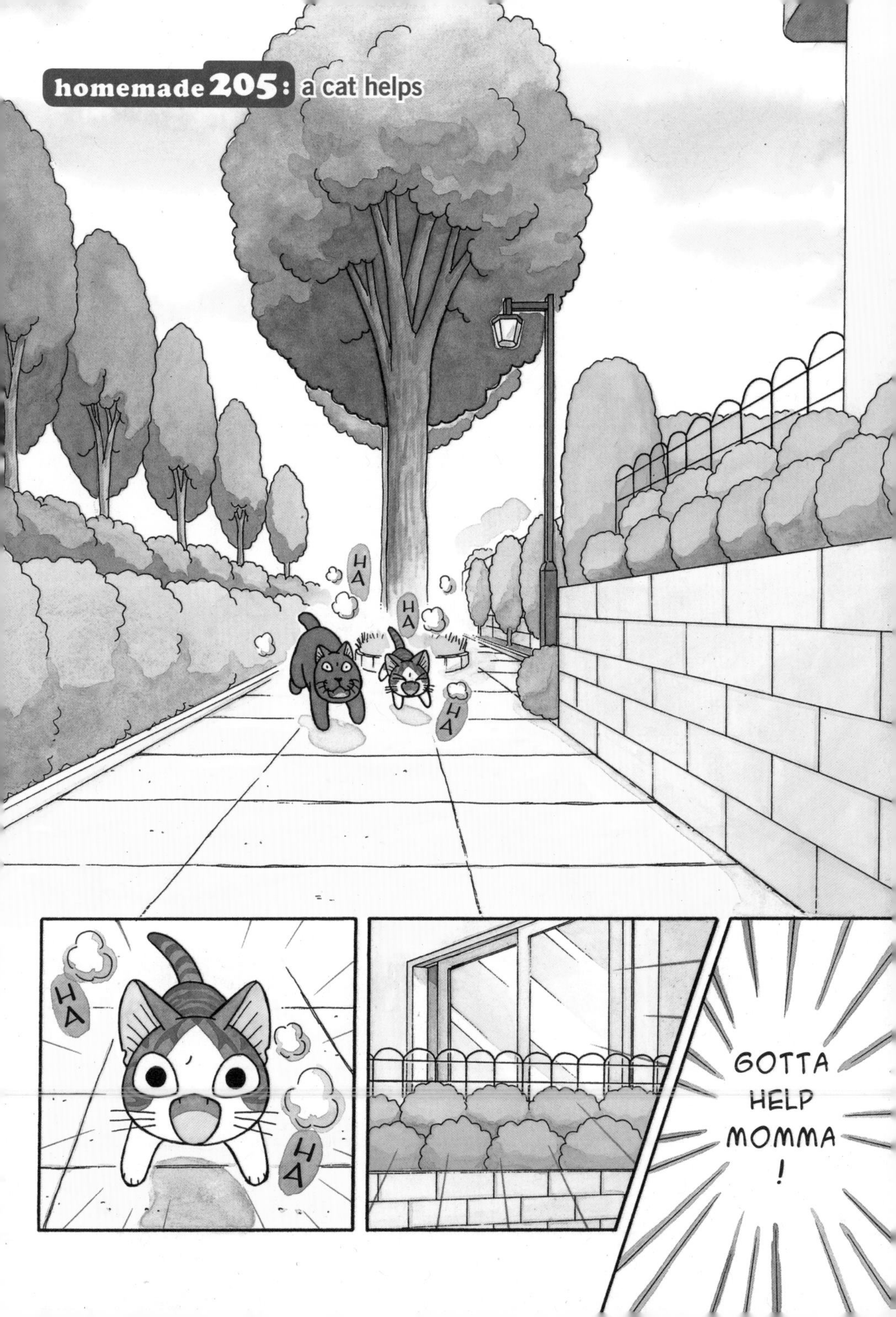
HA
HA
HA
HA
HA
HA
HA
GOTTA HELP MOMMA!

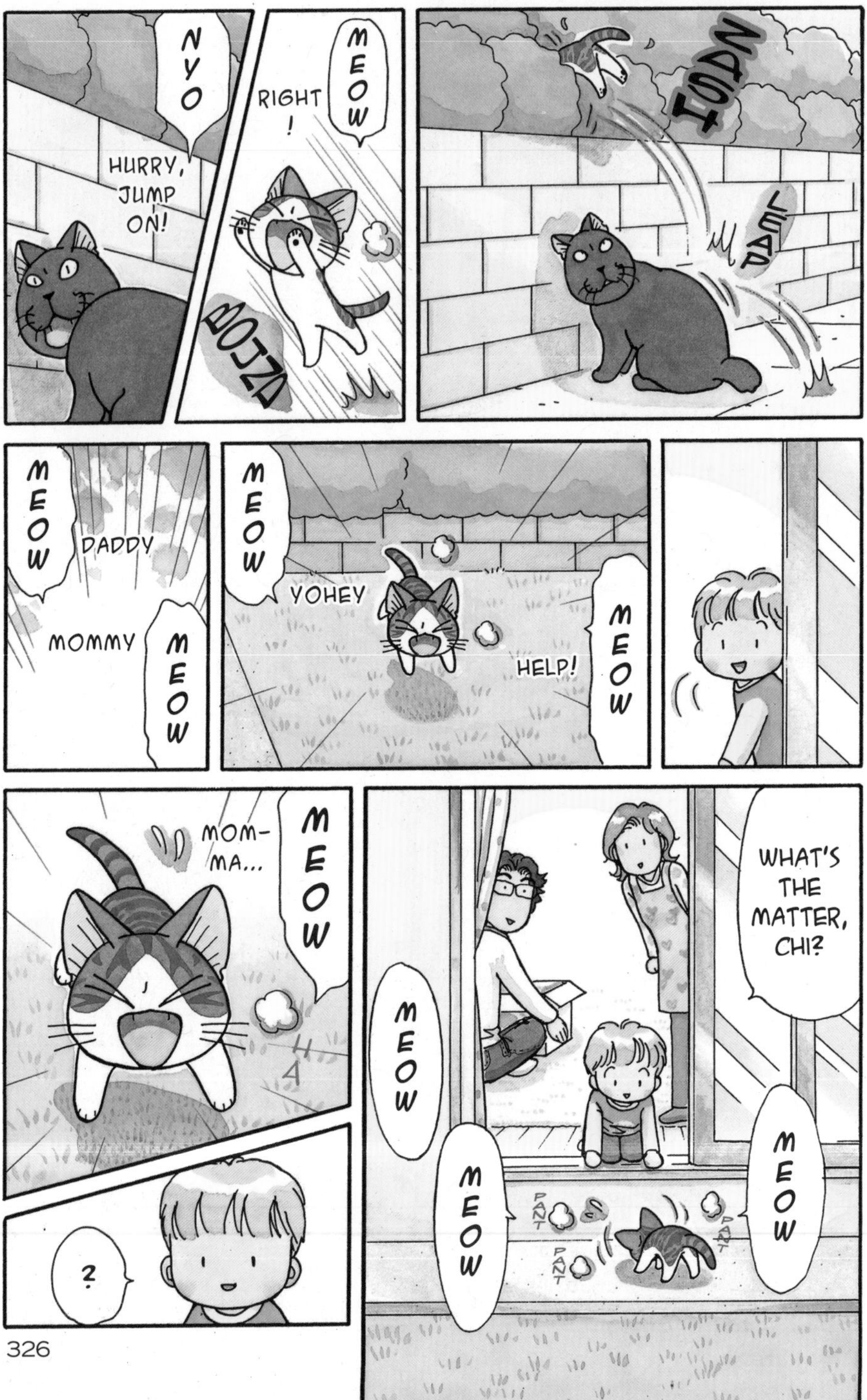
NYO
HURRY, JUMP ON!
MEOW
RIGHT!
LEAP
MEOW
DADDY
MOMMY
MEOW
MEOW
YOHEY
HELP!
MEOW
MOM-MA...
MEOW
HA
?
WHAT'S THE MATTER, CHI?
MEOW
MEOW
PANT
PANT
PANT
MEOW

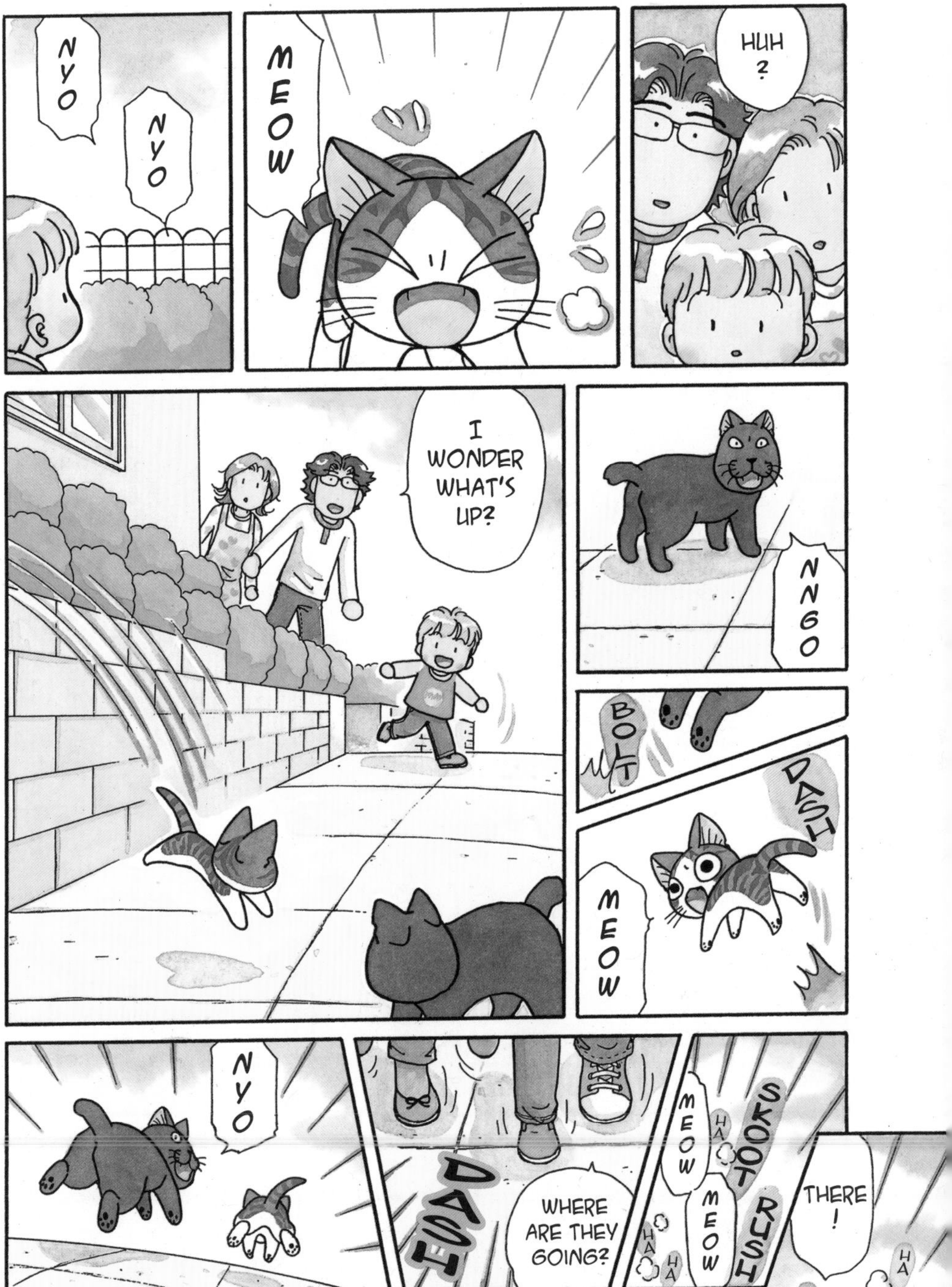

NYO
NYO
MEOW
HUH?
I WONDER WHAT'S UP?
NNGO
BOLT
DASH
MEOW
NYO
DASH
WHERE ARE THEY GOING?
MEOW
HA
SKOOT
MEOW
RUSH
HA HA
THERE!
HA HA HA

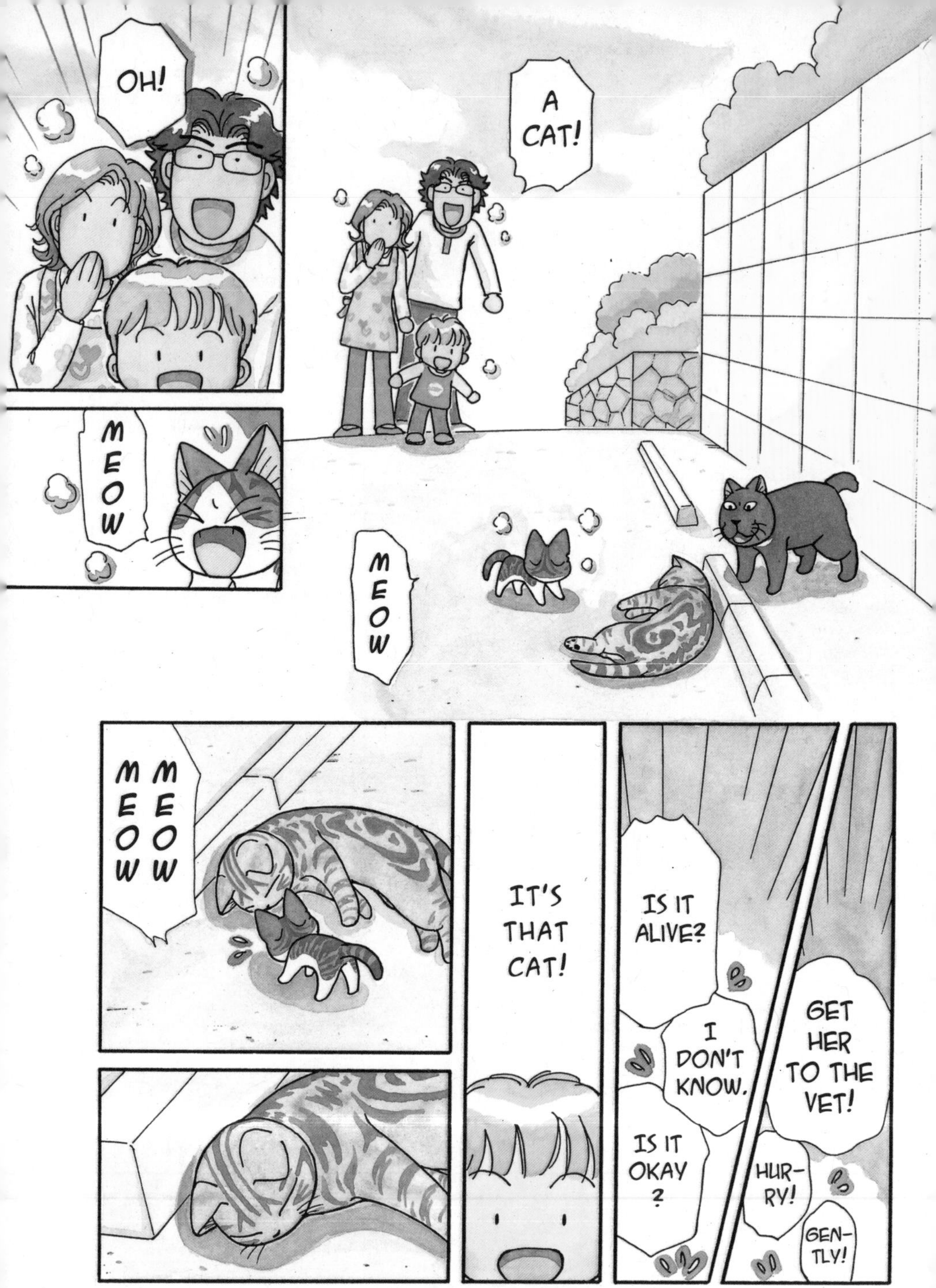
OH!
MEOW
A CAT!
MEOW
MEOW MEOW
IT'S THAT CAT!
IS IT ALIVE?
I DON'T KNOW.
IS IT OKAY?
GET HER TO THE VET!
HUR-RY!
GEN-TLY!

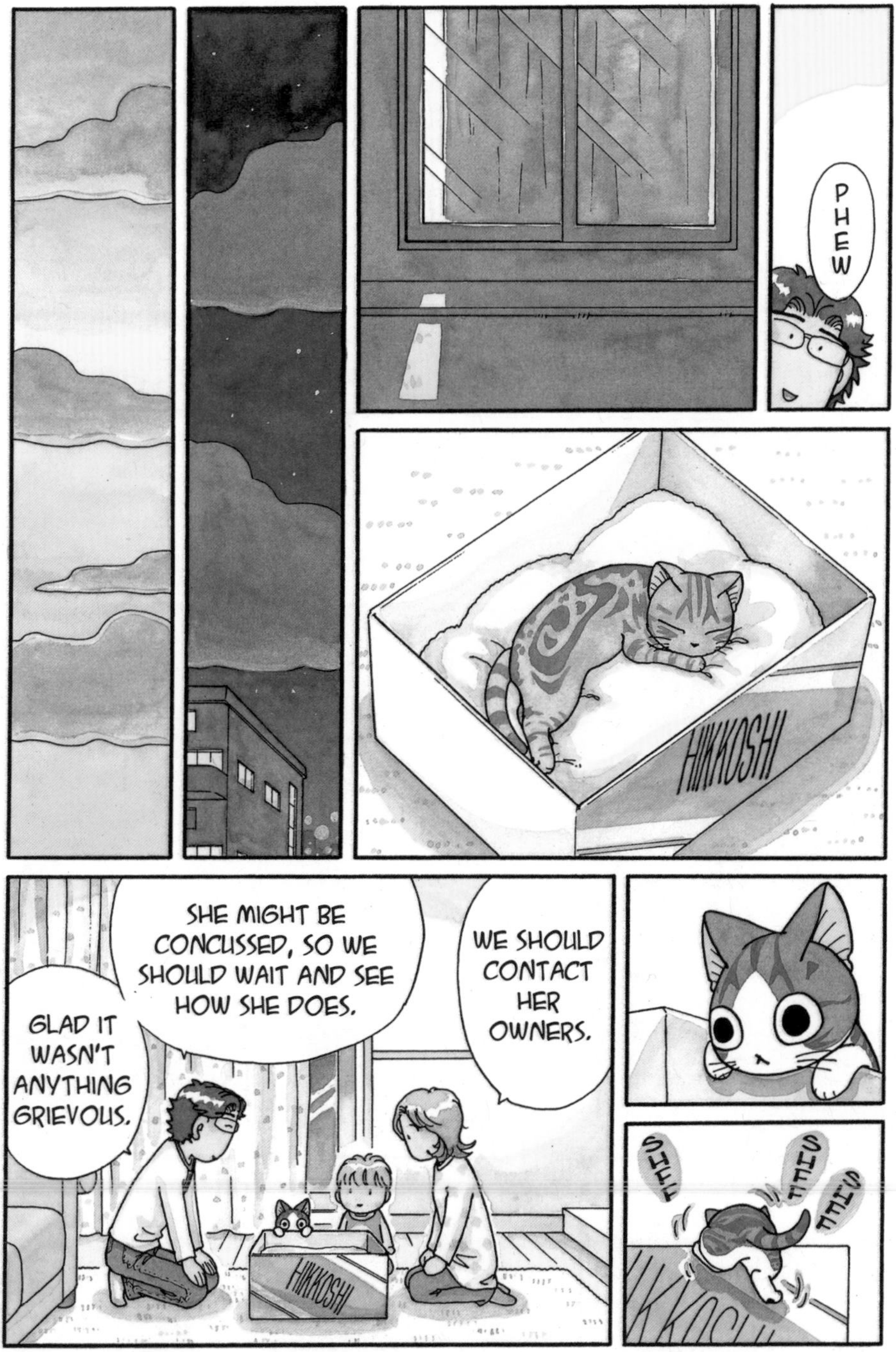
PHEW
HIKKOSHI
SHE MIGHT BE CONCUSSED, SO WE SHOULD WAIT AND SEE HOW SHE DOES.
WE SHOULD CONTACT HER OWNERS.
GLAD IT WASN'T ANYTHING GRIEVOUS.
HIKKOSHI
SHFF
SHFF
SHFF

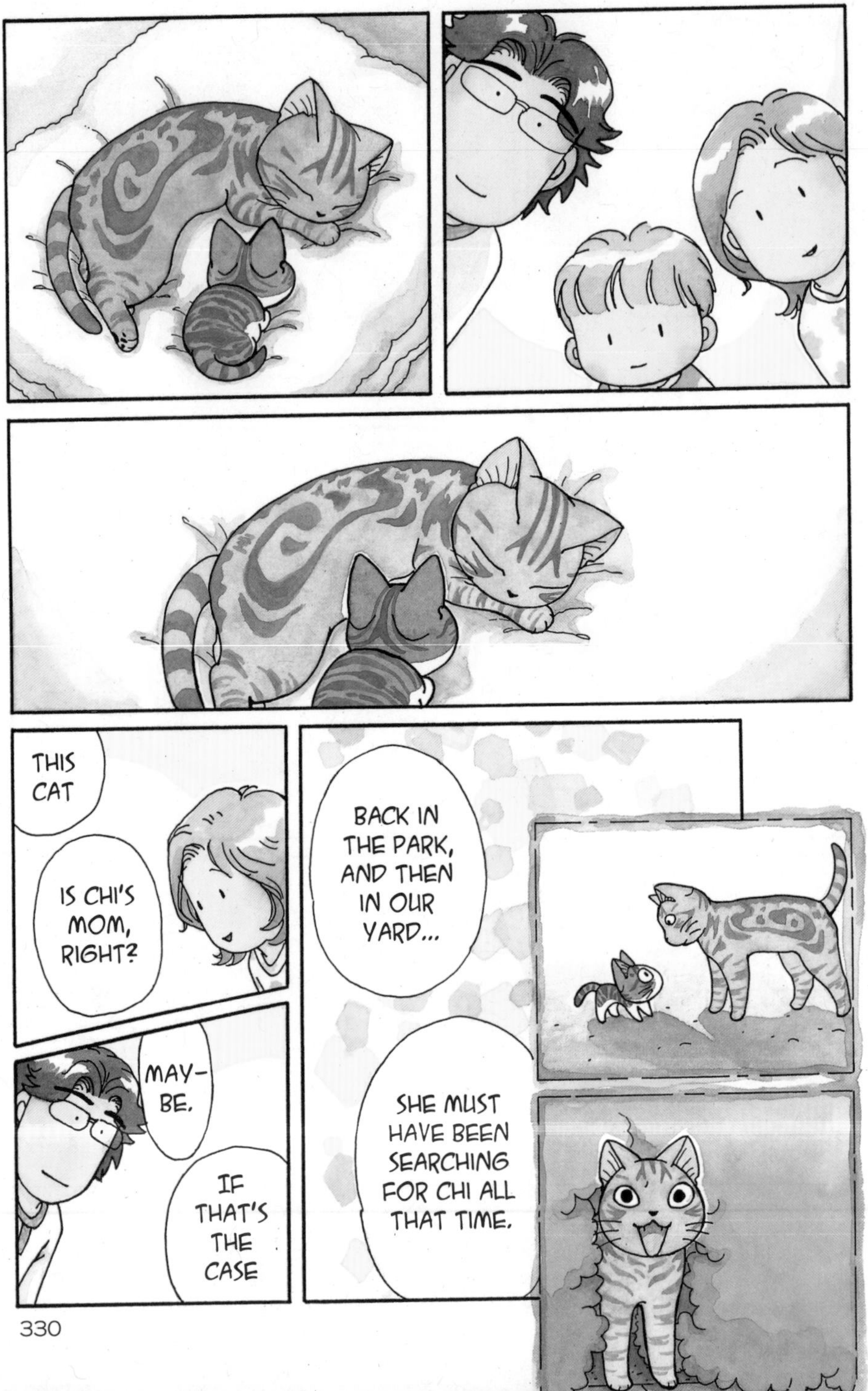
THIS CAT
IS CHI'S MOM, RIGHT?
MAY-BE.
IF THAT'S THE CASE
BACK IN THE PARK, AND THEN IN OUR YARD...
SHE MUST HAVE BEEN SEARCHING FOR CHI ALL THAT TIME.

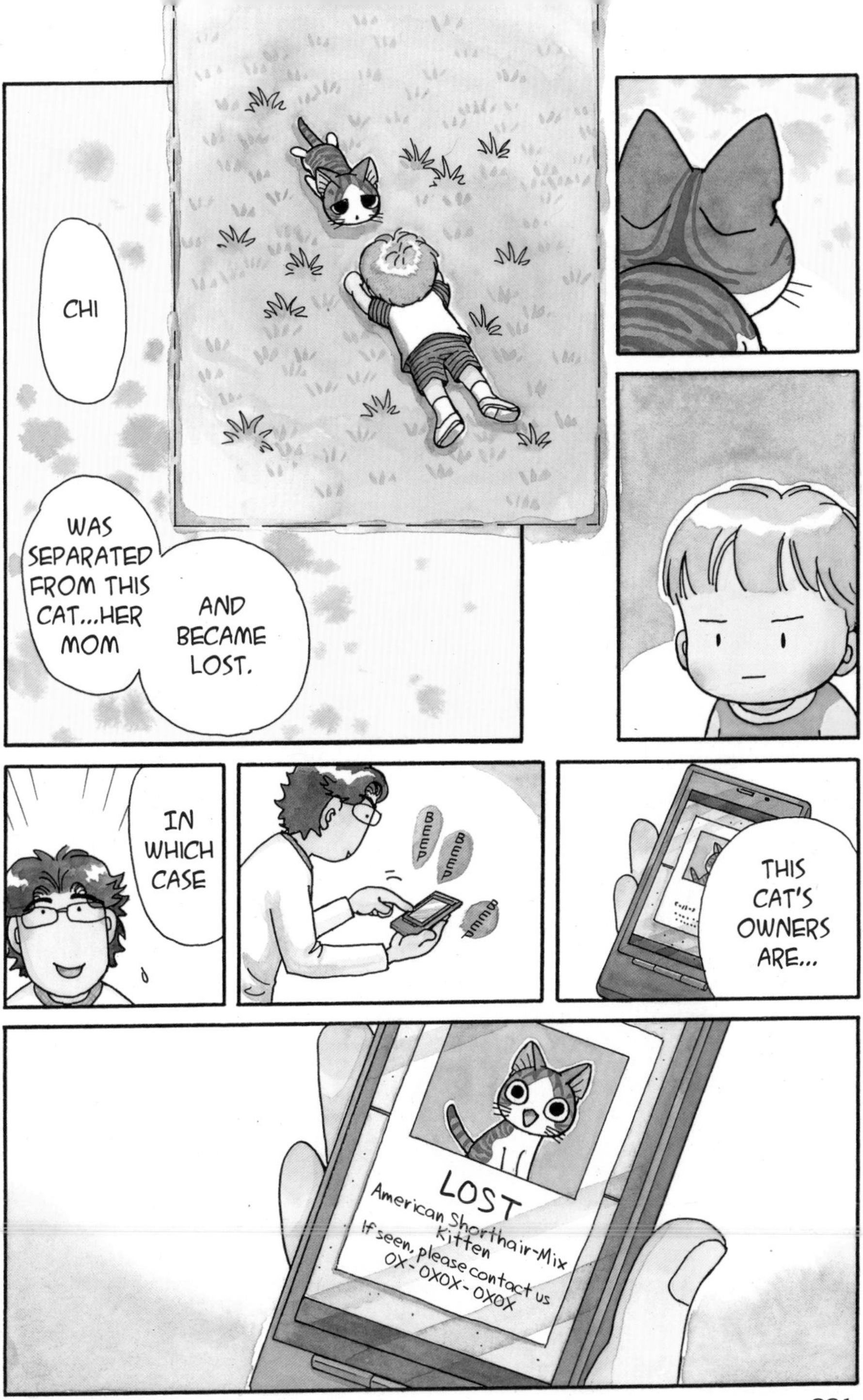
CHI
WAS SEPARATED FROM THIS CAT...HER MOM
AND BECAME LOST.
IN WHICH CASE
BEEP
BEEP
BEEP
THIS CAT'S OWNERS ARE...
LOST
American Shorthair-Mix Kitten
If seen, please contact us
0X-0X0X-0X0X

AND THEY MUST BE THE HOME SEARCHING FOR CHI.

WE MUST CONTACT THEM NOW, RIGHT.

THEN WHAT HAPPENS TO CHI?!

AND WHAT ABOUT CHI?

the end

homemade 206: a cat snuggles

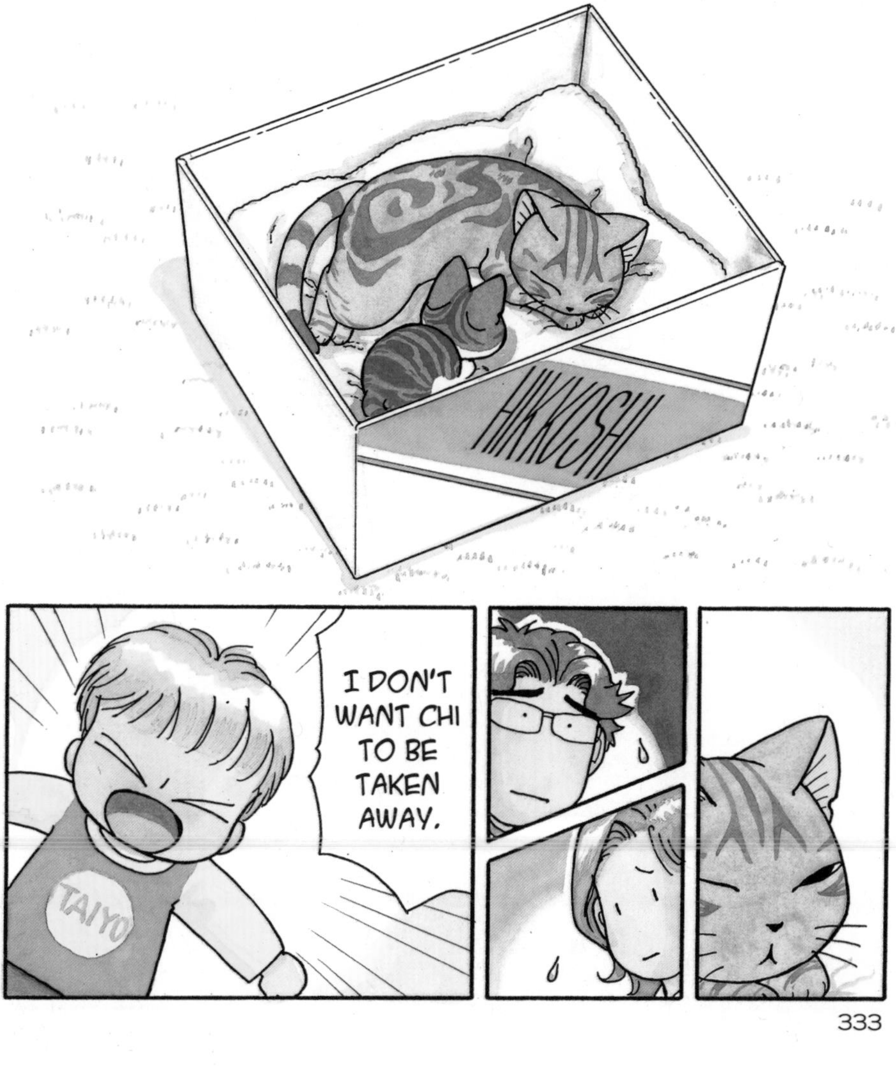
I DON'T WANT CHI TO BE TAKEN AWAY.
TAIYO

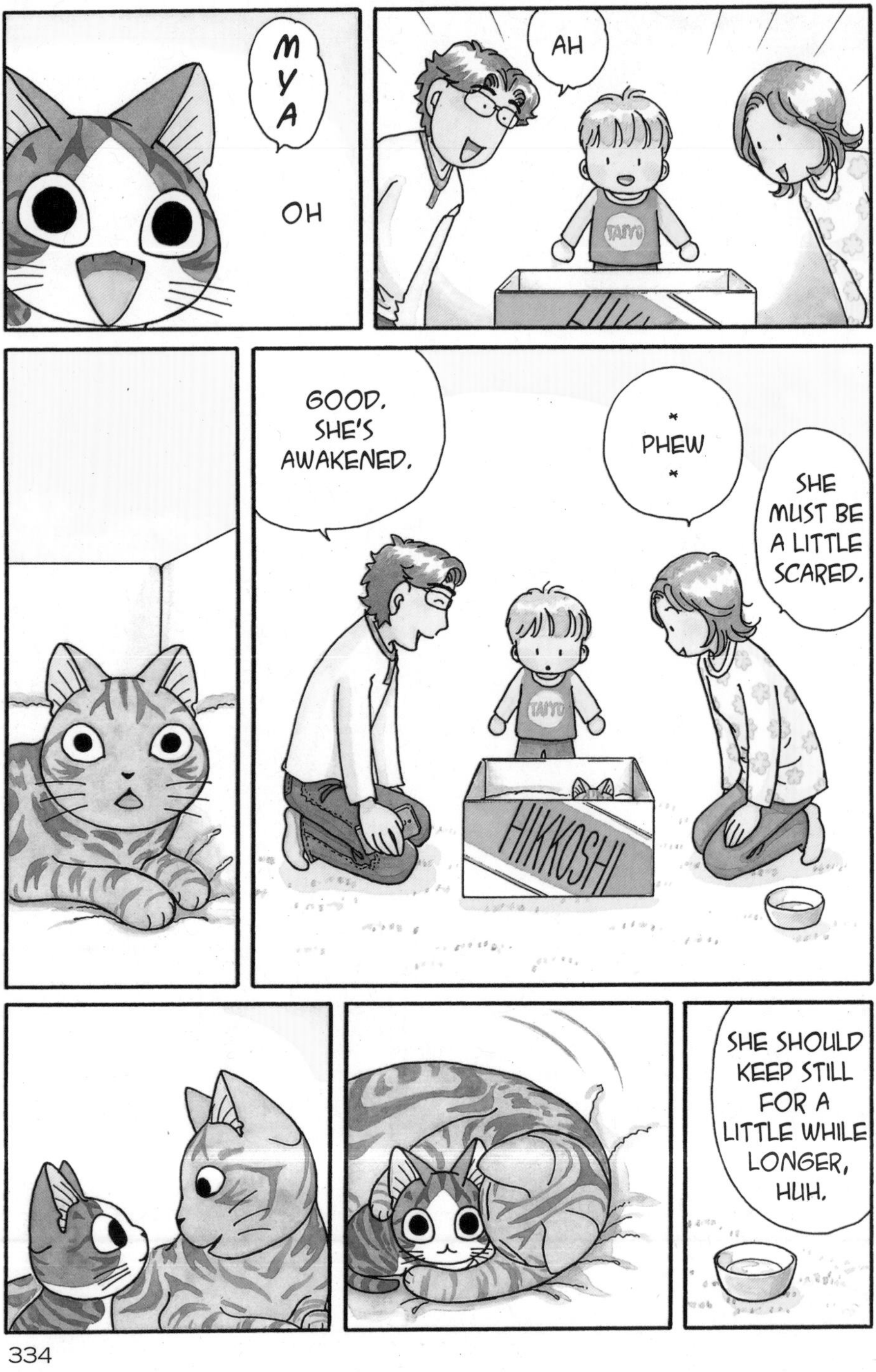
MYA
OH
AH
GOOD. SHE'S AWAKENED.
* PHEW *
SHE MUST BE A LITTLE SCARED.
HIKKOSHI
SHE SHOULD KEEP STILL FOR A LITTLE WHILE LONGER, HUH.

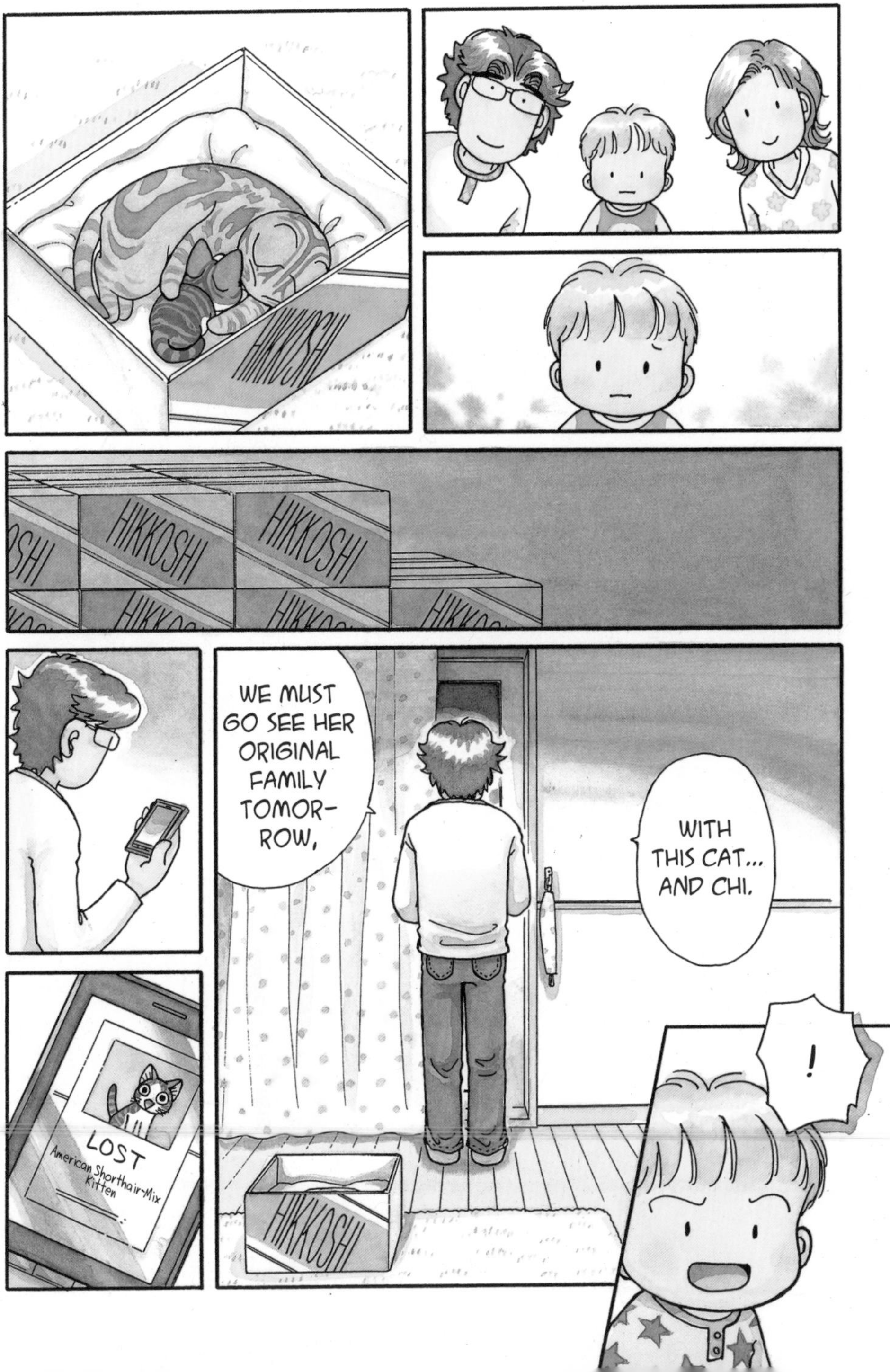
HIKKOSHI
HIKKOSHI
HIKKOSHI
WE MUST GO SEE HER ORIGINAL FAMILY TOMOR-ROW,
WITH THIS CAT... AND CHI.
LOST
American Shorthair-Mix Kitten
HIKKOSHI
!

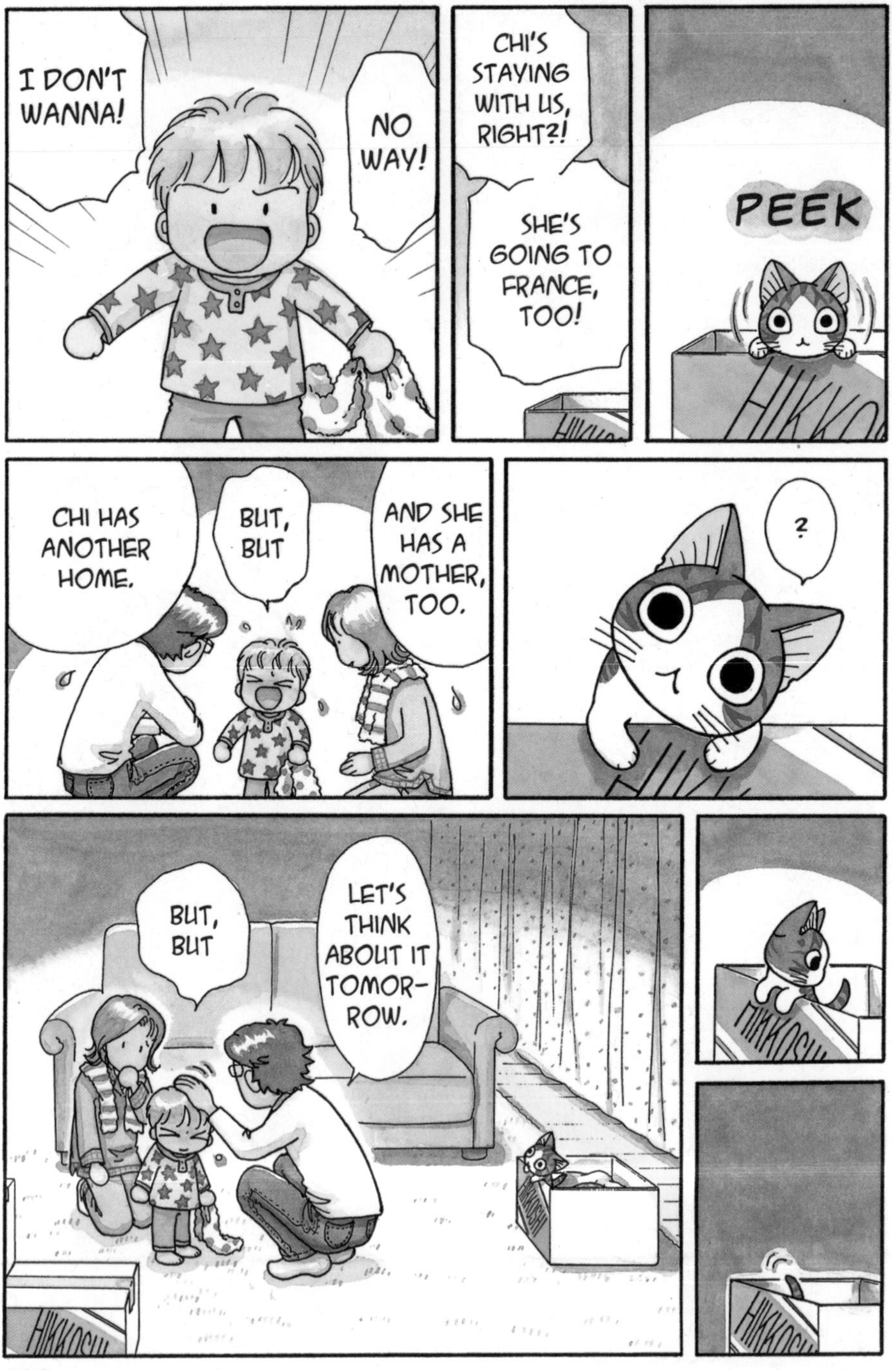
I DON'T WANNA!
NO WAY!
CHI'S STAYING WITH US, RIGHT?!
SHE'S GOING TO FRANCE, TOO!
PEEK
CHI HAS ANOTHER HOME.
BUT, BUT
AND SHE HAS A MOTHER, TOO.
?
BUT, BUT
LET'S THINK ABOUT IT TOMOR-ROW.
HIKKOSHI

FSSH
MWAA
HIKKOSHI
TMP
TMP
TMP
HIKKOSHI

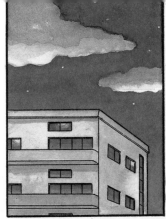

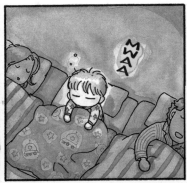

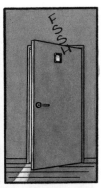

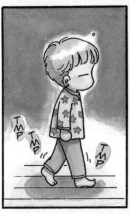

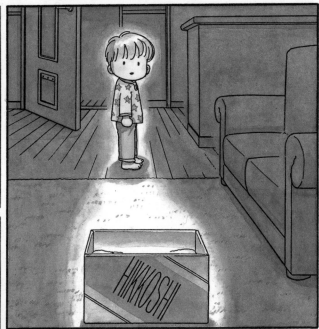

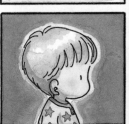

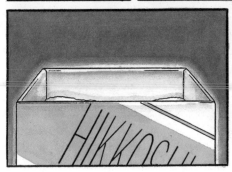

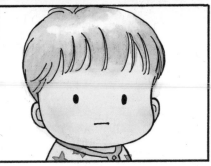

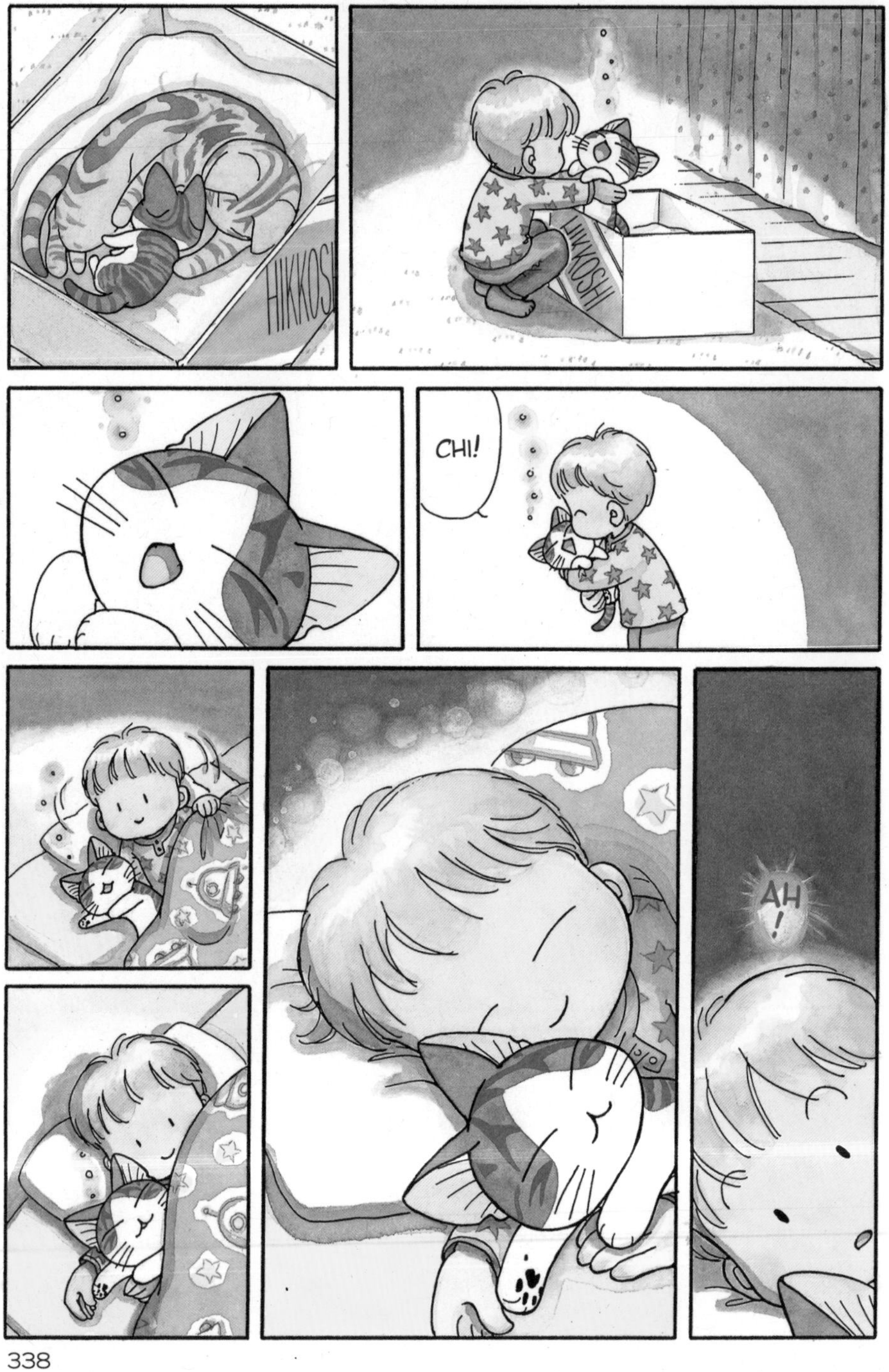
HIKKOSHI
HIKKOSHI
CHI!
AH!

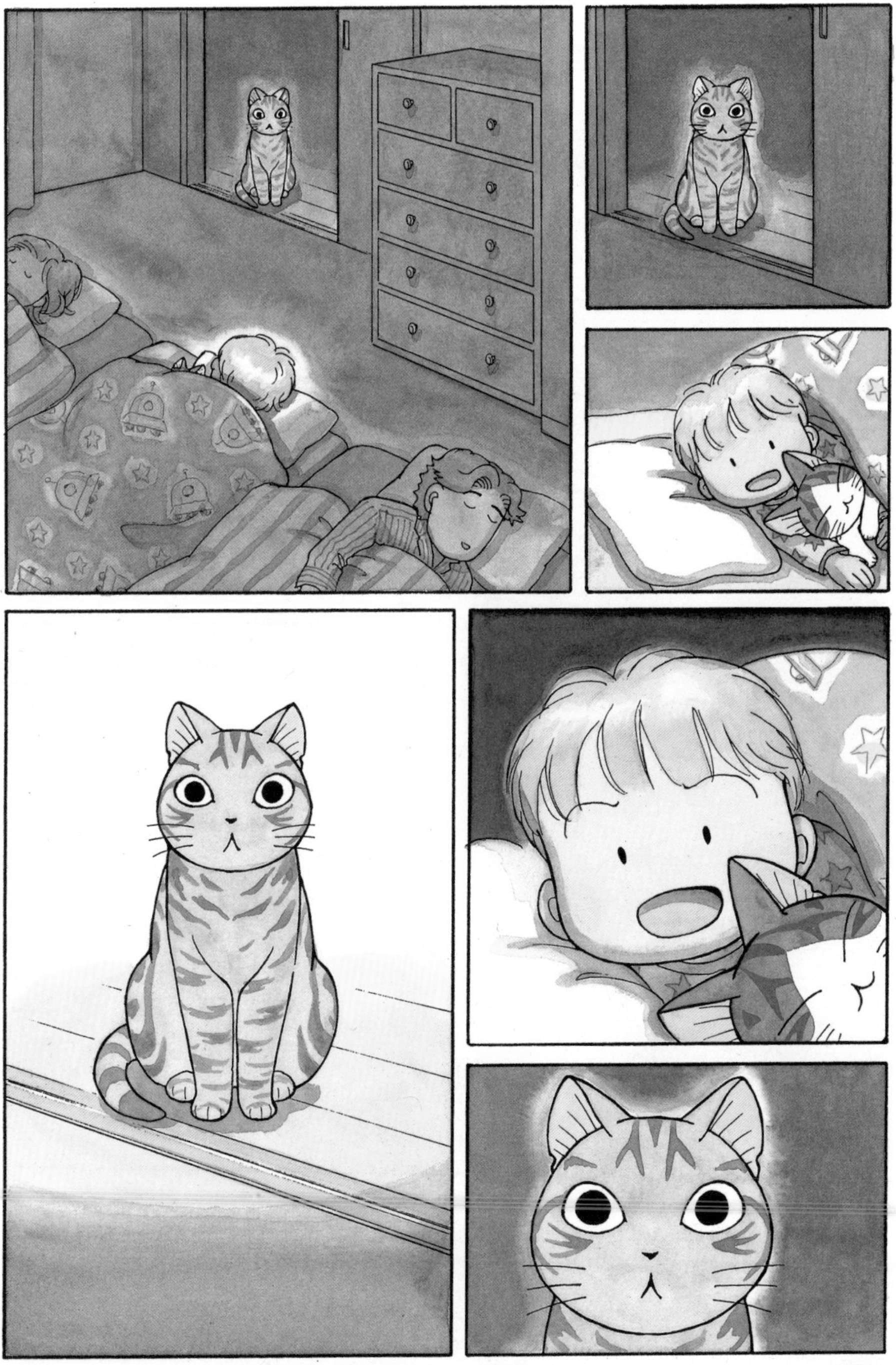

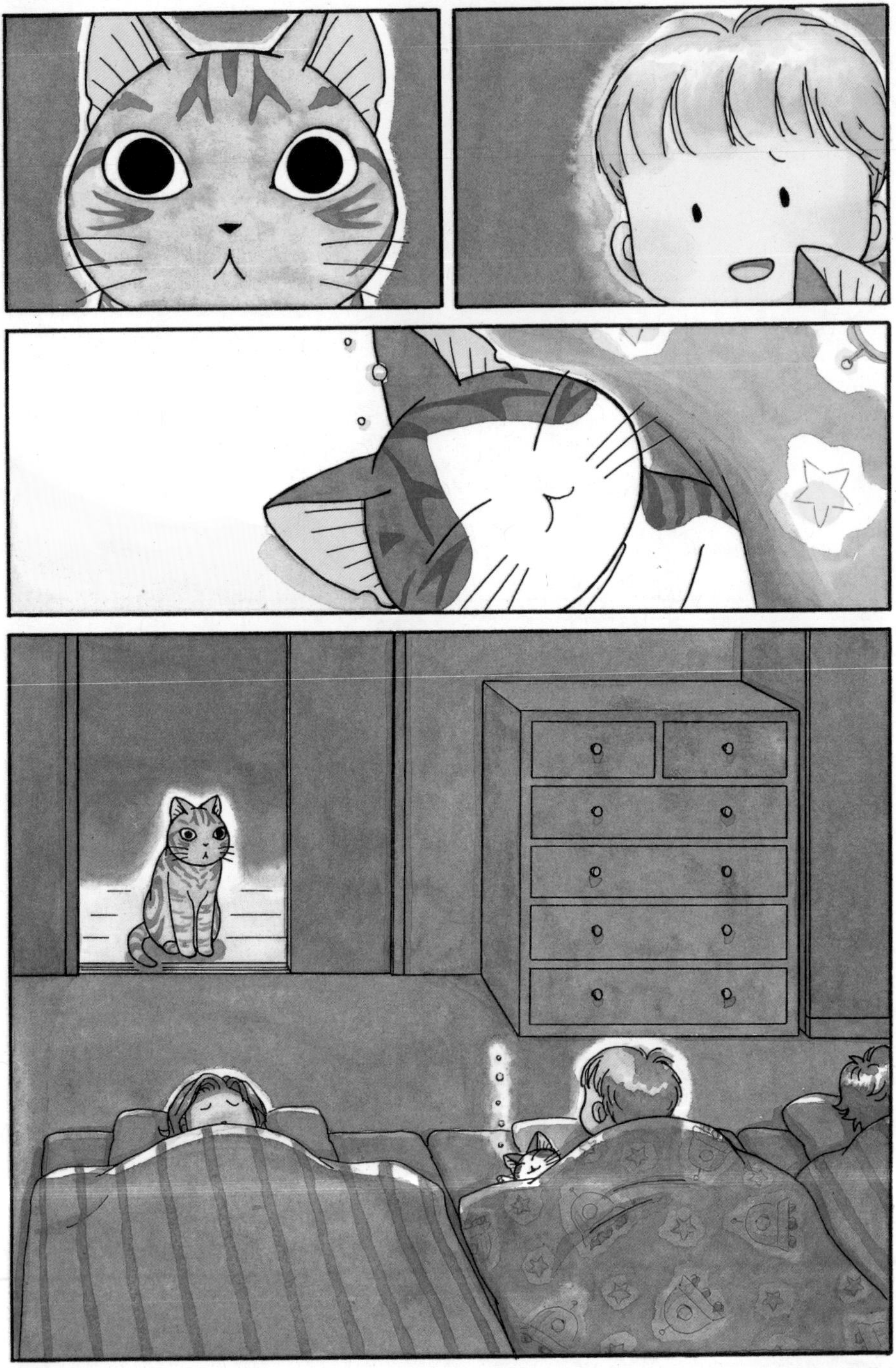

the end

homemade 207: a cat bonds

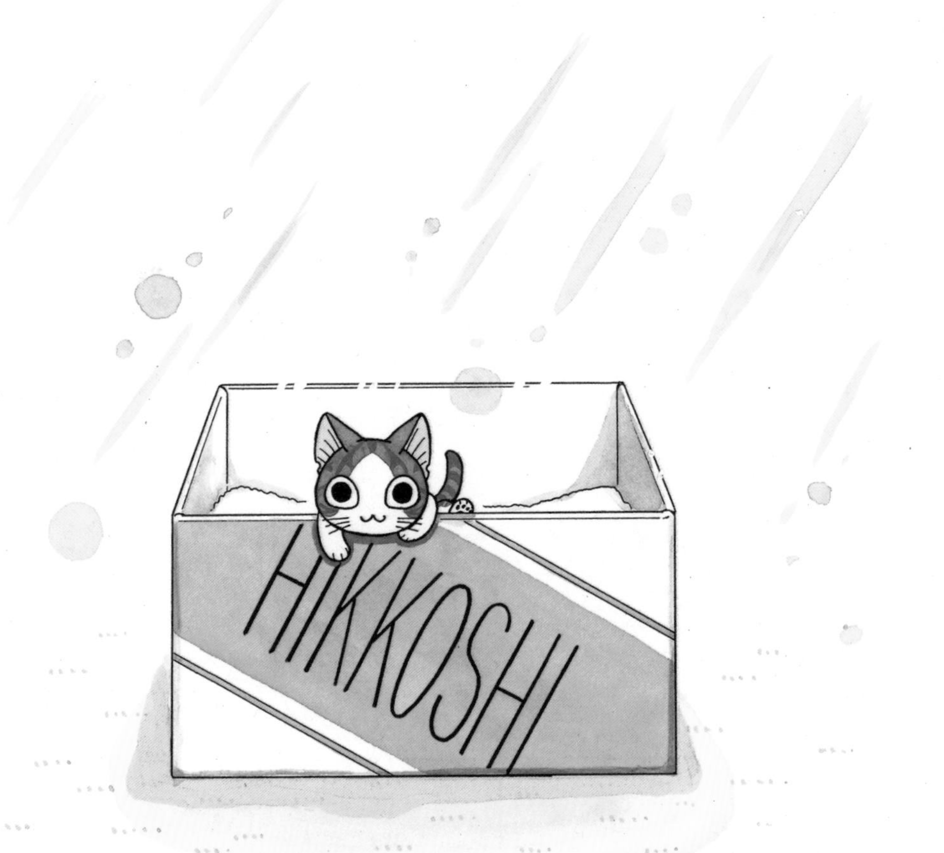
HIKKOSHI

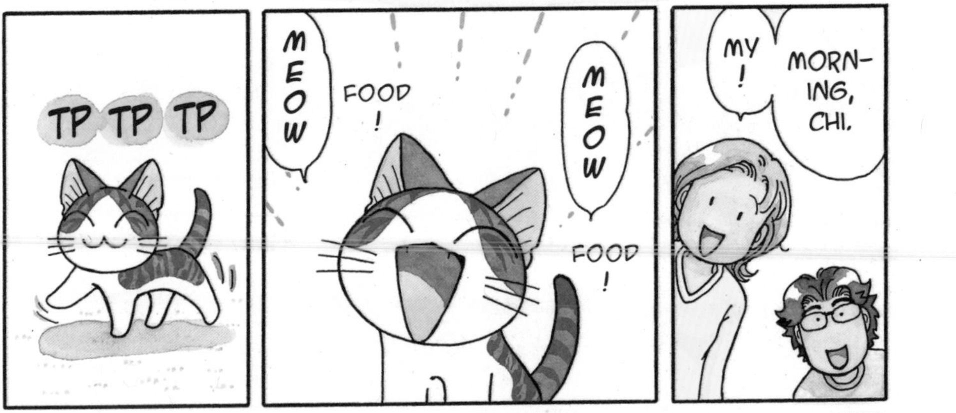
TP TP TP
MEOW
FOOD!
MEOW
FOOD!
MY!
MORNING, CHI.

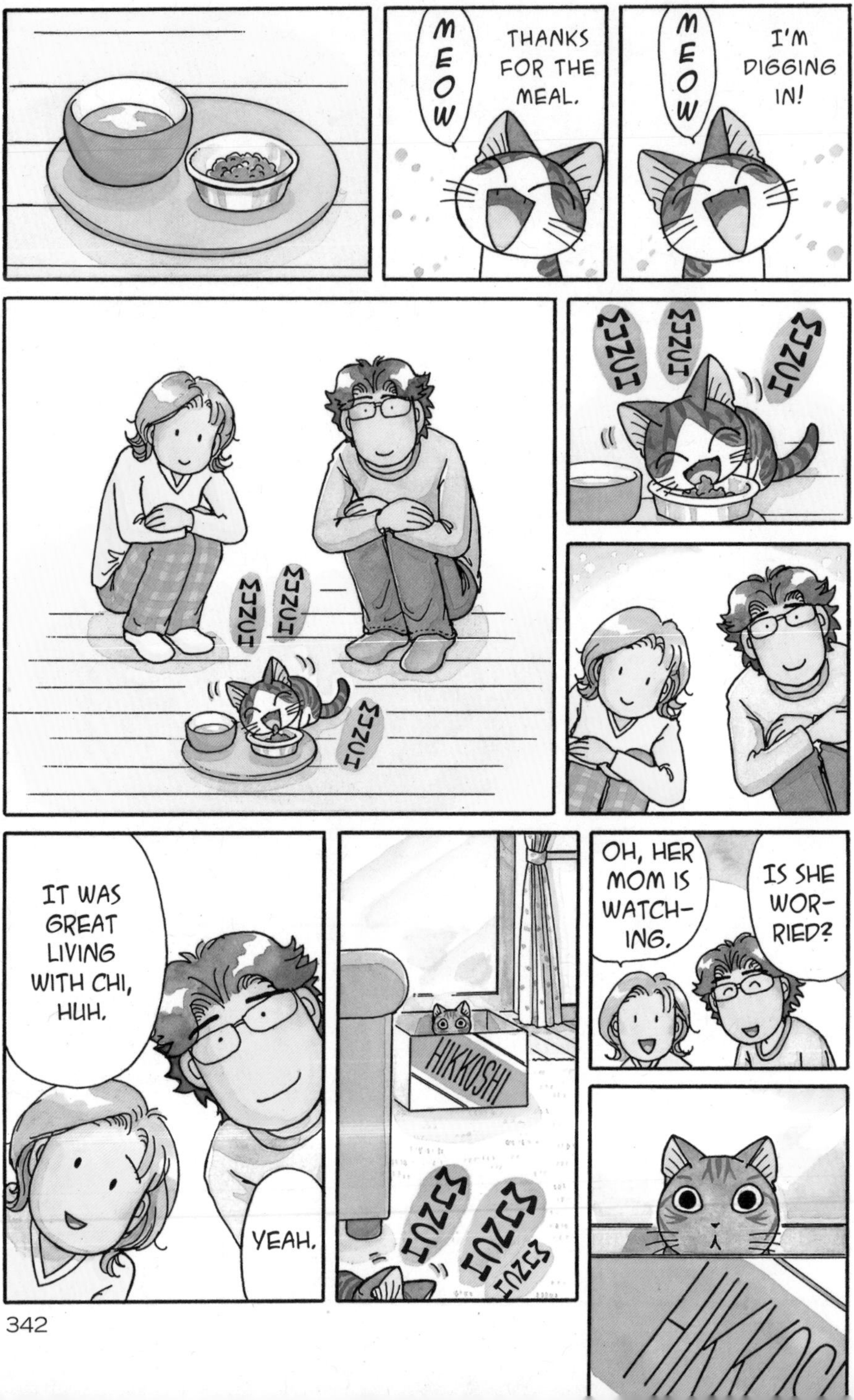
MEOW
THANKS FOR THE MEAL.
MEOW
I'M DIGGING IN!
MUNCH
MUNCH
MUNCH
MUNCH
MUNCH
MUNCH
IT WAS GREAT LIVING WITH CHI, HUH.
YEAH.
HIKKOSHI
MUNCH
MUNCH
MUNCH
OH, HER MOM IS WATCH-ING.
IS SHE WOR-RIED?

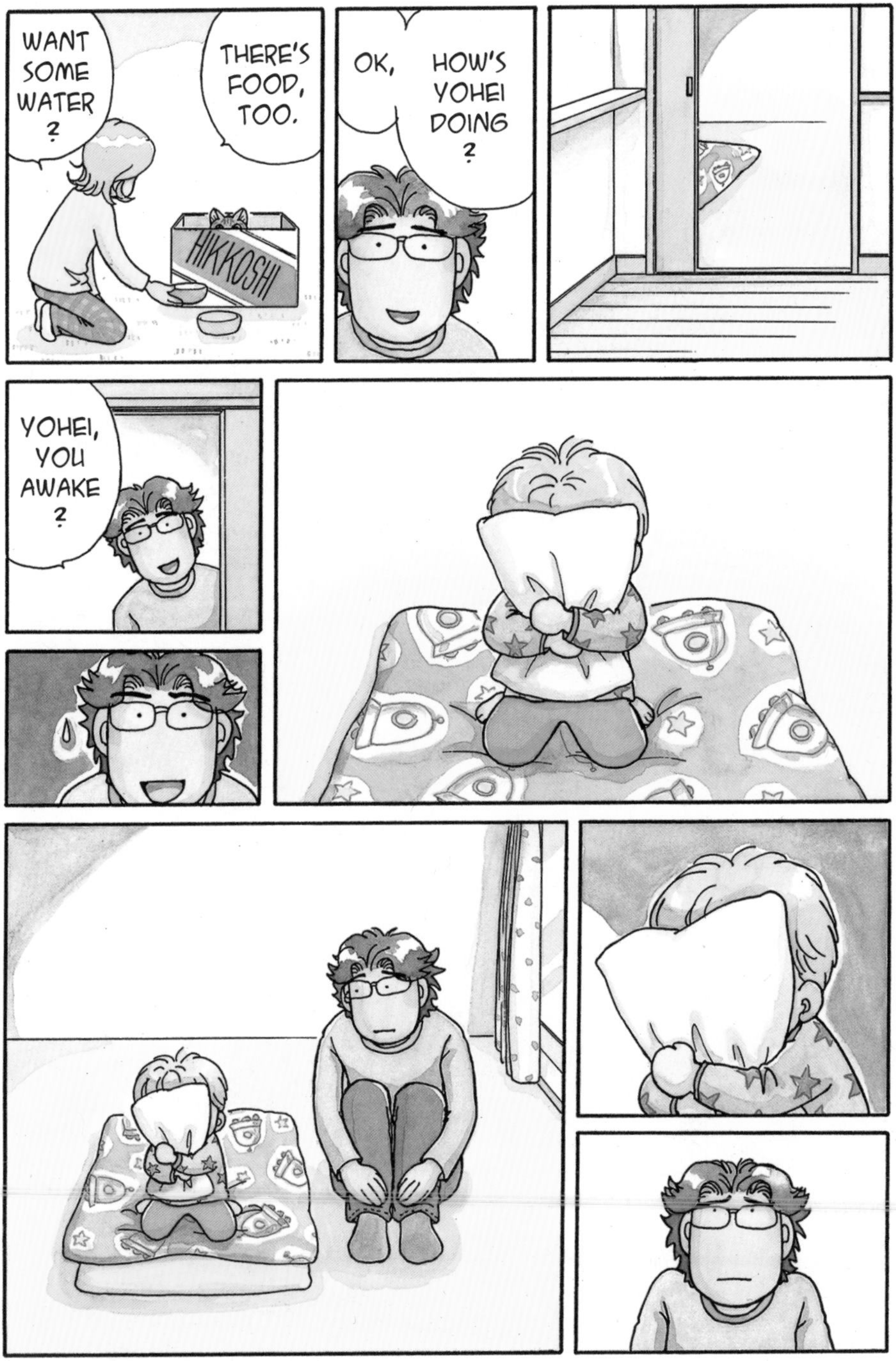
WANT SOME WATER?
THERE'S FOOD, TOO.
OK,
HOW'S YOHEI DOING?
YOHEI, YOU AWAKE?
HIKKOSHI

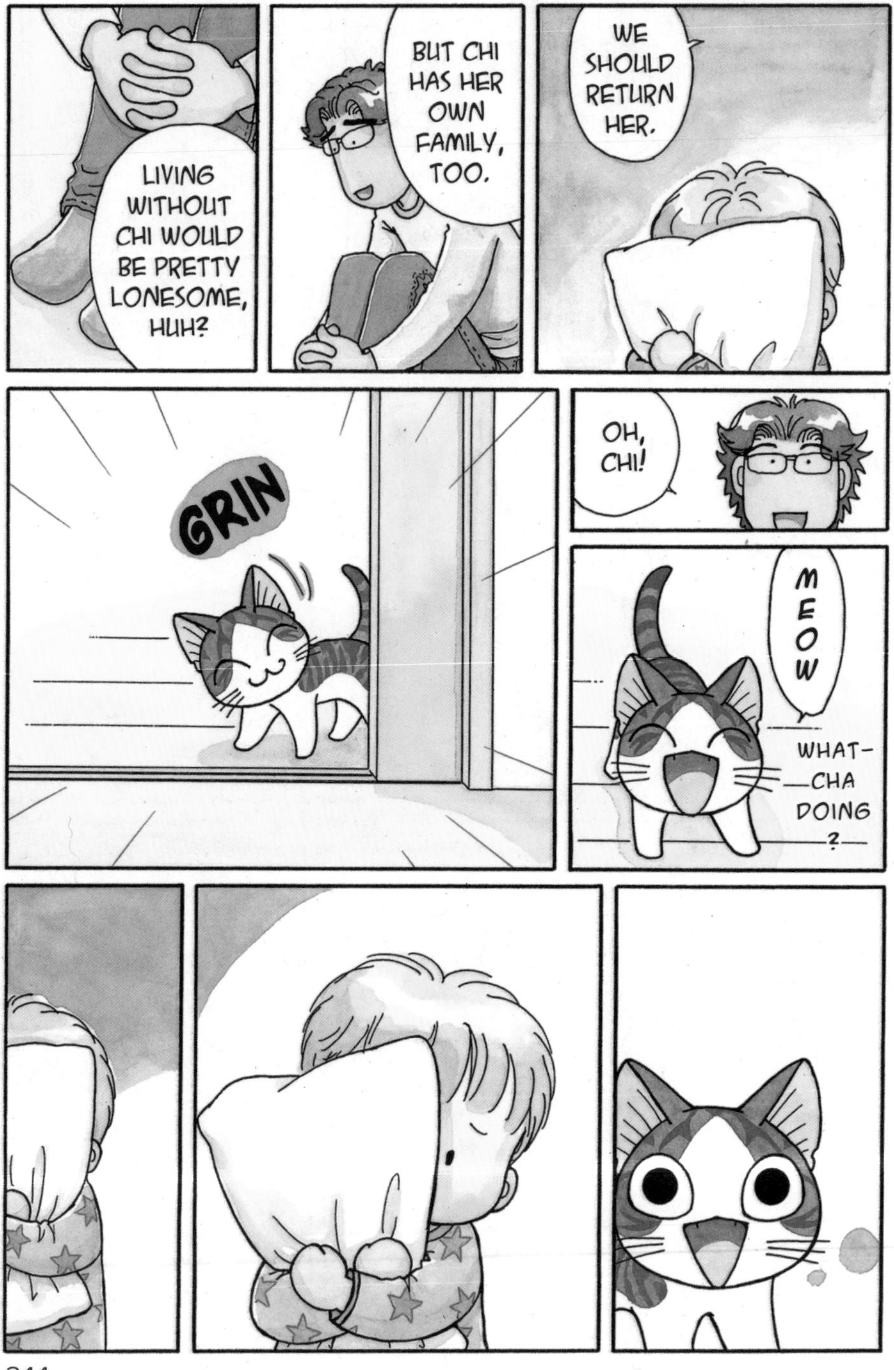
LIVING WITHOUT CHI WOULD BE PRETTY LONESOME, HUH?
BUT CHI HAS HER OWN FAMILY, TOO.
WE SHOULD RETURN HER.
GRIN
OH, CHI!
MEOW
WHAT-CHA DOING?

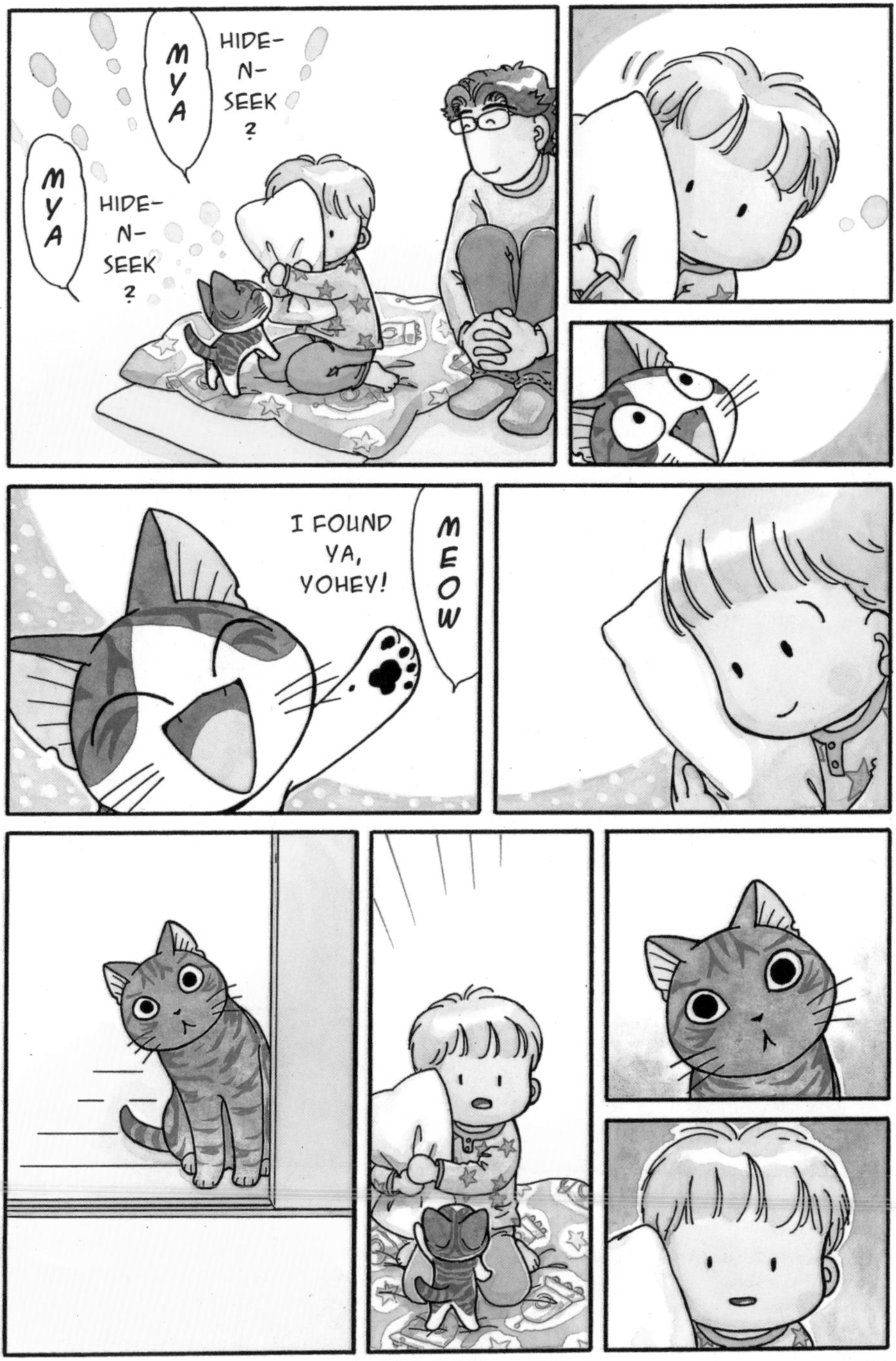

MYA
HIDE-N-SEEK?
MYA
HIDE-N-SEEK?
I FOUND YA, YOHEY!
MEOW

MEOW

WHAT'S THE MATTER?

PAT PAT

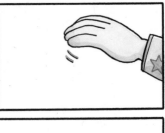

NYAN

346

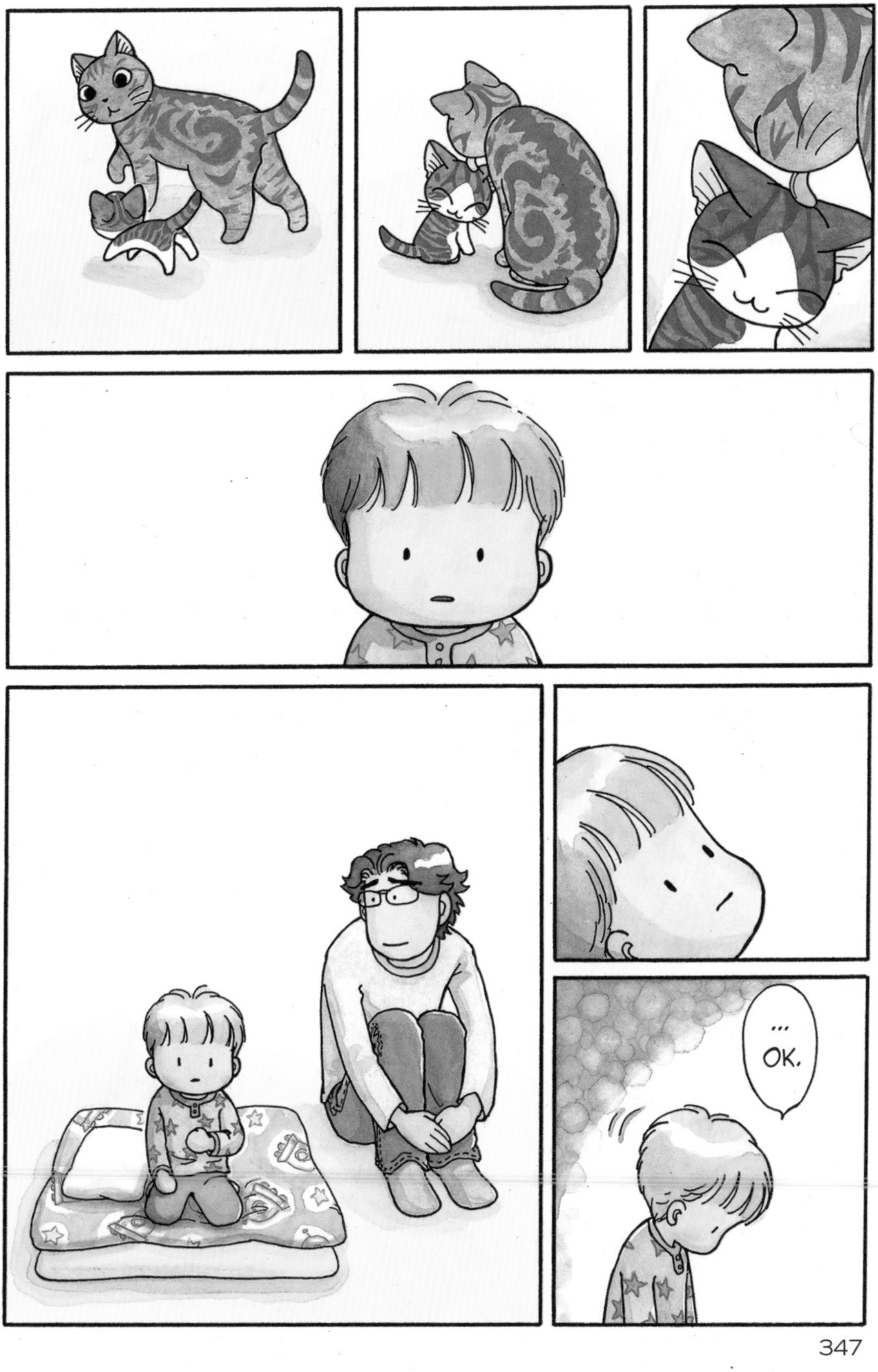
... OK.

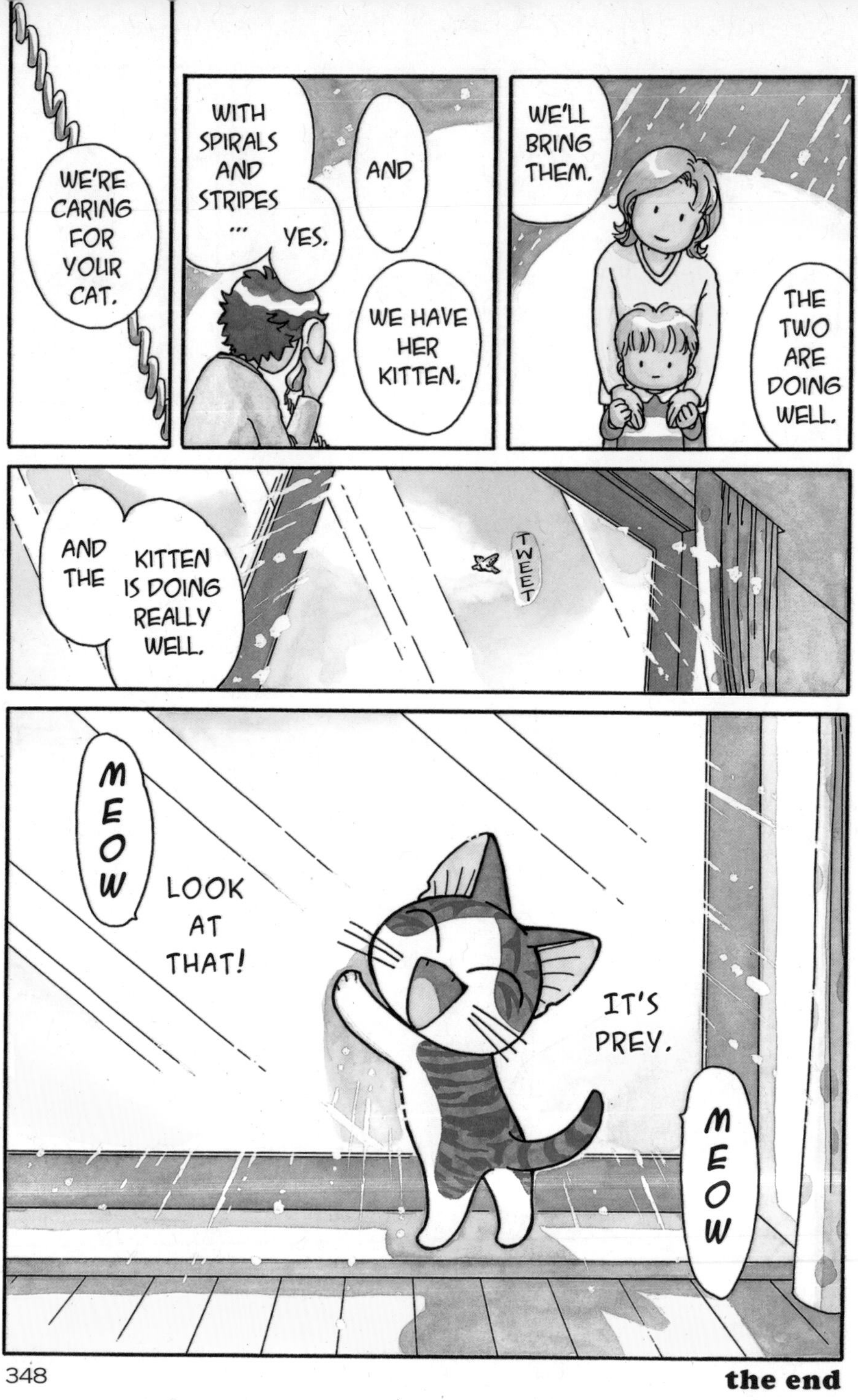
WE'RE CARING FOR YOUR CAT.
WITH SPIRALS AND STRIPES ...
YES.
AND
WE HAVE HER KITTEN.
WE'LL BRING THEM.
THE TWO ARE DOING WELL.
AND THE KITTEN IS DOING REALLY WELL.
TWEET
MEOW
LOOK AT THAT!
IT'S PREY.
MEOW

the end

homemade 208: a cat goes back

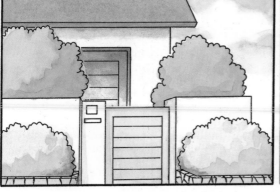

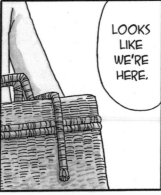

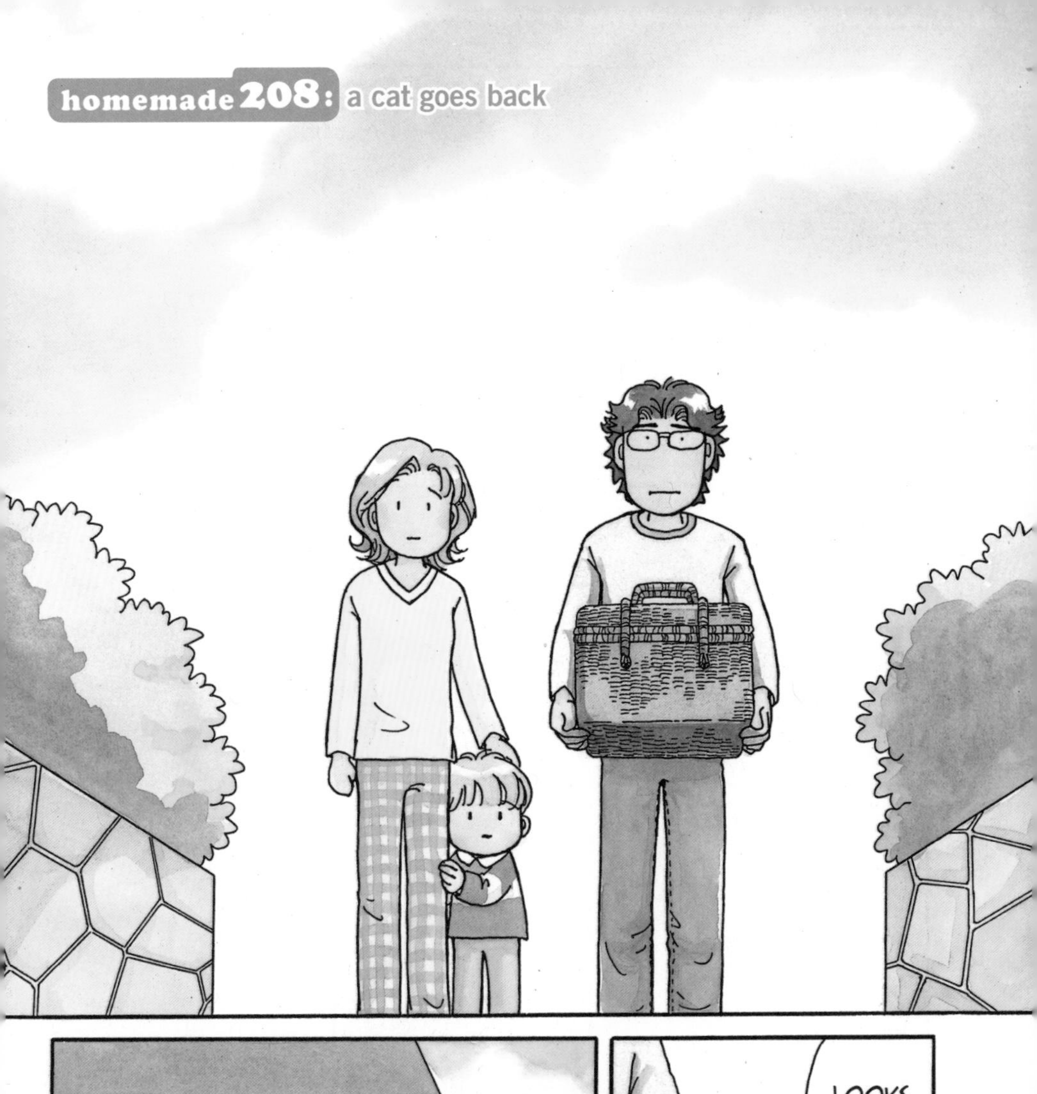
LOOKS LIKE WE'RE HERE.

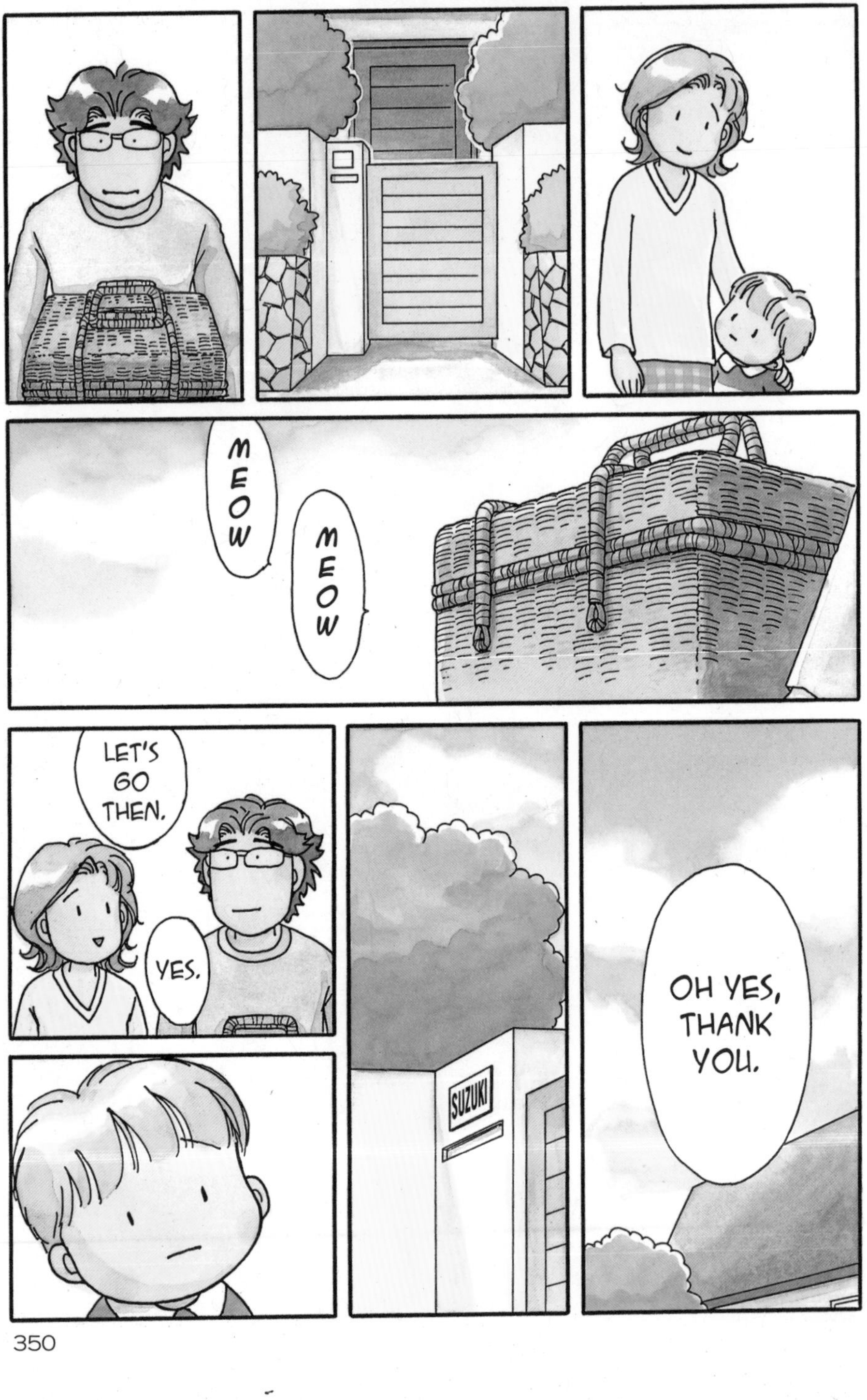
MEOW
MEOW
LET'S GO THEN.
YES.
SUZUKI
OH YES, THANK YOU.

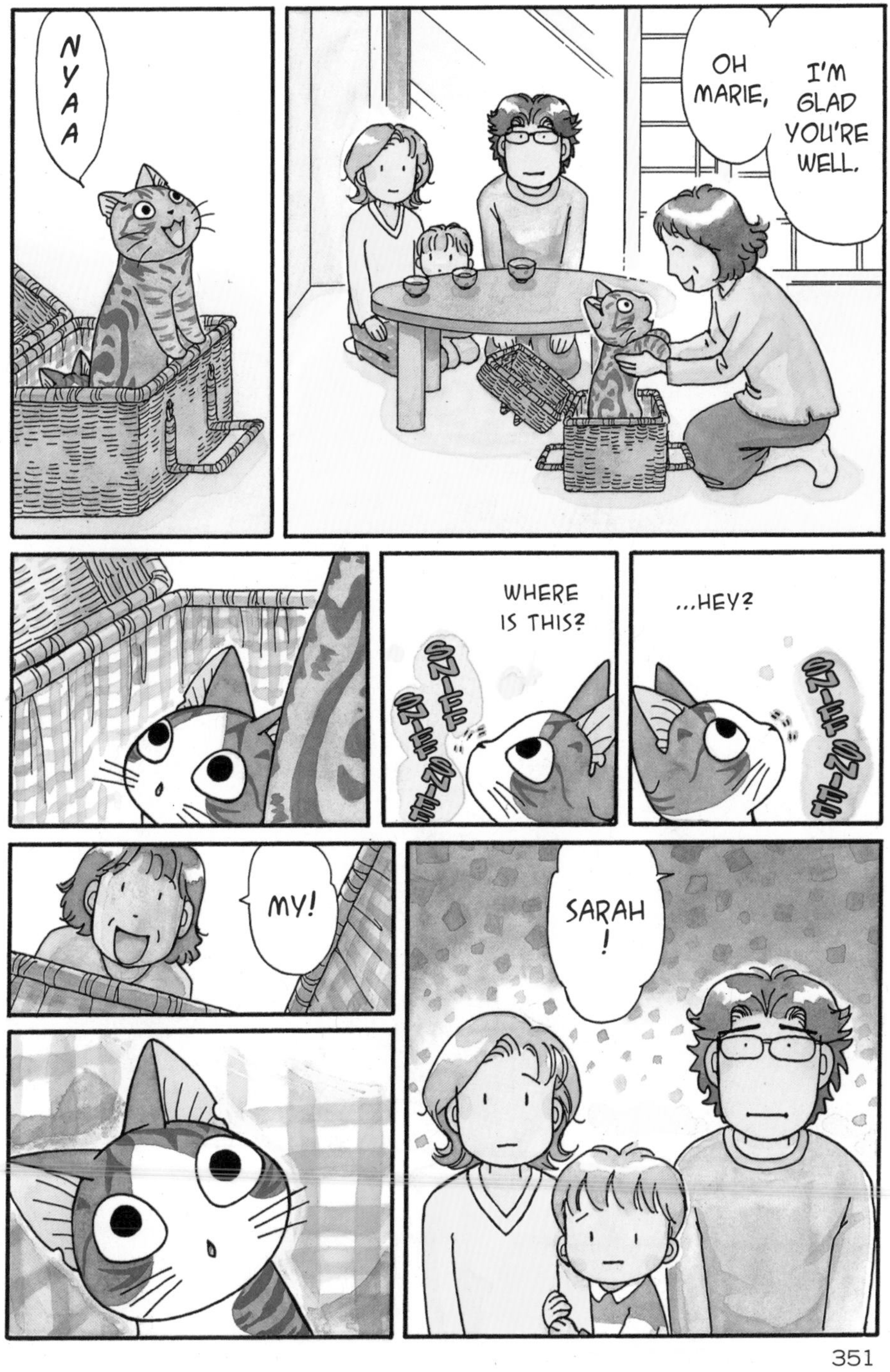
NYAA
OH MARIE,
I'M GLAD YOU'RE WELL.
WHERE IS THIS?
SNIFF SNIFF SNIFF
...HEY?
SNIFF SNIFF
MY!
SARAH!

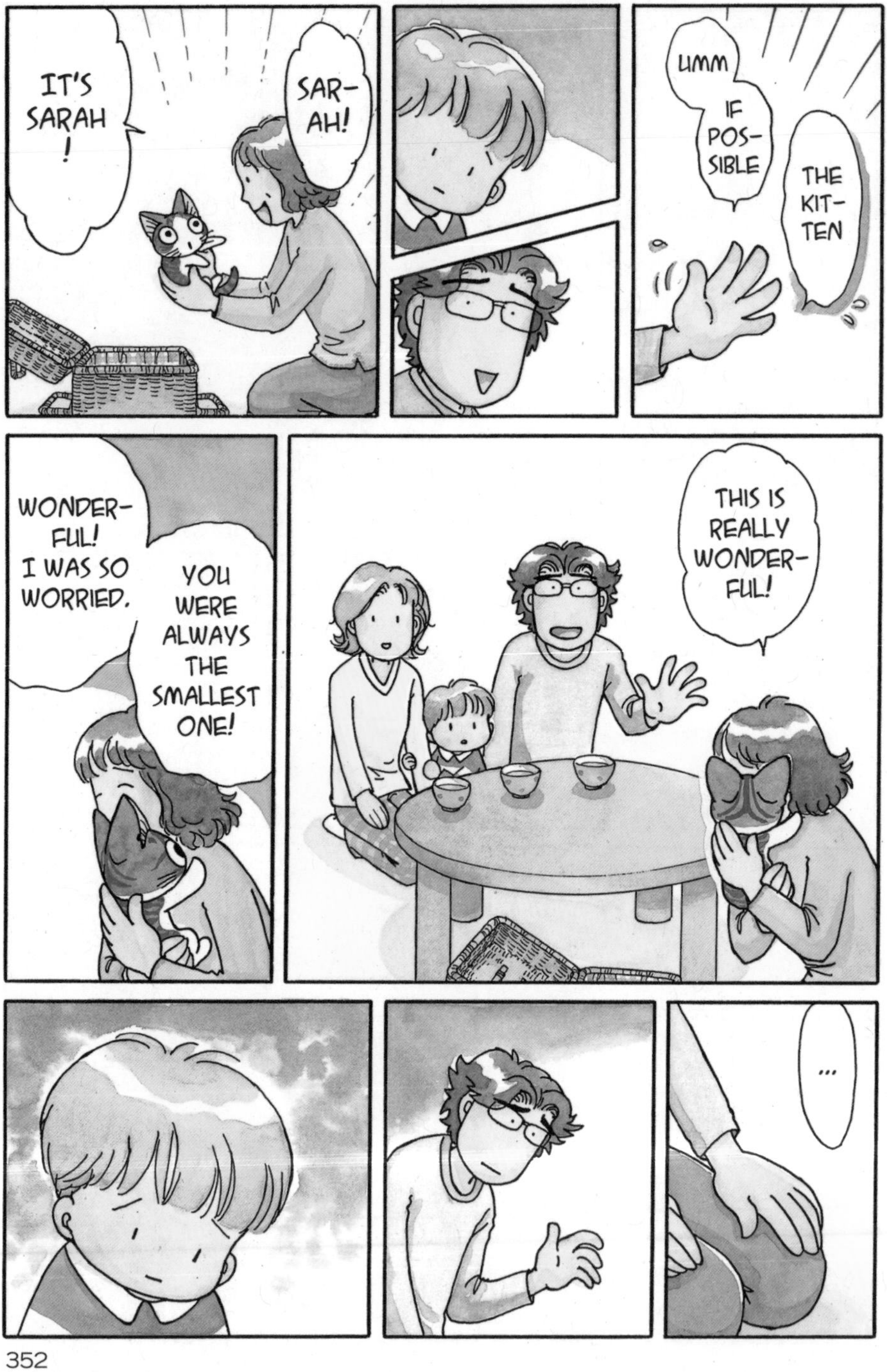
IT'S SARAH!
SAR-AH!
UMM
IF POS-SIBLE
THE KIT-TEN
WONDER-FUL! I WAS SO WORRIED.
YOU WERE ALWAYS THE SMALLEST ONE!
THIS IS REALLY WONDER-FUL!
...

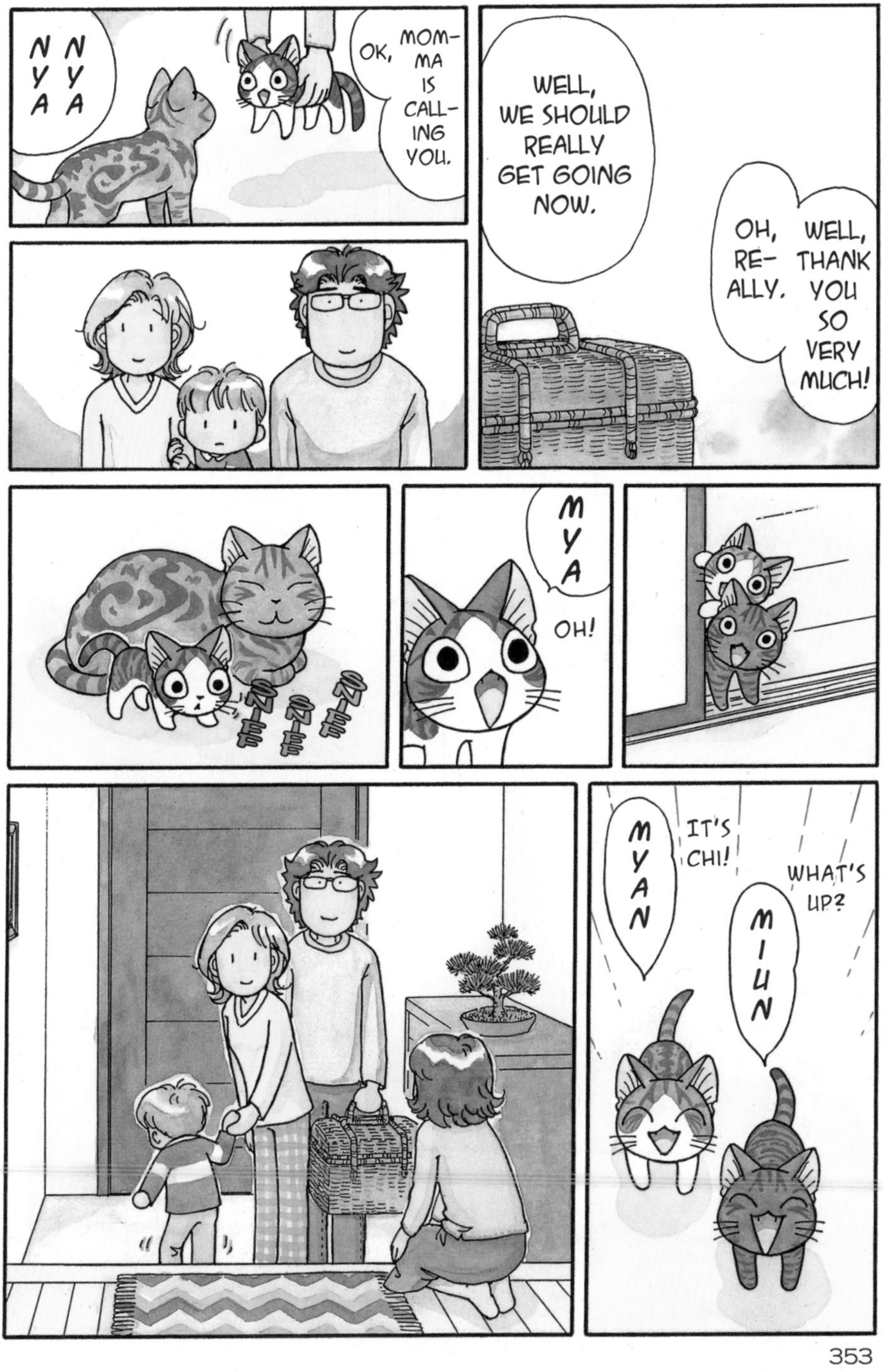
NYA NYA
OK, MOMMA IS CALLING YOU.
WELL, WE SHOULD REALLY GET GOING NOW.
OH, REALLY. WELL, THANK YOU SO VERY MUCH!
SNIFF SNIFF SNIFF
MYA
OH!
MYAN
IT'S CHI!
MIUN
WHAT'S UP?

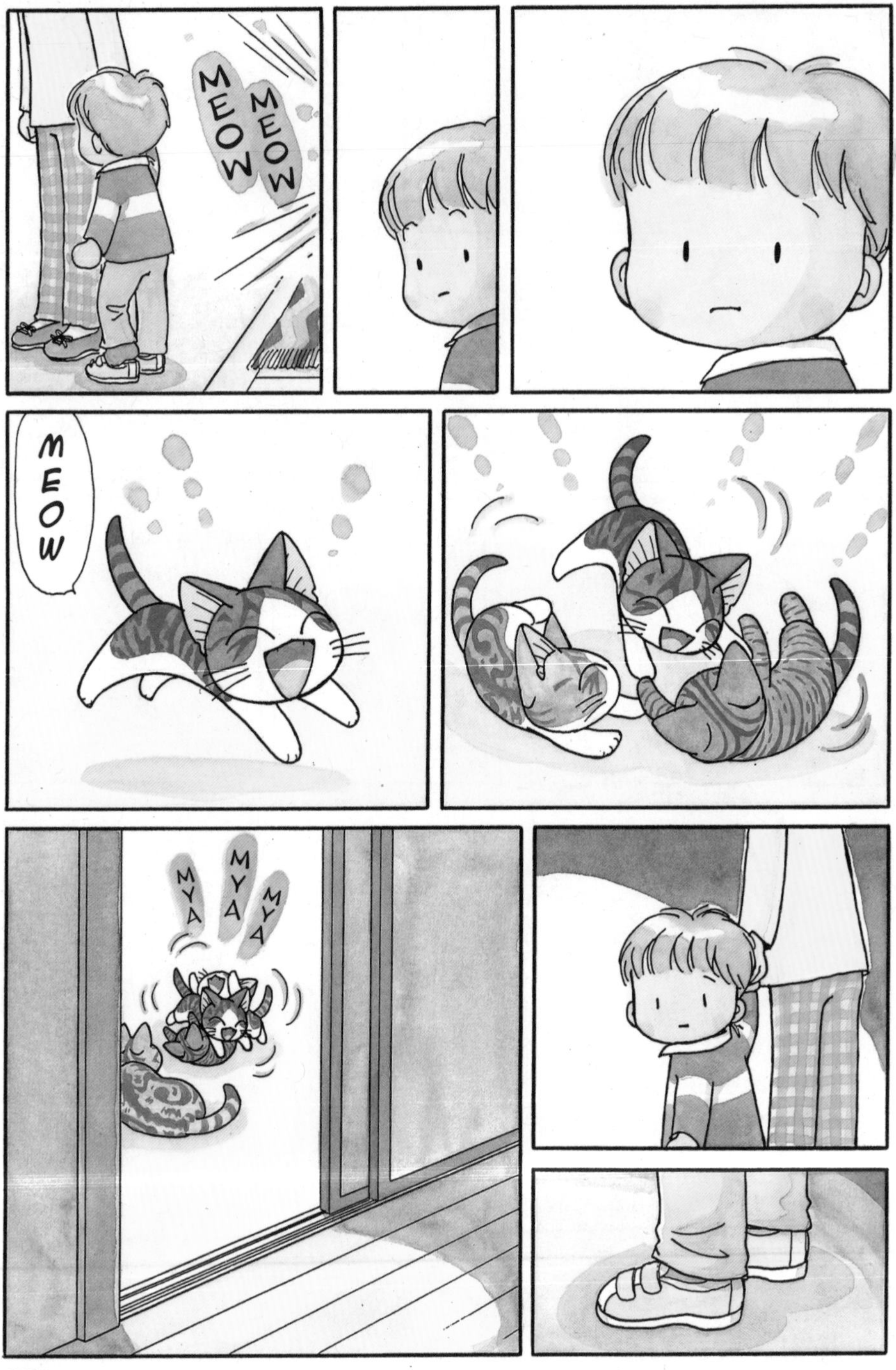
MEOW
MEOW
MEOW
MYA
MYA
MYA

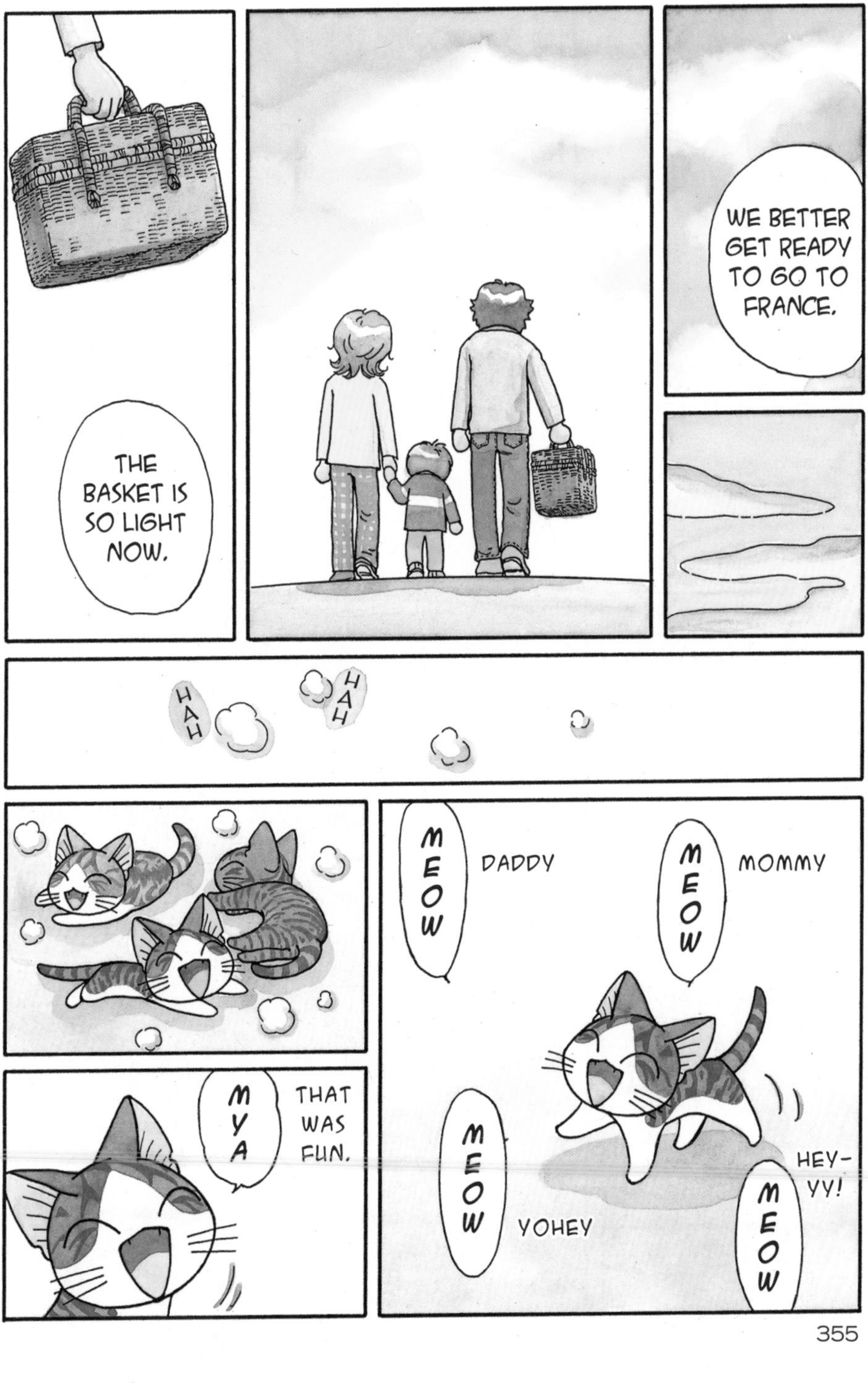
THE BASKET IS SO LIGHT NOW.
WE BETTER GET READY TO GO TO FRANCE.
HAH
HAH
MYA
THAT WAS FUN.
MEOW
DADDY
MEOW
MOMMY
MEOW
YOHEY
MEOW
HEY-YY!

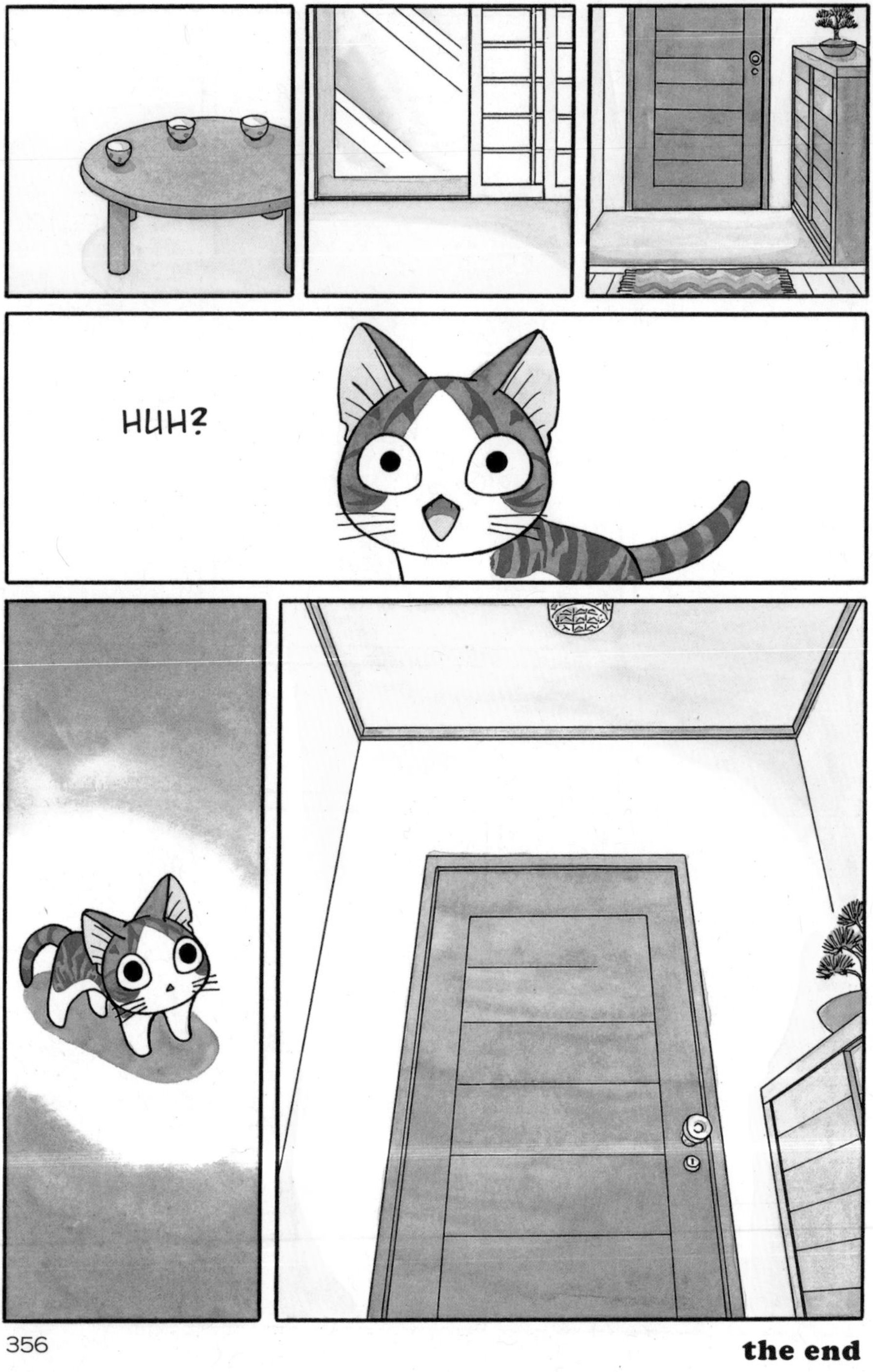
HUH?

the end

homemade 209: a cat accepts

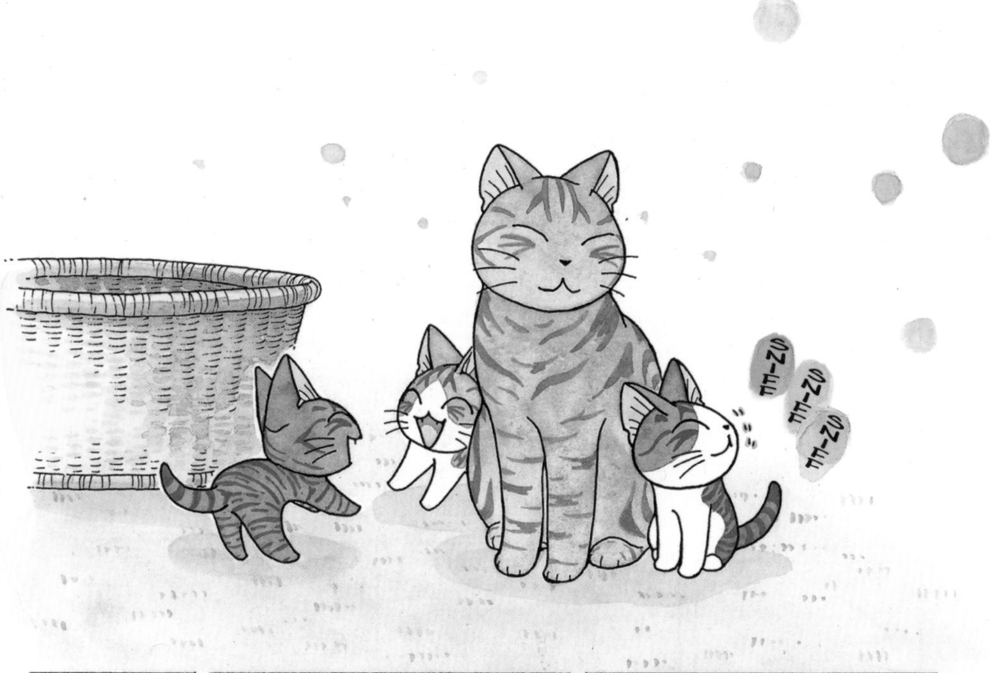
SNIFF
SNIFF
SNIFF

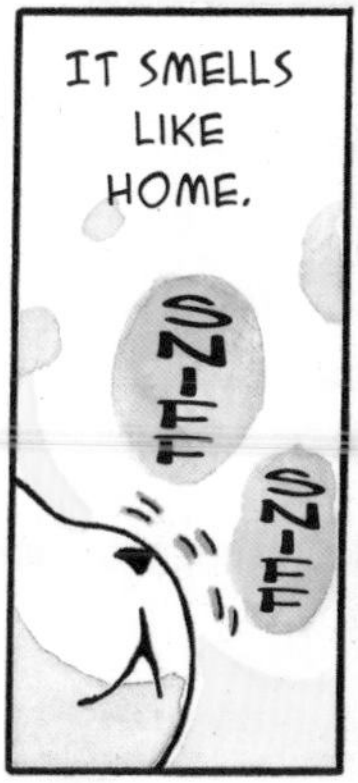
IT SMELLS LIKE HOME.
SNIFF
SNIFF

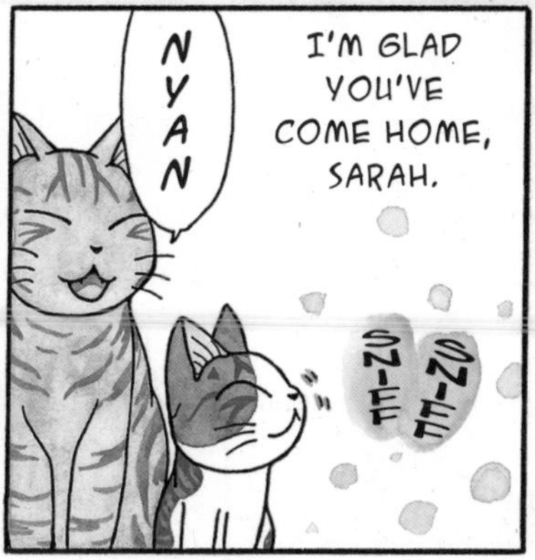
NYAN
I'M GLAD YOU'VE COME HOME, SARAH.
SNIFF
SNIFF

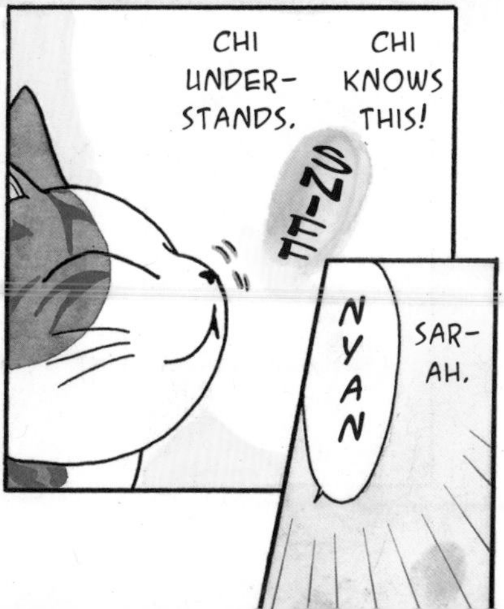
CHI KNOWS THIS!
CHI UNDER-STANDS.
SNIFF
NYAN
SAR-AH.

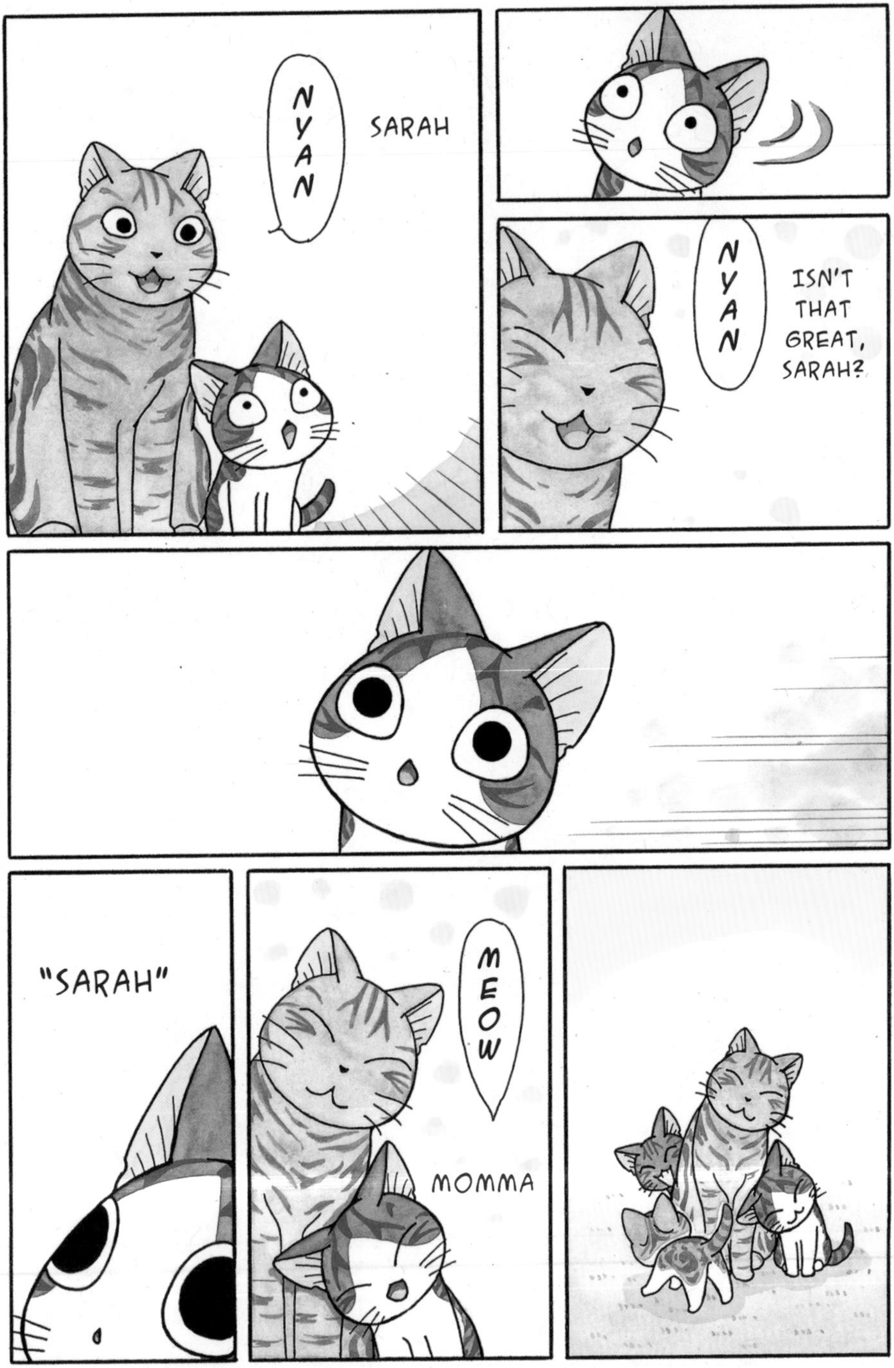
NYAN
SARAH
NYAN
ISN'T THAT GREAT, SARAH?
"SARAH"
MEOW
MOMMA

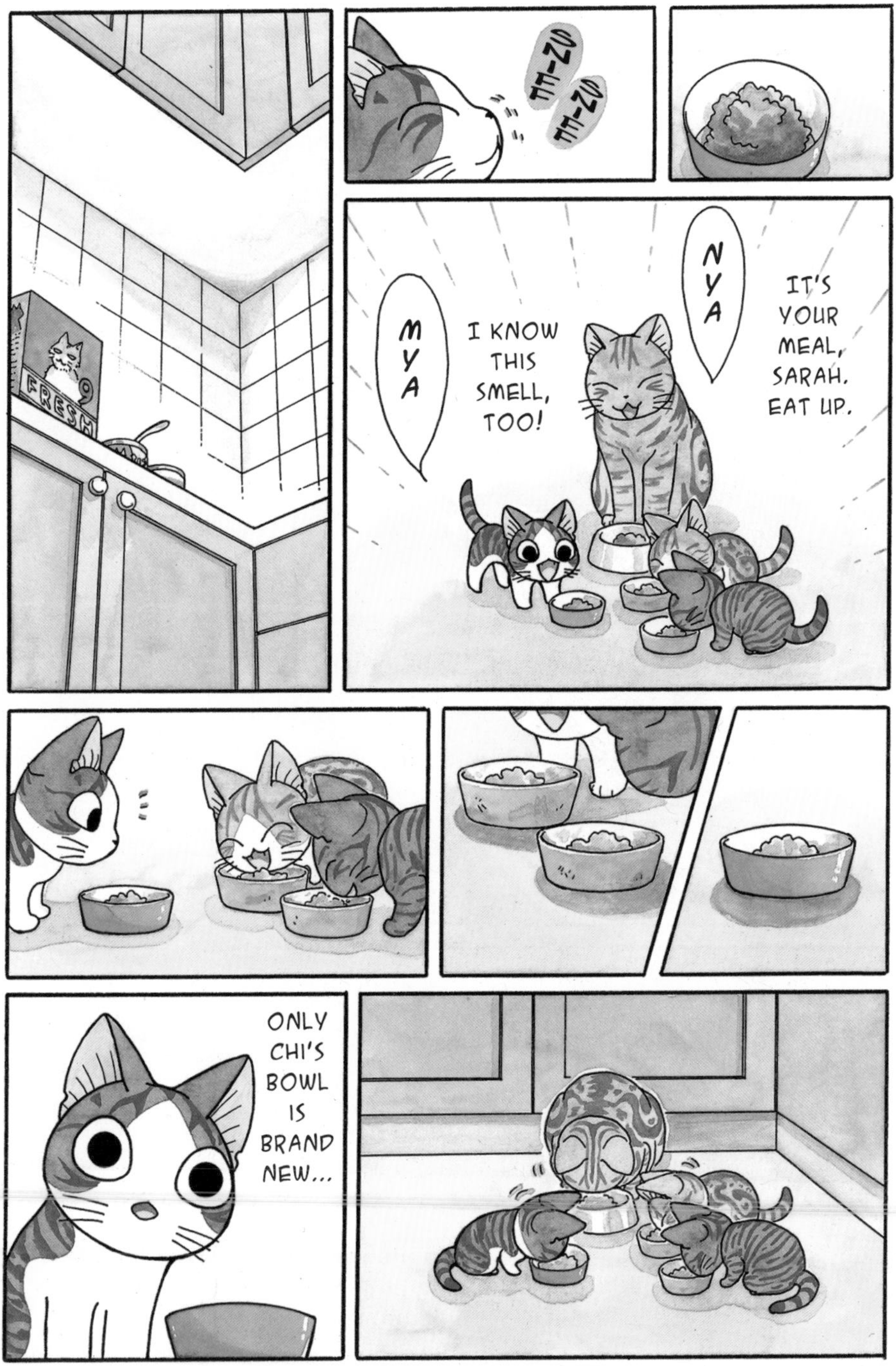
FRESH
SNIFF SNIFF
MYA
I KNOW THIS SMELL, TOO!
NYA
IT'S YOUR MEAL, SARAH. EAT UP.
ONLY CHI'S BOWL IS BRAND NEW...

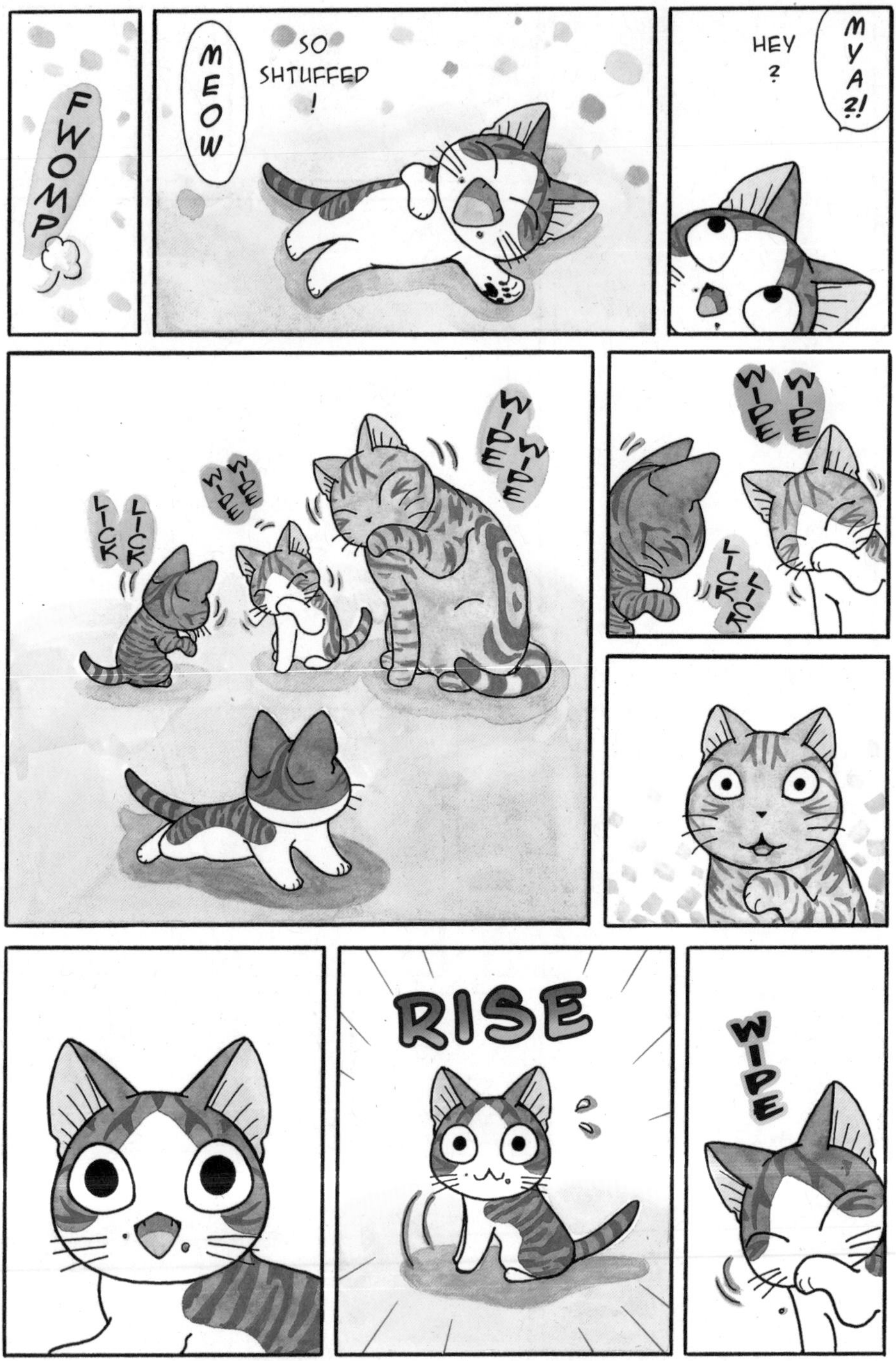
FWOMP
MEOW
SO SHTUFFED!
HEY?
MYA?!
LICK LICK
WIPE WIPE
WIPE WIPE
WIPE WIPE
LICK LICK
RISE
WIPE

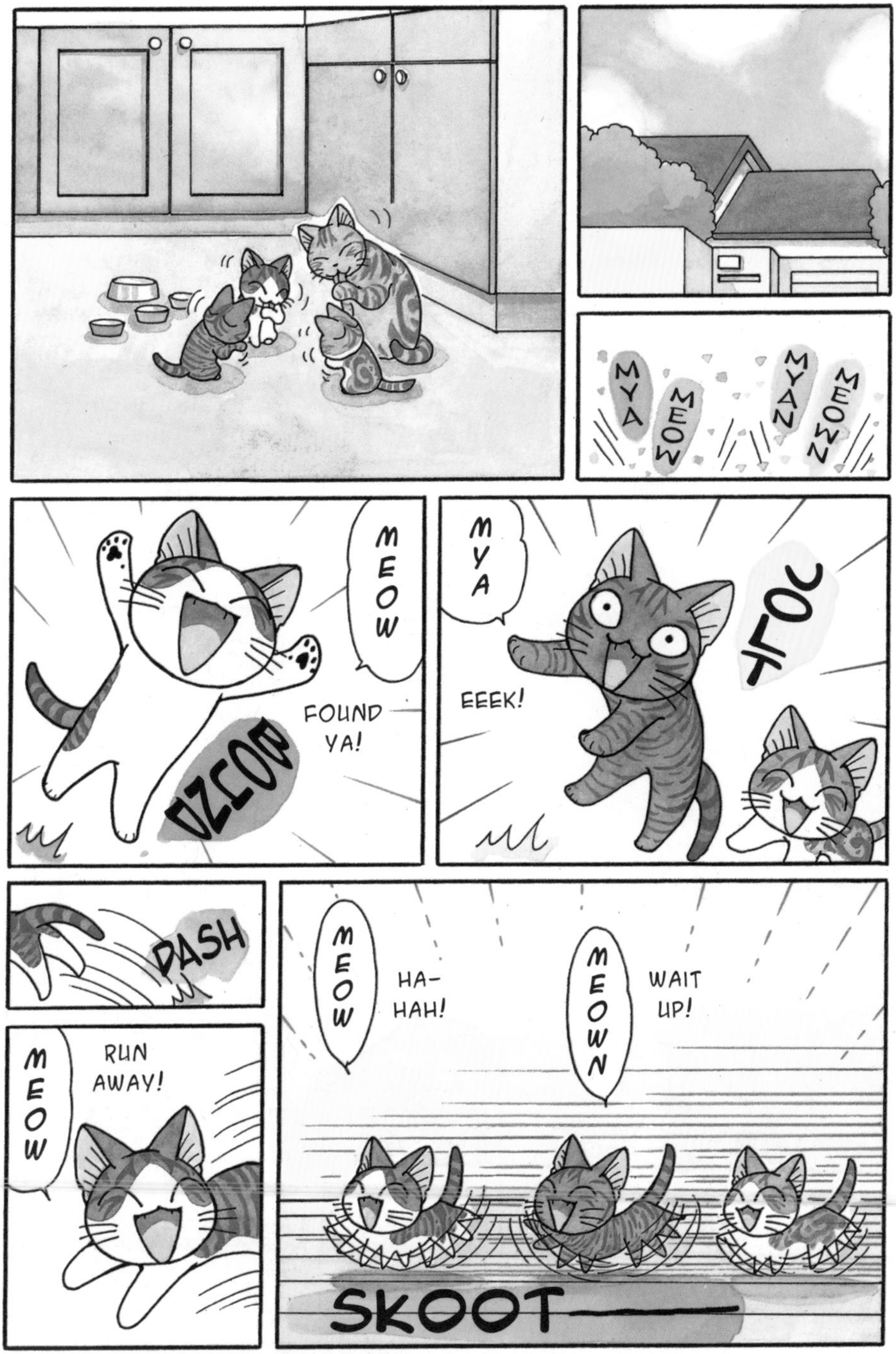
MYA
MEOW
MYAN
MEOWN
MEOW
FOUND YA!
DZOOM
MYA
EEEK!
TOC
DASH
MEOW
RUN AWAY!
MEOW
HA-HAH!
MEOWN
WAIT UP!
SKOOT——

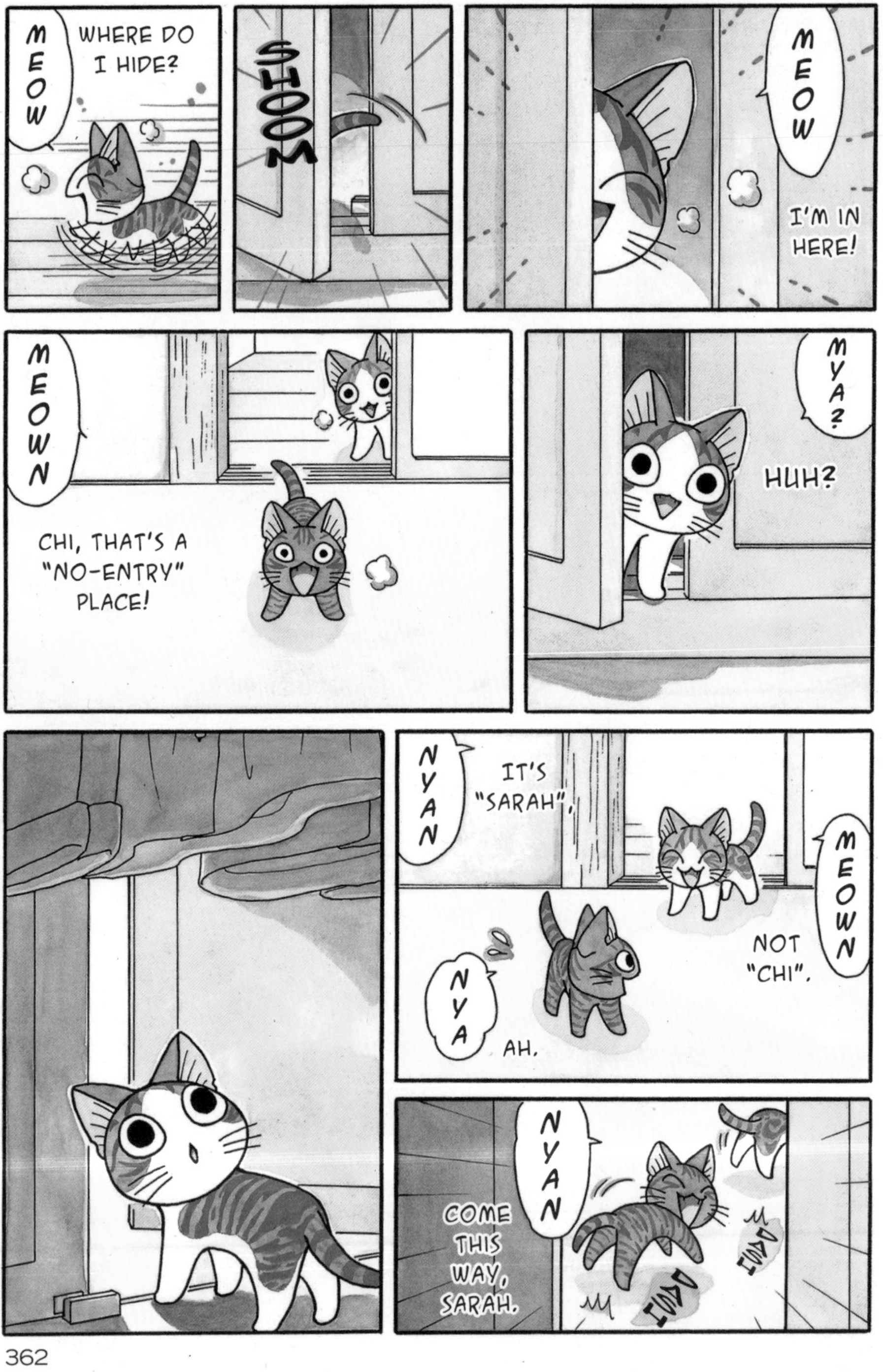
MEOW
WHERE DO I HIDE?
SHOOM
MEOW
I'M IN HERE!
MEOWN
CHI, THAT'S A "NO-ENTRY" PLACE!
MYA?
HUH?
NYAN
IT'S "SARAH",
MEOWN
NOT "CHI".
NYA
AH.
NYAN
COME THIS WAY, SARAH.

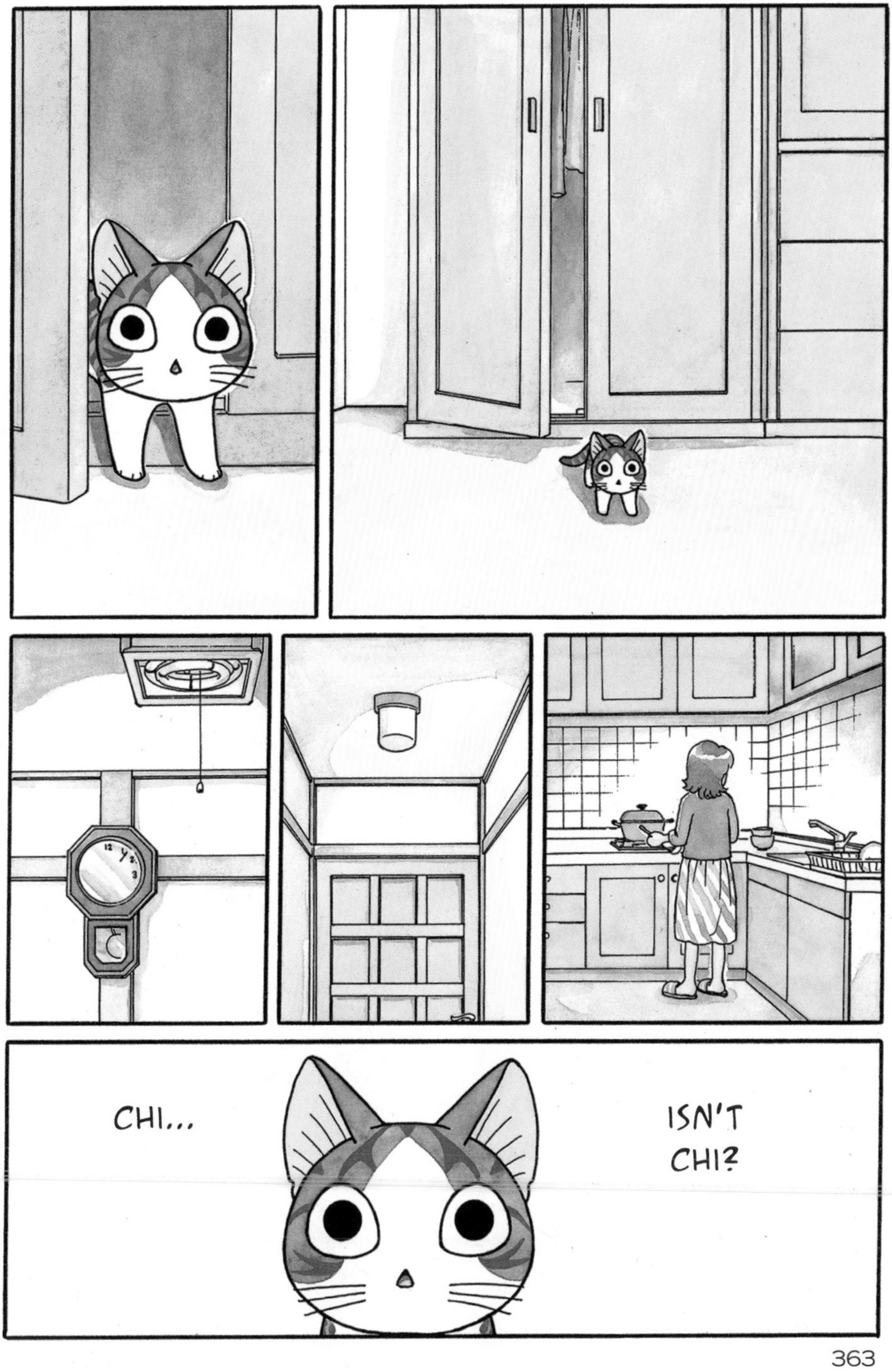
CHI...
ISN'T CHI?

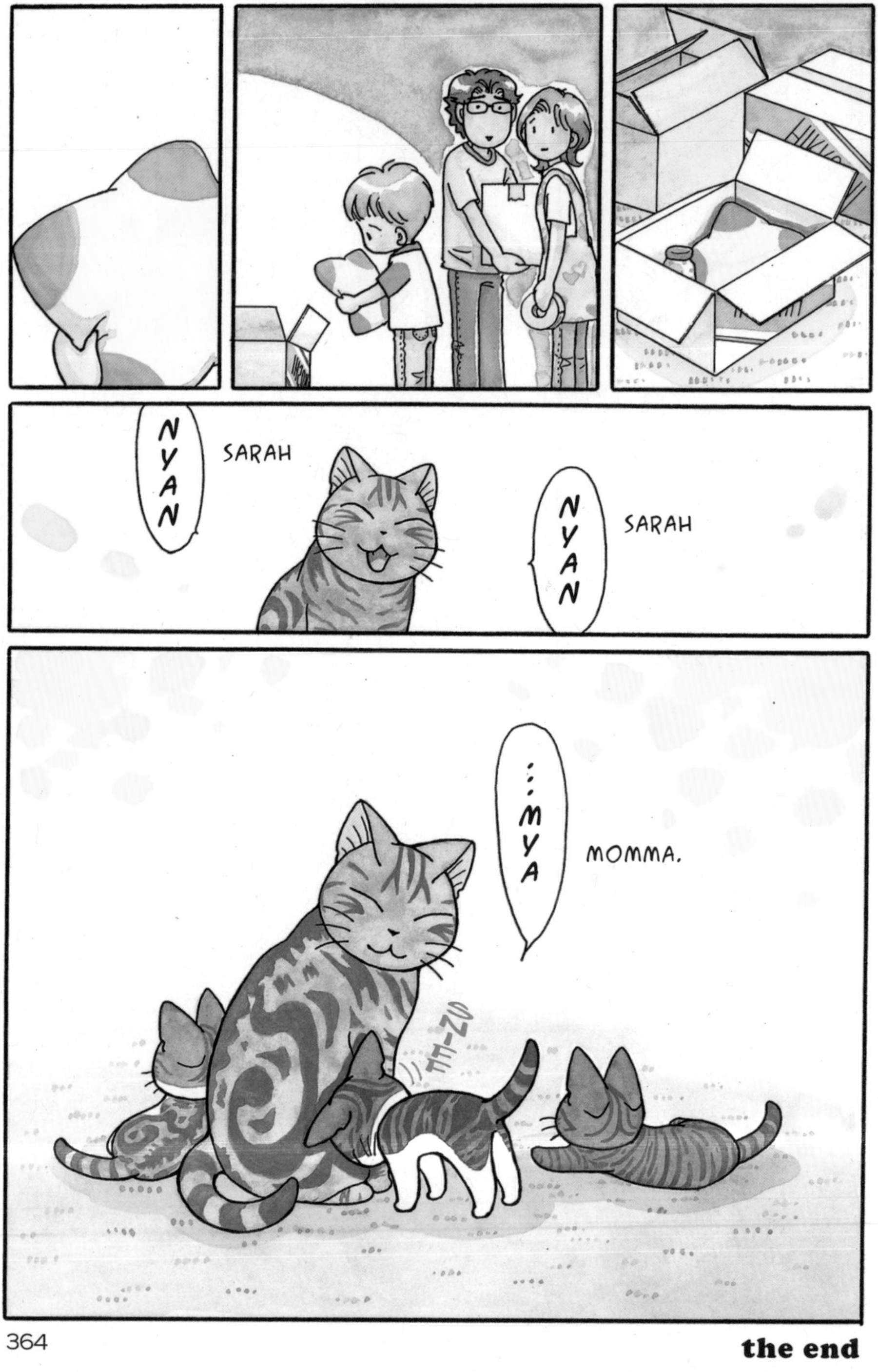
NYAN
SARAH
NYAN
SARAH
...MYA
MOMMA.
SNIFF

the end

homemade 210: a cat fits in

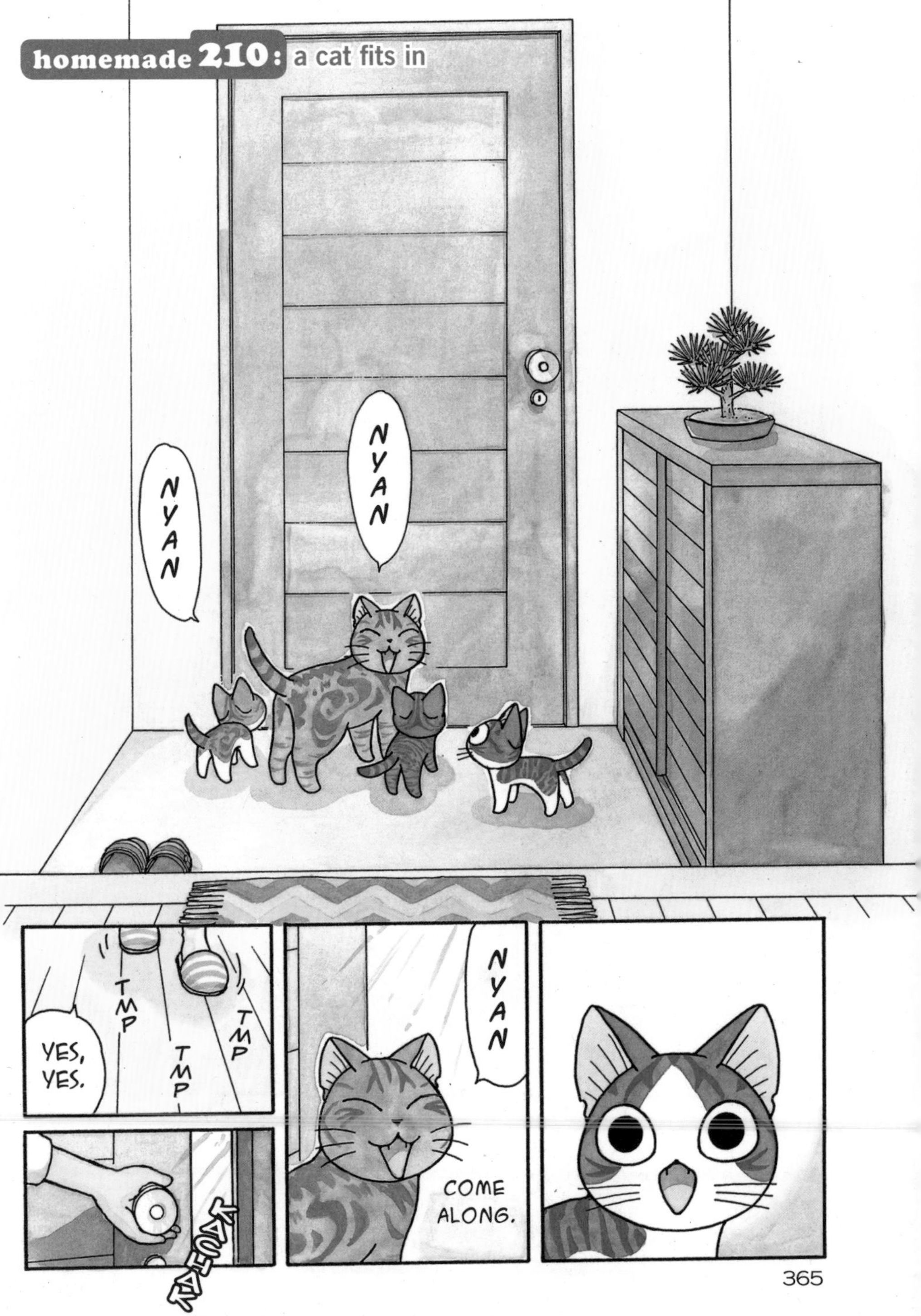
NYAN
NYAN
YES, YES.
TMP
TMP
TMP
KACHAK
NYAN
COME ALONG.

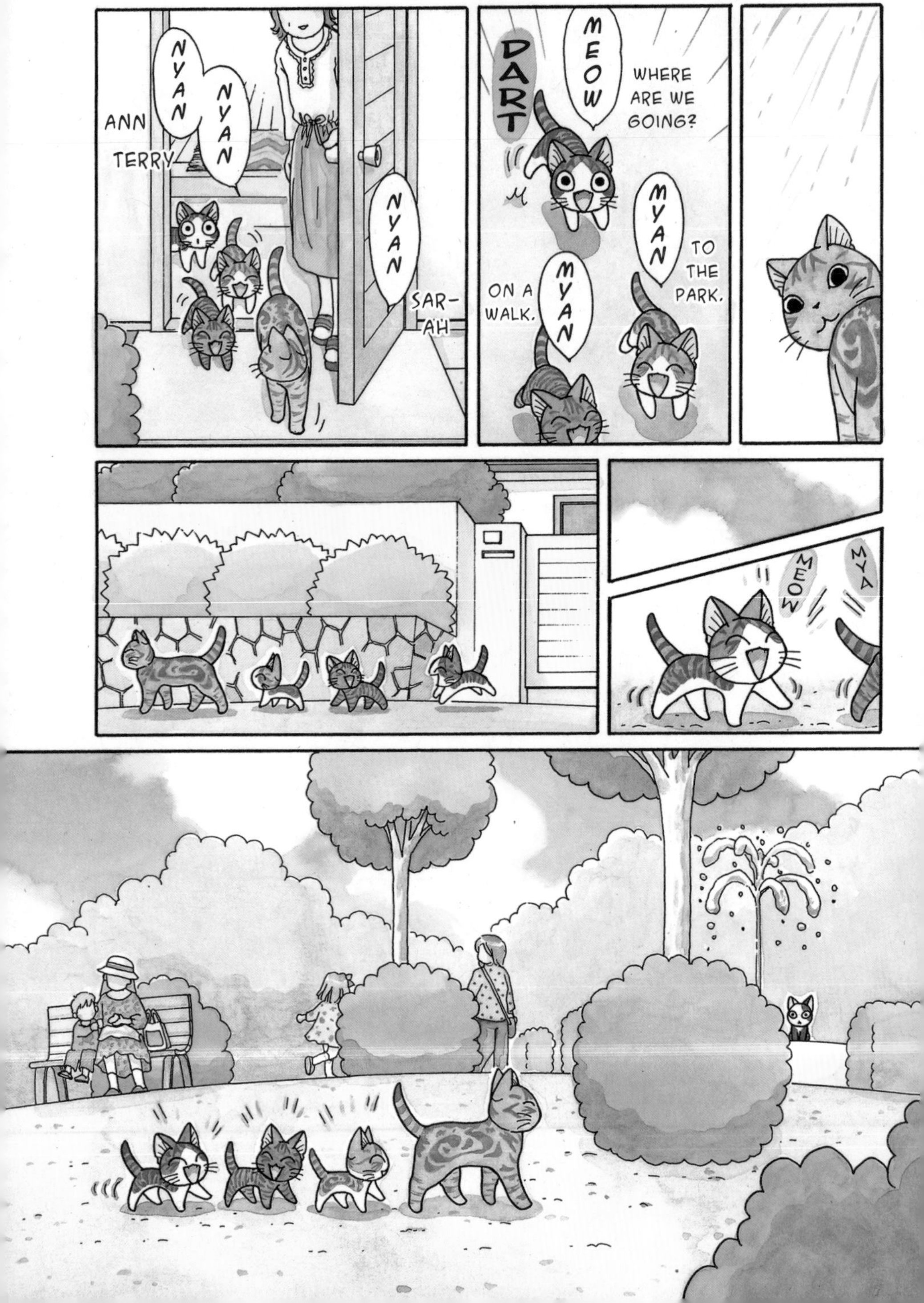
NYAN
NYAN
ANN
TERRY
NYAN
SAR-AH
DART
MEOW
WHERE ARE WE GOING?
MYAN
TO THE PARK.
ON A WALK.
MYAN
MEOW
MYA

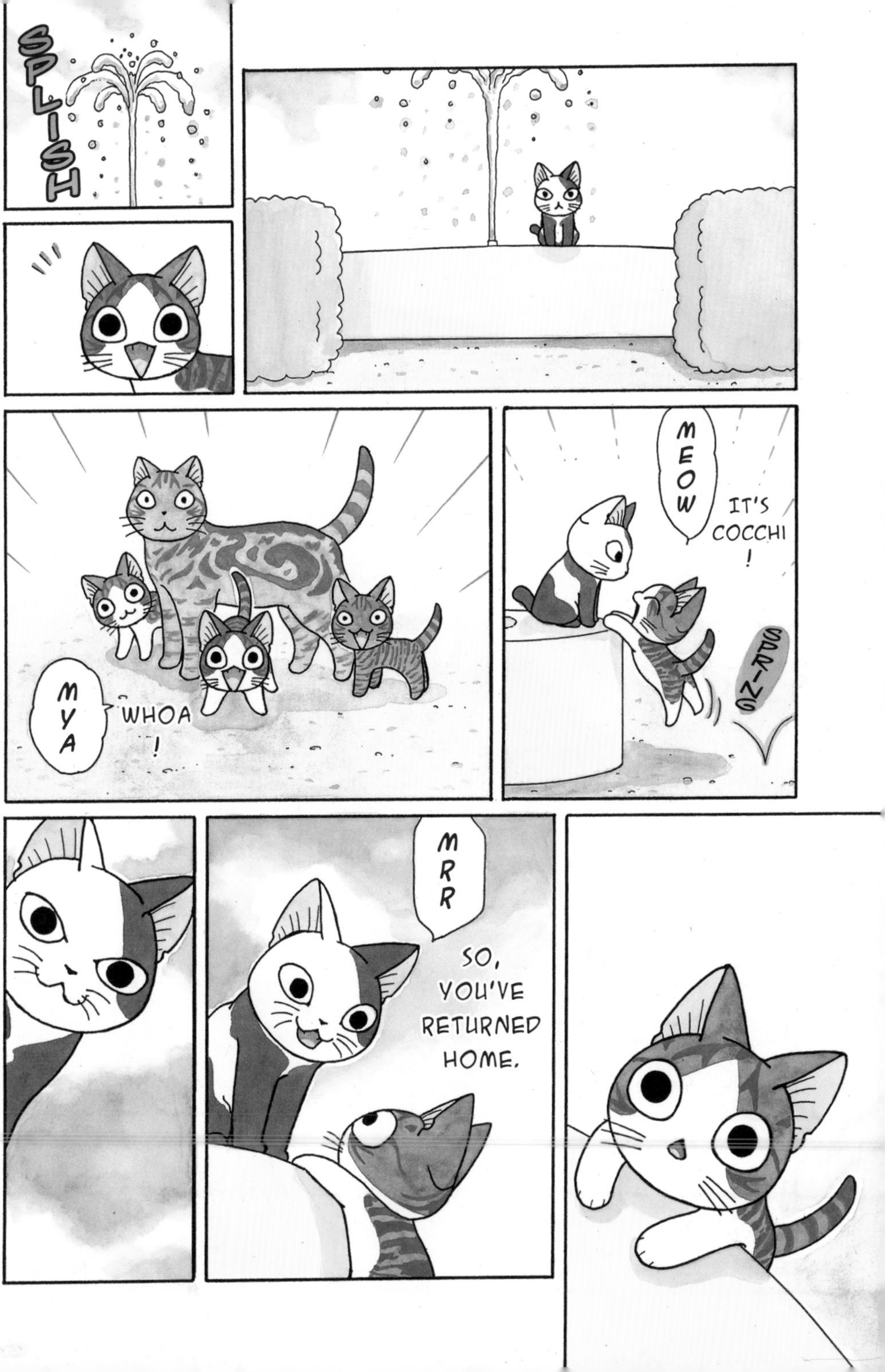
SPLISH
MYA
WHOA!
MEOW
IT'S COCCHI!
SPRING
MRR
SO, YOU'VE RETURNED HOME.

MRR

THAT'S GREAT!

MOMMA

MEOW

CHI'S RETURNED.

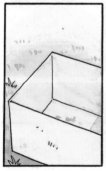

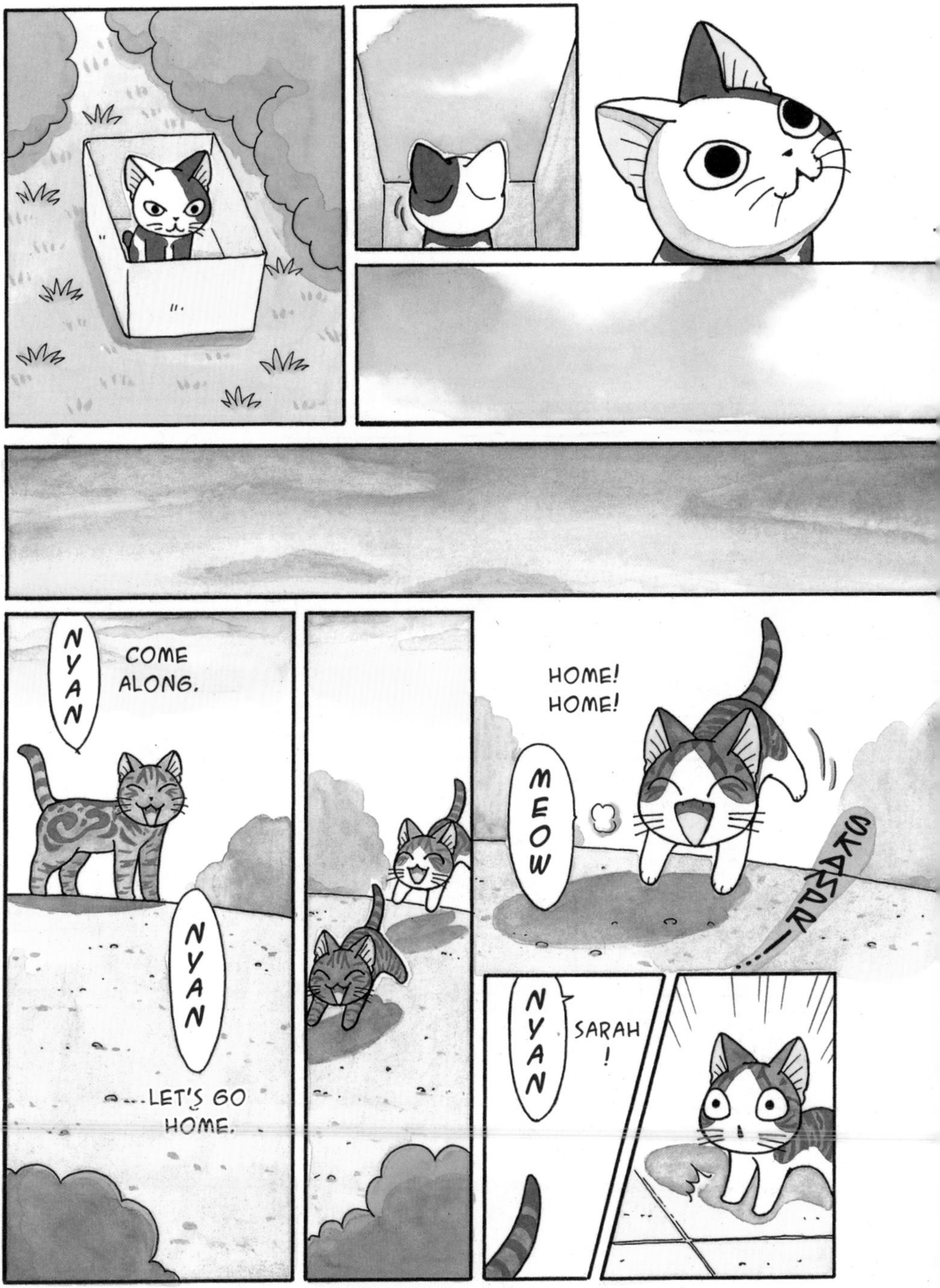
NYAN
COME ALONG.
NYAN
...LET'S GO HOME.
HOME! HOME!
MEOW
SKASPR—...
NYAN
SARAH!

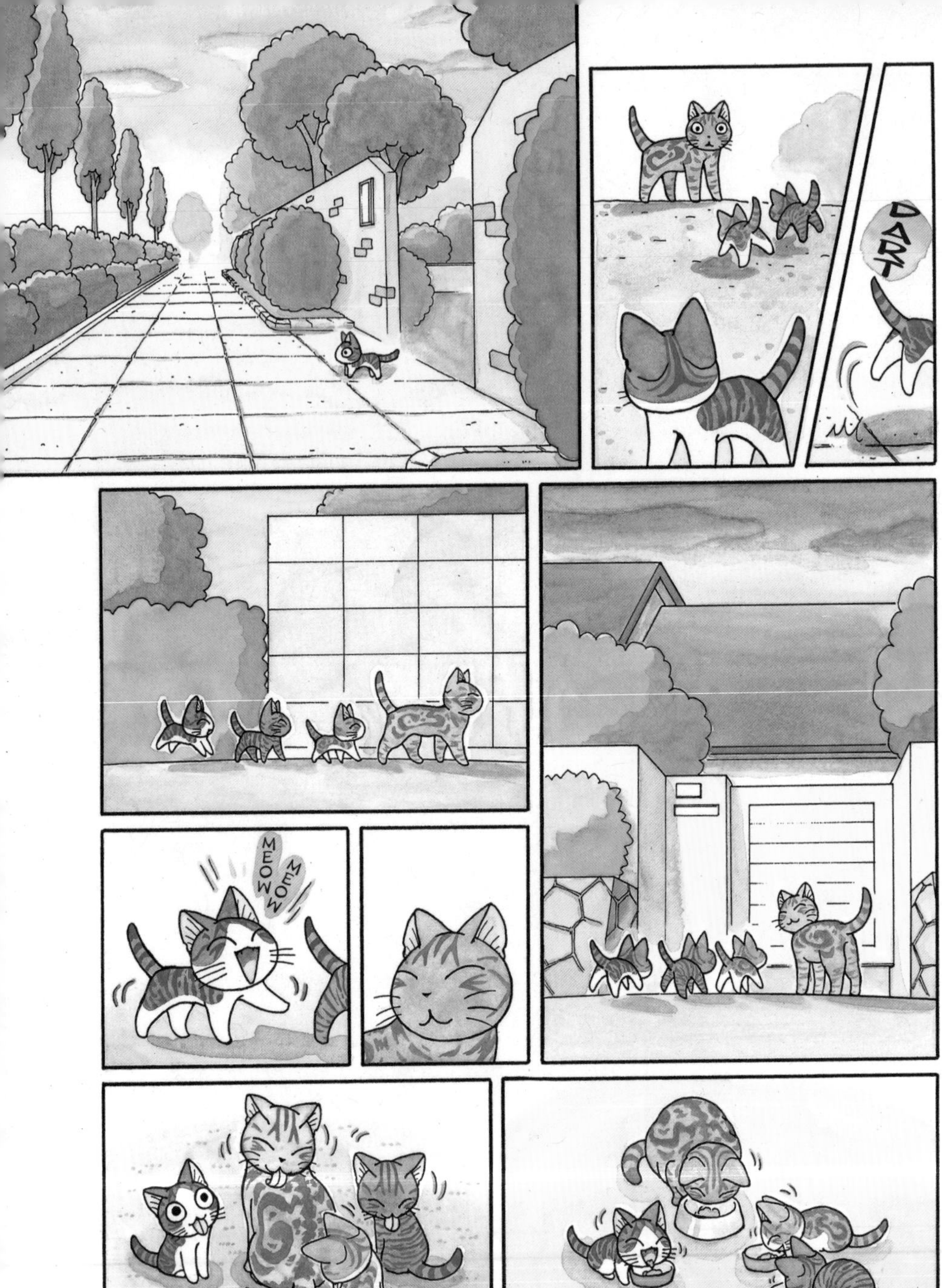
DART
MEOW MEOW

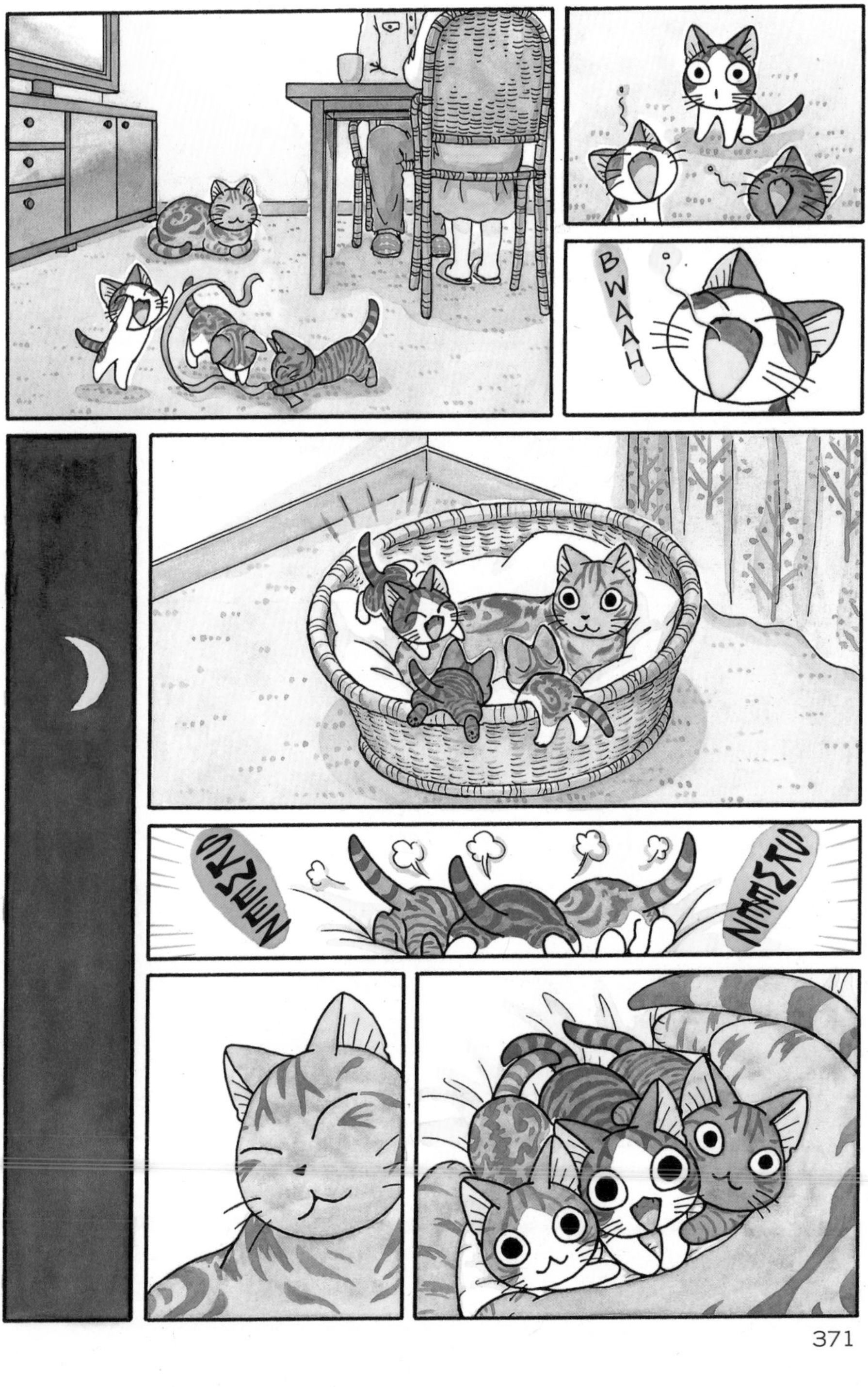
BWAAH

NYAN

GOOD
NIGHT.

ANN
TERRY
SARAH

SO
COMFY.

the end

homemade 211: a cat separates

HIKKOSHI
HIKKOSHI
HIKKOSHI
HIKKOSHI
HIKKOSHI
SHLK SHLK SHLK
SHLK
NYO
HUH?
HIKKOSHI
FRAGILE FRAGILE
THEY'RE MOV-ING?!

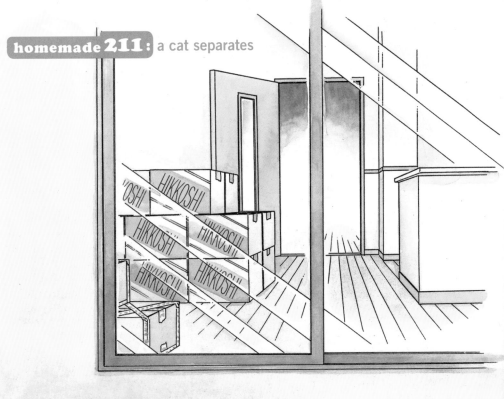

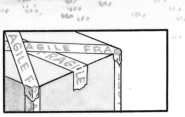

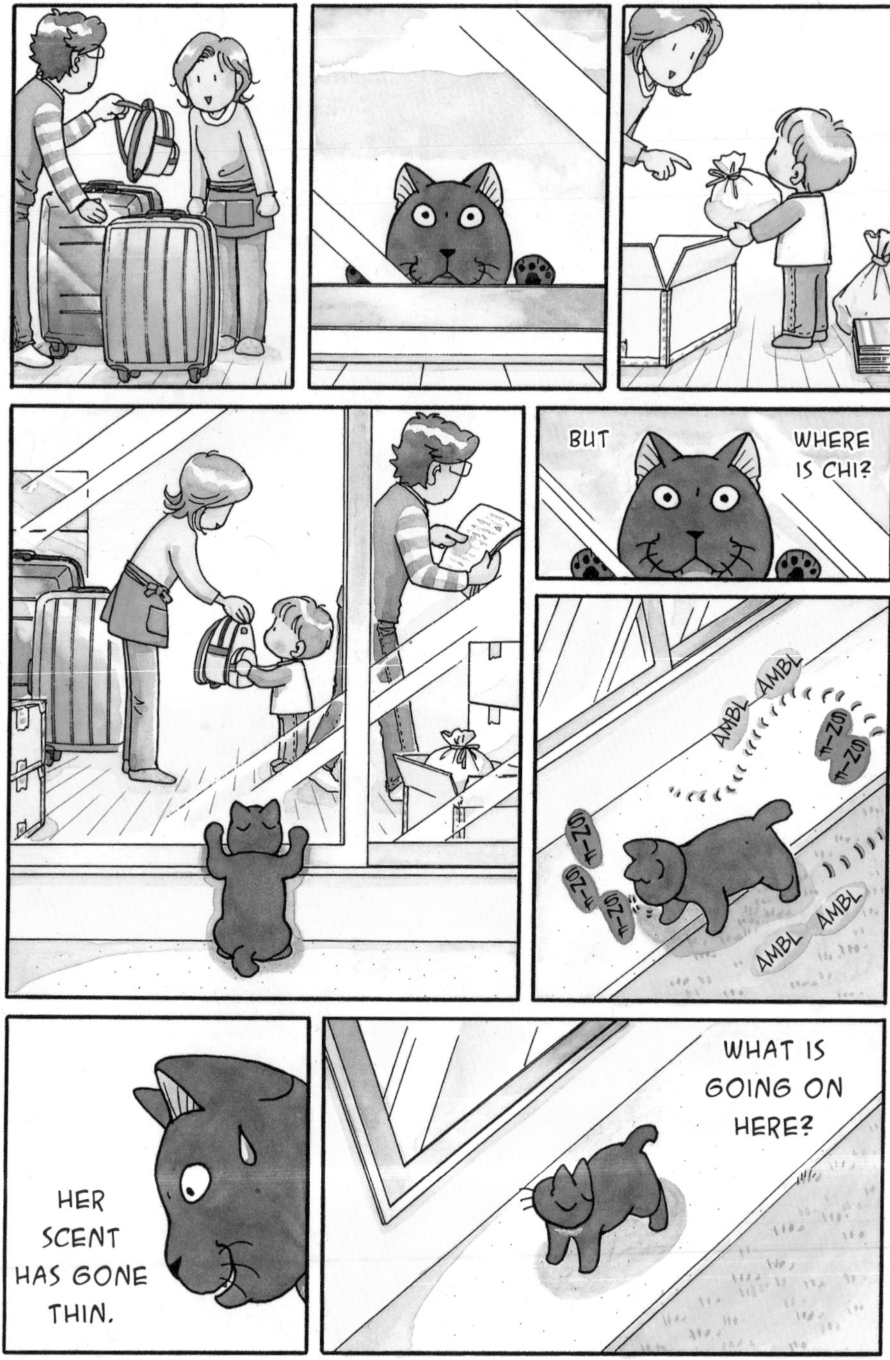
BUT
WHERE IS CHI?
AMBL AMBL
SNIF SNIF SNIF
AMBL AMBL
HER SCENT HAS GONE THIN.
WHAT IS GOING ON HERE?

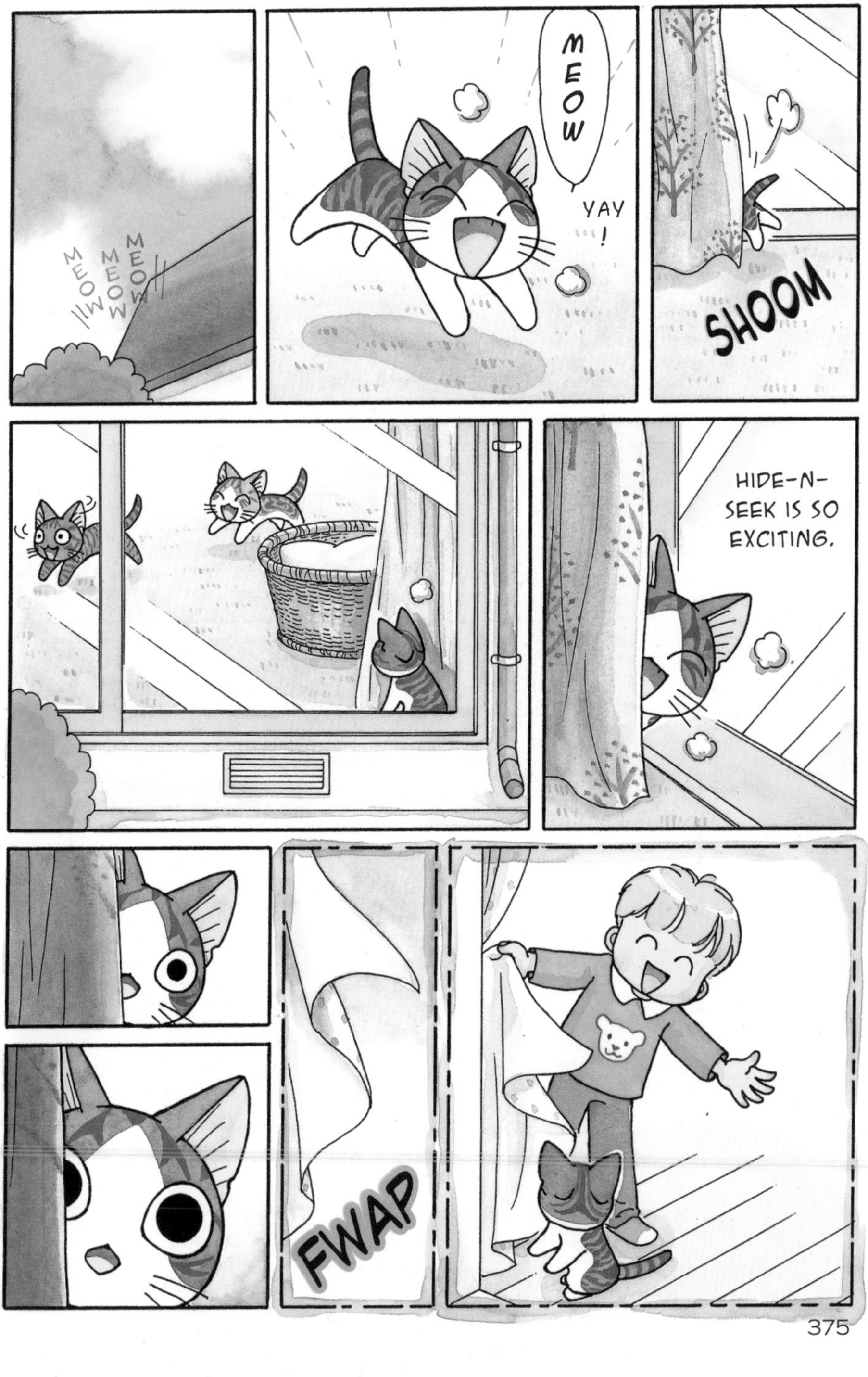
MEOW MEOW MEOW!!!
MEOW
YAY!
SHOOM
HIDE-N-SEEK IS SO EXCITING.
FWAP

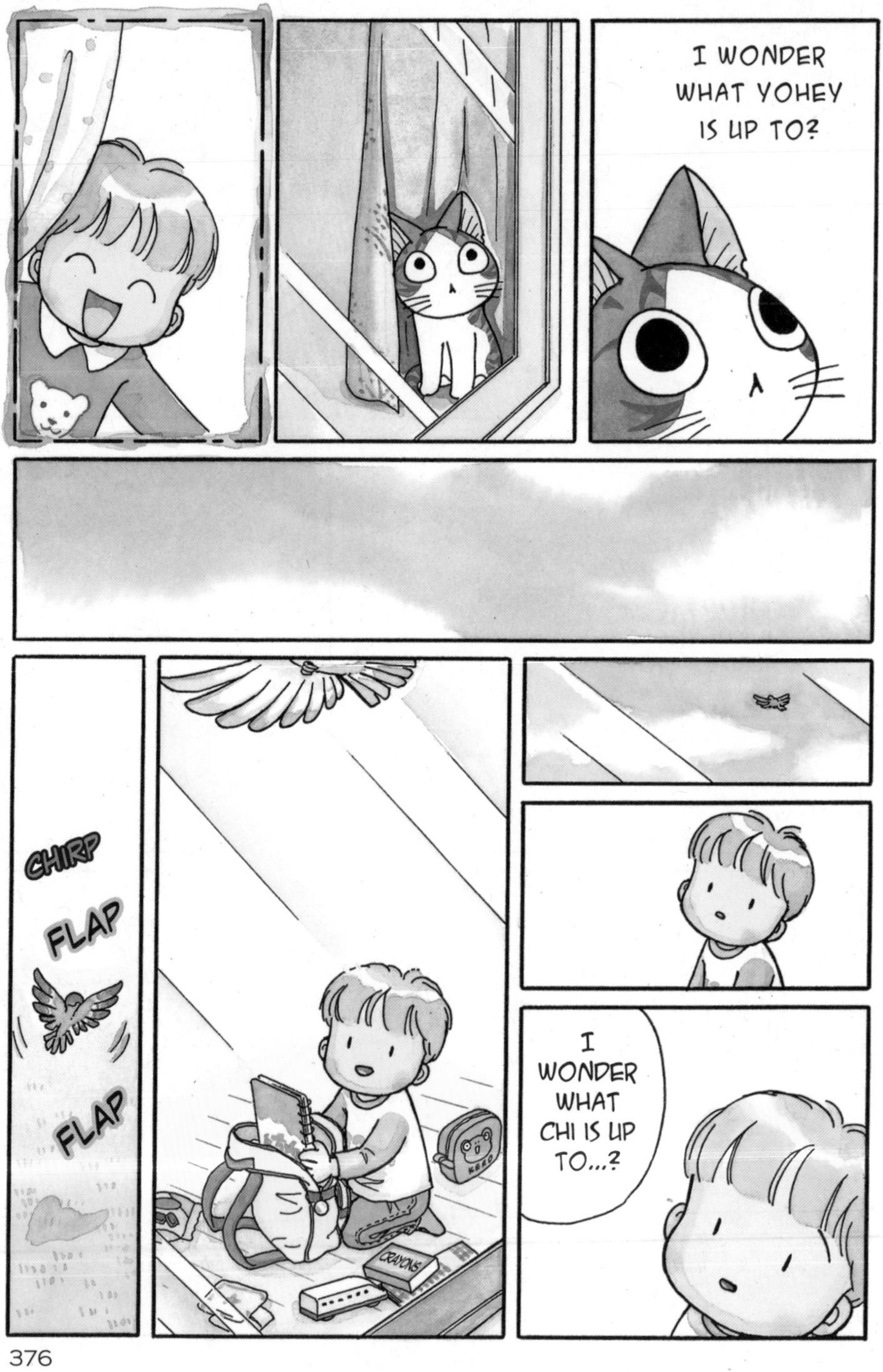
I WONDER WHAT YOHEY IS UP TO?
CHIRP
FLAP
FLAP
CRAYONS
I WONDER WHAT CHI IS UP TO...?

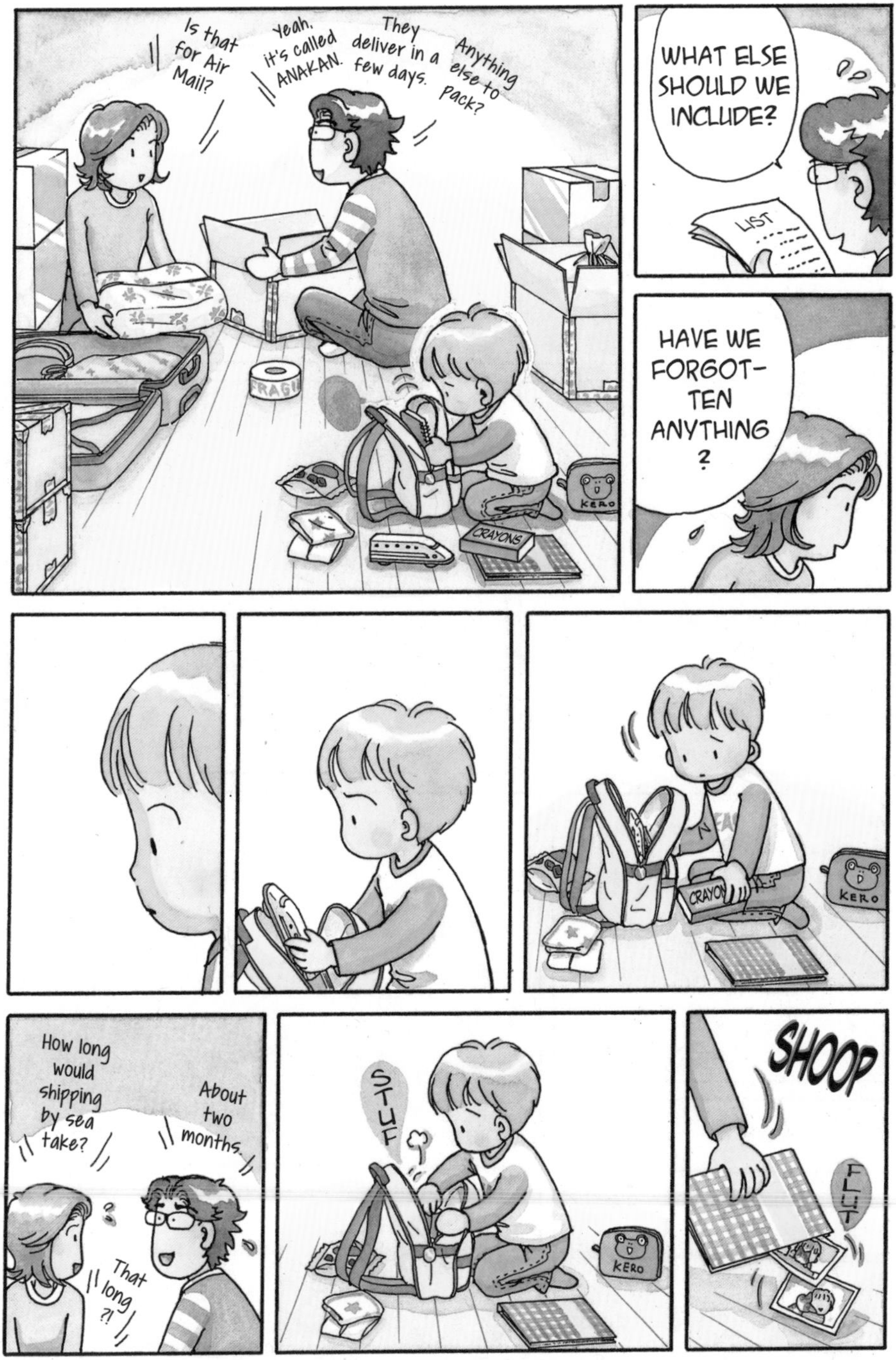
Is that for Air Mail?
Yeah, it's called ANAKAN.
They deliver in a few days.
Anything else to pack?
FRAGI
CRAYONS
KERO
LIST
WHAT ELSE SHOULD WE INCLUDE?
HAVE WE FORGOT-TEN ANYTHING?
CRAYON
KERO
How long would shipping by sea take?
About two months.
That long?!
STUF
KERO
SHOOP
FLUT

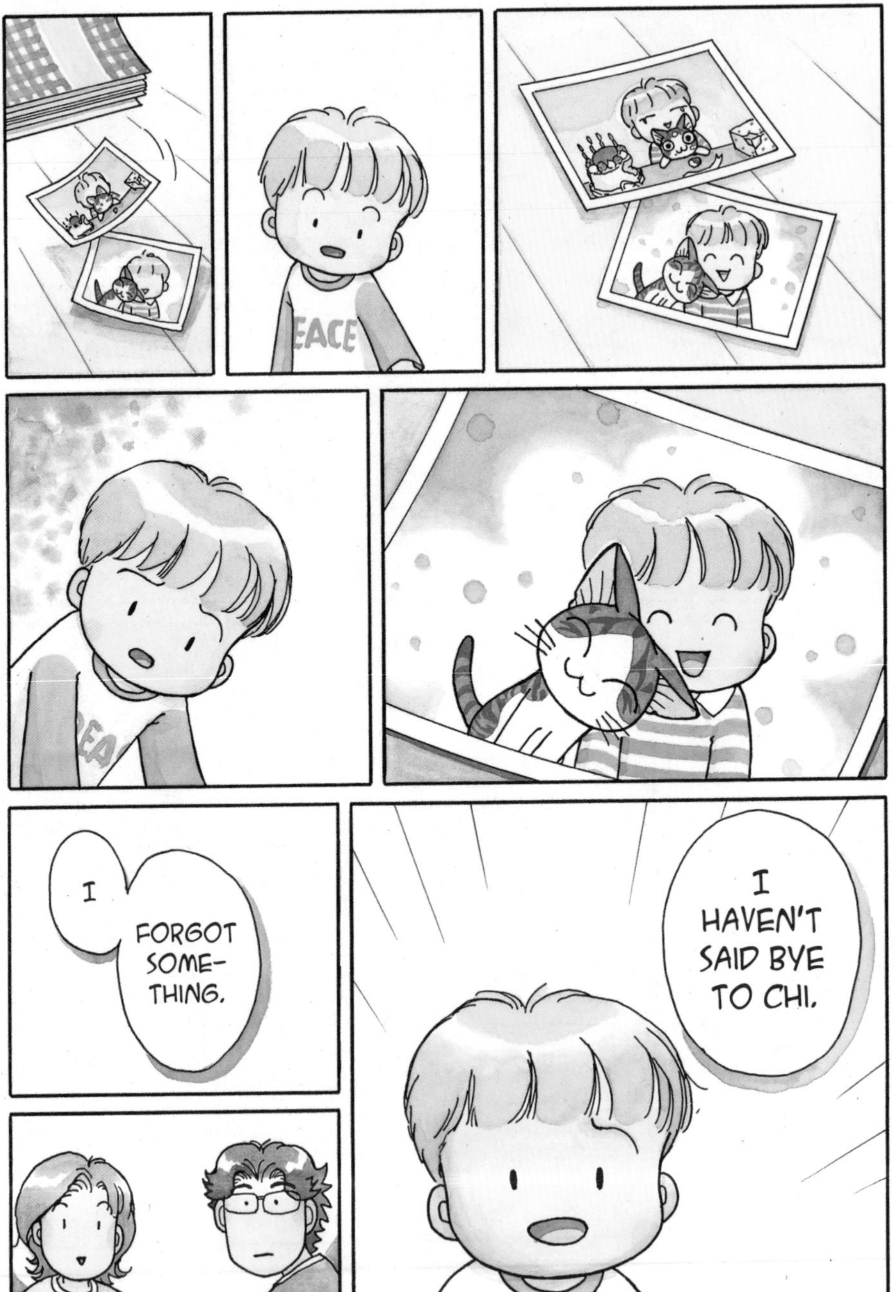
PEACE
PEA
I FORGOT SOMETHING.
I HAVEN'T SAID BYE TO CHI.

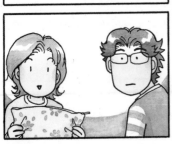

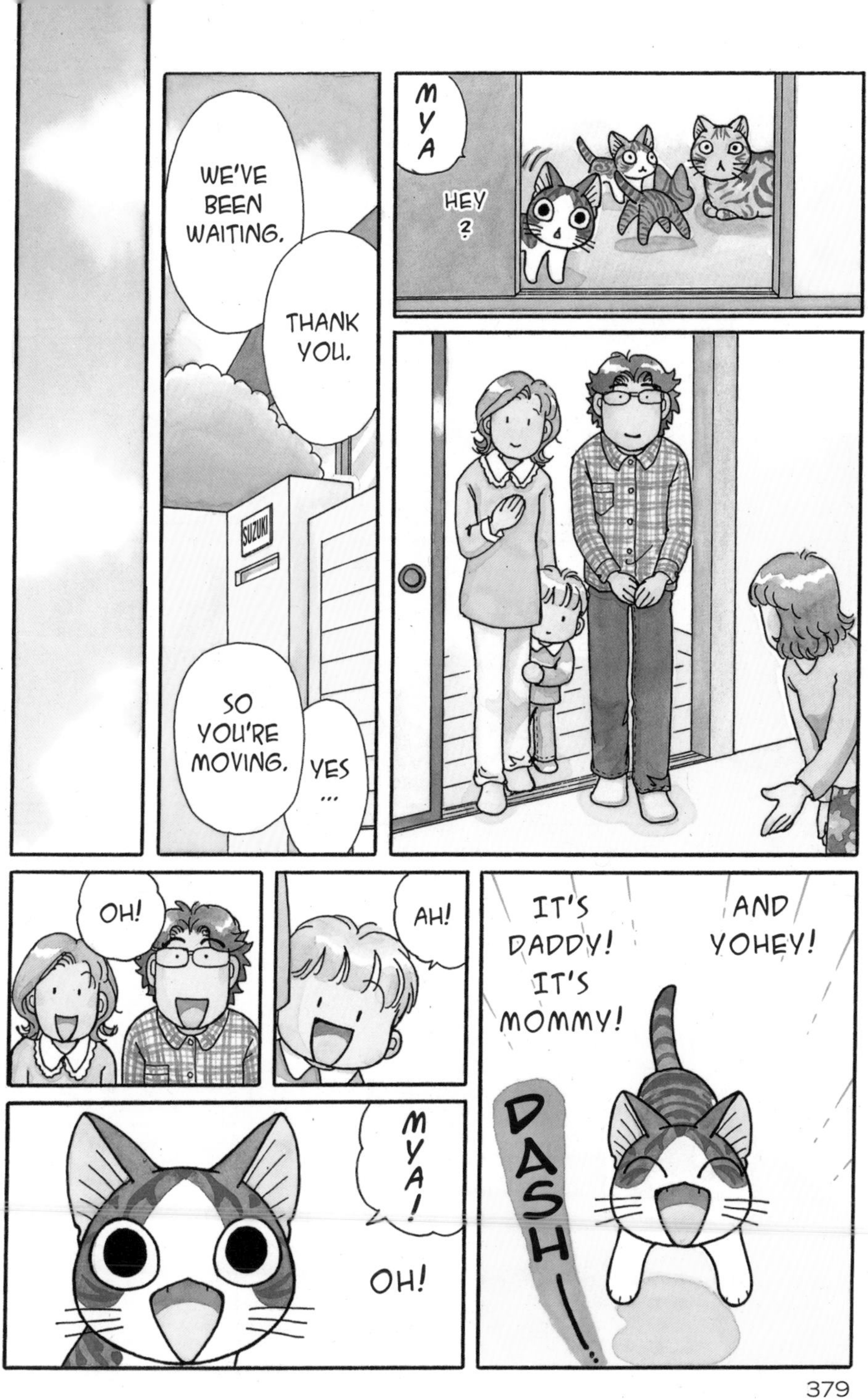
WE'VE BEEN WAITING.
THANK YOU.
SO YOU'RE MOVING.
YES ...
MYA
HEY?
OH!
AH!
IT'S DADDY! IT'S MOMMY!
AND YOHEY!
MYA!
OH!
DASH

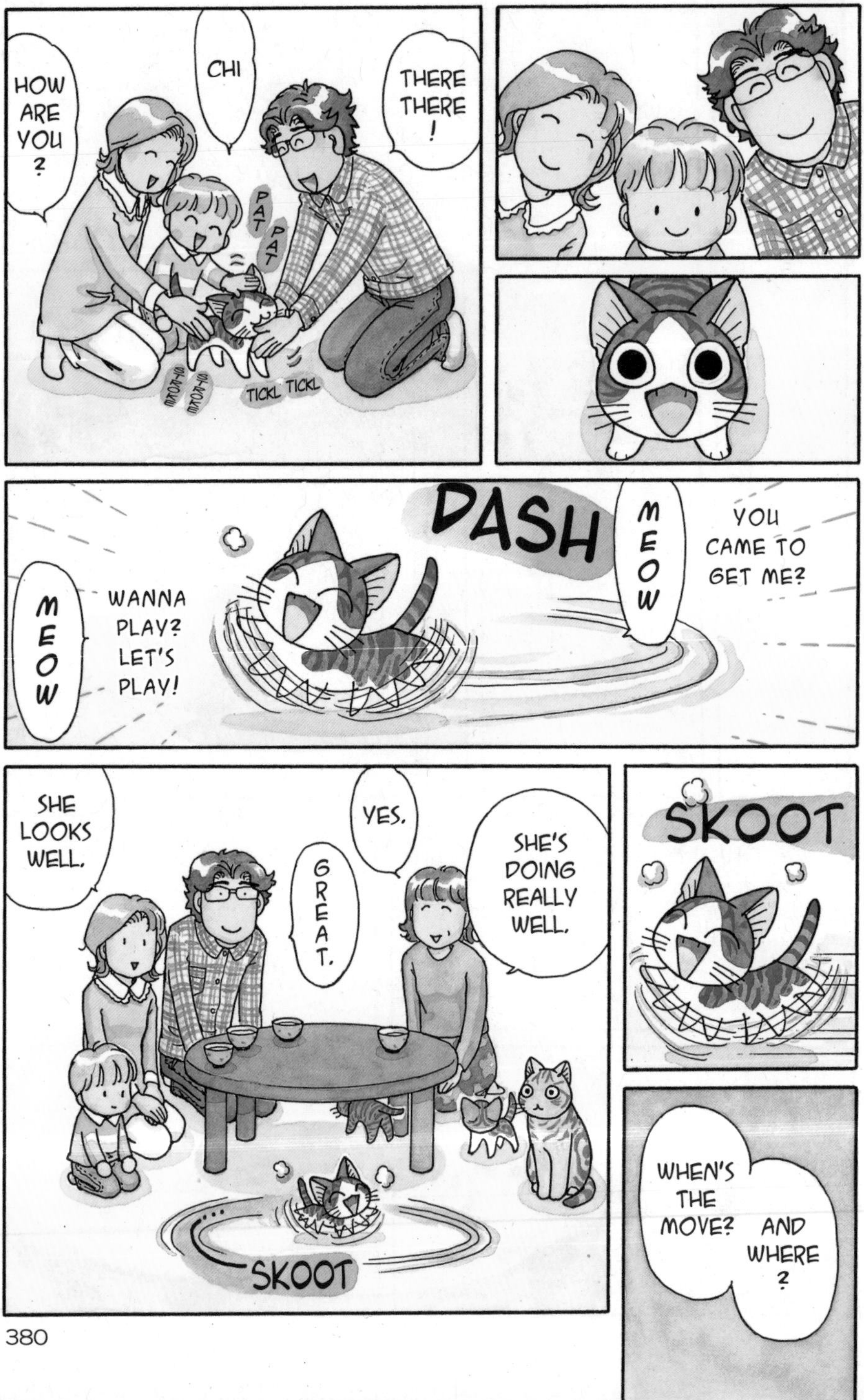

HOW ARE YOU?
CHI
THERE THERE!
PAT PAT
TICKL TICKL
MEOW
WANNA PLAY? LET'S PLAY!
DASH
MEOW
YOU CAME TO GET ME?
SHE LOOKS WELL.
YES.
GREAT.
SHE'S DOING REALLY WELL.
SKOOT
SKOOT
WHEN'S THE MOVE?
AND WHERE?

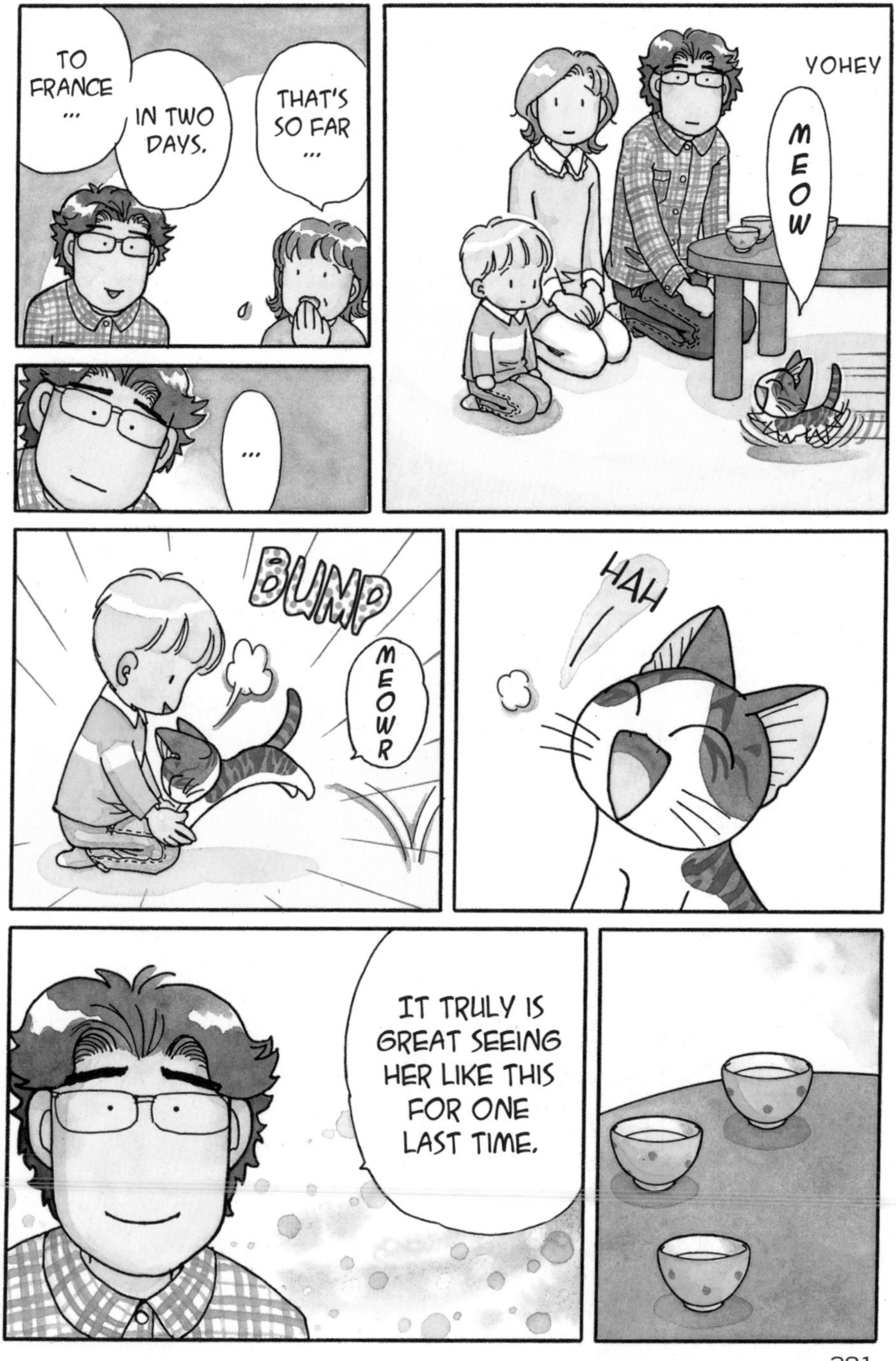
TO FRANCE ...
IN TWO DAYS.
THAT'S SO FAR ...
...
YOHEY
MEOW
BUMP
MEOWR
HAH
IT TRULY IS GREAT SEEING HER LIKE THIS FOR ONE LAST TIME.

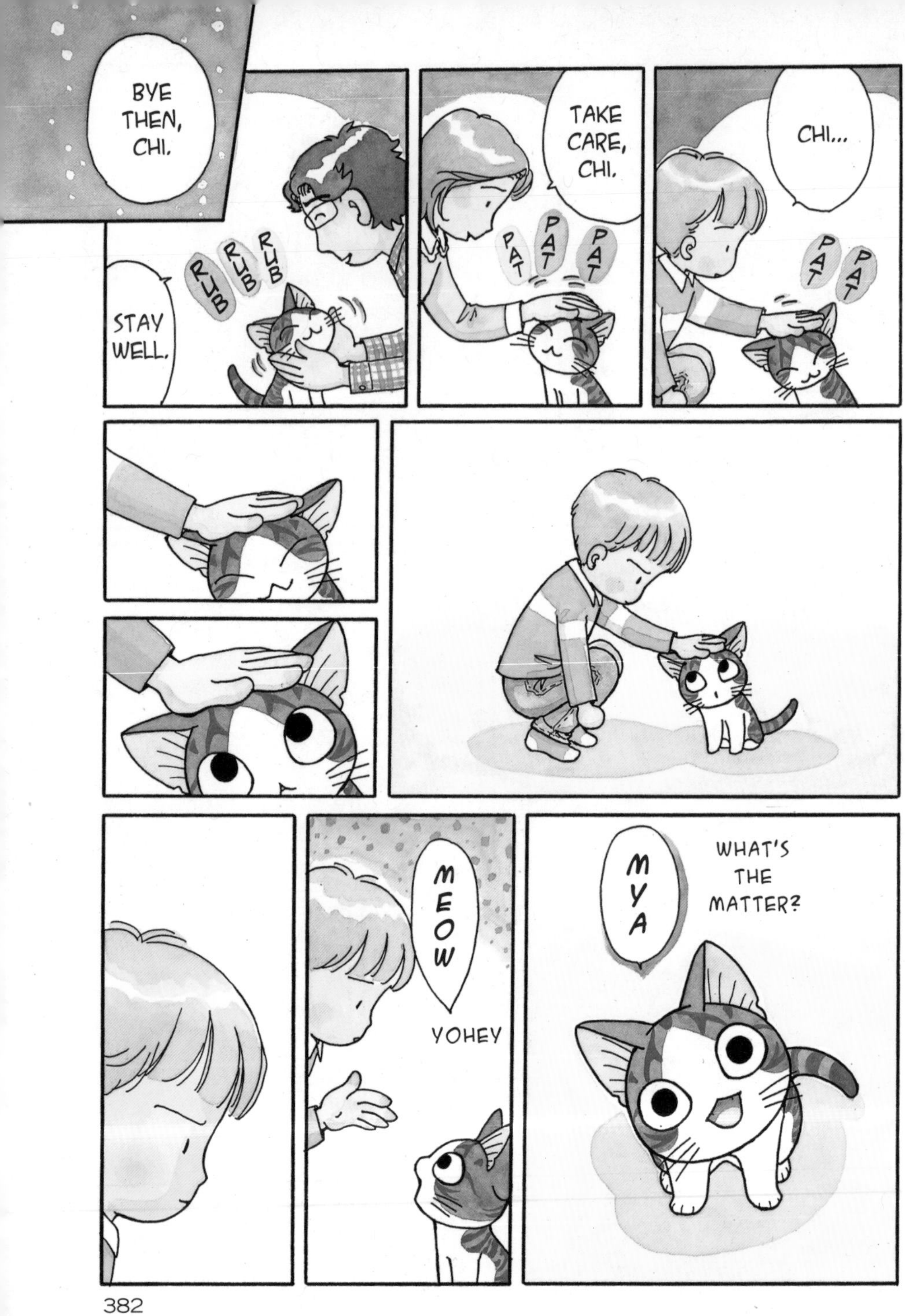
BYE THEN, CHI.
RUB RUB RUB
STAY WELL.
TAKE CARE, CHI.
PAT PAT PAT
CHI...
PAT PAT
MEOW
YOHEY
MYA
WHAT'S THE MATTER?

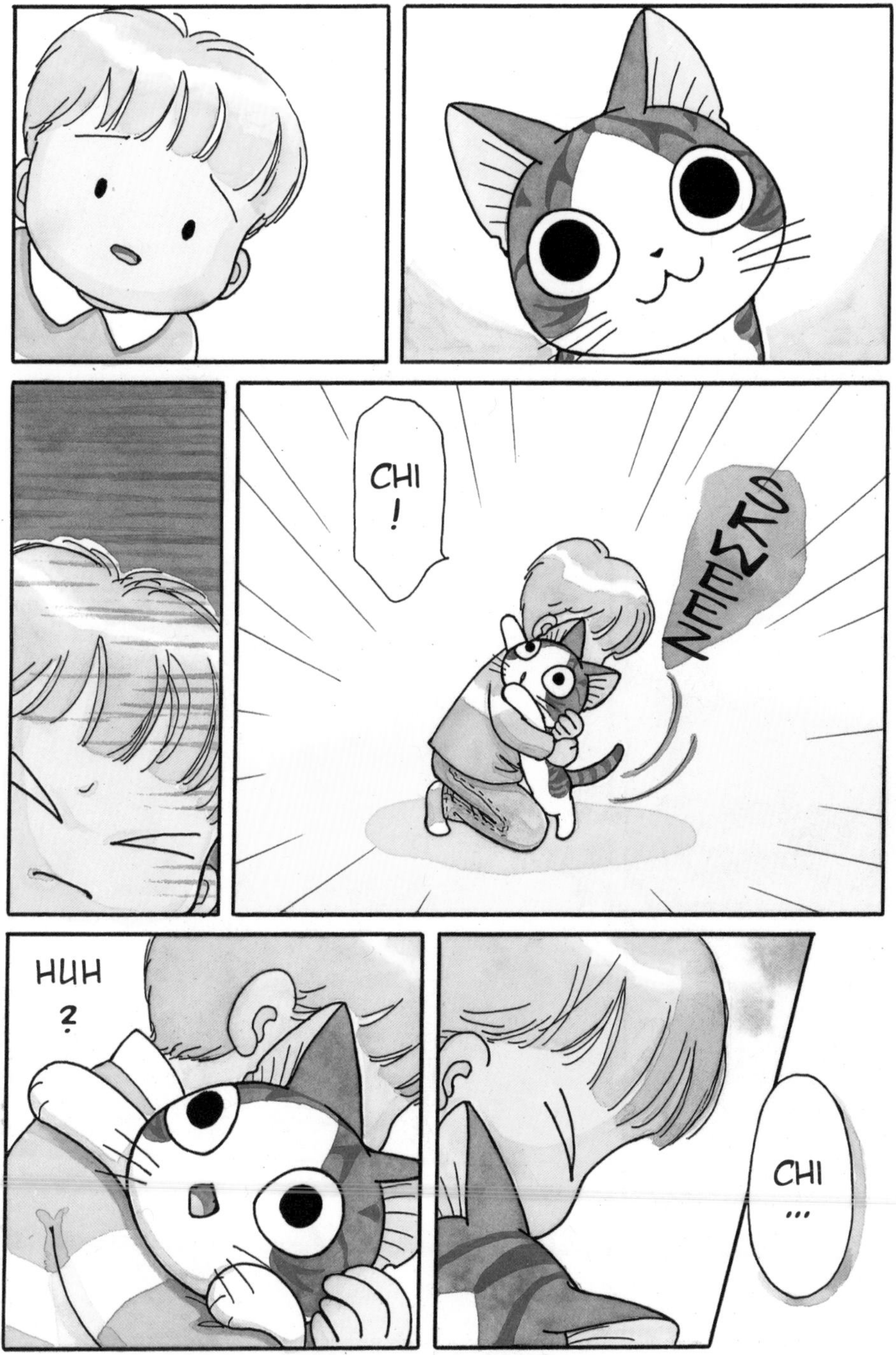
CHI !
HUH ?
CHI ...

PLIP

GOOD-BYE, CHI.

384

the end

homemade 212: a cat confirms

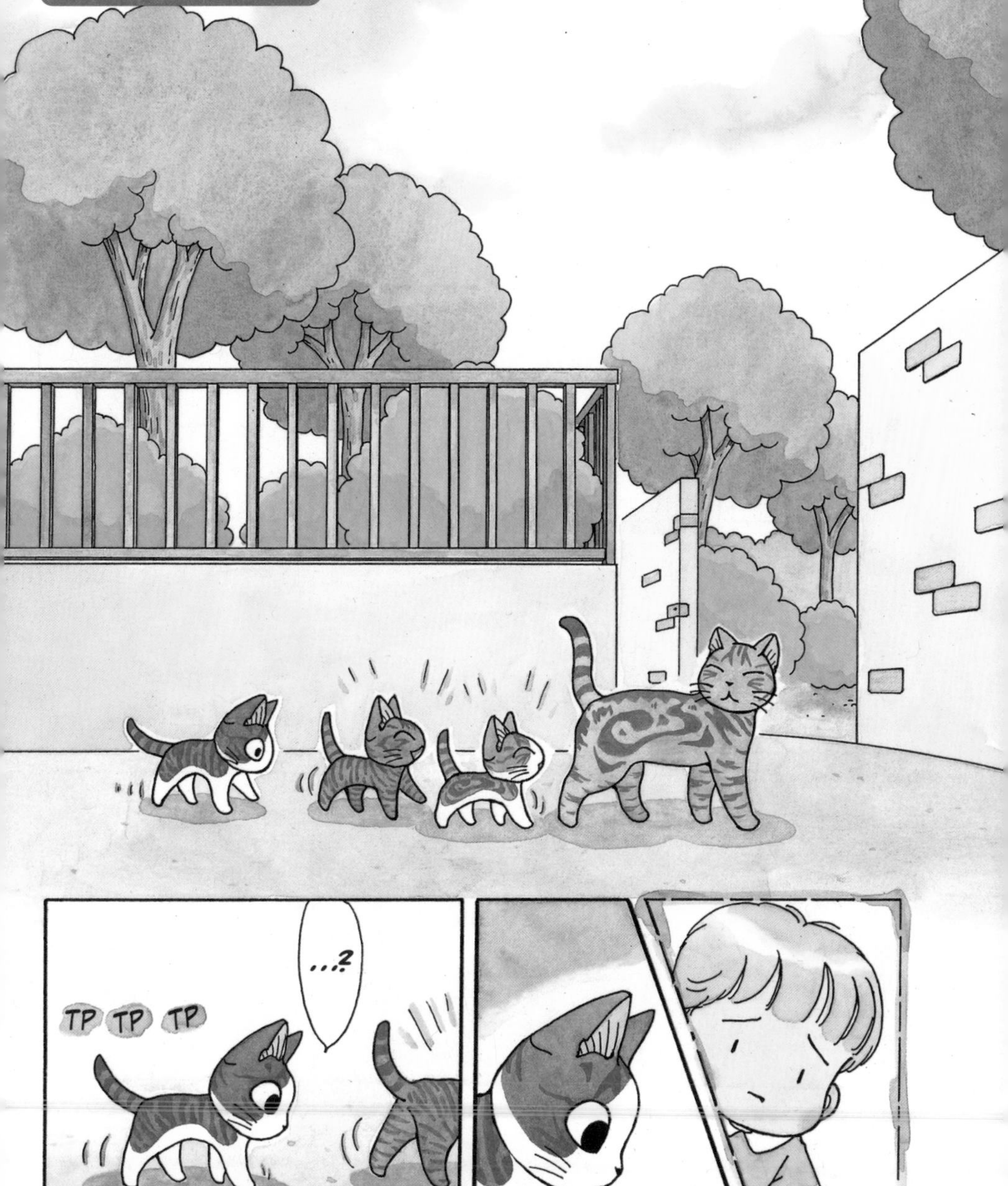
TP TP TP
...?

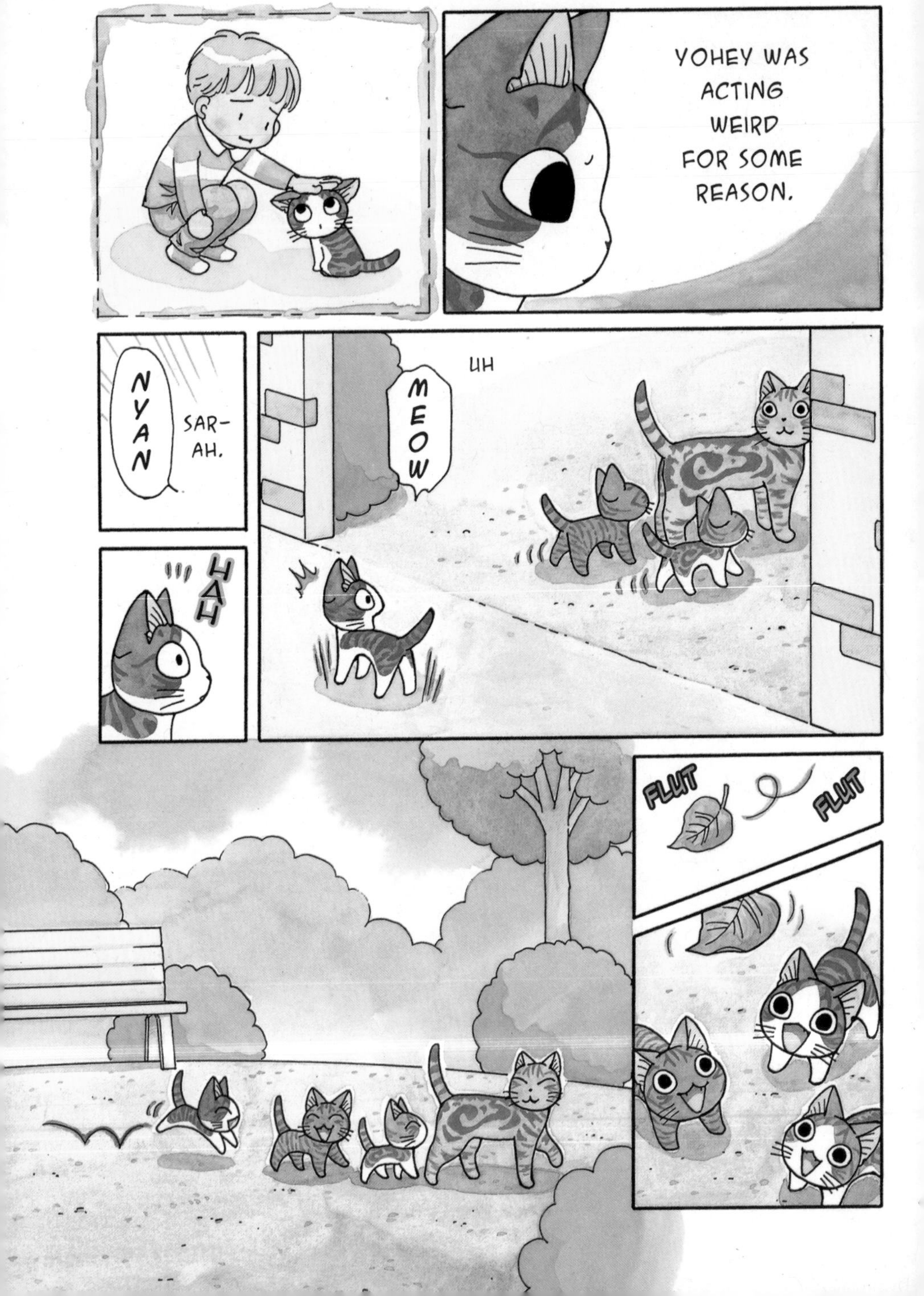
YOHEY WAS ACTING WEIRD FOR SOME REASON.
NYAN
SAR-AH.
HAH
MEOW
UH
FLUT
FLUT

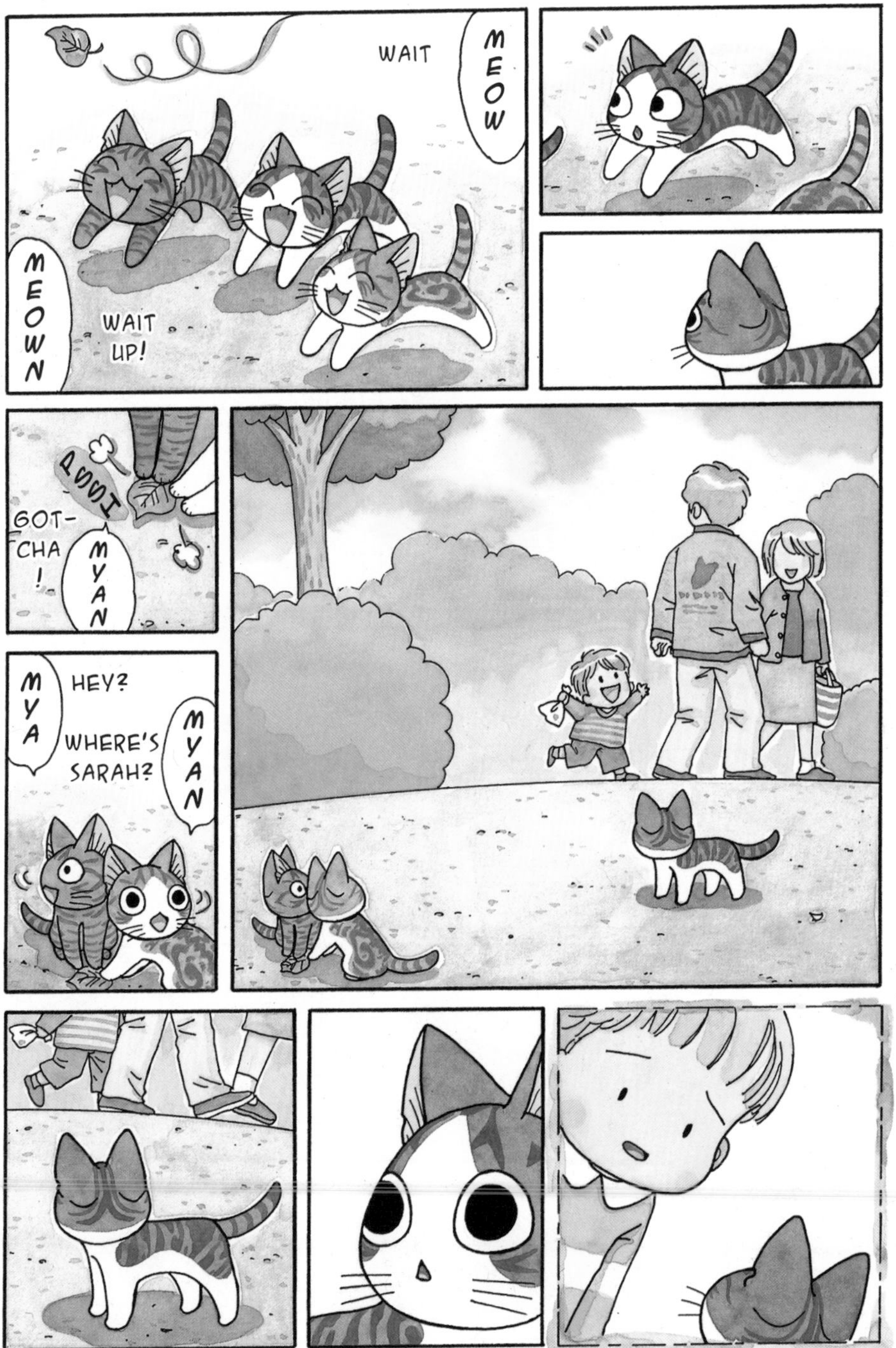
WAIT
MEOW
MEOWN
WAIT UP!
GOT-CHA!
MYAN
MYA
HEY?
WHERE'S SARAH?
MYAN

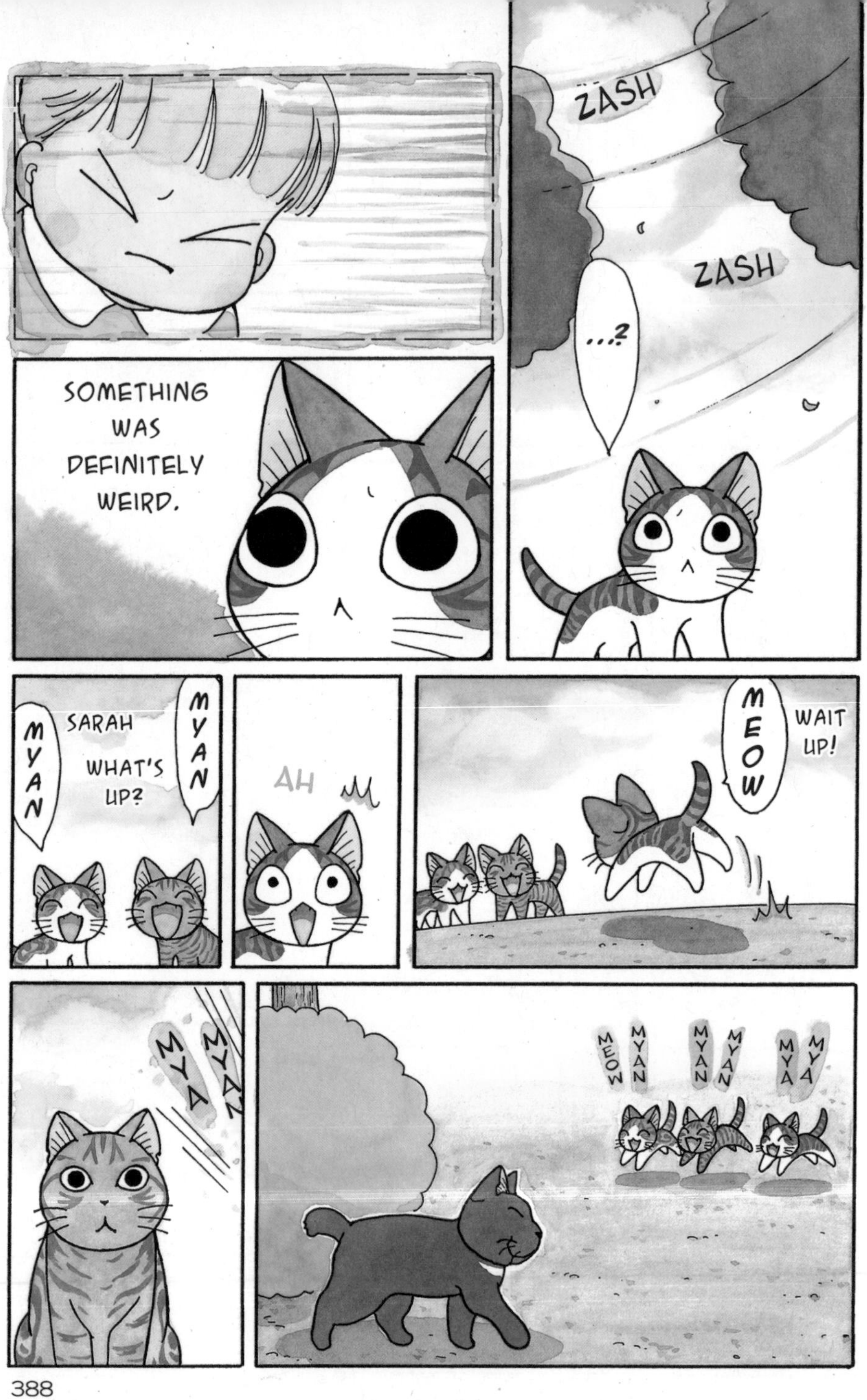
SOMETHING WAS DEFINITELY WEIRD.
ZASH
ZASH
...?
MYAN
SARAH
WHAT'S UP?
MYAN
AH
MEOW
WAIT UP!
MYA
MYAN
MEOW
MYAN
MYAN
MYAN
MYA
MYA

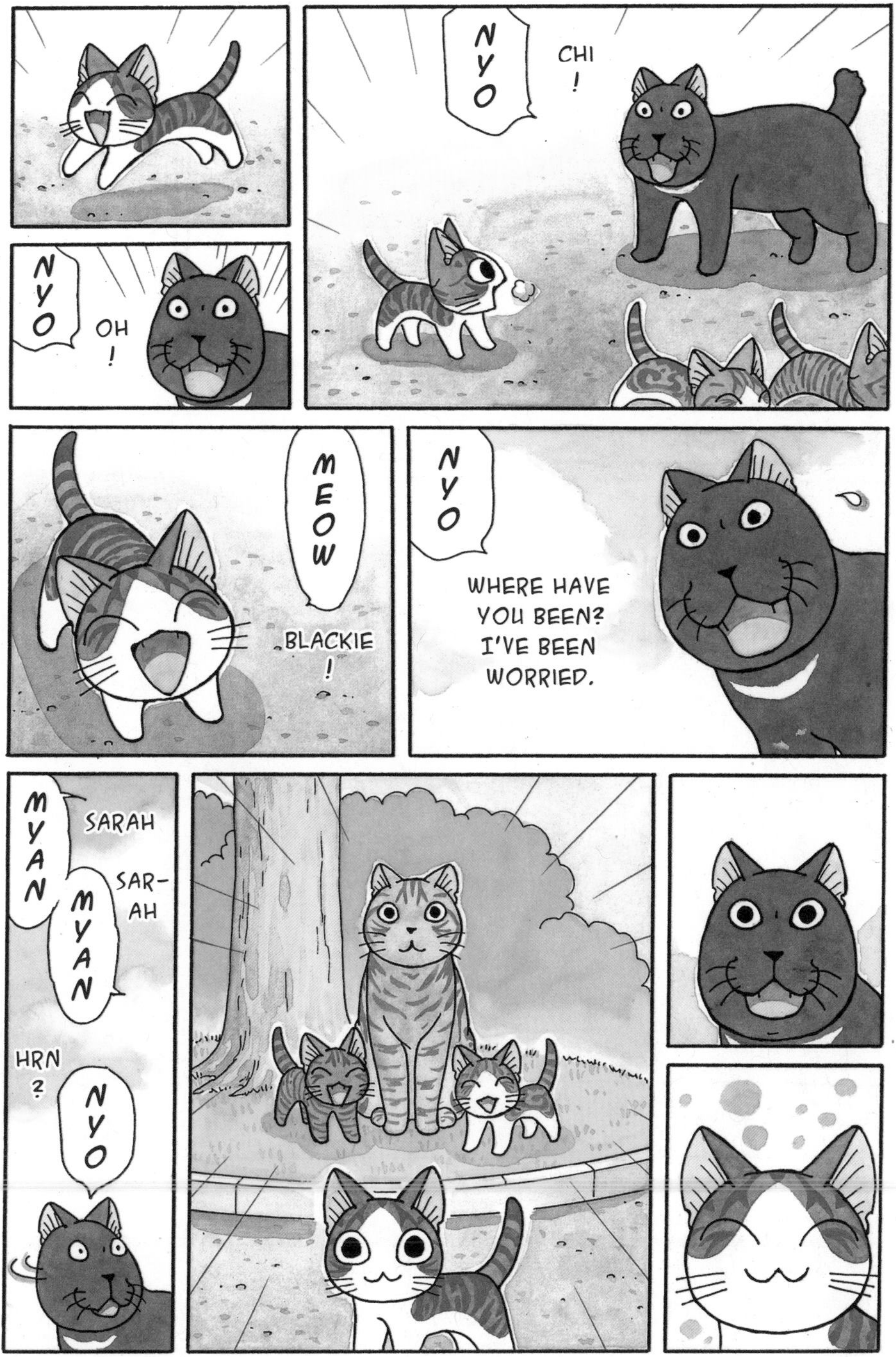
NYO
OH!
NYO
CHI!
MEOW
BLACKIE!
NYO
WHERE HAVE YOU BEEN? I'VE BEEN WORRIED.
MYAN
SARAH
MYAN
SAR-AH
HRN?
NYO

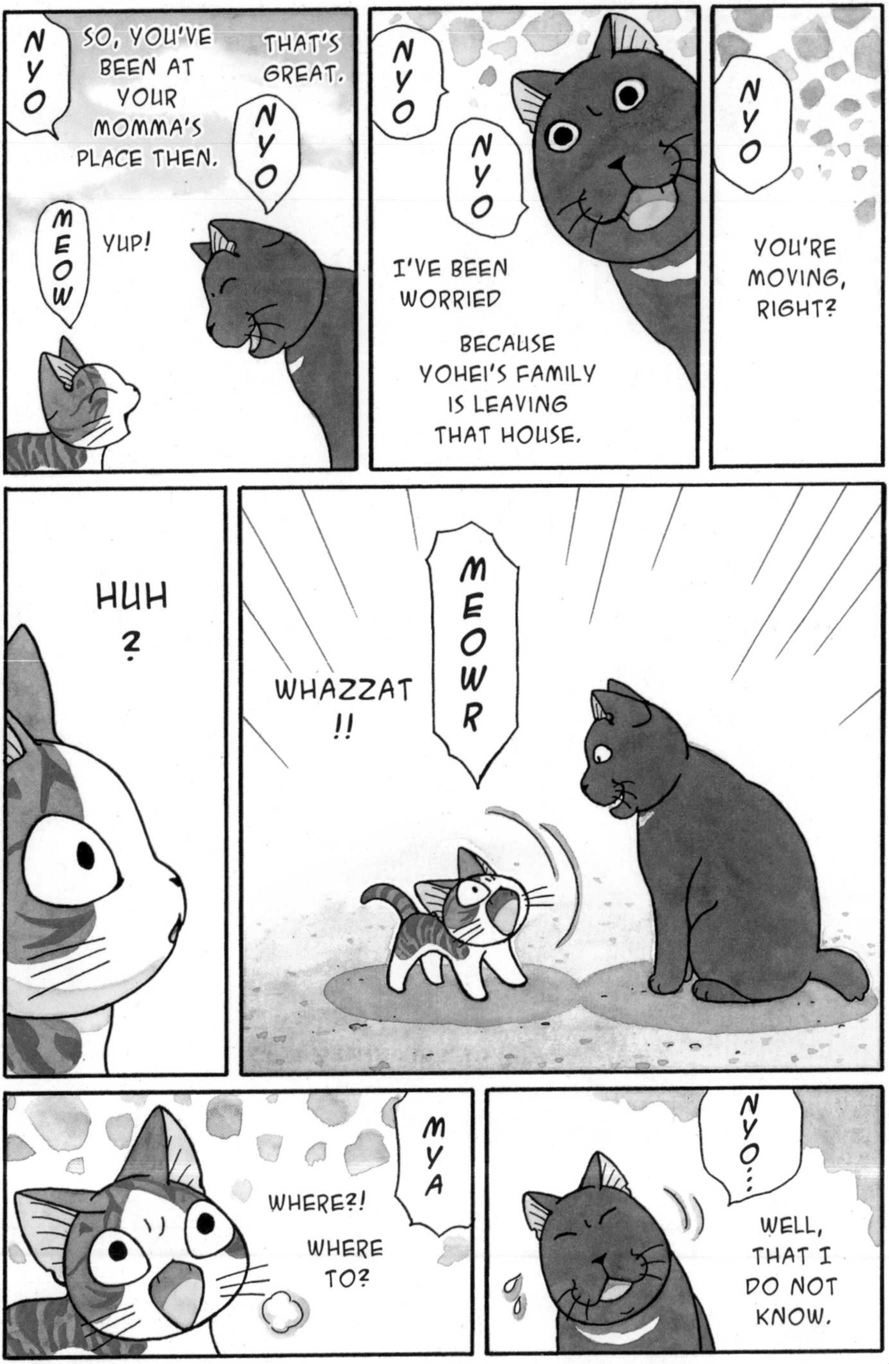
NYO
SO, YOU'VE BEEN AT YOUR MOMMA'S PLACE THEN.
THAT'S GREAT.
NYO
MEOW
YUP!
NYO
NYO
I'VE BEEN WORRIED
BECAUSE YOHEI'S FAMILY IS LEAVING THAT HOUSE.
NYO
YOU'RE MOVING, RIGHT?
HUH ?
WHAZZAT !!
MEOWR
WHERE?!
WHERE TO?
MYA
NYO...
WELL, THAT I DO NOT KNOW.

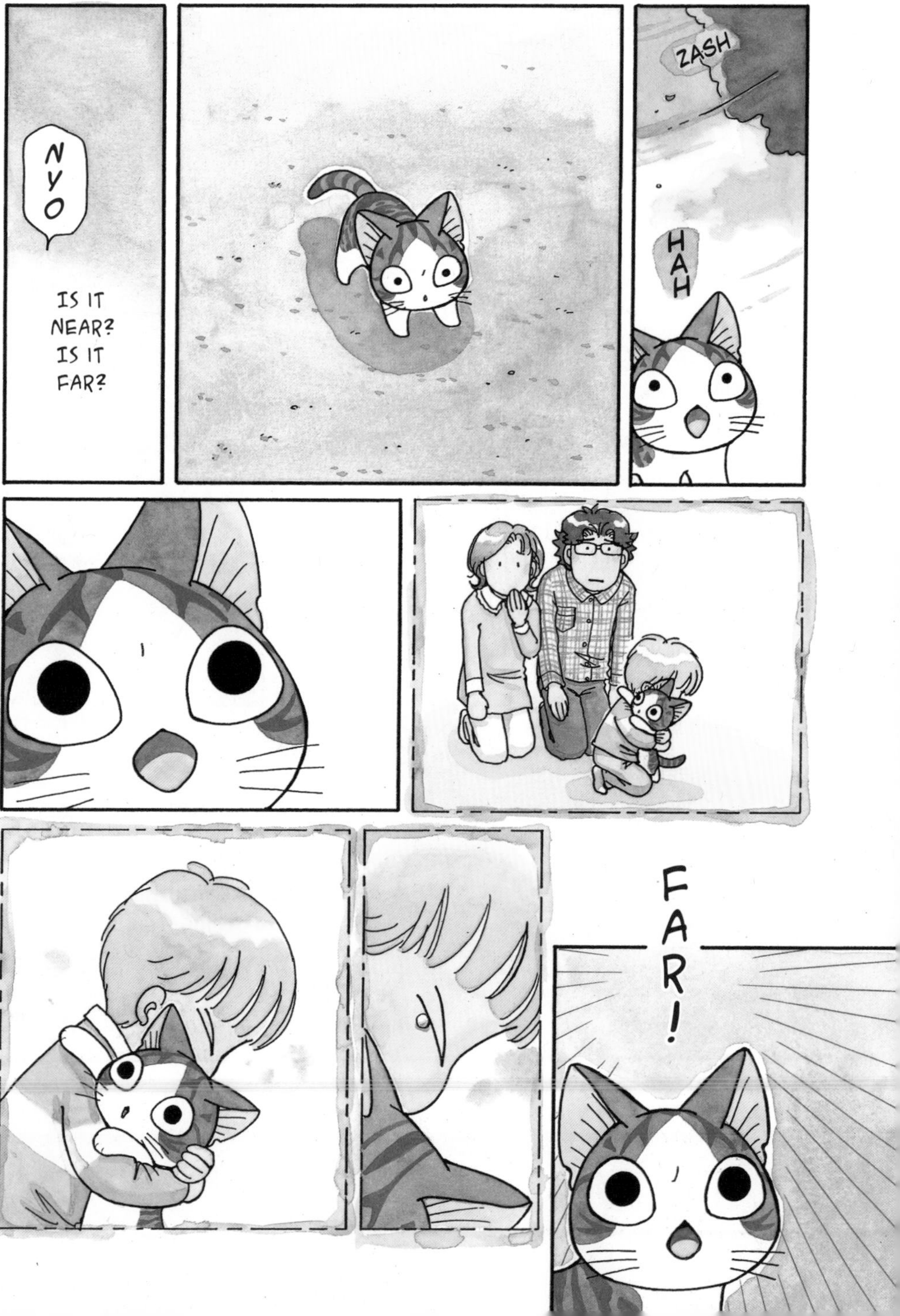
NYO
IS IT NEAR? IS IT FAR?
ZASH
HAH
FAR!

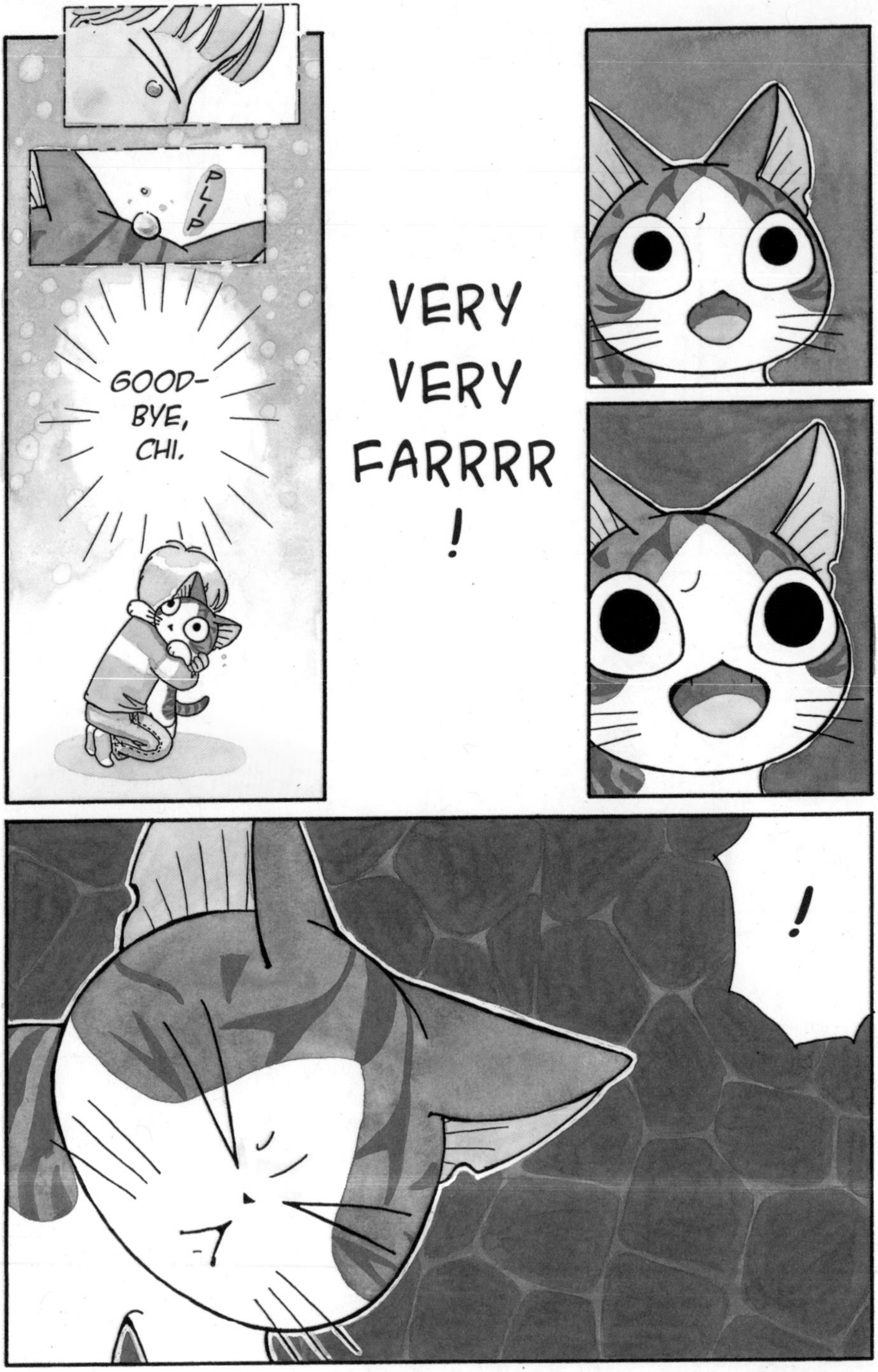
PLIP
GOOD-BYE, CHI.
VERY VERY FARRRR !
!

the end

homemade 213: a cat has to pick

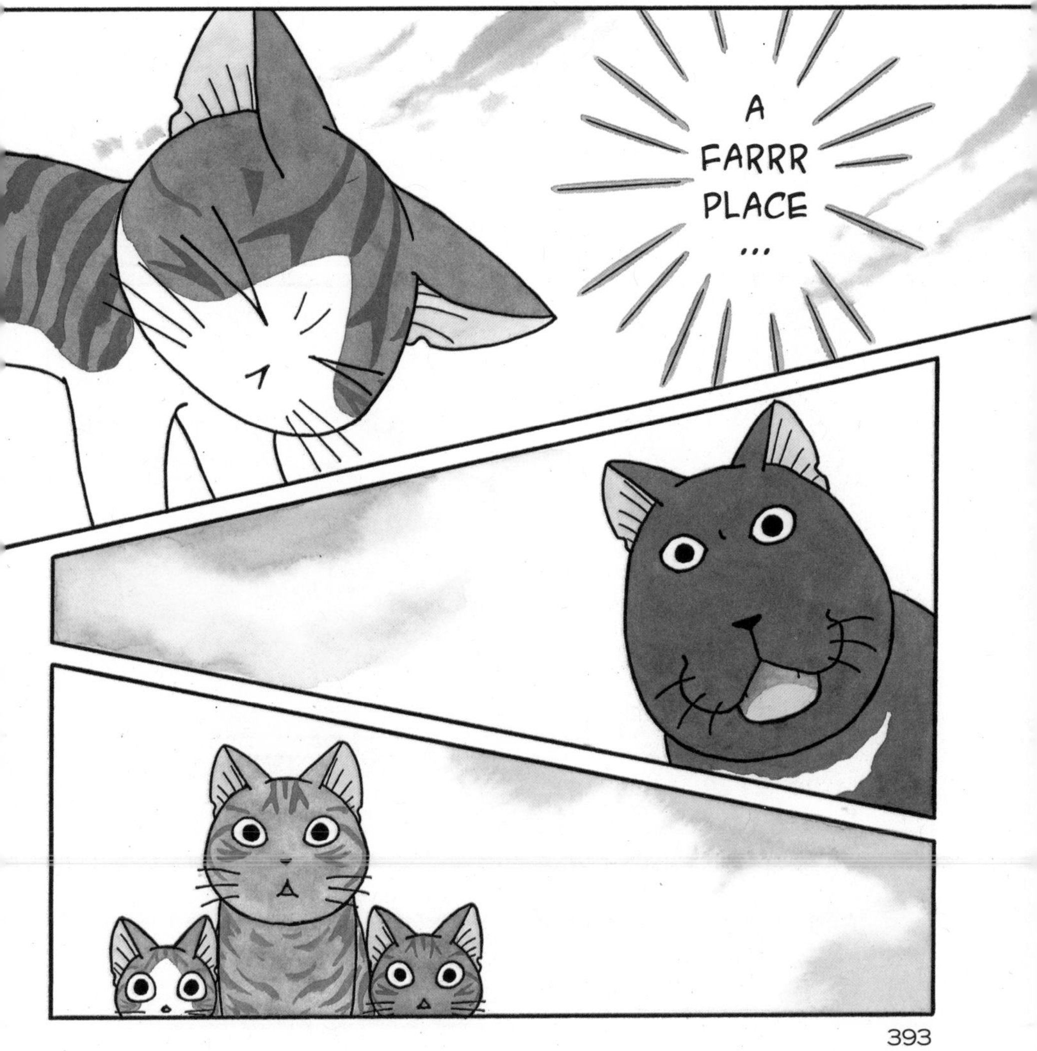
A FARRR PLACE ...

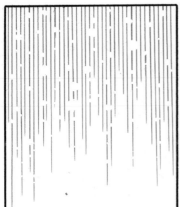

DADDY
MOMMY

YOHEY

BONK

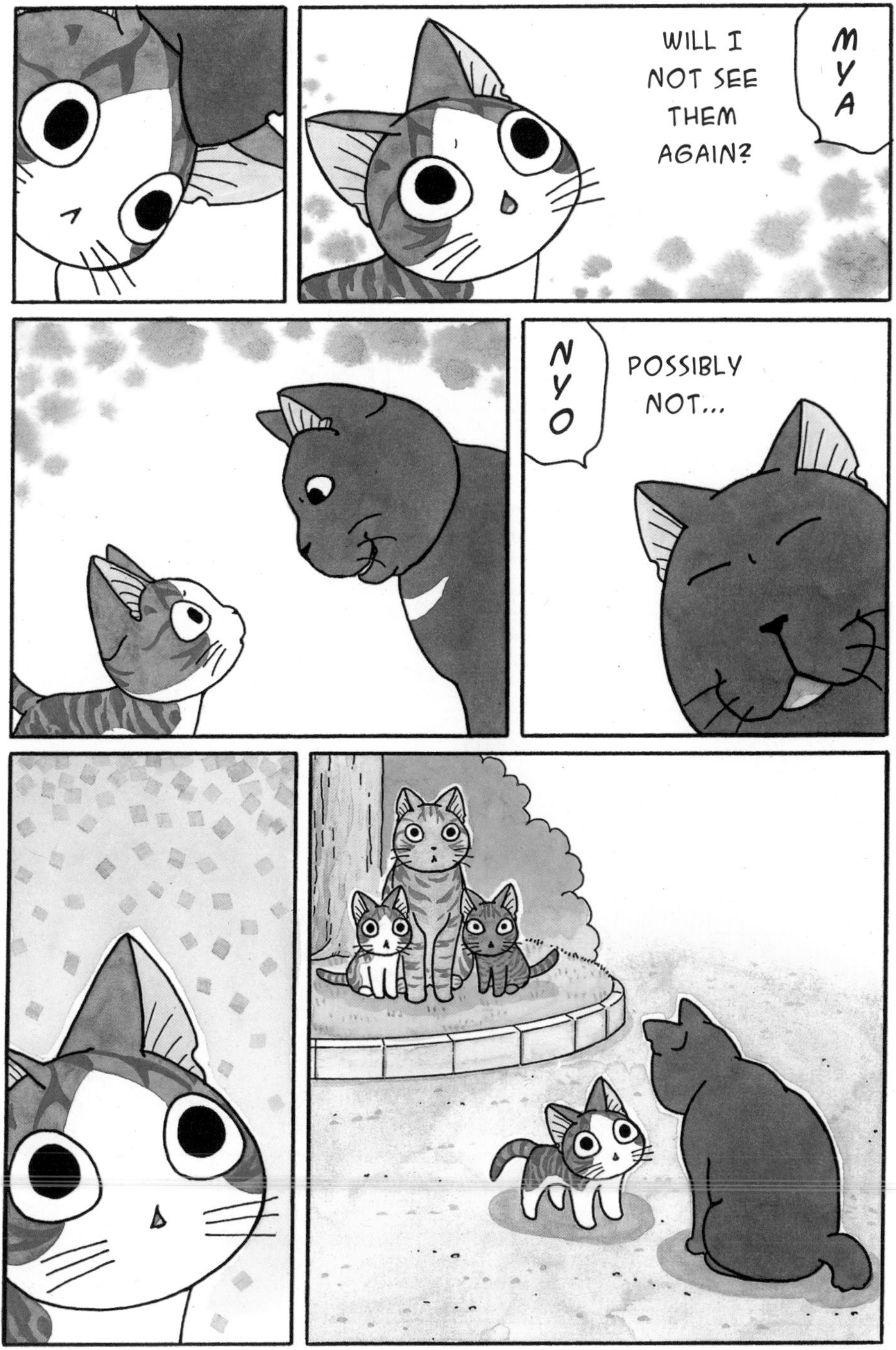
WILL I NOT SEE THEM AGAIN?
MYA
NYO
POSSIBLY NOT...

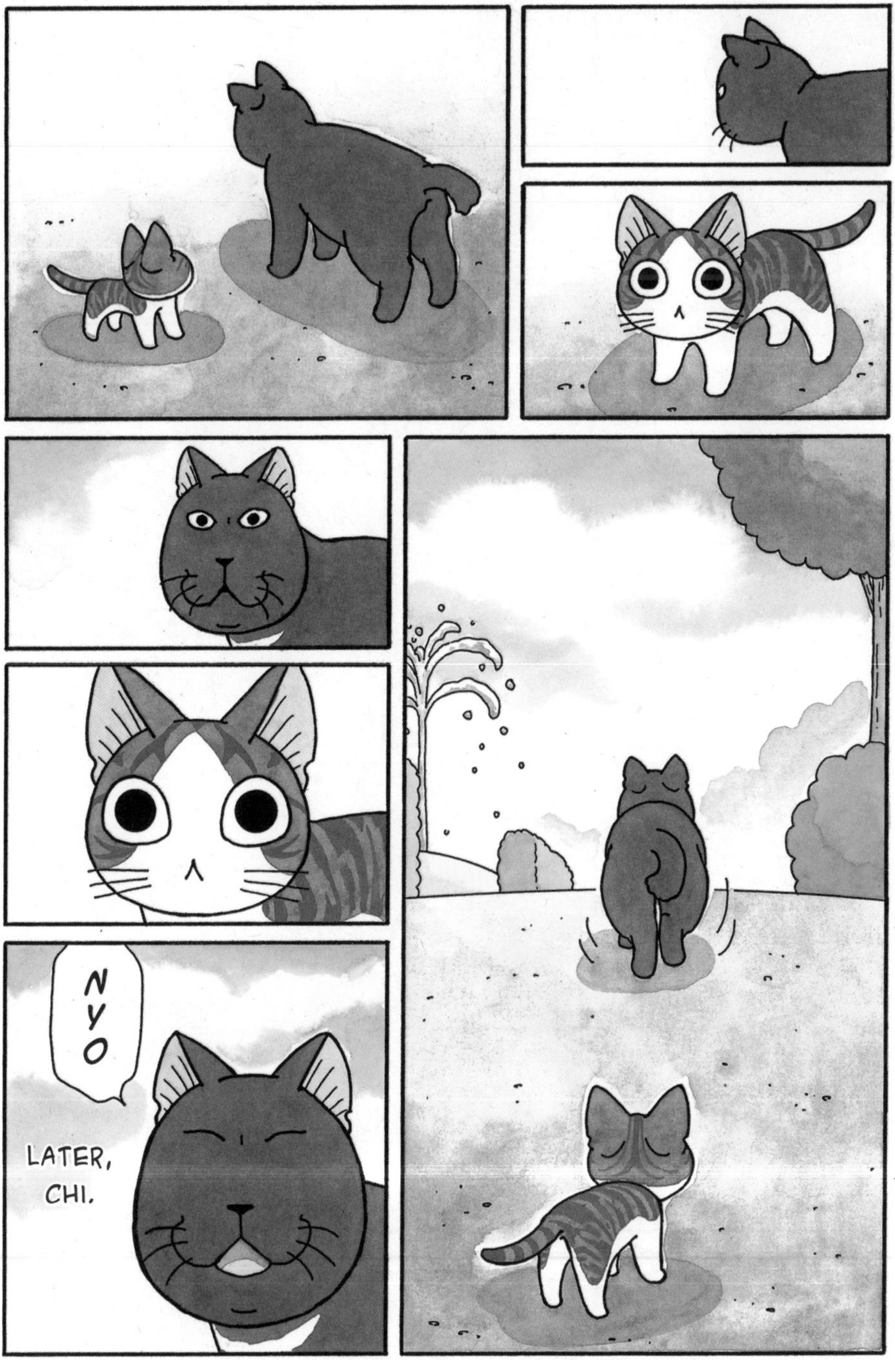
NYO
LATER, CHI.

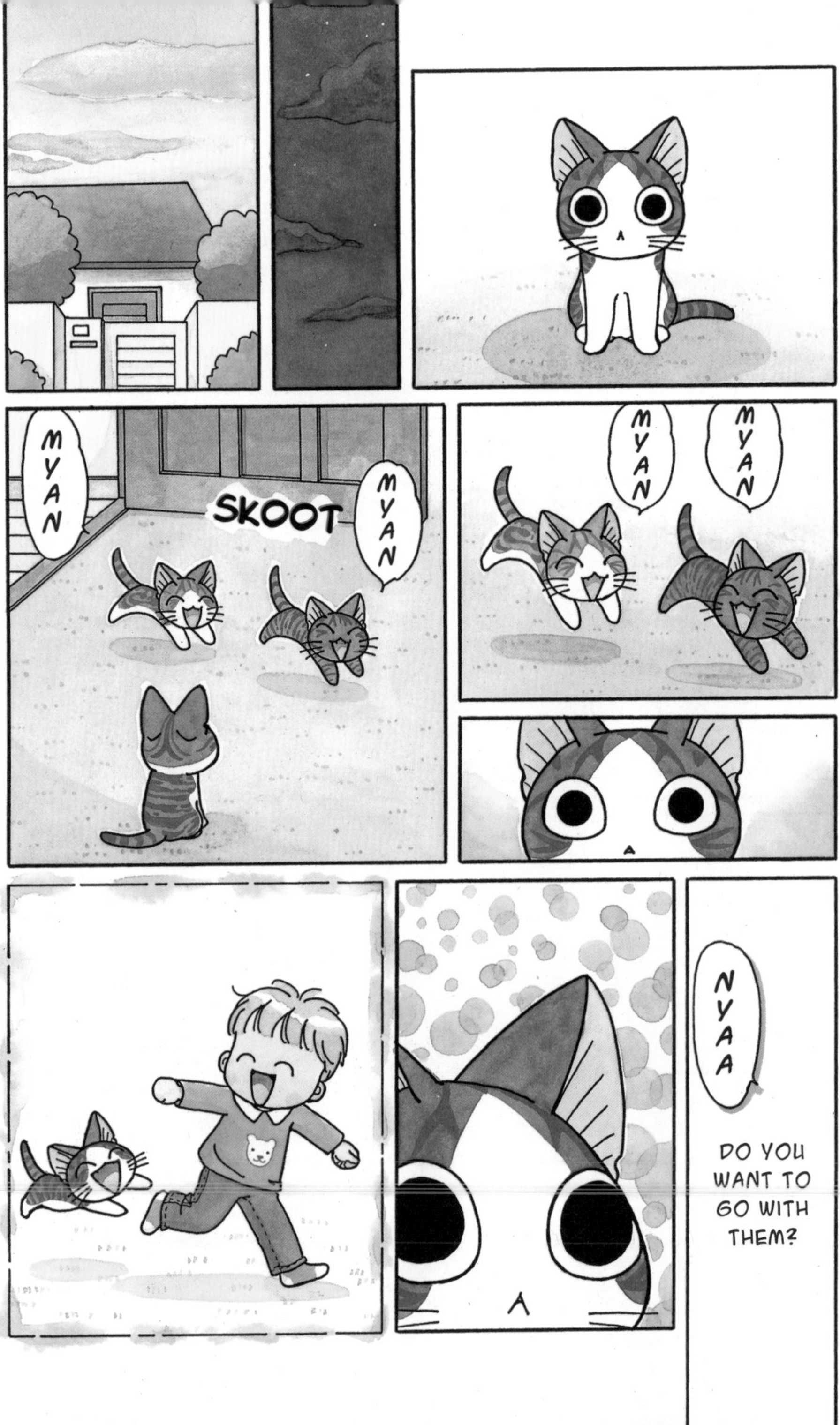
MYAN
SKOOT
MYAN
MYAN
MYAN
NYAA
DO YOU WANT TO GO WITH THEM?

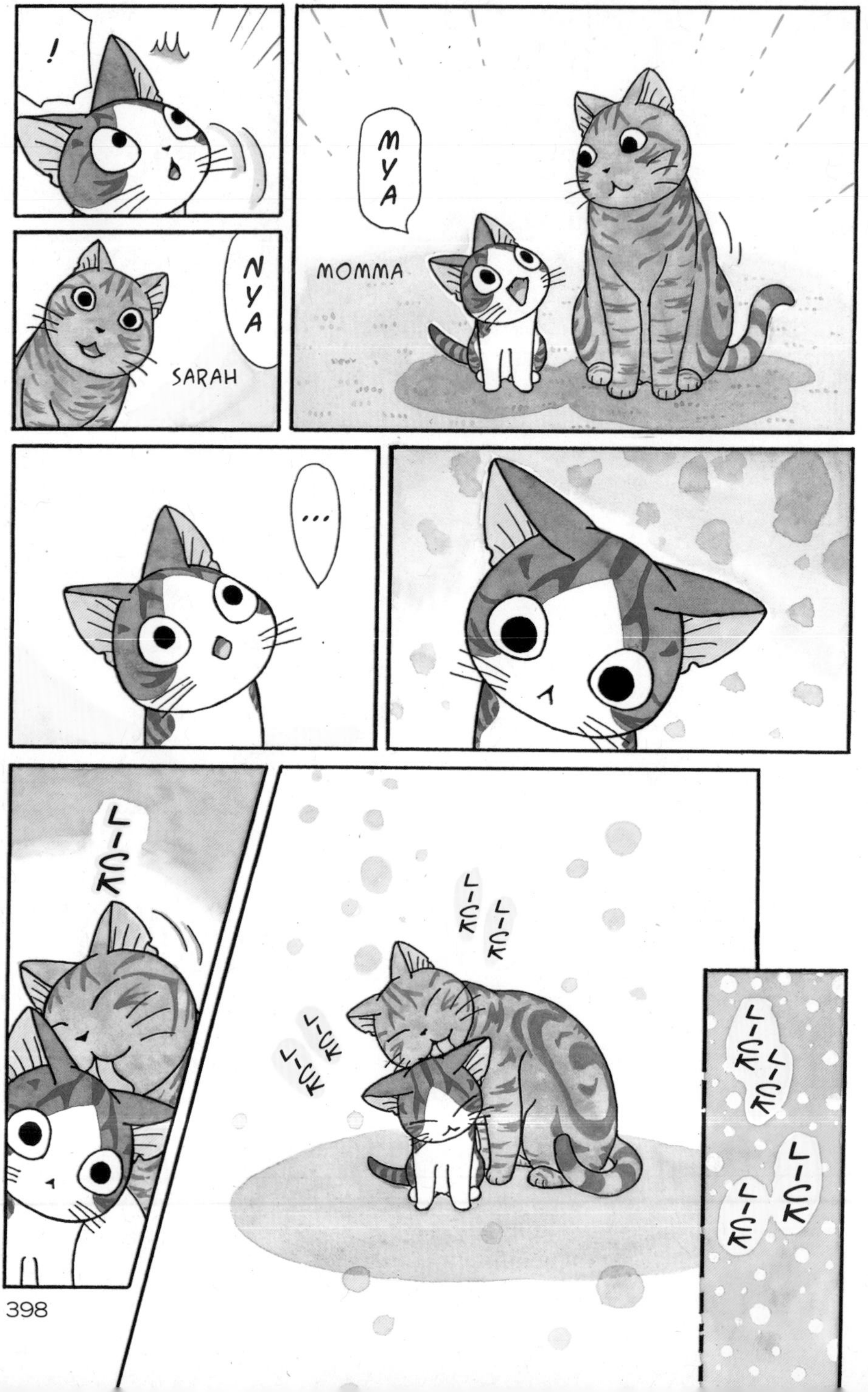
!
MYA
MOMMA
NYA
SARAH
...
LICK
LICK
LICK
LICK
LICK
LICK
LICK
LICK
LICK
LICK

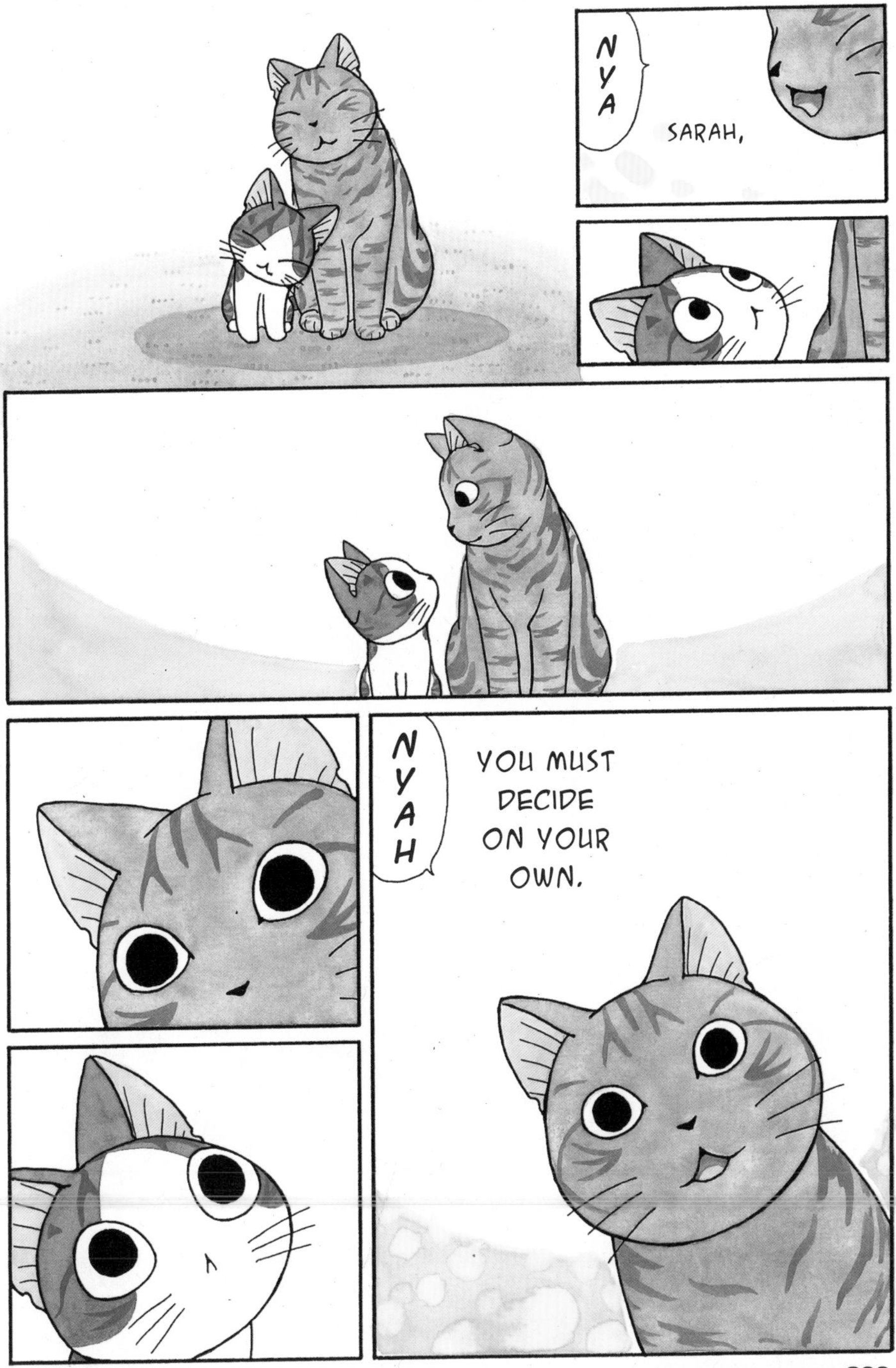
NYA
SARAH,
NYAH
YOU MUST DECIDE ON YOUR OWN.

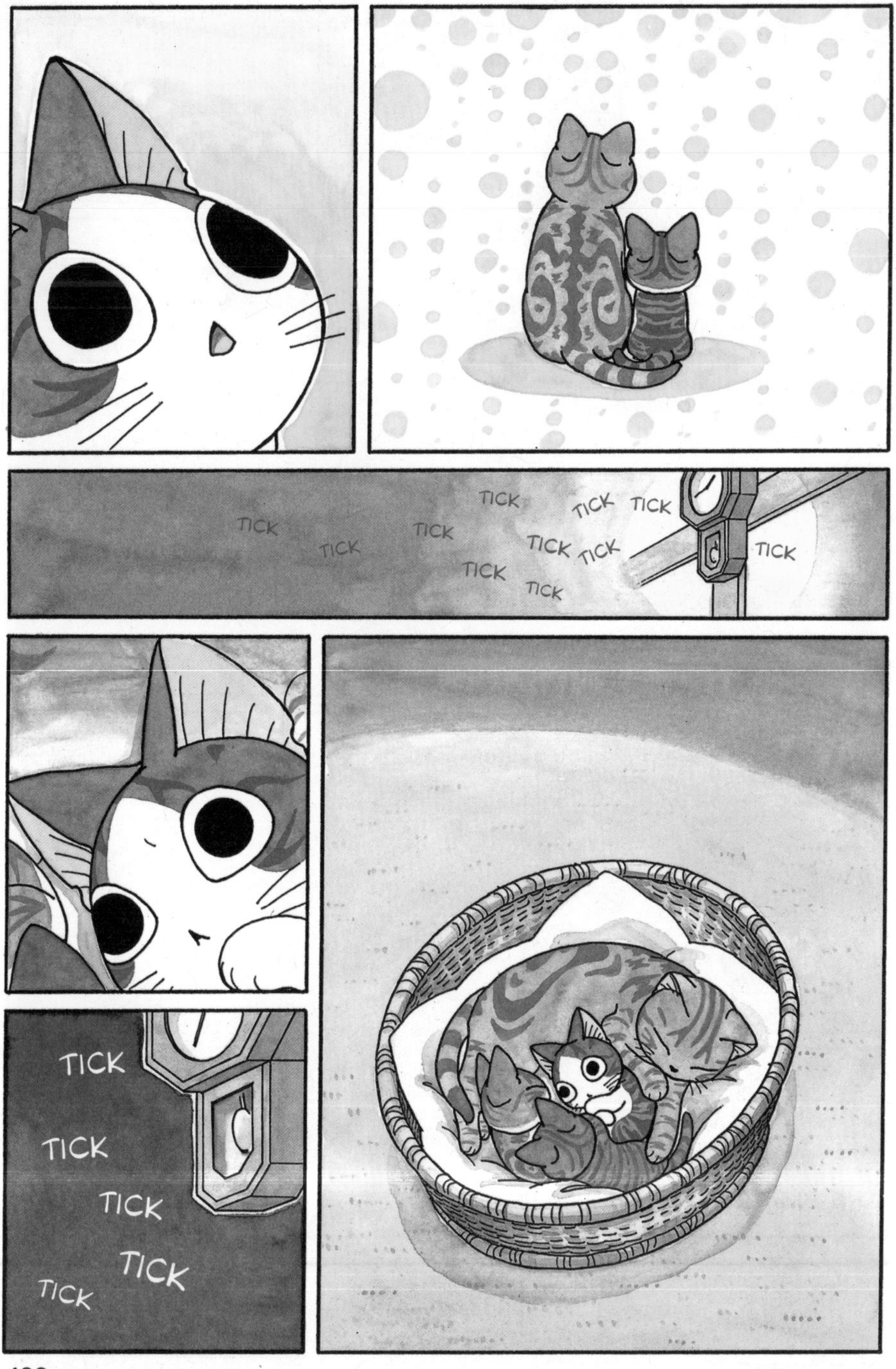
TICK
TICK
TICK
TICK
TICK
TICK
TICK
TICK
TICK
TICK
TICK
TICK
TICK
TICK
TICK
TICK

the end

homemade 214: a cat makes up her mind

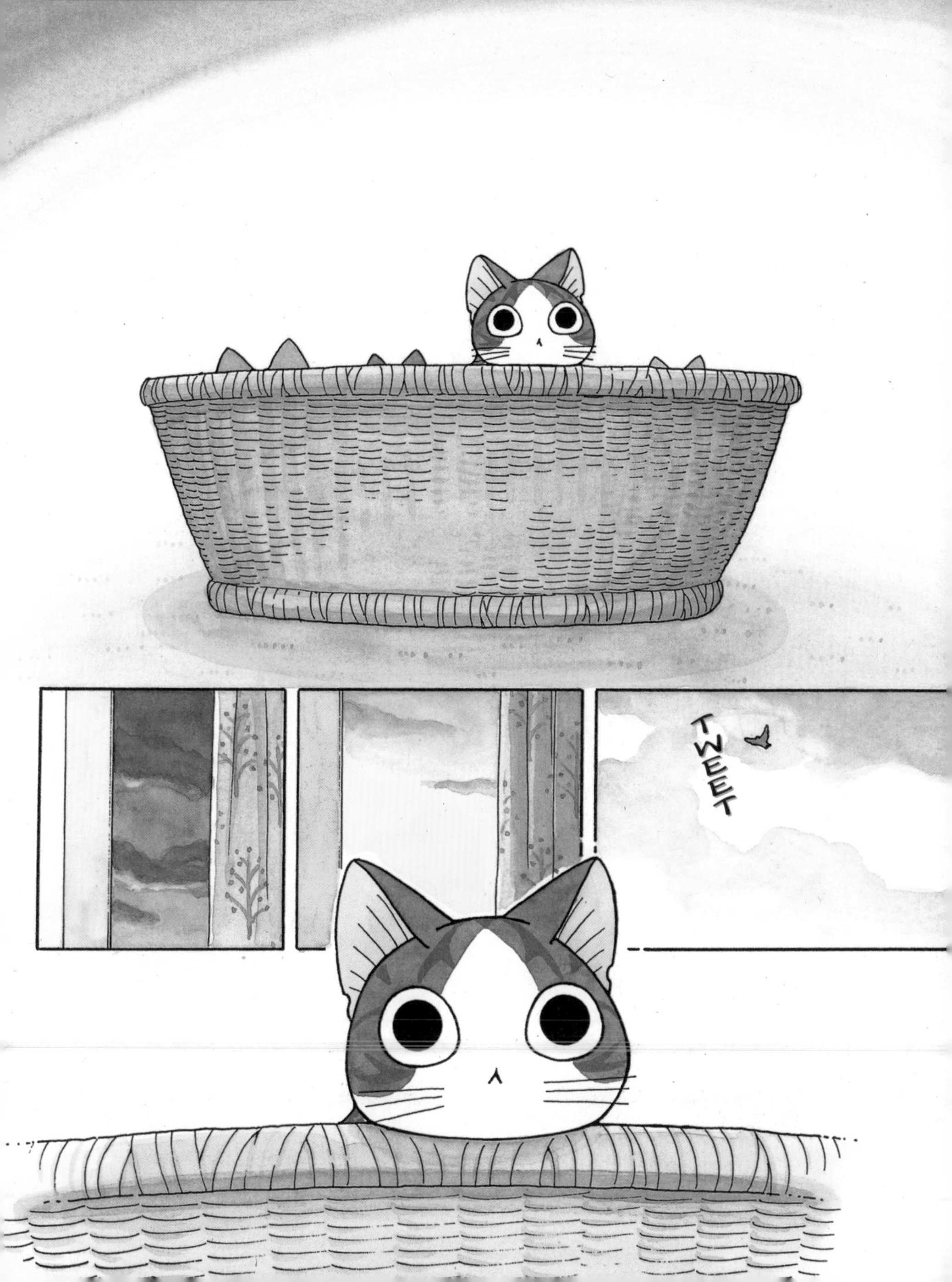
TWEET

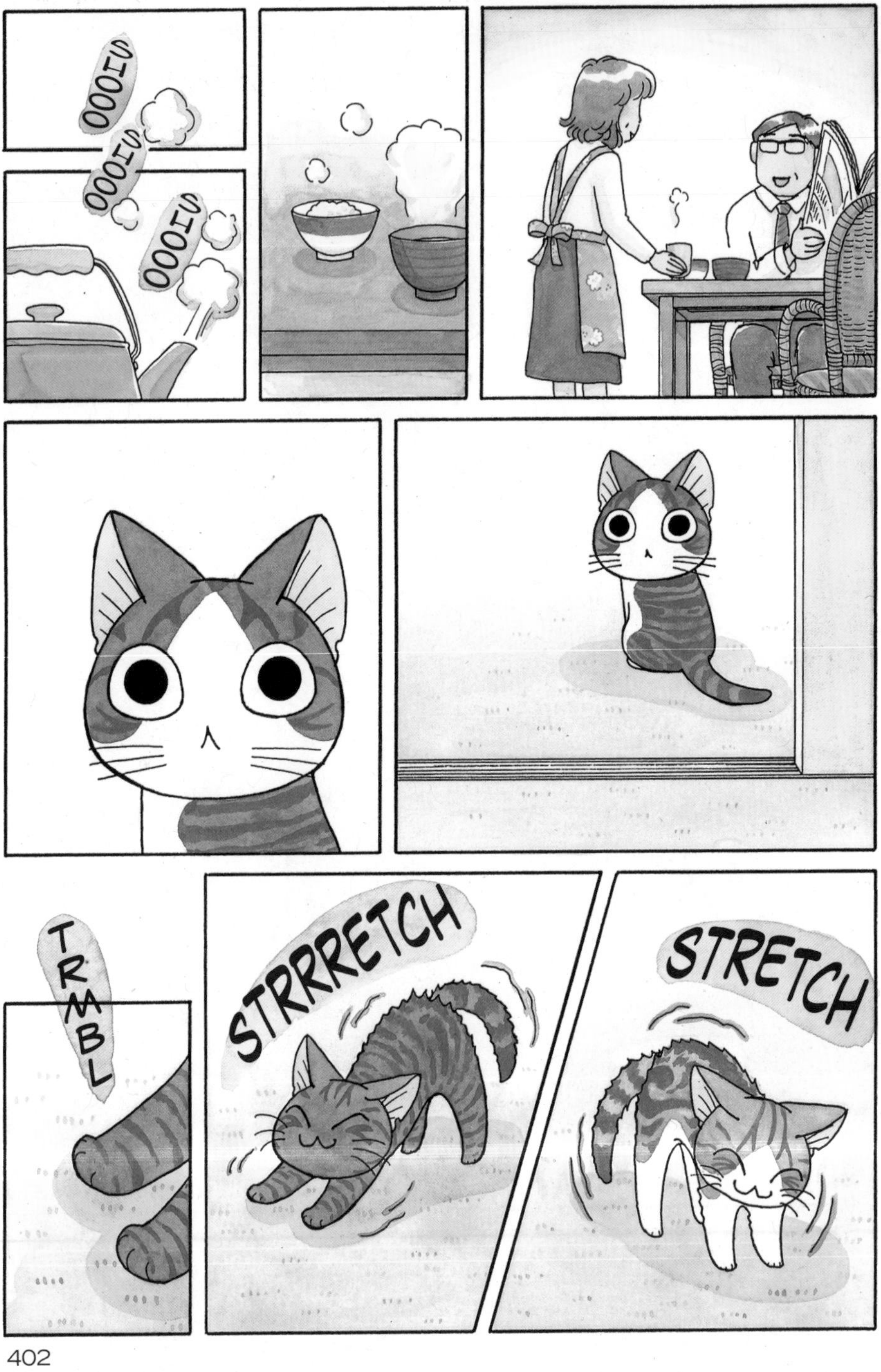
SHOOOO
SHOOOO
SHOOOO
TRMBL
STRRRETCH
STRETCH

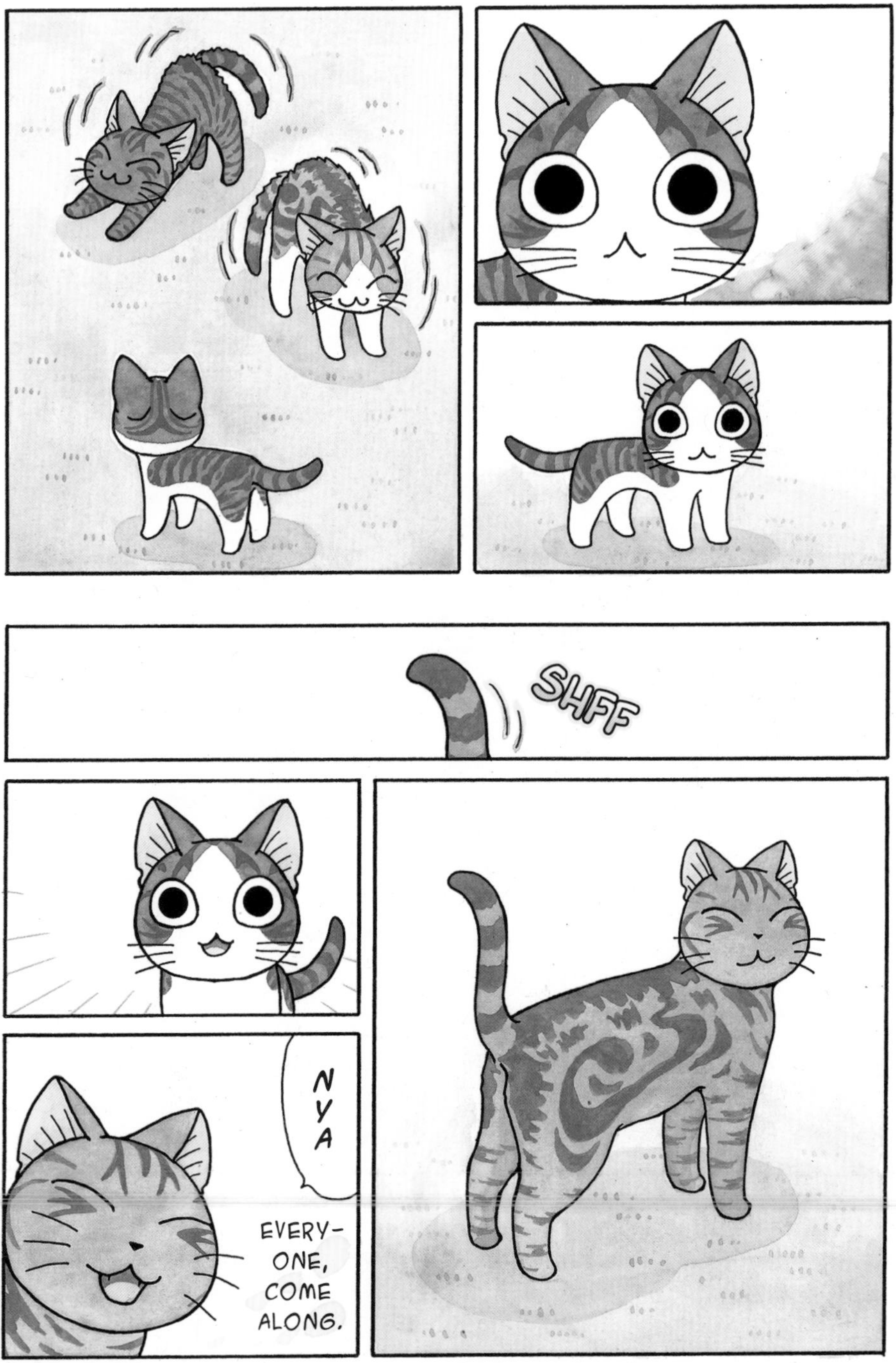
SHFF
NYA
EVERY-
ONE,
COME
ALONG.

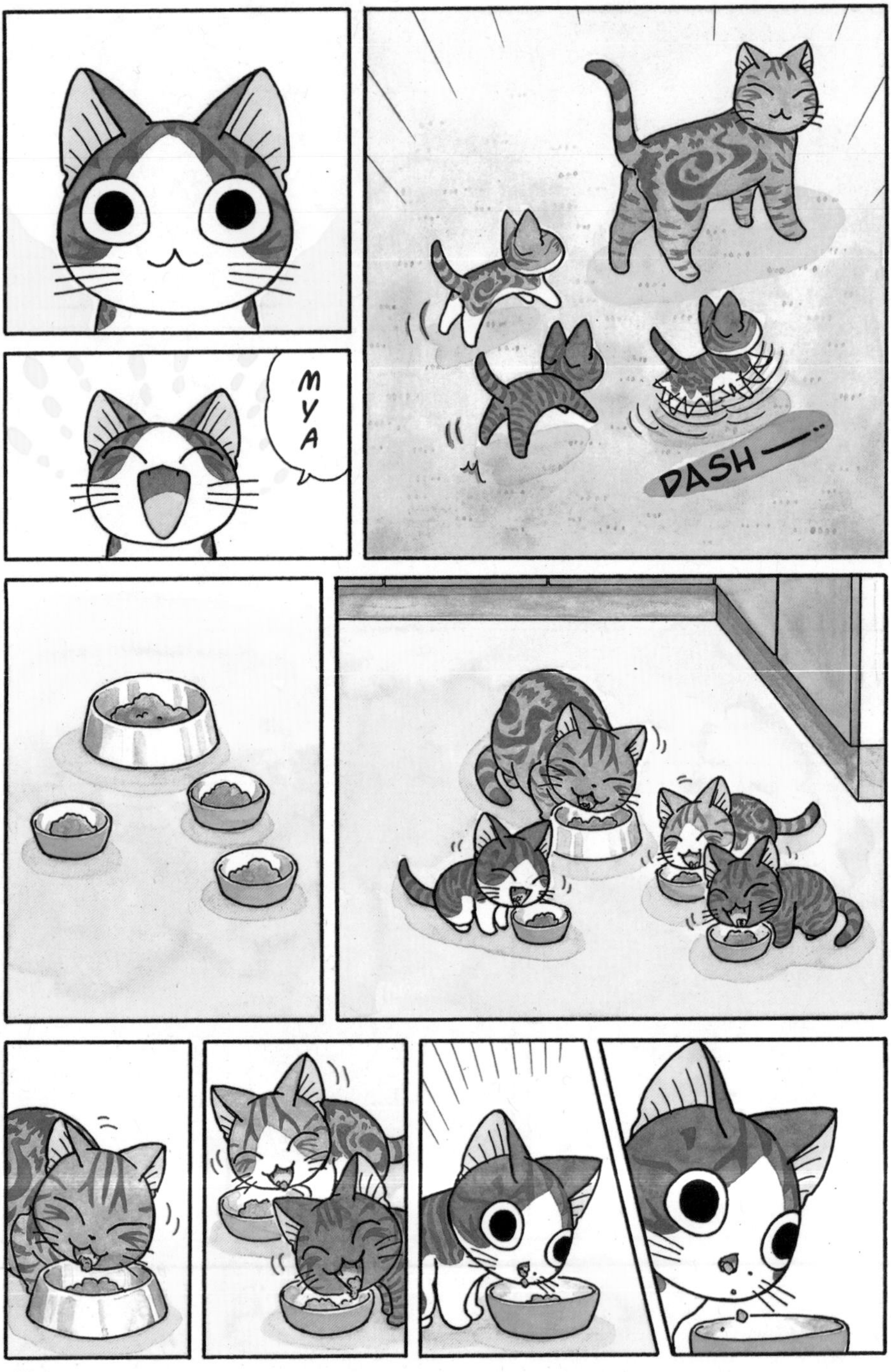
MYA
DASH

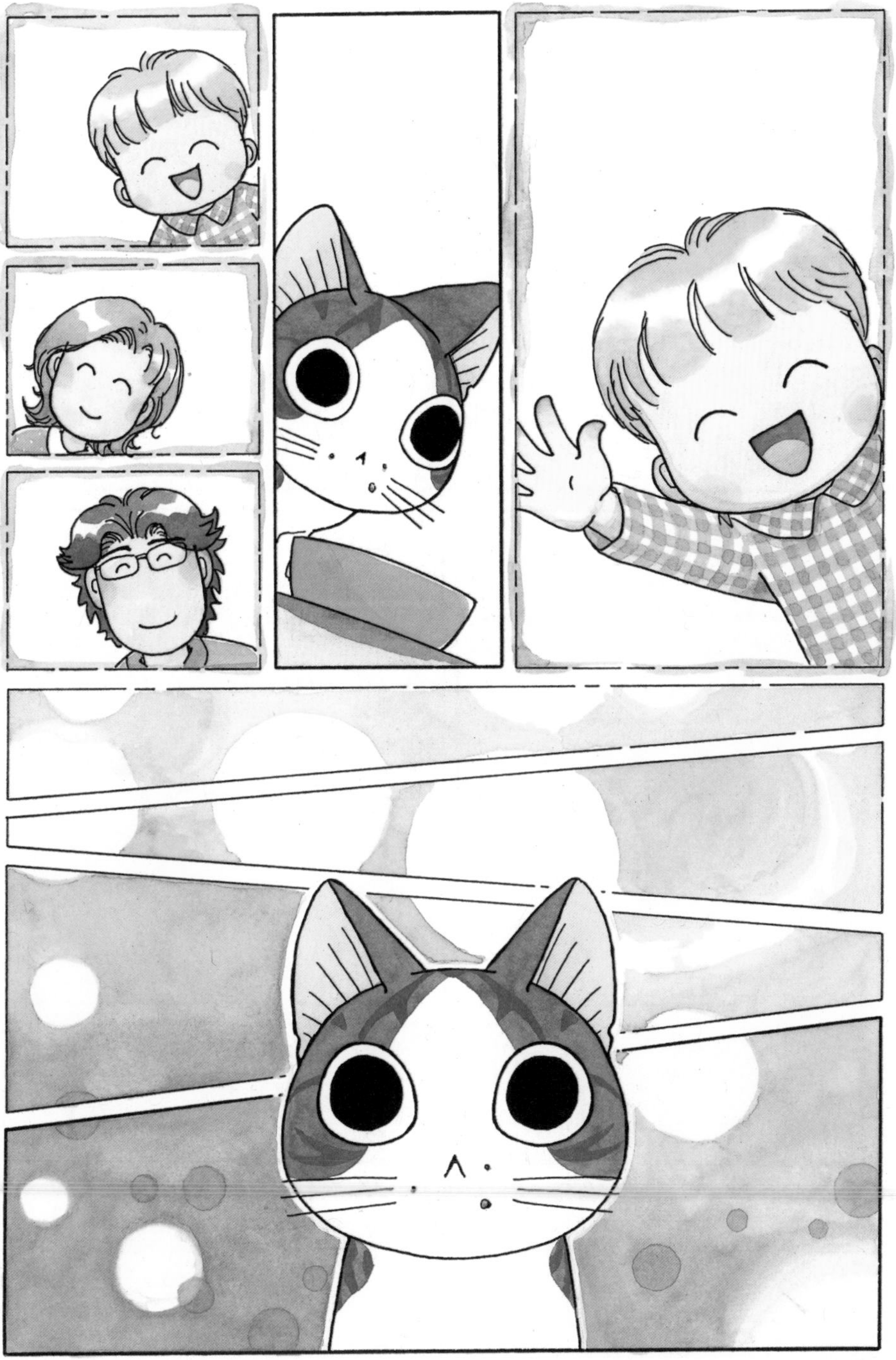

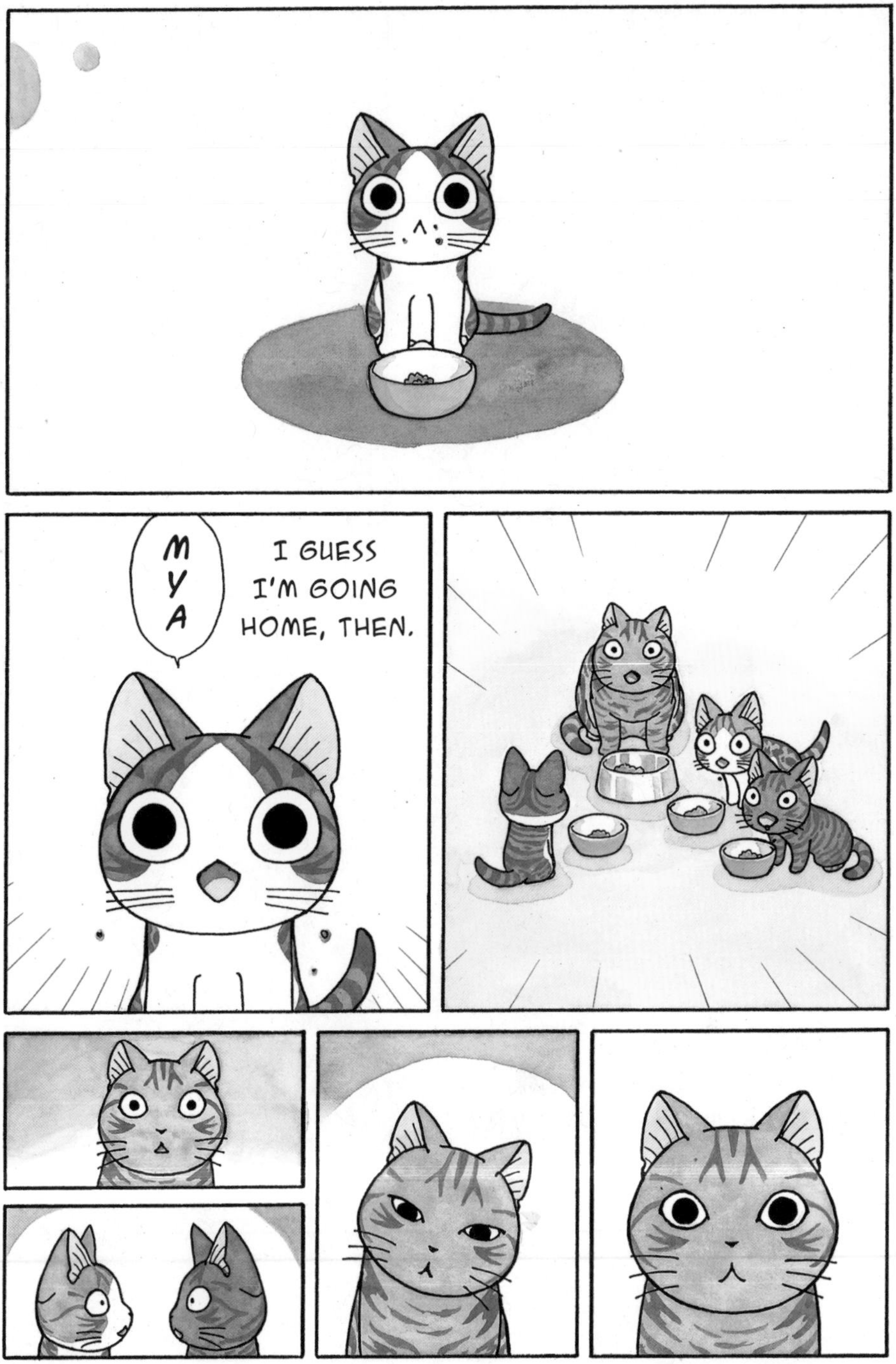
MYA
I GUESS I'M GOING HOME, THEN.

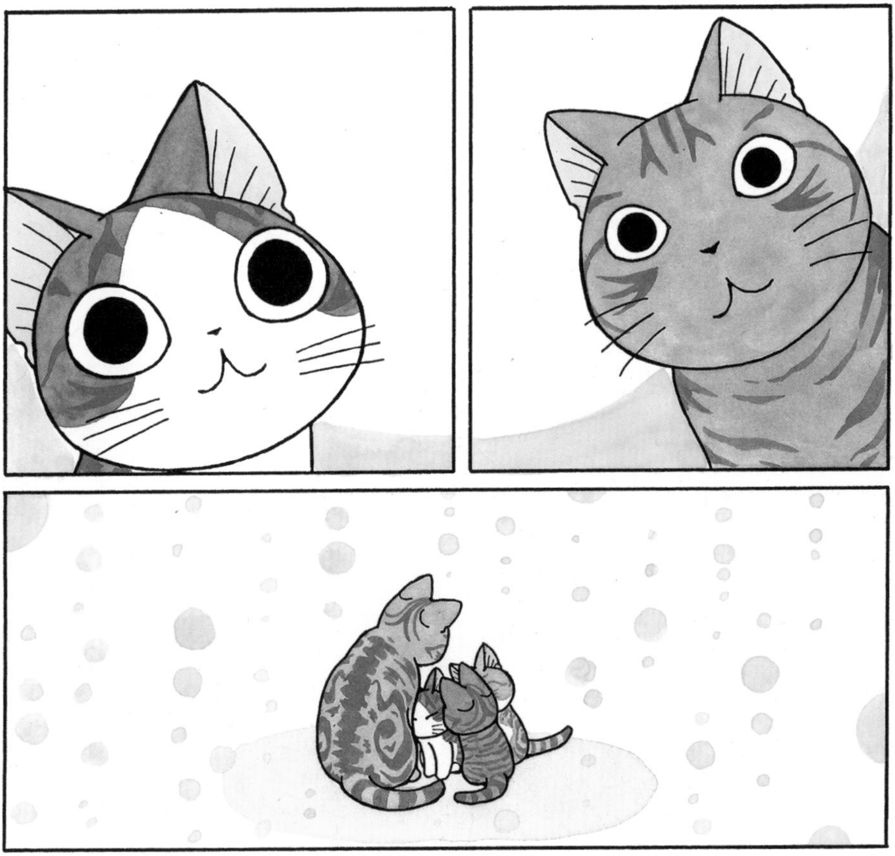

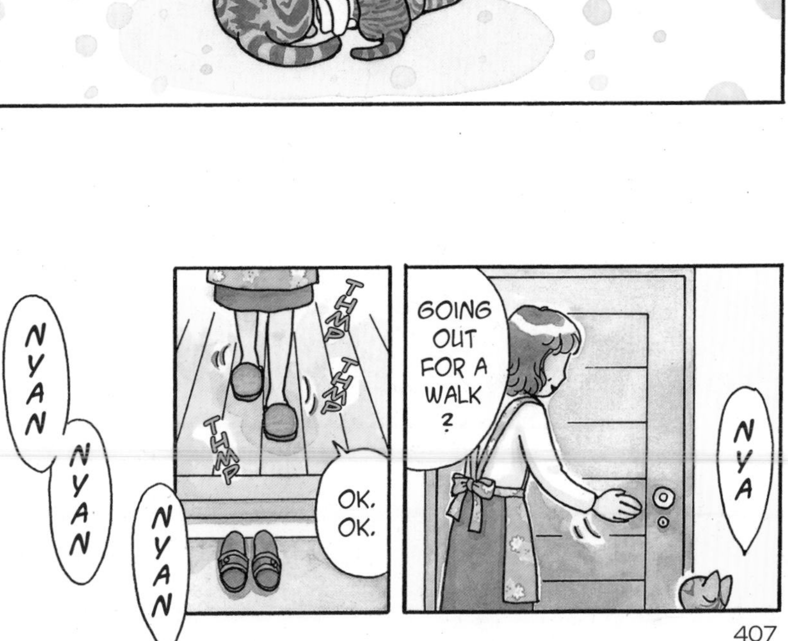
NYAN
NYAN
NYAN
THMP
THMP
THMP
OK. OK.
GOING OUT FOR A WALK?
NYA

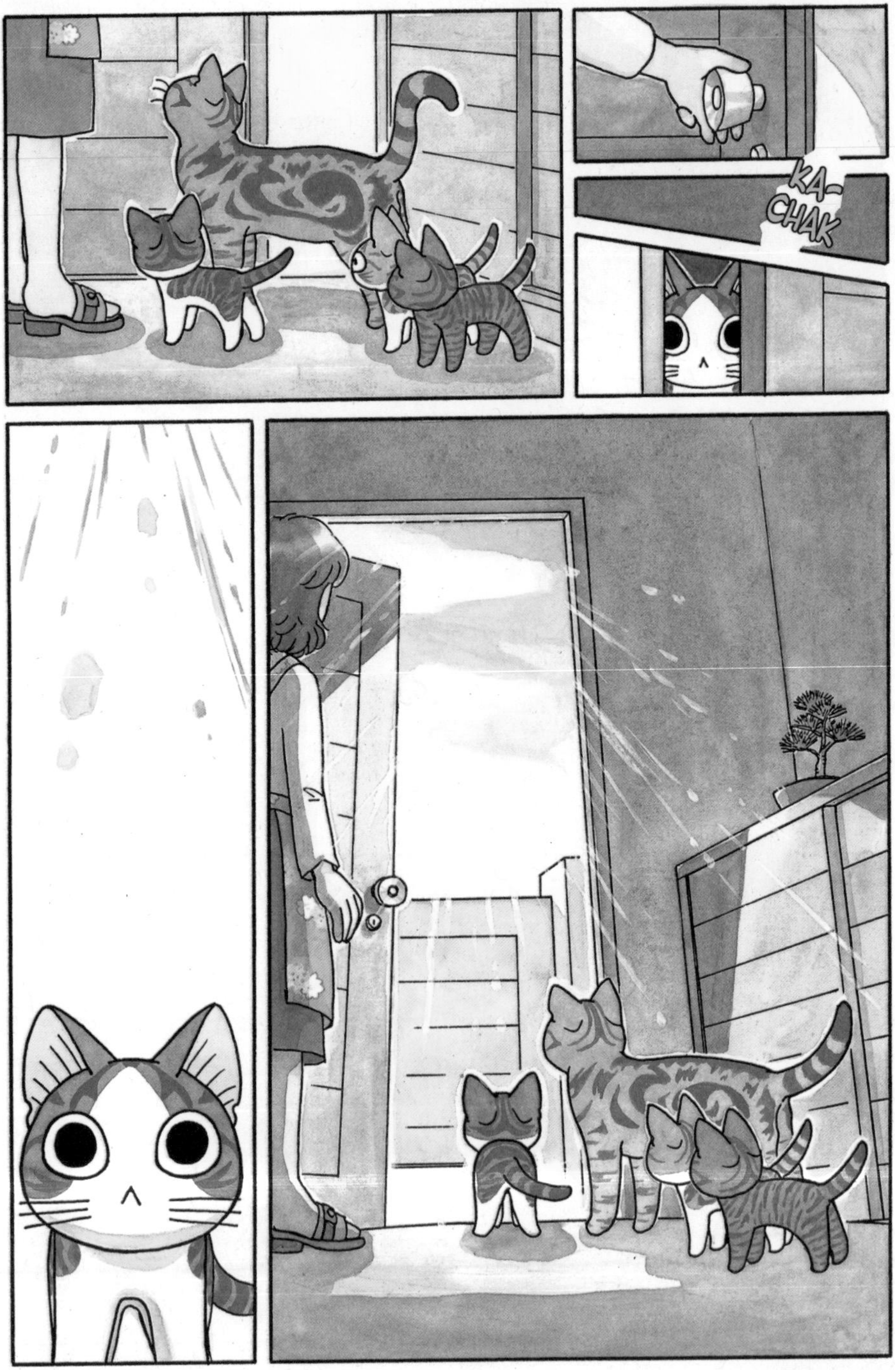
KA-
CHAK

the end

homemade 215: a cat runs off

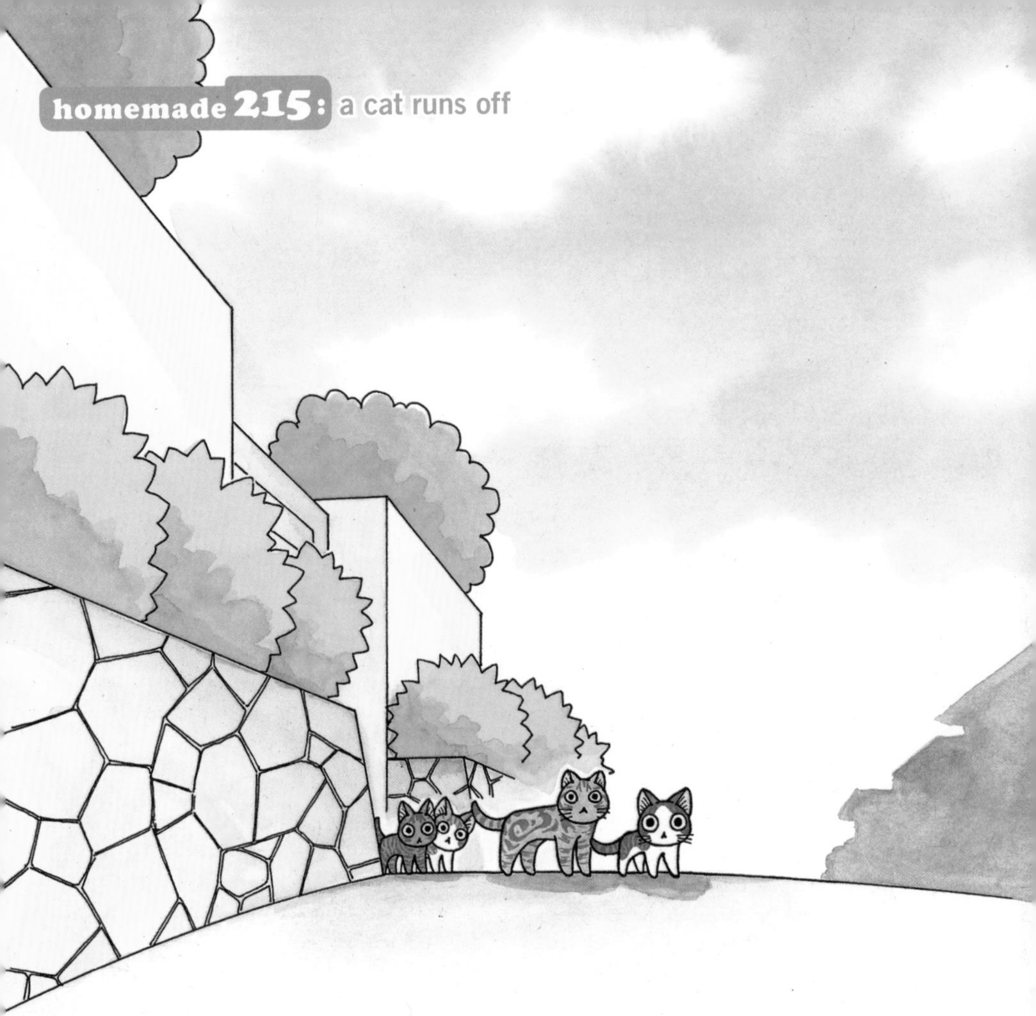

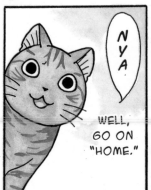

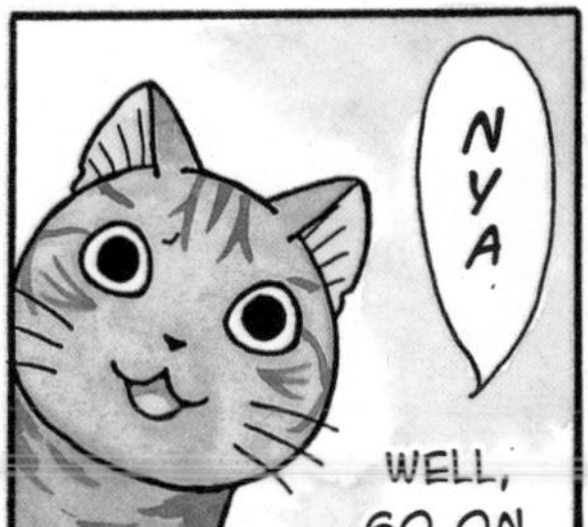
NYA
WELL, GO ON "HOME."

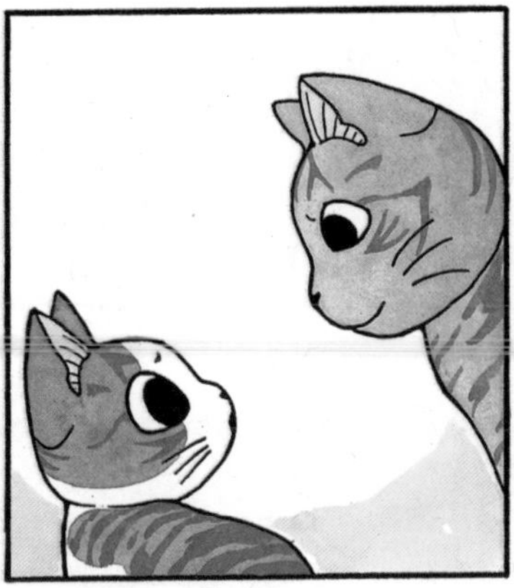

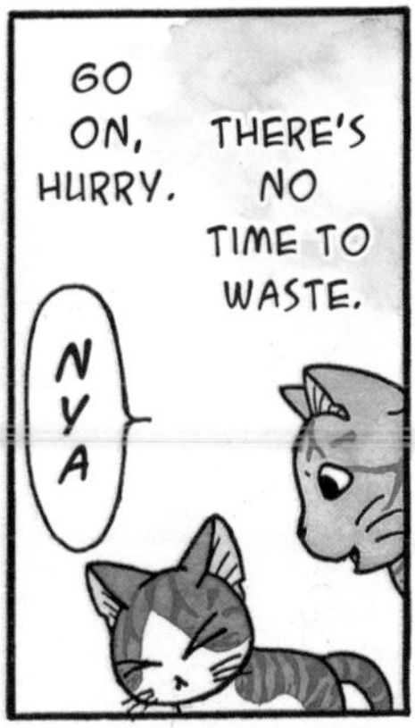
GO ON, HURRY.
THERE'S NO TIME TO WASTE.
NYA

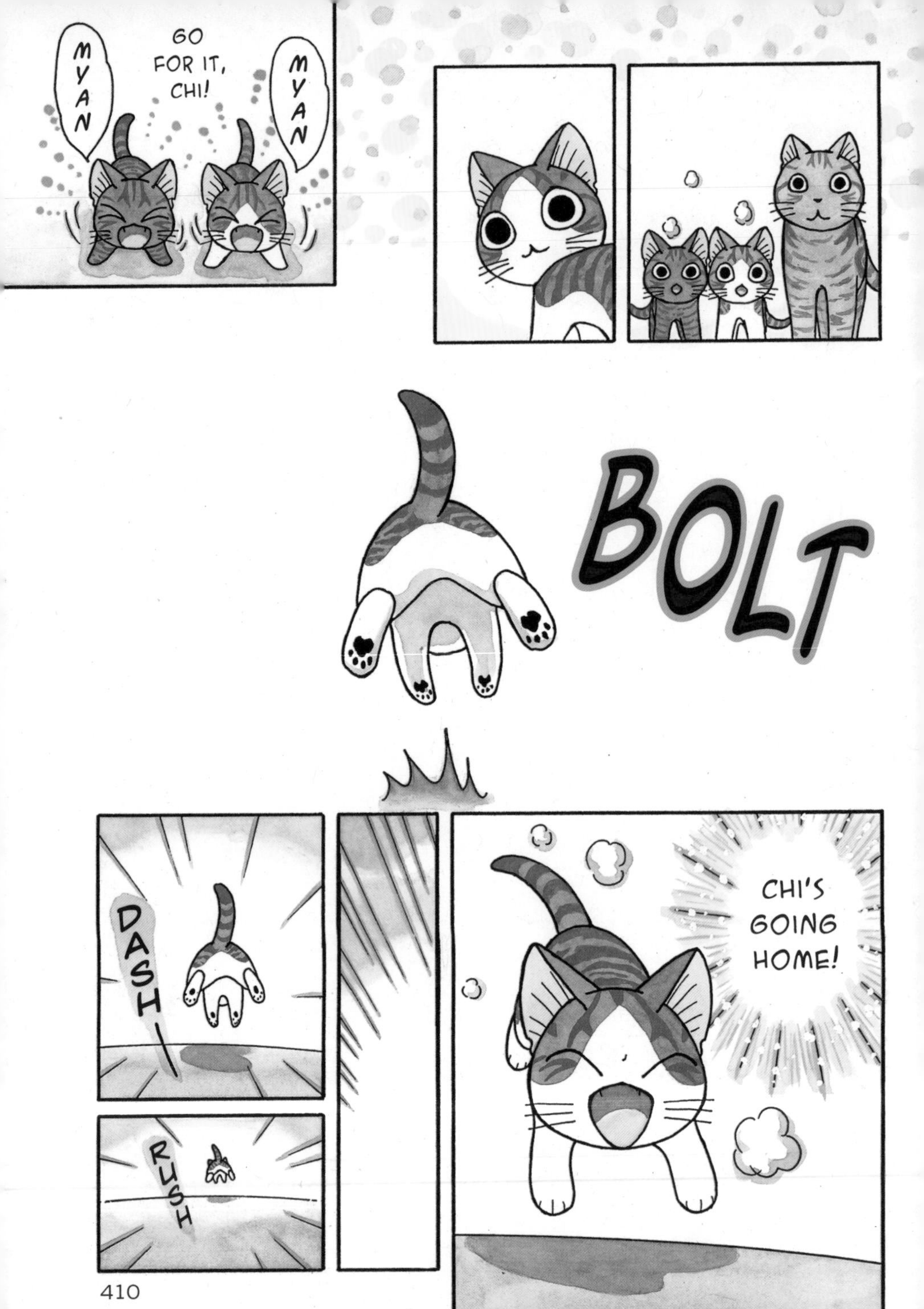
MYAN
GO FOR IT, CHI!
MYAN
BOLT
DASH
RUSH
CHI'S GOING HOME!

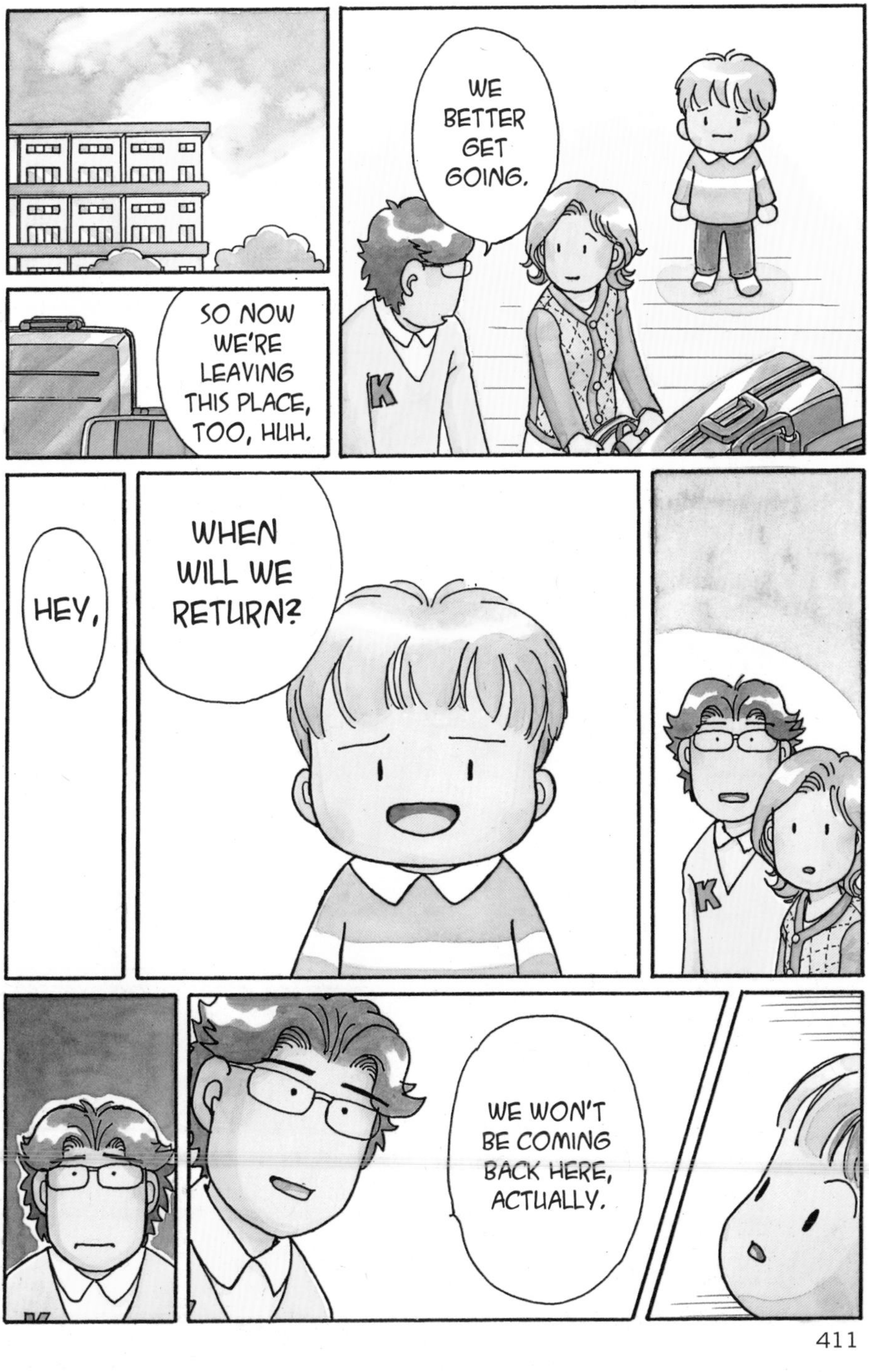
SO NOW WE'RE LEAVING THIS PLACE, TOO, HUH.
WE BETTER GET GOING.
HEY,
WHEN WILL WE RETURN?
WE WON'T BE COMING BACK HERE, ACTUALLY.

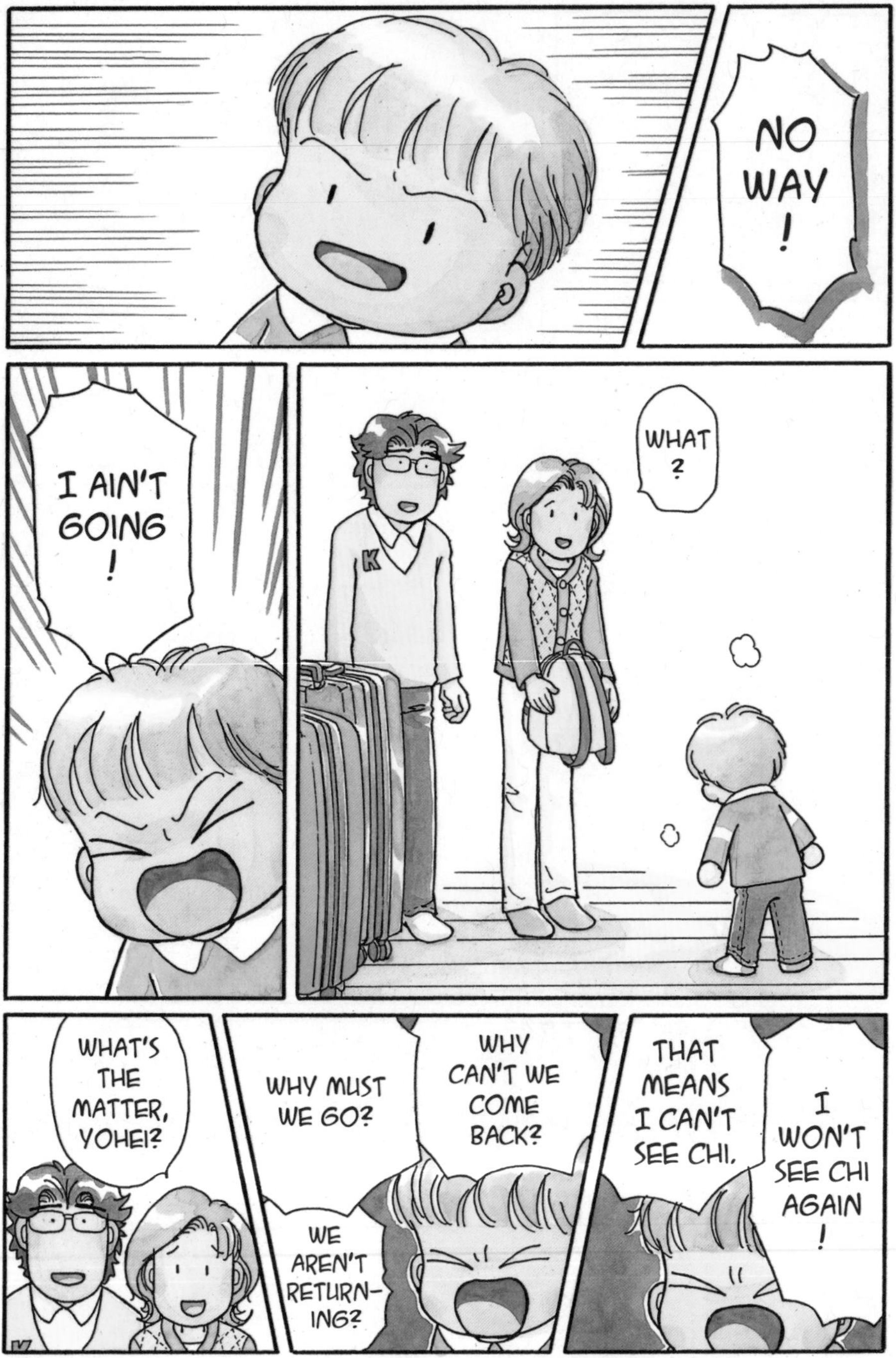
NO WAY!
I AIN'T GOING!
WHAT?
WHAT'S THE MATTER, YOHEI?
WHY MUST WE GO?
WHY CAN'T WE COME BACK?
WE AREN'T RETURNING?
THAT MEANS I CAN'T SEE CHI.
I WON'T SEE CHI AGAIN!

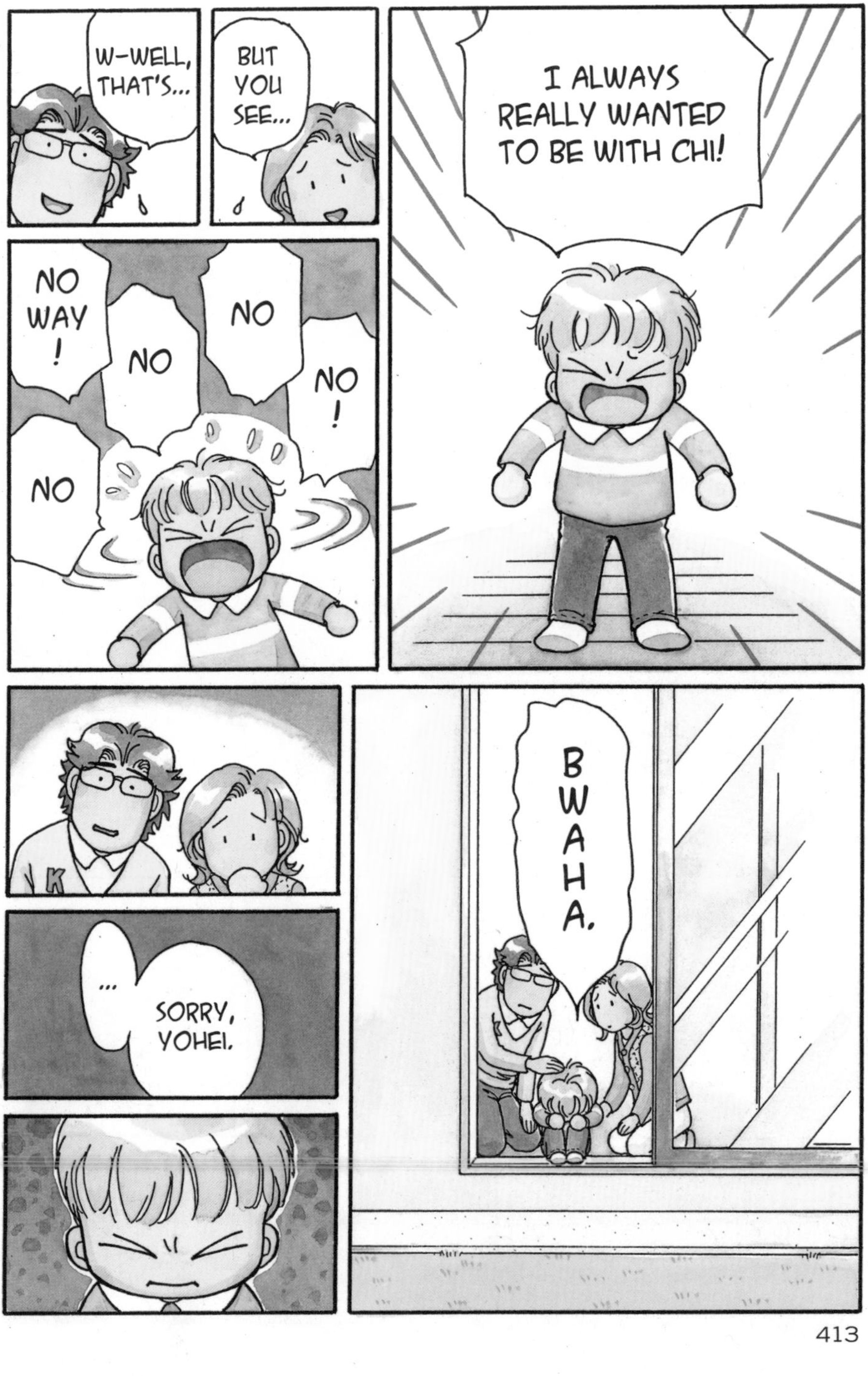
W-WELL, THAT'S...
BUT YOU SEE...
NO WAY!
NO
NO
NO!
NO
I ALWAYS REALLY WANTED TO BE WITH CHI!
... SORRY, YOHEI.
BWAHA.

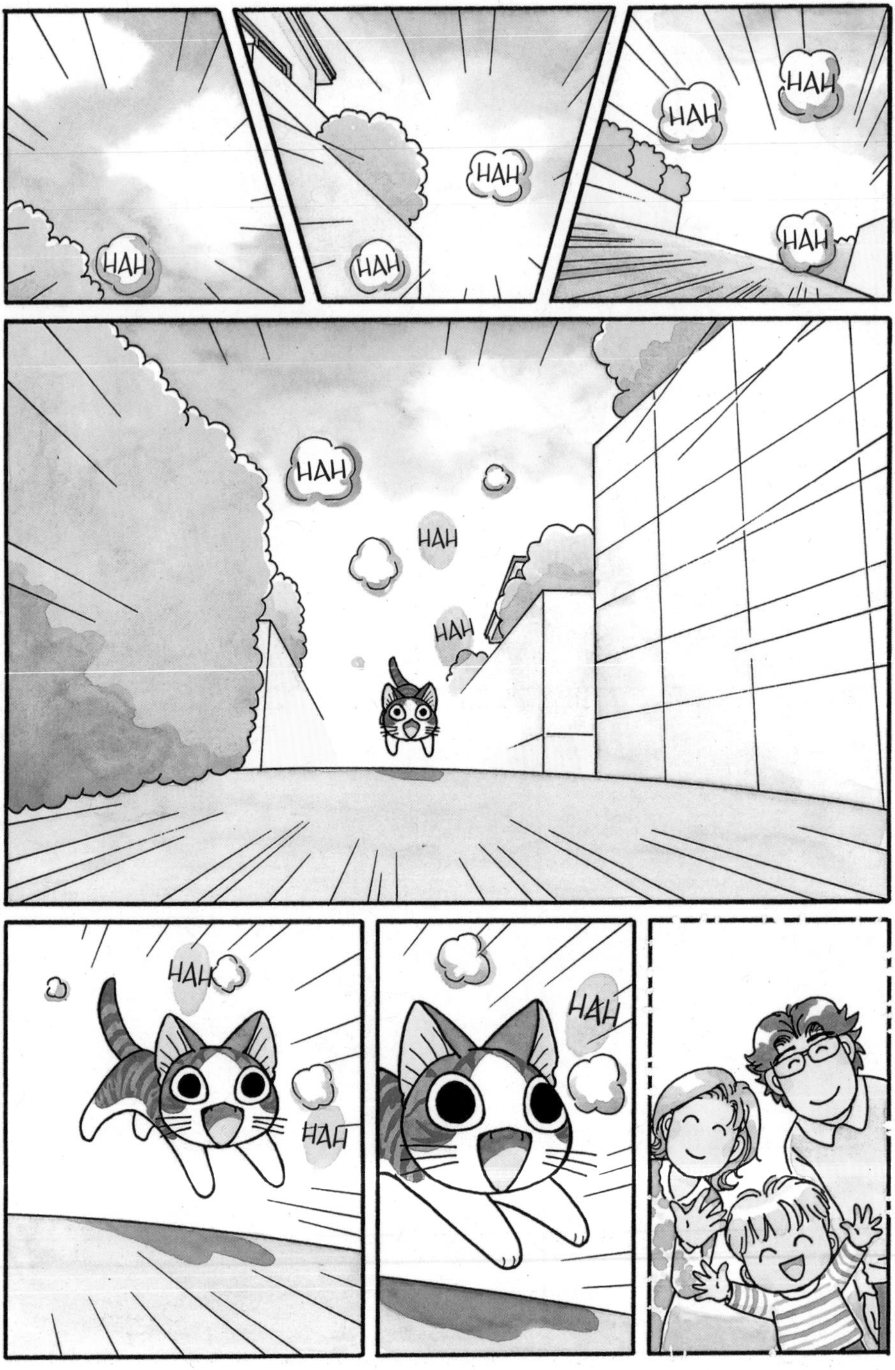
HAH
HAH
HAH
HAH
HAH
HAH
HAH
HAH
HAH
HAH
HAH
HAH
HAH

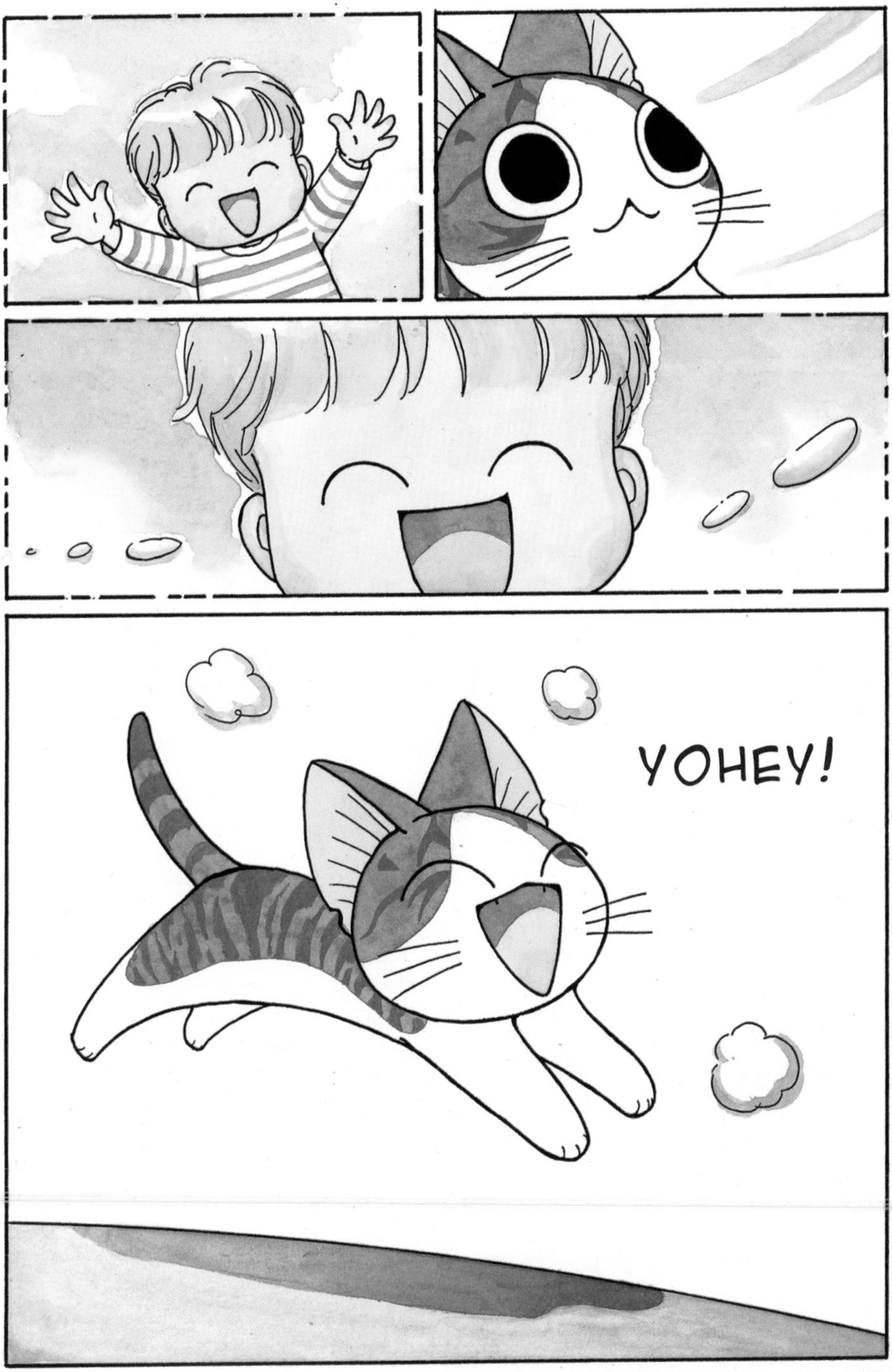
YOHEY!

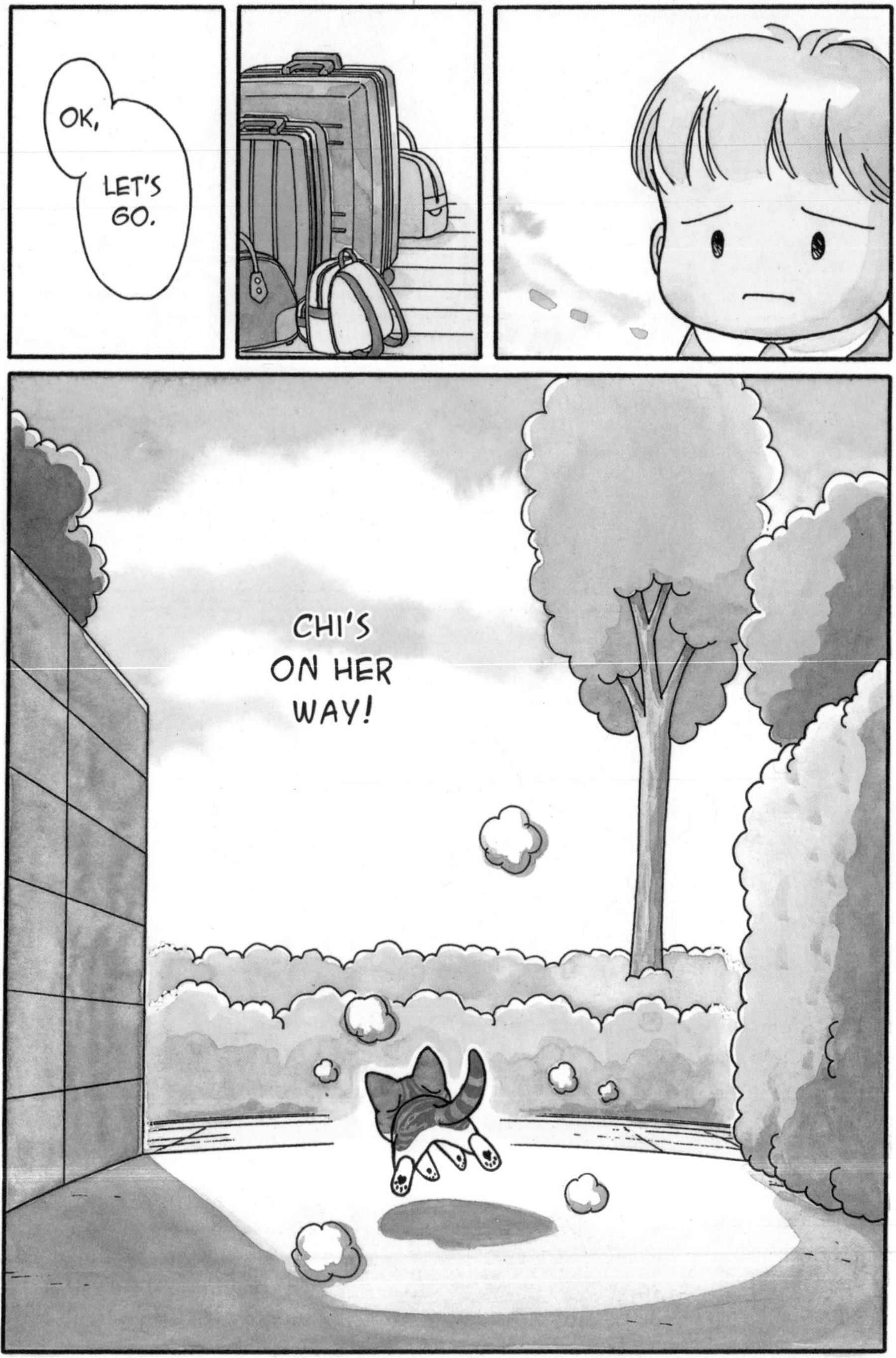
OK, LET'S GO.
CHI'S ON HER WAY!

the end

homemade 216: a cat continues to run

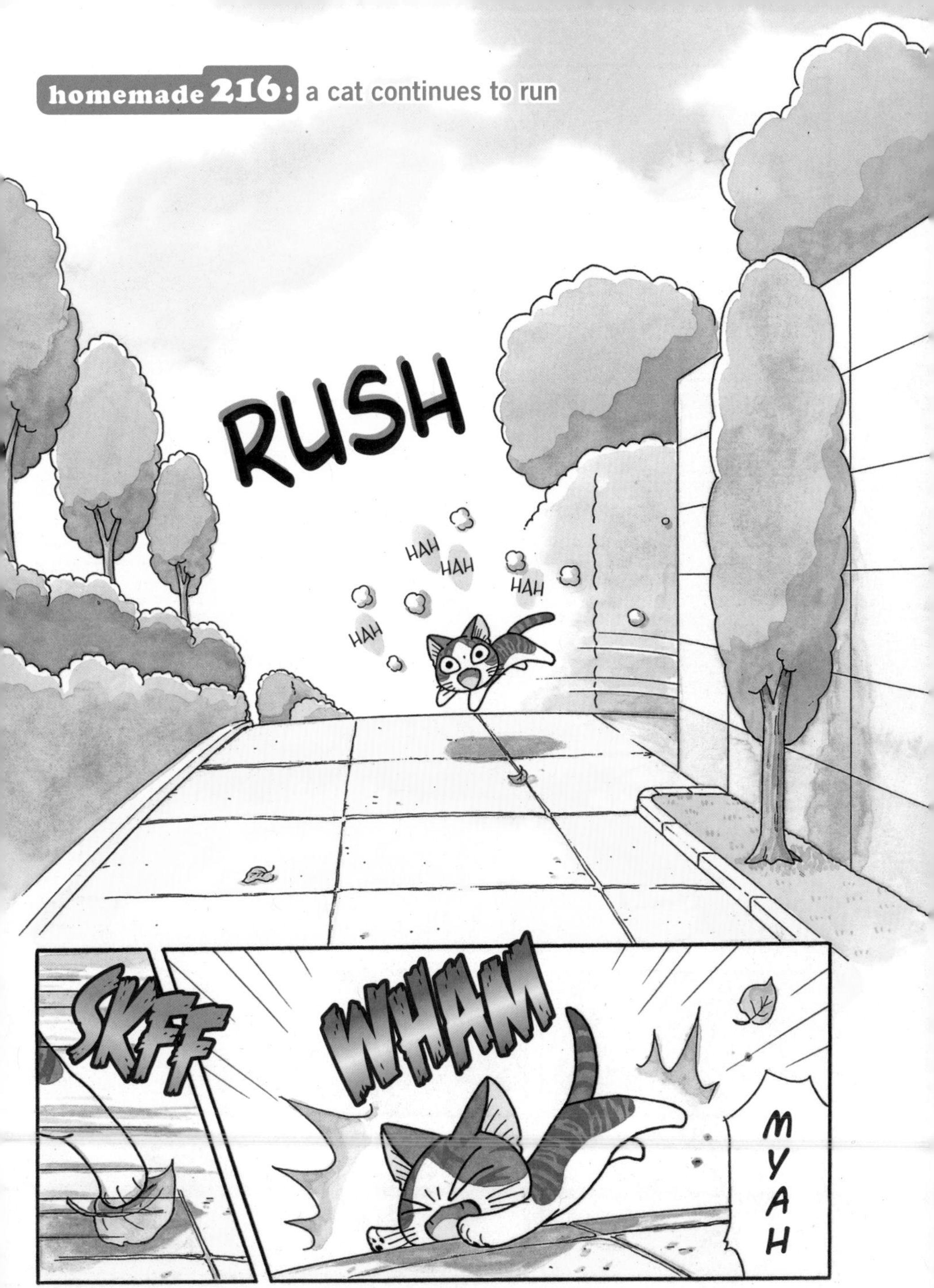
RUSH
HAH
HAH
HAH
HAH
SKFF
WHAM
MYAH

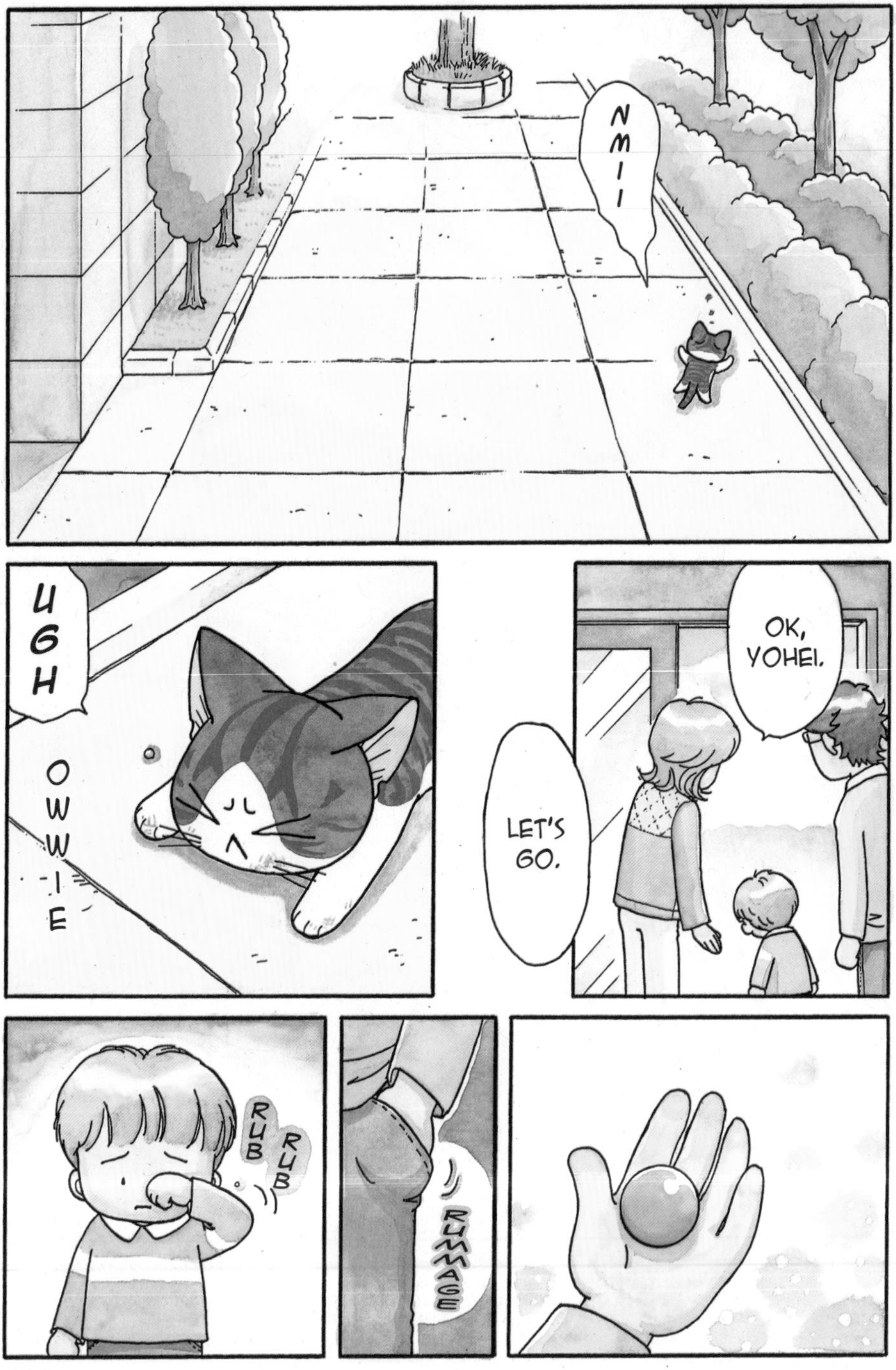
NMII
UGH
OWWIE
OK, YOHEI.
LET'S GO.
RUB RUB
RUMMAGE

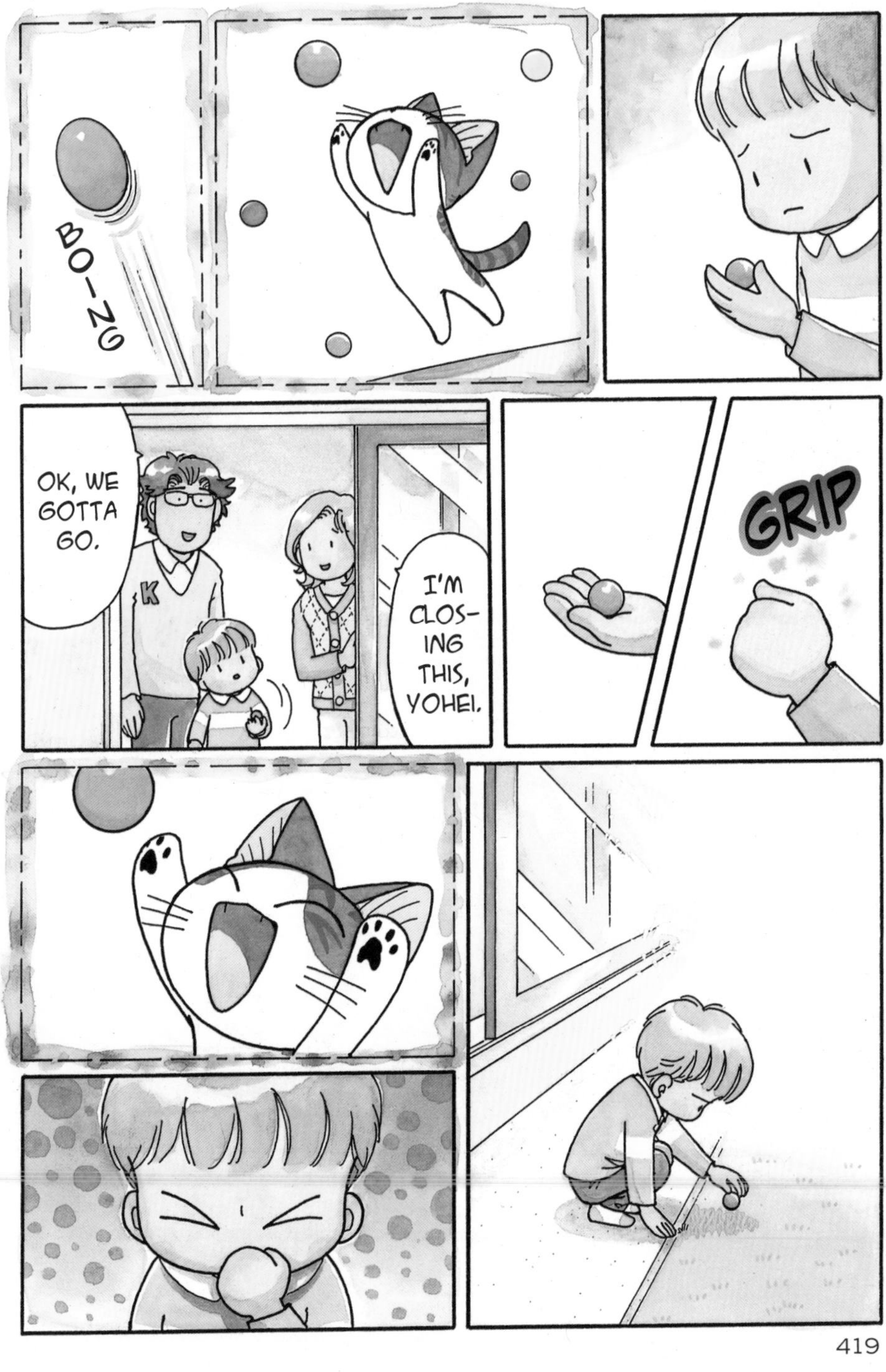
BO-I-NG
OK, WE GOTTA GO.
I'M CLOSING THIS, YOHEI.
GRIP

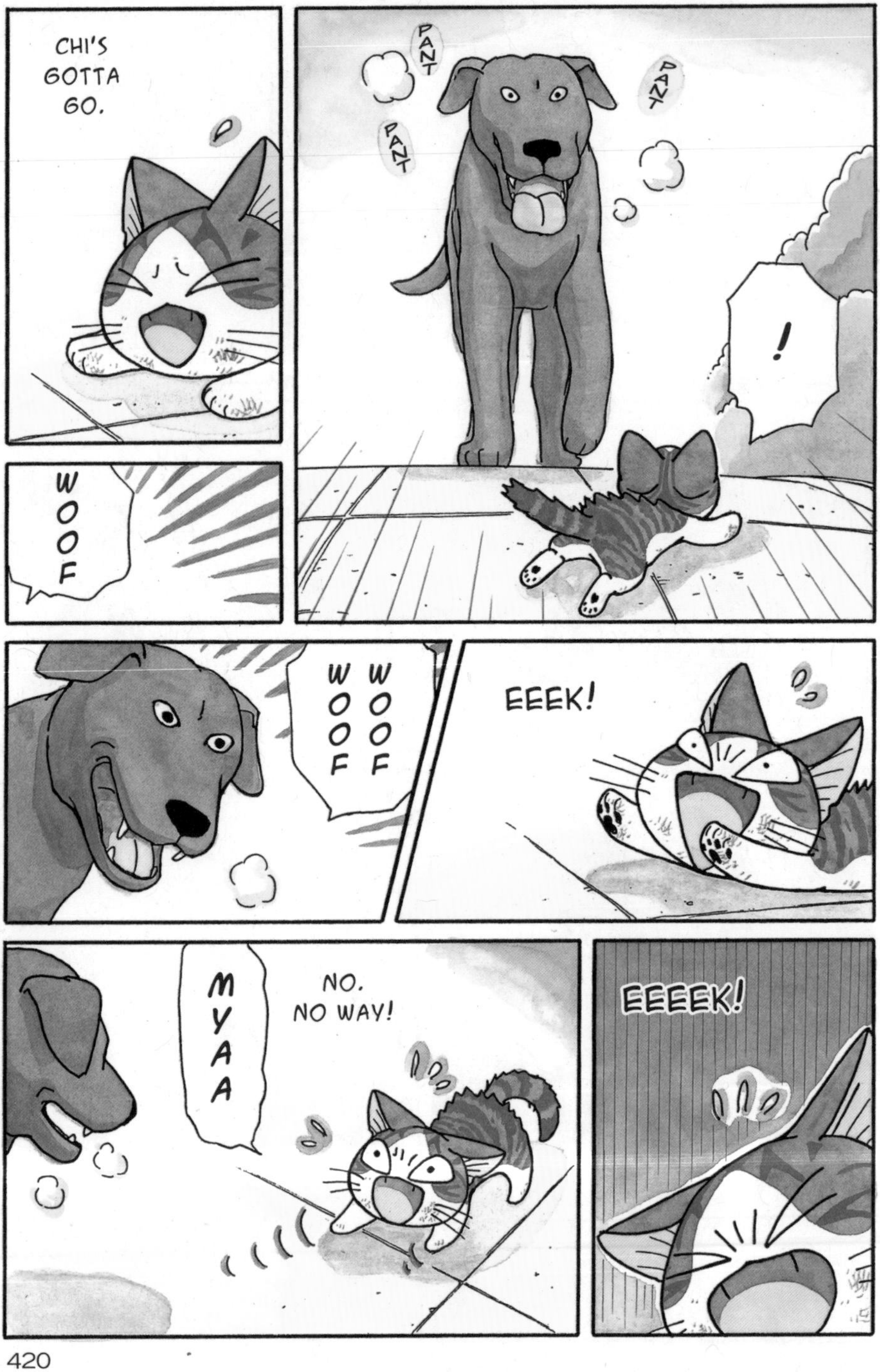
CHI'S GOTTA GO.
PANT
PANT
PANT
!
WOOF
WOOF WOOF
EEEK!
MYAA
NO. NO WAY!
EEEEK!

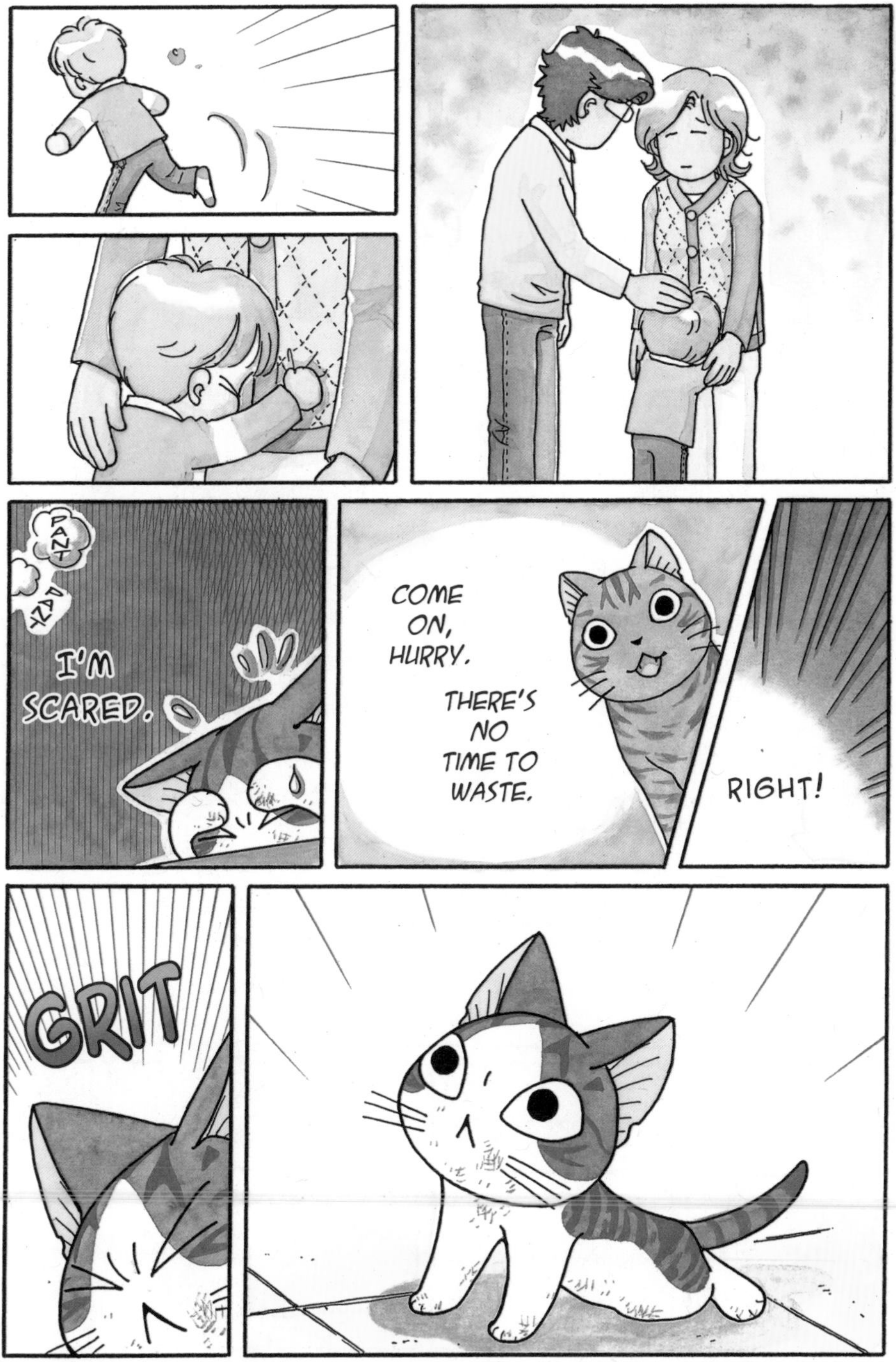
PANT
PANT
I'M SCARED.
COME ON, HURRY.
THERE'S NO TIME TO WASTE.
RIGHT!
GRIT

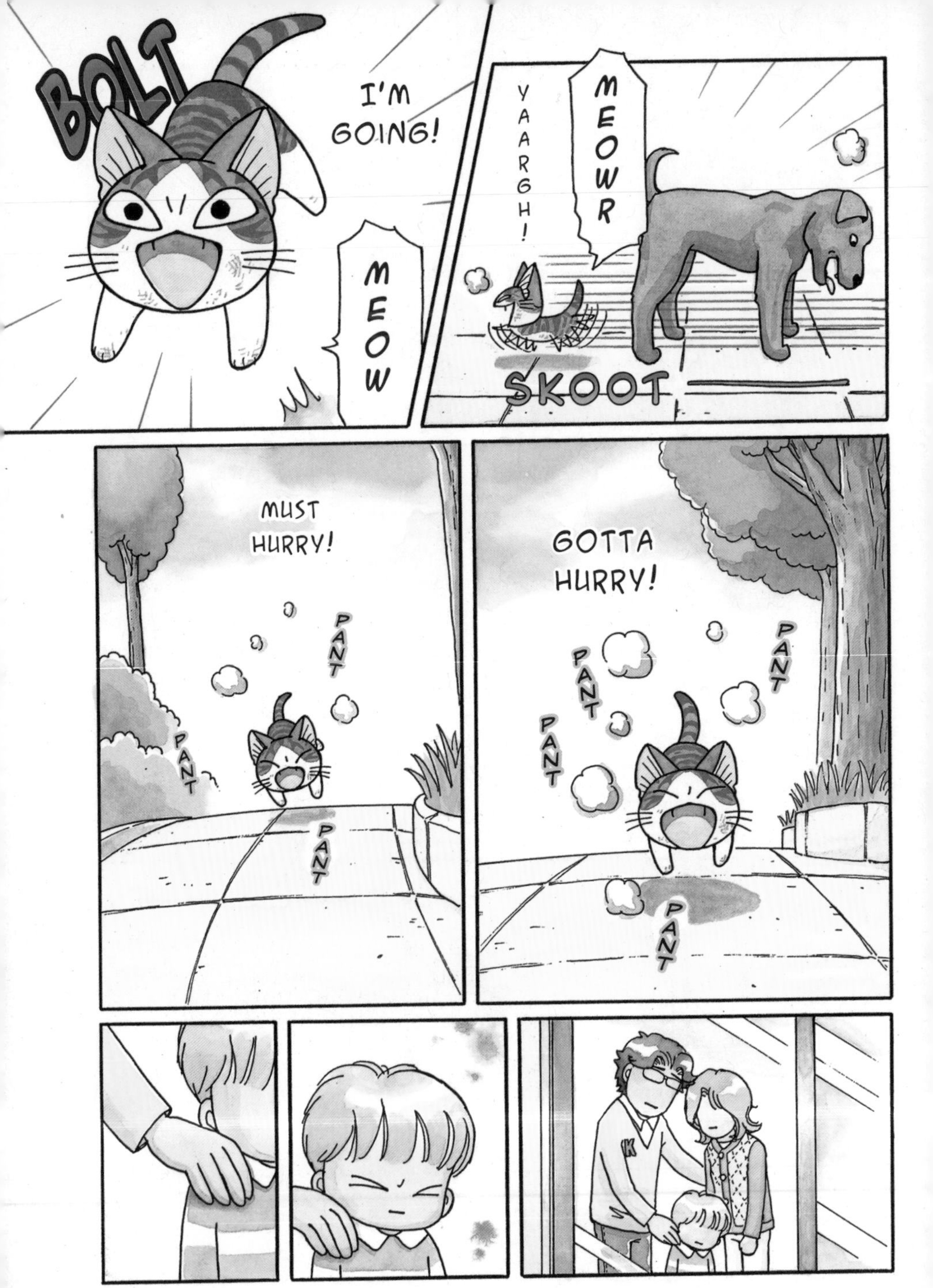
BOLT
I'M GOING!
MEOW
YAARGH!
MEOWR
SKOOT
MUST HURRY!
PANT
PANT
PANT
GOTTA HURRY!
PANT
PANT
PANT
PANT

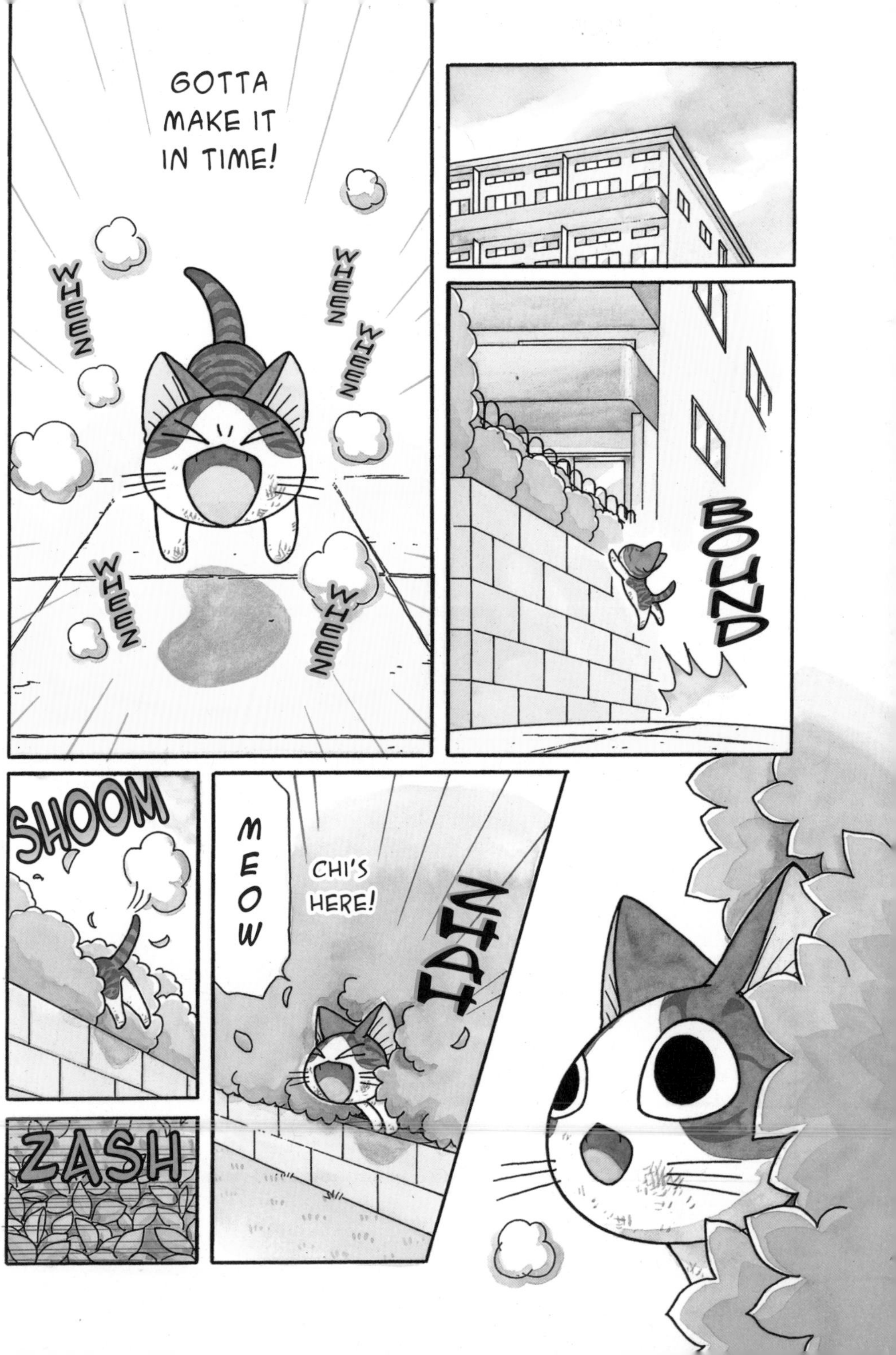
GOTTA MAKE IT IN TIME!
WHEEZ
WHEEN
WHEEN
WHEEZ
WHEEN
BOUND
SHOOM
ZASH
MEOW
CHI'S HERE!
HAHZ

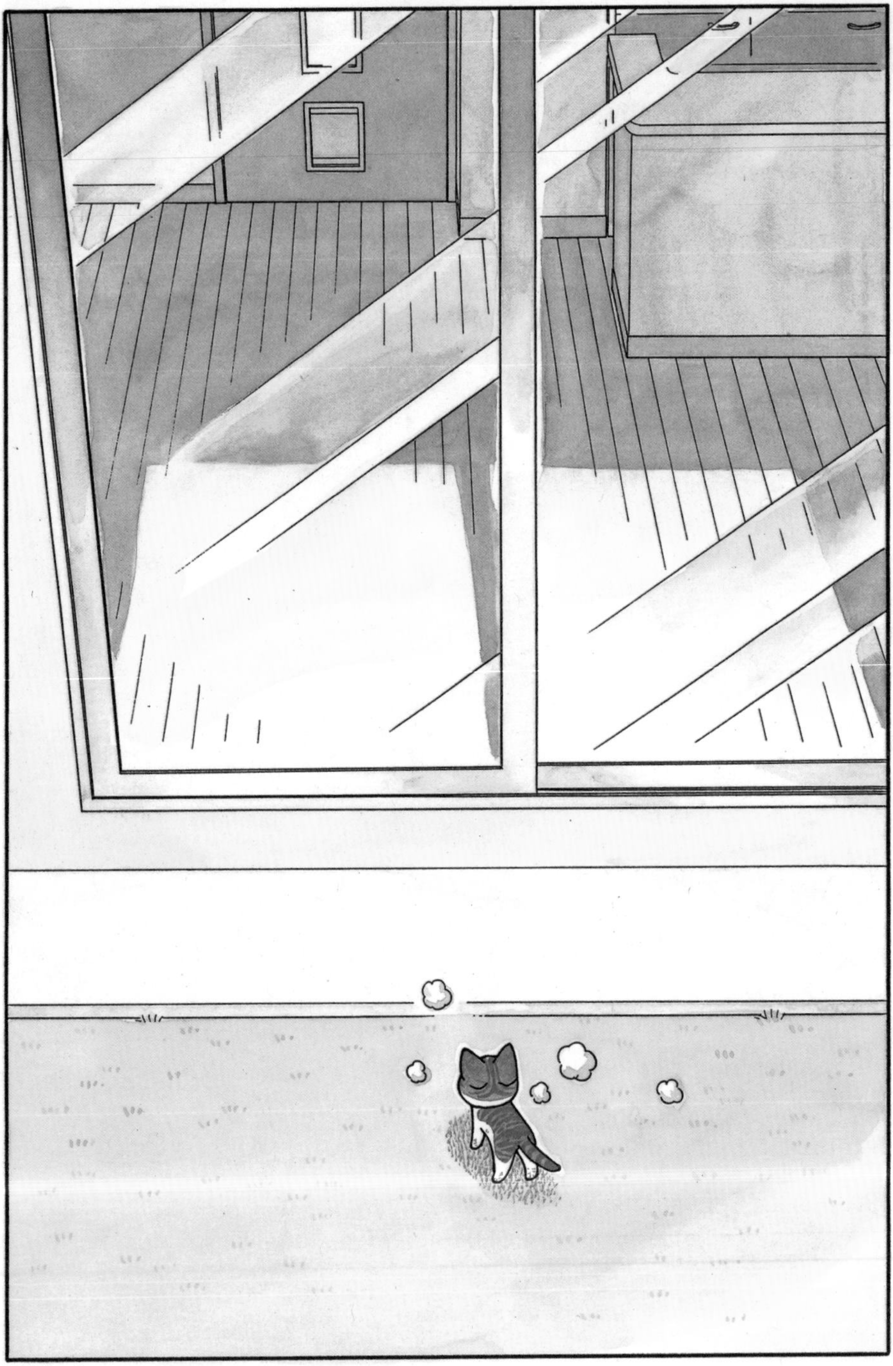

the end

homemade 217: a cat dwells

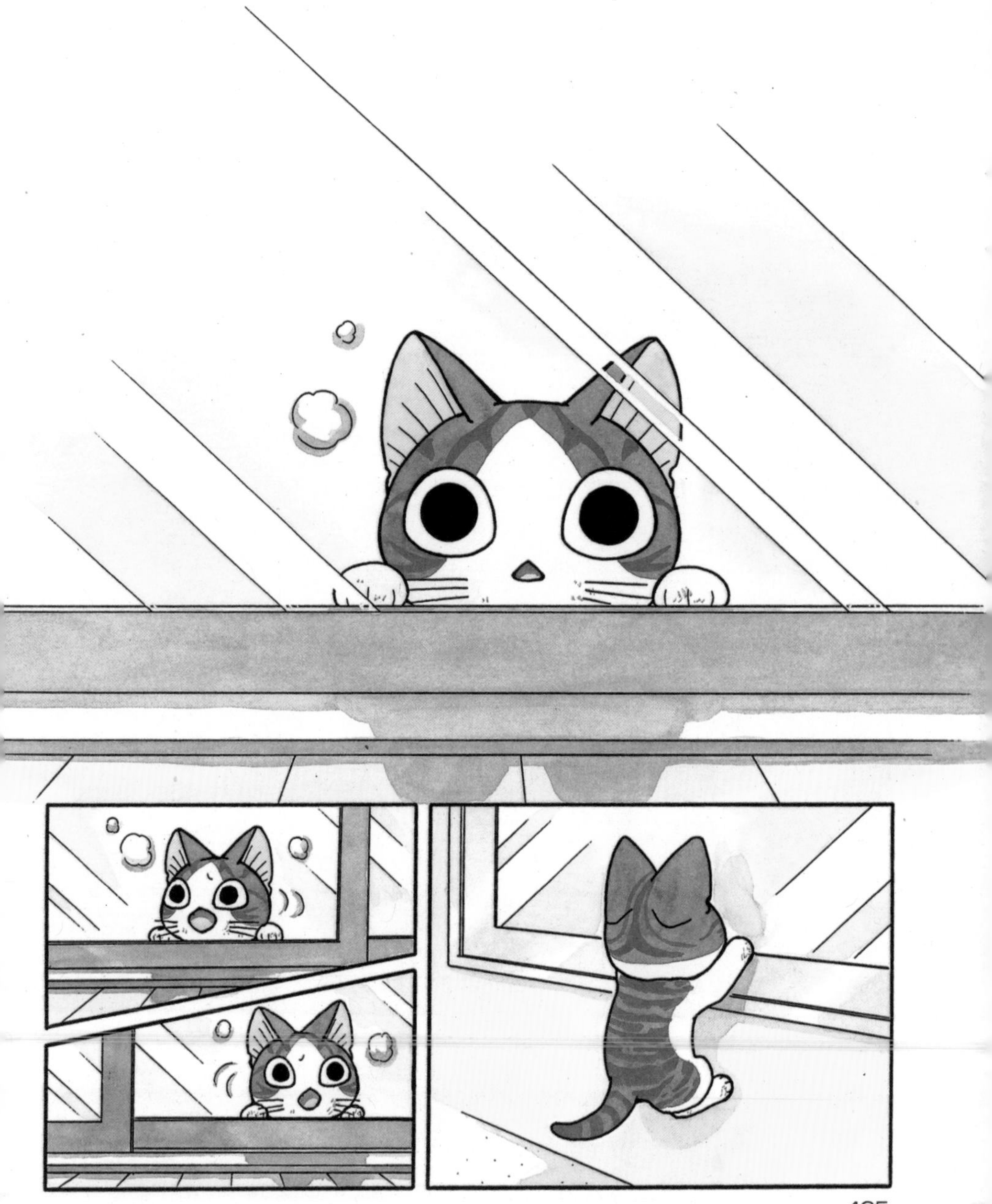

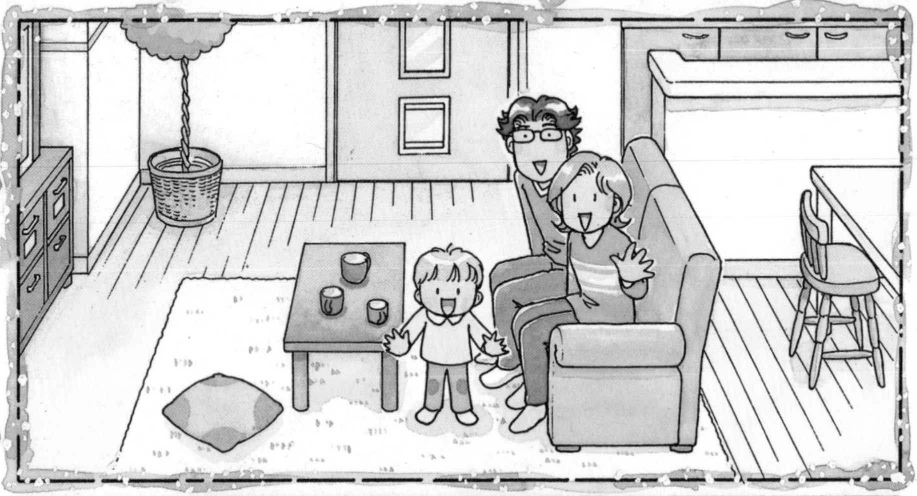

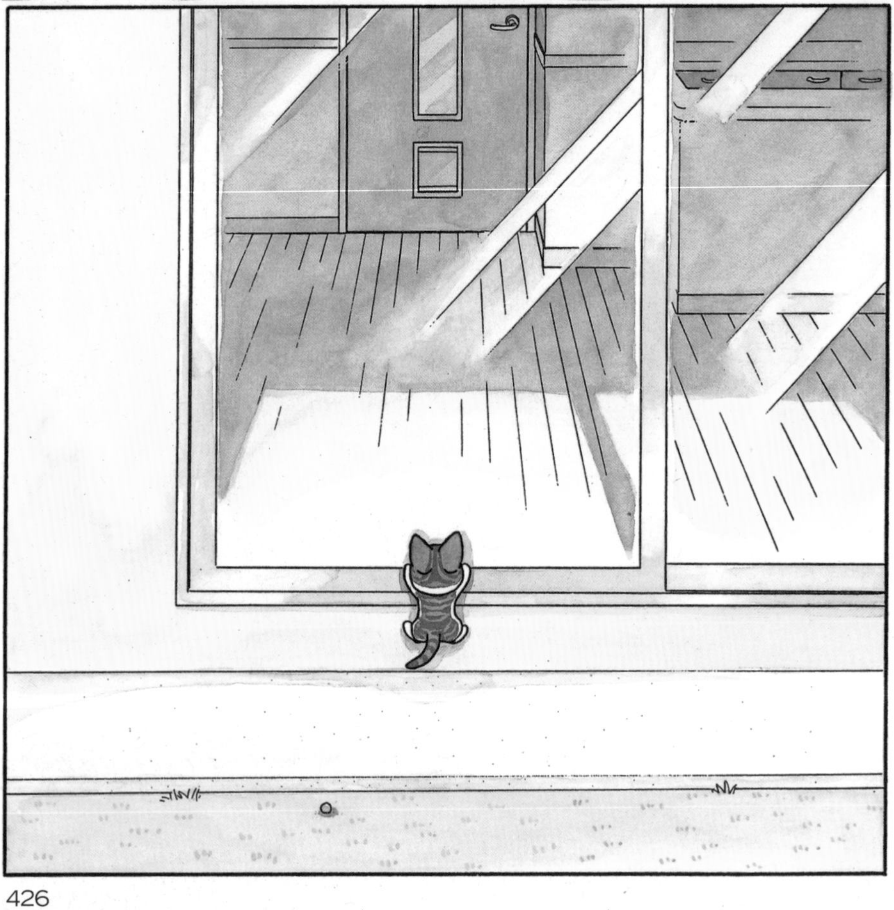

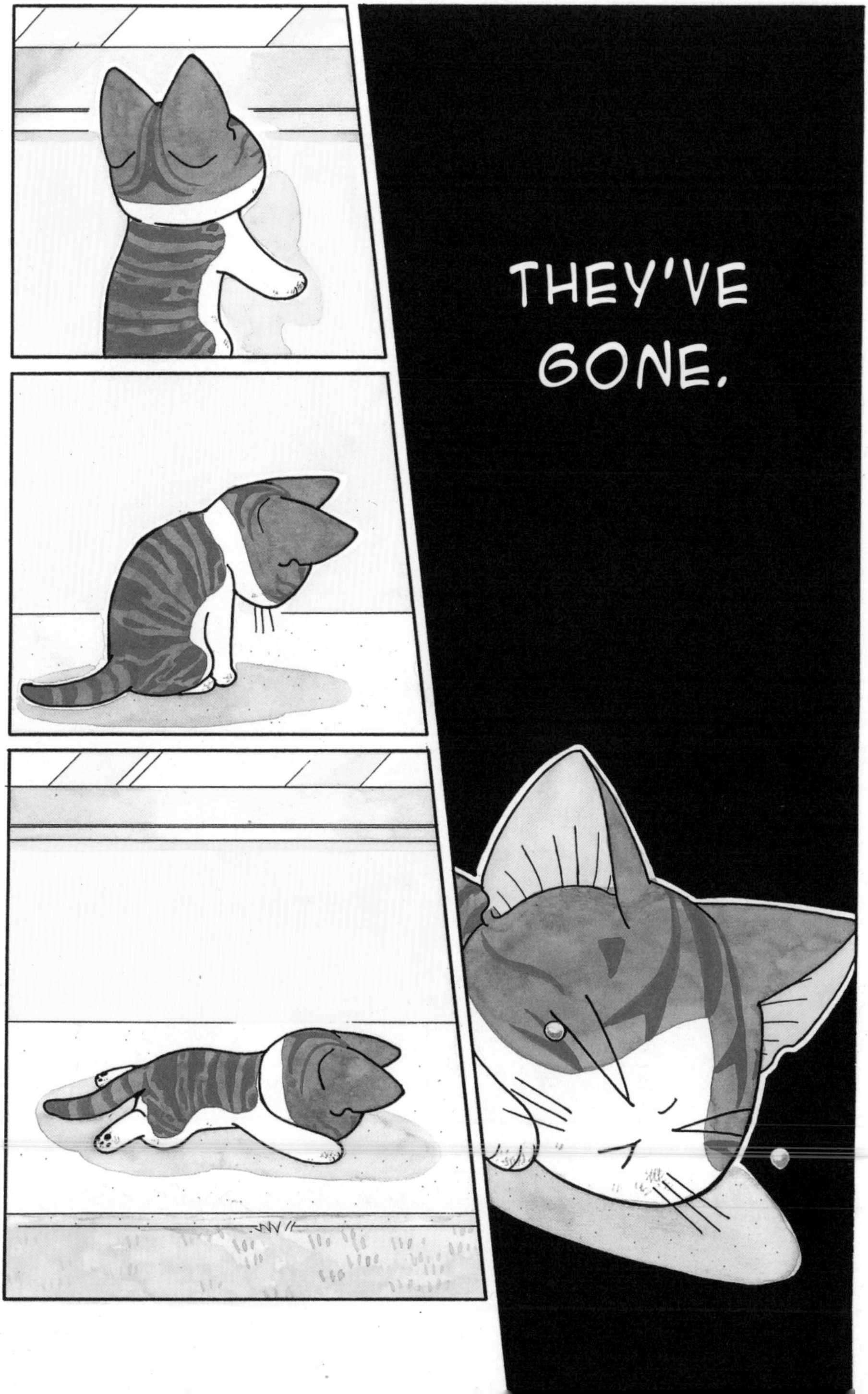
THEY'VE GONE.

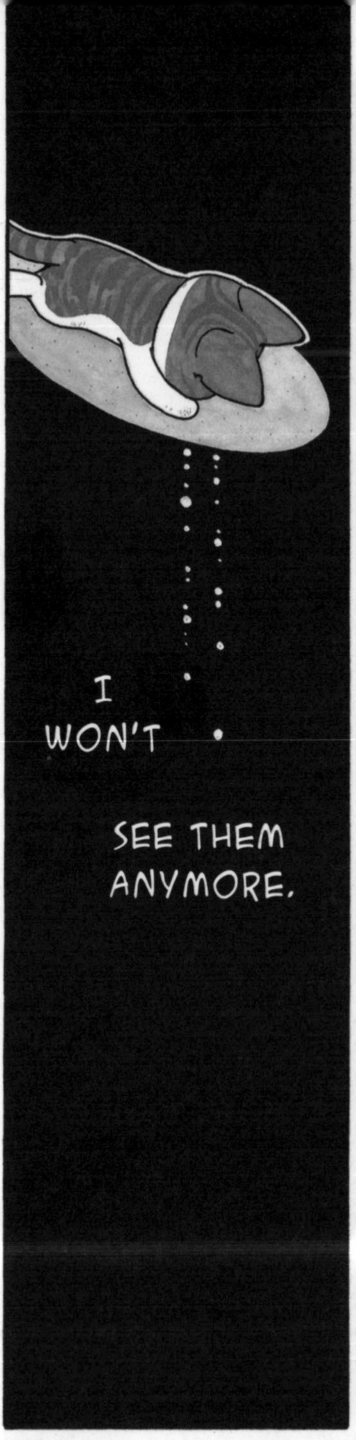
I WON'T
SEE THEM ANYMORE.
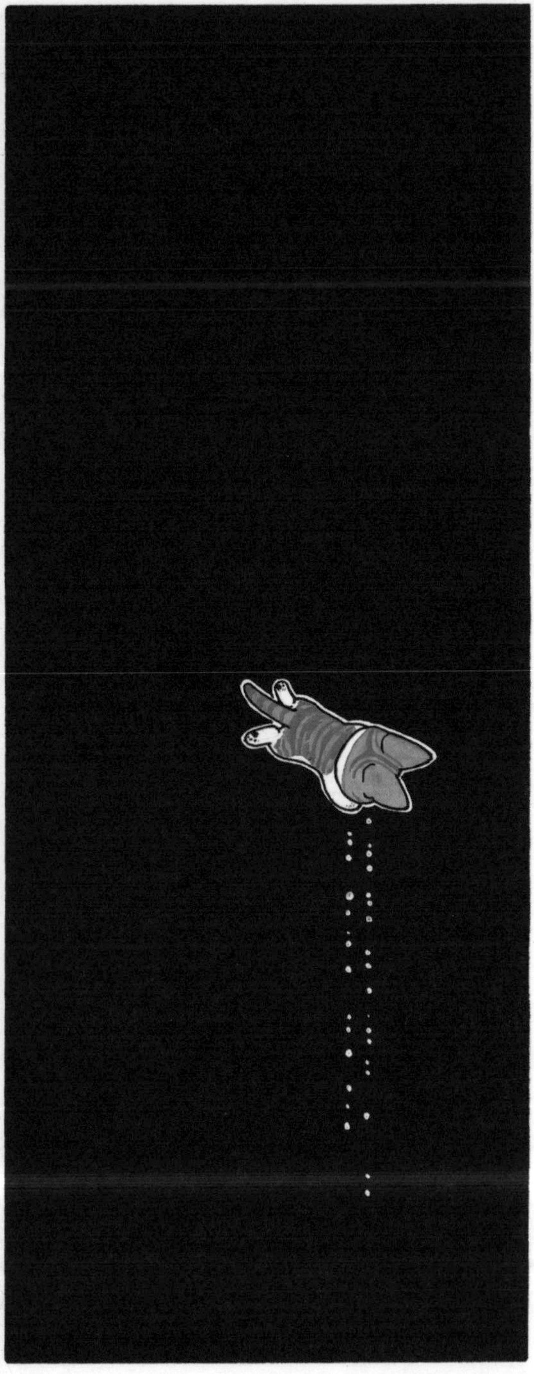

[redacted]

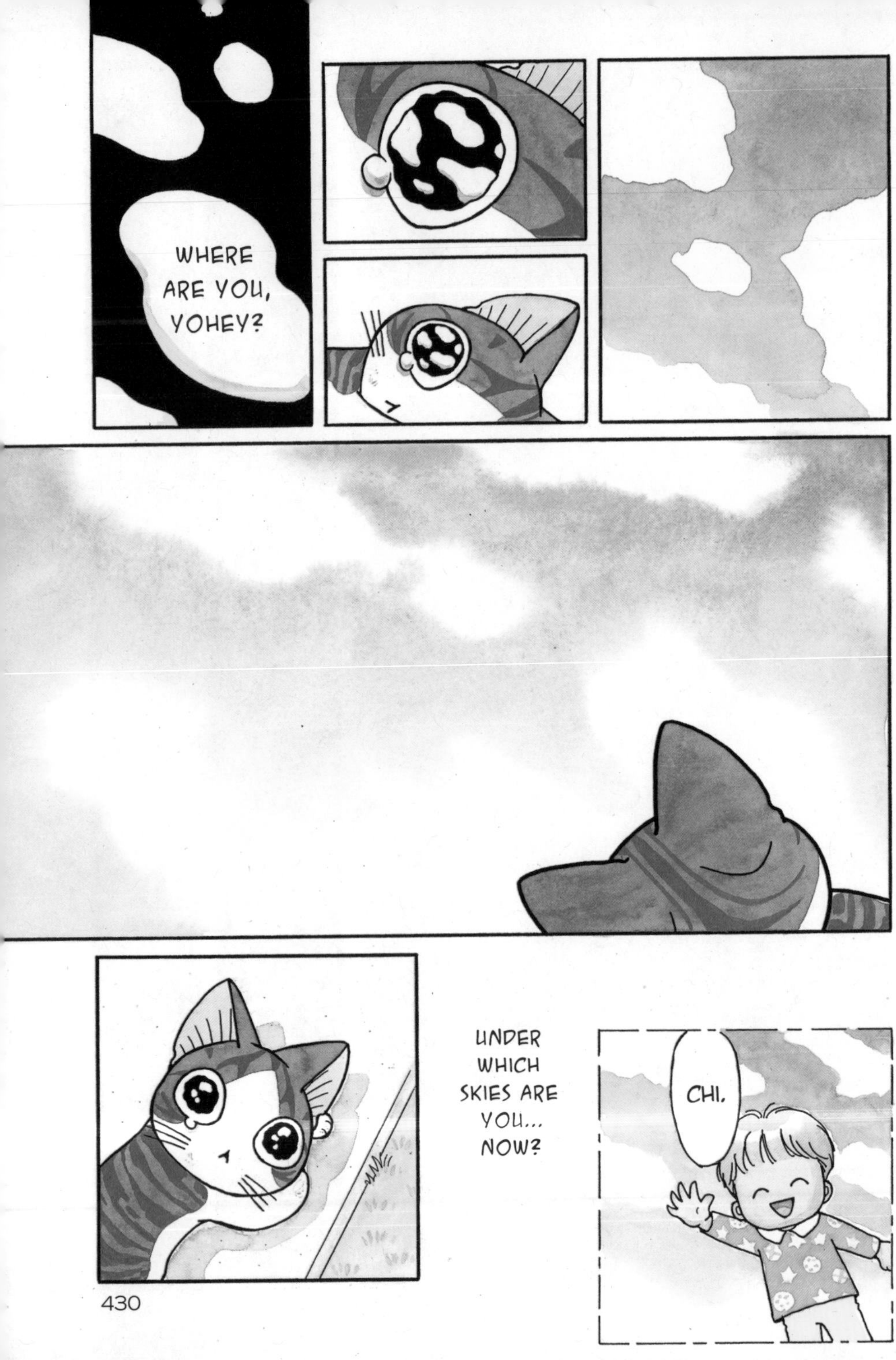
WHERE ARE YOU, YOHEY?
UNDER WHICH SKIES ARE YOU... NOW?
CHI.

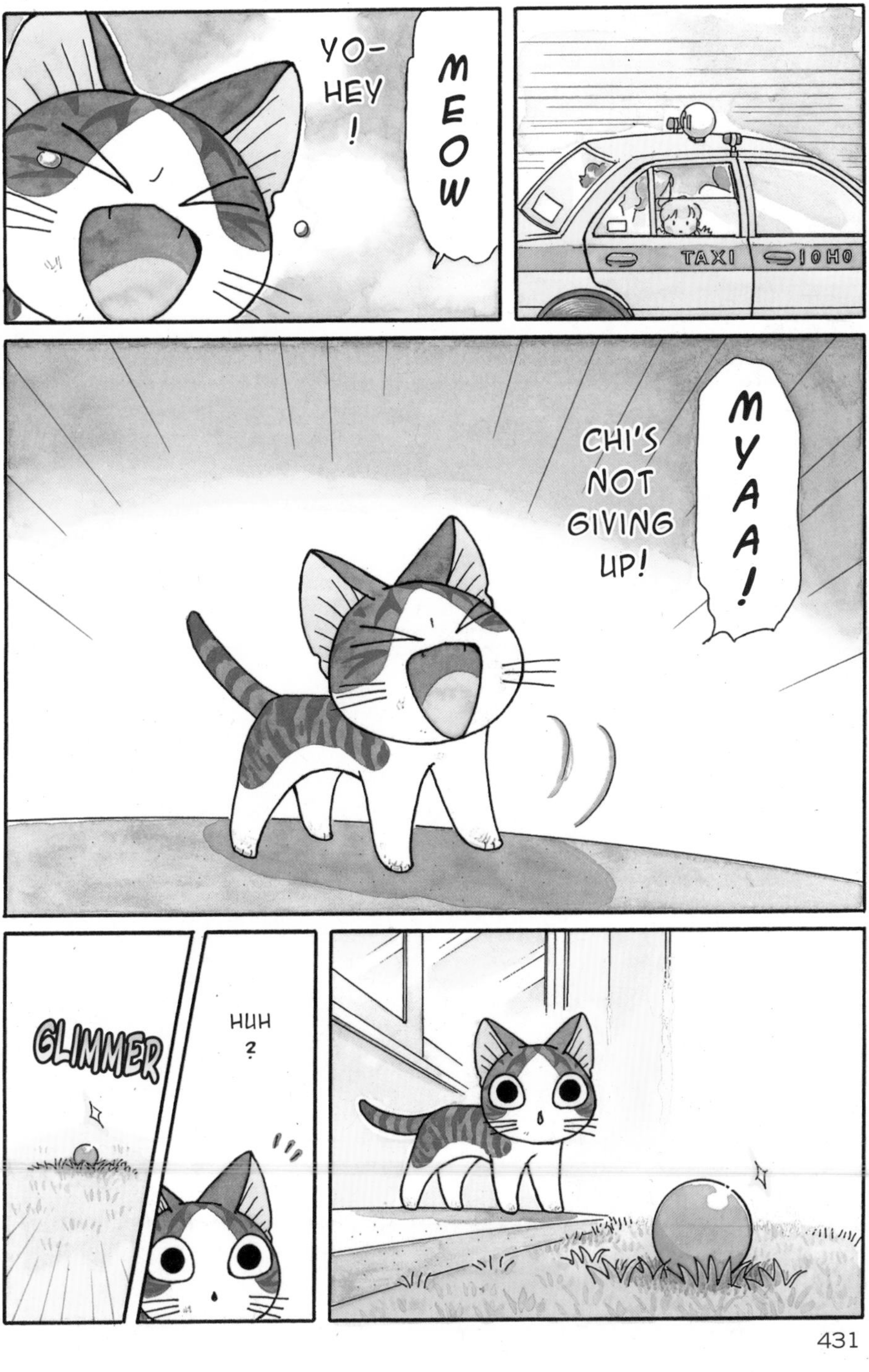
YO-HEY!
MEOW
TAXI
CHI'S NOT GIVING UP!
MYAA!
GLIMMER
HUH?

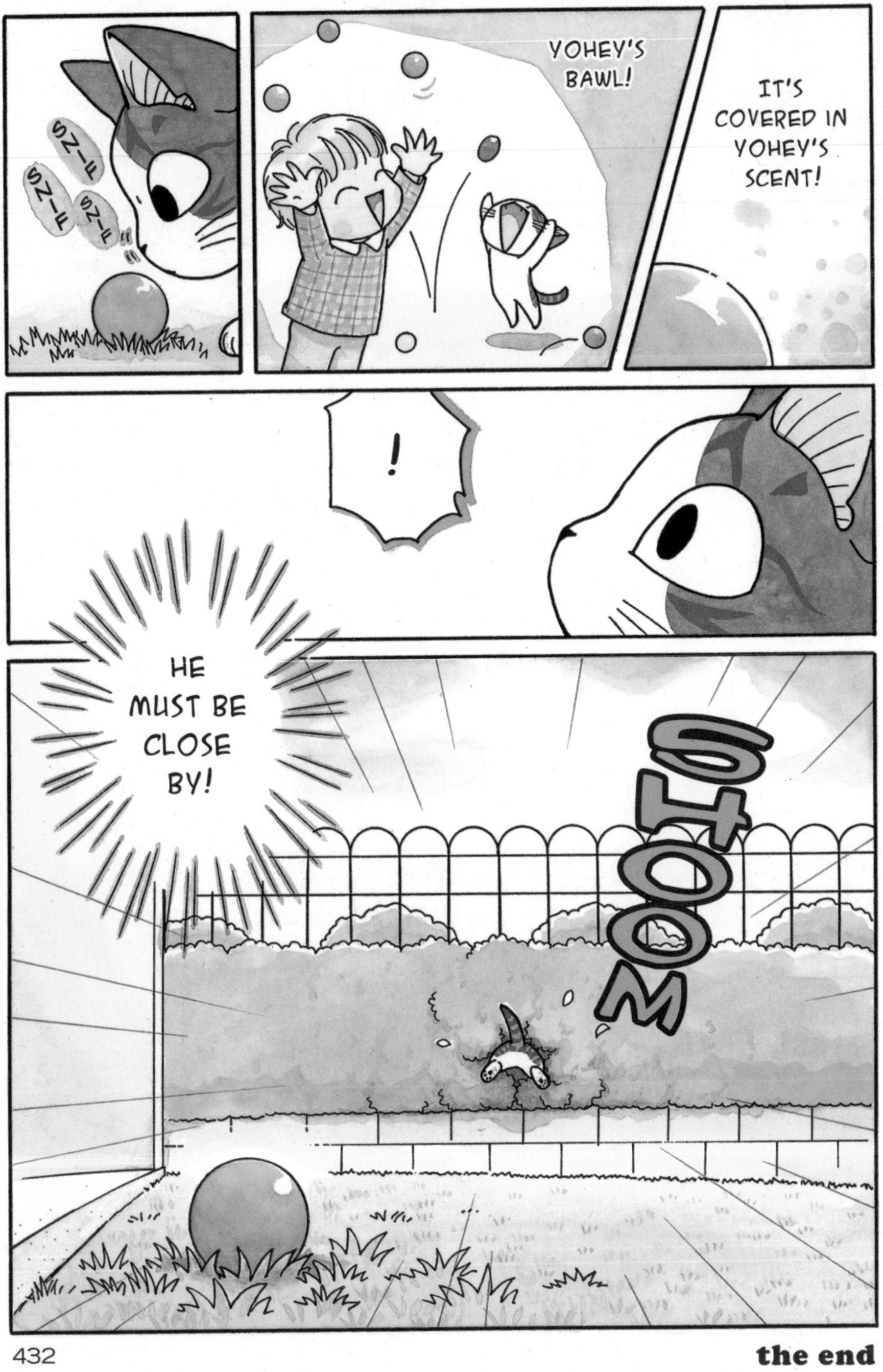
SNIF
SNIF
SNIF
YOHEY'S BAWL!
IT'S COVERED IN YOHEY'S SCENT!
!
HE MUST BE CLOSE BY!
SHOOM

the end

homemade 218: a cat comes home

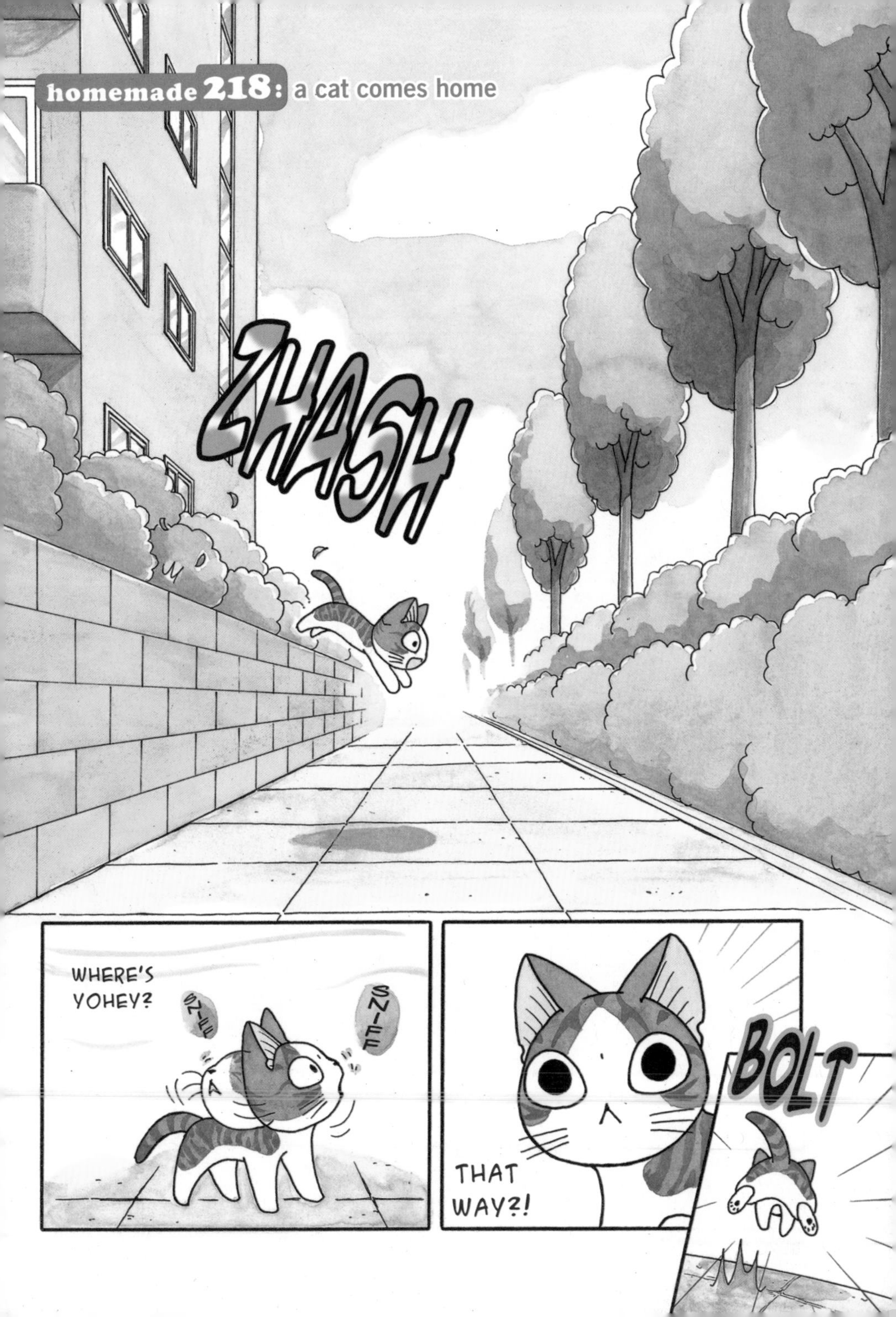
ZHASH
WHERE'S YOHEY?
SNIFF
SNIFF
THAT WAY?!
BOLT

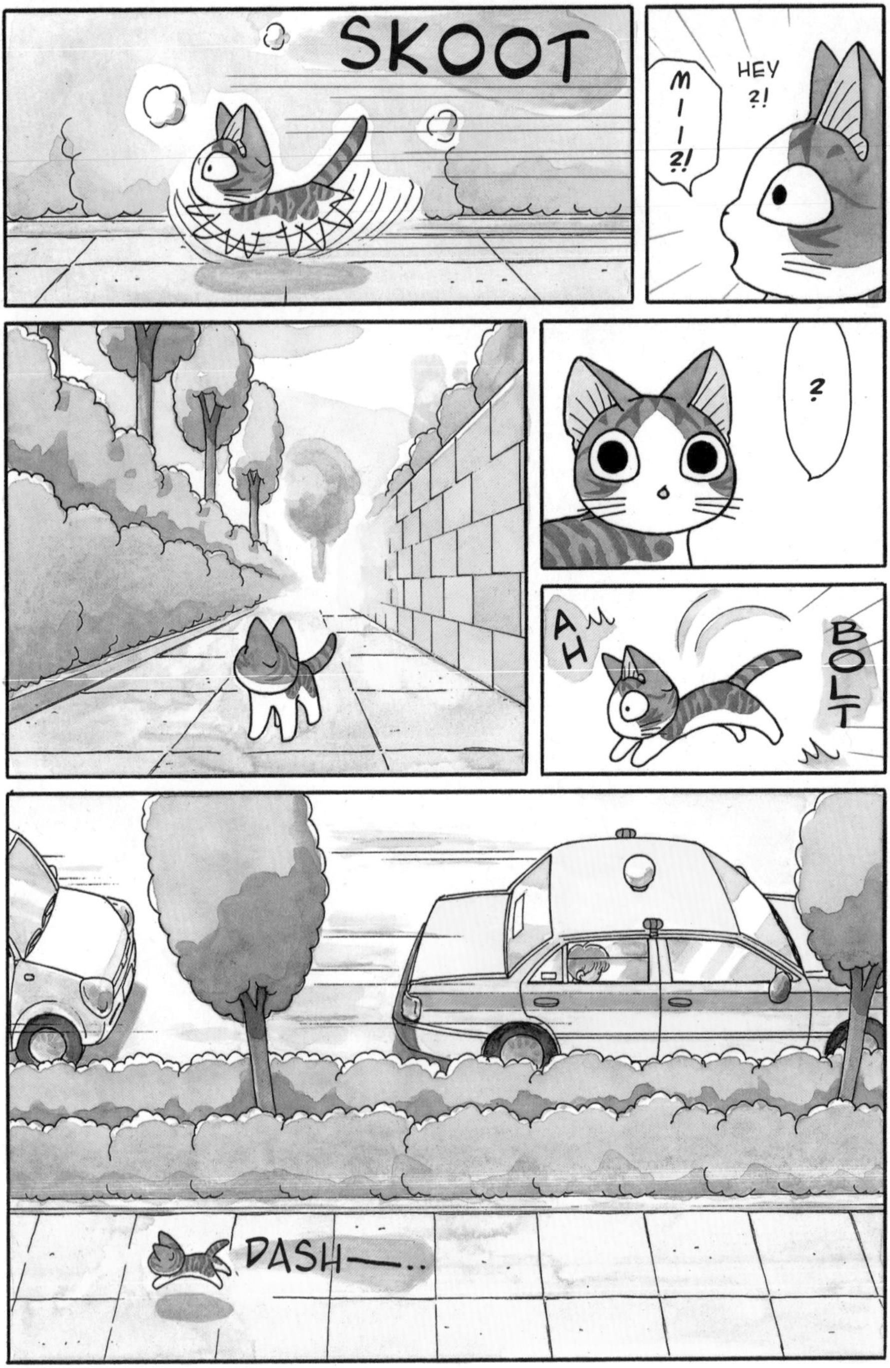
SKOOT
MII?!
HEY ?!
?
AH
BOLT
DASH—..

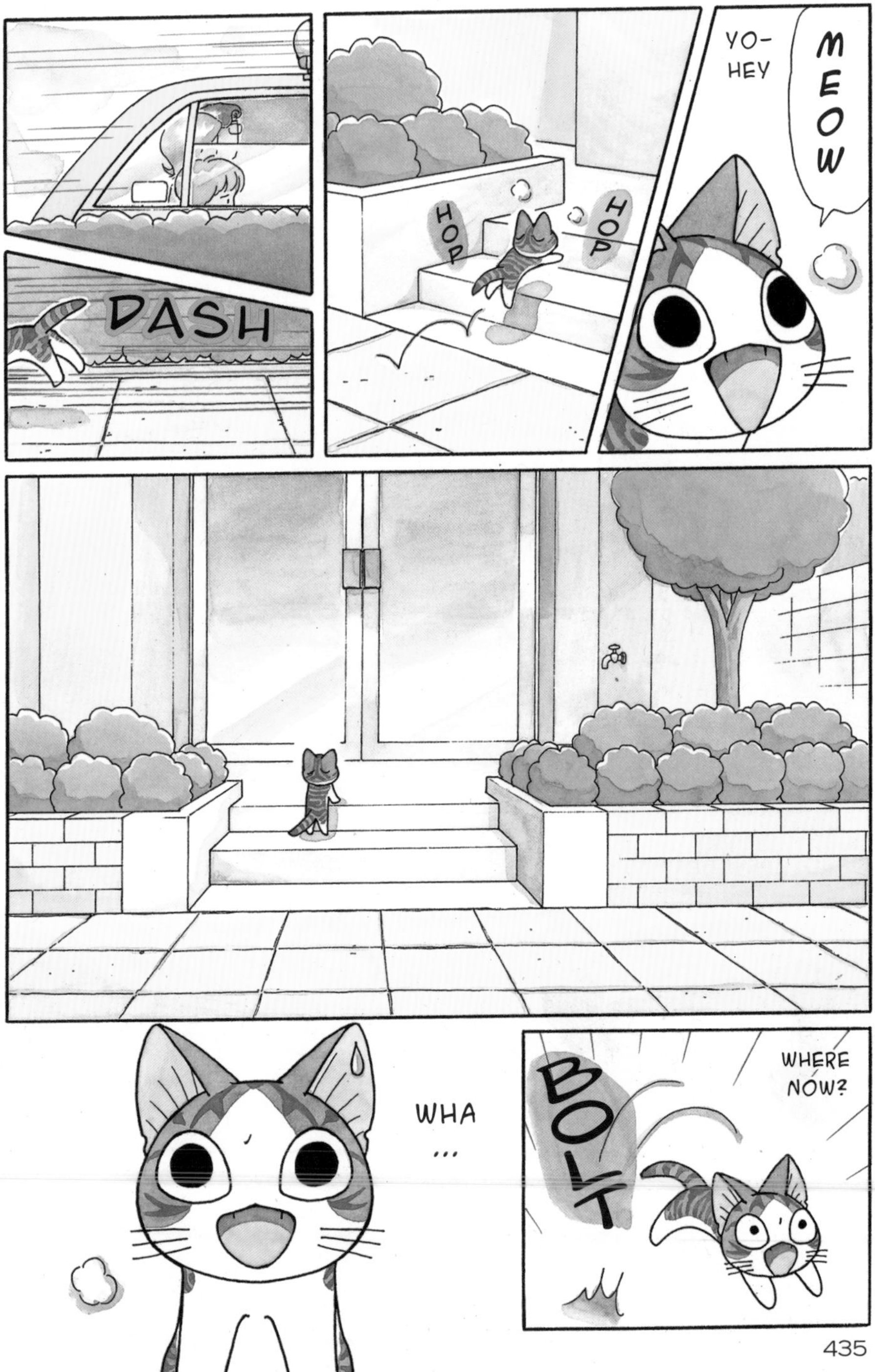
DASH
HOP
HOP
YO-HEY
MEOW
WHA ...
BOLT
WHERE NOW?

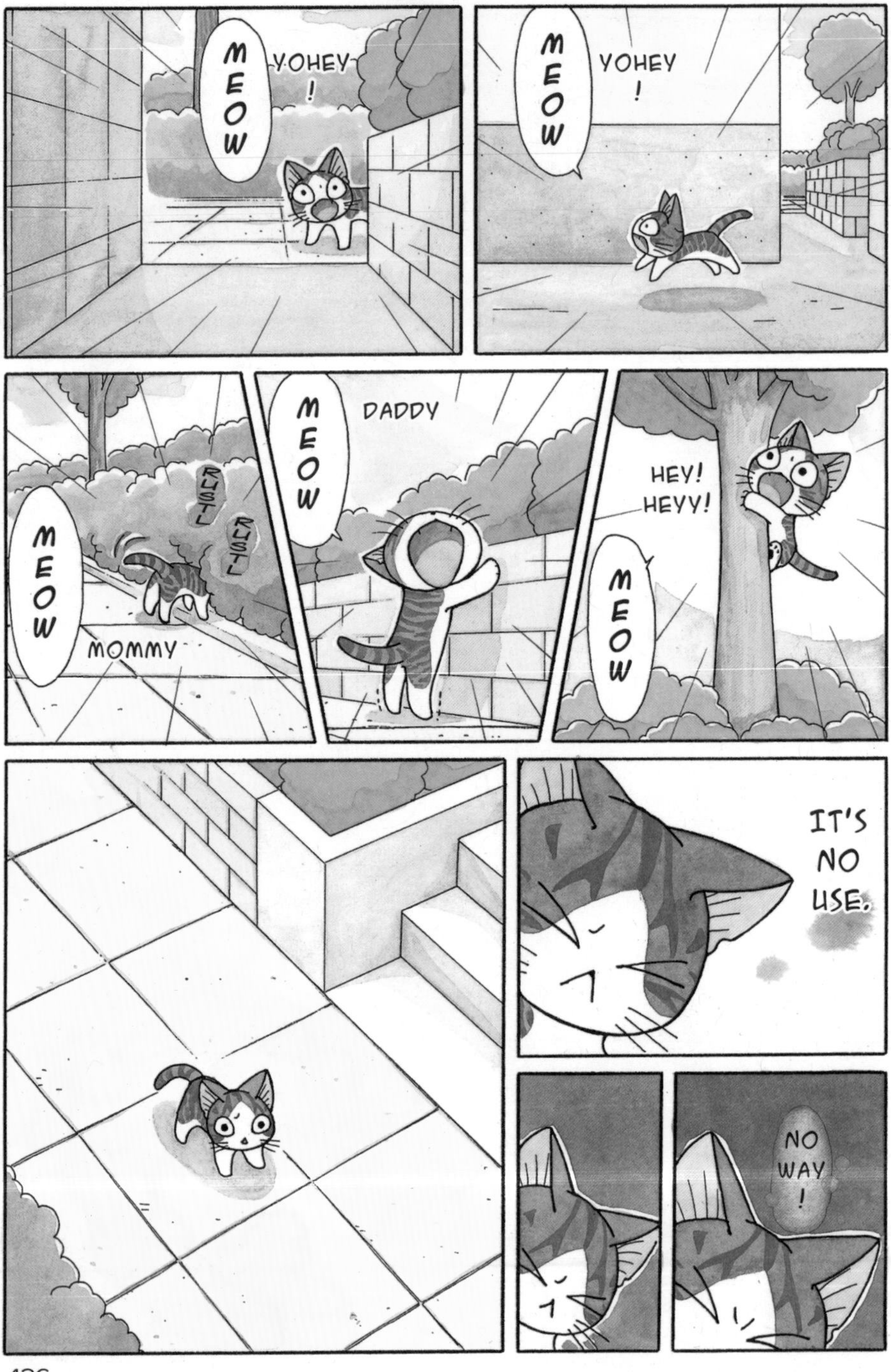
MEOW
YOHEY!
MEOW
YOHEY!
RUSTL RUSTL
MEOW
MOMMY
MEOW
DADDY
HEY! HEYY!
MEOW
IT'S NO USE.
NO WAY!

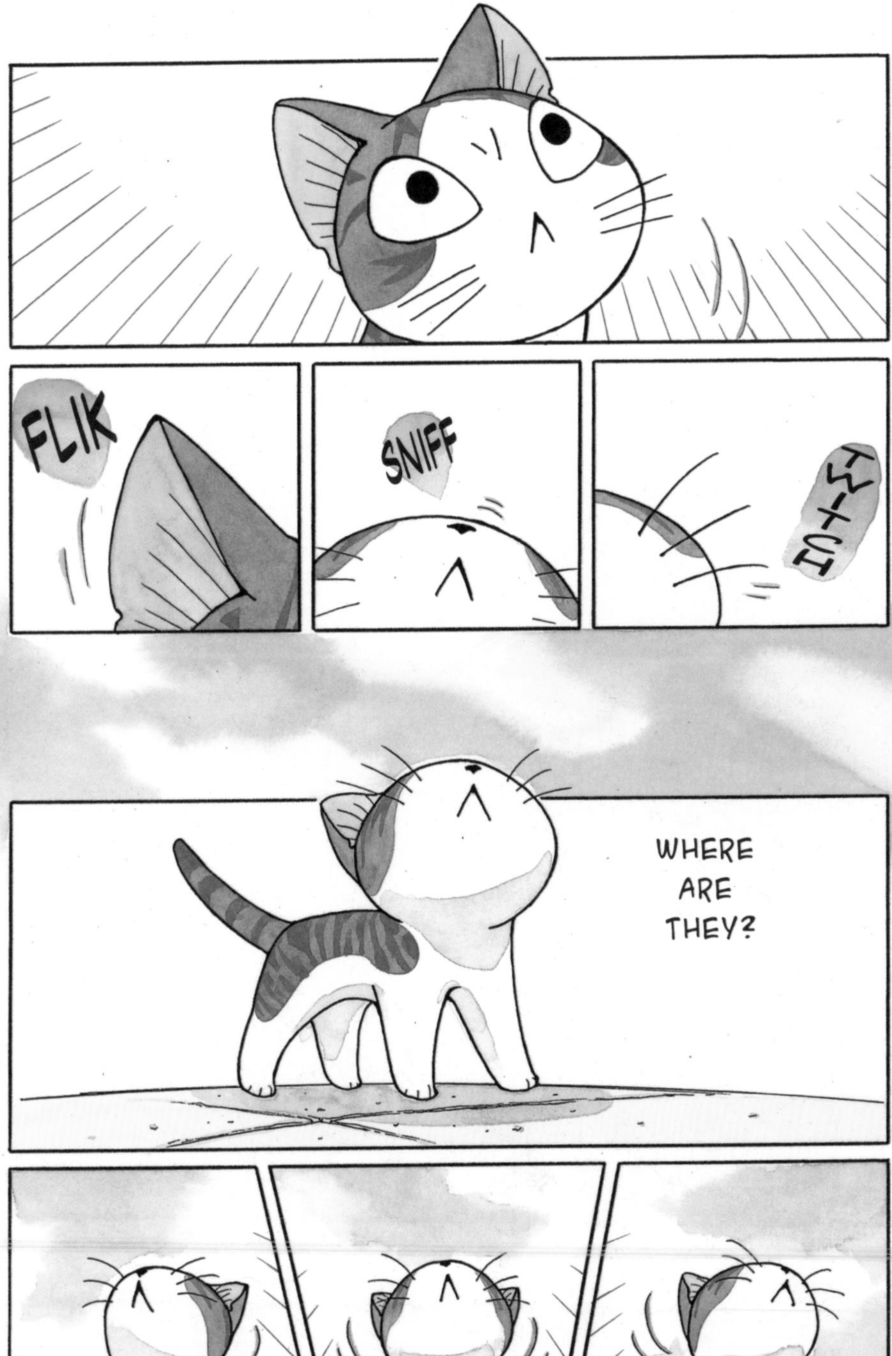
FLIK
SNIFF
TWITCH
WHERE ARE THEY?

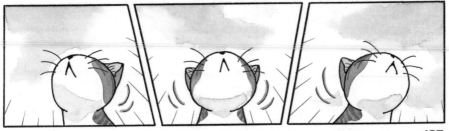

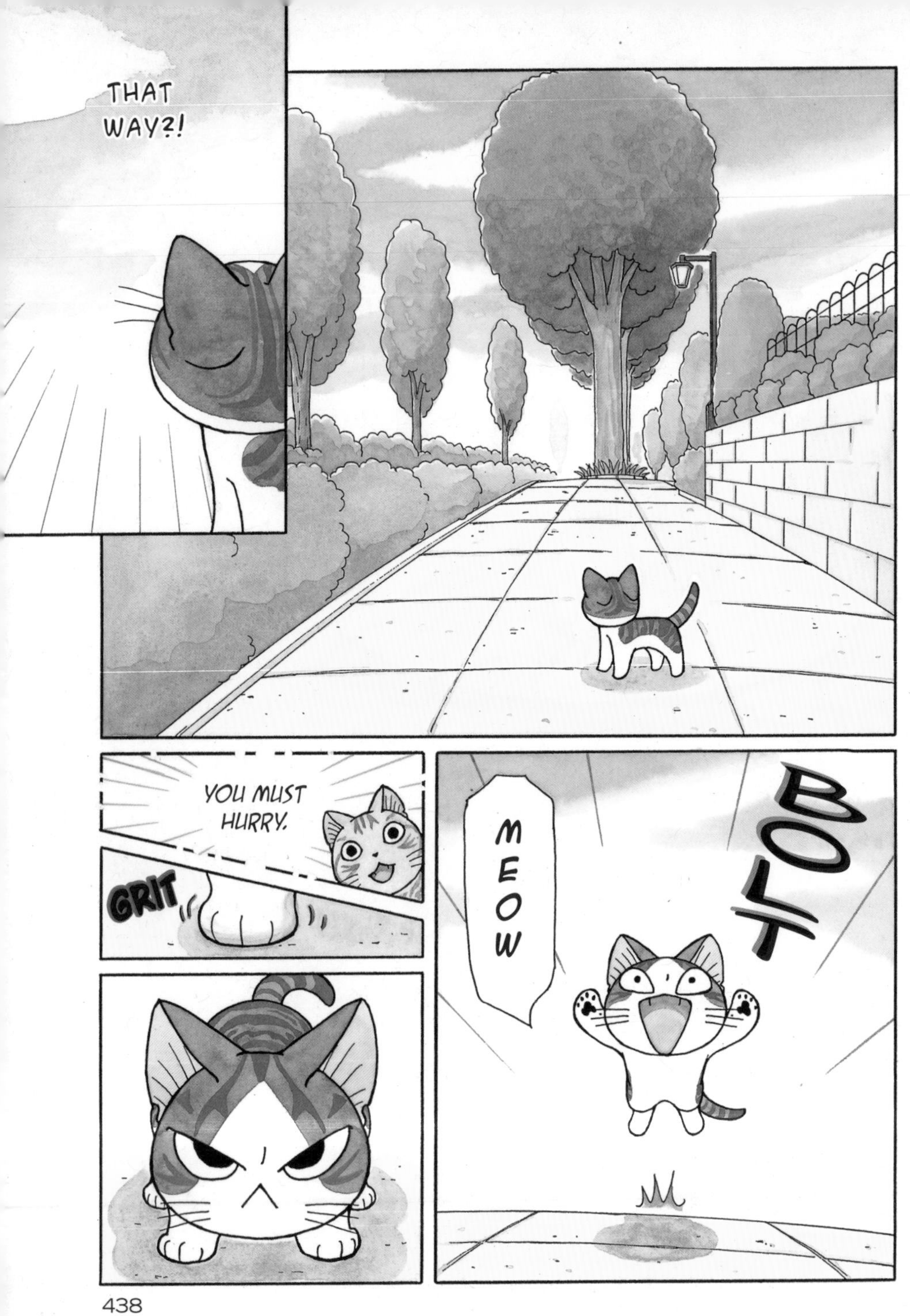

THAT WAY?!
YOU MUST HURRY.
GRIT
MEOW
BOLT

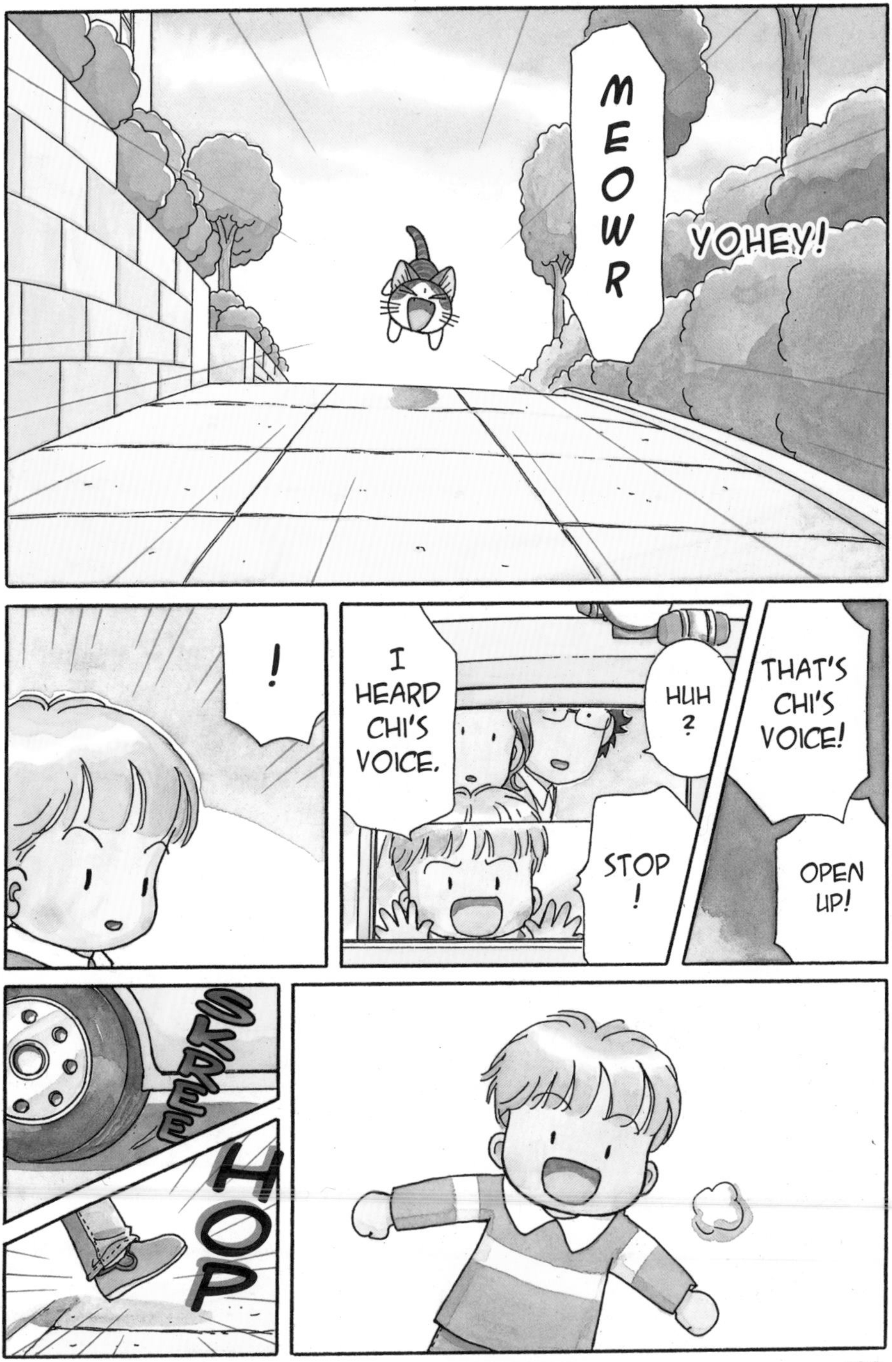
MEOWR
YOHEY!
!
I HEARD CHI'S VOICE.
HUH?
STOP!
THAT'S CHI'S VOICE!
OPEN UP!
SKREE
HOP

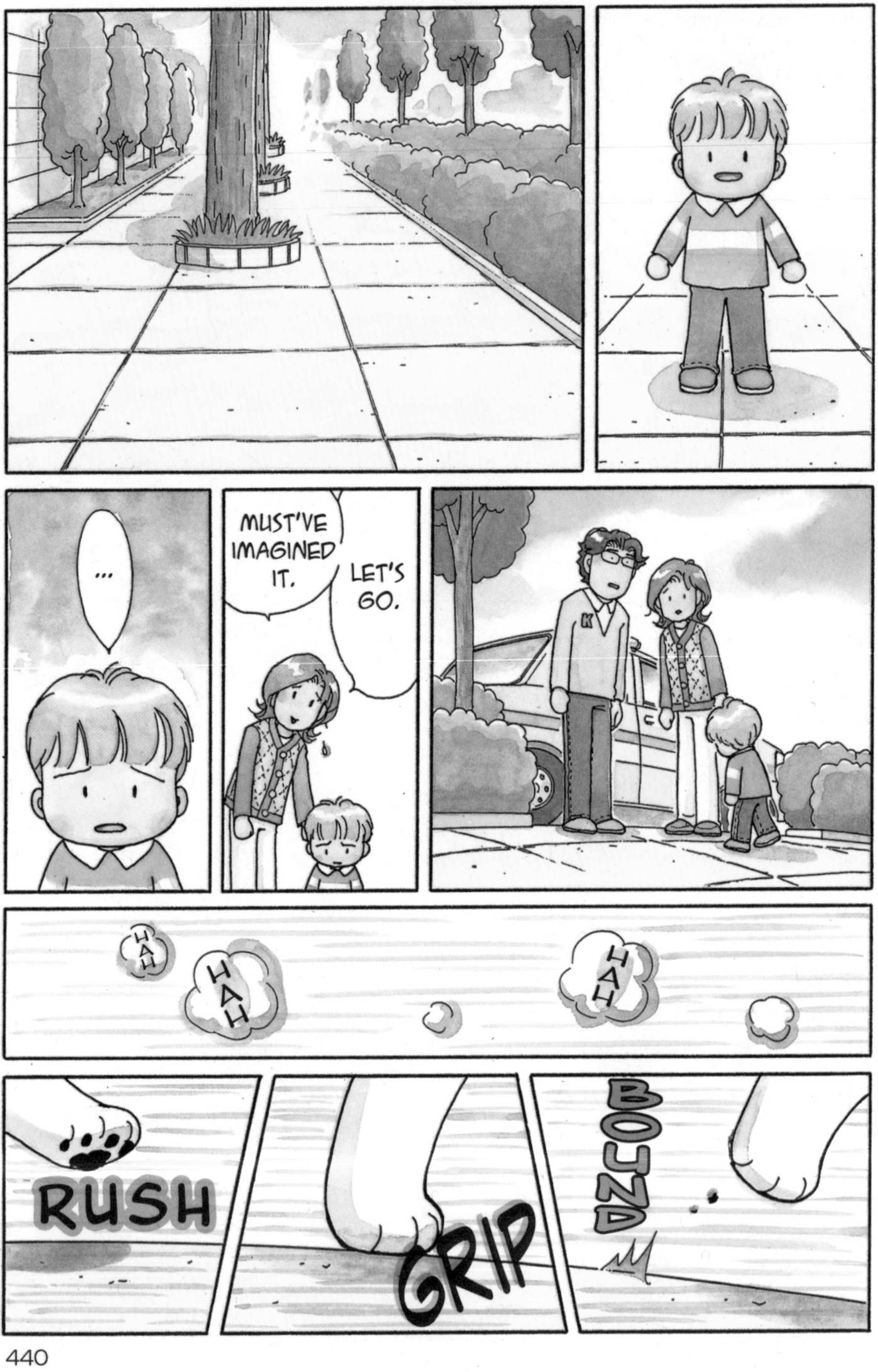
...
MUST'VE IMAGINED IT.
LET'S GO.
HAH
HAH
HAH
RUSH
GRIP
BOUND

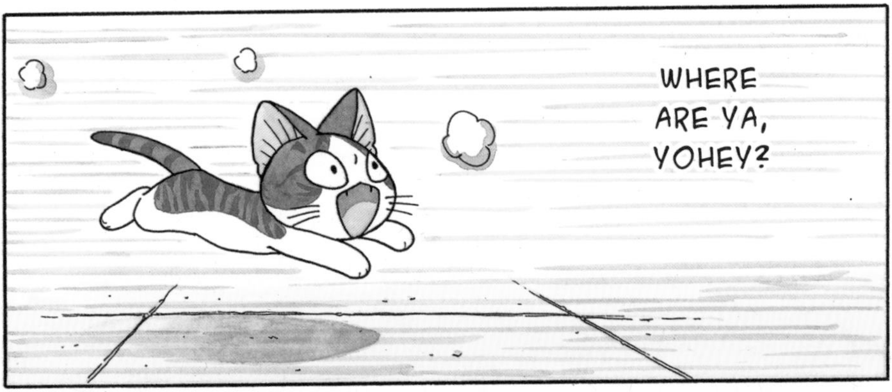
WHERE ARE YA, YOHEY?
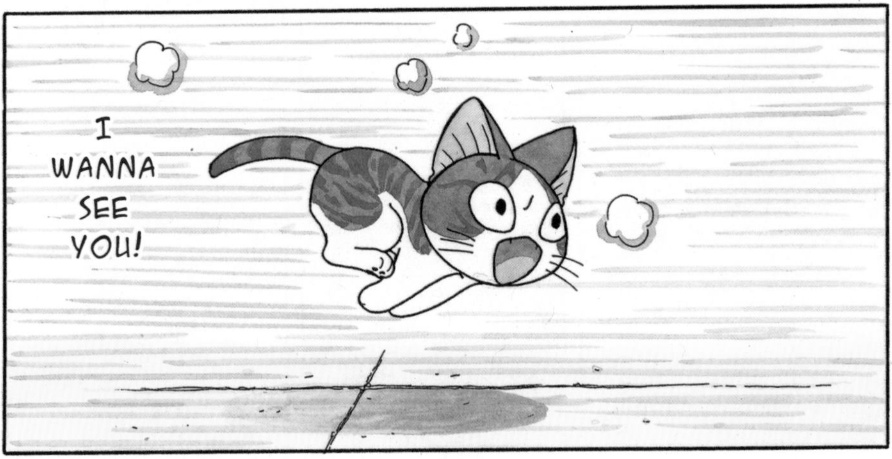
I WANNA SEE YOU!
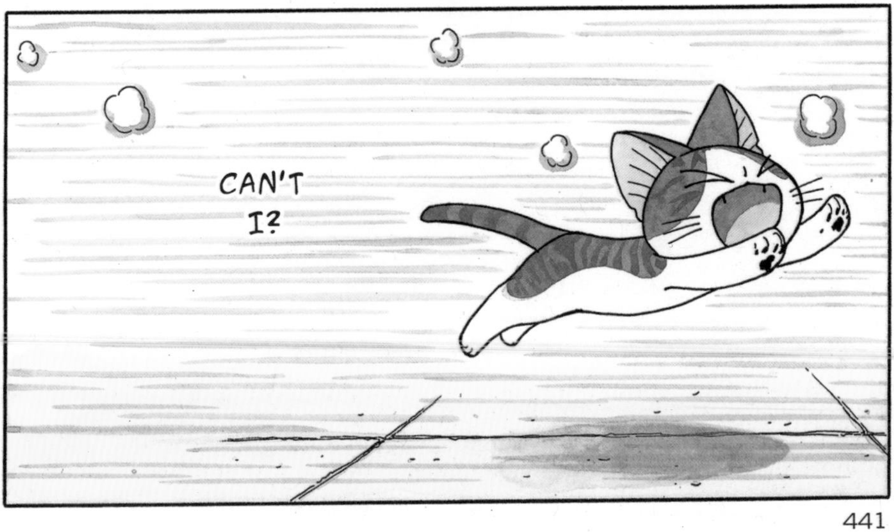
CAN'T I?

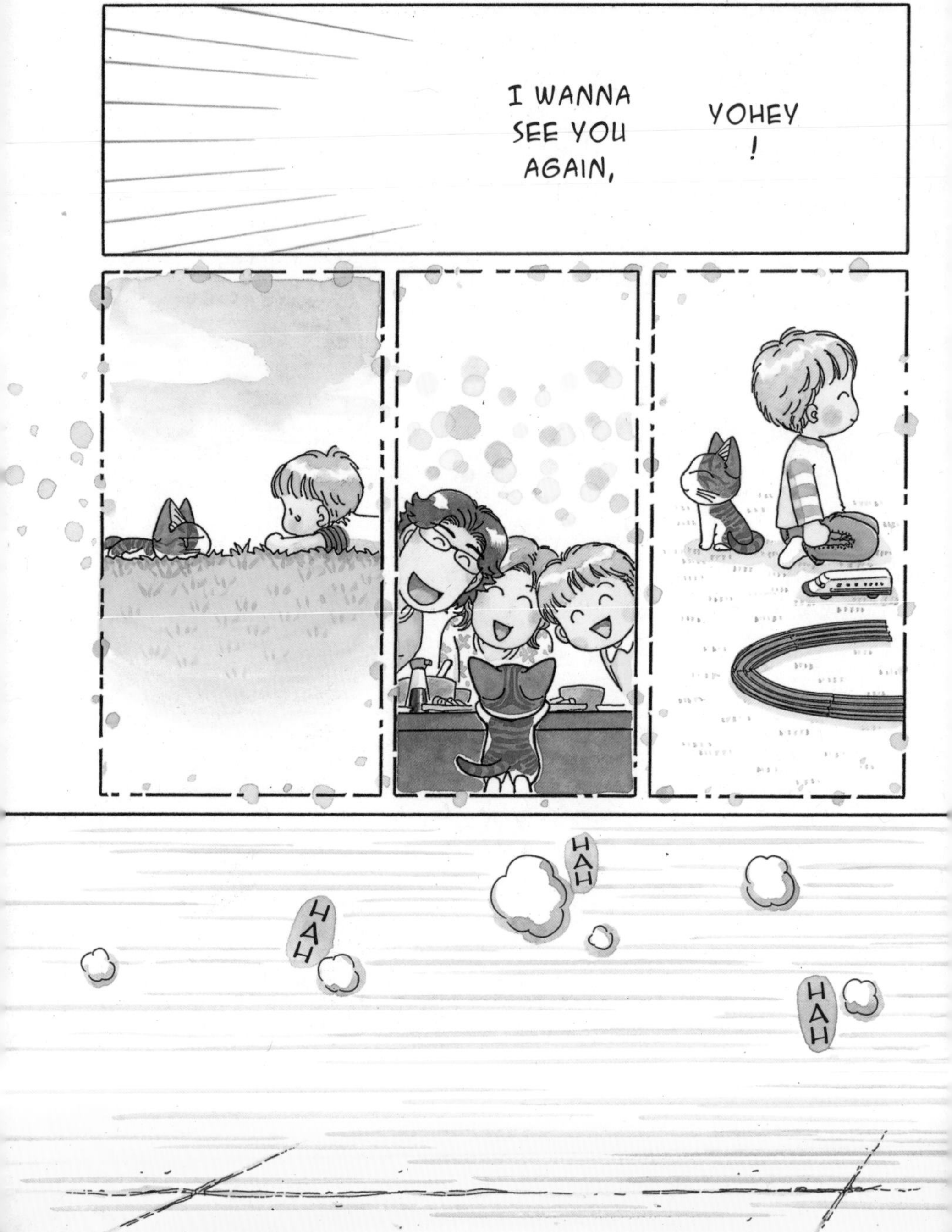
I WANNA SEE YOU AGAIN,
YOHEY!
HAH
HAH
HAH

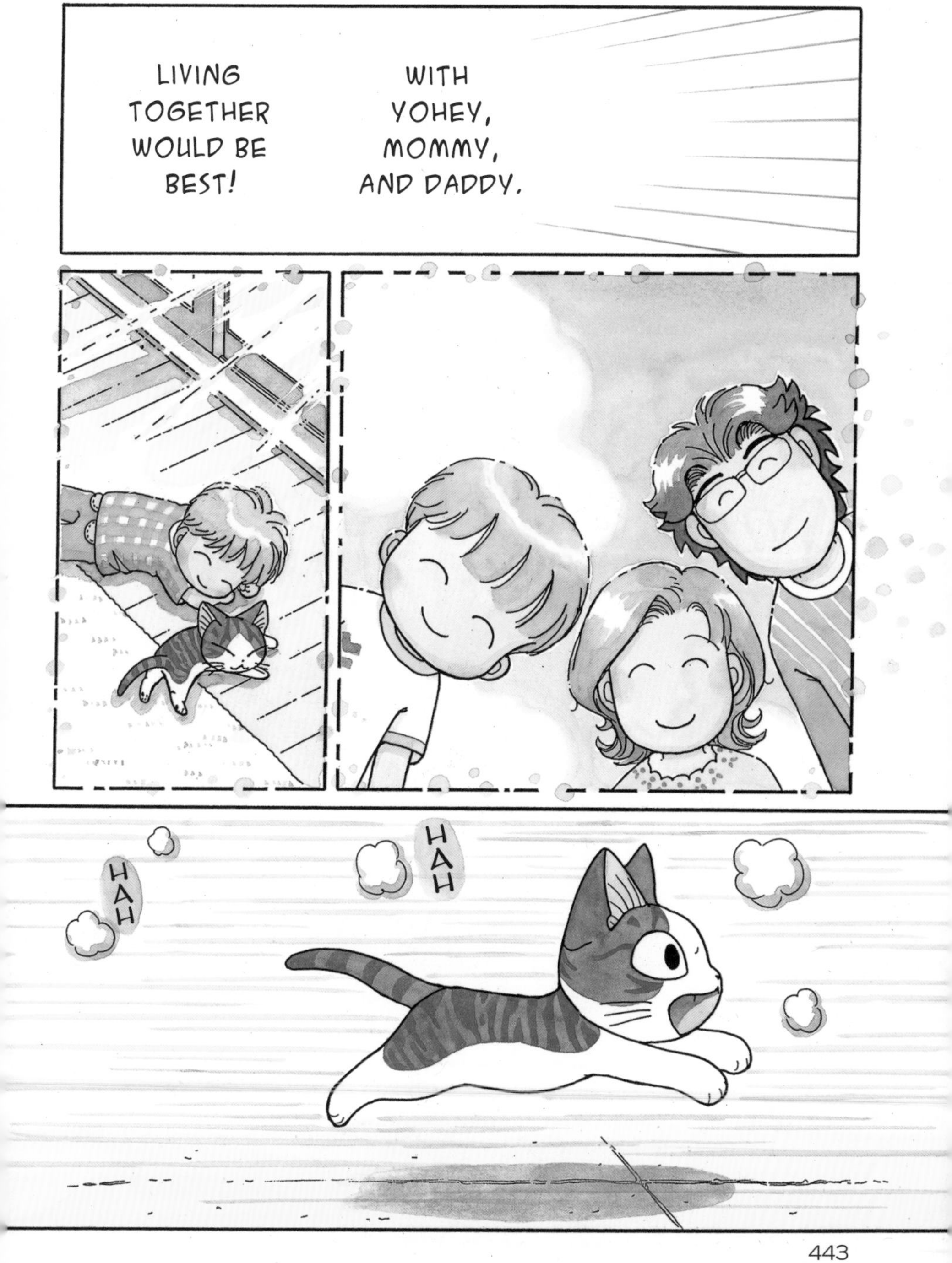
LIVING TOGETHER WOULD BE BEST!
WITH YOHEY, MOMMY, AND DADDY.
HAH
HAH

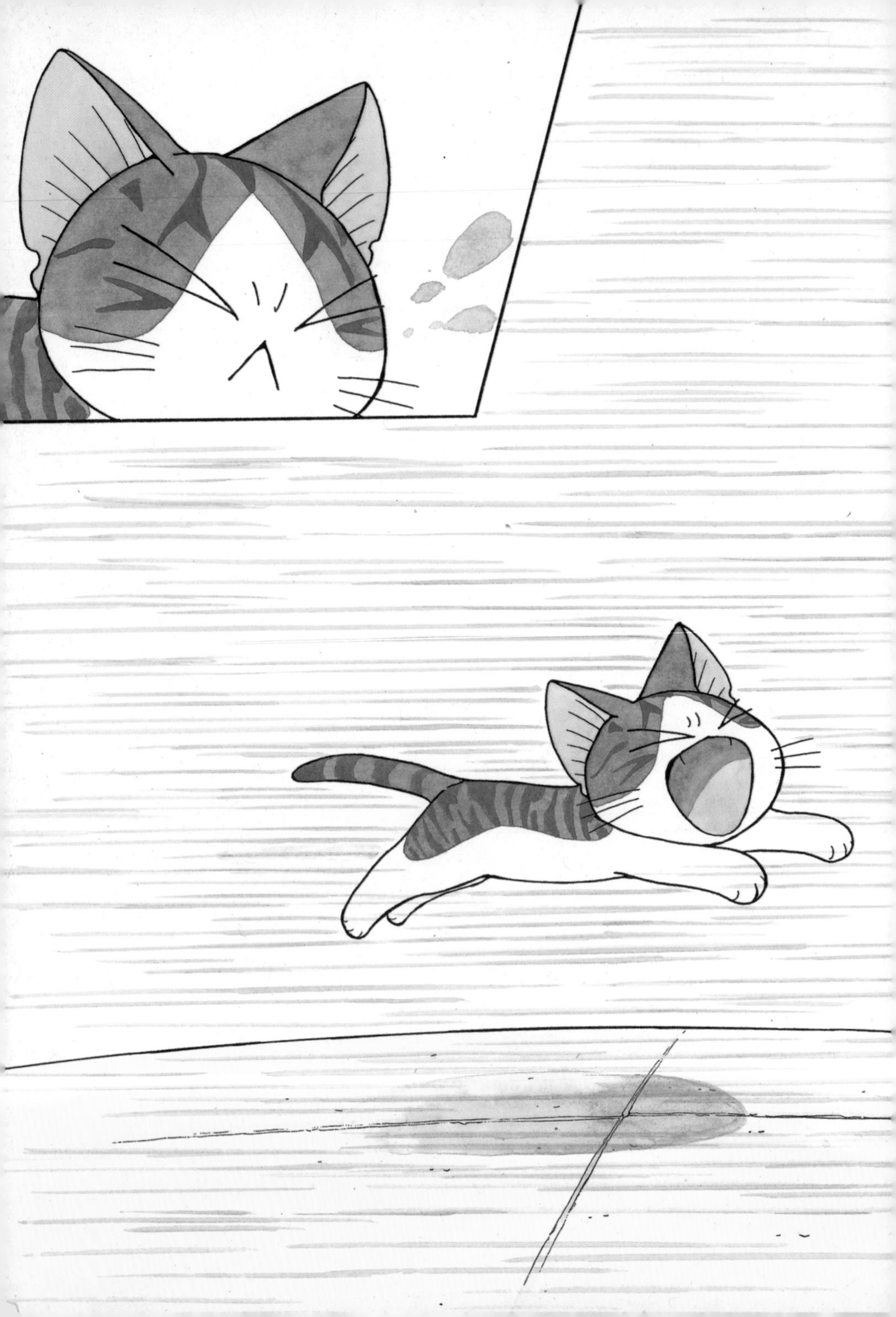

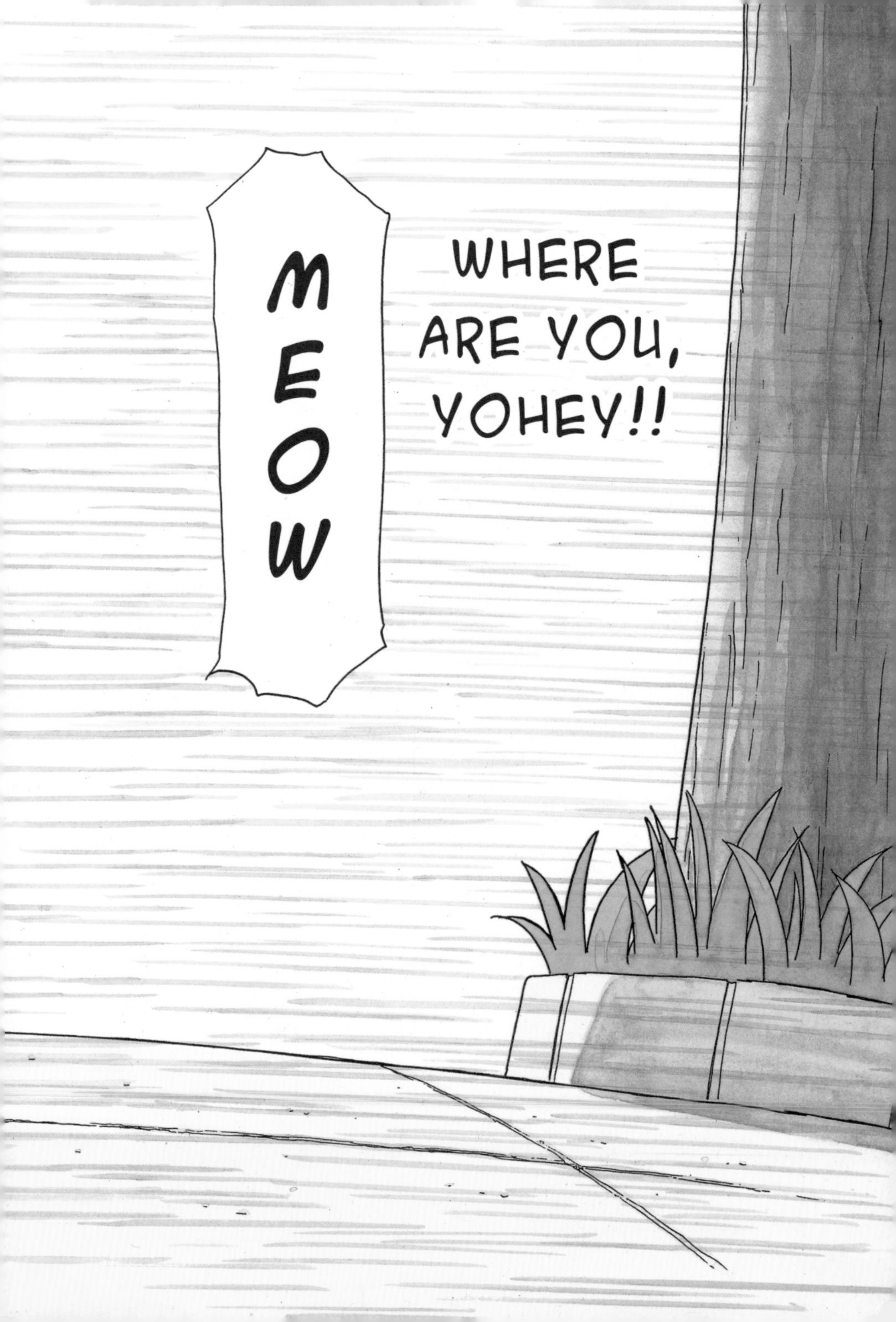
MEOW
WHERE ARE YOU, YOHEY!!

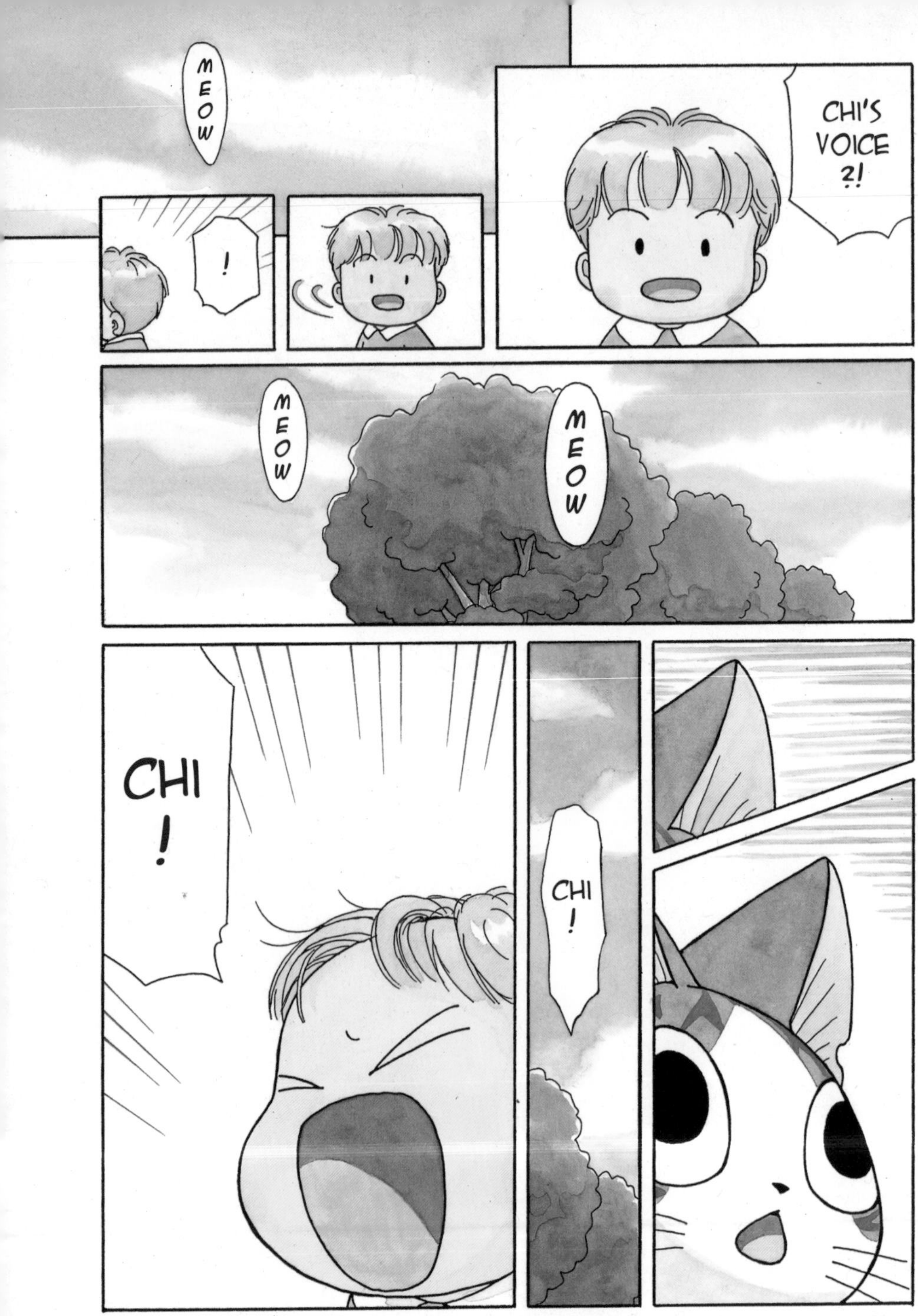
MEOW
!
CHI'S VOICE ?!
MEOW
MEOW
CHI!
CHI!

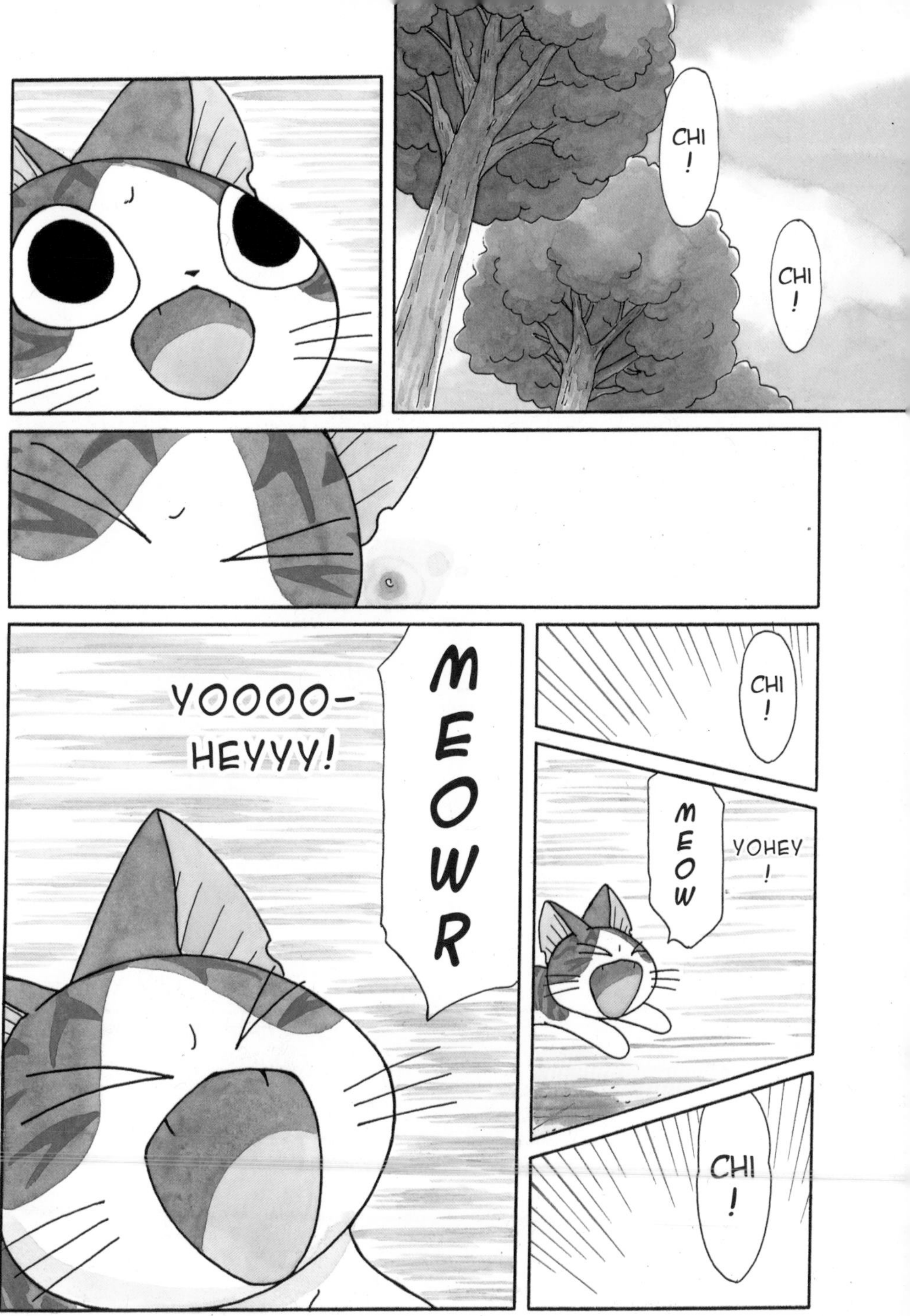
CHI!
CHI!
YOOOO-HEYYY!
MEOWR
CHI!
MEOW
YOHEY!
CHI!

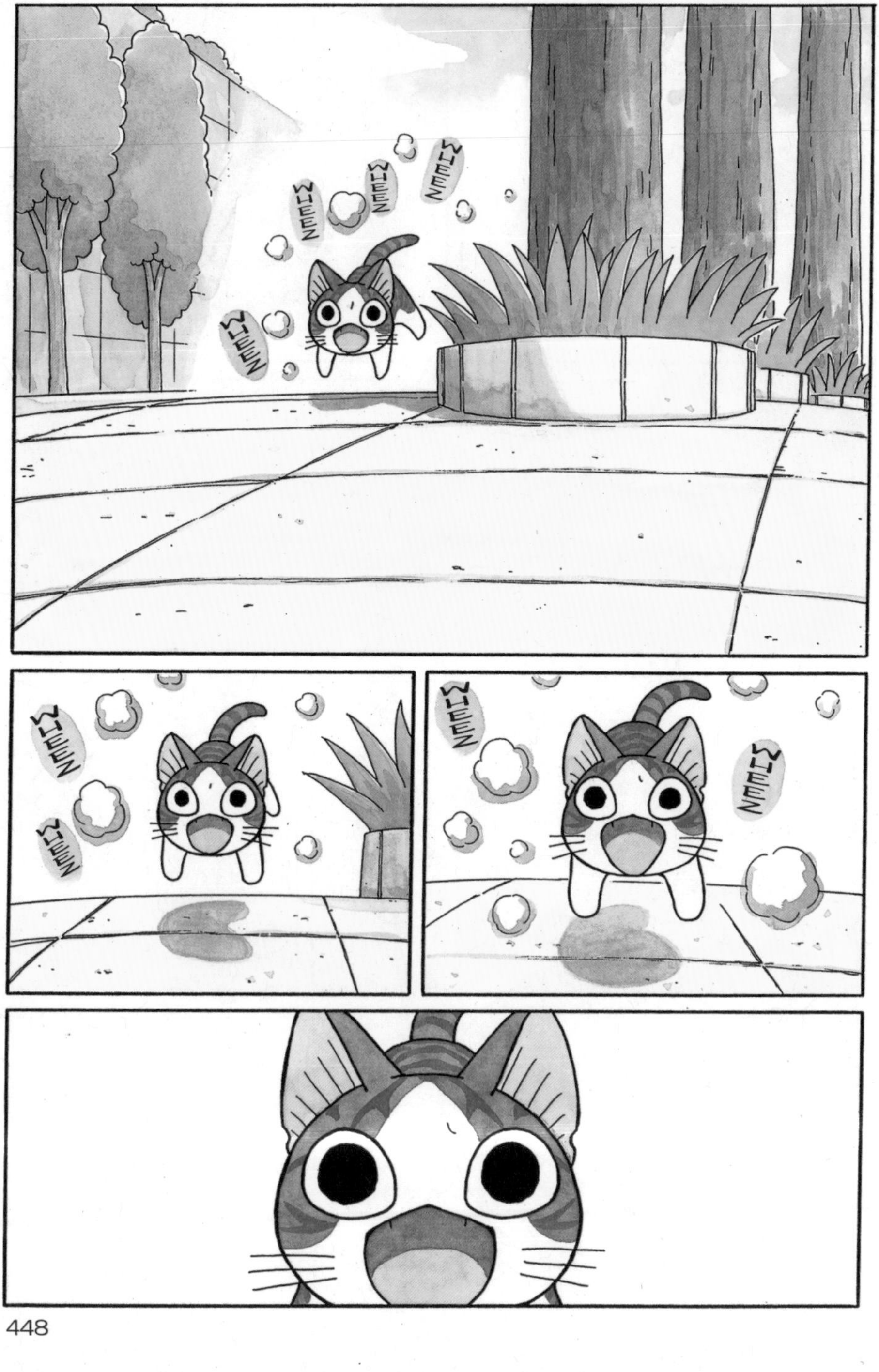
WHEEZ
WHEEZ
WHEEZ
WHEEZ
WHEEZ
WHEEZ
WHEEZ
WHEEZ

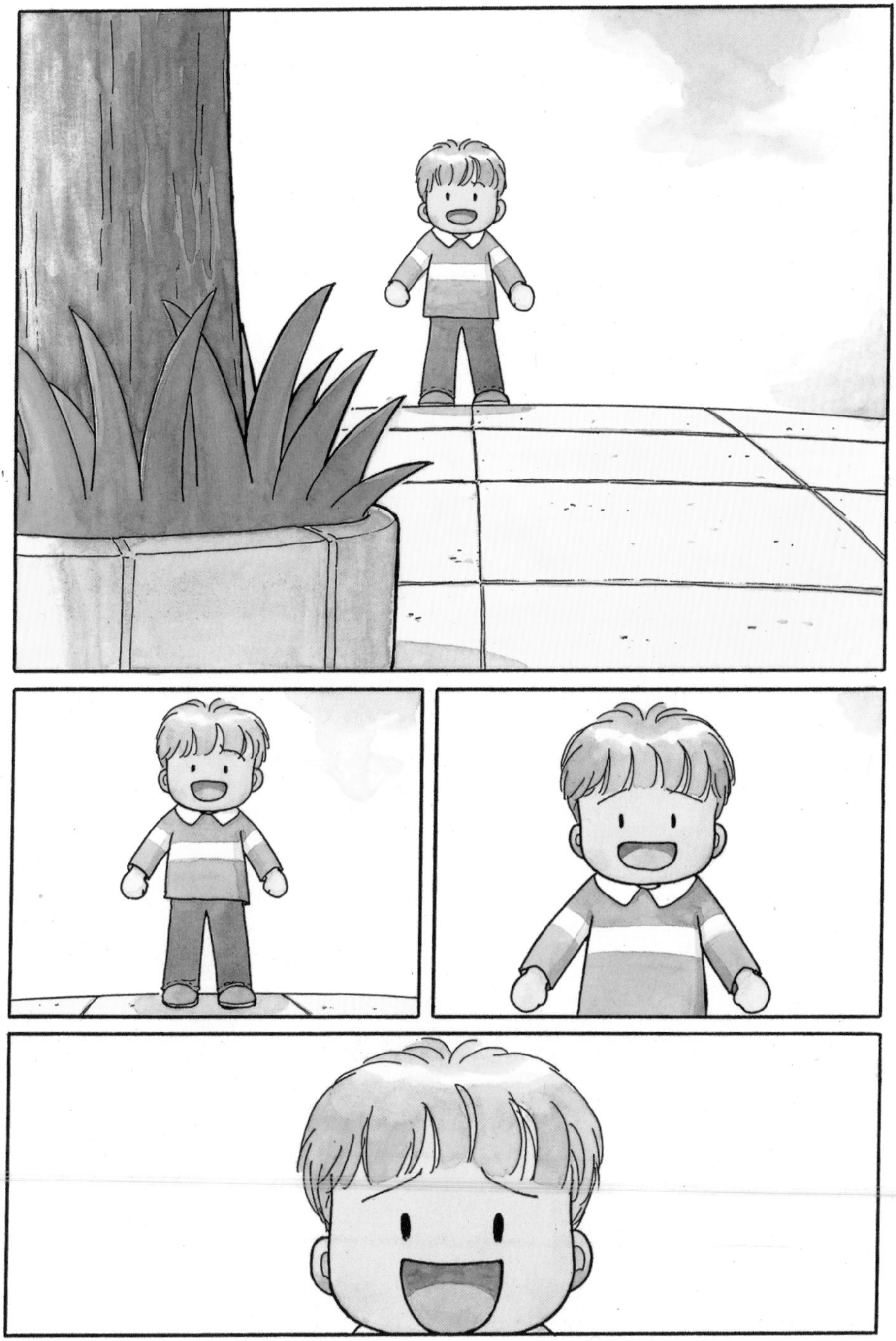

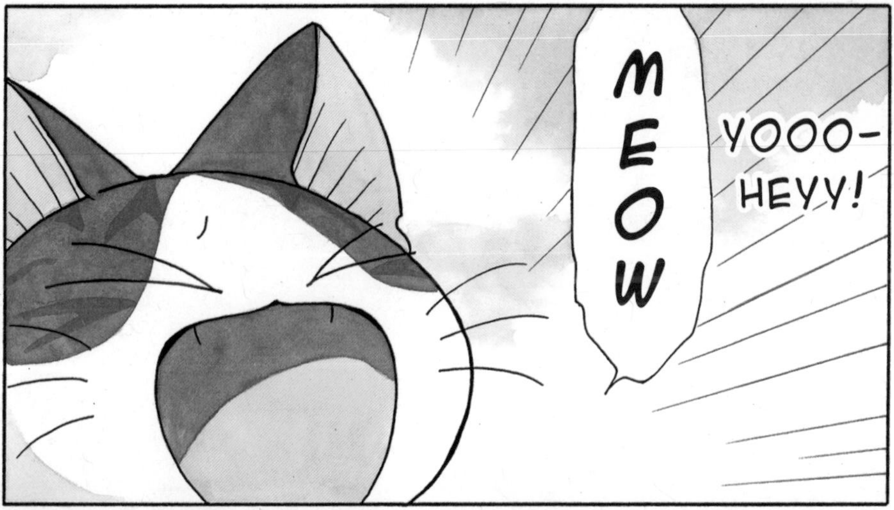
MEOW
YOOO-HEYY!

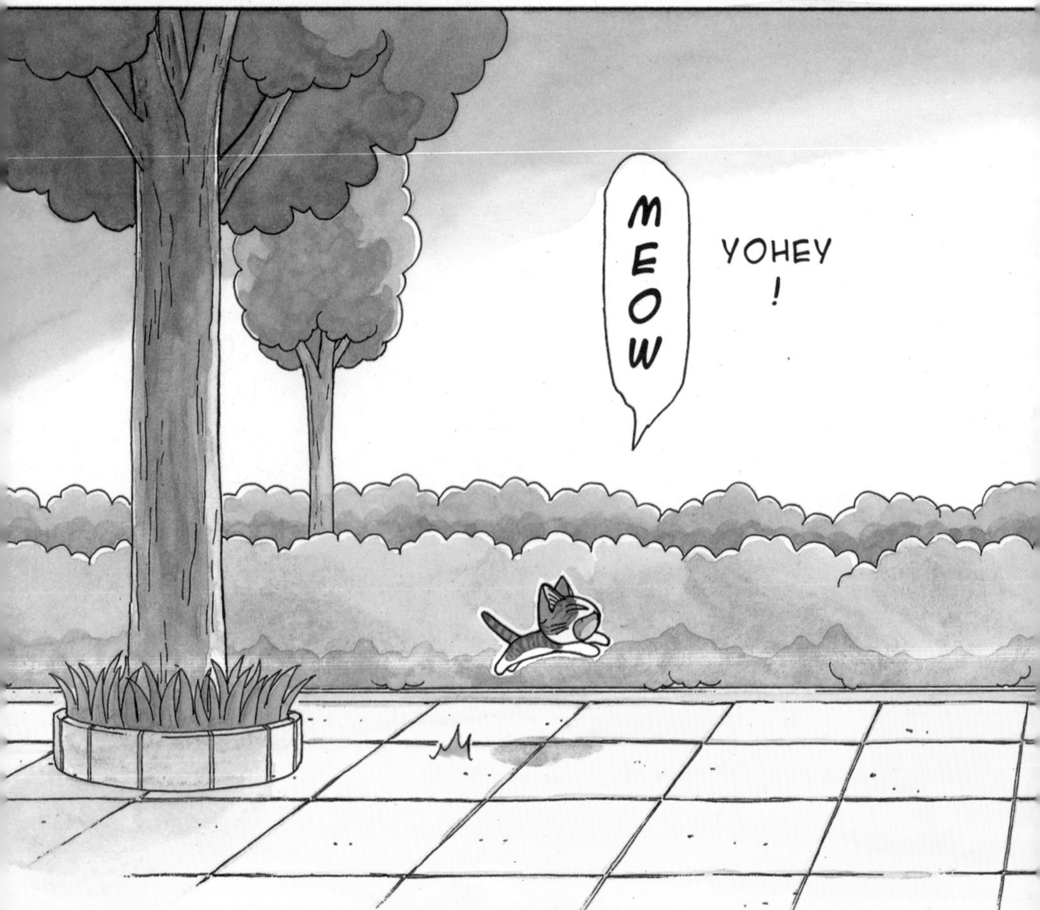
MEOW
YOHEY!

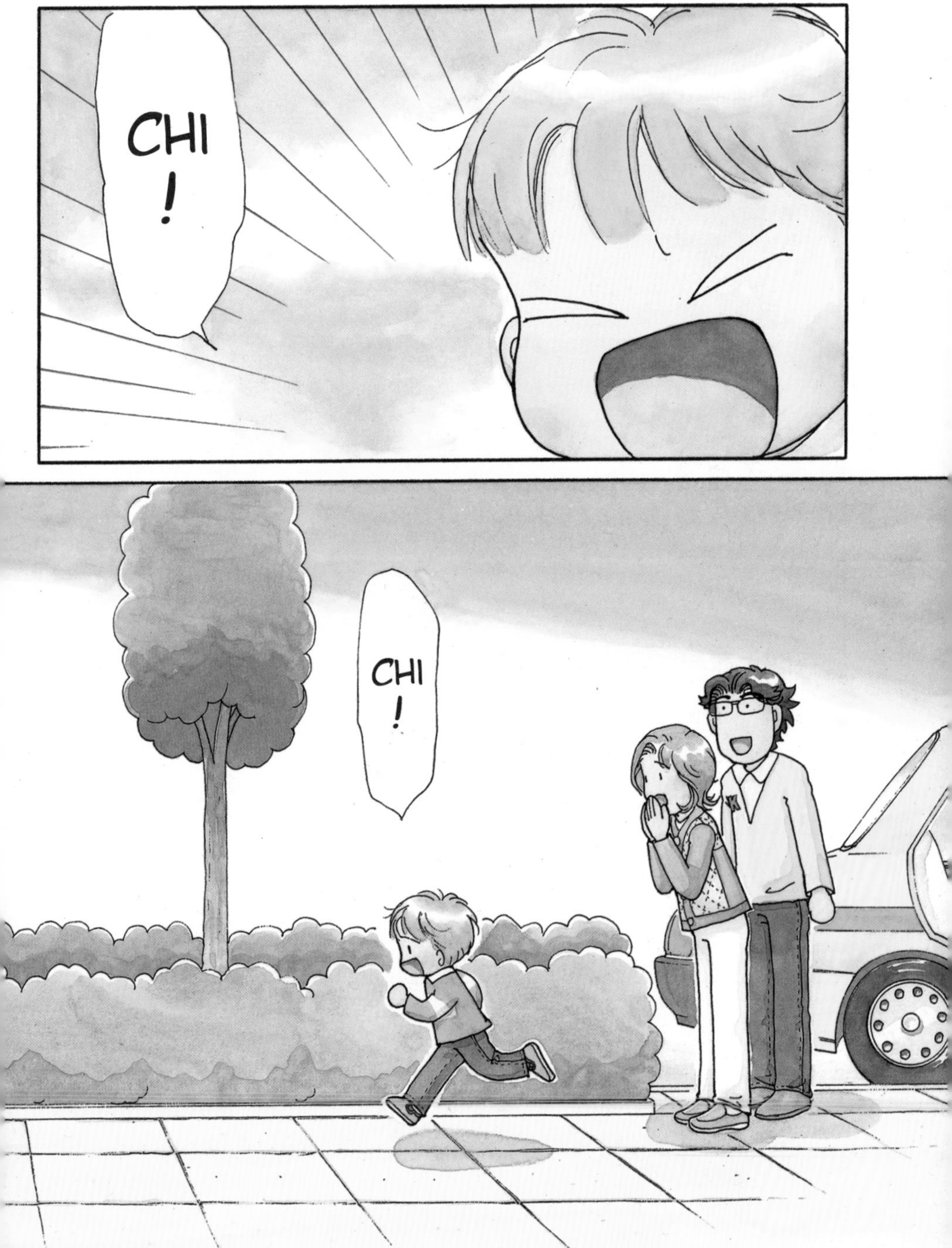
CHI!
CHI!

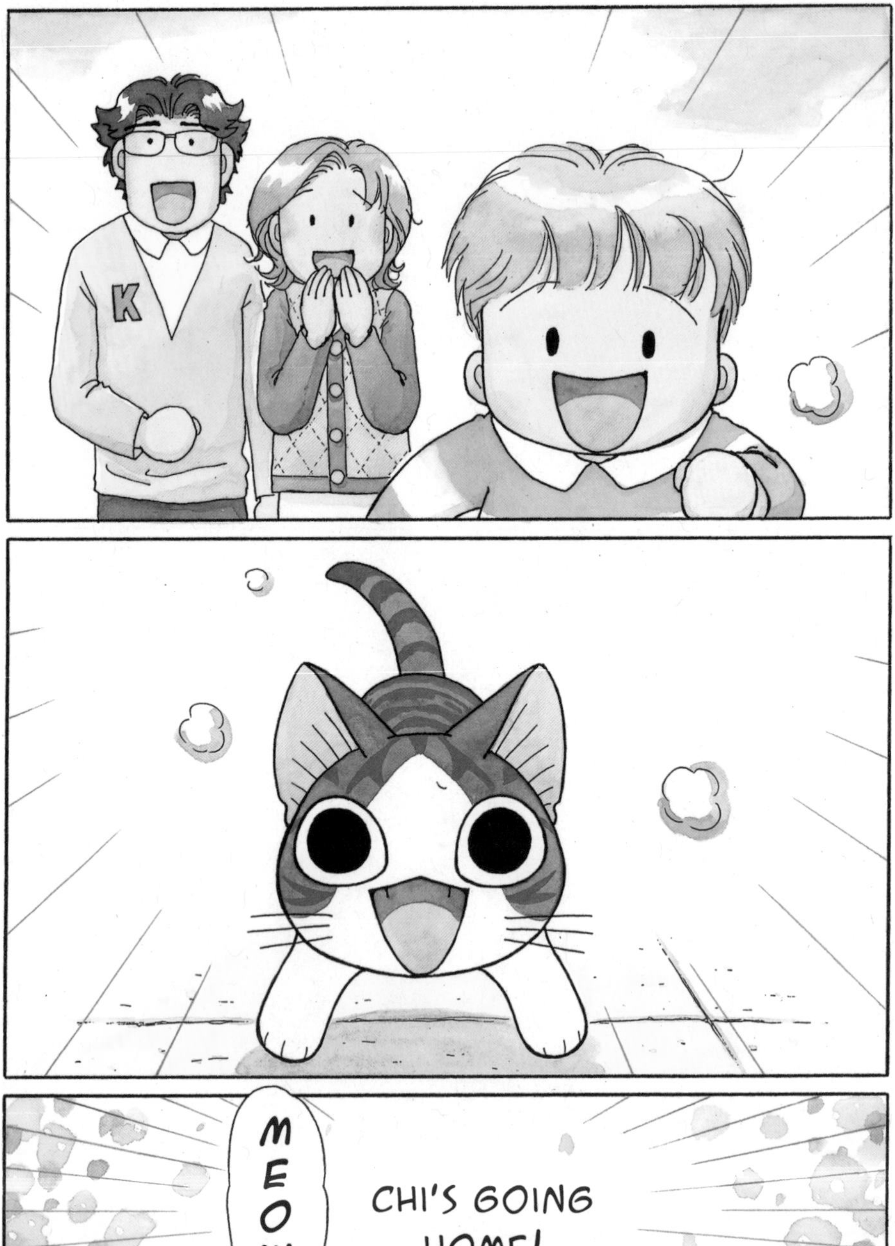
MEOW
CHI'S GOING HOME!

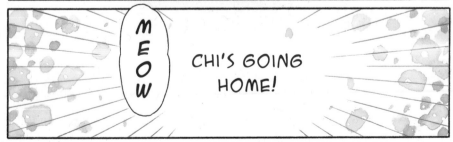

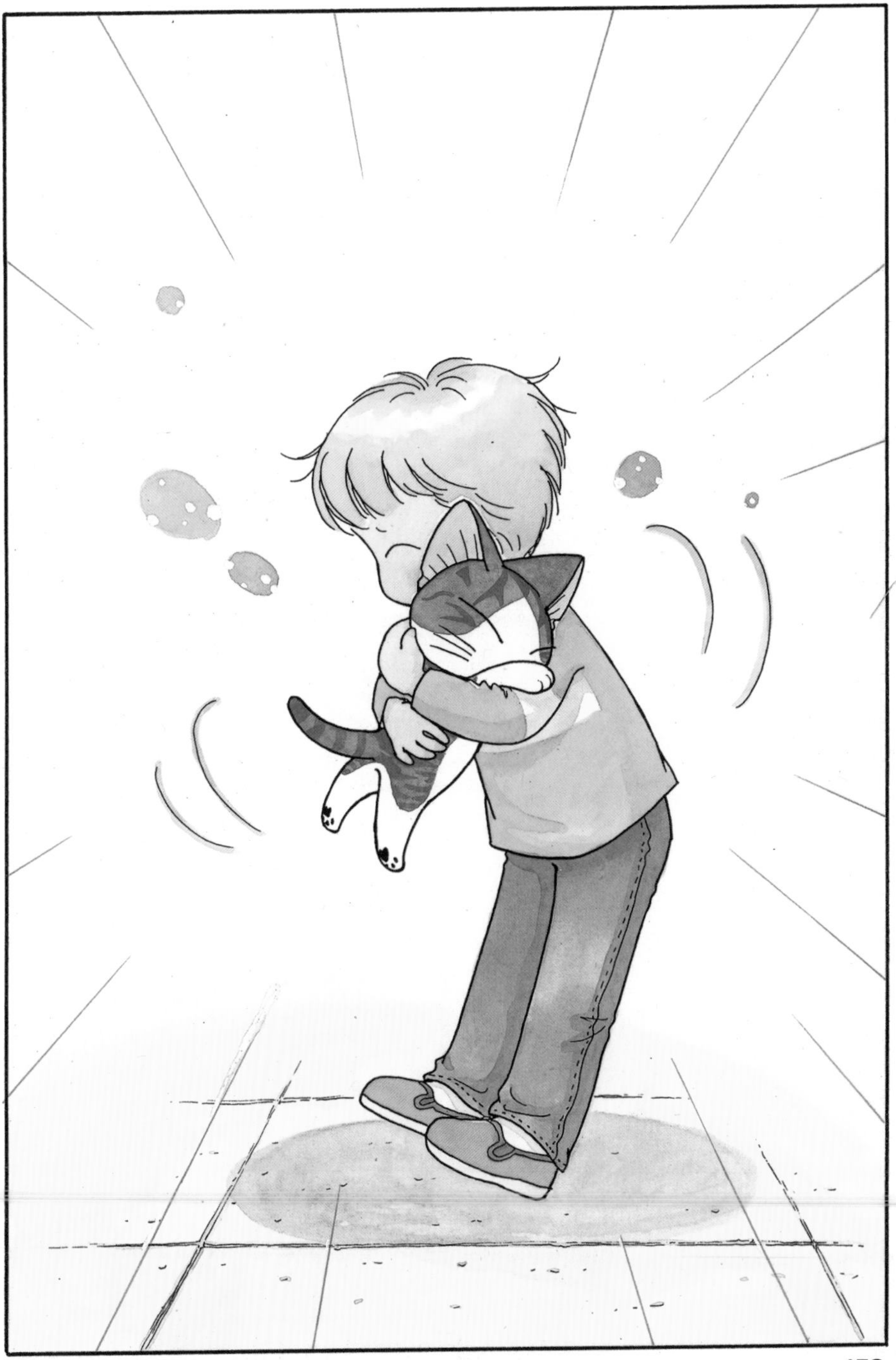

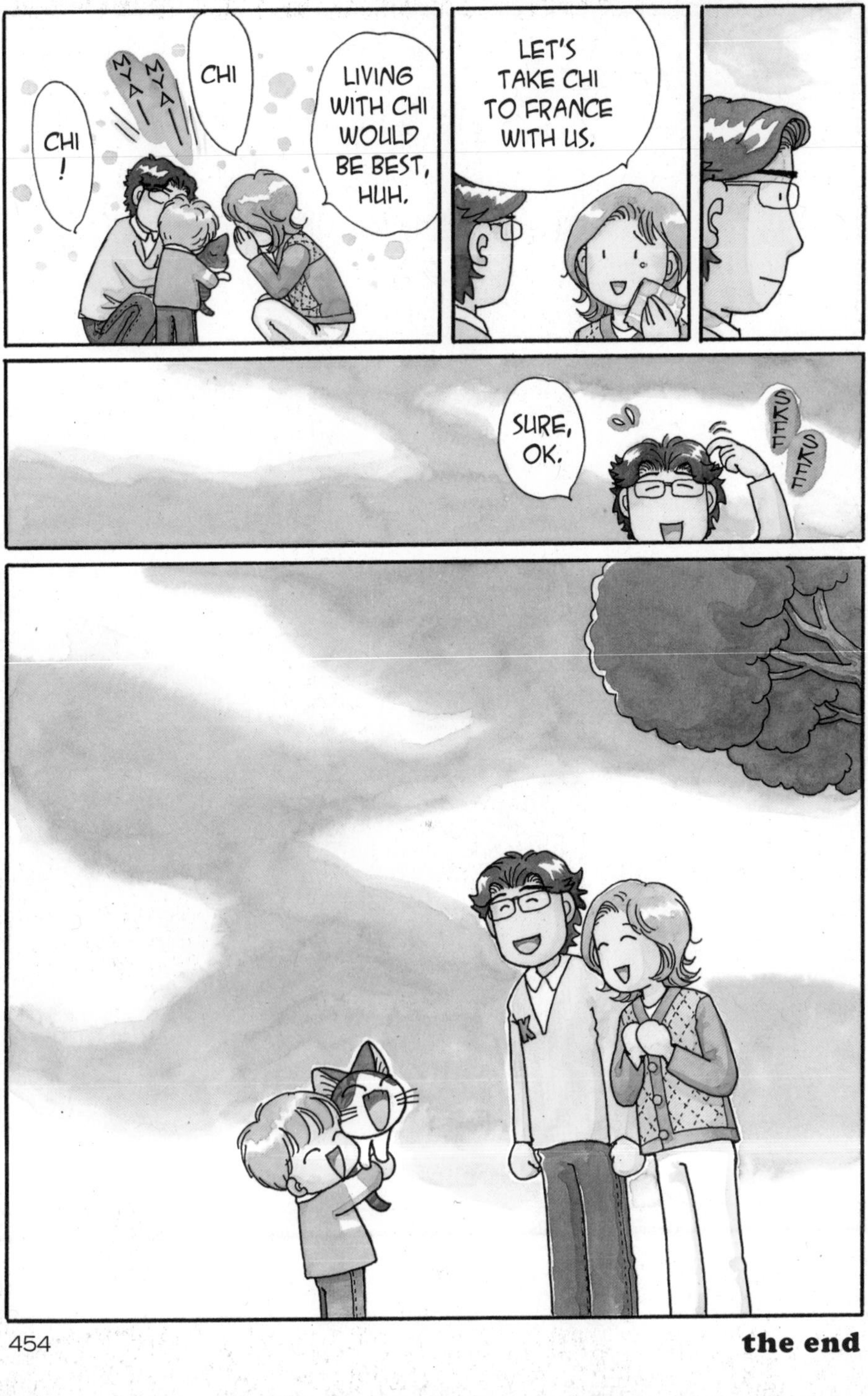
CHI!
MYA MYA
CHI
LIVING WITH CHI WOULD BE BEST, HUH.
LET'S TAKE CHI TO FRANCE WITH US.
SURE, OK.
SKFF SKFF

the end

BOW
BOW
MYA
MYA
412
Quarantine
Inspection

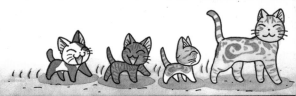

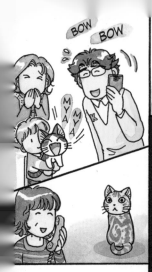

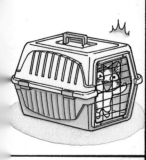

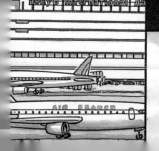

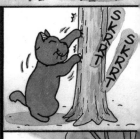

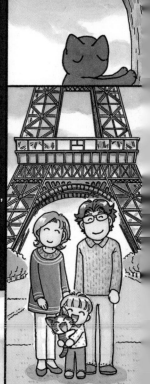

Special Thanks to:

JP Production Staff:
Kasumi Misuto
Masanori Mizuochi
Junko Tanaka

JP Production Support:
Mutsumi Tanaka
Riko Inaba

Design:
Kei Kasai
Megumi Shirakihara

US Production Staff:
Hiroko Mizuno
Aryaan Razzaghi
Grace Lu
Nicole Dochych
Laura Kovalcin

Others:
Press and Events,
Anime Production,
Goods Makers, Foreign
Publishers and Anime Localizers,
Foreign Merchandise,
and Many Others

And to the Readers:
Thank you so much for
our long time together.

SKRRT
SKRRT

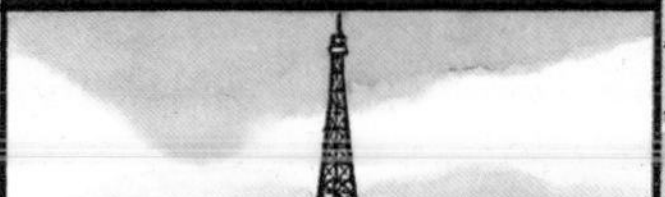

Chi's Sweet Home

Celebrating the Conclusion

Konami Kanata Interview

—Chi's Sweet Home: Where it's been and where it's going—

"Ugo. Nyago, nyagogo. Ugo, ugougo.
Nyangogo, ugo, ugo, nya—ugo."

—(translation) Hello, Blackie here. How did you like the ending of "Chi's Sweet Home"? Chi started publication in 2004, was serialized for 11 years in the magazine Morning, and now, finally we've reached the final chapter. This is solely due to the support of you, the readers. Even though it's the final volume, for the first time in a long while, we're publishing an interview with the creator and author, Konami Kanata. I hope that you enjoy it.

Blackie: Ugo. Nyago, nyaago. (Alright, Konami. It's been a long time.)

Konami (hereafter KK): It has been a long time. When was the last time, I wonder?

Blackie: Ugo, nyago. (The last interview was compiled in the volume 2 release in 2005, so about 10 years ago.)

KK: Wow, 10 years. I'm shocked. Somehow all that time just flew by.

Blackie: Ugo, nyago? (So you've finally reached the final chapter, how are you feeling now?)

KK: Well. I don't actually have any strong feelings about it yet, it's a weird sensation. Somehow, I was finally able to struggle through, and I'm really

The picture of Pi-chan and Konami's son (4) attached to Konami's work desk. Like Chi and Yohei, they are sibling-like best friends.

Drawn especially for use in bookstore promotional displays: Chi being held tightly by Yohei.

happy that I was able to carry out my duty. A feeling like that, I guess.

Blackie: Nya, nya, nya. (That's so Konami, LOL). At the time of the volume 2 interview as well, you answered, "I want to continue to draw steadily and diligently so that I won't miss my deadline.")

KK: Did I really? Well, As far as I'm concerned, it really was a big ambition for me (laugh).

 A photo attached to Konami's work desk.

Blackie: Ugo, nyago. Ugo? (Because this is the final volume, let's take a look back on the eleven years of Chi. What was your inspiration for wanting to draw this story?)

KK: Morning's editor-in-chief at that time, Mr. Kutomi, asked me if I would draw something for the magazine, but what would I draw? Thinking about it, I thought I might try to draw a story about a kitten next. About 3 years earlier, a good friend of mine told me that her cat had just had three kittens, did I want one? It was the first time in my life that I owned a kitten.

"I'll keep the smallest but cutest one for you," my friend told me, and when I went to go see, it really was cute. Up until that point, I'd only ever taken care of adult cats, so I was uneasy about whether or not I could actually care for a kitten, but I planned to seriously give it my all, and accepted the kitten. I named it Pi-chan. She had only been born about 2 months before but she was really friendly, reckless, naughty, and more so than I expected, a cute beast.

At the time, my son was not yet 4 years old, and when the two of them were together, even though they were human and cat, they were like siblings. Everyday is fun, I thought, to the extent that our spirits rose and the feelings of myself, my husband, and everyone in our family became quite cheerful. Thinking it would be good if I could bring the fun of living with a cat to a manga, I decided to make a kitten the main character of the story.

Blackie: Ugo, ugogo? (The picture above was taken at that time, wasn't it?)

KK: Yes. That picture was on my work desk the whole time I drew the manuscript.

Blackie: Ugogo, nya~go? (In the volume 2 interview, you talked about taking a picture capturing the little beast's expressions?)

KK: Right, right. At that time, my son and Pi-chan were still small, but now the two of them have gotten bigger, and Pi-chan has completely settled down and now she has become like a grandma cat.

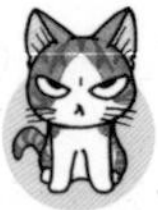

Friends of Chi around the World

Blackie: Nyago, nyago~. (The model for Chi's story was indeed Konami's family. From there, anime, foreign translations, and goods have come out. Chi really has gone on a big adventure, hasn't she?)

KK: Yes, she has. Basically, because the manuscript was drawn on my desk the whole time, I had the feeling that my world was just the desk in front of my eyes. It didn't really sink in that Chi was being read even in foreign countries, but then I went to events in places like Canada, France and Switzerland, and for the first time I met readers who were there for the events. I was astonished when I found out that it wasn't just the world on top of my desk.

Blackie: Nyago, ugo, ugogo. (In 2014, Chi also made an appearance in the global company Apple's TV ad spot, right?)

KK: Yes! The first time I heard about it was from the editor in charge of me. "A TV CM appearance inquiry came from the computer company Apple, and I'm guessing it's that Apple, but are you interested?" Unbelievably, it

Anime Chi.
Her stomach
is full, plump,
and soft.

The illustration
of Chi used by
Apple for a TV
ad spot.

really was that Apple that extended an offer to me. I couldn't believe it.

Blackie: Ugo, ugogo, nyago. (Chi would be appearing together with world famous characters like Mickey Mouse, Snoopy, and Hello Kitty (Laugh))

KK: It was an honor. When Chi got to make an appearance on TV while eating an apple, it was a really great feeling.

 In the anime, Chi became an old man?!

Blackie: Ugo, ugogo, nya? (What did you think when you first saw the anime?)

KK: The way that Chi talked was really cute, so I was very happy. I was asked about my image of Chi's voice by the people at MadHouse, who were in charge of the anime production, and when I answered "Korogi Satomi", a voice actress I love, they made it a reality for me.

Blackie: Nyago, nya. (The way Korogi Satomi portrayed Chi's voice was quite cute.)

KK: From the yawning to the voice used for humming, it's fantastic. And I love the way the anime deals with Chi's movements, especially the tummy-related actions. In the manga, when Chi's tummy was full, she'd just slump and lie down, but in the anime, she thumps her side like some old guy, it's original and fantastic.

Blackie: Nya. Ugogo. (Certainly. After the anime, even in the manga, Chi turned into more of a lazybones.)

Chi's Art Director: Kei Kasai

Blackie: Nyago, nyanya. (All around the world Chi has books and anime, as well as a development of goods, but a lot of the designs are so wonderful.)

KK: That's right. Especially the design of the French products is really pretty and makes me happy. That Chi came to be this loved across the world owes a lot to Kei Kasai, who made me a cover design with the book's worldview in mind. When the editor in charge conveyed the image of a cake box, and soft colors in Scandinavian style, she polished off the design fantastically for me. Along with Ms. Megumi Shirakihara, who did the design for the text in the volumes, the two of them have been in charge of Chi's design since publication started.

Blackie: Ugogo, ugo. (I'm glad that you were blessed with a fortunate meeting.)

KK: Yes. And that's not all. Because I met Ms. Kasai, Blackie was born.

Blackie: Nya, nya? (Eh, is that so?)

KK: At the time, Ms. Kasai had a black cat named Higuma. But, Higuma was slender and handsome, so maybe if you saw him you wouldn't think he was the model (Laugh).

Blackie: Nya, nya?! Nyagogogo! (Wh-What?! That's so rude!)

KK: Sorry (Laugh). But because of similar meetings, others were born, like Alice and Mi-chan.

Blackie: Ugogo. Nyago? (The amount of friends just increased, huh? What about Cocchi?)

KK: Cocchi was, well, he started from a few words of my son. One day, he said, "Chi is lucky because she got picked up and became a house cat, but if she wasn't she'd have been a stray." In life, luck and misfortune exists, and it's sometimes hard to say which is which. Chi was picked up, but I wondered what might have happened if Chi hadn't been picked up, and that was how I came to imagine Cocchi.

Blackie: Ugo, ugogo. Nyago. (Cocchi saw Chi reunited with her family and his view of the world seemed to change just a bit. Because in the end, Cocchi was there with Chi's mom and siblings.)

Higuma who became Blackie's model. Ms. Kasai's house cat. A lot slimmer than Blackie!

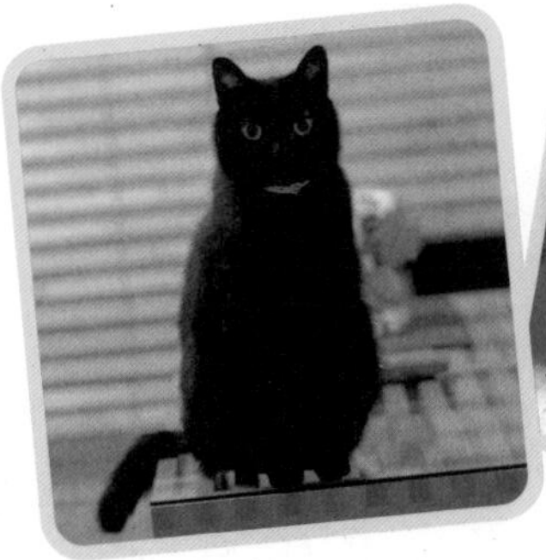

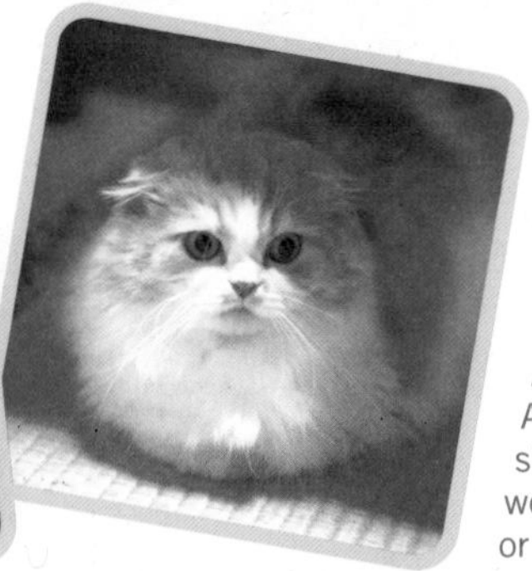

The editor in charge (at the time)'s cat who would be Alice's model. Apparently, she wasn't so well-mannered or polite.

KK: Cocchi loves his freedom as a stray, but now because he has friends, I think he can be even happier.

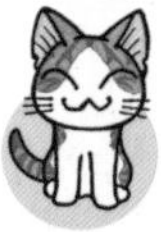

Having Finished the Story

Blackie: Nyago, ugogogo, nygo. (Well, how about a message for those readers that read until the end?)

KK: These books aren't about animals that are just well-behaved, but mischievous and free too, so if I was able to convey the fun of such animals, I'm happy. Another thing, the whole time I was drawing, I tried to respect the fact that cats are cats, and people are people. Because they are not the same species, they cannot communicate with words. Of course, because this is a manga, there is an abundance of human expressions, but, as much as possible, I wanted them to not be human-like, but animal-like looks. So I had to think what's the best way to express that, and it was difficult.

For Chi and the Yamada family, the words they use can't be understood by the other so there might be misunderstandings, but as friends and family, might not they be tied through their feelings? Together they have fun or they cry, and how nice if they ended up precious to each other. Supported by lots of people, I gave it my all and somehow got this far—that's how I feel. I think I was allowed to go beyond my real abilities. Thank you for reading over such a long time.

Interview & Setup: Yoshiko Tezuka

Chi's On Social Media!!

Even with the end of the manga series, Chi's adventures will continue. Fans of Chi can get news and information about the Chi anime, goods, international events and promotions via the four official Chi's Sweet Home accounts. Get to know more about Chi and experience more cute kitty art on these platforms!

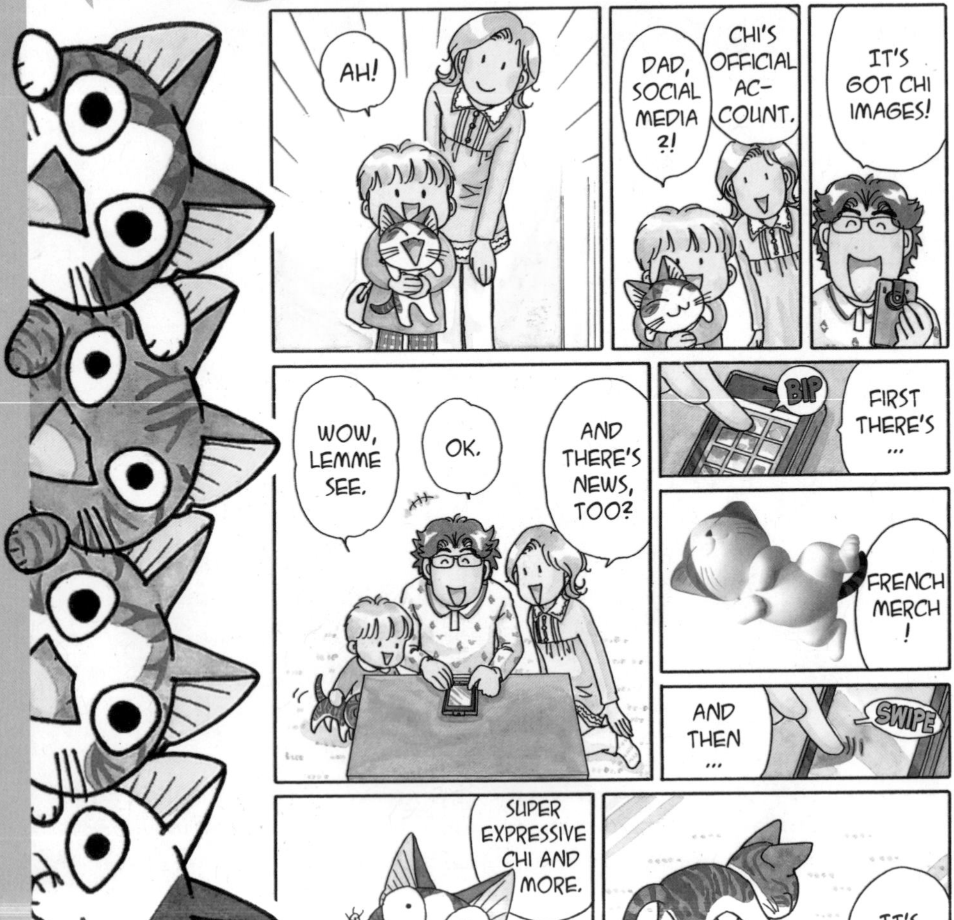
AH!
DAD, SOCIAL MEDIA ?!
CHI'S OFFICIAL AC-COUNT.
IT'S GOT CHI IMAGES!
WOW, LEMME SEE.
OK.
AND THERE'S NEWS, TOO?
BIP
FIRST THERE'S ...
FRENCH MERCH !
AND THEN ...
SWIPE
SUPER EXPRESSIVE CHI AND MORE.
IT'S FULL OF CHI NEWS!

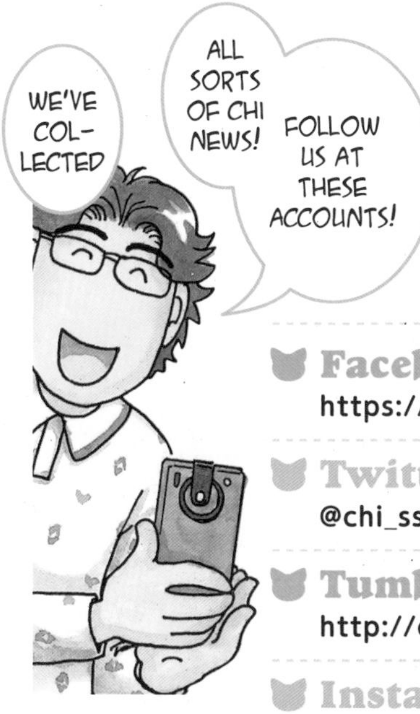
WE'VE COL- LECTED
ALL SORTS OF CHI NEWS!
FOLLOW US AT THESE ACCOUNTS!

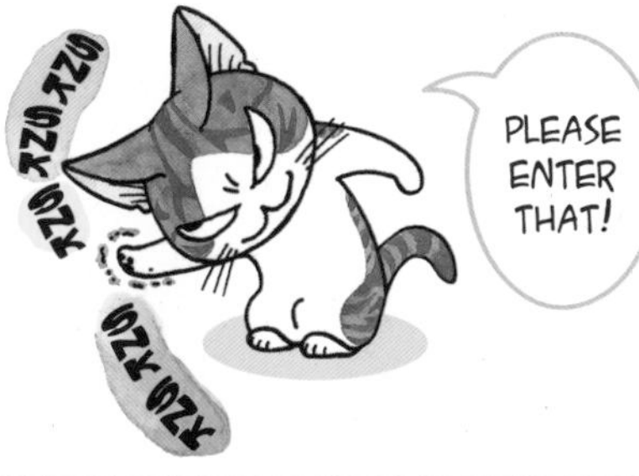
PLEASE ENTER THAT!

Facebook Chi's Sweet Home—Chi's Page
https://www.facebook.com/chissweethomeofficial

Twitter Chi's Sweet Home Official Account
@chi_ssweethome

Tumblr Chi's Sweet Home Official Tumblr
http://chi-sweethome.tumblr.com/

Instagram chi.ssweethome
https://instagram.com/chi.ssweethome/

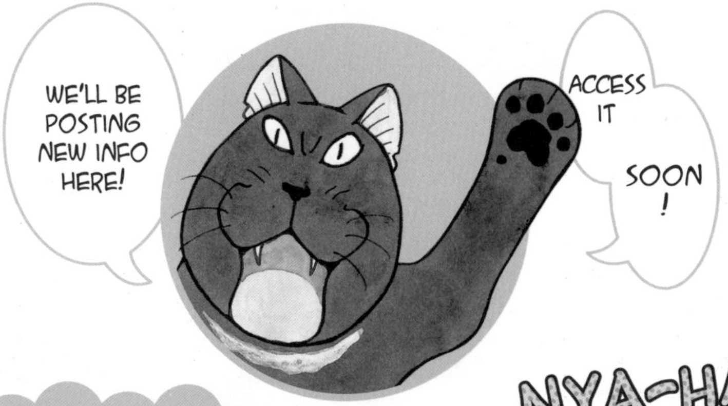
WE'LL BE POSTING NEW INFO HERE!
ACCESS IT
SOON !

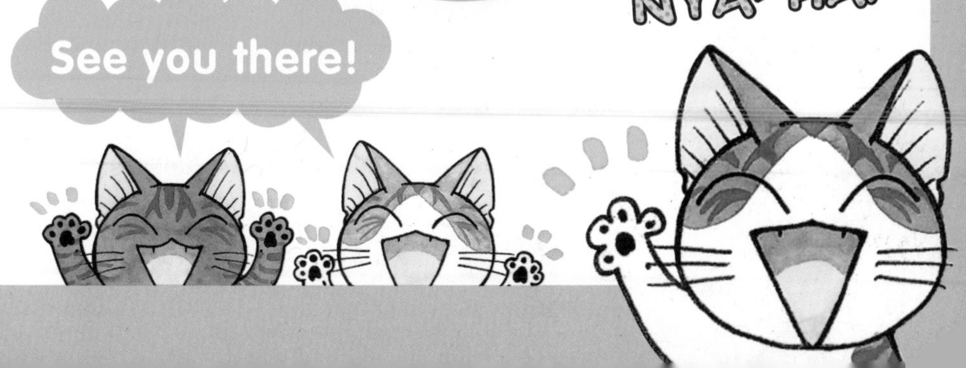
NYA-HA!
See you there!

Chi volumes are now available in eBook format!

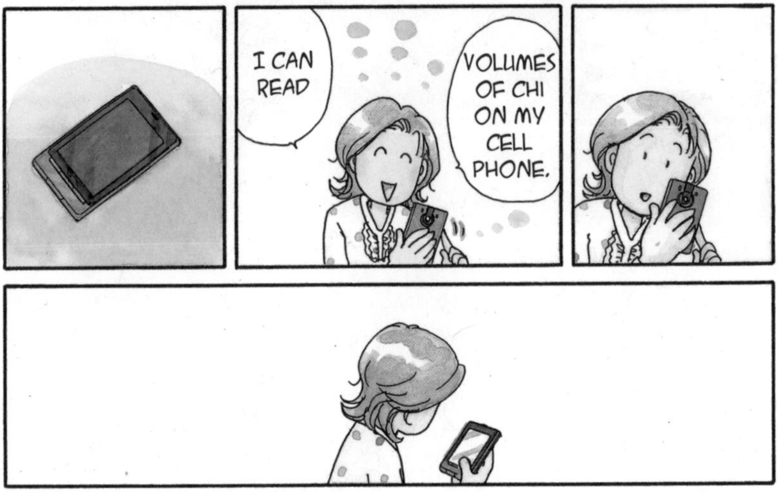
I CAN READ
VOLUMES OF CHI ON MY CELL PHONE.

With this new option how can you stop reading?! All twelve volumes of *Chi's Sweet Home* can now be enjoyed on your tablet or cell phone. Just access your favorite eBook retailer—Kindle, Nook, iTunes Bookstore, Google Play and more—and search for *Chi's Sweet Home*.

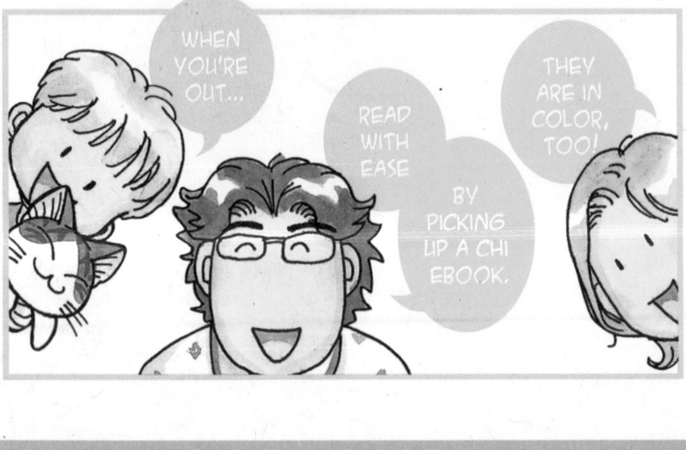
WHEN YOU'RE OUT...
READ WITH EASE
BY PICKING UP A CHI EBOOK.
THEY ARE IN COLOR, TOO!

Chi's Sweet Extras

Message Cards: Cut out and give to friends!

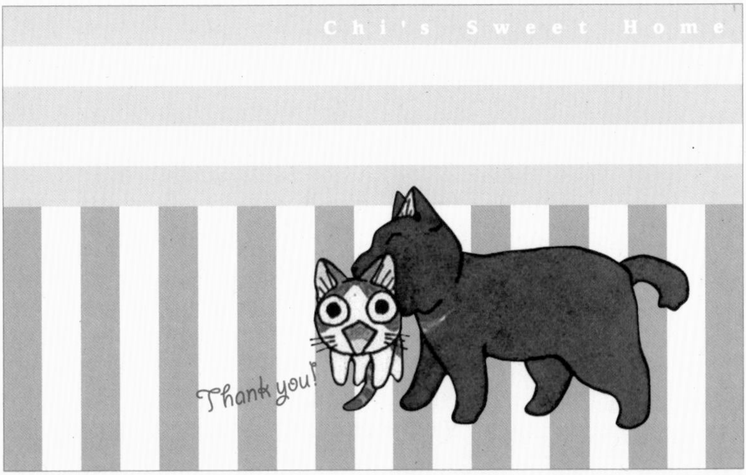
Chi's Sweet Home
Thank you!

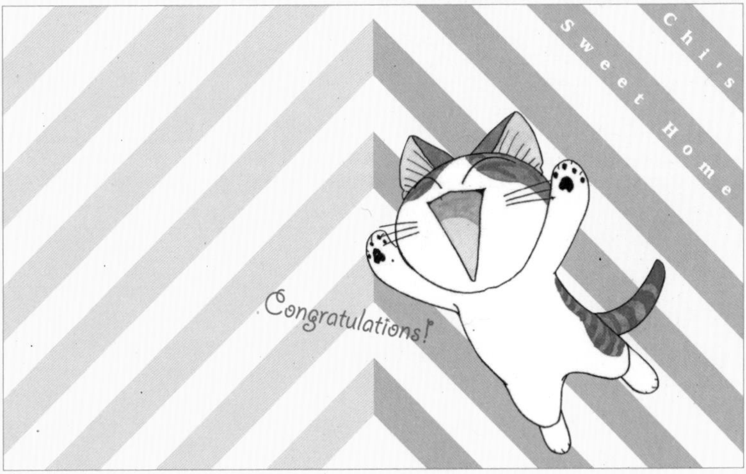
Chi's Sweet Home
Congratulations!

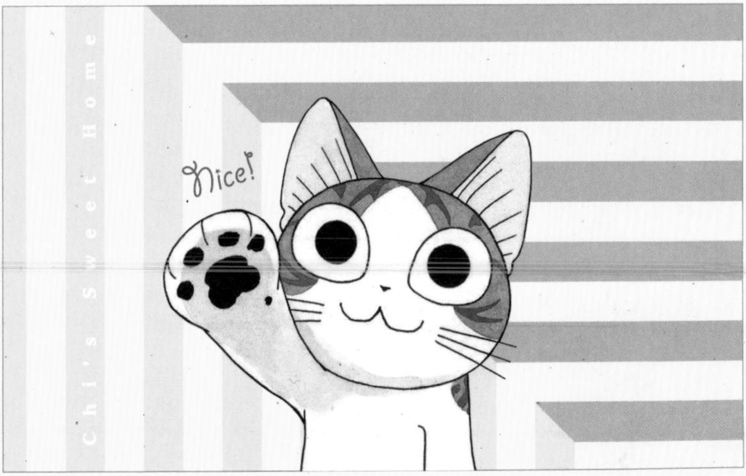
Chi's Sweet Home
Nice!

Chi and Cocchi Spinning Fan

★ Cut out images
★ Tape both to a stick (like a chopstick)
★ Spin it between your hands!

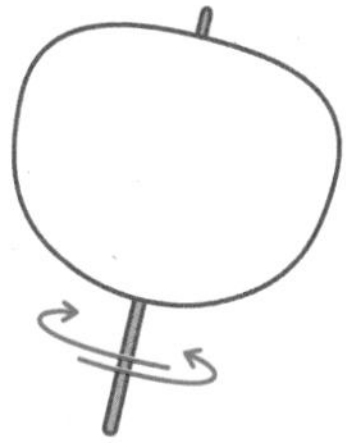

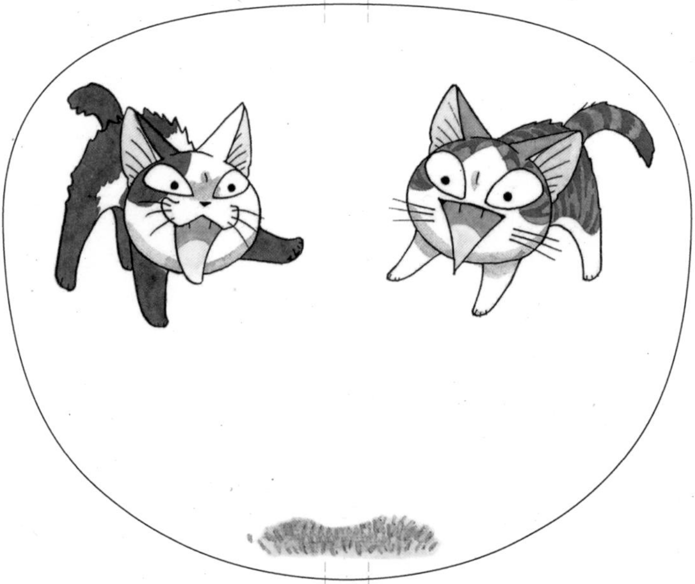

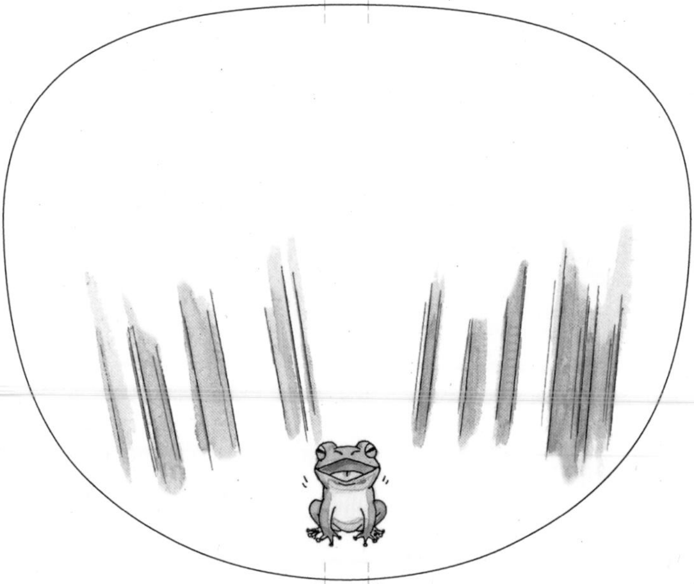

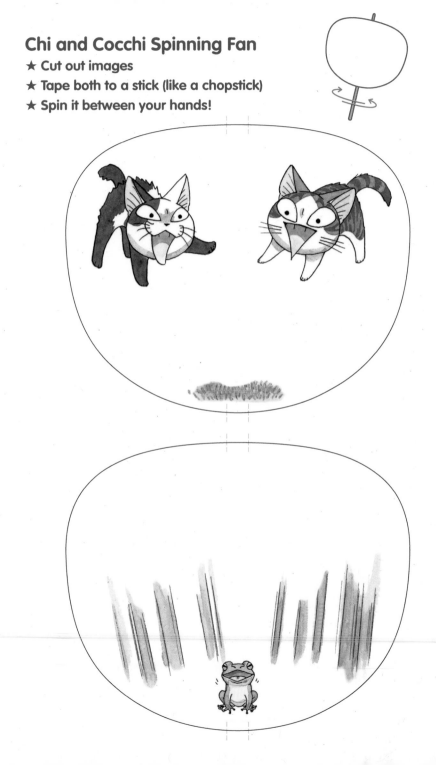

Chi's Sweet Coasters: Cut out and prevent water rings!

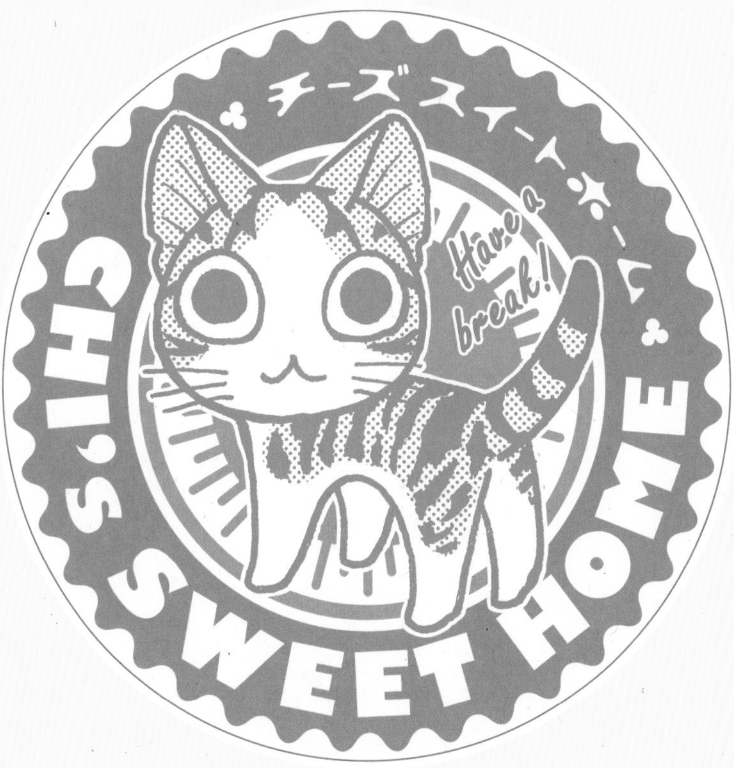
CHI'S SWEET HOME
チーズスイートホーム
Have a break!

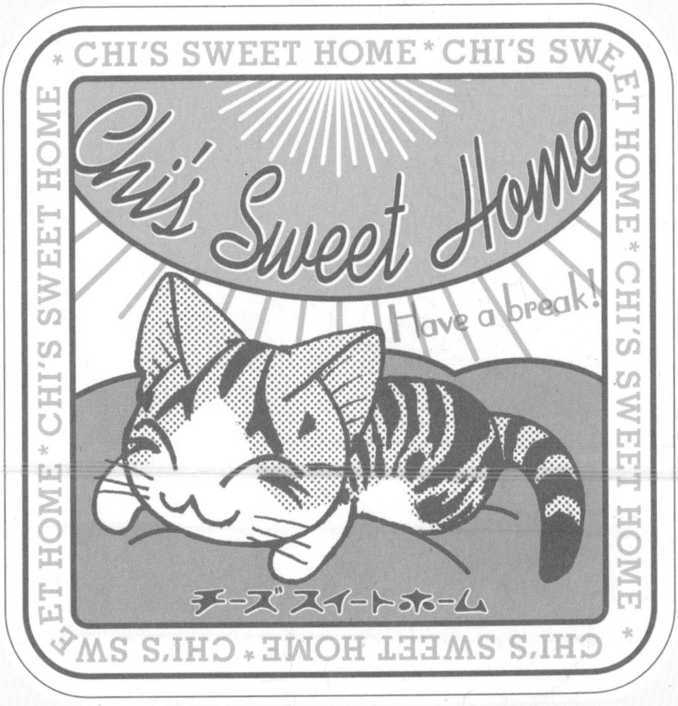
CHI'S SWEET HOME * CHI'S SWEET HOME * CHI'S SWEET HOME * CHI'S SWEET HOME *
Chi's Sweet Home
Have a break!
チーズスイートホーム

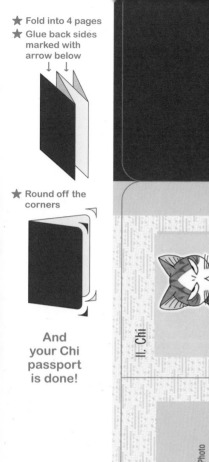

★ Fold into 4 pages
★ Glue back sides marked with arrow below

★ Round off the corners

And your Chi passport is done!

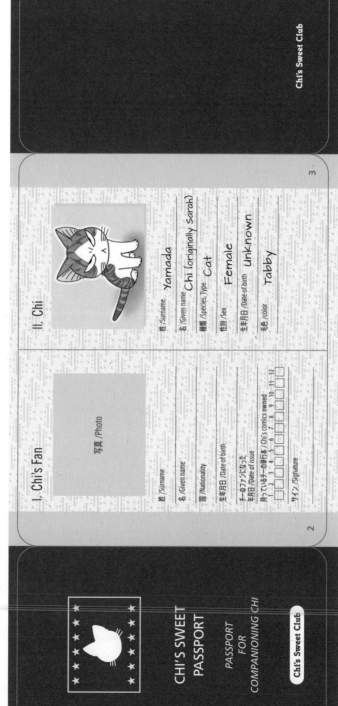

CHI'S SWEET PASSPORT

PASSPORT FOR COMPANIONING CHI

Chi's Sweet Club

I. Chi's Fan

写真 /Photo

姓 /Surname

名 /Given name

国 /Nationality

生年月日 /Date of birth

チーのファンになった
年月日 /Date of issue

持っているチーの単行本 / Chi's comics owned

1 2 3 4 5 6 7 8 9 10 11 12
□ □ □ □ □ □ □ □ □ □ □ □

サイン /Signature

II. Chi

姓 /Surname Yamada

名 /Given name Chi (originally Sarah)

種類 /Species, Type Cat

性別 /Sex Female

生年月日 /Date of birth Unknown

毛色 /color Tabby

Chi's Sweet Club

The Kitten and the Mole

FUKU FUKU

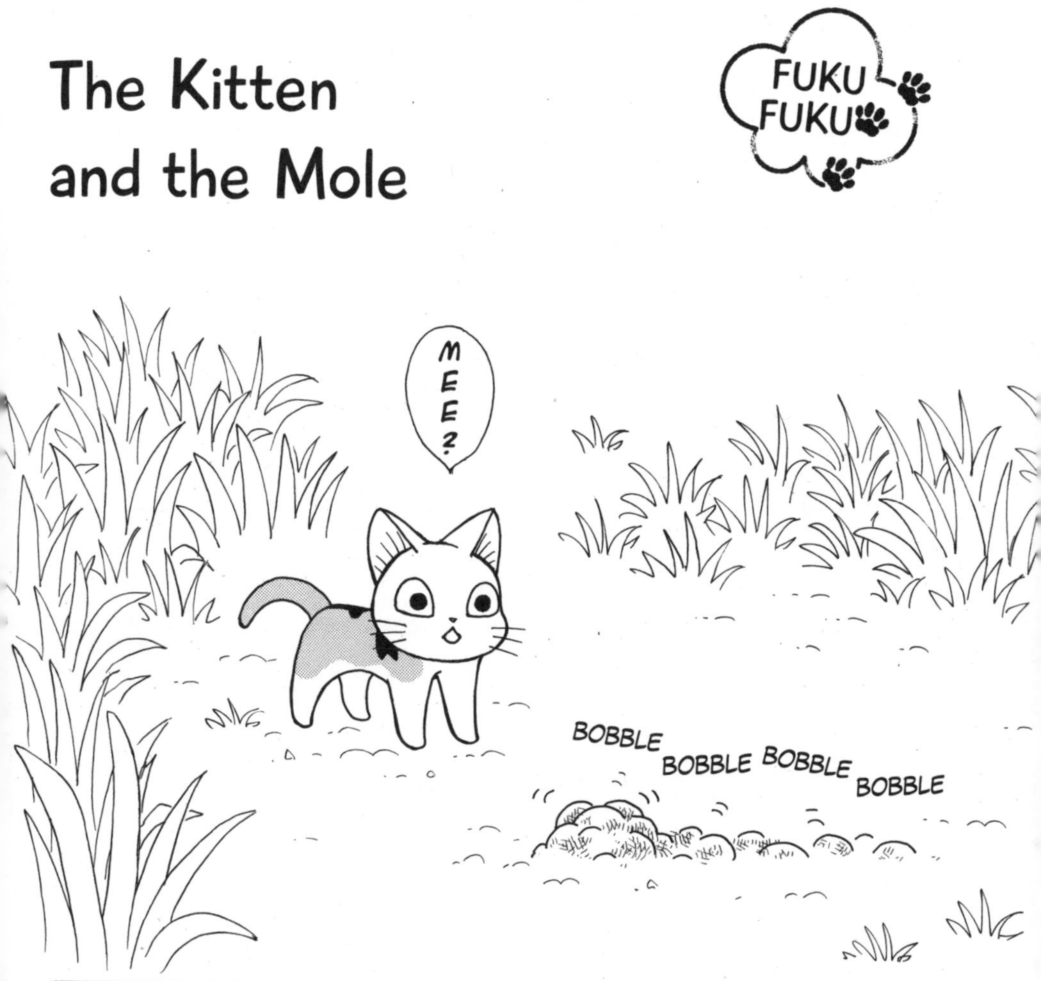
MEE?
BOBBLE BOBBLE BOBBLE BOBBLE

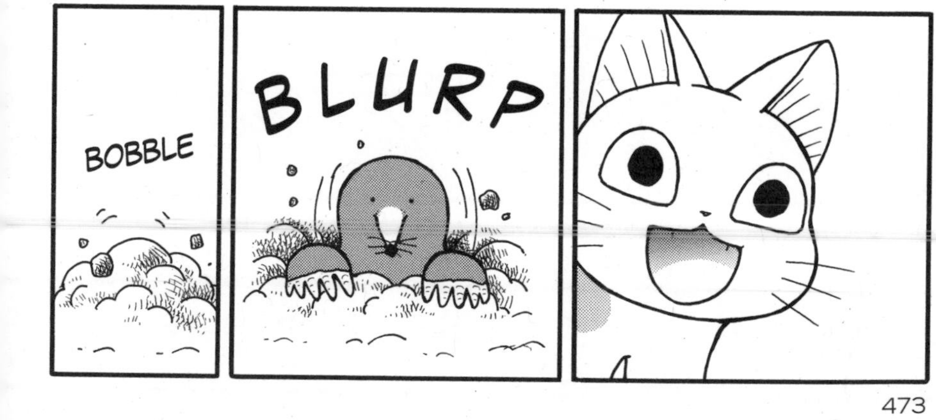
BOBBLE
BLURP

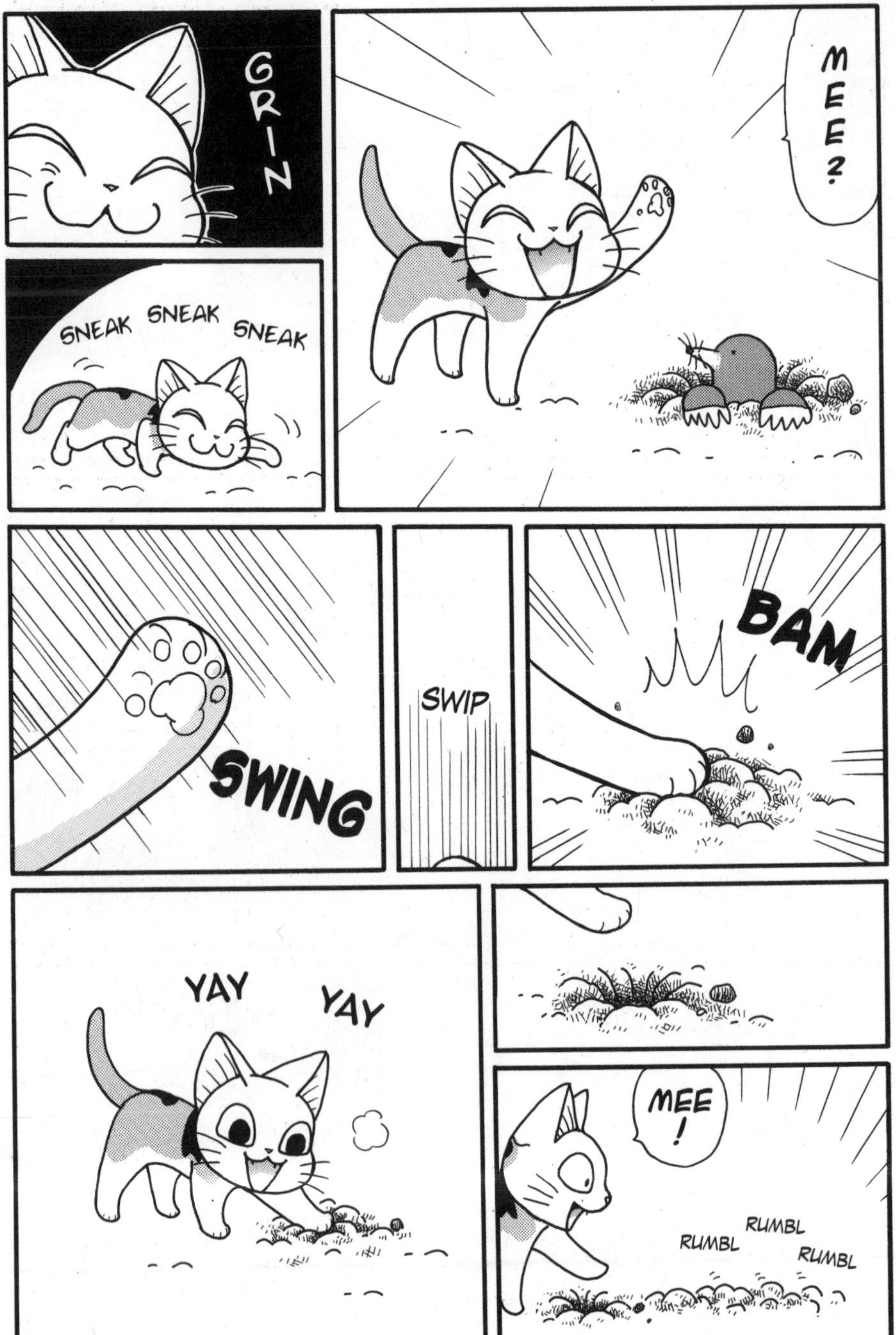
GRIN
SNEAK SNEAK SNEAK
MEE?
SWING
SWIP
BAM
YAY YAY
MEE!
RUMBL RUMBL RUMBL

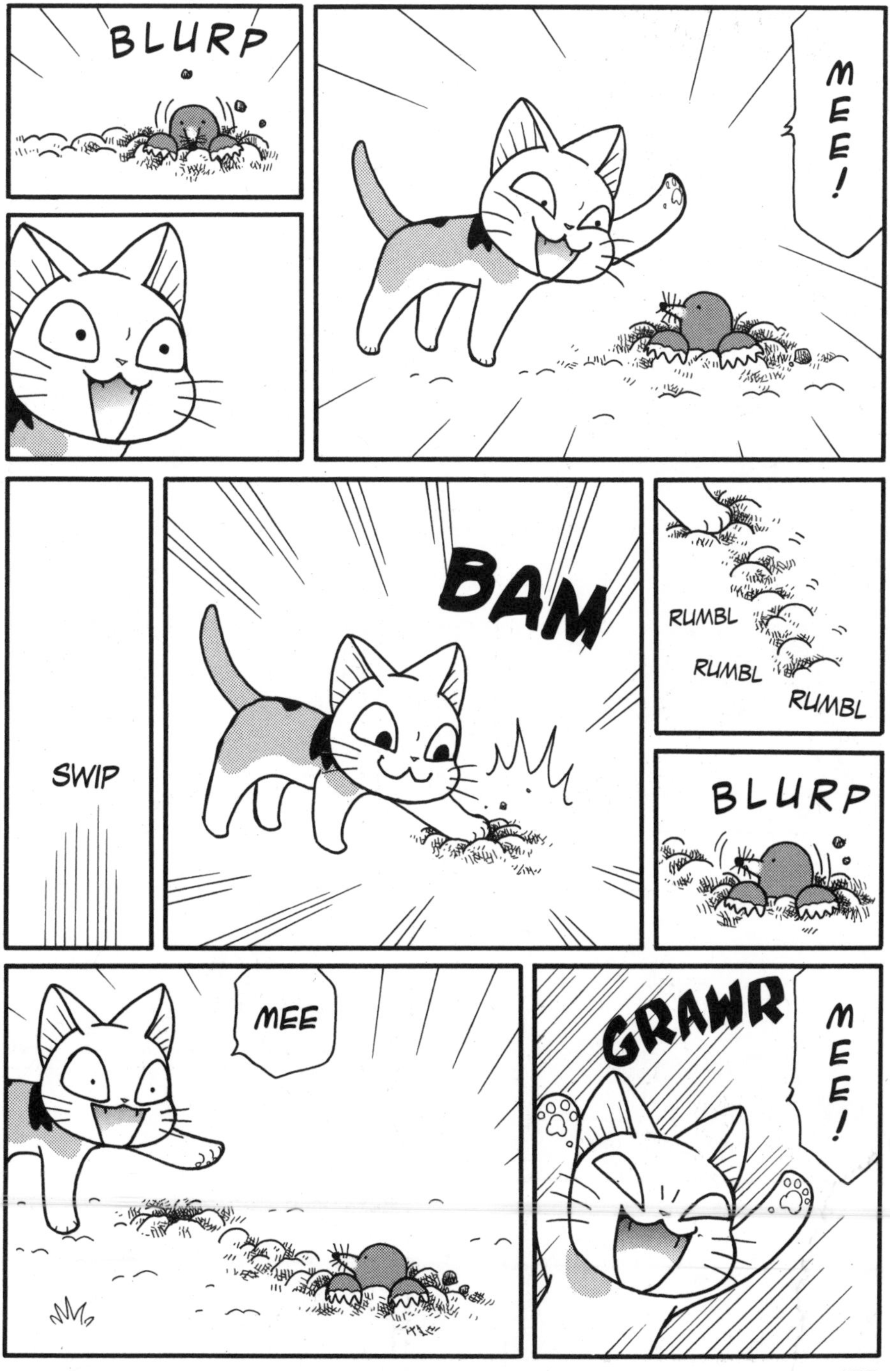
BLURP
MEE!
BAM
RUMBL
RUMBL
RUMBL
SWIP
BLURP
MEE
GRAWR
MEE!

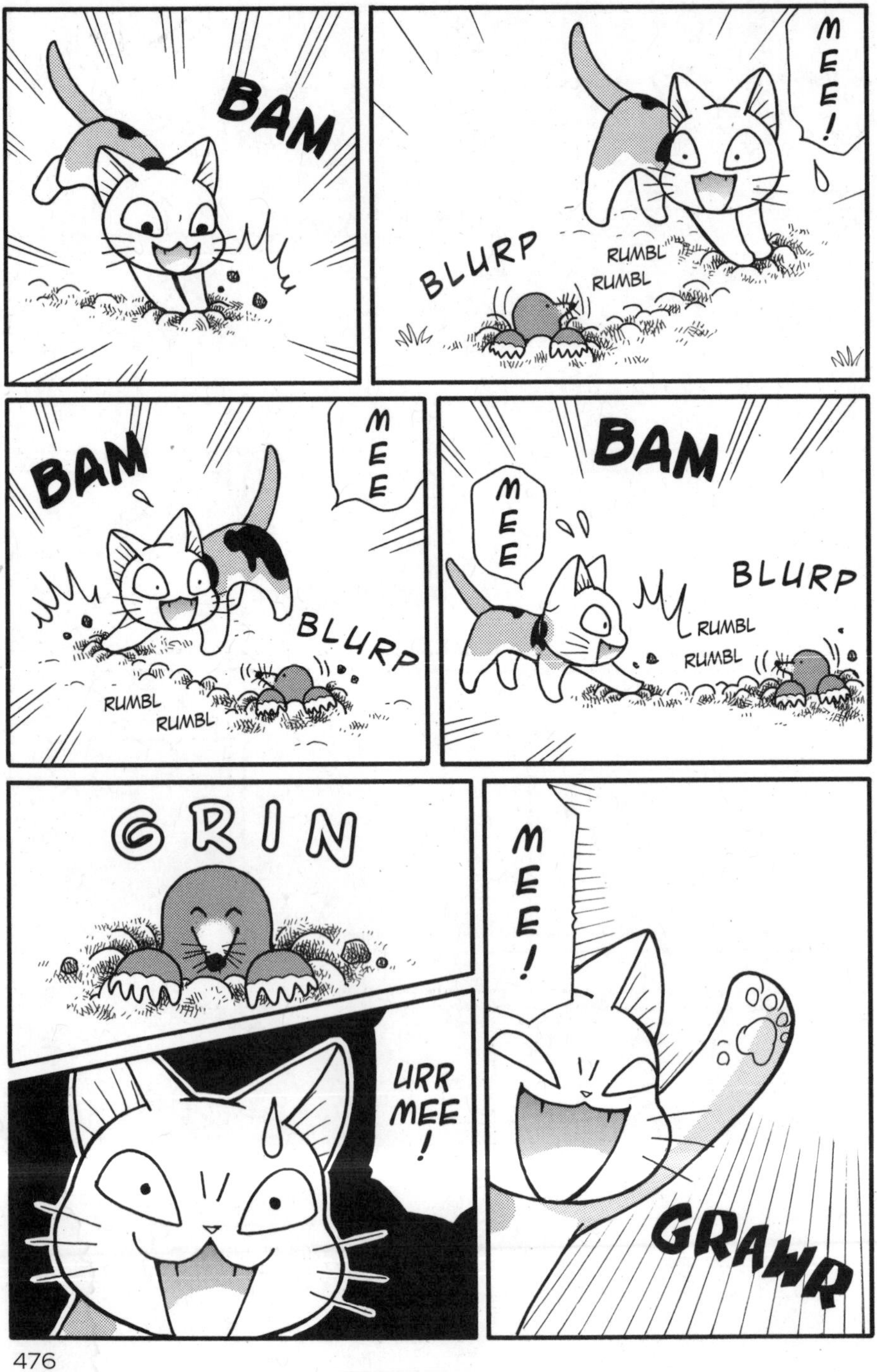
BAM
MEE!
BLURP
RUMBL
RUMBL
BAM
MEE
BLURP
RUMBL
RUMBL
BAM
MEE
BLURP
RUMBL
RUMBL
GRIN
URR MEE!
MEE!
GRAWR

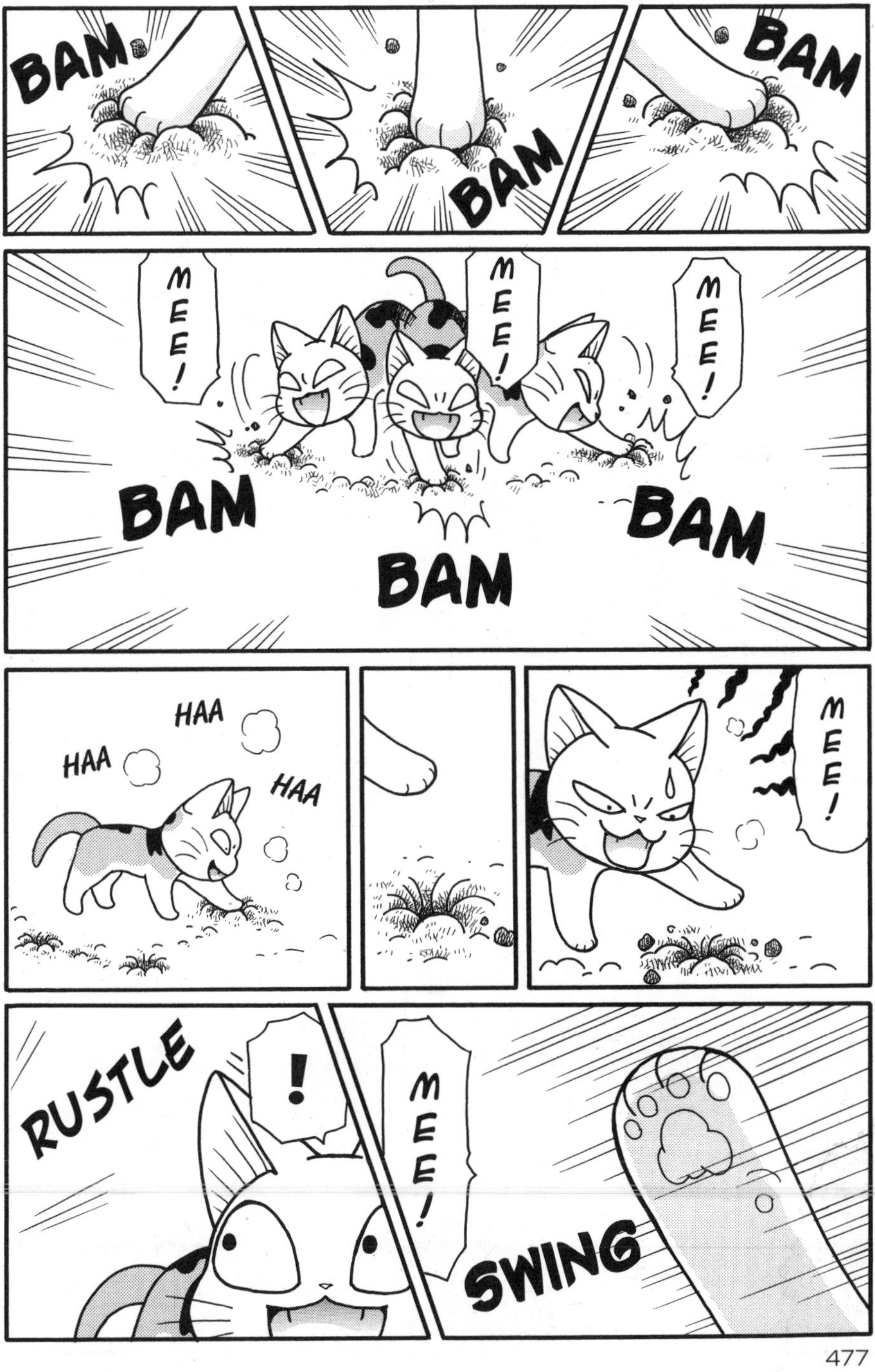
BAM
BAM
BAM
MEE!
MEE!
MEE!
BAM
BAM
BAM
HAA
HAA
HAA
MEE!
RUSTLE
!
MEE!
SWING

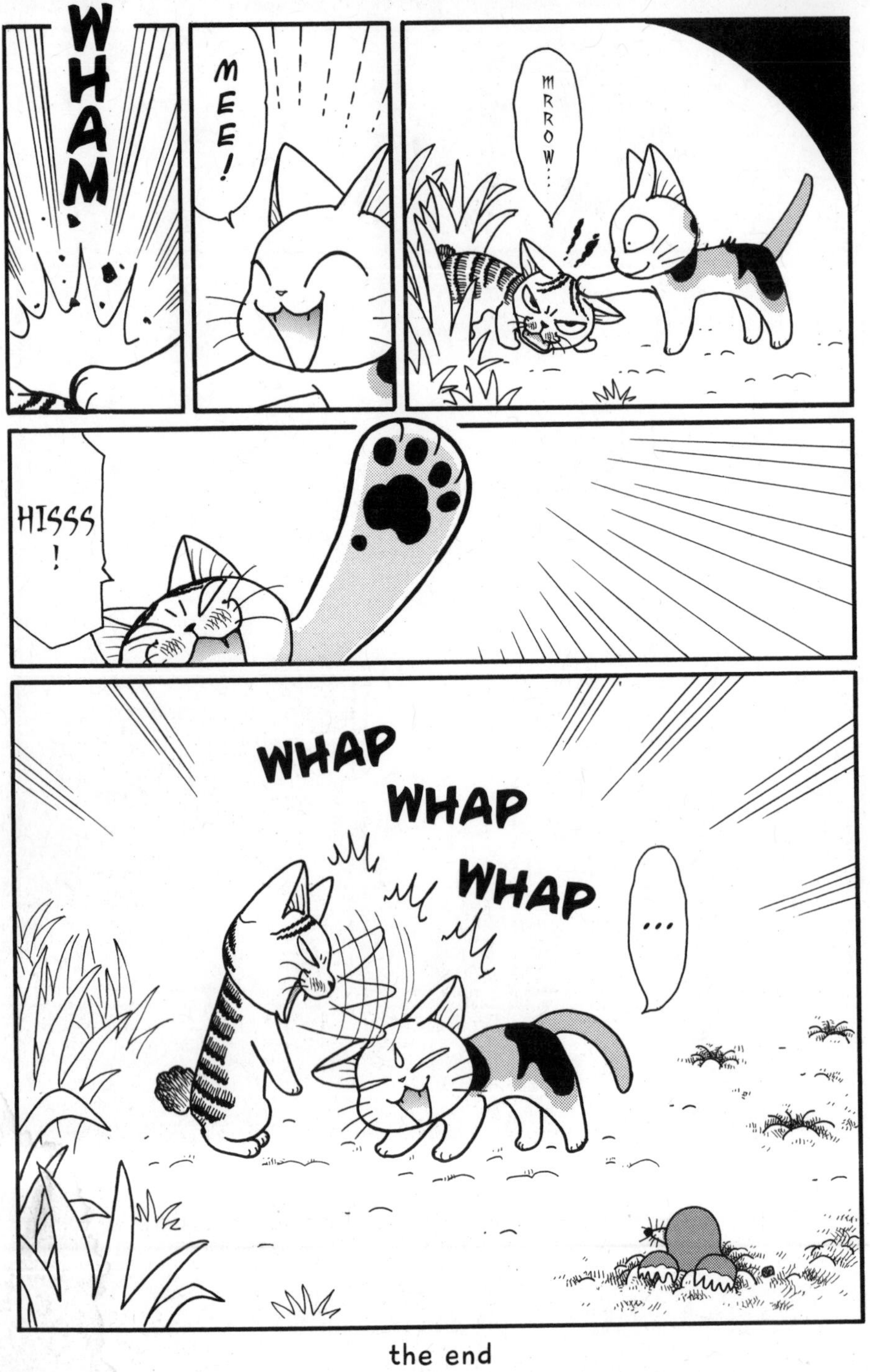
WHAM!
MEE!
MRROW...
HISSS!
WHAP
WHAP
WHAP
...

the end

Chi's
Sweet Adventures

Created by Konami Kanata
Adapted by Kinoko Natsume

Chi is back! Manga's most famous cat returns with
a brand new series! Chi's Sweet Adventures collects dozens
of new full-color kitty tales made for readers of all ages!

Volumes 1-4 On Sale Now!

The Complete
Chi's Sweet Home, Part 4

Translation - Ed Chavez
Marlaina McElheny
Production - Grace Lu
Hiroko Mizuno
Anthony Quintessenza

First published in Japan in 2013, 2014, 2015 by Kodansha, Ltd., Tokyo
Publication for this English edition arranged through Kodansha, Ltd., Tokyo
English language version produced by Vertical Comics,
an imprint of Kodansha USA Publishing, LLC.

Published by Kodansha USA Publishing, LLC., New York

Originally published in Japanese as *Chiizu Suiito Houmu 10-12* by Kodansha, Ltd., 2013-2015
Chiizu Suiito Houmu first serialized in *Morning*, Kodansha, Ltd., 2004-2015

FukuFuku: Kitten Tales 2 chapter 22 originally published in Japanese as *FukuFuku Funya~n Ko-neko da Nyan 2* by Kodansha, Ltd., 2015
FukuFuku Funya~n Ko-neko da Nyan first serialized in *Be Love*, Kodansha, Ltd., 2013-2015

ISBN: 978-1-942993-57-5

Manufactured in Canada

First Edition

Fifth Printing

Kodansha USA Publishing, LLC.
451 Park Avenue South, 7th Floor
New York, NY 10016
www.vertical-comics.com

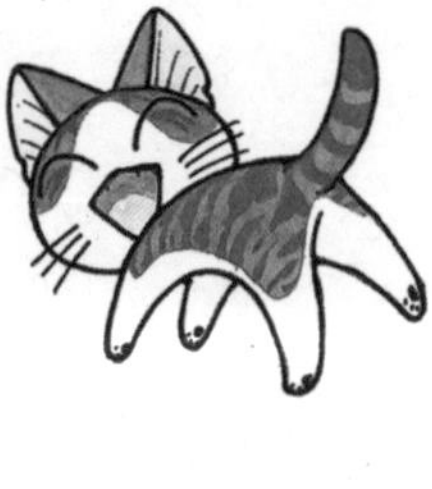

Special thanks to K. Kitamoto

Vertical books are distributed through Penguin-Random House Publisher Services.